W9-BRR-447

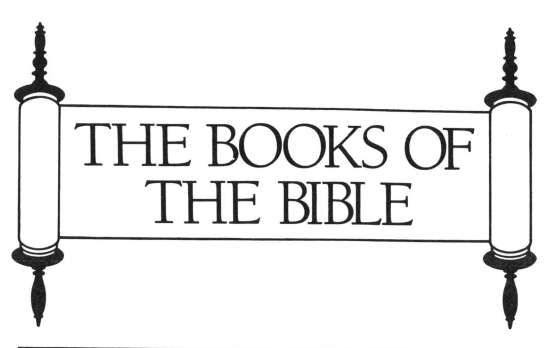

THE BOOKS OF THE BIBLE

The Apocrypha and The New Testament

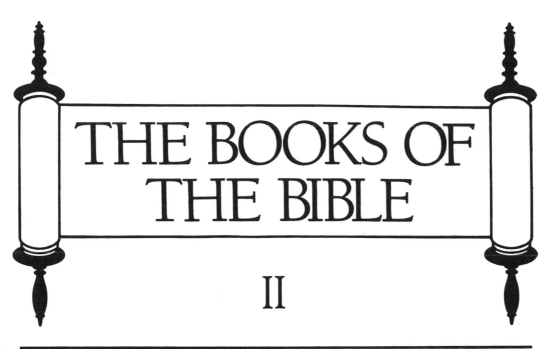

THE BOOKS OF
THE BIBLE

II

The Apocrypha and The New Testament

Bernhard W. Anderson, Editor

CHARLES SCRIBNER'S SONS

NEW YORK

COPYRIGHT © 1989 BY CHARLES SCRIBNER'S SONS
AN IMPRINT OF MACMILLAN PUBLISHING COMPANY

All rights reserved.
No part of this book may be reproduced or transmitted
in any form or by any means, electronic or mechanical,
including photocopying, recording,
or by any information storage and retrieval system,
without permission in writing from the Publisher.

Charles Scribner's Sons
Macmillan Publishing Company
866 Third Avenue, New York, NY 10022

Collier Macmillan Canada, Inc.

Library of Congress Catalog Card Number: 89:10074

PRINTED IN THE UNITED STATES OF AMERICA

printing number

2   3   4   5   6   7   8   9   10

The Books of the Bible/Bernhard W. Anderson, editor.
    p. cm.
   Bibliography: v. 1, p.
   Includes indexes.
   Contents: v. 1. The Old Testament/The Hebrew Bible—v. 2. The
Apocrypha and the New Testament.
   ISBN 0-684-18487-7 (set: alk. paper)—ISBN
0-684-19098-2 (v. 1: alk. paper)—ISBN 0-684-19099-0
(v. 2: alk. paper)
   1. Bible—Criticism, interpretation, etc.   I.   Anderson,
Bernhard W.
BS540.B62   1989
220.6'1—dc20   89-10074
                                                              CIP

The paper in this book meets the guidelines
for permanence and durability
of the Committee on Production Guidelines
for Book Longevity of the Council on Library Resources.

Memorial Library
Mars Hill College
Mars Hill, N. C.
DISCARD

Editorial Staff

Managing Editors
Daniel J. Calto and John Fitzpatrick

EDITORIAL

Associate Editors
Lesley Ann Beneke   Ilene Cohen   Michael Scott Cooper   Eric Haralson
Karen Ready   Irina Rybacek   Joan Zseleczky

Proofreaders
Emily Garlin   Carol Holmes

Editorial Assistant
Brigitte M. Goldstein

Indexer
AEIOU, INC.

PRODUCTION

Director
Matthew M. Kardovich

Book Designers
A Good Thing, Inc.   Mike McIver
(text)   (case)

Production Assistant
Frederick A. Aiese

R
220.61
B 724a
V.2

901528

901258

Contents

CONTENTS

PART TWO: THE NEW TESTAMENT

CONTENTS

Chronology

600–400 B.C.E.	The former kingdom of Judah becomes a Persian satrapy (538).
	The Greeks repel the Persian fleet at Salamis (480).
400–200	The Persian empire succumbs to the armies of Alexander of Macedon (334–330). Judah comes under Greek rule (332).
	Alexander dies (323); his successors, the Ptolemies in Egypt and the Seleucids in Syria and Mesopotamia, engage in a protracted struggle for control of the empire.
	The Seleucids are defeated at the battle of Gaza (312), and Judah comes under Ptolemaic rule.
	Hellenistic Alexandria becomes a center of Jewish learning; its library is established around 280.
	The Septuagint, a Greek translation of the Bible, is produced by Jewish scholars in Alexandria (3d century).
	The Galatians, a Celtic people, establish the kingdom of Bithynia in Asia Minor (279).
	Rome overthrows Carthage in the Punic Wars (264–146).
200–100	War between the Seleucids and Ptolemies continues.
	Judah falls to the Seleucids (183), who impose Greek customs and religious practices on the Jewish population.
	Judas Maccabeus leads a successful revolt against Antiochus IV Epiphanes' attempt to erect a shrine to Zeus at the Temple of Jerusalem (168).
	John Hyrcanus consolidates Hasmonean rule over Judah and surrounding areas (135–104).
	Rome, victorious in the Macedonian Wars (215–148), emerges as the undisputed power in the Mediterranean.
	The Book of **Daniel** achieves its final form (167–164).
	Several books of the Apocrypha date from the period: **Tobit** (*ca.* 180), **Sirach** (*ca.* 170), **Judith** (*ca.* 150), **I Esdras** (150–100), **I and II Maccabees** (134).
	The Essenes, an ascetic Jewish sect, establish a community at Qumran near the Dead Sea (*ca.* 105).
100 B.C.E.–0	Jerusalem is captured by the Roman legion of Pompey; Hasmonean rule ends (63).
	Julius Caesar is assassinated (44).
	Herod of Idumaea (Edom) is made king of the Roman province of Judaea (37).
	The Roman republic comes to an end (31).
	Octavian takes the name Augustus and reigns as first Emperor of Rome (27 B.C.E.–14 C.E.).
	Jesus Christ is born in Judaea (6 or 4 C.E.).
0–100 C.E.	**Herod Antipas** is tetrarch of Galilee (4 B.C.E.–39 C.E.).
	The Roman procurator **Pontius Pilate** governs Judaea (26–36).
	John the Baptist preaches against **Herod Antipas** (27–29).
	Jesus preaches in Judaea and is crucified about 30–33.
	Paul has a conversion experience while on his way to Damascus (*ca.* 33–*ca.* 35).

Peter is imprisoned by **Herod Agrippa** (*ca.* 41–*ca.* 44).

Paul missionizes in Asia Minor and Greece (47–54).

The Roman emperor Claudius expels the Christians from Rome (41).

Paul is arrested in Jerusalem (56). He arrives in Rome about 60.

Paul's letters to the **Thessalonians, Galatians, Corinthians,** and **Romans** are formulated (50–60).

Nero orders the first state persecution of the Christians (64).

The Jewish inhabitants of Judaea engage in a protracted struggle against Roman rule (66–73).

Jerusalem and the Temple are destroyed by the Roman legion of Titus (70).

The **Gospel of Mark** is written about 68–70.

Several epistles attributed to **Paul,** among them **Ephesians,** are composed (75–100).

2 Esdras is written during the reign of Domitian (81–96).

Matthew, Luke-Acts, and **John** are written (85–100).

Revelation of John dates from about 90–95.

100–400 The "Pastoral Epistles" (**1 and 2 Timothy** and **Titus**) are written (*ca.* 110–*ca.* 140).

The Old Latin translation of the Bible is produced in North Africa during the second century.

Bar Kokhba leads a last, unsuccessful revolt against Rome in Judaea (132–135).

Marcion is excommunicated by the church of Rome for repudiating the Old Testament (144).

The Muratorian Canon, the first Christian list of canonical books, is compiled around the 180s.

Jerome produces a Latin version of the Bible known as the Vulgate (383–405).

The canon of the New Testament receives its final form at the Council of Carthage (397).

List of Abbreviations

BIBLICAL BOOKS

Genesis (Gen)
Exodus (Exod)
Leviticus (Lev)
Numbers (Num)
Deuteronomy (Deut)
Joshua (Josh)
Judges (Judg)
Ruth
1 Samuel (1 Sam)
2 Samuel (2 Sam)
1 Kings (1 Kgs)
2 Kings (2 Kgs)
1 Chronicles (1 Chron)
2 Chronicles (2 Chron)
Ezra
Nehemiah (Neh)
Esther (Esth)
Additions to Esther (Add Esth)
Job
Psalms (Ps, Pss)
Proverbs (Prov)
Ecclesiastes (Eccl)
Song of Solomon (Song)
Isaiah (Isa)
Jeremiah (Jer)
Lamentations (Lam)
Ezekiel (Ezek)

Daniel (Dan)
Additions to Daniel (Add Dan)
Hosea (Hos)
Joel
Amos
Obadiah (Obad)
Jonah
Micah (Mic)
Nahum (Nah)
Habakkuk (Hab)
Zephaniah (Zeph)
Haggai (Hag)
Zechariah (Zech)
Malachi (Mal)
1 Esdras (1 Esdr)
2 Esdras (2 Esdr)
Tobit (Tob)
Judith (Jdt)
Wisdom of Solomon (Wis)
Sirach (Sir)
Baruch (Bar)
Letter of Jeremiah (Let Jer)
Prayer of Manasseh (Pr Man)
1 Maccabees (1 Macc)
2 Maccabees (2 Macc)
Matthew (Matt)
Mark

Luke
John
Acts
Romans (Rom)
1 Corinthians (1 Cor)
2 Corinthians (2 Cor)
Galatians (Gal)
Ephesians (Eph)
Philippians (Phil)
Colossians (Col)
1 Thessalonians (1 Thess)
2 Thessalonians (2 Thes)
1 Timothy (1 Tim)
2 Timothy (2 Tim)
Titus
Philemon (Phlm)
Hebrews (Heb)
James (Jas)
1 Peter (1 Pet)
2 Peter (2 Pet)
3 Peter (3 Pet)
1 John
2 John
3 John
Jude
Revelation (Rev)

TRANSLATIONS

Ancient Near Eastern Texts (ANET; non biblical)
Authorized Version (AV; informally known as the King James Version, KJV)
Jerusalem Bible (JB)
Jewish Publication Society (JPS)
New American Bible (NAB)
New English Bible (NEB)
New International Version (NIV)

New Jerusalem Bible (NJB)
New Jewish Version (NJV; published as *Tanakh* by the JPS)
Revised Standard Version (RSV)
Revised Version (RV)
Today's English Version (TEV; also known as the Good News Bible)

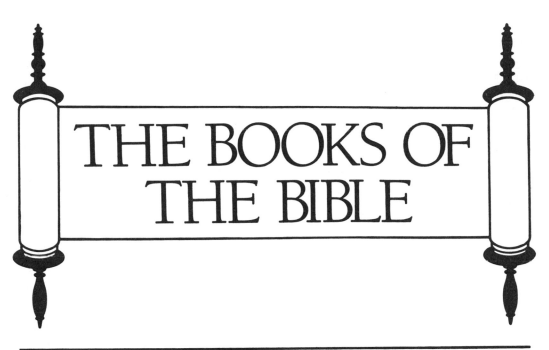

THE BOOKS OF THE BIBLE

The Apocrypha and The New Testament

The
Apocrypha

Introduction to the Apocrypha

INTRODUCTION

Definition and Contents

THE TERM "APOCRYPHA" (Greek: "hidden things") designates a collection of Jewish writings composed between 250 B.C.E. and 100 C.E. Scholars dispute when and why these writings came to be called "hidden things," but most would agree that they are valuable for what they reveal about the religion and culture of Judaism between Ezra and the early part of our era.

The collection consists primarily of texts that were included in the major manuscripts of the Greek translation of the "Old Testament" (the Septuagint), but excluded from the Hebrew canon established by the rabbis in the second century C.E. These texts are: 1 Esdras, Tobit, Judith, additions to the Book of Esther, the Wisdom of Solomon, the Wisdom of Sirach (Ben Sira), Baruch, the Letter of Jeremiah, the Prayer of Azariah and the Song of the Three Young Men, Susanna, Bel and the Dragon, the Prayer of Manasseh, and 1 and 2 Maccabees. Also included among the Apocrypha, although it is not found in extant manuscripts of the Greek Bible, is the apocalypse known as 2 Esdras (or 4 Ezra).

A Christian Collection

The writings of the Apocrypha were first preserved in Jewish circles. Texts composed in Greek were copied; others (Tobit, Sirach, Judith, and 1 Maccabees) were translated from Aramaic and Hebrew and then copied in their Greek form. For some time, in circumstances that we can no longer reconstruct in detail, the Semitic and Greek forms of these texts continued to circulate in Jewish circles. In spite of this continued Jewish interest, it was primarily Christians who preserved and used the Apocrypha.

The early Christian use of the Apocrypha eludes easy description. The extant writings of the early teachers and theologians of the church indicate a preference for quoting the books contained in the Hebrew canon, especially texts from the Torah, Prophets, and Psalms. Certain of the Apocrypha were also quoted and alluded to, although this need not imply canonical authority. Developing scribal practice was more inclusive. The Apocrypha were included in the great fourth- and fifth-century Greek manuscripts of the Old and New Testaments, which were produced by Christian copyists who doubtless used earlier Christian manuscripts. The practice of copying these works in biblical manuscripts continued in other versions that were translated from the Greek. In the Western tradition, the apocryphal writings were taken over into the "Old Latin" translations made in the second and third centuries. Toward the end of the fourth century, Jerome also included these works in his new Latin edition (the Vulgate), although he emphasized in his prefaces that the Jewish community did not accept them as canonical. In 1546 the Council of Trent decreed that all of these works except 1 and 2 Esdras and the Prayer of Manasseh were part of the Old Testament. Subsequently, the Roman Catholic church distinguished between the protocanonical books (the Hebrew canon) and the deuterocanonical books (the Apocrypha except for 1 and 2 Esdras and the Prayer of Manasseh), which were considered authoritative, but of later date. This authoritative status is reflected in modern Roman Catholic editions of the Bible, which place the deuterocanonical works in roughly the same sequence in which they appear in the manuscripts of the Septuagint (see, for example, *The Jerusalem Bible* and *The New American Bible,* and the Old Testament canon table in the first volume of *The Books of the Bible*). Editions of the Bible prepared by the Eastern Orthodox churches, also following ancient tradition, include the deuterocanonical books, as well as 1 Esdras, Psalm 151, the Prayer of Manasseh, and two other works found in the Greek Old Testament: 3 Maccabees and 4 Maccabees (the latter placed in an appendix).

Protestant practice contrasts remarkably with this long-standing tradition in Roman Catholicism and Eastern Orthodoxy. For the Reformers (who wrote before the Council of Trent formalized the longer canon), the Hebrew canon was definitive. One could read the apocryphal writings with profit, but they were not authoritative. In part, this viewpoint was a reaction against the Roman Catholic use of 2 Maccabees to support the doctrine of purgatory and prayer for the dead. This Protestant attitude was reinforced in subsequent centuries, when the Apocrypha came to be excluded from many of the editions of the Bible produced by English-speaking Protestantism. In recent decades, the renewed interest in the study of early Judaism has reversed this trend, and the Apocrypha appear once more in many English-language Protestant editions of the Bible. Nonetheless, reflecting their noncanonical status, they are gathered as a separate collection and placed either between the Old and New Testaments or after the New Testament.

As these brief observations suggest, the deuterocanonical or apocryphal works are of considerable interest for the history of both the Christian communities that included these writings in their Bibles and those that made a point of excluding them. In this essay, however, we shall focus on their value as windows into the world of early Judaism—as witnesses to the religion and culture of the Jewish writers and communities responsible for their composition and initial preservation.

THE APOCRYPHA AS HISTORICAL WITNESSES TO EARLY JUDAISM

The Context: A Time of Transitions

The period between the late fourth century B.C.E. and the end of the first century C.E. was crucial in several respects. The conquests of Alexander the Great (336–323 B.C.E.) brought profound and permanent changes to Judaism. The destruction of Jerusalem and the Temple (70 C.E.) was an integral and perhaps inevitable part of the history of this period; in turn it introduced other permanent changes. Moreover, the appearance of Jesus of Nazareth and the rise of early Christianity created a whole new direction within the apocalyptic wing of Judaism, which had itself been profoundly influenced by changes in the Greco-Roman period. Both early rabbinic Judaism and early Christianity must be interpreted in the context of the developing Judaism of the Hellenistic and early Roman period.

The Collective Value of the Apocrypha

Among the writings of the Hebrew canon, only Daniel and perhaps Esther and Ecclesiastes derive from this period. Thus, the Apocrypha loom large as a resource for our knowledge of this crucial era in the history of Judaism. Viewed collectively, they underscore two basic facts.

1. Jewish religious practice and thought in the early Roman period was more diverse than the contents of the Hebrew canon might suggest and less firmly fixed than this closed canon from a later period might indicate. Jews between 100 B.C.E. and 100 C.E. preserved and transmitted the apocryphal texts; they had not yet limited or canonized the category of texts that came to be known in the Hebrew Bible as "The Writings" (Psalms, Job, Proverbs, Ruth, the Song of Solomon, Ecclesiastes, Lamentations, Esther, Daniel, Ezra, Nehemiah, and Chronicles). In the period

under consideration, the writings that we call Apocrypha were still for many Jews a significant and useful part of their religious literature. They had not yet become noncanonical.

2. Contrary to some Christian stereotypes, the Greco-Roman period is neither an obscure time in the history of Judaism, nor is it marked by a lack of religious vitality and creativity. The Apocrypha are the products of the Jewish communities that preserved what came to be the Hebrew scriptures and that transmitted the faith of Israel into which Jesus of Nazareth and the earliest Christians were born. As the Epistle to the Hebrews observes (11:32–38), the history of Israel runs its continuous course from the exile through the Hellenistic period to the turn of the era. The Apocrypha are one strand in that ongoing history.

The Limitations of the Apocrypha's Witness

Nonetheless, these books present a limited witness. They are only a small part of a much larger and more diverse religious literature that was generated by Jews in the Greco-Roman period. The extent of that literature is suggested by the massive volume of texts that have been preserved among the "Pseudepigrapha," the Dead Sea Scrolls, and the writings of Philo of Alexandria and Josephus. In addition, preserved fragments of lost works and allusions to still other works indicate that an even larger volume of literature was produced during this period. Thus, in the present essay, we shall occasionally allude to the Apocrypha's limitations as historical witnesses and make reference to other texts that help to broaden our perspective.

The Types of Historical Evidence in the Apocrypha

Explicit historical information. The Apocrypha provide direct and explicit historical information about Judaism in the Greco-Roman period. In fact, 1 and 2 Maccabees, both written within a century of the events they describe, are our only extensive contemporary literary witnesses to events in Palestine between 200 and 125 B.C.E. Although each of these histories has its own bias, together they provide the basic data for a reconstruction of second-century Palestinian Jewish history and the rise of the priestly and royal dynasty of the Hasmoneans (the brothers of Judas Maccabeus and their descendants).

Indirect historical evidence. The Maccabean histories are also indirect witnesses to the history of the period; indeed, they are constitutive parts of that history. 1 Maccabees is a propagandistic instrument of the Hasmonean dynasty or its partisans; 2 Maccabees is critical of the achievements of the brothers of Judas Maccabeus. The many differences between these interpretive accounts of the same events underscore the fact that second- and first-century Judaism was not a political, social, or religious monolith.

The historical value of the Apocrypha is not limited to texts that recount history. All of the Apocrypha—because they were created in time and place—testify indirectly to the many-faceted history of early Judaism. These texts reflect their historical contexts and express their authors' interactions with those contexts and their articulation of their religious and cultural heritage. This information must be "teased" from the texts with great caution, and the historian must honestly admit that the evidence is indirect and the conclusions tentative. With these caveats expressed, however, the remainder of this essay will offer some synthetic observations on aspects of this historical witness.

LITERARY HISTORY

The Apocrypha are a part of Jewish literary history, and as such, they constitute a significant component of that people's broader cultural history. Literary forms are cultural artifacts that reflect important aspects of the lives of the people who created and used them. In the Apocrypha we see the Jews of the time reflecting on their past and interacting with their present environment. We hear them teaching and preaching, praying to and praising their God. In order properly to interpret and evaluate this material, we must employ the tools of literary analysis. The authors of the Apocrypha did not simply accumulate knowledge and compile lists of ideas. They expressed their knowledge, ideas, and beliefs through the use of specific literary genres and sometimes in texts of mixed genres.

Literary Forms and Genres

History and historical fiction. A substantial part of the Apocrypha purports to record past events. A few of these texts deal with recent history, but in very different literary styles and genres. Writing in Hebrew, the author of 1 Maccabees recounts Hasmonean history in a way that is reminiscent of the historical biblical books. The author of 2 Maccabees imitates gentile Greek models. In a similar vein, 3 Maccabees presents a legendary account of a conflict in Ptolemaic Egypt. 4 Maccabees retells the stories in 2 Maccabees 6–7 in a heavily philosophical form.

Other authors composed historical fiction that was set in earlier times (1 Esdras, Tobit, Judith, Bel and the Dragon, Susanna). The connections between this fiction and the times and events described in the Bible are tenuous and usually involve only a setting in the exile or postexilic Judaea and interaction (usually conflict) with some gentile king mentioned in the biblical histories. Nonetheless, the setting was indispensable to the authors' purposes, which were, in some sense, religious edification and moral exhortation. These writers did not teach (except incidentally) by explicit precept. Instead they employed narrative forms to portray heroines and heroes of the past as models of good or appropriate behavior. Continuity was crucial; Israel's identity in the present was bound up with its religious history.

Proverbial and philosophical wisdom. The teaching and exhortative functions implicit in Jewish historical fiction are explicit in the "wisdom" texts of the Apocrypha. These works are noteworthy for their development of biblical forms and traditions and their use of non-Israelite philosophical thought. The Wisdom of Sirach instructs primarily by means of proverbs. Differing from its canonical counterpart (Proverbs), however, it presupposes throughout an identification of wisdom and Torah; it reflects an interaction with Greek philosophy (mainly Stoicism); and it intersperses literary forms (such as prayers and hymns) that are rare in the earlier wisdom literature. The form of the proverb also appears in a piece of historical fiction on the lips of Tobit, and outside of the Apocrypha it recurs in the pseudonymous Testaments of the Twelve Patriarchs. The Wisdom of Solomon is noteworthy for its mixed use of Jewish and Greek forms and traditions. The story of the persecuted righteous one (chaps. 2 and 5) reflects a narrative form found in the Joseph story (Gen 37–40) and the

Daniel cycle (Dan 1–6), which has been recast under the influence of a traditional apocalyptic interpretation of Isaiah 52–53. As a whole, however, the Wisdom of Solomon instructs by means of the Hellenistic form known as the protreptic (a treatise that made an appeal to follow a meaningful philosophy as a way of life), and much of its message is cast in conceptions and rhetoric at home in eclectic Hellenistic philosophy.

Hymns and prayers. Hymns and prayers are a small but important component in the Apocrypha. Their significance is historical and literary. Historically, they reveal developments in the form, religious content, and function of "liturgical" genres known from the Bible (mainly the Psalms). They also provide glimpses of how religious people perceived and interacted positively and negatively with God. More concretely, these texts testify to moments of private devotion and institutionalized occasions of public worship. These liturgical pieces are also important for the literary analysis of the nonliturgical texts in which they are embedded. In non-narrative or marginally narrative texts (Sirach, Wisdom of Solomon, Baruch), they are integral to the exposition of the author's thought or worldview. In narrative texts like Tobit, Judith, and Susanna, they advance the plot and provide a realistic touch that mirrors an essential aspect of the pious life. In Daniel 3 and Esther they have been interpolated into a narrative in order to enrich the story and, in the case of Esther, to change its tone.

An apocalypse. The Hellenistic period saw the development and proliferation of texts that claimed to be revelations of hidden things. Authors writing in the name of ancient patriarchs and seers claimed to mediate knowledge of God's hidden world—in heaven or in the recesses of the cosmos—and to reveal the "secrets" or "mysteries" of God's hidden future (Dan 2:27–30; *cf.* Mk 4:11). The corpus known as Pseudepigrapha has preserved a considerable number of such texts ascribed to Enoch, Baruch, Ezra, Abraham, and others. The canonical status of the apocalypses is a complex problem. Some of the early teachers of the church (e.g., the author of the Epistle of Barnabas and Tertullian) alluded to these works and quoted them as authoritative Scripture. The manuscript tradition is another matter. Paradoxically, the Hebrew canon contained an apocalypse (the Book of Daniel), whereas the additional books in the manuscripts of the Greek Old Testament include no apocalypse. Nonetheless, 2 Esdras, a late apocalypse composed *ca.* 100 C.E. in the wake of the destruction of Jerusalem, was included in the Old Latin version and the Vulgate. Its popularity in the second and third centuries may reflect the fact that, despite its apocalyptic form, 2 Esdras takes a dim view of the kind of cosmic speculation that is essential to other revelatory works like the Books of Enoch. Its popularity among Christians was surely also due to the chapters added to the beginning and end of the original apocalypse, which may be Christian in origin and were compatible with negative Christian interpretations of the destruction of Jerusalem.

Authorship, Anonymity, and Pseudonymity

The public statement of authorship was much rarer in antiquity than it is today. Of all the Apocrypha, only two texts reveal their author's real name: the collection of proverbs by the scribe Jesus the son of Sirach (Sir 50:27), and 2 Maccabees, which is mainly an anonymous epitome of a history by a certain Jason of Cyrene (2:23). Of the remaining texts, 1 Esdras, Judith, Susanna, Bel and the Dragon, and 1, 3, and 4 Maccabees do not identify their authors. More intriguing are 2 Esdras, Tobit, the Wisdom of Solomon, Baruch, the Letter of Jeremiah, and the Prayer of Manasseh. These follow the literary convention of pseudonymity found in the Bible in some of the Psalms, Proverbs, Ecclesiastes, the Song of Solomon, and Daniel. All were written in the name of a figure from the past. With the exception of Tobit, the alleged author is a known figure. The ascription allows the real author to suggest a parallel between the present time and that of the alleged author, and, in some cases, to claim authority in the name of the earlier figure. Such authoritative pseudonymity is a typical feature of the apocalypses of the Pseudepigrapha.

JUDAISM IN INTERACTION WITH ITS GENTILE ENVIRONMENT

The discovery of new data and the renewed critical study of the Hebrew Bible have begun to reveal the many complex ways in which the people of Israel interacted with their Near Eastern gentile environment. Israelite life and religion did not exist and develop in a cultural vacuum. Its contexts were Canaan, Egypt, and Mesopotamia. The reforms of Ezra notwithstanding, this trend to interact with its environment continued in the Judaism of the Greco-Roman period. Two major new factors were the size of the Jewish population outside the land of Israel and the hellenized character of the gentile environment. Both factors loom large in the Apocrypha. One might speak here about social and cultural history, but as we shall see, the Jews' response to their environment also had a significant religious dimension.

The Diaspora as a Fact of Life

Although the largest part of the Hebrew scriptures was composed, collected, or edited either in the Babylonian exile or subsequent to it, few of these texts envision dispersion as an ongoing fact of life. In this respect Esther and Daniel are exceptions that form a transition to the apocryphal texts. For the Apocrypha, the Diaspora is either a long-standing problem in need of resolution or a fact of life that challenges the religious and cultural resources of a people who see themselves as special and different.

Where the Diaspora is an issue for the writers of the Apocrypha, it is primarily a problem in need of resolution. The land is essential to the covenantal promises. Tobit begins his memoirs by recalling how as a northerner he had made pilgrimages to Jerusalem. He concludes his book with a hymn and a deathbed revelation that anticipate the return of the Diaspora, the restoration of Jerusalem, and the conversion of the gentiles. Baruch begins with a prayer of confession for the sins that have led to exile, continues with a poem that identifies divine wisdom with the Torah that has been violated, and concludes with an extensive exhortation that proclaims the return of the children of Mother Zion.

Other texts address the problems of living in a gentile environment. For the Wisdom of Solomon, the Letter of Jeremiah, and Bel and the Dragon, the major issue is idolatry. In 3 Maccabees, the Egyptian Jews must choose between cultural and religious accommodation and gentile hostility. Tobit also reflects such hostility and counsels marriage within the tribe as a means of preserving one's Israelite identity.

Life in Hellenistic Palestine

Interaction with Hellenism was not limited to the Diaspora. Palestine itself was also extensively hellenized. 1 and 2 Maccabees sketch the events of the first third of the second century B.C.E. that led to a bitter confrontation between extreme Jewish hellenizers and pious Jews who opposed such accommodation. The situation is described as a crisis of monumental proportions that threatened the existence of traditional Israelite religion and culture in the Jewish homeland itself. The pseudepigraphic Book of Jubilees agrees with this analysis.

Affirmative Interactions
Between Judaism and Its Environment

The Jewish writers of the Diaspora and Palestine do not speak with one voice about Hellenistic culture, however. Although the author of 2 Maccabees clearly sides with the pious Jews who opposed the hellenizers, he tells his story using the rhetoric and literary forms of Hellenistic historiography. For all his invective against the Hellenistic king Antiochus IV, the author of 4 Maccabees interprets the Torah in the idiom of Greek philosophy. The Jerusalem scribe Jesus the son of Sirach equates true Wisdom with Torah, but he also utilizes the ideas and mythic expressions of Hellenistic philosophy and religion. The author of the Wisdom of Solomon, despite his criticism of gentile kings and the folly of idolatry, employs the conceptions of Greek philosophy to mediate what he claims to be the wisdom of an Israelite king.

Thus, the Apocrypha attest to a remarkable spectrum of Jewish attitudes toward the non-Jewish environment; individual authors incorporated what they deemed acceptable and beneficial, and rejected what they considered objectionable and incompatible with their Israelite heritage.

Judaism in Crisis:
Difficult Times and Speculation About
Divine Justice

As they lived in their gentile environment, Jews of the Greco-Roman period experienced an ongoing series of political, economic, social, cultural, and religious crises. We can list only some of the issues: a succession of foreign overlords; the importation and imposition of Hellenistic cultural forms and institutions; times of severe persecution in connection with the latter; sectarian religious strife, notably as a result of the rise of the Hasmonean dynasty; internal social tensions and oppression; and the revolt against Rome in 70 C.E., which brought devastation of the land and destruction of the Jerusalem Temple.

How these facts and events constituted crises for various sectors of the Jewish people is a complicated question with few certain answers. The Apocrypha and especially other contemporary Jewish writings, however, attest to the efforts of Jewish religious thinkers to deal creatively with the perceived problem of theodicy. How does one explain the disparity between the fundamental assertion that the God of the covenant is just and faithful and the persistent experience of injustice? The question was probed in depth and in classical form in 2 Esdras.

For whom is God's justice a problem? Facts and events are always subject to human interpretation. One person's problem is a cause of joy and celebration for another. The complexities of Jewish history in the Greco-Roman period amply document this. Some hellenizing Jews in the 170s and 160s enjoyed freedom, prestige, and prosperity, and, to the extent that they cared, they saw these as blessings from the God of Israel. For others hellenization was either a flagrant sin or an evil that God unleashed on a sinful people. For these people, the victories of Judas Maccabeus and his brothers embodied the triumph of divine retribution. But the ways soon parted among these Jews, and here the literary evidence is fascinating. 1 Maccabees interprets the rise of the Hasmonean dynasty as the historical realization of divine justice and the fulfillment of God's ancient promises. For the authors of the Dead Sea Scrolls and the pseudepigraphic Psalms of Solomon, the Hasmoneans were usurpers. Their claims to kingship violated God's covenant with David, and their conduct of the high priesthood transgressed divine laws and polluted the Temple. In either case, divine justice would inevitably resolve the problem, which 1 Maccabees saw as no problem at all. One can multiply similar examples of sharply differing perceptions of what did or did not constitute a challenge to God's justice.

When does God act? As our previous example

illustrates, divine retribution and deliverance have a time factor. The authors of 1 Maccabees and Judith saw the enactment of justice and salvation in specific historical events in the past. For many others, salvation and retribution take place both in the present and in the future. According to Tobit, God helps pious people here and now, but the great act of deliverance—the glorification of Jerusalem and the return of the Diaspora—was yet to be realized. The author of the Book of Baruch has a similar vision of the future, as does Jesus the son of Sirach. For the latter, God's retribution occurs perhaps daily for the righteous and sinners, but the scribe includes in his collection of proverbs a prayer for the destruction of Israel's enemies and the return of the Diaspora (36:1–17). For the author of 2 Esdras, the destruction of Jerusalem was God's punishment on the Jews, but a great day of judgment lay in the future.

Divine justice for individuals and the community. As the prophetic and wisdom literature of the Hebrew Bible attests, Israel's religious thought developed from views of national retribution to a concern for individuals as the objects of divine justice. Tobit and Sirach indicate that this was not a simple, permanent, one-way development. For Tobit, God's chastisement and merciful deliverance of pious individuals constituted a paradigm. The dispersion and return were the present chastisement and future deliverance of the nation as a whole.

Resurrection and eternal life. The most striking instance of the belief in individual retribution appears in the rise of Jewish speculation about resurrection and eternal life. God delivers people not only from sickness and mortal danger, but also from unjust death. The precise origins of such beliefs are obscure. However, early texts like 1 Enoch, Daniel, and 2 Maccabees indicate that ideas about resurrection and eternal life are rooted in the conviction that God is just. Moreover, these particular expressions of faith blossomed in situations like the persecution by Antiochus. The pious see that, contrary to traditional teaching, righteous conduct can lead to death and apostasy can save one from death. Of necessity, therefore, divine justice will occur after death.

Early Jewish speculation about post-mortem retribution varies greatly with respect to the scope, timing, and nature of this retribution. Who will rise from the dead: some or all of the righteous, some or all of the wicked? Will there be a resurrection of the body or of the spirit? Will the dead rise on a future day of judgment, or do they receive their reward immediately after death?

Messianic belief and the lack of it. Christian readers of the Bible tend to suppose that *the* Jews awaited *the* Messiah, a future ruler from the house of David, who would drive Israel's enemies from the land and establish his reign in Jerusalem. Evidence for such speculation can be found, notably, in the seventeenth of the Psalms of Solomon.

In the light of such assertions, it is instructive to observe that among the Apocrypha only 2 Esdras expresses such a belief. Otherwise, these authors develop scenarios of future divine deliverance and retribution without positing the presence of a future Davidic king. Other texts in the Pseudepigrapha and Dead Sea Scrolls complicate the problem. Agents of divine deliverance have a variety of pedigrees: a Davidic messiah; an anointed high priest; a pair of messianic figures, or one figure who is both king and priest; a prophet (so also 1 Maccabees); the archangel Michael; or a transcendent heavenly figure who combines features attributed to Second Isaiah's Servant of the Lord, the Davidic king in Isaiah 11 and Psalm 2, and "one like a son of man" in Daniel 7. Still other texts await the final, unmediated appearance of God as judge. Thus, in the case of "messianic" speculation, the Apocrypha belie a common stereotype of early Judaism, but they also reveal only a small part of a complex picture (see further, Nickelsburg and Stone, 1983, 161–201).

TRADITION AND SCRIPTURE: THE DEVELOPMENT OF ISRAEL'S RELIGIOUS HERITAGE

As the writers of the Apocrypha interacted with their environment and historical circumstances, they drew on the long religious heritage embodied in the Torah and the Prophets. In a way they were interpreting and expounding texts that were in the process of becoming canonical Scripture. Such exposition, however, grew out of a living tradition. One did not simply go to a text, quote it, and interpret it. Rather, the Apocrypha, Pseudepigrapha, and Dead Sea Scrolls reflect moments in a long, continuous process of religious reflection, speculation, and interpretation. This process was closely tied to texts that were gradually taking on authority as Scripture, but these texts themselves were crystallizations of earlier tradition.

The Torah

The Apocrypha attest the centrality of the Torah and some of the new and different ways that Torah was construed in the Greco-Roman period. It is true, of course, that the Jerusalem hellenizers of *ca.* 200–165 B.C.E. made many concessions regarding the Mosaic Torah and that more compromise followed when Antiochus IV forbade the observance of the Torah. Nonetheless, according to the view that prevailed, the Torah was a sine qua non of Jewish existence and identity.

How Torah was understood and interpreted is another matter. Traditional bodies of legal interpretation certainly existed, but the Apocrypha only hint at these. The Book of Judith reflects kinds of piety that move beyond the letter of the Pentateuch. Tobit emphasizes the importance of almsgiving and other responsible use of one's wealth. Remarkable in both Tobit and Sirach is the use of proverbs to exhort one to pious conduct. The focus is not on *halakhah*—specific prescriptions for right conduct in specific instances. Rather, the sage uses poetic proverbial forms to encourage obedience to the commandments and to stress the reality of divine reward and punishment. In a more "intellectual" vein, other writers embody their ethical advice and exhortation in the forms of Greek philosophy.

What the Apocrypha do not indicate with any clarity is the great diversity in the early Jewish understanding of the Torah. Jews agreed in principle that the divine will had been expressed and that Torah was to be obeyed, but they often disagreed on what constituted the specifics of Torah. The author of the Book of Jubilees and some of the Essene writers of the Dead Sea Scrolls propounded specific interpretations of the Mosaic Torah stricter than those that were current elsewhere in Judaism or that would appear later in Pharisaism. Moreover, they asserted that these

interpretations were divine in origin, and, in the case of Jubilees, written from eternity on heavenly tablets. Other writers maintained that long before Moses brought the Torah from Mount Sinai, the patriarch Enoch had ascended to heaven and had been given revelations of the divine will, which he recorded in documents that constituted a Torah parallel to the Mosaic Torah.

One common Christian stereotype requires brief comment here. It is the idea that Judaism in the Greco-Roman period was sterile, legalistic, and perfectionistic—in contrast to both the vital religion of the prophets and the Christian emphasis on the centrality of faith. The texts of the Apocrypha belie this notion. Obedience to the Torah is encouraged without quoting the minutiae of the laws. The righteous one makes no claims to perfection and finds adequate resources for atonement and forgiveness. Faith is not opposed to Torah obedience; indeed, such obedience is often portrayed as the enactment of one's faith in the God who demands faithful conduct and rewards it.

Traditional Sources for Speculation About Divine Justice

Like their interpretations of Torah, the Jews' speculations about divine deliverance and justice are rooted in their religious past. Even in their most innovative forms, these beliefs were understood to derive from the Mosaic and prophetic texts.

In some cases, references to biblical texts are explicit. The authors of Baruch and 2 Maccabees cite Deuteronomy to explain their present predicament and future hope. The prayer in Daniel 9 interprets a passage in Jeremiah.

Elsewhere dependence is clear even if it is not explicit. Although Deuteronomy may not be cited, its retributive scheme of sin-punishment-repentance-salvation is evident in many texts. Moses' words explain not only the exile and the return from Babylon, but also the disastrous events contemporary with the authors of the Apocrypha. Baruch and Tobit use the traditions about Mother Zion in Second and Third Isaiah without explicitly citing or quoting the prophets.

Especially remarkable are texts about resurrection and eternal life. In 2 Maccabees 7, three strands of the theology of Second Isaiah (Isa 40–55) are transformed from a communal reference to exile and return to a description of individual suffering and vindication (Nickelsburg 1981, 120–121). In the resurrection the creator re-creates and redeems, the children of Mother Zion are returned, and the servants of the Lord are vindicated. This last interpretation has also influenced the wording and literary shape of the story of the persecuted and exalted righteous spokesman of God in Wisdom of Solomon 2–5. However, different from the materialistic imagery of bodily resurrection in 2 Maccabees 7, in Wisdom it is the immortal souls of the righteous that will be vindicated after death. This notion draws on Greek religious and philosophical speculation. Thus Jewish interpretation of sacred tradition is expressed in gentile idiom and conception. The mixture is typical of that syncretistic age.

CONCLUSION

The literature of the Apocrypha is unique in the compass of the works discussed in these volumes because, unfortunately, it is little studied and its significance is scarcely appreciated. History tends to move in continuous increments and not by leaps and bounds. For the Jews and Christians the texts of the Apocrypha witness to a crucial period of history, in which the ancient heritage developed and new transformations—whether rabbinic or Christian— were facilitated. A careful study of these transitional texts and their contexts helps to provide a healthy corrective to the inaccurate, romanticizing claims for one's own tradition and the unfair, stereotypical devaluation of the other's that have often marred Jewish-Christian interactions.

One's religious heritage and inclinations aside, these texts give access to fixed points in the history of Western humanity. Through the window they provide, one can perceive and experience significant moments in the human past. Occasionally, the story can touch or irritate or provoke us, the aesthetics can delight us, and the speculation and reasoning can stimulate new insights or challenge old ones. Such occasions help to justify the reading of the Apocrypha as a humanistic undertaking.

Bibliography

Texts

Charlesworth, James H., ed. *The Old Testament Pseudepigrapha.* 2 vols. Garden City, N.Y., 1983–1985. Annotated translations of the Pseudepigrapha with introductions. Includes works of both Jewish and Christian authorship, as well fragments of otherwise lost texts.

May, Herbert G., and Bruce M. Metzger, eds. *The New Oxford Annotated Bible with the Apocrypha.* Revised Standard Version. Expanded Edition. New York, 1977. The texts of the Apocrypha can be found in most recent English editions of the Bible, and frequently under separate cover. This edition is especially useful because it contains the works accepted by the Eastern Orthodox churches. Its excellent general introduction complements the present essay.

Nickelsburg, George W. E., and Michael E. Stone. *Faith and Piety in Early Judaism: Texts and Documents.* Philadelphia, 1983. Selections from early Jewish texts arranged topically to illustrate the variety in early Judaism.

Sparks, H. F. D. *The Apocryphal Old Testament.* Oxford, 1984. A handy pocket edition of the Pseudepigrapha. Not nearly as extensive a collection as that edited by Charlesworth.

Vermes, Geza. *The Dead Sea Scrolls in English.* 3d edition. Harmondsworth, 1987. English translation of most of the major published Scrolls.

Introductions

Kraft, Robert A., and George W. E. Nickelsburg, eds. *Early Judaism and Its Modern Interpreters.* Philadelphia, 1986. A history of post–World War II scholarship on early Judaism, which documents many of the generalizations in this essay.

Nickelsburg, George W. E. *Jewish Literature Between the Bible and the Mishnah.* Philadelphia, 1981. An introduction to almost all the Apocrypha and the major Pseudepigrapha and Dead Sea Scrolls. Discussed in their historical context with special emphasis on literary matters.

Schürer, Emil. *The History of the Jewish People in the Age of Jesus Christ (175 B.C.–A.D. 135).* Revised and edited by Géza Vermès, Fergus Millar, Matthew Black, and Martin Goodman. 3 vols. Edinburgh, 1973–1986. Introduction to the history and literature of Judaism. Volume 3, in two parts, is even more exhaustive than Compendia 2.2.

Stone, Michael E., ed. *Jewish Writings of the Second Temple Period.* Compendia Rerum Iudaicarum ad Novum Testamentum 2.2. Philadelphia, 1984. Introduction to a wide selection of Jewish writings, discussed by genre or author rather than in historical context.

GEORGE W. E. NICKELSBURG

I Esdras

THE GREEK BOOK of 1 Esdras covers the history of Israel from the reform of Josiah to the reading of the law by Ezra. It contains an alternate form of the text of 2 Chronicles 35–36, Ezra 1–10, and Nehemiah 7:73–8:13 and an account of a contest in the court of Darius (1 Esdr 3:1–5:6) not attested elsewhere in the canonical Bible. The verse numbers employed throughout the discussion are those used in English Bibles; there are minor differences in versification in the Hebrew and Greek Bibles.

The book is called Esdras *a* (1 Esdras) in the Septuagint, where it is distinguished from Esdras *b* (2 Esdras), a literal Greek translation of the canonical books of Ezra and Nehemiah. 1 Esdras is called 3 Esdras in the Vulgate, where it, the Prayer of Manasseh, and 4 Esdras (2 Esdras in the RSV) are printed as a supplement to the New Testament. Jerome, the translator of the Vulgate, expressed himself in a way that explains this supplemental position: "You bring before me an apocryphal book which, under the name of Esdras, is read by you and those of your father. . . . I have never read the book: for what need is there to take up what the church does not receive?" (quoted in Myers 1974, 18).

The Greek text of 1 Esdras, though it is a relatively free translation, is based on an older and often shorter form of the Hebrew and Aramaic biblical text. Esdras *b* in the Septuagint is based on a Semitic text that closely resembles the later Masoretic text. The two translations are basically independent of one another (Hanhart 1974, 17–18).

The Book of 1 Esdras was used by Josephus for his account of the postexilic period in the *Antiquities* (11.1–158; for quotations of 1 Esdras by early Christian authors, see Myers 1974, 17–18), but the vocabulary and free translation style of 1 Esdras suggest that it may have been translated in the second century B.C.E. Unlike Esdras *b* in the Septuagint, 1 Esdras does not consistently employ the same Greek word as an equivalent for a given Hebrew or Aramaic word in the original text. The apparent correlations of 1 Esdras 4:40 with Daniel 2:37, and of 1 Esdras 4:59 with Daniel 2:22–23, support a second-century date. Charles Cutler Torrey (1910) identified Apame, the concubine of the king (1 Esdr 4:29), with the Persian wife of Ptolemy I and suggested a date of about 300 B.C.E. for the composition of 1 Esdras, but this identification of Apame did not gain general acceptance. The provenance of the book, in fact, is unknown and is not likely to be determined until the original extent and purpose of 1 Esdras are discovered.

The book may be outlined as follows:

1. The last years of Judah; the first years of the restoration (1:1–2:30)
   Josiah's passover (1:1–22)
   Reason for the fall of Judah (1:23–24)
   Death of Josiah (1:25–33)

Successors of Josiah and the destruction of
Jerusalem (1:34–58)
Cyrus' permission for the Judean exiles to go
home (2:1–5a)
The return under Sheshbazzar (2:5b–15)
Letters to and from Artaxerxes (2:16–30)
2. The contest of the bodyguards (3:1–5:6)
Debate about what thing is the strongest
(3:1–17)
Speech of the first bodyguard (3:18–24)
Speech of the second bodyguard (4:1–12)
Speech of the third bodyguard (4:13–41)
Zerubbabel's prize (4:42–57)
The Jewish response (4:58–63)
The leaders of the return (5:1–6)
3. The building of the Temple (5:7–7:15)
List of those who returned to Jerusalem
(5:7–46)
The altar and the Temple foundation
(5:47–65)
The building of the Temple stopped by
opponents (5:66–73)
The Temple completed (6:1–7:15)
4. The career of Ezra (8:1–9:55)
Ezra's trip to Jerusalem (8:1–67)
Crisis over mixed marriages (8:68–9:36)
Ezra's reading of the Law (9:37–9:55)

The relationship between 1 Esdras and other
portions of the canon may be diagramed as follows:

1:1–22   ≈ Chr 35:1–19
1:23–24 (without canonical parallel)
1:25–58   ≈ 2 Chr 35:20–36:21
2:1–5a   ≈ 2 Chr 36:22–23, Ezra 1:1–3a
2:5b–15   ≈ Ezra 1:3b–11
2:16–30   ≈ Ezra 4:7–24
3:1–5:6 (without canonical parallel)
5:7–73   ≈ Ezra 2:1–4:5
6:1–9:36   ≈ Ezra 5:1–10:44
9:37–55   ≈ Neh 7:73–8:13a

VARIATIONS FROM
THE CANONICAL TEXT

Except for the last pericope above, 1 Esdras omits
all of the Book of Nehemiah. Nehemiah 7:73–8:13a
is treated in 1 Esdras, probably correctly, as a part of
the story of Ezra, without mention of Nehemiah. The
reference to Nehemiah in Nehemiah 8:9 is often
considered secondary, and the name is lacking at the
corresponding verse in 1 Esdras (9:49). Nehemiah is
mentioned in 1 Esdras 5:40, but this reference too is
secondary (see Rudolph 1949, 20). The major addition to the canonical text in 3:1–5:6 recounts the
wisdom of Zerubbabel and explains why Darius, the
Persian king, authorized the return of the Jews from
Babylon to Jerusalem and their rebuilding of the
Temple, and why Darius supported financially and
legally the postexilic cult in Jerusalem. It also exalts
Zerubbabel and, implicitly, the Davidic line.

According to Ezra 4:7–24, criticisms from the
enemies of the Jews during the days of Artaxerxes I
(465–424 B.C.E.) led to the cessation of work on the
Temple, and this stoppage lasted until the time of
Darius I (522–486 B.C.E.), even though Artaxerxes
ruled *after* Darius. 1 Esdras partially unscrambled this
confusion by structuring the text, placing Darius'
efforts to stop the Temple (2:16–30; *cf.* Ezra 4:7–24)
before his decision to permit Zerubbabel to rebuild the
Temple (3:1–5:6). The confusion *within* 2:16–30
remains, although Josephus corrects the chronology
of the Persian kings by replacing Artaxerxes with
Cambyses and inserting Xerxes between Darius and
Artaxerxes (*cf. Antiquities* 11.21, 30, 120). In Ezra
both 4:8–24 and 5:1–6:18 are written in Aramaic
instead of Hebrew, and this suggests that the arrangement of materials in Ezra, despite its many historical
problems, is more original than that of 1 Esdras.

WHAT IS 1 ESDRAS?

To some scholars (Torrey, Pohlmann, Cross) 1
Esdras represents a fragmentary copy of an earlier
arrangement of the Chronicler's history. In this view
a translation of all or part of 1 Chronicles 1 through 2
Chronicles 34 has been lost from the beginning of 1
Esdras, and Nehemiah 8:13b–18, or even larger
portions of the book from the end. Frank Moore
Cross, for example, reconstructs three editions of the
Chronicler's history:
1. 1 Chronicles 10 to 2 Chronicles 36 plus Ezra 1:1 to
3:13;
2. 1 Chronicles 10 to 2 Chronicles 36 plus Ezra 1–10
and Nehemiah 8, that is, 1 and 2 Chronicles and
the text preserved in 1 Esdras;

3. 1 and 2 Chronicles, Ezra, and Nehemiah.

In his view, 1 Esdras is a fragment of edition 2, beginning with 2 Chronicles 35 and ending at the equivalent of Nehemiah 8:13 in the middle of a sentence ("And they came together . . ."). If 1 Esdras represents an earlier form of the Chronicler's history, the reading of the law at the conclusion of the restoration of the Temple and its cult in Nehemiah 8 (possibly continuing originally through the equivalent of Neh 8:18) could be seen as a religious reform analogous to the reforms of Hezekiah (2 Chr 29–30) and Josiah (2 Chr 35). Hezekiah's reform is linked to Solomon (2 Chr 30:26), Josiah's to Samuel (2 Chr 35:18), and Ezra's to Joshua and the events of the Exodus and conquest with which he is associated (Neh 8:17; *cf.* Pohlmann 1970, 147–148).

Subsequent studies, however, questioned whether there ever was a Chronicler's history consisting of a unified account of 1 and 2 Chronicles and Ezra (or Ezra and Nehemiah). H. G. M. Williamson argues that Nehemiah 8 was never the direct continuation of Ezra 10 in any other document except 1 Esdras, though he grants that it was associated historically with Ezra 7–10. Torrey proposed that Nehemiah 8 originally stood between Ezra 8 and Ezra 9. This produces a coherent chronology within the seventh year of Artaxerxes' reign: fifth month (Ezra 7:9), seventh month (Neh 7:73), ninth and tenth months (Ezra 10:9, 16). As commentaries and histories of Israel will make clear, there is a vigorous debate about whether this seventh year is from the time of Artaxerxes I or Artaxerxes II. The former would be 458 B.C.E.; the latter, 398 B.C.E. 1 Esdras betrays some knowledge of other parts of Nehemiah in addition to chapter 8. It contains a translation of Ezra 2–3, and these chapters presuppose the connection of all of Nehemiah 7 with Nehemiah 8. These connections contradict the idea that 1 Esdras represents a form of the Chronicler's history to which the Nehemiah materials had not yet been added (H. G. M. Williamson 1987, 38–42). Williamson and others, therefore, treat 1 Esdras as a document that has been *compiled* from the materials now in 1 and 2 Chronicles, Ezra, and Nehemiah. Proponents of the compilation hypothesis are divided on the question of whether 1 Esdras represents a complete book or whether it is only a fragment. Karl-Friedrich Pohlmann, who believes that 1 Esdras represents an early form of the Chronicler's history, offers arguments on the basis of form and content to suggest that the book must have begun with an equivalent of 2 Chronicles 34 (as does Williamson, who rejects the notion of a Chronicler's history) or even of all of 1 and 2 Chronicles (Pohlmann 1970, 32–33). Pohlmann also discounts the numerous attempts to identify the present ending as the original ending (1970, 34–35). Tamara Eskenazi finds an analogy to 1 Esdras' ending in mid-sentence in the ending of 2 Chronicles itself.

Those who affirm the integrity of the present book seek to understand what its author or editor might have wanted to say by the present arrangement of materials. Eskenazi, for example, believes that the author of 1 Esdras wanted to conform the books of Ezra and Nehemiah to the ideology of the books of Chronicles by giving special emphasis to the centrality of David, the inclusive characteristics of Israel, the doctrine of retribution, the need to obey the prophets, and the Temple and its cult. In her view 1 Esdras is a distinct composition by the persons, circle, or school responsible for the Books of Chronicles.

The centrality of David—so important in 1 and 2 Chronicles—is seen in 1 Esdras (3:1–5:6), where Zerubbabel is identified as a descendant of David (5:5), who played a decisive role in the return of the Jews to Jerusalem and the rebuilding of the Temple. In Ezra and Nehemiah, Zerubbabel is identified only as the son of Shealtiel without connecting the latter to the Davidic line (for support of the connection to David, see 1 Chr 3:17–24, Hag 2:23, and Zech 3:8). In 1 Esdras it is only after Zerubbabel's appearance in the story that a large number of Jews returned to Jerusalem. The royal heir, Zerubbabel, is responsible for everything good that happens; failures and false starts characterize the period before him. 1 Esdras also omits the disparaging comment about Zerubbabel's ancestor Solomon in Nehemiah 13:26. As is well known, there is no mention of Solomon's faults in 1 and 2 Chronicles.

Eskenazi finds a more hospitable attitude to foreigners in 1 Esdras than in Ezra-Nehemiah. When 1 Esdras describes the first meeting between those who had returned from exile and the peoples of the land (5:48–50; *cf.* Ezra 3:2–3), the author adds a crucial sentence that transforms the significance of the passage: "And some joined them from the other peoples of the land." 1 Esdras also softens the opposition to the returned exiles in 2:16–30. Jacob Myers observes, "The extended description of the opposition in Ezra 4:9–10 is curtailed; only the few bare essentials are given—almost as if the interracial character of the Samaritan community were deliberately played down" (Myers 1974, 42).

The emphasis on retribution and the need to obey the prophets is provided by a small modification in 1:28, where 1 Esdras reads: "Josiah . . . did not heed the words of Jeremiah the prophet from the mouth of the Lord." The corresponding passage in 2 Chronicles 35:22 reads: "Josiah . . . did not listen to the words of Neco from the mouth of God." 1 Esdras stresses that Josiah died because he did not listen to divine words mediated through a prophet, unlike the Chronicles text in which the mediator is Neco, an Egyptian king. Retribution is also a central theme in 1:23–24.

By omitting the Nehemiah memoirs, 1 Esdras keeps the reader's focus more closely on the Temple and its cult. The Temple is mentioned forty-seven times in chapters 1–7, compared with forty-one times in the parallels of Chronicles and Ezra.

Anne E. Gardner has attempted, less successfully in my judgment, to relate 1 Esdras as a complete book to the events and people of the Maccabean crisis. In her view the reinterpretation of the death of Josiah in 1:23–24, shows that this disaster, too, like the persecution of the Jews in the second century B.C.E., was the result of sin and not of divine caprice. The insertion of the story of the three bodyguards was to show that all the riches and power in the world are of no interest compared to rebuilding the Temple. The Temple's central importance is also emphasized by the fact that the book begins and ends in the Temple, or at least in its vicinity. Most of the material in Nehemiah, according to this hypothesis, was left out because it had little relevance to the Maccabean crisis.

Harold W. Attridge has speculated that the continuity between the old and new Temples, emphasized in 1 Esdras, may have played some role in the polemics of the second century between the Jerusalem Temple and its rivals, the Oniad temple at Leontopolis in Egypt and the Tobiad temple at Araq-el-Amir in Transjordan.

THE CONTENT OF THE MAJOR ADDITIONS

Whether the book is fragmentary or complete, whether its order represents an earlier form of the Chronicler's history or a compilation drawn from the canonical books, this much is certain: the additions in 1:23–24 and 3:1–5:6 would seem to offer the best clues to the document's significance.

The words of 1:23–24 are a supplement based on 1 Kings 13:2, 32 (a prophecy of the rise of Josiah) or 2 Kings 23:24–27 (a summary of Josiah's reign, including a reference to the wickedness of Manasseh that made the destruction of Judah inevitable). They explain that the evil of the *people* at the time of Josiah was so great that the judgmental words of God eventually had to rise up against Israel. Without these verses a reader might conclude that the great piety of Josiah ought to have prevented the final destruction of Jerusalem, which occurred a few years after his death. Torrey believed that these two verses were part of the original text of Chronicles and were accidentally dropped out of the text.

The addition in 3:1–5:6 places great emphasis on the Davidide Zerubbabel and explains why the Persian Darius was moved to authorize the rebuilding of the Temple. Most scholars agree that the passage was originally composed in a Semitic language, probably Aramaic. (The frequent use of the Greek word "then" seems a literal translation of an Aramaic expression and is not idiomatic in the Greek language.) Pohlmann suggests that the passage was added to the book some time after the original translation was made, since he detects differences in word choice between the original translator and the interpolator (1970, 50–51, 150–151). W. Th. In der Smitten, however, believes this section was always an integral part of the Book of 1 Esdras.

The contest of the bodyguards in 3:1–5:6 is perhaps the most memorable portion of 1 Esdras. King Darius prepares a great banquet for all the officials of the Persian empire, which stretched from India to Ethiopia (3:1–17; *cf.* Esth 1:1, 8:9). While there is a hint that the king was bothered by insomnia (3:3), he seems to be asleep during the initial contest among the bodyguards (3:13). Strangely, the bored bodyguards determine for themselves what prizes the king will award in the contest (3:5–7). Whoever comes up with the wisest answer about what is strongest is to receive fine clothing, a gold bed, and an exalted position as "kinsman" of the king. In his narration of this story the historian Josephus has the king himself propose the contest and promise the rewards (*Antiquities* 11.34–36).

The bodyguards decide to put their proposals under the king's pillow and to abide by the decision about the winner that he and the three nobles of Persia will make. The first two bodyguards propose wine and the king as the two strongest things in all the world. The third suggests that women are the strongest but then changes his answer and proposes that truth is strongest, since it is the victor over all things.

When the king wakes up and learns about the contest, he summons all his officials and orders the three bodyguards to explain the reasons for their opinions. Each speech of the bodyguards has a common introductory formula ("Gentlemen," followed by a rhetorical question), and each ends in a similar way ("He stopped speaking").

The first bodyguard argues that wine demonstrates its strength by equally leading astray the mind of all classes in society. Wine makes people forget sorrows or poverty, but it also makes people forget to be friendly. People drunk with wine fight, and when they sober up, they cannot remember what they have done. After exploring the ambiguities of wine, the wise bodyguard concludes that it must be the strongest thing since it forces people to do the things he has just described (3:18–24).

References to men as the strongest (4:2; *cf.* 4:14) lead some commentators to conclude that a speech about the strength of men is missing from the text. The second bodyguard's speech, however, concentrates primarily on the ambivalent qualities of kings. Kings get people to fight for them blindly and to turn over all their booty to the royal treasury. Soldiers hardly ever wonder whether the goal of the king's war justifies the supreme sacrifice. Farmers, too, are controlled by the king, who forces them to pay taxes on their produce. The word "obey" is prominent in this speech (see 3:3–12). People fight and farm for the king, even though he is only a man (3:7). In addition, the king eats, drinks, and sleeps like anyone else, and thus he is vulnerable. Yet people do not attack the king directly, nor do they abandon the king in order to take care of their own business (3:11). Seven times in verses 7–9, the second bodyguard notes that whatever the king commands, that is what his subjects do (4:1–12).

The speech of Zerubbabel, the third bodyguard (4:13–41), is the climactic moment in the book. The fact that Zerubbabel's name suddenly appears in verse 13 probably means that the contest among the bodyguards once served another (non-Jewish?) function before it was included in 1 Esdras. Zerubbabel first reviews the previous proposals about the strength of the king, men, and wine before turning to consider women and their strength. Since women are the originators of kings and other rulers by giving them birth, they are clearly superior to these political figures. Women also raise the men who plant vineyards, which in turn produce wine. Women make men's clothes and affect their reputations. Men who have accumulated all sorts of treasures drop them in open-mouthed amazement when they gaze at a beautiful woman. Men leave their parents and their native lands to live out their lives with their wives. Hence, the third bodyguard argues, women rule over men (4:22).

While soldiers are forced by the king's power to fight, men voluntarily undertake all sorts of military and dangerous adventures for the women they love. They face wild animals or even take up lives of crime so that they can lay their trophies at the feet of a woman. Many lose their minds because of women (4:26), while wine merely leads minds astray (3:18); many become slaves because of them, and perish or sin because of them.

Zerubbabel even dares to contrast the strength of women with that of King Darius (4:28–32). Although foreign lands fear the Persian king, his concubine Apame playfully takes his crown and puts it on her head and slaps the king with her left hand. The king looks at her in open-mouthed amazement like the rich men noted above (4:19). He laughs when she laughs; when she becomes angry, he flatters her. This defense of the strength of women is an incisive, if implicit, critique of the second bodyguard's proposal about the strength of kings.

Just when it seems as if the case is to be closed, while the king and his nobles look at one another, astonished at Zerubbabel's boldness and ready to make their decision (4:33), he begins to assert the superiority of truth as the strongest of all phenomena (*cf.* Pss 117:2, 146:6). Truth may connote rightness, steadfastness, and uprightness in addition to its usual meanings. Truth is a quality of God. Earth and heaven call upon and bless truth; all the previous candidates for the title of "strongest thing"—wine, theking, women, the sons of men and their works— are deemed unrighteous or deceptive. Because of their unrighteousness people die, but truth is strong and prevails forever and ever. Truth controls the strength, kingship, power, and majesty of all the ages (4:40; *cf.* 1 Chr 29:11–13 and the doxological conclusion to the Lord's Prayer). Truth is an impartial judge. That is why Zerubbabel was able to tell the truth about the king's subordination to his concubine in 1 Esdras 4:29–32. The praise of truth disarms any objections anyone might have to the bodyguard's comments on the king's conduct. Finally, Zerubbabel prays, "Blessed be the God of truth!" This prayer hints that God himself may even be stronger than truth (*cf.* 4:34–35a). Zerubbabel's speech leads the people to acclaim his answer. The Latin rendering of their cheer—"Magna est veritas et praevalet" (Great is truth and it will prevail)—has became a well-known proverb. In closing, Darius recognizes Zerubbabel as the wisest of his bodyguards and honors him as a kinsman (4:42; 3:7).

Thanks to the story of the three bodyguards, Zerubbabel becomes in 1 Esdras the most important person of the postexilic era (see Josephus). He is wise and pious, and loves the people. God gives him the wisdom that won the contest. As in Daniel, a Jew pits his wisdom against that of gentile rivals, he wins both the contest and the king's favor. His personal success and his favor with Darius do not make him forget his duty. Zerubbabel reminds the king of vows that he had made to rebuild Jerusalem and the Temple (a vow ascribed to Cyrus in 1 Esdr 2:1–9) and of Cyrus' plan to return the cultic vessels there. Though 1 Esdras 1:55 (≈2 Chr 36:14) reports that the kings of the Chaldeans destroyed the Temple, 1 Esdras 4:45 also

blames that action on the Edomites (*cf.* Ezek 36:5, Obad 11–14).

In his favorable reply Darius combines elements of the decree of Cyrus (Ezra 1:2–4, 6:3–5), his own affirmation of this decree (Ezra 6:6–12), and Artaxerxes' authorization of Nehemiah (Neh 2:5, 8). He grants Zerubbabel and the other returnees safe conduct, provides cedar wood from Lebanon to rebuild the Temple, and exempts the Jews from governmental searches of their houses. Darius also excuses the Jews from taxes and expels the Idumeans (Edomites) from their territory. He provides for annual grants for rebuilding the Temple and for maintaining the regular worship, perhaps hoping that sacrifices and prayers will be made for him and his sons (1 Esdr 6:31, Ezra 6:10). Like his predecessor Cyrus (Ezra 6:5), he commands that the Temple vessels be restored. In 1 Esdras and Ezra, the Temple vessels are returned by Sheshbazzar (1 Esdr 2:14–15 [≈Ezra 1:11], 1 Esdr 6:18–19 [≈Ezra 5:14–15]), in addition to Zerubbabel. The commandment to offer seventeen daily sacrifices (6:52) is unattested elsewhere in the Old Testament.

Zerubbabel (called only the "young man" in 4:58) offers appropriate thanksgiving to the King of Heaven, who granted him wisdom. When he shares the good news with other Jews in Babylon, they rejoice for seven days, a response more enthusiastic than historically seems to have been the case (4:58–63).

Darius provides the caravan with a cavalry escort of 1,000 and sends them off with martial music. The names in 5:5 show some confusion. Jeshua is the high priest of the early postexilic period (Ezra 3:2). The other figure, as the text should be read, is the governor, "Zerubbabel, son of Shealtiel, son of Jehoiachin, of the house of David" (1 Esdr 5:5). In the canonical Book of Ezra, as noted above, no mention is made of Zerubbabel's Davidic ancestry, perhaps because of the book's anti-eschatological stance, which was willing to accept Persian domination and had no salvific hopes tied to the house of David.

1 Esdras 5:57 is also an addition to the Hebrew text of Ezra 3:8: "And they laid the foundation of the temple of God on the new moon of the second month *in the second year* after they came to Judea and Jerusalem." Wilhelm Rudolph explains this as a gloss

that attempted to clarify chronological difficulties, though the italicized words were added even later and frustrated the author's intentions (1949, p. xii). The words "we found the elders of the Jews who had been in captivity building in the city of Jerusalem" in 1 Esdras 6:8–9 should be restored as original to the text of Ezra 5:8 (*cf.* Rudolph 1949, 50).

The supplementary materials in 1 Esdras have two primary purposes: they explain why God's judgment of Judah was necessary despite the piety of Josiah; and they attribute Darius' motivation in authorizing the rebuilding of the Temple to the heroic wisdom of Zerubbabel, a descendant of David.

Bibliography

Attridge, Harold W. "Historiography." In *Jewish Writings of the Second Temple Period.* Compendia Rerum Iudaicarum ad Novum Testamentum 2.2, edited by Michael E. Stone. Philadelphia, 1984. Pp. 157–160.

Crenshaw, James. "The Contest of Darius' Guards." In *Images of God and Man,* edited by David M. Gunn. Sheffield, England, 1981. Pp. 74–88.

Cross, Frank Moore. "A Reconstruction of the Judean Restoration." *Journal of Biblical Literature* 94 (1975): 4–18.

Eskenazi, Tamara C. "The Chronicler and the Composition of 1 Esdras." *Catholic Biblical Quarterly* 48 (1986): 39–61.

Gardner, Anne E. "The Purpose and Date of I Esdras." *Journal of Jewish Studies* 37 (1986): 18–27.

Hanhart, Robert. *Text und Textgeschichte des 1. Esrabuches.* Göttingen, 1974.

In der Smitten, W. Th. "Zur Pagenerzählung im 3. Esra (3 Esr. III,1–V,6)." *Vetus Testamentum* 22 (1972): 492–495.

Klein, Ralph W. "Studies in the Greek Texts of the Chronicler." Ph.D. diss., Harvard University, 1966.

Myers, Jacob M. *I and II Esdras.* Anchor Bible, vol. 42. Garden City, N.Y., 1974.

Nickelsburg, George W. E. "The Bible Rewritten and Expanded." In *Jewish Writings of the Second Temple Period.* Compendia Rerum Iudaicarum ad Novum Testamentum 2.2, edited by Michael E. Stone. Philadelphia, 1984. Pp. 131–135.

Pohlmann, Karl-Friedrich. *Studien zum dritten Esra.* Göttingen, 1970.

———. *Historische and legendarische Erzählungen: 3. Esra-Buch.* Jüdische Schriften aus hellenistisch-römischer Zeit 1. Gütersloh, 1980.

Rudolph, Wilhelm. *Esra und Nehemia samt 3. Esra.* Handbuch zum Alten Testament, vol. 20. Tübingen, 1949.

Torrey, Charles Cutler. *Ezra Studies.* Prolegomenon by W. F. Stinespring. 1910. Reprint. New York, 1970.

Williamson, H. G. M. *Ezra and Nehemiah.* Old Testament Guides. Sheffield, England, 1987.

RALPH W. KLEIN

II Esdras

THE APOCALYPSE OF EZRA was forged out of the fires set to the Temple in Jerusalem by the Romans (70 C.E.). The Temple had been desecrated the and burnt before during the preceding half-millennium, but this time the Romans did their work thoroughly and it has not been rebuilt since.

Long considered canonical by the Western church, this work is known as 4 Esdras or 4 Ezra in the Vulgate ("Esdras" is a Greek form of Ezra). It does not survive in Greek, and its status in the other Christian churches varies. The book was deleted from the Roman Catholic canon by the Council of Trent. Protestants consider it part of the Apocrypha under the title of the Second Book of Esdras, and it is as 2 Esdras that I shall refer to it here.

The creative interpretation of the destruction of the Temple in the generation that experienced it determined the future shape of Judaism. However, 2 Esdras, an extraordinary record of the religious experience of an individual faced with incomprehensible crisis, was not part of the heritage that Judaism carried into its long exile. It was nonetheless quickly adopted by Christianity and influenced many of the Christian churches. A similar fate befell several other Jewish works, called the Apocrypha and Pseudepigrapha.

The basic force driving the author of 2 Esdras was the problem of the justice of God. The Temple was the central, common institution of the whole Jewish people of Israel. How could a just God permit the destruction of his Temple and the suffering of his people? The book stands out from most contemporary treatments of this subject for its profundity and sensitivity, but it is written in a genre and style that are strange to modern men and women. We must learn to appreciate them before we can understand the book.

Second Esdras is an apocalypse, a type of Jewish religious literature that arose probably in the fourth or third century B.C.E. The apocalypses are reports of visions or revelations in which God or an angel imparts secrets of heaven and earth, of time and the cosmos, of creation and redemption. Although they arise from biblical prophecy, the apocalypses constitute a distinct genre with literary conventions and forms bizarre to many of us. They are virtually never attributed to the person who wrote them, but to ancient biblical heroes. Moreover, the revealed information is often said to have been seen by this pseudepigraphical hero in a symbolic form or an allegory, often as a vision or a dream. Thus, even an author of intensely personal writings hides behind a mask and expresses his ideas in the form of dreams and symbols.

The core of 2 Esdras is a single composition, the fruit of one creative mind. Chapters 1 and 2 as well as 15 and 16 were added long after the original work was composed, when 2 Esdras was adapted for Christian use. The writer of the original used some preexisting sources, and he certainly operated within a rather rigid literary tradition, which he subordinates to his own plan and intention. He set forth his experience as seven visions, each distinct and separate from one another. The first three visions present the seer's movement from his initial quandary, pain, and bewilderment to a measure of understanding. This pattern is abruptly broken and brought to crisis and resolution in the powerful experience of the fourth vision. Two dreams follow, at the end of which Ezra sings the Almighty's praise. The seventh vision, the story of the revelation of Torah to Ezra, concludes the book.

EZRA'S VISIONS

Vision 1 (3:1–5:20)

At the very beginning, the pain and the problem break forth. Chapter 3 is an address by Ezra to God. It is not a prayer for God's mercy—rather Ezra is hurt and angry. It is thirty years after the destruction of Jerusalem. He is in Babylon on his bed lamenting the destruction of Zion when he feels inspired to speak "fearsome things" before the Most High.

Each of the first four visions commences with a similar description: Ezra is weeping and mourning; suddenly inspiration seizes him and he speaks to God. He is not said to be among the people or in a public place but on his bed at night. Yet what befalls him is not a dream but a different type of experience. Later, when he does dream (in Visions 5 and 6), he is quite conscious of it.

Ezra reproaches God for Zion's fate. You created humankind, he says in effect; you allow humans to sin and then you punish them for sinning. You continually gave them hope—you saved Noah, elected Abraham, redeemed Israel, even descended to reveal the Torah to them. However, you did not grant them the ability to observe the Torah and to fulfill their hope, and then you punished them for disobeying. Your way of running the world, Ezra declares, leads directly to the destruction of Zion.

Suddenly Ezra stops. What things he has said! What an indictment! In Scripture, it is usually God who blames Israel for sinning, and God's punishment of Israel for disobedience is considered both just and justified. How different is Ezra, as he angrily rebukes the Creator. "Terrible words" they truly are, for they challenge the basic axiom of Israelite and Jewish

thought: that God is just in his dealings with humans. God's past actions toward Israel, Ezra says, do not show divine grace but exhibit divine injustice. They have led directly to the destruction.

Even on relative grounds, he argues, Israel should not have been punished. Is Israel worse than Babylon? Has any nation been wholly righteous? At least Israel has tried (3:28–36)!

Ezra has made his accusation and an angel appears to respond to it (4:1). No dramatic events surround the angel's appearance—suddenly he is there reproaching Ezra for wishing to understand the "way of the Most High," God's way of governing the world (4:2). He does not desire to know that, Ezra responds, but rather simple things—why the fate of Israel is what it is (4:22–25)? Some people have argued that the angel and Ezra represent two different groups within Judaism—a skeptical one (Ezra) and a traditional one (the angel). More persuasive is the view that the whole of the discussion with the angel is an externalization of Ezra's internal conflict. He both confronts the tradition and affirms it; the drama of the first part of the book is Ezra's move from complete doubt to partial acceptance of the divine decree.

Ezra's dialogues with the angel throughout the first three visions may be divided into two types—disputes in which he argues with the angel and predictive dialogues in which he asks simple questions to elicit information about the future. The structures of the first three visions are parallel. They open with Ezra's address, go on to a dialogic dispute, move from that to dialogic predictions, and conclude with a direct prediction set in the mouth of the angel.

The basic solution that the angel offers Ezra is that the way of the Most High will prove just at the end of days. The dialogic prediction of Vision 1 (4:26–52) turns on the question of when the end will come. Again and again the angel tells him that it is predetermined. Like a woman's womb, the world will birth its future when its term is full. By the end of the dialogue Ezra has accepted the truth of this. Now he asks: if there is to be an end and if its coming is predetermined, what signs will indicate that it is close? The angel tells him of the terrible events that will precede the end, expressing the widely held belief that evil would reach an unprecedented peak before the coming of redemption.

Vision 2 (5:21–6:34)

The second vision is preceded by a fast and by Ezra's inspired address. This time, the election of Israel is the issue, and it is discussed in language of love and hate: "If thou dost really hate thy people, they should be punished at thy own hands" (5:30; RSV). A dialogue ensues, and although Ezra has partially accepted the idea that events are fixed in advance, he cries once more for vindication. Again he is told that the end cannot be hastened; the process of judgment was created with the world, and it is inherent in the very course of world history.

In the dialogic parts of this vision, Ezra does not argue as strongly as in Vision 1. The opening address is in poetic diction. In a delicate way, using repetitive formulaic language, the election of Israel is described. Each image represents the choicest of a species (the vine, the lily, the Jordan, Zion, the dove, and the sheep). Yet these symbols are skillfully chosen, for they simultaneously evoke imagery used in the Bible to talk about Israel (5:23–28). The predictive dialogue also concludes with a poem on creation marked by a repetitive series of lines beginning with the word "before" (6:1–5). God's reminder that before creating all the world "I planned these things [i.e., judgment] and they were made through me and not through another" (6:6) culminates in a prediction of the end of the age and redemption.

One might think that at this point the author had achieved his goal. Starting in Vision 1 from a problem of theodicy, questioning God's justice in governing the world, he came to accept the idea that God's way in the world is incomprehensible. He became concerned as to when the vindication would come and was provided with signs of its approach (Vision 1).

Vision 2 seems to regress; the problem of Israel is reformulated in terms of election rather than divine justice. But has not the issue already been resolved in Vision 1? It seems not. Ezra certainly does not again exhibit the acute questioning he did in Vision 1, but his mind is clearly not at ease. In one sense, the revelation of redemption with which Vision 2 concludes already bears within it the answers to all the questions that have been asked and will be asked. Yet the book is not a systematic theology but the odyssey

of a soul, and though the answer has been proffered, Ezra's soul is not yet ready to accept it. Instead the seer launches into the address that opens the unusually long third vision.

Vision 3 (6:35–9:25)

The third vision is composed of three "subvisions," each of which is structured like Visions 1 and 2. The writer's artistry, combining literary balance and conceptual insight, once again is evident. Vision 2 opened with a poem on election and its dialogues concluded with a poem on creation highlighting the idea of election. The seer's address at the beginning of Vision 3 is a recital of creation that climaxes in the idea of election: "If the world has indeed been created for us, why do we not possess our world as an inheritance?" (6:59).

The same emphasis on creation and the relation between creation and election recurs in the monologue and prayer with which the third subvision opens (8:4–36). Creation and election form a pair of sustained thematic motifs that hold the whole together. The combination of creation and election is significant. Often people contrast two dimensions of Jewish teaching about the future—the universal, touching on all human beings, and the national, relating to the fate of Israel. Yet, these two concepts never existed separately. God's future redemptive activity was always seen through the patterns of God's two great past acts of redemption, the creation and the Exodus, one universal and the other national. The two are tightly intertwined in the author's thought for together they express God's grace. At the conceptual and developmental level, this evocation of the prior themes indicates that, though Ezra has accepted the idea of predestination and of the future vindication, he is still not at peace.

In the dialogue (7:1–25) that follows the initial address of Vision 3, the author moves from a preoccupation exclusively with Israel to a concern with the righteous and the wicked. Two parables of the broad and the narrow are told. The world that was created for Israel, they hint, may be the world to come and not this world at all. The angel concludes by stressing that the wicked disobeyed God's commandments, and therefore "empty things are for the empty, and full things are for the full" (7:25).

No questions ensue; nothing intervenes between the dialogue and a remarkable prophecy of the coming Day of Judgment, when the righteous will receive their reward and the wicked their punishment (7:26–44). In this eschatological prophecy the author's ideas about the end of days are set forth systematically. It complements the prophecies of woe and redemption with which the first two visions had concluded. The heavenly Jerusalem, the ideal city preserved on high, will be revealed. Then the Messiah will come and rule over all the righteous of the last generation for four hundred years. He will then die, together with all those whom he ruled, and the earth will revert to primordial chaos from which, after seven days, a new world will issue. The resurrection of all the dead, both righteous and wicked, will take place. God will appear in judgment to reprove the wicked and praise the righteous. There follows a remarkable description of that Day of Judgment—all the natural seasons and luminaries will disappear, only the splendor of the glory of the Most High will remain, by which all shall see what has been prepared for them. It will last seven years, we are told.

This description combines the "national" elements of the Messiah ruling the righteous in the land of Israel, and the "universal" elements of the general resurrection and the Day of Judgment, when all people are judged for their deeds.

Ezra has advanced one more step. He accepts the fate that awaits the righteous and wicked, and he has learned that fate in detailed and graphic form. He questions neither divine justice nor the course of events. But his acceptance of the idea of reward and punishment raises the issue that is to dominate the rest of the long vision, that of the few and the many (7:45–74). How is it, Ezra asks, that God created so many people in the world and will redeem so few? The apparent inequity has become terribly acute precisely because reward and punishment have been promised. Few will be saved but many will perish, the angel informs him, and God rejoices over the precious few and does not grieve over the many sinners who perish (7:49–61).

Ezra responds not with a question, but with a lament. What a terrible fate this is! No note of argument is to be found, no questioning of God's justice is explicit, only distress (7:62–69). The angel

asserts, once more, that the wicked are responsible for their own fate (therefore, he implies, what is Ezra upset about?).

Ezra seeks some respite for the many who will suffer (7:75–99). What will be the state of the righteous and wicked, he asks, after death, but before resurrection? The angel replies that they will straightway enter into reward and punishment respectively. This remarkable passage sets forth an additional aspect of the author's teaching about eschatology by describing in detail the postmortem fate of souls. Although no similar descriptions are known, the passage reads as if it was drawn from a manual or handbook, since it starts and concludes with clear teaching formulas (7:78 and 7:99). It offers no relief from the sternness of the decree.

Again Ezra tries to find a basis for moderating this severity. Will there be intercessory prayer on the Day of Judgment? Can the righteous pray for the wicked on that day? This possibility for alleviating the fate of the wicked is also closed to him (7:100–115). True, intercession and prayer have an important role in *this* age, the angel tells him, but on the Day of Judgment each person must bear the consequences of his or her own deeds.

Again the seer laments, asking what the purpose of reward is when "we" have sinned (7:116–126). Once more the angel asserts that humans have a choice, the wicked bear the responsibility for their own fate. In all this discussion, then, from 7:45 on, the angel repeats his initial words to the seer: on the Day of Judgment the righteous will be rewarded for their deeds, the wicked punished for theirs. There is no escape.

The seer is not at peace yet, so he takes another tack. Instead of argument or questions, he resorts to petition and prayer. In 7:132–140 he expounds the famous verses from Exodus 34:6–7 that came to express so much of the Jewish concept of God (the "13 *Middot*"). God is called merciful, Ezra propounds, because he *is* merciful; consequently, there must be mercy for the wicked. The angel responds, "Many have been created, but few shall be saved" (2 Esdr 8:3). Then Ezra prays, asserting that God is responsible for the creation of human beings, for their wondrous complexity, and for their education and training (8:4–19). Why did God create human beings only to destroy them? Humans have sinned, and the judgment is inexorable. Therefore, Ezra prays, please grant mercy.

The famous Prayer of Ezra ensues, in which he combines praise of God's might, confession of sins, and an impassioned appeal for divine mercy (8:19b–36). The angel responds to this prayer in 8:37–62. Most humans have sinned, they bear the responsibility for their sin, and they will be punished. God will rejoice over the few who are saved, that is what is significant rather than the multitude that will perish. The position of the angel (God's representative, who often speaks as if he were God) has not changed throughout the whole vision. The unique element here is that Ezra and those who are like him, that is, the righteous, will be rewarded.

In the course of all this questioning and arguing, Ezra does not question the way God conducts the world, "the way of the Most High" (except rather mildly in 8:4–36). He has assented to the angel's basic teachings. Yet the lot of humans seems to him pointless and out of tune both with God's character as merciful and with the actual work of creation. Humans were formed with God's own hands. Will God treat them like seed, some of which germinates and some of which does not? Ezra even implies that just as God is responsible for the rain that determines the fate of the seeds, so God is responsible for the conditions that determine the fate of human beings.

The angel stresses and restresses the fact that God rejoices in the reward of the righteous and does not grieve over the fate of the sinners. He rejects Ezra's argument from creation, posed in 8:4–19, with the words "I will not concern myself about the fashioning of those who have sinned . . . but I will rejoice over the creation of the righteous" (8:38–39).

The conditions of this world are irrelevant for those who will inherit the world to come, the angel says (8:46). You, Ezra, he continues, are one of those and although your concern expresses love for humankind, you love them much less than God, whose love is expressed in his very rejoicing over the righteous and his rewarding them (8:46–47). Your concern for the wicked is misplaced; you should instead rejoice in your own reward and that of the other righteous. That reward is detailed in a list of the elements of eschatological goods (8:51–54). Again the angel repeats his

argument—the wicked have determined their own fate; not only did they act wickedly, they despised and denied the Most High and they persecuted the righteous (8:57). They did this, knowing the fate that awaited them: "For just as the things which I have predicted await you, so the thirst and torment which are prepared await them" (8:59).

Ezra's appeal for compassion in the final judgment is rejected. Until the judgment, the complementary qualities of mercy and repentance are active and available. In judgment they are withdrawn. In judgment, humans bear the responsibility for their own sins, and in judgment God does not grieve for their fate. Nor should Ezra; he should rejoice in the reward of the righteous. The theme of Ezra's own righteousness is raised and strikingly repeated in 8:47–62. This is the point of the passage, as is indicated by Ezra's docile acceptance of it and his turning, in 8:63, to detailed questions about signs of the end. In the first two visions, such requests for signs indicated that Ezra had reached a new understanding. This is the first such request in the long third vision. It signifies that the issue of the few and the many is moving toward a resolution. A new stage has been reached here in Ezra's understanding. The promise of reward to Ezra and to those like him is part of this process. Therefore he is willing and eager to receive the revelation of further details about the signs.

The emphasis on Ezra's righteousness is worth considering. In 7:76 Ezra is told not to reckon himself among the wicked. The angel emphasizes his position as a paradigmatic righteous one (the righteous are those "who are like him"). His own fate, his eternal life, is predicted. The problem of the few and the many is resolved—the many perish not as God's responsibility but as their own. The few will be rewarded, and Ezra is one of them.

Two classical apocalyptic themes, which often occur at the end of apocalyptic revelations, conclude the pericope. The end is near, and only to Ezra and the few righteous alone have the signs of its coming been revealed (9:1–22).

Vision 4 (9:26–10:59)

The fourth vision is a turning point in the book. It is connected in many ways with that which preceded, but clearly signals that new events are also going to happen. In its introduction the familiar themes of the seer's distress and the onset of speech can be observed, yet Ezra is now in a new location, in a field outside the city, where he remains throughout Visions 5, 6, and 7. The pattern of seven days is maintained as before the three preceding visions (see 5:13 and 6:35; a seven-day fast before the first vision is not mentioned in 3:1–2, but is clearly implied by 6:35). He no longer fasts, however, but abstains from meat and wine, partaking solely of the flowers of the field. This practice stands between the complete fasting that precedes the first three visions, and the absence of any dietary discipline at all in the fifth and sixth.

When the inspiration comes upon him, he addresses God about the concept of Torah. He patterns his exhortation partly on biblical expressions, such as "Hear O Israel" (Deut 5:1, 6:4, 9:1, 20:3), giving it a very solemn atmosphere. His concern is refocused. He has left behind the difficulties flowing from the divine governance of the world, the issues of the few and the many, or those of theodicy, and has accepted the angel's position presented in the previous visions. Yet his mind is not completely at ease, and he raises questions of anomalies inherent in the concept of Torah.

Torah was given but not observed. That fact has affected only the vessel that receives and contains the Torah (the human heart), for the Torah, given by divine glory (3:19) to glorify humans (9:31), remains in its glory even if the humans perish (9:37). Torah is a divine gift; it has a heavenly essence yet it is disobeyed, and humans will perish on account of their disobedience.

Most strikingly, the vision that ensues does not constitute a response to these real issues in the writer's thought. This fact is inexplicable on literary grounds in a composition by a very skilled author, and perhaps it reflects an actual change in his real experience, for suddenly the unexpected happens.

Ezra, in the field (9:38), sees a woman weeping, with rent clothing and ashes on her head, the traditional signs of mourning. "Then I dismissed the thoughts with which I had been engaged and turned to her" (9:39, cf. 10:5), Ezra says, and abandons the subject of the Torah. Indeed, it is not just his train of thought about Torah that he abandons, but the very

questions that have preoccupied him since the start of the book. A turning point has been reached. The woman explains that she is grieving sorely. Barren for thirty years, she prayed to God, who eventually granted her a son. She, her husband, and their neighbors rejoiced greatly, and raised him with care. But on the joyous evening of his nuptials, he entered the bridal chamber and fell down dead. She mourned until the second evening, when she fled to the field, resolved to fast there and to mourn until her death.

This tale, which resembles the biblical story of the birth of Samuel (1 Sam 1), has been thought to have been drawn from folklore. It was apparently taken over without its original ending, which might have included the revival of the son (compare 10:16 and 2 Kgs 4:18–37).

The parallels between the woman and Ezra are most suggestive. Redemption is promised to Ezra after thirty years (3:1), just as the woman receives the grace of a child after the same period of time (9:43). Moreover, her fasting, weeping, and mourning her loss are exactly like Ezra's conduct described in the narratives intervening between Vision 1 and 2 and between Visions 2 and 3. Later the parallel is completed: not only does the woman play Ezra's former role, but Ezra plays the angel's. He changes from the one comforted to the one who gives comfort.

Ezra's new role as comforter is skillfully indicated by a series of close literary parallels between his function and that formerly held by the angel (10:6 ‖ 4:2, 5:33, 10:9 ‖ 7:54, 10:12–14 ‖ 5:51–55, 10:15–17 ‖ 5:13, 6:30–34, 9:23–25). This reversal of roles became possible once Ezra accepted fully what the angel said to him in the previous visions. Even at the very end of Vision 3, Ezra still had difficulty in assenting unquestioningly to the clear implications of the angel's teachings about the few and the many. In 10:10, however, he comforts the woman with the words that "almost all go to perdition, and a multitude of them are destined for destruction." Since this is the fate of most humans, and since Zion is mourning her children, how can she grieve so for the loss of a single child? What is striking is that this teaching Ezra offers to the woman is precisely that which he refused to accept at the end of the previous vision, that is, that few are saved and many damned.

Ezra's acceptance of the consolation the angel

offered him earlier is even more thoroughgoing than first appears. He declares: "For, if you acknowledge the decree of God to be just, you will receive your son back in due time" (10:16). In the wonderful address with which Vision 1 opens Ezra had cast deep doubt on the justice of God's action; he now holds out God's very justice to the woman as the beginning of comfort. Recognition of God's justice will bring her son back "in due time." Ezra's promise of restoration of the woman's son here corresponds to the angel's predictions of future redemption. He offers wholeheartedly that comfort that he himself was unable to accept fully when it was extended to him. How profoundly he has changed since the beginning of his quest!

Once he accepted all that he was taught, the issue of the few and the many withdrew to the background, and the mourning for Zion reasserted itself more poignantly. Vision 1 had opened with Ezra's pain over the destruction of Zion and the abundance of Babylon (3:2), and the same theme completely dominates this fourth vision. It is the meaning of the woman's tale that becomes the mainspring of Ezra's comfort afterwards. Ezra's deep distress over the destruction of Zion was channeled by the presence of the woman's grief and the human need to console her. The act of reaching out was the catalyst for him to internalize his newly integrated worldview. Deep psychological insight permeates this episode.

Suddenly (10:25–27) the woman is transformed before his very eyes into a city with huge foundations. Her countenance becomes bright and shining, and flashes like lightning; she utters a loud cry, and finally the earth shakes. Ezra's powers of vision, his hearing, and his very physical orientation are disturbed. He is deeply frightened by what he is experiencing; he loses consciousness and, as he faints, he calls for his angelic guide, crying that his prayer for illumination has brought about his death.

A very powerful experience is being described. The seer's reactions to the revelations in the first three visions do not resemble this. Nor do those which follow upon the dreams in Visions 5 and 6. There is nothing like it in the other Jewish apocalypses. In its intensity this experience complements the pressure of unrelieved stress evident in the first part of the vision. It resembles the major sort of reorientation of personality usually associated with religious conversion. The stress precipitated this intense experience that resulted in the reorientation of the seer's worldview.

The same angel reappears, linking this unusual vision experience to the earlier visions, and interprets the vision to Ezra (10:38–54). The woman is Jerusalem; the thirty years of barrenness are the three thousand years before sacrifices were offered in it; the birth of the son is the building of the Temple; his death, the city's destruction. Ezra comforts her, and is shown her true, future glory. Here, for the first time in the book, the revelation to Ezra is described as "great secrets." This term is otherwise applied only to the esoteric revelations received by Abraham (3:14) and Moses (14:5, *cf.* also 14:46). A change has taken place, and from this point on Ezra receives more and deeper revelations of secrets and takes on a full prophetic role.

Ezra is not to fear, for the Most High has chosen him for the revelation of wonders. He is told to go in and see the building (10:55). The building is still there (so already in 10:32, "I saw, and still see"); the vision is not a dream, but a waking experience. Ezra's visit to the heavenly city is not described; the angel says only that he will see and hear as much as his physical capabilities will allow. These mysterious words may hint at the full revelation of consolation that resolves the issue of justice raised at the start of Vision 1. If so, then the resolution of the issue is not made explicit verbally, but remains on the level of direct experience (10:55–56). The author of 2 Esdras clearly saw the limits of the revelation of secret knowledge, and that may be at play here as well.

In the concluding injunctions of Vision 4, Ezra is told to remain in the field for two nights. There he will experience dream visions that will concern "what [God] will do to those on earth at the end of days" (10:59).

The fifth and sixth visions, which follow, are the most traditional from the perspective of Jewish apocalyptic writing. Both relate complex symbolic dreams that the seer experiences, of a kind that are foreign to modern sensibilities.

Vision 5 (11:1–12:51)

The fifth vision (11:1–12:39) is of a fantastic eagle with wings, little wings, and three heads. Ezra's psychological state is not described here, nor is the onset of inspiration, only the fact that he had a dream. The eagle, the central symbol of the dream, is linked to prior apocalyptic tradition by the observation that it is the fourth beast of those the Most High revealed to Daniel (Dan 7:7–8; see 2 Esdr 11:40, 12:11). The dreamer sees a complicated, many-limbed eagle (11:1–35), whose judgment (11:36–46) and destruction (12:1–3) he watches.

The vision begins with the eagle, with twelve feathered wings and three heads, rising from the sea (11:1). It opens its wings over the whole earth; all the winds blow upon it, and clouds gather about it (11:2). The dream describes the fate of the numerous wings and heads. There are twelve ordinary wings, eight little wings, and three heads. The wings start to rule, and in 11:13–17 special note is made that the second wing rules twice as long any other. All twelve wings and two of the little wings rise; they rule one after the other and disappear; only the three heads and six of the little wings remain (11:23).

Two little wings separate from the six and stay under the right head (11:24). Two of the remaining four disappear and the other two plan to reign together (11:25–28). The rule of the little wings is more ephemeral than that of the ordinary wings, and the heads are more important than both of them. The symbolism is graded to the significance of the rulers.

The largest, middle head awakens and, allied with the other two, gains control of the earth and holds power longer than all its predecessors (11:29–32). It then disappears (11:33) and, of the two heads remaining (11:34), the right-hand one devours the left-hand one. The history of the eagle approaches its end. A roaring lion issues from the forest indicting and sentencing the eagle by saying that God had established it as last of the beasts so that the end might come through it (11:37–39). The eagle had conquered all preceding beasts and held sway with oppression and deceit. It judged the earth untruthfully, afflicted the meek, and loved the wicked. Its insolence and pride had come up to the Most High (11:40–43). The time allotted to it had ended, and therefore it would disappear with all its parts, and the earth, refreshed, would await its creator (11:44–46). The grim sentence is immediately executed: the last little wings disappear, the eagle is burned, and the whole earth is terrified (12:3). Note that although the lion indicts and pronounces sentence, in the vision the execution of the sentence remains in God's hands.

The dream is powerful; Ezra awakens and reacts to it with bewilderment, fear, and petitions for enlightenment. He experiences physical weakness and prays to be strengthened (12:3–6; similar are 5:14, 10:25, 10:28, 10:30–31, 13:13b). Such reactions probably reflect real responses to vision or dream experiences. He turns dramatically and upbraids his own mind, "You have brought this upon me because you search out the way of the Most High" (12:4). Wearied by all this searching, which precipitated exhausting and terrifying experiences (including the dream), he beseeches the Most High for help. He recalls God's grace extended to him in the past, and asks for the interpretation of the vision.

In 3:14 and 14:5 reference is made to an esoteric tradition of revelation to Abraham and Moses about "the end of the times." Here, significantly, Ezra describes what has been revealed to him as "the end of the times." He clearly recognizes the change in his own status, which is signaled by what is revealed to him. He no longer deprecates his own worthiness but accepts it and bases his petition to God on it (12:7–9). These features form a clear contrast with the preceding vision.

The angel comes to interpret the dream. The eagle is the fourth kingdom that had been revealed to Daniel, but the revelation to Ezra is superior to Daniel's. "Behold the days are coming," Ezra is told, in a phrase that sets a predictive tone (12:13; see also its use in 5:1, 6:18, and 7:26). First general and then detailed interpretations follow. The chief of these are set off by introductory phrases like "as for your seeing," a standard procedure in such interpretations.

The idea, drawn from chapters 2 and 7 in Daniel, is that there will be four great empires, and that the fourth will achieve peaks of wickedness surpassing all its predecessors'. After the fall of the fourth empire, the kingdom of the righteous or the saints or the angels will ensue. This view was shared by several eastern peoples who were conquered by the Greeks under Alexander. For them, the Greeks were the fourth empire and they hoped for the restoration of their native rule after the fall of the Greeks. Second Esdras reinterprets Daniel's vision by seeing Rome as the fourth kingdom. The eagle is the symbol of the Roman legions and traditionally the Lion of Judah signifies the Messiah. The point of the vision is that the Roman kingdom will reach a peak of evil and then will be destroyed and the kingdom of Israel will be restored (12:10–35).

The various limbs of the eagle are taken to be Roman emperors. The twelve wings will be twelve kings, and of them the second will rule twice as long as any other. The little wings are eight kings who will rule briefly; the three heads will renew many things and their rule will be very oppressive, for which reason they are called heads. The disappearance of the large head means (for no reason evident from the vision symbolism) that one of these three kings will die on his bed in agony (12:26), a reflection of real history. Similarly, in 12:27–28 the one head is said to kill the other, and an important additional fact is added: the killer will himself be killed by the sword. The lion is identified as the Messiah, son of David (12:32). He will denounce the wicked kings and set them up in judgment, reprove them, and destroy them.

The eagle vision is a close-up view of a particular part of the eschatological process, the waning days of the world empire and its destruction. The climax is to be the appearance of the Messiah and the inception of his kingdom. The Messianic kingdom expected is a temporary one, to be followed eventually by the Day of Judgment (12:34). Similarly, each of the preceding and following visions focuses on a particular element of redemption.

History is presented as a schematic whole, and the author's interest is not academic, but to know exactly where he stands in that process. For scholars, moreover, such historical recitals, which are common in apocalypses of the Second Temple period, are particularly important. Although, in his pseudepigraphic persona, the author can relate events actually past as if they were of the future, there is a point at which he is forced to abandon the "prediction" of the actual course of past events and must foretell future happenings. This is the point of time at which he lived. Thus, the identification of this point yields an indication of the actual lifetime of the author.

This technique has been used extensively in study of 2 Esdras, and in particular of the eagle vision. The central point in any unraveling of the symbolism

is the identification of the three heads, for the end of history is expected during the days of the third head. The wings and little wings are identified with various emperors, and the second wing, the one that ruled longest, is Augustus. The most persuasive theory interprets the heads as Vespasian, Titus, and Domitian, for the details admirably suit current knowledge of these emperors. The book was thus composed in the time of Domitian (81–96), probably in the latter part of his reign, when his cruelty and oppression reached unprecedented proportions.

The final part of the vision is composed of two elements: the formal conclusion with the associated injunctions, and a narrative dealing with the reassurance of the people after Ezra's prolonged absence (12:35–50).

The book consistently holds that eschatological secrets are a proper subject of revelation. Thus when Ezra receives revelations about them, he is told to record them and transmit them secretly to the wise among the people (12:37–38), just as Abraham and Moses did. In pseudepigraphic books, such commands supply an explanation for the transmission of the books and so authenticate them.

Ezra is instructed to remain in the field for seven days. If all the days of fasting, partial abstention, and remaining in the field from Vision 1 to Vision 6 are counted, they make a total of forty days (taking the "three weeks" in 6:35 as implying also a seven-day period preceding Vision 1). Again, Ezra becomes a second Moses (see chap. 14), and when he goes to receive the Torah in chapter 14 he fasts for forty days (cf. Exod 34:28). Thus, the first six visions—of forty days' duration—parallel the giving of the Torah (also of forty days' duration). The Torah encompasses the revelation of the same secrets as the first six visions. The author makes this profound point using a mechanical indicator, the two periods of forty days.

Vision 6 (Chapter 13)

After seven days Ezra dreams in the night, just as he did in the preceding vision. In his dream Ezra sees a wind arising from the sea and stirring its waves. Then "something like the figure of a man" arises from the sea and "flew with the clouds of heaven," and his look and voice evoked terror: "all who heard his voice melted as wax melts when it feels the fire (13:3–4;

RSV). Dream symbols frequently take their meaning from cultural context. In the world of 2 Esdras, the sea is one of the primordial elements of creation, an ancient monster. Traditionally, it is God's appearance that makes his enemies melt like wax (Ps 97:5, Mic 1:4), and in Daniel 7:13 a human figure (the "Son of man") flies on the clouds into the presence of divinity. The mention of these features therefore evokes a striking atmosphere of particular solemnity.

The man thus presented, the action begins (13:5–7). An innumerable multitude assembles from all directions to make war upon him. He carves out a great mountain and flies upon it. The forces are drawn up, and though the innumerable host fear the man flying upon the mountain, they attack. The man holds no weapons (13:9) but breathes out a fiery stream that consumes the onrushing host. Only ashes and the smell of smoke remain (13:11). Biblical images of God as fierce warrior infuse this description. God uses fire to destroy enemies (Ps 97:3–7; 1 Kgs 19:12; 2 Sam 22:9). God needs no weapons!

Redemption follows victory. A peaceful multitude comes, some joyous and some sad, some bound and some bringing others as offerings (13:13).

The passage 13:13b–20 links the dream to the interpretation. In 12:3–9 Ezra had described his fear and disorientation on receiving the dream. Here, in contrast, he asserts his worthiness and immediately asks for the interpretation. At the end of Vision 3 the angel had assured Ezra energetically that he was not to reckon himself among the sinners (8:47–62). The angel takes up Ezra's worthiness again in 10:38–39 and 10:50–59; Ezra himself mentions it in 12:7–9. By the time of the present vision, Ezra unconditionally asserts his own worthiness, and can even venture to draw his own conclusions from the vision.

Throughout the book Ezra has rung changes on the view that "it were better not to have been born, or having been born to die." Here he asserts, drawing conclusions from his own interpretation of the dream vision, that those who are alive in the last days are more fortunate (or less unfortunate) than those who are dead. In his new role as prophet (cf. 12:42), with his new self-consciousness and new eschatological hope, Ezra no longer despairs of this world and of life.

The angel confirms that those who survive in the last generation are indeed more blessed than those who have died. It is still preferable to be one of the surviving remnant, who "have works and have faith in the Almighty" (13:23). Elsewhere in the book, the righteous are described as those who have works or those who have faith, and the two terms also occur together in 9:7. This is an important reminder that Paul's use of these terms (for example, in Gal 2:15–3:29) is a special application of a less specific usage found in contemporary Jewish literature. God, who has brought about the messianic woes and their perils, can also save people from them.

The interpretation of the dream follows—it is about the Messiah, the attack on him by a host of hostile nations, his victory and annihilation of them, and, finally, the ingathering of the multitude of the redeemed. The man is the Messiah, precreated by God, as were many eschatological things (cf. 6:6 and 9:8). There will be chaos and confusion when the time comes for the Most High to approach and deliver those upon the earth. The internecine strife will reach a peak when all the wicked unite to attack the Messiah. The "mountain carved out" by the man (13:6) is an image most likely drawn from Daniel 2:34–35. The mountain is interpreted as Zion, which appears as a fully built city, indicated by the mountain's being carved without hands.

The man, on Zion, will destroy the multitude by his reproof. This interpretation of his fiery breath gives it a judicial rather than a military meaning. The very reproof of the enemies brings about their destruction.

The close correlation in the previous vision between the content and sequence of the dream and the interpretation is missing here. Furthermore the tight, coherent dream in this vision contrasts with its complicated, diffuse, and somewhat incoherent interpretation. For example, the only element of 13:1–4 that is interpreted—and it is mentioned three times—is the fact that the man came up from the sea. The winds that stirred up the sea, his flying on the clouds, and the effect of his gaze and his voice are ignored. There are also portions of the interpretation with little if any basis in the dream. The most striking is he long and complex tradition about the nine and one-half tribes (13:40–47), which is only loosely-linked to the image of the peaceable multitude. Even this tradition is not sufficient for the author, who appends, in 13:48–49, a new prediction about "those who are left of your people" referring to the Messiah's defense of the remnant of Israel. This action is not even hinted at in the vision.

The problematical relationship between this dream and its interpretation leads to the conclusion that the author drew the dream itself from a preexisting narrative, allegory, or even dream report, and composed an interpretation for it. There are real differences between the presentation of the redeemer figure in the dream and in the interpretation. The views propagated by the interpretation are congruent with the view of the Messiah and salvation presented elsewhere in the book (for example, 9:8 and 12:34), while those of the dream vision are very different. They reflect the idea of a cosmic redeemer with important analogies elsewhere in Jewish literature of the Second Temple period, but quite unique within 2 Esdras. This dream narrative, originating separately from the interpretation, may originally have expressed ideas very different from those it now stresses in context.

The literary complexity of this vision can be seen in the passage dealing with the nine and one-half tribes, one of the earliest instances of this widespread idea. It is clearly drawn as a whole from another source and bears only a very general relationship to its context.

The interpretation concludes with an assertion of Ezra's worthiness to receive this revelation and the conclusion of Vision 6 (13:53–58). Particularly intriguing is the change of perspective about Ezra that is again accentuated in this section. Previously Ezra was praised for his virtue or humility (8:46–51) and his grief for Zion and his general righteous conduct (10:39, 50). Here he is praised for his devotion to God's ways, an interesting twist on the theme of the search for the way of the Most High that was so dominant in Vision 1. He is enjoined to wait here three more days, to receive another revelation. This passage then not only concludes the sixth vision but also forms the end of the dream visions and of the major revelatory strand of the book.

Quite unlike anywhere else in the book in similar contexts, Ezra is said to rise to his feet (he does this previously only to receive a prediction in 6:13 and

6:17). Once on his feet, he keeps on walking in the field and praises God.

The first vision opened with Ezra accusing God. The six great visions conclude with him praising the Most High "because he governs the times and whatever things come to pass in their seasons" (13:58). The very first stage of his illumination in Vision 1 was the recognition of God as arbiter and master of the course of events. That recognition began the development that led from Ezra's accusation to unreserved praise. It was, however, only in the fifth and sixth visions that Ezra reached a fuller understanding. He realized that the times determined the promise of redemption, involving the destruction of Rome (Vision 5) and of evil in general (Vision 6).

Vision 7 (Chapter 14)

Ezra remains in the field, not lying on the grass, but sitting under an oak tree (*cf.* Gen 14:13, 18:1; Judg 4:5) opposite a bush from which the divine voice issues. This is a deliberate evocation of Moses and the burning bush (Exod 3:1–6), which is explicitly reinforced by 14:3: "I revealed myself in a bush and spoke to Moses." Ezra receives this vision in the mood of exultation and assurance of illumination that permeated his prayer and activities at the end of Vision 6. Nothing is said in the introduction to Vision 7 about his mental or emotional state, or about any inspiration coming upon him. He is in the field, giving great glory to God, when he is summoned. Most significantly, it is God who directly addresses Ezra from the bush—no angel is mentioned here or anywhere else in the chapter. Ezra declares himself ready and rises to his feet (14:2). God's direct participation makes this vision distinct from the first six and endows it with a particular solemnity.

The vision opens with an address, but instead of Ezra addressing God (as in all the preceding instances), God addresses Ezra. God's speech from the bush (14:3–18) first retells the history of the revelation to Moses. "I revealed myself" to Moses, and "I sent him" to bring the people out of Egypt. "I led him" to Sinai. "I kept him with me." "I told him" secrets. "I commanded him." Vision 1, too, had opened with a historical account, but what a difference there is! The first recital was placed in the seer's mouth, and it was marked by the repeated "Thou" as the seer indicted God for having created the world. Here God's "I" is a celebration of God's action on behalf of Israel. This strikingly encapsulates the change that has taken place in the course of the book.

After narrating the history, the divine speaker moves to predictions about Ezra's personal fate (14:9) and about the future of the age (14:10–12). Both predictions imply Ezra's imminent passing from the world. Ezra is told that he will be taken up to live with the Messiah and with the saints who have been taken up alive. This promise is directly connected to the divine assertion in 13:52 that "no one on earth can see my Son or those who are with him, except in the time of his day." The times, he is told, have grown old (see also 14:17). The age of the world is divided into twelve parts, of which nine and one-half have passed (14:11–12). Although it was a widespread idea that the world age is divided into a fixed number of parts that can be revealed to a seer, this is the only hint at such a view in 2 Esdras and it is rather obscure.

The address concludes with injunctions relating both to the people and to Ezra, followed by a recapitulation of the reasons for the belief that the end of the world is at hand. He is to lay up in his heart "the signs that I have shown you, the dreams that you have seen, and the interpretations that you have heard" (14:8). These are the chief eschatological prophecies of the book. "Signs" refers to the messianic woes, while "dream" and "interpretations" are the dream visions (10:59, 12:35).

Ezra is informed explicitly by God of the coming woes. The greater part of the world age has passed, and he himself is to be translated. He is told, therefore, a substantial portion of the very events he had been instructed to search out earlier in the book (9:1–2). It is unclear, however, whether Ezra sees himself living at the end of the world age. He is told that there are still two and one-half parts of the world age to come, that the earth had grown old, and that the woes will start. Therefore he is being translated, as a sign of grace, in order to escape the suffering. On the basis of this passage, therefore, what seems to be immediately expected is Ezra's translation to heaven (14:14), with the great upheavals of the Messianic woes and the end of the world still somewhat in the future.

The theme of secret revelation has been intro-

duced here into the vision (14:6), and it forms one of its leitmotifs. It was already hinted at in 3:14, but there it had no direct application to Ezra and his actions. It was first applied to Ezra in 12:37–38 and will arise once more in another particularly important context (14:45–46).

Ezra responds by accepting the commands that God has laid upon him (14:19–22). He will "reprove the people who are now living" (see 14:13). At the end of 14:20, however, true to character, Ezra has a question to pose to God. His reproof will be received by those now alive, but what about those who have not yet been born? This question too seems to imply that Ezra does not expect that the end will come in his own generation.

Ezra follows up this question with a request. He asks for the Holy Spirit to be sent into him and to enable him to write down "everything that has happened in the world from the beginning, the things which were written in thy law . . . that those who wish to live in the last days may live" (14:22). Nowhere else in the book does Ezra ask for inspiration. When it comes upon him, it is involuntary. The assumption that the Torah was lost or burnt is used by the author to structure his views about Ezra, Moses, and the new giving of the Torah. The Torah is to be given anew so that people can gain eternal life (cf. 9:31).

God tells Ezra to gather the people and instruct them not to seek him for forty days (14:23–26). Again the image of Moses is evoked. Ezra, to whom the scriptures are to be revealed, is to go away for forty days, the same period of time that Moses was on Mount Sinai. Moreover, as was mentioned earlier, this figure is equivalent to the total number of days in which the first six visions took place. Afterward Ezra reached a new stage of revelation. Thus the second forty days complements and balances the first set, providing a climax of revelation before Ezra's assumption to heaven.

Ezra is also to prepare writing tablets and to take five skilled scribes with him. These two elements explain in "naturalistic" terms how the revelation was recorded, adding a measure of verisimilitude to the story. Moreover, they distinguish Ezra from Moses; the two are similar but deliberately not identical.

The final element in God's response is that the

revelation Ezra will receive will be partly for public distribution and partly secret. The special, dual nature of the revelation of revealed and secret books is again made clear.

EZRA'S MISSION

As he has been instructed, Ezra addresses the people (14:27–36). He tells the people of their history, setting forth each stage as God's grace and Israel's unfaithfulness. The Exodus and the giving of the Torah are mentioned, and in immediate counterpoint Israel's transgression in the past and present (14:29–30). Next the gift of the land is celebrated, but again, "you and your fathers committed iniquity" (14:31). They sinned, and because God is judge he took their land and now they were in exile (14:32–33). Then follows an exhortation: If they are good, the people are told, they will be rewarded, for after death there is judgment and recompense.

The message here does not take up the themes of the destruction of Zion and its restoration, which were the major focus of the first six visions. The concern here is almost solely with the Torah and its function. On the one hand, Ezra talks of the Torah having been burnt, of humankind not knowing its redeeming knowledge. On the other, it is called a "law of life," and in its renewal human beings will find the way to life. The first six visions, with their forty days, brought Ezra to the role of prophet. In them were resolved the issue of the destruction of Zion through the idea of its predetermined redemption and the concern for the suffering of the righteous in the concept of their eschatological redemption. The present chapter recounts the renewal of "the law of life." This revelation transcends and complements those of the preceding dream visions, not as an authentication of the book as has often been claimed, but as its completion.

Now the climax of the revelation of the secret and public books to Ezra (14:37–48) ensues. First, Ezra recounts how he took the five men and went and stayed in the field (14:37). The next day he had a waking experience. First he heard a voice saying, "Drink what I give you to drink!" (14:38). Then he saw a cup and took it and drank its clear, fiery contents (14:39–40). Upon this drinking he felt

himself to be inspired. The actual start of the inspiration is described in language that in some ways resembles that used earlier in the book, but is much more explicit. It includes the onset of the inspiration, the feeling of enlightenment, the retention of the content of the enlightened knowledge, and the ability to articulate or dictate this retained content. In all the previous instances the speech that comes upon him is a bitter or argumentative one. Here it is the revelation of scripture.

The words and books that Ezra dictates in his inspired state are written down. The five scribes are also said to be inspired, although clearly their experience is not comparable to Ezra's. One sign of this is the odd comment that they wrote in "characters they knew not" (14:42). This may be a reference to the tradition known to the rabbinical sages that the square Aramaic script (used since the Second Temple period for Hebrew) was brought back by Ezra from Babylon. This tradition perhaps retains a historical memory of the introduction of the Aramaic script. At the same time, this wondrous writing serves to validate yet another aspect of the creation or transmission of the scriptures. Ezra dictates, and the scribes write, ninety-four books in the stipulated forty days. God then instructs Ezra to publish twenty-four of them. Twenty-four is one of the traditional numbers for books of the Hebrew Bible, and this is its first occurrence. He is to hide the seventy, for they are the books that contain true knowledge and wisdom and are to be transmitted only to the wise among the people.

The comment that the esoteric books are those that contain saving knowledge reveals attitudes common to both written scriptures and esoteric writings. Just what the seventy secret books were is unknown. They might include 2 Esdras itself, and perhaps other eschatological or apocalyptic writings, as is hinted in 12:36–38, where Ezra is commanded, in terms like those used here, to transmit eschatological teaching secretly. Clearly, this revelation is an event of very great importance to the author. It is central to the structure of the chapter, which focuses on the issue of the revealed writings. It is central to the whole book, for this is the revelation that Ezra received once he achieved the status of prophet. It is the revelation of the scriptures that "those who wish to live in the last days may live" (14:22) and of the tradition and corpus of esoteric and exoteric writings. At one level, this vision relates the revelation of the ninety-four books; at another level it tells of the esoteric knowledge that Ezra himself has become worthy to receive. In most versions of the book, the last verse of the chapters concludes with Ezra's assumption to heaven.

The message of the book is, in the final analysis, a rather traditional one. In spite of the destruction of the Temple, God's justice and his eschatological vindication of the righteous and punishment of the wicked are asserted. The overthrow of detested Rome, the ingathering of the exiles, the Messianic kingdom, and the Day of Judgment are the building blocks of the author's hope. The author's great artistry has produced a rich and complex work, filled with issues of universal religious faith. But, far more than this, the book is a powerful and moving odyssey of "Ezra's" soul, and the calm haven it reaches is the inner message of this remarkable writing. That voyage is presented with insight and sensitivity.

Bibliography

Selected Editions

Bensly, R. L., and M. R. James. *The Fourth Book of Ezra.* 1895. Reprint. Nendeln/Liechtenstein, 1967.
Stone, M. E. *The Armenian Version of 4 Ezra.* Philadelphia, 1979.
Violet, B. *Die Esra-Apokalypse I: Die Überlieferung.* Leipzig, 1910.

Translations and Commentaries

Box, G. H. *The Ezra-Apocalypse.* London, 1912.
———. "4 Ezra." In *Apocrypha and Pseudepigrapha of the Old Testament*, edited by R. H. Charles. Oxford, 1913.
Gry, L. *Les dires prophétiques d'Esdras.* 2 vols. Paris, 1938.
Gunkel, H. "Das vierte Buch Esra." In *Die Apokryphen und Pseudepigraphen des alten Testaments*, edited by E. Kautzsch. Tübingen, 1900.
Knibb, M. A., and R. J. Coggins. *The First and Second Books of Esdras.* Cambridge, 1979.
Metzger, B. M. "The Fourth Book of Ezra." In *Old Testament Pseudepigrapha*, edited by J. H. Charlesworth. Garden City, N.Y., 1983.
———. "The Second Book of Esdras." In *The New Oxford Annotated Bible with the Apocrypha*, Revised Standard Version. Expanded Edition, edited by H. G. May and B. M. Metzger, New York, 1977.
Myers, J. M. *1 and 2 Esdras.* Anchor Bible, vol. 42. Garden City, N.Y., 1974.
Schreiner, J. *Das 4. Buch Esra.* Gütersloh, 1981.

Stone, M. E., and T. A. Berzoen. "2 Esdras." In *Harper's Bible Commentary*, edited by J. L. Mays. San Francisco, 1988. Pp. 776–790.
Violet, B. *Die Apokalypsen des Esra und des Baruch in deutscher Gestalt.* Leipzig, 1924.

Selected Studies

Brandenburger, E. *Die Verborgenheit Gottes im Weltgeschehen.* Zürich, 1981.
Breech, E. "These Fragments I Have Shored Against My Ruins: The Form and Function of 4 Ezra." *Journal of Biblical Literature* 92 (1973): 267–274.
Faye, E. de. *Les apocalypses juives.* 1892.
Harnisch, W. "Die Ironie der Offenbarung: Exegetische Erwägungen zur Zionvision im 4. Buch Esra." *Zeitschrift für die alttestamentliche Wissenschaft* 95 (1983): 75–95.
———. *Verhängnis und Verheissung der Geschichte.* Göttingen, 1969.
Hayman, A. "The Problem of Pseudonymity in the Ezra Apocalypse." *Journal for the Study of Judaism* 6 (1975): 47–56.
Hilgenfeld, A. *Die jüdische Apokalyptik in ihrer geschichtlichen Entwicklung.* Jena, 1857.
James, M. R. "Ego Salathiel qui est Ezras." *Journal of Theological Studies* 18 (1917): 167–177.
Keulers, J. "Die eschatologische Lehre des vierten Esrabuches." *Biblische Studien* 20, nos. 2–3 (1922).
Knibb, M. A. "Apocalyptic and Wisdom in 4 Ezra." *Journal for the Study of Judaism* 13 (1982): 56–74.
Kraft, R. A. "'Ezra' Materials in Judaism and Christianity." In *Aufstieg und Niedergang der römischen Welt* 19.1, edited by W. Haase. New York, 1979. Pp. 119–136.
Society of Biblical Literature 1981 Seminar Papers, edited by K. H. Richards. Chico, Calif., 1981. Contents include L. L. Grabbe, "Chronography in 4 Ezra and 2 Baruch"; A. F. J. Klijn, "Textual Criticism of 4 Ezra. State of Affairs and Possibilities"; J. R. Mueller, "A Prolegomenon to the Study of the Social Function of 4 Ezra"; P. G. R. de Villiers, "Understanding the Way of God: Form, Function, and Message of the Historical Review in 4 Ezra 3:4–27."
Stone, M. E. "The Concept of the Messiah in 4 Ezra." In *Religions in Antiquity*, edited by Jacob Neusner. Leiden, 1968. Pp. 295–312.
———. "The Metamorphosis of Ezra: Jewish Apocalypse and Medieval Vision." *Journal of Theological Studies* 33 (1982): 1–18.
———. "Coherence and Inconsistency in the Apocalypses: The Case of 'the End' in 4 Ezra." *Journal of Biblical Literature* 102 (1983): 229–243.
Thompson, A. L. *Responsibility for Evil in the Theodicy of 4 Ezra.* Missoula, 1977.

MICHAEL E. STONE

Tobit

THE THEME OF the entertaining and popular narrative of Tobit is that piety and charity will be rewarded by God despite appearances to the contrary. This message is conveyed through a story of God's mercy on two pious but oppressed Jews of the Diaspora, Tobit and Sarah, whose experience is an example for all other Jews as well. The plight of Tobit and Sarah is relieved in the course of a journey made by Tobit's son, Tobias, and the angel Raphael, whose identity is unknown to the characters until his purposes have been achieved. Their ignorance, combined with the knowledge the narrator gives the reader, produces humorous ironies that have contributed strongly to the popularity of this ancient tale.

The ancient popularity of the Book of Tobit is reflected in the substantial number of surviving copies written in several languages. The very popularity of the book, however, raises two problems for modern readers. First, although the copies all present essentially the same story, it survives in basically two different forms, a long one and a short one, requiring us to choose which form we will read. Second, sometimes one copy and sometimes another will present a reading closer to the original, so that we have to choose which copy we will read, and in which translation.

The first problem is the easiest to solve. While earlier English translations such as the Revised Standard Version (RSV) were based on the short form

known from two Greek translations (Codex Alexandrinus and Codex Vaticanus), the long form is now seen to be the more original and the short form an abbreviation of it. First attested by another Greek translation (Codex Sinaiticus) and the Old Latin translation of it, as well as by the Latin Vulgate, the greater antiquity of the long form is supported by portions of five copies, four in Aramaic and one in Hebrew, found after World War II among the Dead Sea Scrolls. These still unpublished Semitic texts also show that the original language of the story was probably Aramaic, and that the original contained all fourteen chapters, thus setting aside some earlier doubts about the originality of chapters 13 and 14. The long form is the basis for more recent translations such as the New English Bible (NEB) and the Jerusalem Bible (JB), and for the major English-language commentary by Frank Zimmermann. We will use the long form.

The second problem, concerning the wording, is more difficult. Because some translations (e.g., NEB) are based on only one or two Greek texts and others (e.g., JB) on a wider range of texts, including the Old Latin, we have to choose between translations. We will follow the Jerusalem Bible. But because the English translations often use different English words to translate the words of the original texts, there are places where the New English Bible or even the Revised Standard Version may represent a better translation than the Jerusalem Bible. For this reason, while following the Jerusalem Bible we will on occasion use the English from one or more of the other translations. For example, a key word in the text is one that the Jerusalem Bible renders as "pity," whereas other translations better render it as "mercy." On the other hand, the Jerusalem Bible better translates an equally significant related word in the Greek as "almsgiving," while the New English Bible renders it as "charity." Unfortunately, no English translation can reveal the linguistic relationship between the two Greek words in question. Therefore, while we will refer to the story in the Jerusalem Bible translation, it is often helpful to consult other translations and commentaries like Zimmermann's, which provide both another translation and notes on variant readings and original meanings.

The popularity of the Book of Tobit also raises the question of the source of its appeal. Traditionally, scholars have posed the question of sources in terms of other texts used by the anonymous author of the book. For example, because he refers to events in the life of a man named Ahiqar, it is probable that he knew the popular story of the Ahiqar (text in Charlesworth) who, like Tobit, was a suffering and delivered righteous hero. Similarly, folklorists long ago noted that Tobit contains the well-known folklore themes of the grateful dead and the dangerous bride, which the author merges, developing the former in connection with Tobit and the latter in connection with Sarah (cf. Pfeiffer, Zimmermann). A classicist (Fries) has further argued that similarities between the episodes involving Tobias and Raphael and those involving Odysseus' son, Telemachus, and the goddess Athena in Homer's *Odyssey* (books 1 to 4) are based on a no longer extant earlier story. And biblical scholars, too, have identified the author's use of biblical texts, motifs, and themes, and of later Jewish prayers, aphorisms, and ideas (Pfeiffer, Zimmermann, Nickelsburg, Ruppert). All of these possible dependences of the author are useful in helping us to locate the story in its cultural-historical context, and they are equally useful in helping us to understand certain things in the text itself.

Unfortunately, the exact nature of this context is still disputed, and there is as yet no commentary that brings all of the suggested influences to bear on the story. Nevertheless, all of the alleged dependences can also be viewed from another angle, one that focuses on the story itself, which is our concern, rather than on its sources. For all of the alleged dependences represent the kinds of things in the story that appealed to its readers. Its author manipulated already popular themes, motifs, and even literary forms and devices to produce one of the most delightful stories to survive from antiquity. Indeed, Tobit represents a consummate use of humor as a vehicle for religious education and edification. Our concern is with the way in which the vehicle and its "load" appear in the story of Tobit and his family. To satisfy that concern, we will present a summary of the story that is also an interpretative reading of it.

THE STORY OF TOBIT AND HIS FAMILY

An unidentified third-person narrator introduces the central character, Tobit, by describing his genealogy, his origins in Thisbe of Galilee, and his present status as an exile in Assyria, following Assyria's conquest of Israel's northern kingdom in the eighth century B.C.E. (1:1–2). The narrator therefore pretends to be giving a historical account, but all of the evidence suggests that Tobit is a fictional character. The story is about one time and for another, although just what other time is unclear. From predictive references to the return to the land of Israel and to the rebuilding of the Temple after the Babylonian exile in the sixth century, and from the lack of reference to cataclysmic events in the second century, scholars locate the time of writing roughly between 400 and 200 B.C.E. Where it was written is yet another problem, although the exilic context and the message of the story suggest that it was written in exile for Diaspora Jews. Somewhere in the area of Syria around 200 seems the current best estimate, but it is only an informed guess.

Throughout the story, Tobit is located in Nineveh in Assyria, and the narrated actions both begin (chaps. 1–5) and effectively end there (chaps. 11–14), though they are interrupted by a journey to Media undertaken by Tobit's son, Tobias, and his ambiguous guide, Azarias, who is also the angel Raphael (chaps. 6–10). The story actually ends with Tobias back in Media after his parents' death (14:12–

15), but all of the action takes place between Nineveh and Media. The main plot line of the story, which concerns Tobit, corresponds to the geographical sequence of Nineveh-Media-Nineveh because the complication of the plot (Aristotle's *desis* or "binding") is generated in chapters 1 through 5; its working out (*peripeteia*) is described in chapters 6 through 10; and its resolution (*lysis*) is presented in chapters 11 through 12, with supplementary material being given in chapters 13 and 14. The complication of the subplot, concerning Sarah, is also introduced in chapters 1 through 5, but its resolution occurs in chapters 6 through 10.

The geography of the story also bears on its content, which has to do with maintaining Israelite identity while in exile not only from the land of Israel, but also from Jerusalem, the dwelling place of Israel's God. Tobit's personal problem is therefore also exiled Israel's collective problem, and his story is thus a paradigm for the story of exiled Israel. The relationship between the personal and the collective comes to the fore in chapters 13 and 14.

After the narrator's introductory words, the story begins (1:3) with the first-person autobiographical words of Tobit himself. This continues until 3:7, when the initial narrator takes over to tell about events taking place at the same time as Tobit's prayerful lament in 3:1–6, but some distance away in Media and centering on Sarah, whose plight leads her to a similar lament in 3:11–15. Then, in 3:16–17, this narrator tells the reader that the laments of both Tobit and Sarah were heard in heaven and that Raphael, an angel whose name means "God heals," was sent to heal them of their respective problems. Raphael is therefore the agent who will undo the complications and resolve the story's two plot lines. But more of this later. For the moment, it should be noted that the narrator who speaks in 3:7–17 continues to speak to the end of the story, except when quoting the characters' speech. For this reason, Tobit's autobiographical narration in 1:3–3:6 is hard to explain. Tobit 12:20 provides a partial explanation when Azarias/Raphael tells Tobit to write down all that has happened, but because Tobit does not continue in a retrospective first-person account from 3:7 on, we have to look at what the author has achieved with the change of narrative voice.

The change of voice produces results that could not have been achieved by retaining the first-person voice of Tobit. The first clue is that Tobit is ignorant of Sarah's travails going on simultaneously with his own but in distant Media (3:7–15). The second clue is that Sarah and Tobit are equally unaware that their prayers have been heard in heaven, and that the angel Raphael has been sent to heal them (3:16–17). And the third clue is that no one but the reader knows that the man who will appear to the characters as Azarias is in fact Raphael (chaps. 5–12). Consequently, from 3:7 until 12:11–21, when Raphael discloses his identity, none of the characters knows what the reader knows, indeed is given to know by the third-person narrator who takes over from Tobit in 3:7.

This narrative device of playing with the relationship between two levels of knowledge, the characters' and the readers', is widely employed in Greco-Roman, Jewish, and Christian literature of antiquity, and almost invariably in connection with the appearance of a divine being in human form. This device was popular precisely because it produced both (1) expectations on the part of readers (that the ignorant characters will come to understand what the readers already do) and (2) delightful ambiguities, ironies, and humor, as when the characters in Tobit utter the truth but do not realize it. In this light, we must alter our earlier question and ask not why the autobiographical narration ended, but why it ever began in the first place. Perhaps the best answer is that this is one of the few compositional deficiencies in his story. On the other hand, it may stem from the author's having had in mind the story of Ahiqar, which he knew (see 1:21–22, 2:10, 11:18, and especially 14:10), for this story, too, is told in the autobiographical first person. Whatever the reasons may be, however, the voice that takes over in 3:7 presupposes what the first-person voice of Tobit has said.

Tobit's righteousness is one of the two main themes of his autobiographical statement in 1:3–3:6. Before the exile he, unlike other northerners, had maintained his allegiance to the law that bound all Israel to Jerusalem and its Temple, "God's dwelling place." He made his pilgrimages to it and offered there the tithes ordained in the law of Moses. He also married a kinswoman, named Anna, who bore him a son, who was called Tobias.

In exile, his piety continued. In addition to giving alms to his brothers and countrymen, he refused to eat pagan food. His piety was rewarded by his God, whom he saw as responsible for the Assyrian king Shalmaneser's appointment of him as head of supplies. Not incidentally, this conviction already represents Tobit's confidence that the God who dwells in Jerusalem can also be effective for exiles outside of the land of Israel.

Tobit's appointment gave him freedom to travel, and in the course of his travels, he left money with a man named Gabael at Rhages in Media. In a development of consequence to both reader suspense and plot complication, Tobit was denied access to the money when, after Sennacherib replaced Shalmaneser, the roads to Media were closed (1:14–15). When Tobit later becomes impoverished, he sends his son to retrieve the money. Thus the casual reference to the leaving of the money in Media supplies a motive for the journey that ultimately resolves the story's two plot lines.

Tobit now goes on to say that he persevered in his almsgiving, and that he also embarked on a new venture that was in violation of the king's law but in accordance with Israelite law: he stole the bodies of Israelites slain by Sennacherib and left to rot, and he properly buried them. Betrayed to Sennacherib, who would kill him for his offense, Tobit fled, and in his absence all of his goods were confiscated, leaving him, Anna, and Tobias impoverished. Then, after Esarhaddon replaced Sennacherib, and one Ahiqar, whom Tobit claims as a relative, assumed a high office under the new king, Ahiqar intercedes with the king on Tobit's behalf and Tobit is permitted to return to Nineveh. Back home, Tobit and his family celebrate the feast of Pentecost, but the meal is interrupted when Tobit learns that yet another Israelite body has been found. Again following his own people's laws, Tobit secretly buries the corpse. Afterward, while he is resting from his activities by the courtyard wall, the droppings of sparrows fall into his eyes and incurably blind him.

With Tobit blind, Anna has to get a job, which leads to a misunderstanding between them that results in her taunt that his piety has gotten him nothing but poverty and blindness. The reader sees that Tobit has given mercy but received none, not even from his wife.

Such is his dismay at his plight that Tobit now offers a prayerful lament to God, in which he asks God to deliver him from his afflictions by allowing him to die. He has had enough of misery and reproach unrelieved by mercy. His prayer contains praise for God's justice, a plea for God's mercy, and a confession of Israel's sins, for which God has punished the people by giving them over to their enemies for exile and reproach (3:1–6). Tobit's situation is Israel's, yet his personal plea is for his own death, for despite his own confession he maintains that his plight is without cause. To him death seems better than a life without mercy.

With the end of Tobit's lament, the third-person narrator now takes over to describe the simultaneous plight of Sarah, the daughter of Raguel, in Ecbatana of Media (3:7–15). She also suffers the insults of those around her. She had been given in marriage seven times, only to have each husband killed by the demon Asmodeus before the marriage could be consummated. Her maids insult her by wrongly claiming that she has killed her husbands. So great is her grief that she contemplates suicide. Realizing, however, the sorrow and shame this would bring to her father, Sarah, like Tobit, prays to the God of mercy to deliver her from reproach by granting her death. Part of Sarah's grief is that she is her father's only heir, and thinks she has no other kinsman left alive whom she might marry. This, too, later proves to be relevant to the plot, for it turns out that Tobit's son is the sole eligible kinsman left, and that he is fated to show up on Sarah's doorstep while on his way to pick up his father's money in Rhages, also in Media. Her marital misfortune becomes therefore also a potential threat to the resolution of the two plot lines. If Tobias dies, then all is lost for all concerned—which would not make for a very happy story.

With the end of Sarah's lament, we now have under way two plot lines concerning pious, righteous characters who, despite Tobit's confession, are suffering unjustly in a merciless world and who pray for God's merciful deliverance through death. But now (3:16–17) the narrator tells the reader that their deliverance, and therefore the resolution of the plots, will come not through death but through "healing." Their prayers found favor before the glory of God, and an angel, Raphael, was sent to heal them by restoring Tobit's sight ("so that he might see God's light with his own eyes"), by giving Sarah as bride to Tobit's son, Tobias, and by ridding her of the demon Asmodeus. Having thus informed readers of what has happened in heaven unknown to the characters, the narrator returns to their actions on earth.

Assuming that in response to his prayer he is about to die, Tobit delivers a farewell speech or last testament to his son, Tobias (chap. 4). The speech is linked to Tobit's plot line by references to the family's poverty (4:21) and to the money Tobit had left with Gabael at Rhages some twenty years previously (4:1–2, 4:20, 5:3). But in light of Sarah's thinking she was without an eligible kinsman to marry (3:15) and the narrator's noting that Raphael would give Sarah to Tobias because she belonged to him by right (3:17), one of Tobit's comments also bears on Sarah's plot line (4:12–13). He enjoins Tobias to take a wife from his father's tribe, as Israel's ancestors did from the very beginning. Tobit, too, took a wife from among his kin (1:9), and now Tobias must marry a kinswoman. Here the identity and the hope of Israel are at stake. For Israel to inherit the earth (4:12), Israelites must remain Israelites and not dilute the race or undermine its hope by marrying outsiders.

In addition to this point, Tobit's injunctions comprehend a wide range of ethical behavior. The motive for doing what is enjoined is self-interest (4:5–6, 14). Religiously, do what you are supposed to do and God will reward you (4:7); socially, follow the "golden rule": "Do to no one what you would not want done to you" (4:15). But perhaps more to the thematic point of the book, acts of mercy like almsgiving will lead to God's mercy for the doer: "Never turn your face from any poor man and God will never turn his from you" (4:7; cf. 3:6, 15). Ironically, Tobit here enjoins upon his son the very behavior that has failed to produce for him the results he promises his son. Even in his death wish, Tobit's piety is unflagging, for his death would be a sign of God's mercy. Unlike the author of Ecclesiastes, to whom personal experience gives no evidence of intercourse between God in heaven and man on earth, Tobit believes absolutely in God's control of things on earth. And the narrator has assured the reader of this

control in his account of Tobit's and Sarah's prayers and Raphael's mission (3:16–17). Beginning in chapter 5, the narrator shows how, as Tobit believed, God responds to the righteousness of his people, even in ways that are not immediately apparent to them.

Chapter 5 is a gem of humorous double meaning. Father, son, and mother discuss Tobias' journey to collect the much-needed money left with Gabael at Rhages in Media. They are concerned with how Tobias and Gabael will recognize one another, whether Gabael will give him the money, which route he should take, and how he can proceed in safety. The solution is to find a knowledgeable and trustworthy guide. The narrator introduces the guide by telling the reader that he is really Raphael, and the narrator henceforth refers to him as such, except when quoting the other characters, who call him either Azarias or "brother" or "friend." Consequently, the characters see, hear, and understand—and so speak about—one thing, while the reader knows and understands another. As a result, the reader, who is presumed to know something about angels, finds great humor in the relationship between Raphael and the others. For example, in the Bible God or an angel will often say, "Fear not, I am with you." One need not fear anything if God or one of his agents is present, and such divine beings are also omniscient. The reader thus finds a long series of humorous double meanings, especially in chapter 5, and also begins to wonder how long it will take the other characters to catch on to Raphael's identity. The narrator's granting of special knowledge to the reader generates expectations as well as humor.

The narrator says that when Tobias encounters Raphael he does not realize that he is an angel (5:4–5). The reader has to chuckle when Tobias asks him where he comes from and which family and tribe he belongs to, as well as when Tobit says that Raphael comes from a good and honorable line and that his brothers are worthy men. Indeed! The irony is that what is true of Azarias is even truer of Raphael, about whom Tobit and Tobias, but not the reader, are ignorant.

But the reader may be a bit perplexed—unless he or she has read similar stories, like the *Odyssey* (especially books 1–4)—when in response to Tobit's questioning Raphael blatantly lies about his identity, family, and homeland. Obviously, the angel lies to conceal his identity, but less obvious—since, as in most Jewish angel stories, he did not have to lie—is the simple narrative motive of heightening the reader's appetite both for double meaning and for the ultimate moment of recognition. So Raphael claims to be one of Tobit's kinsmen and to know Gabael, to whom Tobias is being sent. Raphael has also been to Media often and knows the way by heart. In his capacity as an angel, he knows and assures Tobit that "before long God will heal" him, for this is part of Raphael's mission (5:9; cf. 3:16–17). He knows, too, as well he should, that the whole journey will go just fine.

Further humor results when Raphael tells Tobias that he will wait for him, "but do not be long." Tobit is concerned that his son's companion be reliable. Raphael says that he will go with Tobias and that Tobit should "be not afraid," both of which are traits of Jewish theophanies and angelophanies. And Tobit prays that God will protect Tobias and send an angel to go with him, ironically assuring Anna, too, that a good angel will go with their son.

With both the characters and the readers thus prepared, the uncommon couple set off for Media from Nineveh to fulfill Tobit's wishes and resolve the story's two plot lines. That these are uppermost in the narrator's mind is disclosed in the very first episode on the road (6:1–9), when Tobias is attacked by a fish while washing his feet in a river. Raphael ("God heals") orders Tobias to capture the fish and remove the gall, heart, and liver because they have curative powers. After Tobias does as ordered, and is back on the road, he asks Azarias about the these powers. The angel replies that by burning the heart and liver, smoke is created that completely does away with afflictions caused by a demon or evil spirit. The gall, on the other hand, is used as an eye ointment for people (like Tobit) who have white spots on their eyes. "After using it, you only have to blow on the spots to cure them" (6:9). Interestingly enough, Tobias not only lacks the knowledge to connect the first cure with Sarah, but he also fails to connect the second with his father. Nevertheless, the reader now knows that two of Raphael's three tasks are on their way to completion. But the third task, the safe marriage of Sarah to Tobias, is also prepared for because Tobias unwittingly possesses the anti-demon medicine that

will save his life and make his marriage possible. All that remains is for Sarah and Tobias to meet, and that is the subject of the rest of the chapter and on through chapter 10.

While on the way to Rhages for the money, the travelers stop on the outskirts of Ecbatana and Raphael tells Tobias that that night he will meet Sarah, a kinswoman upon whom he has sole claim according to the law of Moses (6:10b–18). The angel's words resonate with Sarah's lament about being her father's only heir and having no eligible kinsman left for her to marry. Not only is Tobias eligible, but Sarah belongs to him before anyone else. Indeed, she was destined for him from the beginning. Anxiously, however, Tobias reports his knowledge of her past history with husbands, which makes him "a little afraid." Raphael reassures Tobias that all will go well if on their wedding night Tobias first puts the heart and liver of the fish on the burning incense in Sarah's bedroom, and then, before consummating the marriage, he and Sarah stand by the bed and pray for God's grace and protection. Anxiety removed, a now-sentimental Tobias falls madly in love with the woman he has yet to meet.

In Ecbatana, Tobias and Azarias go to Raguel's home and meet him and his wife, Edna. When the hosts learn that Tobias is a kinsman, they rejoice greatly and prepare a welcoming meal. The subject of marriage is broached and Tobias' claim is acknowledged, but not without Raguel's warning about the previous seven husbands. Tobias persists, however, and Raguel, virtually in Raphael's own previous words to Tobias, consents, promptly gives Sarah to him, and then draws up the marriage contract prescribed in the law of Moses.

The meal ended, all prepare for bed. Tobias does with the fish's heart and liver as Raphael directed, causing the demon such distress that he flees through the air to faraway Egypt, whence Raphael pursues him and binds him in shackles. So much for Asmodeus! The demon gone, Tobias gets Sarah out of bed so that they can offer a thankful prayer to God for creating the institution of marriage, and can ask for God's mercy on them both into their old age. Meanwhile, a pessimistic Raguel is outside with his servants digging a grave for Tobias, hoping to avoid further embarrassment by burying him before the neighbors awaken and learn about groom number eight. He quickly learns, however, what the reader already knows, and in relief he offers a thankful blessing to God for his mercy on the young couple.

In his joy, Raguel now demands that Tobias spend two weeks with his new family before returning home with half of Raguel's wealth in addition to his daughter. With Sarah's double problem resolved by the arrival of the only eligible kinsman and the departure of the demon, her plot line is resolved and two of Raphael's chores are completed. But the two-week stay delays the completion of his job and the end of the story. To speed things up, Tobias sends Raphael on to Rhages to secure his father's money and bring the trustworthy Gabael back to Ecbatana to celebrate the marriage. Raphael does as ordered, but Tobias remains anxious to return to his father, still without connecting the curative gall with his father's blindness.

Finally, the feast ends and Tobias manages to get back on the road home, after the mandatory parental blessings, gifts, and, of course, advice. Then, nearing Nineveh, and mindful of Tobit's state, Raphael suggests that he and Tobias go on ahead of Sarah and her entourage, and he instructs Tobias how to anoint Tobit's eyes with the fish's gall. They meet the anxiously waiting parents, and Tobias promptly performs the cure on his father's eyes, whereupon Tobit, like Raguel, blesses God for his mercy, which turns out to involve restoration rather than death. This done, Tobias reports on his journey and Tobit goes out to the gate of Nineveh to greet his new daughter.

With everyone's troubles ended, there remains only the payment of Azarias for his services. But this raises the question of his true identity, which is the last item of unfinished business in the story. Father and son discuss the amount due Azarias, but Raphael, still unrecognized, takes them aside and utters words whose piety governs the Book of Tobit and that are indeed a variant of Tobit's own testament in chapter 4:

Bless God, utter his praise before all the living for all the favors he has given you. Bless and extol his name. Proclaim before all men the deeds of God as they deserve, and never tire of giving him thanks. It is right to keep the secret of a king, yet right to reveal and publish the works of God. Thank him worthily. Do what is good, and no evil can befall you. Prayer with fasting and alms with right conduct are better than riches with iniquity. Better to practice almsgiving than to hoard up gold. Almsgiving saves from death and purges every kind of sin. Those who give alms have their fill of days; those who commit sin and do evil, bring harm on themselves. (12:6–10)

Raphael then takes up the theme of the propriety both of keeping the secret of a king and of revealing the works of God, using it as the basis for his disclosure of knowledge the reader has enjoyed since early on in the story. Thus he says that he has been involved since the time of Sarah's and Tobit's laments, and even of Tobit's burying of the dead, when he brought their words and deeds before God. Then he openly identifies himself as Raphael, "one of the seven angels who stand ever ready to enter the presence of the glory of the Lord" (12:15). His presence among Tobit and his family was the will of God. And what they saw in Azarias, even his eating—angels do not eat—was an appearance or vision, no more. Before returning to God, Raphael enjoins Tobit to write down all that has happened. Then, as divine beings usually do after completing their tasks, he rises in the air and disappears.

The story proper ends in chapter 12, yet the book contains two more chapters whose relationship to the story has long been questioned. Their originality to the story is supported by the earliest versions of it found among the Dead Sea Scrolls, where both chapters are represented. But their originality is also suggested by the fact that although the personal problems of the characters have been resolved in the first twelve chapters, the problem of exiled Israel, with which the book began (see also 3:3–5), has yet to be addressed. This is the concern of later chapters.

The resolution of Israel's problem is the subject of Tobit's prayer in chapter 13 and of his second farewell speech in chapter 14. The eternal God who is the Lord of history has punished Israel through exile, but he will also be merciful, both restoring the scattered exiles (13:5), as he has mercifully restored Tobit, and restoring Jerusalem and Israel's Temple (13:9–10, 16–17). Indeed, Tobit summons Israel to do as he has done (13:5–8) in order to experience the deliverance he has experienced.

Similarly, his story in chapter 14 is a lesson for

Israel. On his deathbed in great old age, Tobit tells Tobias to flee from Nineveh to Media because the process of Israel's deliverance is about to begin with the destruction of Assyria that was announced by the prophets. To be sure, there will be yet another exile and further destruction, but God will once again have mercy and restore all Israelites to the land of Israel, where they will rebuild Jerusalem and the Temple (14:3–7). When Tobit and then Anna die, Tobias and Sarah return to her family in Ecbatana, and before his death Tobias witnesses the beginning of the fulfillment of prophecy in the destruction of Nineveh. God has mercifully begun to turn his face toward his exiled people. So the story ends. Tobit and Sarah have been healed, and Israel's healing has begun, inevitably to be completed.

Bibliography

Fries, Carl. "Das Buch Tobit und die Telemachie." *Zeitschrift für wissenschaftliche Theologie* 53 (1910–1911): 54–87. Considers many striking relationships between the Book of Tobit and portions of the *Odyssey* dealing with Telemachus.

Lindenberger, J. M. "Ahiqar." In *The Old Testament Pseudepigrapha*, edited by J. H. Charlesworth. Vol. 2. Garden City, N.Y., 1983–1985. Pp. 479–507. Introduces and translates the Story of Ahiqar (Ahikar) referred to in Tobit.

Milik, J. T. "La Patrie de Tobie." *Revue Biblique* 73 (1966): 522–530. Cites the passages from Tobit found in the Qumran manuscripts and discusses the geographical provenance of the story.

Nickelsburg, George W. E. *Jewish Literature Between the Bible and the Mishnah.* Philadelphia, 1981.

———. "Stories of Biblical and Postbiblical Times." In *Jewish Writings of the Second Temple Period*, edited by Michael E. Stone. Compendia Rerum Iudaicarum ad Novum Testamentum 2.2. Philadelphia, 1984. Pp. 33–87. Treats Tobit in the context of its contemporary Jewish literature and history.

Pfeiffer, Robert H. *History of New Testament Times, with an Introduction to the Apocrypha.* New York, 1949. Pp. 258–284. Discusses Tobit in the context of previous research and is especially valuable for his treatment of folkloric elements in the story.

Ruppert, Lothar. "Das Buch Tobias: Ein Modellfall nachgestaltender Erzählung." In *Wort, Lied und Gottesspruch: Beiträge zur Septuaginta*, edited by J. Schreiner. Würzburg, 1972. Pp. 109–119. Relates Tobit to the biblical story of Joseph.

Simpson, D. C. "Tobit." In *The Apocrypha and Pseudepigrapha of the Old Testament*, edited by R. H. Charles. Vol. 1. Oxford, 1913. Pp. 174–241. Provides an earlier but still useful introduction and translation with critical notes.

Zimmermann, Frank. *The Book of Tobit.* Philadelphia, 1958. Provides an English translation with an extensive introduction and commentary.

NORMAN R. PETERSEN

Judith

THE BOOK OF JUDITH is one of the extrabiblical books found in the Septuagint. Written in Greek, Judith was never included in the Hebrew canon. Protestants regard it as part of the Apocrypha. Roman Catholic and Eastern Orthodox Christians recognize Judith as part of the canon of the Old Testament, listing it as one of the historical books (Joshua, Judges, 1–2 Samuel, 1–2 Kings, 1–2 Chronicles, Ezra-Nehemiah, Tobit, Judith, Esther).

Judith is an anonymous book. Nothing is known about its author except what can be deduced from the story itself. The author writes in Greek but imitates Hebrew idiom and syntax. The author is familiar with Palestinian, Assyrian, Babylonian, Persian, and Greek history and geography, and most especially with Jewish religious customs of the second century B.C.E. Most scholars describe the author as a Pharisaic Palestinian Jew.

The story mixes political and geographic details in such a fashion that there can be no doubt that Judith was meant as didactic fiction, not factual history. No author as attentive to compositional details as the writer of Judith could have mistakenly portrayed Nebuchadrezzar, the Babylonian king responsible for the fall of Jerusalem in 587 B.C.E., as an Assyrian.

A reference to Judith in the first epistle of Clement of Rome in the first century C.E. makes it clear that the story was composed before this time.

The exact date of the composition cannot be determined. The historical data in the book are at the service of the storyteller's fiction, which intermingles references from five centuries of real history, including Assyrian, Babylonian, Persian, and Greek antecedents. It seems most likely that Judith was composed early in the first century B.C.E. during the late Hasmonean period.

The story suits the reign of John Hyrcanus (135–105), who served as both king and high priest of Jerusalem. Early in Hyrcanus' reign, after Jerusalem had been under siege for a year, he agreed to pay a heavy tribute to the Seleucid king, Antiochus VII Sidetes. On the death of Antiochus in 128, Hyrcanus ceased paying the indemnity and expanded the borders of his territory. He forced the Idumeans (the old Edomites) to become Jews. Fear of military domination and struggle over which God should be served are important components in the story of Judith.

Judith is a fictional narrative which imaginatively tells a story that encourages exclusive worship of the one God of Israel. The story addresses fear of external and internal threats to the faith. Most of the story takes place in a little town to the north of Jerusalem called Bethulia. The town, which is described as being in the region of Samaria, is otherwise unknown in Palestinian geography. Judith, whose name means "Jew," is a courageous woman also known only from this story.

CONTENT AND STYLE

Part 1 (1:1–7:32) tells the story of a military and religious struggle that begins in Persia and makes its way to the little Israelite town of Bethulia. Nebuchadrezzar's political sovereignty over all the nations of the world and Yahweh's divine sovereignty over Israel come into direct conflict. The fearful Israelites nearly capitulate to their enemy. Part 2 (8:1–16:25) tells how a widow, Judith, delivers the people of Israel from their own fears and destroys the enemy who threatens their continued existence.

The two parts of the narrative are balanced and proportional. Each is structured internally by a threefold chiastic pattern in which certain narrative components are repeated in reverse order.

Structure of the Narrative

Judith 1–7 includes a description of Nebuchadnezzar's Persian campaign and a threefold chiastic development of events in the Assyrian camp and in Israel. It describes Nebuchadnezzar's eastern campaign and revenge against the disobedient western vassal nations (1:1–7:32):

1. Introduction to Nebuchadnezzar and his campaign against Arphaxad (1:1–16).
2. Nebuchadnezzar commissions Holofernes to take vengeance on the disobedient vassal nations (2:1–13).
3. Holofernes attacks the western nations (2:14–7:32).
   - A. Holofernes leads the campaign against the disobedient nations; the people surrender (2:14–3:10).
   - B. Israel hears and is "greatly terrified"; Joakim orders war preparations (4:1–15).
   - C. Holofernes talks with Achior; Achior is expelled from the Assyrian camp (5:1–6:11).
   - C'. Achior is received into Bethulia; he talks with the people of Israel (6:12–21).
   - B'. Holofernes orders war preparations; Israel sees and is "greatly terrified" (7:1–5).
   - A'. Holofernes leads the campaign against Bethulia; the people want to surrender (7:6–32).

Judith 8 to 16 is similarly organized by a threefold chiastic pattern with the climactic scene of Holofernes' beheading at its center:

- A. Introduction to Judith (8:1–8).
- B. Judith plans to save Israel (8:9–10:9a).
- C. Judith and her maid leave Bethulia (10:9b–10).
- D. Judith overcomes Holofernes (10:11–13:10a).
- C'. Judith and her maid return to Bethulia (13:10b–11).
- B'. Judith plans the destruction of Israel's enemy (13:12–16:20).
- A'. Conclusion about Judith (16:21–25).

The Content of the Narrative

The story opens as Nebuchadnezzar attacks Arphaxad in his impenetrable capital, Ecbatana in Persia. Nebuchadnezzar had requested auxiliary troops from his western vassal nations. Their disregard of his order occasioned the political revenge that led to the attack against Israel.

Holofernes, commander in chief of the Assyrian troops, leads the expedition against the rebel vassal nations. Despite their surrender, Holofernes demolishes their cultic sites and destroys their gods, "so that all nations should worship Nebuchadnezzar only, and all tongues and tribes should call upon him as god" (3:8; translations from Revised Standard Version except as noted). The Israelites are understandably terrified as they watch the approach of the Assyrian troops.

In part 1 (1–7), "fear" or its denial propels the development of the story. The western nations refuse Nebuchadnezzar's orders because they do not "fear him" (1:11; Au. trans.). As Holofernes moves against these nations they experience "fear and terror" (2:28). The Israelites in turn are "greatly terrified" (4:2). When the Israelites prepare for war, the Assyrians boast that they "do not fear" them (5:23; Au. trans.). As the Assyrian army closes in on the Bethulians, they are "greatly terrified" (7:4).

Fear is coupled with a contest over the one true God. Nebuchadnezzar specifically instructs Holofernes to require only political submission from the nations (see 2:5–13, Nebuchadnezzar's only words in the entire story). Holofernes goes beyond his sovereign's command, destroys the religious centers of the subjugated nations, and demands that they worship his king (3:8). When Achior, the Ammonite, suggests that the God of Israel might defeat the Assyrian army if provoked (5:21), Holofernes rages, "Who is God except Nebuchadnezzar?" (6:2). After thirty-four days of siege with no water, the Bethulians lose heart and declare, "We have no helper, for God has sold us into their hands" (7:25; Au. trans.). Crisis makes apostasy and slavery look appealing to the besieged Bethulians.

Judging themselves guilty of some sin (7:28), the Bethulians ask their leaders to surrender to Assyria. Uzziah suggests a compromise that gives God five days to deliver them. As part 1 ends, the Israelites, who "were very dejected" (7:32; Anchor Bible) temporarily postpone what seems inevitable surrender, destruction of their sanctuary, and worship of Nebuchadnezzar. It seems the narrative needs only to describe the five-day wait and the final conquest of Israel. Two sections balancing the introductory description of Nebuchadnezzar's campaign against Arphaxad and his subsequent commissioning of Holofernes would finish the story in style. But no such sections appear.

Instead Judith enters the story, and in part 2 (8–16) "beauty" conquers fear. Judith, the "beautiful" widow of Manasseh (8:7), lays aside the sackcloth of her three-year-and-four-month widowhood in order to make herself "very beautiful, to entice the eyes of all who might see her" (10:4; Au. trans.). The leaders of Bethulia (10:7), the Assyrian patrol (10:14), the entire Assyrian camp (10:19), and, most important, Holofernes (10:23) marvel at her "beauty." Holofernes and his servants acclaim her "beautiful in appearance" and "wise in speech" (11:21, 23). "This beautiful womanservant" so arouses Holofernes that he instructs his eunuch Bagoas to persuade Judith to eat and drink with them so that he might have an opportunity for sexual intercourse with her (12:11–12; Au. trans.). Judith, who "fears God exceedingly" (8:8; Au. trans.), proves more than equal to his seduction and to the theological confusion that had brought her own community to within five days of surrendering to the enemy.

Judith reprimands the leaders of Bethulia for putting "God to the test" (8:12). She defends God's freedom to protect or to destroy (8:15) and argues that faith means to "wait for deliverance" (8:17), not to coerce God. Judith reminds the Bethulian officials that since their generation had not sinned by knowing other gods, they had every reason to hope that God would not disdain them (8:18–20). She argues that they are being tested (8:25), just as Abraham, Isaac, and Jacob were tested (8:26). She exhorts them to serve as examples of confidence in God, reminding them that the safety of the sanctuary, Temple, and altar rests upon their and her actions. She herself promises to deliver Israel within the allotted five days by a secret plan (8:32–34).

After praying that God give her the strength to crush the arrogance of the Assyrians by the deceit of her lips (9:10), dressing alluringly, and preparing a bag of ritually pure food, Judith and her maid go to the enemy camp. She explains to Holofernes that she has come to reveal the moment when he can successfully capture Jerusalem (11:5–19).

For three days Judith follows a routine of praying, bathing nightly outside the camp, and eating her own food. On the fourth night she is invited to the tent of Holofernes for a party (12:13). When the two are alone, Holofernes falls asleep because he is drunk (13:2). Judith seizes the opportunity of the moment, prays, takes his sword, prays a second time (13:7), and, with two mighty strokes, cuts off his head (13:8). She puts his head into her food bag; then she and her maid walk out of the camp. She arouses no suspicion because such is her nightly custom. This night, however, she does not bathe; she returns to Bethulia.

The townspeople and officials praise Judith's great deed (13:17–20). She outlines a plan of attack for the next morning and asks that Achior, the Ammonite, whom Holofernes had condemned to share the fate of the Bethulians, be brought to her (14:1–5). Achior, overwhelmed at the sight of the head of the enemy general, converts and is circumcised that very night (14:6–10). The next day, the Israelites successfully rout the Assyrians (14:11–15:7).

Joakim, the high priest of Jerusalem, comes to praise Judith's great victory for God (15:8–10). And after plundering the enemy camp for thirty days, the

Israelites follow Judith in a triumphal procession of dance and song to Jerusalem for a three-month celebration (15:11–16:20).

When they return home, Judith's fame spreads and many men desire to marry her (16:22). Judith chooses to live alone for the remainder of her long life. Before she dies, she frees her maid and distributes her property. She is buried with Manasseh and is mourned by Israel for seven days (16:24). The book closes with the note that for a long time after her death no one spread terror among the people of Israel (16:25).

THEOLOGICAL DISCLOSURES

The governing perspective of the Book of Judith is theological. Seven closely related theological disclosures in the story merit particular attention.

Judith as Resistance Literature

The Book of Judith is designed to counter fear and to affirm the sovereignty of the God of Israel. Its primary lesson is that "fear of the Lord" is worth all costs, and that the faithful are those who fight the good fight. In a day of hard choices, part 1 teaches that ultimately devastation does not count, and part 2 that survival does not matter. Judith insists that right resistance involves allowing God radical freedom to deliver or destroy (8:15). This story disarms fear of external and internal enemies. It models resistance to any power that would impede or dictate God's actions.

Personal Prayer

The practice of personal prayer is important to Judith. She is the only character in the story who regularly prays alone. She comes into the story as one accustomed to dwelling alone in a shelter on the roof of her house (8:5), and she retires to solitude at the close of the story (16:21–23).

Before every action in the story, Judith prays. It is her habit of personal prayer that allows her to walk out of the enemy camp when her work there is done. She tells Holofernes that she is "devout and serves the God of heaven day and night" (11:17; Au. trans.). She explains that she will go out into the valley every night and pray to God so that she will know when Holofernes ought to attack Jerusalem (11:17–19).

When she leaves the enemy camp the night she beheads Holofernes, the soldiers simply assume she has gone out to pray.

Her personal prayers, as distinguished from her communal prayers, are composed of laments and petitions. She implores God to be with her as she prepares to go into the enemy camp (9:4, 12) and again as she lifts the sword to chop off Holofernes' head (13:4b–5, 7b).

In her opening prayer in chapter 9, Judith asks three things of God: that God hear her prayer (9:4), that God break the strength of the Assyrians (9:8), and that God give her the strength to crush the arrogance of the Assyrians by the deceit of her lips (9:10, 13).

Trust is the hallmark of all Judith's prayers. As she prays, so she acts. Implicit in her every action is the conviction that faithfulness counts more than life. Her sure hope is that God will not disdain the people (8:20). She trusts God to deliver the people through her hand (8:33). But more important than any result is right fear of the Lord and right service of God. She urges the town officials of Bethulia to join her in setting an example for the people (8:24): "Let us give thanks to the Lord our God, who is putting us to the test" (8:25).

Lying

The lies of three characters stand out in this story. Judith lies for the sake of the covenant community, and Holofernes and Uzziah lie out of self-interest. Judith asks God to make her a good liar: "By the guile of my lips, smite slave with prince and prince with his servant. Break into pieces their high estate by the hand of a female" (9:10; Au. trans.). By "deceit" (9:10, 13) she intends to destroy the enemy. Once in the Assyrian camp, she systematically sets about deceiving the Assyrians. Her words in 10:11–13:10a are sometimes true in a factual sense (11:10), are sometimes true in the sense of having double meanings (11:6, 16), and are sometimes outright lies (11:8, 19).

Holofernes, "who had been biding his time to deceive her" (12:16; Au. trans.), lies when he tells her she has nothing to fear because he is "not one to harm anyone who serves Nebuchadnezzar" (11:1; Au. trans.). He conveniently forgets his destruction of the sanctuaries of seacoast peoples who had sent him envoys to sue for peace (3:1–8). Holofernes is not interested in truth; he wants to seduce Judith (12:12).

Uzziah lies through self-deception. He most likely believes his words to Judith that from her earliest days all had recognized her good sense and sound judgment (8:29). But flattery is not esteem. His failure to consult her about the crisis in Bethulia, especially when the people cry, "We have no one to help us" (7:25), suggests that he does not seriously value her judgment. It is not true, as he lamely pleads to Judith (8:30), that the people "forced" him to vow that he would hand over the city in five days if God did not deliver them (see 7:23–28). He proposes the five-day delay himself (7:30). He counts his plan an inviolable vow (8:30).

Faithfulness to a human vow is surely rendered meaningless in comparison to faithfulness to God. But Uzziah's comments to Judith show that he does not see it that way: "The people were very thirsty and they compelled us to do for them what we have promised, and made us take an oath which we cannot break. So pray for us, since you are a devout woman, and the Lord will send us rain to fill our cisterns and we will no longer be faint" (8:30–31). He hopes for magic and miracles, thinking rain will fill the cisterns during the rainless months (4:5, 7:20).

Judith tells Uzziah and the other elders of Bethulia that their advice is unsound. She pointedly accuses them of setting themselves above God by planning to surrender the town: "You are putting the Lord Almighty to the test, but you will never know anything! If you cannot plumb the depths of a human heart or understand the thoughts of his mind, then how can you fathom God, who made all these things, or understand his mind, or comprehend his reasoning?" (8:13–14; Au. trans.). Uzziah's theological judgments are false, and Judith challenges the lie of his putting himself in God's place.

In the Book of Judith lying is justifiable when it is congruent with righteousness and the honest maintenance of the covenant. What matters most is fulfilling the covenantal responsibilities. Righteousness and honesty with regard to the covenant are the marks of the lies Judith told for the faith. Truth is not factual. Truth is personal, relational, and revealed in process.

Faithfulness and the Order of Creation

Judith lies in this narrative because it is necessary for the good of the community. Faithfulness involves neither magic nor quietism. Faithfulness is measured in terms of active participation in the process of shaping tradition. No standard except the covenant with God is absolute. By right of God's created order, which calls men and women alike to responsible relationship with God, Judith models a radical faithfulness that goes to any length to overcome oppression. Her bold style of faithfulness creates a congruence between self-understanding, understanding of God, and action. She does not tell God how to be God.

She "fears God exceedingly" (8:8) and knows that faithfulness means "waiting for deliverance" (8:17). Destruction or deliverance are of no real importance. Her conviction that God is free from human manipulation corrects and transforms the fear of her people. Judith's best gift to the people is the freedom and courage of right "fear of the Lord." The story ends with the statement that "there was no longer any who spread fear among the Israelites during the days of Judith or for many days after she died" (16:25; Au. trans.).

Societal Conventions

No biblical woman is as unconventional as Judith. None is as punctiliously pious in observing ritual dietary restrictions (see her preparations for her time in the enemy camp [10:5]; her explanation to Holofernes that she has to use her own things [12:2–4]; and her consumption of only her own food at the party to which Holofernes invites her on the fateful fourth night in the enemy camp [12:19]). No other woman shatters the fetters of narrow orthodoxy in more startling ways.

Judith is unconcerned about societal conventions suitable to the maintenance of patriarchy. She summons the male leaders of her town, challenges their actions, and accuses them of putting themselves in the place of God (8:9–34). She delegates the management of her household to a woman, not a man (8:10). She chops off a man's head (13:8). She lies for the sake of her people and the sanctuary of their God. Even though childless, she refuses to remarry (16:22).

On her account Achior joins the house of Israel (14:6–10). The terror-stricken eunuch Bagoas shouts, "One Hebrew woman has brought disgrace upon the house of King Nebuchadnezzar! For look, here is Holofernes lying on the ground, and his head is not on him!" (14:18). Joakim, the high priest of Jerusalem, testifies, "You are the exaltation of Jerusalem, you are the great glory of Israel, you are the great pride of our nation! You have done all this singlehanded; you have done great good to Israel, and God is well pleased with it. May the Almighty Lord bless you for ever!" (15:9–10; Au. trans.).

Communal Prayer

Part 1 is like a communal lament gone awry. When the covenant people appear for the first time in the narrative in chapter 4, they gather because they have heard of Holofernes' destruction of the temples from their neighbors: "They were therefore very greatly terrified at his approach, and were alarmed both for Jerusalem and the temple of the Lord their God" (4:2). Joakim, the high priest of Jerusalem, orders the people to fortify all the passes that lead to their hilltop towns (4:7), which they do (4:8). And then in a great voice they cry to God, fast, sprinkle ashes on their heads, and put sackcloth everywhere—on the men, women, and children (including the alien residents, hired laborers, and purchased slaves), on the cattle, and even on the altar itself (4:10–11). They petition God to "look with favor upon the whole house of Israel" (4:15).

They pray and God listens: "The Lord heard their prayers and looked upon their affliction" (4:13). But God does not answer their prayer as they wish, so they lose heart. Their complaint then shifts from identifying the Assyrians as their enemy to identifying God's vengeance as the problem (7:28). In response to the people's cry, "We have no one to help us; God has sold us into their hands" (7:25), the equally confused town leaders of Bethulia come up with the plan to postpone surrender for five days.

In part 2, when Judith prays with the community, it is first a silent prayer as she leaves the town to go to the enemy camp (10:8). When she returns with the head of Holofernes, she calls out jubilantly, "Open, open the gate! God, our God, is still with us, to show his power in Israel, and his strength against our enemies, even as he has done this day!" (13:11). In a loud voice she urges the people, assembled to witness the triumph, to "Praise God, O praise him! Praise God, who has not withdrawn his mercy from the house of Israel, but has destroyed our enemies by my hand this very night!" (13:14). The final chapter of the book includes a communal liturgy of thanksgiving led by Judith. In a scene suggestive of a triumphant procession to Jerusalem (see 16:18), Judith and the people sing of God's great victory. Together they confess that their God "crushes wars" (16:3). Final resolution is achieved by their acknowledgment that "to those who fear you, you will show mercy" (16:15; Au. trans.).

Trust in an invisible, all-powerful God has been put to the test. In part 1, it seems as if all is lost. In part 2, the people, through the deed of the woman Judith, find voices to praise God with the renewed confidence that the one "who fears the Lord shall be great for ever" (16:16).

God

God is the holy warrior who crushes wars (16:3) and all opponents. The whole book addresses the question of the identity of the true God for Israel. In the end the transcendent, holy one of Israel, championed by Judith as a God "not like a man, to be threatened, nor like a human being, to be won over by pleading" (8:16), triumphs. God is reliable; God sees those things which bind the people of Israel, and God provides for their deliverance. God never abandons the people to a future with no hope. But God's ways are mysterious. God is free of human dictates.

In her personal prayer before going into the enemy camp, Judith says it all: "For your strength depends not upon numbers, nor your might upon powerful men; for you are God of the lowly, helper of the insignificant, upholder of the weak, protector of the despairing, savior of those without hope. Please, please, God of my father, God of the inheritance of Israel, ruler of heaven and earth, creator of the waters, king of all your creation, hear my prayer!" (9:11–12; Au. trans.). The ten titles for God embedded in this prayer sum up well who God is for the author of the Book of Judith.

CONCLUSION

All is well that ends well, but it is not the ending that counts most in the Book of Judith. Daily faithfulness to the covenant in all its mystery claims allegiance in this story. Judith reinterprets the crisis her people face as God's test of faithfulness, not God's punishment or abandonment of the people. No enemy, fear, or anxiety can dictate or impede the way of righteousness. Covenant faith is a dynamic, continuous choice of direction and movement toward the divine-human congruence God holds out to all creation.

The Book of Judith is a triumphant tale that models militant faithfulness in the face of adversity. Together part 1 and part 2 disclose fresh interpretations of what it means to serve only one God, to turn to this God for an easing of life's plights, and to trust God without reserve. This finely crafted fictional story tells again the ancient truth that by vocation and God's design the covenant people are free if they "fear God" only and rely wholeheartedly on the covenant.

Bibliography

Alonso-Schökel, Luis. "Narrative Structures in the Book of Judith." In *Protocol Series of the Colloquies of the Center for Hermeneutical Studies in Hellenistic and Modern Culture*, edited by Wilheim Wuellner, Berkeley, Calif., 1974, no. 11, 1–20. This article is followed by seven written responses and the minutes of the colloquy.

Craven, Toni. "Artistry and Faith in the Book of Judith." *Semeia* 8 (1977): 75–101. An article detailing the compositional components of the Book of Judith.

———. *Artistry and Faith in the Book of Judith*. Chico, Calif., 1983. A literary/rhetorical analysis of the external design of the Book of Judith and its internal compositional patterns.

———. "Tradition and Convention in the Book of Judith." *Semeia* 28 (1983): 49–62. A comparison of Judith, Esther, and Ruth.

———. "Women Who Lied for the Faith." In *Justice and the Holy: Essays in Honor of Walter Harrelson*, edited by Douglas A. Knight and Peter J. Paris, forthcoming. An article about seven women for whom truth was not fact, but rather a personal and relational process.

Dancy, J. C. *The Shorter Books of the Apocrypha*. Cambridge, 1972. Includes a brief but insightful commentary on the theology and text of Judith.

Enslin, Morton S. *The Book of Judith: Greek Text with an English Translation, Commentary, and Critical Notes*. Leiden, 1972. Very helpful commentary.

Moore, Carey A. *Judith: A New Translation with Introduction and Commentary*. The Anchor Bible, vol. 40. Garden City, N.Y., 1985. A detailed study of the Book of Judith with a sensitive new translation. Includes full bibliography.

TONI CRAVEN

The Wisdom of Solomon

THE WISDOM OF Solomon is one of the Apocrypha or deuterocanonical books, accepted as part of Scripture by the Roman Catholic church (and some Eastern Orthodox Christians) but rejected by Protestantism. In antiquity it was more widely accepted as canonical than any other book of the Apocrypha. It was quoted as authoritative from the end of the second century C.E. onward, and was clearly regarded as Scripture by Clement of Alexandria, although Origen, in the third century, admitted that it "is not held by all to have authority" (*On First Principles* 4.4.6). Oddly enough, the Wisdom of Solomon was listed with the books of the New Testament in the Muratorian Canon, which originated in Rome about 200: "Further an epistle of Jude and two with the title John are accepted in the Catholic Church, and the Wisdom written by friends of Solomon in his honor." It has been suggested that the reference to "friends of Solomon" is a mistake by the Latin translator of a Greek original, which read, "the Wisdom of Solomon, written by Philo in his honor" (Winston, 68), referring to the Jewish philosopher who lived in Alexandria at the time of Christ. Its inclusion within the New Testament list would then be explained by the tradition that Philo had been converted to Christianity.

The ambiguity of the status of the Wisdom of Solomon in the early church reflects the circumstances of its composition. As the author of the Muratorian Canon was aware, it is not a work of King Solomon, but a pseudepigraphon composed in his honor. (Origen sometimes referred to it as "The Wisdom attributed to Solomon"; Winston, 68). It was rejected by Protestantism because it was not included in the Hebrew Bible—a fact deriving both from its original language, Greek, and from its late date of composition. There is no evidence that the work ever enjoyed the status of Scripture in Judaism. It is a product of the Greek-speaking Jewish Diaspora, most probably in Alexandria, and is, with 2 Maccabees, one of the very few products of this branch of Judaism that was ever accorded canonical status. Its peculiar importance arises from its location at the intersection of Jewish tradition and Hellenistic culture, and also from its similarity to later examples of the Christian appropriation of Greek philosophy to conceptualize religious faith.

STRUCTURE AND CONTENT

The book falls into three main parts: the "book of eschatology" in 1:1–6:21, the "book of wisdom" proper in 6:22–9:18, and the "book of history" in chapters 10–19. The threefold division of the book is universally accepted, but the boundaries between the divisions are disputed. Some scholars define the "book of eschatology" as chapters 1–5 (Georgi, 393) and regard chapter 10 as part of the middle section of the book (Winston, 10–12; Dimant, 246; Georgi, 393). The ambiguity of the transitional passages (6:1–21 and chap. 10) will be evident from the following outline of the contents.

"The Book of Eschatology" (1:1–6:21)

The book begins with an exhortation to the rulers of the earth to love righteousness (1:1), supported by several assertions about wisdom and the spirit of God, and culminates with the statement that righteousness is immortal (1:1–15).

The relation between righteousness and immortality is illustrated by a contrast between the respective fates of the righteous and the wicked (1:16–5:23). The section 1:16–2:24 sets out the "unsound reasoning" of the wicked, who argue that "hereafter we shall be as though we had never been" and who consequently think that might is right and proceed to oppress the righteous. In 3:1–9 the author asserts that the righteous only seem to die, but are at peace, and in 3:10–4:6 he contrasts the righteous and the wicked with respect to sterility and children. Even the person incapable of procreation, if righteous, is really blessed. The section 4:7–20 contrasts the deaths of the righteous and the wicked. Virtue is more important than length of years. And then, in 5:1–23, the author describes the vindication of the just at the final judgment.

The book ends with an exhortation to kings and judges to learn wisdom (6:1–21), and includes a description of wisdom in 6:12–16 and of how it leads to a kingdom (6:17–20).

"The Book of Wisdom" (6:22–9:18)

The section 6:22–25 promises, in the first person, to tell "what wisdom is and how she came to be" (6:22). Then, in 7:1–9:18, the exposition of wisdom follows: 7:1–22a gives an autobiographical account of how the author (ostensibly Solomon) came to acquire wisdom; 7:22b–8:1 lists the attributes of wisdom; 8:2–21 explains the attraction of wisdom for Solomon; and 9:1–18 contains Solomon's prayer for wisdom.

"The Book of History" (chaps. 10–19)

The initial section, 10:1–14, lists several examples of how wisdom saved "the righteous man." The examples are transparently biblical, ranging from Adam ("the first-formed father of the world") to Joseph ("when a righteous man was sold"), but no names are mentioned. In 10:15–21, the author describes the deliverance at the Exodus, and in 11:1–19:22 he demonstrates divine justice by a series of seven contrasts between the plagues of Egypt and the blessings of Israel in the wilderness. There are also two extensive excursuses, one on divine mercy (11:15–12:27) and one on idolatry (13:1–15:19).

The transitional passage between the first two parts, 6:1–21, is presented as a direct exhortation to the rulers of the earth. It thus parallels 1:1–15 and forms an *inclusio* for the "book of eschatology." It also anticipates the following part by giving a brief description of wisdom in 6:12–16. The theme of kingship is continued through chapters 7–9.

Chapter 10 evidently begins the perusal of biblical history that continues in chapters 11–19. It is true that wisdom is the divine agent in this chapter, whereas chapters 11–19 speak more directly of God. In 11:1, however, the third-person agent that caused the works of Israel to prosper is most probably wisdom. God is usually addressed in the second person throughout chapters 11–19.

The very difficulty of deciding the boundaries of the main parts is an argument for the unity of the book. The section 6:1–21 is a transitional passage that refers back to the opening address but also introduces the main theme of the following chapters. Similarly, chapter 10 continues to highlight the figure of wisdom, which dominated 6:22–9:18, but introduces the discussion of history, and specifically of the Exodus, that dominates the final section.

LANGUAGE AND UNITY

In the late eighteenth and early nineteenth centuries, it was customary to ascribe different parts of the book to different authors (Winston, 12–13). In 1860, however, the commentary of Carl Grimm went far toward establishing the unity of the book on the basis of language and style. Theories of diverse authors were revived in the early twentieth century. The most influential arguments were those of Friedrich Focke, who held that chapters 1–5 were originally composed in Hebrew, and that the translator of these chapters added chapters 6–19. His main arguments concerned the supposed lack of Greek philosophy, the relative absence of the personified figure of wisdom in chapters 1–5, and the increased tone of nationalism in chapters 10–19.

Most commentators, however, have continued to defend the unity of the book, and the originality of the Greek language throughout. In fact there is no lack of Greek philosophical terminology in chapters 1–5. The "spirit of the Lord," which fills the world and holds all things together (1:7), is clearly identical with the spirit (*pneuma*) wisdom, which loves human-kind (1:6) and is further described in 6:22–9:18. The doctrine of immortality in chapters 1–5 is also indebt-ed to Greek philosophy. Several Greek expressions in chapters 1–5 have no obvious equivalent in Hebrew (e.g., *to synechon ta panta*, "that which holds all things together," 1:7, *aphtharsia*, "incorruption," 2:23; see further Winston, 13). The Greek style is excellent throughout, and several thematic terms recur in the various sections (Winston, 16). The more nationalistic tone of chapters 10–19 is related to the subject matter of those chapters and need not be taken as an indication of different authorship.

GENRE

The coherence of the different parts of the Wisdom of Solomon must be understood in terms of the genre of the whole. This is variously identified as the *logos protreptikos* or exhortatory discourse (Reese 1970, 117–121; Winston, 18–20) or as an encomium (Gilbert, 307). In either case it is a rhetorical work, drawing on philosophical arguments, that advocates a course of action and tries to show that it is expedient and good. In this case the subject of the exhortation is love of righteousness (1:1) and wisdom (6:9). The "book of eschatology" shows what is at stake by presenting the arguments of the opponents and show-ing their inadequacy. It also presents the author's most basic argument for the value of righteousness: it leads to vindication in a judgment after death. The

"book of wisdom" is the encomium proper. It de-scribes the origin and nature of wisdom and the manner in which it is attained. This part has an autobiographical component that strengthens the ar-gument by the testimony of personal experience. The final part of the book (chaps. 10–19) elaborates the theme by well-known examples. Biblical history, especially the Exodus story, is expounded to show that the efficacy of righteousness is guaranteed by the universe itself. The author makes plentiful use of *synkrisis*, comparison and contrast, to show the su-periority of righteousness to its opposite. One distinc-tively Jewish feature of the last section is that the author repeatedly addresses God in the second person.

THE BOOK OF ESCHATOLOGY

The opening part of the book presents the doctrine of immortality, which is of crucial impor-tance for the commendation of wisdom and righteous-ness. It also provides a major example of the intersec-tion of Greek and Hebrew traditions. While the thesis that chapters 1–5 are translated from Hebrew cannot be maintained, it is likely that the author drew some of his ideas from a Semitic source (or translation thereof). This is most clearly the case in chapter 5, where the immortality of the righteous is portrayed in the context of an apocalyptic judgment scene, which finds its closest parallels in the Enoch literature, originally composed in Aramaic (Nickelsburg, 70–78).

The understanding of immortality in the Wis-dom of Solomon is indebted to apocalyptic traditions in two respects. First, immortality pertains to "the mysteries of God" (2:22). The idea of mystery (Ara-maic *raz*) appears prominently in the Book of Daniel and in the Dead Sea Scrolls. It refers to matters that are ordinarily inaccessible to human knowledge, but are made known through special revelations. Such revelations form the subject matter of the apocalypses. The Hebrew wisdom tradition, in contrast, shows little interest in mysteries or special revelations and relies primarily on tradition and common human experience. Traditional Hebrew wisdom (Ecclesiastes, Sirach) also rejected any belief in a reward after death. The expectation of a meaningful afterlife (as opposed to the survival of a shade, which was the traditional

Israelite belief) first entered Jewish tradition in the apocalyptic literature, specifically in 1 Enoch and Daniel.

Second, in Wisdom 5, immortality takes the form of fellowship with the angels, who are referred to as "saints" or "sons of God." The idea that righteous people who are afflicted on earth will hereafter share the glory of the angels is clearly expressed in 1 Enoch 104:2–6:

> Be hopeful! For you were formerly put to shame through evils and afflictions, but now you will shine like the lights of heaven and will be seen, and the gate of heaven will be opened to you . . . for you will have a great joy like the angels of heaven . . . and now do not be afraid, you righteous, when you see the sinners growing strong and prospering in their desires, and do not be associated with them . . . for you shall be associates of the host of heaven.

The promise of Daniel 12:3 that the wise will shine like the stars forever should likewise be understood to refer to an association with the angels after death. The term "saints" or "holy ones" is often used to refer to angels in apocalyptic literature (Daniel, 1 Enoch, the Dead Sea Scrolls). It is noteworthy that the early, pre-Christian apocalyptic idea of an afterlife does not clearly imply the resurrection of the body (although that idea is implied in 2 Maccabees 7 and appears clearly in later apocalyptic writings, e.g., 2 Esdras 7:32, *Sibylline Oracles* 4:181–182). Even Daniel 12:2 (those who sleep in "the land of dust") may refer to Sheol or the netherworld rather than the grave, and so does not necessarily imply bodily resurrection. The apocalypses envisage the exaltation of the spirit rather than of the body. Paul probably reflects the typical Semitic idea when he speaks of "a spiritual body" (1 Cor 15:44) that is different from a physical body but is not yet the same as the philosophical idea of the soul, which later Christian theology adapted from Greek philosophy.

In the Wisdom of Solomon these apocalyptic ideas of life after death are woven together with the more philosophical concepts of the Greeks. The ways of life of the righteous and the wicked are contrasted as two different philosophies. The philosophy of the wicked is rather eclectic. The motif of being born by chance (2:2) is typical of Epicureanism; the equation of reason with a spark (2:2) is Stoic; the determina-

tion to "crown ourselves with rosebuds ere they wither" (2:8) is a commonplace of popular philosophy from the Epic of Gilgamesh on, although the reference to rosebuds is distinctly Greek. (This motif was made famous in English literature by Robert Herrick's verse "Gather ye rosebuds while ye may" in his poem "To the Virgins, to Make Much of Time.") The treatment of the righteous man is reminiscent of Plato's description of the purely righteous man: "Let him be the best of men, and let him be thought the worst; then he will have been put to the proof and we shall see whether he will be affected by the fear of infamy and its consequences." Further, "after suffering every kind of evil he will be impaled" (*Republic* 2.361). In the spirit of Plato, the Wisdom of Solomon also affirms a contrast between what seems to be and what really is. In this case the righteous only seem to die, but in fact are at peace (3:2–3). There is no mention here of resurrection, either from the grave or from Sheol. Instead the author seems to be influenced by the Platonic belief in the immortality of the soul.

There has been endless debate as to whether Wisdom accepts the Greek dichotomy of soul and body, and thus understands immortality accordingly (Larcher 1969, 237–327). The parallelism of soul and body in 1:4 ("Wisdom will not enter a deceitful soul, nor dwell in a body enslaved to sin") suggests that either body or soul can stand for the person. The statement in 8:19–20 is more problematic: "As a child I was by nature well endowed and a good soul fell to my lot; or rather, being good, I entered an undefiled body." Commentators disagree as to the precise significance of this verse (Larcher 1969, 273–274; Winston, 26). It seems to presuppose some form of the preexistence of the soul. Such an idea has no precedent in Hebraic tradition but bears evident resemblance to Plato's doctrine of preexistence. There are, of course, differences. There is no suggestion in Wisdom of Solomon that souls are eternal, or uncreated, and there is no room here for the transmigration of souls, or for the theory of recollection of knowledge from a former life. On some of these points, the Platonic tradition had itself been modified by the first century B.C.E. (see Dillon, 96–102, on Cicero), but Wisdom was also constrained by the biblical tradition. Accordingly, the basis for the doctrine of immortality is not the inherent nature of the soul but the belief that "God made man for incorruption and made him in the image of his own eternity" (2:23). The ultimate warrant is derived from Genesis, but requires a distinctively Hellenistic interpretation of the scriptures. The term *aphtharsia* (incorruption) is borrowed from Epicurean philosophy and suggests that immortality does indeed pertain to the nature of the soul through the design of the creator. In the Book of Wisdom, however, that design can be thwarted. The realization of immortality depends on righteousness. In this respect Platonic philosophy is modified by the apocalyptic tradition.

The Wisdom of Solomon, then, uses both the imagery of the apocalypses and the more philosophical idiom of the Greeks. The two traditions are intertwined rather than fully integrated. The righteous after death can be envisaged as immortal souls or as fellows of the angelic sons of God. There is an underlying conviction that both traditions were expressing the same truth, although the formulations cannot be fully reconciled. Christianity later adopted a similar uneasy compromise between its apocalyptic heritage and Greek philosophy. Perhaps the greatest historical importance of Wisdom lies in the fact that it accepted the immortality of the soul as a valid expression of biblical faith and thereby paved the way for the synthesis of Hebrew and Greek traditions that followed.

THE FIGURE OF WISDOM

The fusion of Greek and Hebrew thought also complicates the portrayal of personified Wisdom, which occupies a pivotal place in the book. Wisdom provides an assurance of immortality through her laws (6:18). More fundamentally "she reaches mightily from one end of the earth to the other and she orders all things well" (8:1) and is identical with the spirit that holds all things together (1:7). In the review of biblical history in chapters 10–11, Wisdom acts in the place of God to deliver the righteous.

The biblical precedent for this figure is found in Proverbs 8, and it was further developed in Sirach 24. Both passages are declarations placed in the mouth of personified Wisdom. Both may already be influenced by the aretalogies or praises of the Egyptian goddess Isis, in which she sings her own praises. (The parallels with Isis are stronger in Sirach than in Proverbs.) In the Greek translation of Proverbs 8, Wisdom is clearly said to be created by God. (The meaning of the original Hebrew is disputed; it may mean that God acquired, rather than created, Wisdom.) Already in Proverbs, however, Wisdom took part in creation as God's helper. Her way is the way of life, because she is intimately acquainted with the structure of creation.

Sirach 24 goes further. There Wisdom proceeds from the mouth of God, and so can readily be identified with word (*logos*) or spirit (breath, *pneuma*), although these terms are not used. What is elsewhere said of God is there attributed to Wisdom— her throne is in a pillar of cloud, and she alone encompasses the earth. She is then bidden to pitch her tent in Israel, and is ultimately identified with "the book of the covenant of the Most High God, the law which Moses commanded us" (24:23). Wisdom, then, is not equated with God but is a form of divine presence in the world. This conception makes possible a way of speaking of the divine that is more abstract and amenable to philosophy than the anthropomorphic language of the Pentateuch. Sirach establishes a special relationship, even identity, between this universal wisdom of creation and the particular law of Israel.

The Wisdom of Solomon was indebted to this Jewish tradition, but it was also informed by Greek philosophical thought. The Stoics used the terms *logos* (word, reason) and *pneuma* (spirit) to refer to a divine principle immanent in the universe. This principle was conceived as a fiery substance so fine that it permeates all things. It is the rational, organizing principle of the universe. It differs from the Hebrew Wisdom in its material character, in the sense that it is not only a quality but a component of the physical world. It also differs from Hebraic tradition insofar as it is identified with the deity and is fully immanent in the universe (Armstrong, 122–129).

The Wisdom of Solomon is faithful to the Hebrew belief in a supreme, transcendent God who is the creator and donor of Wisdom. The figure of Wisdom, however, takes on the cosmological functions of the Stoic Logos in holding all things together and putting them in order. Its quasi-physical character is most apparent in the hymnlike list of attributes in 7:21–8:1:

For in her there is a spirit that is intelligent, holy, unique, manifold, subtle, mobile, clear, unpolluted . . . all powerful, overseeing all and penetrating through all spirits. . . . For wisdom is more mobile than any motion; because of her pureness she pervades and penetrates all things. (7:22–24)

Because of its power of penetration, Wisdom can enter the souls of the righteous and make them friends of God and prophets (7:27). This, of course, does not happen automatically, but only if the soul is properly disposed. (In Stoicism, too, people had to strive to live in accordance with nature.) The proper disposition is defined as "giving heed to her laws" (6:18). We may assume that these laws included the Law of Moses (in view of the identification of law and wisdom in Sirach, and of the prominence of biblical traditions throughout the book). Yet it is clear that salvation is not conceived here simply in terms of obedience to the law. It involves a transformation of the person through the indwelling of Wisdom, which brings one into harmony with creation. Correspondingly, the world is "saved" through the transformation of individuals: "a multitude of wise men is the salvation of the world" (6:24).

The Wisdom of Solomon does not think of Wisdom only in cosmological terms. It also uses the language of love and desire and speaks of taking her as a bride and living with her (8:2, 16). The praises of Wisdom resemble the praises of the Egyptian goddess Isis, and indeed Wisdom is the closest approximation to a goddess that can be found in the Jewish tradition. Yet, in the Wisdom of Solomon, the cosmological understanding is dominant and the figure of the bride appears to be a deliberate metaphor.

THE REVIEW OF HISTORY

The workings of Wisdom and of God in history are the subject of the last ten chapters of the book. These chapters have been described as a *midrash*, or narrative exposition of a biblical text, in this case primarily Exodus. The designation is at best a loose one (Reese 1970, 91–98). The objective of the author is not to expound the text but to develop his own theme of divine justice, using Exodus for illustration.

These chapters have been more aptly compared to a homily, but we need not infer that they were ever actually delivered in a synagogue.

While these chapters draw heavily on the biblical text, they are also informed by philosophical interests. The author is at pains to show the correspondence between the trials of the Israelites in the wilderness and the plagues of the Egyptians. The correspondence carries a lesson. The Egyptians were killed by the bites of locusts and flies, but the Israelites were not even overcome by poisonous snakes (16:9–10). The Egyptians were properly punished by animals, since they worship animals; the destruction of their children was warranted by their attempt to kill the Hebrew children (18:5). As with the persecuted righteous of chapter 3, reality is often the opposite of what appears to be the case. When "lawless men" thought they held Israel captive, they themselves were prisoners of darkness (17:2). Everything that happens has a place in the providential design. God has "arranged all things by measure and number and weight" (11:20).

Even the apparent miracles of the Exodus are not viewed as disruptions of the laws of nature. Since those laws are fashioned by the spirit of God, it is only appropriate that "creation, serving thee who hast made it, exerts itself to punish the unrighteous, and in kindness relaxes on behalf of those who trust in thee" (16:24), and fights for the just (16:17). The elements change places like the notes on a harp (19:18), but the harmony remains. The author can also use mythological language on occasion, as when God's logos is said to leap from heaven as a mighty warrior (compare the more vivid imagery of Revelation 19), but the warrior language is metaphorical here. The logos, or word, is implicitly identified with wisdom in 9:1–2. The destruction of the Egyptians, then, is the work of the cosmic Wisdom itself. In this interpretation of Exodus, nothing is arbitrary. Everything follows the providential design of the creator.

Since nature so perfectly reflects the designs of its maker, the Wisdom of Solomon argues that it is possible to arrive at the knowledge of God by inference from nature—"for from the greatness and beauty of created things the Creator is recognized by analogy" (13:5). The author vacillates as to whether pagans are culpable for failing to reach this knowledge

(13:1–9) but concludes that they cannot be excused. The argument here is similar to that of Paul in Romans 1, where the gentiles are condemned for immorality, since "what can be known about God is plain to them, because God has shown it to them. Ever since the creation of the world his invisible nature, namely his eternal power and deity, has been clearly perceived in the things that have been made. So they are without excuse" (Rom 1:19–20). This confidence in the power of reason must be qualified by the conviction that wisdom is a gift of God. It does, however, lay the responsibility for ignorance on humanity. (It should be noted that there had been a growing tendency toward monotheism in Greek philosophy since the fifth century B.C.E. and that the Stoics had developed a natural theology. This did not lead to widespread recognition of the God of the Jews, but some enlightened Greeks viewed Judaism with respect. So the Pythagorean Numenius said that the god of Jerusalem was father of all the gods, and that Plato was only "Moses speaking Attic Greek" [Stern 2, 206–216], and the anonymous author of "On the Sublime" said that the opening chapter of Genesis gave appropriate expression to the power of the deity [Stern 1, 364].)

While the author has some hesitation about the guilt of those who fail to recognize the true God, he is scathing toward those "who give the name 'gods' to the works of men's hands" (13:10). There was a long Jewish tradition of polemic against idol-worship, dating back to the time of the Babylonian exile (see especially Isa 44:9–20 and the apocryphal Letter of Jeremiah). The Wisdom of Solomon echoes Second Isaiah's jibe that an idol-maker uses one piece of wood to make a fire and another to make a god (13:11–19, cf. Isa 44:13–17). Worst of all are the "enemies of thy people," who "worship even the most hateful animals" (15:18). The worship of animals was especially characteristic of the Egyptians. We should note, again, that Jews were not alone in their critique of idols. Hellenistic philosophers, Cynics, and Stoics also occasionally derided the worship of images.

The Wisdom of Solomon goes further in its critique of idols than mere derision. Most interesting is its speculation on the origin of the custom. Obviously it was not part of God's creation, so it must have been invented by humanity. Two examples are of-

fered. In one case, idolatry comes from grief for the dead—a bereaved father makes an image of his son and worships him as a god (14:15). In the other case, people make an image "of a king whom they honored, so that by their zeal they might flatter the absent one as though present" (14:17). These examples certainly do not provide an adequate explanation of the origin of idolatry, but they are plausible instances nonetheless. This kind of explanation bears a resemblance to the euhemeristic theory of religion, which takes its name from Euhemerus of Messene (*ca.* 300 B.C.E.), who held that the gods of popular worship were kings or heroes whom people wished to honor.

According to the Wisdom of Solomon, "the idea of making idols was the beginning of fornication, and the invention of them was the corruption of life" (14:12). In part this is an inference from the author's belief that pagan ritual was debauched (14:23: "whether they kill children in their initiation, or celebrate secret mysteries, or hold frenzied revels with strange customs . . ."). More fundamentally, it reflects his conviction that morality depends on right understanding. The situation of the idolaters is essentially the same as that of the wicked in chapter 2, who did not reason rightly—"because they trust in lifeless idols they swear wicked oaths and expect to suffer no harm" (14:29). In contrast, knowledge of God is "complete righteousness" and is "the root of immortality" (15:3). In the author's view, belief in retribution is the underpinning of morality, and it is denied by the idolaters.

Even in dealing with idolaters, however, the God of Wisdom is merciful. The Egyptians, who are guilty of worshiping animals, are not exterminated at once. Instead they are punished gradually, so that they have opportunity for repentance (11:15–12:2). The sufferings of righteous and wicked both serve a constructive purpose, although they differ in degree: God tests the one group as a father, the other as a stern king (11:10). The persistence of the wicked is evidence of the mercy of God. The reason is that God loves everything that exists and hates nothing of the things he has made (11:24).

According to the Wisdom of Solomon, creation is fundamentally good. God, we are told (1:13), did not make death and does not delight in the destruction of the living but created all things that they should exist. Death entered the world "through the envy of the devil" (2:24). There is an implication of dualism here (perhaps influenced by apocalyptic traditions), insofar as death and the devil are powers not created by God. The primary responsibility for evil, however, is placed on "the impious," who invited death by their words and deeds (1:16). The Wisdom of Solomon resolutely affirms human free will, even though God knows that the thinking of the wicked will not change (12:10).

The "book of history" (chaps. 10–19) has often been described as nationalistic since it deals extensively with the destruction of Israel's enemies (Reider, 41). There is an ambiguity here, however. Just as the names of individual Israelites are suppressed, and they are treated as instances of "the righteous man," so the name Israel is not mentioned, and we read of "a holy people" (10:15) or "thy people" (15:14) or even "the righteous" (18:20). There is no doubt that the author is referring to Israel, and, by implication, to the Jewish people of his day, but he defines his people in terms of wisdom and ethical stance rather than simply of nationality. This definition would scarcely include Jews who abandoned the law, but might well include sympathetic, God-fearing gentiles. Such an attitude was broadly typical of Diaspora Judaism (Collins 1983, 244–245), and it is not accurately characterized as nationalistic.

RELATION TO JEWISH LITERATURE

Like most Jewish writings of its time, the Wisdom of Solomon draws heavily on the Jewish scriptures. The examples in chapters 10–19 are drawn directly from the Bible, and the supposedly autobiographical passages in chapters 7–9 draw on the story of Solomon in 1 Kings 3 and 5, and in 2 Chronicles 1. There is obvious continuity with the wisdom tradition, especially in the case of the figure of Wisdom, as we have noted above. It has been suggested that the Wisdom of Solomon 1–9 is modeled on Proverbs 1–9 (Dimant, 247). The two passages have several themes in common: retribution, the antithesis of life and death, the relation of wisdom to kingship, and, of course, the figure of Wisdom herself. (See further Larcher 1969, 97–99; Skehan.) The parallels, however, are broadly thematic and do not determine a

literary structure. The Hellenistic book is much more tightly organized than its Hebrew predecessor. More broadly still, the affirmation of natural theology, or of the possibility of attaining a knowledge of God from nature (Wis 13), is in continuity with the empirical emphasis of the older wisdom literature. Yet the perspective of the Wisdom of Solomon is significantly different both from the Hebrew wisdom literature and from the Hebrew Bible in general in several respects.

The main changes in perspective can be seen by comparison with Sirach, the latest Hebrew wisdom book (Collins 1979). Sirach spoke for the older wisdom tradition and for ancient Israel in general when he said: "Good things and bad, life and death, poverty and wealth come from the Lord" (Sir 11:14). For the Wisdom of Solomon, in contrast, God did not make death (Wis 1:13). Death appears as an independent power, who has a kingdom, although not on earth (1:14), and can make a covenant with his followers (1:16). There is a metaphysical dualism here that is closer to the apocalypticism of the Dead Sea Scrolls than to the Hebrew wisdom books.

For Sirach, death is the decree of the Lord and there is no inquiry or judgment after this life (Sir 41:4). In the Wisdom of Solomon, the judgment after death is all important. Moreover, the death of the righteous is only apparent—they "seem to die" (Wis 3:2). The belief in immortality is the most important illustration of a fundamental philosophical difference between the Hellenistic and the Hebrew book. Hebrew wisdom was fundamentally empirical. Hence the consistent skepticism of Ecclesiastes ("Who knows whether the spirit of man goes upward and the spirit of the beast goes down to the earth?" [Eccl 3:21]). In contrast, Wisdom of Solomon claims to know the mysteries of God, and is convinced of invisible realities. These metaphysical and epistemological differences also lead to different ethical values. Where hope is focused on immortality, long life and fertility become less important (Wis 4:1–20) and wisdom takes on an otherworldly character.

This change of perspective in the wisdom tradition owes something to the use of Jewish apocalyptic traditions in chapters 1–5. More fundamentally, it is influenced by Hellenistic philosophy, which had a strong Platonic component.

Jews of the Hellenistic Diaspora, especially in

Alexandria, had attempted to interpret their scriptures in philosophical categories from the second century B.C.E. on. The earliest surviving examples of this tradition are the exegetical fragments of Aristobulus from the mid second century B.C.E. and the *Letter of Aristeas*, which may be slightly later (see Collins 1983, 175–182). The great master of philosophical Judaism was Philo of Alexandria, who wrote his voluminous works in the first half of the first century C.E. Philo's philosophical position has been characterized as "a mystical Middle Platonism" (Winston, 3). There was considerable interchange between the various philosophical schools around the turn of the era, and the Platonic tradition had absorbed elements of Stoicism and Aristotelianism (see Dillon). While Philo did not strictly follow the teachings of Plato, he was following a philosophical movement of his own day.

Several aspects of the Wisdom of Solomon correspond to Philo's teachings (Larcher 1969, 151–178; Winston, 59–63). For both, Wisdom is something radiant that streams from God and is God's agent in creation. Both also speak of her in erotic terms as bride or spouse. Wisdom governs scientific knowledge and is also the source of prophecy and morality. Both authors equate wisdom and logos. Philo develops the notion of the logos, however, whereas the Wisdom of Solomon does not.

Both authors hold that God created the world out of unformed matter (Wis 11:17; Philo, *On the Creation* 9) rather than out of nothing. Both hold a teleological view of the world—that is, that things are created for specific purposes. Humanity was created for eternal life with God, but only the just achieve this goal. The soul is a preexistent spiritual entity that is weighed down by the body (Wis 8:19–20). Both affirm human responsibility and free will, although they recognize that wisdom is a divine gift. Both accept the four cardinal virtues, taught by Plato and the Stoics (Wis 8:7). Both also engage in polemics against idolatry, but this was commonplace in Hellenistic Judaism.

The philosophical conceptions of the Wisdom of Solomon are much less developed than those of Philo. There is no reference to the Platonic theory of Ideas, or discussion of the powers of God. There is no sustained allegorical exegesis, although particular symbols (Lot's wife in 10:7; the high priest's robe in 18:24) have allegorical significance.

Despite the clear affinities between the Wisdom of Solomon and Philo, it is not possible to prove that either used the other. While Wisdom of Solomon is less developed philosophically than Philo, this fact does not necessarily prove that it was chronologically prior. Not all philosophically minded Jews in the same milieu necessarily reached the same levels of complexity and sophistication. Larcher is undoubtedly right, however, in insisting that the Wisdom of Solomon did come from the same milieu as Philo, and cannot be very far removed from him in date (Larcher 1969, 176).

DATE AND PROVENANCE

Partly because of its resemblance to the work of Philo, the Wisdom of Solomon is usually thought to have been composed in Alexandria. The Egyptian provenance of the work is scarcely disputed. While the allusions to Egypt in chapters 10–19 are inspired by the biblical story, the extended emphasis on the Egyptians, in contrast to the brief treatment of the Canaanites, most readily suggests an Egyptian setting. The polemic against idolatry and the worship of animals also fits the Egyptian context very well. While none of these arguments is conclusive, and the book could in principle have been written elsewhere, there is no evidence at all in favor of any other location.

The date of composition is somewhat more controversial. Some commentators set the date as early as the second century B.C.E. (So most recently Georgi, 395–397, who points to the book's affinities with second-century apocalyptic writings, especially those in *1 Enoch*, and to the fact that its view of wisdom is less developed than what we find in Philo. Georgi locates the composition in Syria.) Arguments for a date in the first century B.C.E. rely heavily on the lack of allusions to Philo (so Dimant, 243), but then the fact that Philo shows no acquaintance with the Wisdom of Solomon becomes problematic. The most probable date is in the early Roman period. Winston (22–23) has pointed to some thirty-five words and usages that do not appear in Greek literature before the first century C.E. Several other aspects of the work fit the early Roman period, notably the contention that idolatry arises from the desire of subjects to flatter a distant ruler (Wis 14:17). The term *kratēsis,* "dominion" (6:3), is used elsewhere specifically for the Roman conquest of Egypt (Winston, 153).

The account of the persecution of the righteous, and the subsequent divine judgment in chapters 2–5, figure prominently in attempts to date the book. In Winston's view this section of the book "could only be called forth by a desperate historical situation" (Winston, 23), and so he suggests the reign of the Roman emperor Caligula (37–41 C.E.) as the most likely period. On that occasion there were riots in Alexandria and the Jews were proclaimed "aliens and foreigners." Whether the book can be tied to such specific events remains questionable, in view of its notorious lack of references to specific dates and places. All we can say is that it presupposes a situation where righteous, observant Jews encountered resentment and their lives were in danger. Such a situation in Alexandria can be more easily posited in the first century C.E., especially from the time of Caligula on, than at any earlier time.

FUNCTION AND MESSAGE

Despite its familiarity with the language of Greek philosophy, the Wisdom of Solomon is clearly not a philosophical treatise. It is rather a rhetorical, hortatory work that makes occasional use of philosophical ideas. There is, throughout, an attempt to present a logically coherent argument, and there is relatively little reliance on imagery and symbol such as we find in the apocalypses. Yet the philosophical interest of the work is subordinated to a hortatory purpose.

The Wisdom of Solomon is often classified as "apologetic literature." The attempt to express Jewish faith in the language of Hellenistic philosophy is often assumed to be an attempt either to win gentile adherents or at least to win the sympathy and respect of the Greeks. The fact that the book is addressed to "the rulers of the earth" lends some support to this view. The author affirms that "the imperishable light of the law was to be given to the world" through God's people (18:4). The lack of reference to distinctive Jewish customs such as circumcision, and the explanation of biblical history in terms of general principles

would presumably facilitate the task of apologetic.

Yet there is a long-standing debate as to whether such literature was primarily intended for gentile readers or was first of all an attempt to formulate the identity of the hellenized Jews (Collins 1983, 1–10). The alternatives are not mutually exclusive. The author would surely have liked to find gentile readers, but he was far more likely to be persuasive to his fellow Jews. Moreover, there was considerable diversity in Hellenistic Judaism, and the book may be read as an attempt to promote one view of Judaism against others.

One possible clue as to the author's intention is the choice of Solomon as a pseudonym. Pseudonymous writings were common in both Jewish and gentile circles in this period, for various reasons. Jews of the Hellenistic Diaspora often attributed their works to pagan figures. We therefore find a collection of oracles ascribed to the Sibyl (a prophetess of Greek and Roman legend), a collection of sayings in the name of Phocylides (a sixth-century poet), and a letter highly laudatory of the Jews that was supposedly written by one Greek, Aristeas, to another, Philocrates. All of these writings are recognized to be Jewish compositions. The pagan pseudonym gave the impression of objectivity; praise of Judaism was more impressive if it came from someone who was not a Jew. We do not know whether any gentiles accepted the supposed authorship of these works, but we may assume that Jewish readers took pride in the apparent support of independent authorities.

In the Wisdom of Solomon, the pseudonymous author is an Israelite king, Solomon. Solomon was an appropriate author for a wisdom book because of his biblical reputation for wisdom (1 Kgs 3–4) and the fact that he was thought to be the author of Proverbs and Ecclesiastes. He was also a cosmopolitan figure, the Israelite king who could most truly claim to stand on a par with the rulers of the earth. Remarkably enough, the book does not mention Solomon by name. His identity is implied through biblical allusions (see Dimant, 251; the allusions include the author's quest for wisdom in preference to wealth [1 Kgs 3–4] and his prayer [1 Kgs 8]). This oblique way of identifying the king presupposes a readership familiar with scripture, and so primarily Jewish. This is also true of the references to biblical history, where names are never mentioned.

Yet the author would have us believe that he is addressing the kings of the earth, at least in the first part of the book. Such an audience is appropriate for Solomon, but it also suggests that the work has political implications. At the conclusion of the first part, in 6:1–10, the rulers are admonished for failing to keep God's law, even though their dominion comes from God and they are servants of his kingdom. In view of this passage, the discussion of righteousness in the preceding chapters is not a purely theoretical discussion but is written with a view to the conduct of Roman and Alexandrian rulers. The righteous one of chapter 2, who upbraids the wicked for sins against the law, is surely the faithful Jew. (In 18:13 Israel is "God's son," just as the righteous one is in 2:18.) The wicked in question include the rulers (*cf.* 6:4). They may also include renegade Jews, but we do not know that Jewish apostates plotted against their fellow Jews, as the wicked plot against the righteous in chapter 2. Responsibility for the persecution and death of the righteous must be attributed to the rulers. These rulers, then, are cautioned that God will "examine your works and scrutinize your deliberations" (6:3; *cf.* 1:6–11, which says that no wickedness will go undetected, because the spirit of the Lord fills the earth).

It is unlikely that any gentile ruler heeded, or even read, these admonitions. Philo's account of the embassy to Gaius (Caligula) in 39–40 is of relevance here. The account is a vigorous denunciation of the emperor. Yet it makes clear that when the Jews (including Philo himself) actually approached the Roman rulers, their tone was one of supplication. In the words Philo ascribes to one Jewish supplicant (*Embassy to Gaius*, 233) "no one is so mad as to oppose a master when he is a slave." The critique of the rulers in a literary work like the Wisdom of Solomon served primarily as confirmation and support for the Jews themselves. On the one hand, it reassures the righteous that they have nothing to fear from their rulers, because at worst they will only seem to die, but will enjoy immortality. (Compare Philo, *Embassy to Gaius*, 117, who says that the Jews accepted death as willingly as if it were immortality.) On the other hand, the book provides assurance that the rulers will be judged in their turn. The consolation and reassur-

ance are most apparent in chapters 10–19, where the Exodus is held up as a paradigm for history, to show that God does not overlook his people but stands by them (19:22).

In reassuring its readers of divine retribution, the Book of Wisdom was encouraging them to persevere in their Judaism. The author's view of Judaism has two facets. On the one hand, it is thoroughly hellenized. The law here does not refer to peculiarly Jewish customs but to the God-given law of nature itself. The author is in line with the common Hellenistic philosophy of kingship when he demands that kings should pursue wisdom and righteousness. The Greeks, too, held that the king must be a wise man and a copy and imitator of God (Sthenidas of Lokri, cited by Winston, 63). There is no necessary tension between Judaism and gentile culture or gentile sovereignty. The ideals of Hellenistic kingship are quite acceptable to Judaism; it is the practice of the actual rulers that is deficient.

LATER INFLUENCE

There is a certain tragic irony in this optimistic view of Jewish-Hellenic relations. In fact those relations had begun to deteriorate in the early Roman period, at the very time when the Wisdom of Solomon was written. There were anti-Jewish riots in the time of Caligula and again in 66. These were largely caused by the resentment of the Egyptian Greeks toward the Jews for refusing to worship the pagan gods and participate fully in civic life, and yet laying claim to equal status with the citizens. Egyptian Judaism suffered the aftereffects of the Jewish war against Rome of 66–70, and was nearly wiped out in the great Diaspora revolt of 115–118. Jewish communities flourished in various parts of the Roman empire after that date, but they produced scarcely any literature that has survived. The attempt to express Jewish religion in Hellenistic literary forms, it appears, virtually came to an end in the early second century. Rabbinic Judaism disregarded the literary heritage of the Diaspora. The Wisdom of Solomon, like the works of Philo, was preserved and transmitted by the Christian church.

The influence of the Wisdom of Solomon on early Christianity is considerable. It is not cited in the

New Testament, and recent commentators have found the arguments for influence inconclusive. There are certainly affinities between the Wisdom of Solomon and several New Testament books. We have already noted the parallel between Romans 1 and Wisdom of Solomon 13 on revelation through nature. There is also a general similarity between the use of the logos and the theme of eternal life in the Gospel of John and what we find in Wisdom. It is not possible, however, to establish literary dependence in these cases. The most intriguing parallel with the New Testament is found in Matthew's passion narrative (Matt 27:41–44). There we are told that Jesus was taunted on the cross: "He trusts in God; let God deliver him now, if he desires him; for he said, 'I am the Son of God.'" In Wisdom the "ungodly men" resent the fact that the righteous man boasts that God is his father. So they resolve: "Let us see if his words are true . . . for if the righteous man is God's son, he will help him." Even here the allusion is disputed, but it seems likely that Matthew had the Wisdom passage in mind. In any case, the similarity between the fate of the "righteous man" and that of Christ is noteworthy. The motif of the vindication of the suffering righteous is, of course, older and finds its paradigmatic expression in the suffering servant of Isaiah 53 (Nickelsburg, 62–66).

The earliest explicit citations of the Wisdom of Solomon are found in Clement of Alexandria at the end of the second century, and there it is clearly cited as scripture. As we noted at the beginning of this essay, its scriptural status was widely, but not universally, accepted. Jerome formally excluded it from the canon, since it was not part of the Hebrew Bible. Augustine, however, favored its canonicity because of its widespread use, and cited it more than eight hundred times. Its canonical status was finally decided, in opposite ways, by the Reformers and the Council of Trent.

The Wisdom of Solomon was of considerable importance for the development of Christian theology. It provided the clearest biblical teaching on the immortality of the soul, as distinct from resurrection. Even more significant, however, was the figure of Sophia, Wisdom, itself. We have noted the correspondence of Sophia and Logos, especially in Philo but also in the Wisdom of Solomon. The New Testament (Gospel of John) chose the term Logos, presumably because of its masculine form. The church fathers, however, restored Sophia to the discussion of theology. Irenaeus identified Wisdom and the Holy Spirit, on the basis of Wisdom of Solomon 1:5–6. More often, Wisdom was identified with the Logos. Origen affirmed that Christ is called Wisdom, and that "the only begotten Son of God is God's wisdom hypostatically existing" (*On First Principles* 1.2.1–2). The Arian heresy, which held that the Son was preexistent but still created, was also indebted to the Jewish tradition of Wisdom as the first creature of God.

In recent times the figure of Wisdom, more than the book, has become a focus of renewed interest for feminist theologians. While all the Jewish wisdom books subordinate Wisdom to God, the figure still represents divine activity in the world. The fact that this figure could be personified as a woman helps put the usual masculine imagery for God in perspective and reminds us of the metaphorical character of all personifications of the divinity.

Bibliography

Armstrong, A. H. *An Introduction to Ancient Philosophy.* 3d ed. London, 1957.

Collins, John J. "Cosmos and Salvation: Jewish Wisdom and Apocalyptic in the Hellenistic Age." *History of Religions* 17 (1977): 121–142.

———. "The Root of Immortality: Death in the Context of Jewish Wisdom." *Harvard Theological Review* 71 (1979): 177–192.

———. *Between Athens and Jerusalem: Jewish Identity in the Hellenistic Diaspora.* New York, 1983.

Dillon, John. *The Middle Platonists.* London, 1977.

Dimant, Devorah. "Pseudonymity in the Wisdom of Solomon." In *La Septuaginta en la investigación contemporánea* (V Congreso de la IOSCS), edited by N. Fernández Marcos. Madrid, 1985. Pp. 243–255.

Focke, Friedrich. *Die Entstehung der Weisheit Salomos.* Göttingen, 1913.

Georgi, Dieter. *Weisheit Salomos.* Gütersloh, 1980.

Gilbert, Maurice. *La Critique des dieux dans le Livre de la Sagesse.* Rome, 1973.

———. "Wisdom Literature." In *Jewish Writings of the Second Temple Period*, edited by M. E. Stone. Philadelphia, 1984. Pp. 283–324.

Grimm, Carl L. *Das Buch der Weisheit.* Leipzig, 1860.

Larcher, C. *Études sur le Livre de la Sagesse.* Paris, 1969.

————. *Le Livre de la Sagesse; ou, La Sagesse de Salomon.* Paris, 1983, 1984.

Mack, Burton. *Logos und Sophia: Untersuchungen zur Weisheitstheologie im hellenistischen Judentum.* Göttingen, 1973.

Nickelsburg, George W. *Resurrection, Immortality, and Eternal Life in Intertestamental Judaism.* Cambridge, Mass., 1972.

Reese, James M. *Hellenistic Influence on the Book of Wisdom.* Rome, 1970.

————. *The Book of Wisdom: Song of Songs.* Wilmington, 1983.

Reider, Joseph. *The Book of Wisdom.* New York, 1957.

Skehan, Patrick W. "The Literary Relationship of the Book of Wisdom to Earlier Wisdom Writings." In *Studies in Israelite Poetry and Wisdom.* Washington, D.C., 1971. Pp. 172–236.

Stern, Menahem. *Greek and Latin Authors on Jews and Judaism.* 2 vols. Jerusalem, 1976, 1980.

Winston, David. *The Wisdom of Solomon.* Anchor Bible, vol. 43, Garden City, N.Y., 1979.

Wright, Addison. "The Structure of the Book of Wisdom." *Biblica* 48 (1967): 165–184.

JOHN J. COLLINS

Sirach (Ecclesiasticus)

T HE WISDOM OF Jesus Son of Sirach belongs to the biblical writings known as wisdom literature. It is frequently mentioned in lists, both ancient and modern, that include Proverbs, Ecclesiastes, the Song of Solomon, and the Wisdom of Solomon. The book by Ben Sira, as the author is called in Hebrew, shares many features with each of these writings, and these common features justify its classification as biblical wisdom literature. A comparison of Sirach with other wisdom literature shows, however, that Ben Sira's book manifests a number of characteristics that are clearly distinctive. These distinguishing features include novelties both in the area of literary performance and also at the level of conceptual achievement.

Distinguishing literary features of significance include acknowledgment of authorship; descriptions of the author's vocation; reflections on the circumstances of the author's times, life, and thought; creative appropriation of traditional literary genres; strikingly imaginative poetry about the figure of Wisdom; a unique epic poetry consisting of an incomparable hymn in praise of the great figures of Israel's history; and most unusual combinations of proverbs, wisdom poetry, psalms, prayers, and hymns of praise. The overall impression made by the book is that of very creative literary activity.

Marks of intellectual pursuit include the development of the concept of wisdom; the use of the concept of wisdom to link the orders of creation and history; a reflection on the identification of wisdom and the Torah, that is, the Pentateuch, or the "law"; a concerted attempt to merge the logic of proverbial wisdom with that of specifically religious practices; a theological rationale for the office of the scribe; a very careful accommodation of Hellenistic popular philosophy; and the creation of an epic etiology for Second Temple Judaism as a social system. The use of proverbial idiom to think abstractly and theologically in these ways may be one of the author's finer intellectual achievements.

These distinctive features of Ben Sira's book of wisdom invite explication and determine the organization of the discussion to follow. The article will unfold in three major sections. The introductory section includes brief descriptions of Ben Sira's authorship, vocation, times, and influence. The second major section is devoted to an analysis of the book's literary composition. Finally, Ben Sira's intellectual achievement is assessed and his theological system reviewed.

INTRODUCTION

Author

Jeshua ben Sira was a learned scribe and teacher who lived in Jerusalem during the turbulent times of transition from Ptolemaic to Seleucid hegemony around 200 B.C.E. His book indicates that he had

65

thought deeply about the quality of life within the society created by the Second Temple state. His view in general was that life under the Temple system was ordered as it should be, that the system itself was divinely ordained, and that the responsibility of its leaders was to ensure its perpetuation. He argued that the skills required to enhance well-being under the system could be learned, for they were expressions of a universal order called wisdom.

Ben Sira was not naive about the uncertainties of the unstable political situation at the time, the reality of cultural changes that were taking place, or the challenge of the times for teachers dedicated to the task of educating the next generation in the principles and values of the Jewish way of life. He therefore approached his educational task with a sense of seriousness and concern. His book of wisdom is marked by a conservative attitude on matters where Jewish values and practices were at stake, and the tone of admonition throughout the book betrays some anxiety lest the lessons should not be persuasive. Though conservative in his approach to traditional values, Ben Sira nonetheless explored the horizons of his world through wide reading and a broadly cosmopolitan experience. From them he crafted a remarkable system of thought, at once philosophically sophisticated and theologically sound, in order to marshal the support of proverbial wisdom and its matter-of-fact ethic for the religious system to which he was loyal. His book of wisdom documents the fruits of this amazing intellectual labor.

The author's name is given in both Greek and Hebrew manuscripts in the subscript at Sirach 50:27. The manuscript traditions disagree in respect to some bits of information, but agree in the mention of three names. The Hebrew reads "Jeshua (Eleazar) ben [son of] Sira." The Greek transliteration reads "Jesus Son of Sirach." In the prologue to the Greek translation prepared by Ben Sira's grandson, the grandson refers to his grandfather as Jesus. In the Greek manuscript tradition, the name Jesus Son of Sirach also appears in an incipit as part of the title of the book.

Title

By custom, Ben Sira's book of wisdom is referred to both as Ecclesiasticus and as Sirach. The title Ecclesiasticus stems from the period of the Christian canonization of the book, its translation into Latin, and its inclusion in the Vulgate. Ecclesiasticus means "churchly" or "belonging to the church." The designation Sirach, on the other hand, stems from the (probably faulty) Greek transliteration of Ben Sira's name, and is an abbreviation from the title of the book as found in most Greek manuscripts.

Although the Greek incipit gives the title of the book as The Wisdom of Jesus Son of Sirach, early Christian references frequently omitted Ben Sira's name. Commonly used designations were simply "Wisdom" or "Guide to Virtue." Since the Hebrew manuscript fragments begin at Sirach 3:6, one cannot be sure of the original designation in Hebrew parlance. In the rabbinic tradition, however, the book is referred to variously as the "Book (or Instruction, or Proverbs) of Ben Sira," or simply as the "Book of Instruction." Modern scholars tend to use either Wisdom of Ben Sira or Book of Ben Sira.

Date

The book was written during the first quarter of the second century B.C.E. Scholars date its completion at *ca.* 180 on the basis of three considerations. The first is that the poem about the high priest Simon (Sir 50:1–21), at the end of the hymn in praise of the ḥasidim (pious ones), assumes that Simon was no longer living. The Simon in question was surely Simeon II, who died *ca.* 200. The second consideration is that neither the circumstances nor the issues of ideology involved in the Maccabean revolt against Antiochus IV Epiphanes in 164 are reflected anywhere in the book. Thus the book was written before that time. The third is that Ben Sira's grandson, who translated the book from Hebrew into Greek, states in his prologue that he decided to do so after he arrived in Egypt in the thirty-eighth year of Ptolemy Euergetes. This must be Ptolemy VII Euergetes II, whose dates are 170–116, putting the grandson's arrival at 132. Allowing for two full generations between Ben Sira's scholarly activity in Jerusalem and his grandson's work of translation in Egypt, the period between 195 and 180 can be determined as the time when Ben Sira flourished.

The Times

Jerusalem had prospered under Ptolemaic hegemony during the third century B.C.E. A relatively autonomous society had been built on the model of the ancient Near Eastern temple-state by assigning royal and civic functions to the priesthood. A remarkable system of production, crafts, banking, taxation, civil service, and cultural cultivation centered in the Temple. Wealthy families controlled landed estates as well as positions of power within the priestly councils. There was time for leisure, literary pursuits, and celebration.

Egypt's defeat in the Fifth Syrian War (202–195) triggered a series of precipitous political scrambles in Jerusalem. The Tobiads, a leading family, were split on the issue of whether their loyalties should be to Egypt or to Syria, then suffered extreme shifts in attitude as political parties sought advantage under the new circumstances. Soon the position of the high priesthood was politicized, setting the stage for the programs of hellenization under Antiochus IV Epiphanes and the Maccabean response.

At the turn of the century the high priest was Simon II, the last to preside over the old arrangements. Ben Sira's hymn in praise of the *hasidim* concludes with a glorious portrayal of Simon presiding on the high holy Day of Atonement (Sir 50:1–21). Since the poem was written after Simon's death (Sir 50:1), and thus during the high priesthood of Onias III, when political battle lines were being drawn, Ben Sira's sympathies are disclosed. He wanted life to continue as it had been under the relative autonomy of the old Ptolemaic rule. It does not appear that he took sides in the current party conflicts, however, or that he was proposing political resistance to the Seleucids. He favored Simon and the old arrangements because he valued the institutions of the Second Temple system and the patterns of life they had sustained. His book of wisdom confirms this assessment of his fundamental commitments, for the instruction offered in it assumes the system of religion and society created in Judaea during the third century B.C.E. Ben Sira viewed that system as ideal and expressed his desire that it should never come to an end (Sir 50:24 [Heb.]).

Ben Sira's Vocation

Scholars imagine Ben Sira as a teacher-priest in a Temple school in Jerusalem. While there is no external evidence that such an institution existed in Jerusalem at the time, nor internal evidence that Ben Sira was a priest, the scholarly consensus is probably correct. His book demands some professional setting, and Ben Sira's own sense of vocation can be understood only by imagining a prominent position for him in the institutional structure of Jerusalem society.

One of the manifestations of his strong sense of vocation occurs in snippets of autobiographical discourse throughout the book. In every instance of personal reflection, the subject is the same. He speaks first of his quest for wisdom, or of his having been filled with wisdom, and then of his desire to share what he has learned with his students (Sir 24:30–34, 33:16–18, 39:12–35, 42:15, 50:27–29). These snippets of self-reflection correspond exactly with the description Ben Sira gives of the work of the scholar-teacher in a most remarkable poem (Sir 39:1–11). He calls the scholar-teacher a "scribe," and compares the work of the scribe with other vocations (Sir 38:24–34). Thus the poem contains a number of clues about Ben Sira's own work that help to explain the nature of the book he wrote. A brief explication of this poem is therefore in order.

The poem unfolds in four movements. The first movement describes the scholar's quest for wisdom. He "sets his mind upon the law of the Most High" and "searches out the wisdom of all the ancients" (Sir 39:1–4, Box and Oesterley). In the second movement Ben Sira mentions that the mark of the scholar's piety is that he is careful to combine his quest for wisdom with his search for God. The latter will take the form of a prayer for mercy, and God's response will take the form of filling the scholar with "the spirit of understanding" (Sir 39:5–6). The third movement follows from this moment of inspiration. The scholar will no longer be occupied only with the study of the discourse of the ancients, but will now "himself declare wise instruction" and "pour forth wise sayings in double measure" (Sir 39:6–8, Box and Oesterley). The result of this activity is described in the final movement. The "congregation" will recognize his wisdom and praise him for it (Sir 39:9–11).

This description of the scribe's vocation does not agree with nuances usually associated with the term "scribe" in modern parlance. Ben Sira's scribe was neither a mere copyist of texts nor an accountant in the bureaucracy of the Second Temple system. He was a scholar-teacher with an amazing aspiration for literary competence, a clear program of research, and a definite educational objective.

The scholar's "texts" included the "law of the Most High," the "wisdom" and "discourse" of all the ancients, and the "good and evil among men," which he also "read" as he traveled through his own social world. The scholar's piety combined the quests for wisdom and for divine approval. The scholar's inspiration came in that moment when his understanding of the wisdom of others could finally be put in his own words. And the mention of the congregation shows that the vocation described was familiar to Ben Sira's contemporaries. It also shows that the congregation was able to recognize outstanding performance in the office defined by that vocation.

Thus the work of the scribe had social significance. His wisdom was pursued in the interest of the culture sustained by the social system. His vocation demanded that his learning combine the proverbial wisdom of life, wherever it might be found throughout the ancient Near East, with those particular documents specific to the social institutions of the Second Temple state. His instruction would be judged, moreover, to see whether the ethic it proposed fit the needs of life within the society ordered by the Second Temple system.

Authorship

Ben Sira clearly took delight in his work and enjoyed authorial consciousness. Traditional to the wisdom literature of the ancient Near East were both the authorial form of introduction ("Listen, my son") and the autobiographical report on experience ("Three things I have seen"). Both are enhanced in Ben Sira's book, the first by a strong authorial presence behind the proverbs of admonition, and the second by the use of the autobiographical report to give an account of his experience as a scholar-teacher. Autobiographical references include, moreover, the mention of writing, and they are all styled in the poetry of praise.

Praise is due to the sage in all aspects of his work, according to Ben Sira, but especially in his work as a scribe (Sir 39:9–11). It was as a scribal sage that Ben Sira composed hymns in praise of God's judgments (Sir 39:12–35; cf. 39:32), the Creation (Sir 42:15–43:33; cf. 42:15), and the ḥasidim (Sir 44–50; cf. 44:1 [Heb.]). He knew that, should the scribe find the right words (should he himself achieve a fine poem), praise would accrue to him as well as to those praised in his poetry. The same phrase is used ("the congregation proclaims praise") for both the scribe and the ḥasidim who were the object of Ben Sira's hymn of praise (Sir 39:10, 44:15).

Modern scholars argue that Ben Sira's sense of authorship is a clear sign of Hellenistic influence. This judgment is undoubtedly right. Ben Sira understood the vocation of the scholar-teacher as being an opportunity for research and writing. Thus his book is more than a collection of ancient proverbial wisdom or a handbook of contemporary ethical instruction. Both of these functions are still served, to be sure. But patient classification and conservative transmission of traditional lore have given way to personal creativity.

Composition

Later studies have suggested that the genre closest to Ben Sira's collection of materials is the Hellenistic teacher's handbook. The teacher's handbook may have supplied the model for the kind of material selected for inclusion in the book, and for some features of the arrangement of Ben Sira's compositions. But many of these compositions surpass the formal requisites for use in mimetic instruction. In Ben Sira's book, pedagogy vies with performance and display. Traditional genres of wisdom literature were clearly expanded upon, taken as forms for experimental literary activity, and combined with literary forms and functions not customary for the tradition. Proverbs, autobiographical references, wisdom myths, meditations on the Genesis account of the creation of Adam, hymns of praise, psalms, prayers, preachments, and admonitions—all are present, and all are presented in a polished poetry that bears the marks of great literary skill and manifests fine intellectual purpose and control. Thus Ben Sira's book builds upon forms, themes, and values traditional to the literature of wisdom. But the wisdom it brings to expression is Ben Sira's own.

At the level of composition, the clue to Ben Sira's thoughtful purposes is his forthright combination of proverbial wisdom with theological poetry. Ultimately, Ben Sira's poetry ushers the reader into serious reflection, not only about the ways of wisdom and folly, but about the purposes of God for Israel. These purposes were manifest, according to Ben Sira, both in creation and in history, if only one could read each order correctly. It was the purpose of his poetry to enable the reader to do that. Thus his poetry was written in the mode of human wisdom, to be sure, but it stood in the service of nothing less than a full theological rationale for Second Temple Judaism.

Conceptuality

Although figurative language abounds, and the mode of composition is poetic, Ben Sira's book is not lacking in the development of concepts and systematic thought. Concepts are created by using images of certain figures frequently throughout the book. This frequent recurrence of a particular image and the variety of perspectives on a given figure eventually define concepts that serve Ben Sira's purpose of thinking clearly about the world, history, Second Temple society, law, and education.

One of the more important concepts developed in Sirach is the idea that the world is an ordered creation. Another is that human societies should be ordered by law. A third is that humans are capable of knowing the order in creation and of understanding the requirements of law. These concepts (creation, society, law, and the human capacity to think) are developed by the ingenious use of imagery. Of critical significance for this process of conceptualization are descriptions of the figure of Wisdom (imagined at the Creation and as appearing within history), references to the "place" where Torah (law, instruction) can be found, and depictions of human figures (including Adam, the *hasidim*, and "the wise") as those engaged in the quest for understanding. Ultimately it is the richly nuanced figure of Wisdom itself that links each of these concepts to the others.

One of the more important themes used to forge these concepts into a systematic view of the world is that of the quest. Both Wisdom and the one who seeks Wisdom are imagined as questers. By using certain sequences from the patterns of questing, such as those of changing location ("He poured her out upon all his works" [Sir 1:9]; "So I took root in an honored people" [Sir 24:12]), or seeking and finding ("Come to her like one who plows, and sows, and wait for her good harvest" [Sir 6:19]), conceptual imagery is manipulated in the interest of systematic constructions. Thus creation and history are linked according to a specific sequence, and wisdom and law juxtaposed in particular configurations. The imagery of location and the slightly narrative notion of relocation are used to great advantage in the definition of a conceptual system.

Scholars generally agree that Ben Sira's poetry was the vehicle for profound reflection on the interrelationships among wisdom, creation, history, law, piety, and practice. Many cite Ben Sira's conceptual achievement as a major contribution to intellectual history, calling it the "nationalization of wisdom" or the "identification of wisdom and law." It has been seen most clearly in the express identification of wisdom, epic, and law at Sirach 24:23. This identification was achieved by using the imagery of the figure of Wisdom to align the concept of wisdom with "the book of the covenant of the Most High God, the law which Moses commanded us." A critical reading of Sirach cannot avoid the questions of how Ben Sira achieved that correlation with his poetry, and for what reasons.

Influence

Apparently Ben Sira's handbook of wisdom was an immediate success. The signs of its popularity are many. The fact that it was translated into Greek within the century is one of them. Another is that the manuscript traditions in both Hebrew and Greek divide by types from a very early period, suggesting widespread copying. A third is the evidence of a very vigorous scribal activity and interest in the book. Emendations, additions, rearrangements, and marginal notations mark the history of transmission and demonstrate the eagerness with which Ben Sira was read, as well as the desire on the part of his readers to see subsequent circumstances reflected in his book and addressed by his wisdom. Citations of the work are a fourth sign of its popularity, documented in both early Christian and rabbinic literatures. And a fifth is that both the rabbis and the early Christian scholars mentioned Ben Sira's book by name in the short lists of writings under consideration for special privilege in the processes known as canonization.

One of the ironies resulting from the period of canonization is that, whereas the rabbis excluded Ben Sira's book from those that "defiled the hands," it was included in the so-called Alexandrine canon by Christians and dubbed "the church's book." Ben Sira's poetry of wisdom was eventually lost to Judaism but was embedded in the Catholic canon and cherished by Christian readers for almost two thousand years as a sourcebook for their devotion, ethical instruction, and theology.

Text

Modern scholarly preoccupation with Ben Sira's book began in the years 1896 to 1899, when Solomon Schecter discovered four fragmentary Hebrew manuscripts of the work in the storeroom (Heb., *genizah*) of an old synagogue in Cairo. Since then additional fragments of the Genizah text have been published, scroll fragments from Qumran have been found, and a scroll from Masada was discovered that contains the Hebrew text of Sirach 39:27–43:30. All together these manuscripts cover approximately two-thirds of the book. They are a precious scholarly treasure because, until they came to light, not a single Hebrew text was known to be extant. Lost to the dominant traditions of rabbinic Judaism sometime during the early medieval period, Ben Sira's book of wisdom was known to modern scholars only in its Greek and Syriac versions and other translations based upon them. With the discovery of the Hebrew fragments, Ben Sira's book has been returned to the corpus of Hebrew scriptures, to be read once again as a document of Jewish learning and piety from the time before the Christian era.

THE LITERARY COMPOSITION

Ben Sira's book consists mainly of proverbs and poems in a style typical of the ancient Jewish sage. Large blocks of material collect and codify proverbial wisdom about human behavior and offer advice for achieving well-being. But attempts to ascertain a single principle of organization for Ben Sira's book have generally failed. Outlines founder for lack of major headings, balance among segments, and clear rules of sequence from segment to segment. Narrative models cannot manage the sheer bulk of non-narrative, didactic, and admonitory discourse. The handbook model breaks down because the various kinds of material are not collected by type (hymns, for instance) and because instructions are not given for the use of materials in the classroom. Nevertheless, most scholars agree that formal characteristics can be identified for much of the material and that, when taken together, these formal characteristics do give the book a certain coherence and structure.

Four observations on formal characteristics have been customary. The first is that proverbs are regularly clustered by theme and that the clusters frequently unfold as integral units of elaboration. The units often form periods or small essays that argue a certain view on a specific matter of ethical concern (e.g., 1:11–2:16, on fearing the Lord; 3:1–16, on honoring parents).

The second observation is that a number of poems interspersed throughout the book focus upon the figure of Wisdom. In this poetry, Wisdom is imagined as a female figure with divine powers and destiny. The range of her activities is quite astonishing, but the set of poems appears nonetheless to have a common theme. It is the theme of her location or, to use the mythic expression, the theme of where Wisdom might be found. This theme can be expressed as Wisdom's own quest to find a place to dwell among humans. These poems appear to mark off sections of proverbial material and to introduce themes for the arrangement of units of proverbs.

A third observation is that the book contains a number of hymns, psalms, and prayers. The function of this poetry for the organization of the book is much more difficult to determine. Much of it appears to have been inserted at various junctures merely in accordance with principles of association or convenience. In some cases, however, the poetry of praise is positioned appropriately for the development of basic themes and concepts. A close look at the conceptuality of this hymnic material may help clarify its contribution to the purpose and arrangement of the book as a whole.

The fourth observation is that the hymn in praise of the pious (*ḥasidim*) is placed at the end of the book. With this poem a sense of climax is reached by celebrating the glory manifest in the specific moment of a central ritual enactment. This climax may serve as a fitting conclusion to affirmations of a more general variety throughout the book about the "presence" of wisdom in "Israel." If the hymn in praise of the pious is read as an answer to the question with which the book opens about the presence of wisdom in the world, the first and last poems can be seen to make a set.

These four speculations about the purposive arrangement of materials in Sirach deserve further explication.

Proverbs

For the wise among the cultures of the ancient Near East, proverbs were the primary unit of observation, insight, expression, and reflection. Proverbs were used to make sense of the relatively typical sequences, relationships, or traits characteristic of all observable phenomena and occurrences. Knowing when to apply proverbs required astuteness in understanding the rhyme and reason of the world constructed by the proverbial imagination, and skill in making judgments about aspects of one's accidental world. Proverbs were the medium of thinking, and proverbial wisdom was the accumulation of a culture's rationalizations.

The ancient Hebrew sage thought in proverbs and created a special kind of poetry based upon their logic. The poetry worked by juxtaposing two or more lines that offered proverbial observations. Scholars call this the "parallelism of members," and they have studied the various relationships possible between parallel lines. Thus the second line may restate the first with a slight nuance, or name a second different instance, or offer an analogy for comparison from another order of discourse, or provide a reason, or a contrast, or even a contradiction. The Hebrew sage played the gaps between the everyday world and the proverbial encasement of typical occurrences. He also explored the lack of fit among differing proverbial assessments of the same kind of occurrence. It was through these gaps in proverbial wisdom and thinking that the Hebrew sages explored the limits of the human capacity to master and understand the world.

Ben Sira was a Hebrew sage who understood about proverbs and the kind of thinking they made possible. In his poem about the wisdom of the scribe, he mentions expressly that "he will seek out the hidden meanings of proverbs, and be at home with the obscurities of parables" (Sir 39:3). Proverbs and parables (comparisons) abound in his own book of wisdom, and he was obviously "at home" with them and skilled in their use. Nevertheless, his poetry is more in the *style* of the proverbial than a collection of priceless proverbs itself. Were one to make a list of the truly striking proverbs in Sirach, proverbs capable of independent transmission because of their memorable clarity and attraction, the bulk of Ben Sira's poetry would not be included. With Ben Sira the aphoristic sentence or memorable maxim has given place to a rhetoric of admonition and praise. The form of the proverb is retained and the poetry of parallel lines is masterful, but the points are not allowed to ride upon a single well-turned phrase and its application to a particular case. Instead, principles are set forth in the form of proverbs, and proverbs are used to elaborate upon the principles. The elaboration takes place by clustering proverbial material around a particular theme.

The blocks of proverbs clustered by theme are easily identified. Thus there are sections on humility (Sir 3:17–28), friendship (Sir 6:5–17), rulers (Sir 9:17–10:5), proper speech (Sir 19:5–16), the training of children (Sir 30:1–13), and table etiquette (Sir 31:12–32:13), among many others. Almost all of the proverbs in Sirach are found in blocks of material joined to one another by theme. Within the blocks, proverbial insights are placed in relation to one another in a variety of ways. Patterns of association for constructing parallel lines in Hebrew poetry are used as well to join verses and form sets of verses. One also detects an overall purpose to a unit consisting of several verses. In addition to the momentary insight created by a given pair of lines in a single verse, each versicle in a block functions in relation to the whole by supplying what the Greek rhetors would have called a supporting argument. Arguments might clarify the point or principle of the unit by means of a comparison, contrast, or example, as well as expand upon the cases in which the principle could be seen to apply. Repetition occurs and instances stack up until the horizon of the reader's imagination is reached and the impression is given that the principle always pertains.

As an example, in Sirach 3:1–16 there is a unit of proverbial material on the theme of honoring one's parents. The unit begins with the traditional formula "Listen to me" and makes a point of identifying the speaker as "your father" (Sir 3:1). The traditional exhortation follows, about doing what one is told so that nothing bad will happen. Then a reason is given: "For the Lord honored the father above the children" (Sir 3:2). The reason appeals to a code of honor rationalized theologically. It appears merely to support the exhortation of the father that his children listen to him, but in fact introduces the theme of honor, equating it implicitly with "listening," and then goes on to expand its applicability as an ethical principle as far as the mind can imagine. Thus the stage is set for what the Greek rhetors would have called an elaboration.

Ten versicles follow. There are three proverbs illustrating that "the one who honors his father" reaps fine rewards (Sir 3:3–6). Two imperatives come next, one positive ("Honor your father") and one negative ("Do not glorify yourself"), each supplied with an additional supporting argument ("For a father's blessing strengthens the houses of the children"; "For a man's glory comes from honoring his father" [Sir 3:8–11]). These verses introduce yet another significant consideration, which is given with the new terminology of blessing and curse, concepts that will serve to good advantage later in the elaboration. The two imperatives in Sirach 3:8–11 function as admonitions, but serve as well to lead the reader through a series of dialectical inversions calculated to give the impression that the logic governing the honor-consequence relation pertains in every case that can be imagined, no matter how construed. With the principle established, the final exhortation can be given.

The son is asked to "help" his father in his father's old age, "even if he [his father] is lacking in understanding" (Sir 3:12–13). The promise is that, when the son has his own day of affliction, his kindness to his father "will be remembered" and "credited against his sins" (Sir 3:12–15). Ben Sira is careful not to promise what he cannot deliver, namely, that the son's sons will surely take care of him in his old age as well. He turns instead to a consideration of rewards (blessings) that only the Lord can grant. Then comes the final verse with its reminder that the Lord can also issue curses (Sir 3:16). The period is complete. The danger alluded to in verse 1 is finally specified only in verse 15, and the reason for the introduction of the language of blessing and curse in verse 8 is now clear. The argumentation is extremely clever, interweaving an old cliché about paying attention to one's teacher with a specific item from the Jewish code of ethics (fifth commandment) and a forceful theological commonplace.

An even closer reading will show that the logic of elaboration governs not only the formation of this unit of proverbs but its placement in relation to other units around it. It is not insignificant that the unit just preceding this one develops the theme of the "fear of the Lord" (Sir 2:1–18) and that both units are preceded by the opening hymn to wisdom in which the wisdom of the created order, the fear of the Lord, and the keeping of the commandments (cf. Sir 1:26–27) are equated. One sees that the various logics of proverbs, poetry, and rhetoric have been used to merge the notions of wisdom and law in support of the specific instances given with the two major divisions of the Ten Commandments. The result is a sense of seriousness about the importance of seeing the ethical principle underlying both the proverbial admonitions and the special code. This sense of seriousness pervades the proverbial material throughout Ben Sira's book. His choice of themes is clearly intended to address ethical issues of real consequence for Jewish society at the time.

Wisdom Poetry

A second type of poetry is dedicated to the figure of Wisdom and develops the theme of the quest. The imagery serves to imagine both Wisdom's quest for human acceptance and the human quest for her. Personified and depicted as if she were a divine creature with cosmic power and destiny, the figure of Wisdom represents the concept of a universal order upon which a rational ethic might be based. There is little interest in exploring the profile of the personification itself. The burning questions have to do with her "location" and the trouble humans seem to have in "finding" it. Thus the poetry ranges from highly imaginary and mythic moments, such as the moment of the Creation itself (Sir 1:1–10, 24:1–7), to descriptions of quite recognizable moments in a person's struggle to discern what is right and to do it. If one does not limit the set of wisdom poetry to only those poems that personify Wisdom and narrate her quest for a place to dwell, but includes as well those that address the question of how to seek and find her, the following list results: 1:1–30 ("All wisdom comes from the Lord"); 4:11–19 ("Wisdom exalts her sons"); 6:18–37 ("My son, from your youth up choose instruction"); 14:20–15:10 ("Blessed is the man who meditates on wisdom"); 16:26–17:14 ("The works of the Lord have existed from the beginning by his creation"); 24:1–34 ("Wisdom will praise herself"); 37:16–26 ("Reasoning is the beginning of every work"); 39:1–11 ("He who devotes himself to the study of the law"; cf. "the wisdom of the scribe" [38:24]); 51:13–22 ("While I was still young"); and 51:23–30 ("Draw near to me").

In this poetry Wisdom is objectified in order to "locate" her in the orders of creation, history, culture (literature), social institutions, human reason, human labor, and human struggle, and especially in the history of Israel, the books of Moses, the Temple in Jerusalem, the ritual of the Temple liturgy, the vocation of the priestly scribe, and the scribal compositions in praise of the divine purposes for the entire arrangement. Nothing is to be left out, except, of course, the fool who does not bother with the quest or cannot meet its demands, and thus lives foolishly.

The poetry of wisdom complements the poetry of proverbs in interesting ways. Thinking in proverbs begins with a particular instance and generalizes about it as a typical case. Generalizations based upon a typical case do not conclude, however, that it must always be so. Thus Ben Sira pressed the logic of proverbial thinking about as far as it could go in his little essays in support of ethical principles. His wisdom poetry starts at the opposite end of the spectrum and runs from the universal to the particular. Its purpose is to create the impression that the behavior recommended in the ethical instructions agrees with the grand design of all that can be imagined. Wisdom is the concept that allows for the overlap and alignment of the two poetries. If a certain type of behavior is seen to be "wise," and if the world can be imagined to have been created "wisely," the recommended ethic receives a strong philosophical or theological support.

Unfortunately, making the leap conceptually from conservative ethic to worldview was not as simple as it might appear. The figure of Wisdom and the slightly narrative imagery of her presence at the Creation and her activities among human societies invited the imagination to generalize in ways that cannot account for differences among cultures and differences within a culture with respect to opinions, patterns of behavior, inequalities, and definitions of well-being. Ben Sira recognized this problem, however, and addressed it in his poems in an interesting way. Invariably, at least two perspectives are brought to bear upon the figure of Wisdom in a given poem. The two perspectives usually address the problem of the universal and the particular by means of some difference in the location of Wisdom or the conditions of her availability. By choosing apt imagery for the figure of Wisdom, and creating a strong poetry to portray Wisdom under a double perspective, Ben Sira portrays Wisdom as a power that belongs in two "places," or forms a bridge between two extremes. Thus she is depicted as being present both in creation and in history, among all peoples but especially in Israel, and in all writings of the ancients but especially in the books of Moses; she is both present and absent in all human labor, seen by the wise but hidden to the fool.

The doubling of perspective on Wisdom's availability can easily be illustrated. In the first poem (Sir 1:1–20), Wisdom is imagined in no less than five "locations": before the Creation, at the Creation, in creation ("poured out upon all his works"), available to all humans ("dwelling with all flesh"), and present in particular "to those who love the Lord." In the second poem (Sir 4:11–19), the contrast is between the manner of Wisdom's presence during and after her disciplining of the seeker, as she changes from a source of anguish to one of joy. In the poem on the creation of the human race in Sirach 17, Wisdom is said to have been given to humans by virtue of both their endowments as creatures and the covenant established with Israel. It is the same with the poem about Wisdom's quest for a dwelling in Sirach 24. After traversing the whole of creation, she took possession of every people and nation before finding a resting place specifically in Zion.

This poetry punctuates Ben Sira's book, providing reminders of the larger frames of reference within which the poetry of admonition is to be heard. It hardly functions as an outline, for the divisions created by it are uneven and the proverbial themes that occur in a division are only loosely related to it. Nevertheless, a close reading shows that some association between the two poetries figured in the selection and arrangement of materials. Following the first wisdom poem, to return to an earlier example, the theme of the "fear of the Lord" as the "beginning" of wisdom is announced, after which units of material emphasize the duties of obedience to God and parents as well as the virtue of humility. The theme of humility appears to set the stage for the next wisdom poem on the two phases of the life with wisdom: initial discipline and eventual exaltation. Various forms of advice against exalting oneself come next, preparing the reader for the exhortation to accept wisdom's yoke in Sirach 6:18–37. Thus the two poetries (the poetry of wisdom and the poetic elaboration of proverbial material) overlap at the point where "wisdom" is at stake. By framing his admonitions with the poetry of wisdom, Ben Sira did not achieve a clear set of headings for the systematic organization of his many ethical themes. But he did provide an imaginary setting for his instructions that could encompass all of creation and history. In doing so, he offered his readers the chance to reflect upon the link between the self-evident truths of the proverbial on the one hand, and what might be discerned of the divine purposes in the created orders on the other.

Psalms and Hymns of Praise

A third kind of poetry can be identified as psalms and hymns of praise. The number of these hymnic poems is not large, but their importance is great. They share features of both style and content with the poetry of wisdom and thus do not seem out of place. They also share features with poetry more traditional to the life and institutions of worship, however, thus serving to shift the focus of Ben Sira's reflection about wisdom onto familiar patterns of meditation. The list includes the following: (1) 18:1–14 ("He who lives for ever created the whole universe"); (2) 22:27–23:6 ("O that a guard were set over my mouth"); (3) 36:1–17 ("Have mercy upon us, O Lord"); (4) 39:13–31 ("Listen to me, O you holy sons"); (5)

42:15–43:33 ("I will now call to mind the works of the Lord"); (6) 51:1–12 ("I will give thanks to thee, O Lord and King").

The list includes three poems that would not be out of place if found in a collection of psalms. Two of these are prayers (2, 3), and one is a psalm of thanksgiving (6). They share the themes of struggle and of the need for divine assistance, themes that are familiar marks of Jewish piety of the period. They follow generally the traditional pattern of request-thanksgiving as it pivots on a moment of rescue. The other three are hymns of praise for the goodness and orderliness of God's creation. These hymns have much in common with the poetry of wisdom and share patterns of thought with it. A gradient curve results that runs from wisdom poetry through the hymns of creation to psalms of thanksgiving and prayers.

The placement of this material within the larger collection of materials in the book does not seem to serve any structural function. Nevertheless, it is important to notice that hymnic material of this type tends to appear later in the collection and to increase in the second half of the book (following chapter 24). Scholars have frequently mentioned that the first half of the book appears to be framed by the two major hymns in praise of wisdom, the opening hymn, which describes how Wisdom was present at the Creation and how she was made available to all people (Sir 1:1–21), and the song Wisdom sings about her quest for a dwelling place in Sirach 24:1–34. It is within this section of the book that the pattern of punctuating proverbs with wisdom poetry is most noticeable. Following chapter 24 it is much more difficult to detect patterned sequences. A variety of new themes and purposes seems to have been unleashed.

Only two of the hymnic poems occur within the first half of the book, a poem about the Creator (1) and a prayer (2). The prayer occurs in the context of admonitions concerning the consequences of certain kinds of speech and behavior. A special sense of seriousness about the codes and consequences of Jewish piety is noticeable in this section. The prayer is appropriate to this section, for it asks divine assistance in order to comply with the admonitions concerning silence and control of the tongue. Thus the prayer serves to heighten the sense of seriousness and bring the entire discussion about wisdom to bear upon the question of obedience to the law.

The occurrence of the hymnic poetry on creation in Sirach 18:1–14 does not disturb the overall pattern, for it belongs to a larger unit of wisdom poetry that runs from Sirach 16:26 to 18:14. This larger unit occurs roughly two-thirds of the way through the first half of the book, focusing upon the very critical issue of the human capacity to discern the wisdom of God. The hymnic poetry in Sirach 18:1–14 is simply an extension of that difficult meditation. The language of praise for God's creation is used, but not to invite the reader to sing. An argument is in process that requires the introduction of the idea of God's transcendence. What God knows and does is set in contrast to the limitations of human existence ("Who can search out his mighty deeds?" [Sir 18:4]). The form of the poem is a hymn to God's creation, but the theme is actually taken from the mythology of wisdom. Wisdom is hidden beyond the reach of the human capacity to find her anywhere in the world (*cf.* Prov 1:28; Job 28; Sir 1:1–6; Wis 9:13–17, 13:1–9; Bar 3:15–31). The argument is that wisdom is nonetheless possible because God graciously revealed the patterns of piety (wisdom) in the system of covenants that govern Second Temple Judaism ("Therefore the Lord is patient . . . and pours out his mercy" [Sir 18:11]). Thus the hymn to the Creator is part of the larger meditation and serves the poetry of wisdom as a supporting argument.

According to Ben Sira, "a hymn of praise should be uttered in wisdom" (Sir 15:10). One notes, therefore, that the other two creation hymns (4, 5) are announced as poetry that Ben Sira himself has written. The first follows directly upon the poem in praise of the scribe. Ben Sira makes the transition from that poem to the hymn in praise of creation with an autobiographical verse ("I have yet more to say, which I have thought upon" [Sir 39:12]), and concludes the hymn with the following statement: "Therefore from the beginning I have been convinced, and have thought this out and left it in writing: The works of the Lord are all good" (Sir 39:32–33). It is the same with the hymn in Sirach 42:15–43:33. The opening line announces, "I will now call to mind the works of the Lord." Thus the inclusion of hymnic poetry in

Ben Sira's book follows from his program of meditation upon wisdom.

The content of the hymnic poetry is not insignificant, for with it is given the theological frame for Ben Sira's system of thought and instruction in piety. Nevertheless, as a matter of meditational and compositional strategy, Ben Sira did not begin with hymnic poetry in praise of God's creation, but with the image of wisdom at the Creation (Sir 1:1–21). Thus, pedagogically, the hymns in praise of the Creator and his creation serve to demonstrate the fruition of Ben Sira's program, not its point of departure. The effect created by this strategy is the illusion that, if one begins a quest for wisdom anywhere in the world of human experience and culture, one will eventually end up in the Temple at Jerusalem with prayers and praise for the Creator's special revelations to Judaism.

Epic Poetry

At the end of Ben Sira's book of wisdom there is a long poem in praise of the *hasidim*. This poem does not fall into a class with other poems in Ben Sira's book, nor with other poetry before Ben Sira's time. It can be described as epic poetry, however, because of its theme and scope: the glory of Israel's heroes from the beginning to the end of Israel's history.

The poem is finely crafted in a distinctive meter (tetrameter, in contrast to the free verse of the preceding material) and segmented in units of uneven length devoted to each of the figures. The figures run from Enoch at the beginning (or perhaps originally from Noah) to Simon, the high priest officiating at the Temple in Ben Sira's own time. A pattern of characterization is used that classifies figures according to office. The offices of father, priest, prophet, and king predominate, with Moses described in terms of several offices, and the judges mentioned at their particular juncture in the history.

The history unfolds according to the following pattern: The first seven figures are taken together as being those with whom the covenants were established at the beginning. They are Noah, Abraham, Isaac, Jacob, Moses, Aaron, and Phinehas. After the entrance into the land under the judges, a long section rehearses the history of the prophets and kings. Kings are classed as good or bad, and the functions of the prophets are described in relation to the type of king with whom each is matched. Figures of the restoration are briefly mentioned (without Ezra) to close the period of struggle with the kings and prepare for the scene of climax. The structure is balanced, the sweep impressive, and the poetry of celebration strong.

The poem belongs in a class by itself because of its distinctive features of style and content. Because of these features, scholars have found its presence in Ben Sira's book of wisdom difficult to explain. When compared with earlier wisdom writings, the anomalies are compounded. They include the epic style, the interest in history, the privilege implicitly granted to the Hebrew scriptures under interpretation, the studied fascination with the figure of the prophets, and the obvious advocacy of Second Temple institutions. None of these interests have appeared appropriate for a sage in the tradition of wisdom.

A number of considerations indicate just the opposite, however, leading to the view that this poem not only belongs among the finer literary accomplishments of Ben Sira but is intentionally placed at the conclusion of his book. A major consideration bears upon the relation of the epic poem to the hymn in praise of creation that immediately precedes it (Sir 42:15–43:33). The two poems are joined together both by poetic devices and by thematic pattern. The opening lines of each make a pair ("I will now call to mind the works of the Lord"; "Let us now praise famous men"), and the terminology appropriate to each of the two types of poetry has been switched (with "praise" used to introduce the epic, and "remember" used to introduce the hymn to creation). The two poems are linked as well by means of the final line of the creation hymn ("And to the godly he has granted wisdom"). This line looks both ways, forming an apt solution to the problem of hidden wisdom (cast as God's inscrutability) with which the hymn comes to a close, as well as a preparation for the new subject to be announced in the next verse. Thematically, the two poems follow the pattern of imagining wisdom first in creation, and then in history. This pattern occurs frequently throughout the book (see 1:1–8/1:9–18; 16:24–30/17:1–11; 24:1–7/24:8–21; 39:12–35/40:1–11). Thus there are good reasons for taking the two poems as a set and regarding them as a fitting conclusion to Ben Sira's book of wisdom poetry.

Two specifications are required if the poetry of wisdom is to be read thematically throughout the book: the notion of "wisdom in creation" and the notion of "wisdom in history." If one reads the wisdom poems with the first notion in mind, a theme is discovered behind Ben Sira's affirmations that wisdom can be discerned in the natural world. It is the theme of Wisdom's hiddenness, a statement of the problem humans have in finding her. On the one hand, her presence in creation is affirmed; on the other, it is denied that anyone can find her there except the Lord, who did so at the time of the Creation. Not every creation poem expresses this thought by portraying wisdom as a cosmic figure, but the dialectic between affirmation and denial is present in all of them. Several poems prefer the imageries of order, obedience, and majesty to celebrate the Creator's wisdom and power, before introducing the refrain of human limitation. In the two poems that do depict Wisdom's presence at the Creation (Sir 1:1–30, 24:1–34), the point is that something else had to happen in addition to creation in order for her to be found by humankind. In the first poem it is said that the Creator gave her as a gift to humankind (Sir 1:9, 1:19); in the second, Wisdom herself is said to have sought a place to dwell among the nations (Sir 24:7).

The creation hymn at the conclusion of the book uses the terminology of "glory," not wisdom, to describe the wonders of the Lord's creation. It is emphasized that the glory is greater than humans can comprehend or bring to expression in song. The use of the term "glory" appears to be fortunate, for it easily sustains the dialectic of wisdom's hidden presence even while preparing the reader for the transition to the epic poetry to follow. In the epic it will be the "glory" of the ḥasidim that will be sung.

If one follows the theme of wisdom's location "in history" throughout this poetry, one notes a gradual specification of moments that were foundational for the history of humankind and Israel. In the first wisdom poem the specification is vague, for the emphasis is upon creation and humankind in general, not upon history. Thus there is mention of wisdom dwelling with "all flesh." A shift occurs within the poem, however, to language that alludes to specifically Jewish thought and piety (such as the specification of "those who love him" or the mention of "the fear of the Lord"). Nevertheless, this happens without making a point of the shift in focus from a general to a particularly Jewish anthropology. Certainly there is no emphasis upon the slight allusion to the historical moments when, according to the Hebrew epic, the gift of wisdom might have taken place—that is, in the Garden or on the occasions when covenants were established. The allusions to the stories in Genesis 1–2 and the Sinai event are much more obvious in the wisdom poem in Sirach 16:26–17:14. Still, the two events are not clearly distinguished, and thus no point is made of the double allusion or the movement it suggests from the more general to the more specific bestowal. The situation is quite different in chapter 24. There wisdom is said first to "have gotten a possession" in every people and nation, and then to have found a special "resting place" in Jerusalem.

If the epic at the end of the book is read as the climax of this set of poems, the claim it makes is startling. Not only would the moments of wisdom's location in Israel have been specified systematically, thus gathering up the earlier allusions to covenant, law, and Jerusalem by rehearsing the entire covenantal history, but Ben Sira would be asking the reader to imagine Second Temple society in his own time as the culmination of the divine purpose in creation and the divine plan for human history. The final scene suggests that Ben Sira may have had exactly that in mind. He celebrates the glory of the high priest in his great moment of covenant enactment by describing the scene as the reflection of the very glory of creation itself. Thus the epic poem and the hymn to creation that precedes it belong to Ben Sira's poetry of wisdom even though the figure of Wisdom is not portrayed as present.

The Structure of the Book

Four types of poetry can be distinguished in Ben Sira's book of wisdom. They differ from one another in both form and content, and relate to one another in different ways. The most important typological difference is between the poetry of proverbs and the poetry of wisdom. One function of the book appears to be the attempt to relate the wisdom associated with the tradition of proverbs with the wisdom abstraction that comes to expression in the poetry of wisdom. This is achieved in part by framing the poetry of

proverbs with the poetry of wisdom in ways that suggest the identification of the two. This strategy dictates the interweaving of the two types of poetry, and may partially account for the selection and arrangement of blocks of proverbs. However, the arrangement of proverbs does not appear to have given the book a clear overarching principle of organization. What little structure the book has derives rather from the wisdom poetry, and it is the poetry of wisdom, not that of the proverbs, that sustains interesting formal and thematic relationships with the other two types of poetry.

One of the other types of poetry, the poetry of psalm and praise, serves to domesticate the poetry of wisdom within hymnic forms traditional to the cult. This effect is important for Ben Sira's grand design, but the arrangement of this poetry does not appear to have structural significance for the book.

In the case of the epic poem, the fourth type of poetry in the book, both its placement and its thematic elaboration of wisdom themes suggest that the poem functions as a climax and conclusion to the book as a whole.

Thus a semblance of structure can be discerned in the arrangement of the types of poetry and the way in which themes from each are interrelated. Nevertheless, clear lines cannot be drawn, either among the various types of poetry, for each shades into the other in certain instances, or among segments of an overall organization, for segments are not clearly delineated or balanced. The bulk of the material remains proverbial and is not easily organized by means of the wisdom poetry. The design in evidence in the first sections of the book is difficult to follow throughout the collection, as large chunks of proverbial material accumulate that bear little relation to the theological concerns of the wisdom poems. If the point of the book is the merger of the two modes of discourse, the execution of the merger is experimental. The structure of the book reduces, finally, neither to a collection of proverbs nor to an essay in poetry on a theological theme.

Later scribes understood this in their own way. On the one hand, they treated the book as one would treat a handbook for teachers in the Hellenistic milieu. This is manifest in the messiness of the manuscript tradition and the evidence it provides of widespread use of the book to collect additional material, reorganize it, and provide headings for easy reference. On the other hand, Ben Sira continued to be viewed as the author of the material, and the material itself as a creative composition, not merely a collection of traditional materials by an anonymous teacher.

The accompanying outline builds upon the fundamental distinction between the blocks of proverbial material and the set of wisdom poems that punctuate the book. In the accompanying outline the four poems of prominence are identified by their first lines (shown in capital letters). Blocks of proverbs have been designated mainly by theme (e.g., On fearing the Lord) and are indented farthest to the right. In some instances, several smaller units have been subsumed under a single heading in order to compress the list of themes and suggest possible principles of organization. Hymnic material (with first lines in italics) and wisdom poems appear in the same column for the reasons given above.

THE CONCEPTUAL ACHIEVEMENT

The analysis of Ben Sira's composition has forced a consideration of literary features that betray deeply embedded, but unexpressed, patterns of thought. These patterns appear to address critical intellectual issues of his time. Some of these patterns have surfaced in the discussion of the relationships among the various types of poetry he produced, and aspects of the intellectual challenge of his times have been touched upon by noting the novelties of his writings and relating them to the social-historical circumstances of his life, thought, and commitments. Another set of reflections is required, however, to determine Ben Sira's place in the mix of traditions and cultures that swirled around him, and to assess his intellectual accomplishments. In order to do this, one needs to see his work in its larger cultural context and to study it in comparison with those traditions that may have influenced it.

Three distinct traditions of cultural transmission can be discerned in Ben Sira's work: (1) the Hebrew wisdom tradition; (2) a certain "priestly" tradition of life and thought cultivated within the institutions of the Second Temple, and drawing upon its scriptures,

OUTLINE

(unnumbered)	Prologue
1:1–10	"ALL WISDOM COMES FROM THE LORD"
1:11–2:18	On fearing the Lord
3:1–16	On honoring parents
3:17–4:10	On humility
4:11–19	"Wisdom Exalts Her Sons" (But first she will test them)
4:20–31	On critical moments
5:1–6:4	On not exalting yourself
6:5–17	On putting friends to the test
6:18–37	"My son, from your youth up choose instruction"
7:1–14:19	On not doing evil (a lengthy section of elaborated admonitions on topics of human relations: family, friends, officials, strangers)
14:20–15:10	"Blessed Is the Man Who Meditates on Wisdom" (She will exalt him above his neighbors)
15:11–20	On keeping the commandments
16:1–23	On the mercy and wrath of the Lord
16:24–18:14	"The works of the Lord have existed" (a hymn to creation and covenant)
18:15–22:26	On wisdom and folly (a large collection of proverbs that compare the wise to the foolish)
22:27–23:6	"O that a guard were set over my mouth"
23:7–15	On swearing
23:16–27	On adultery
24:1–34	"WISDOM WILL PRAISE HERSELF"
25:1–26:18	On things pleasurable; on things disgusting (especially kinds of women)
26:28–28:26	On vices and weaknesses (especially harmful speech)
29:1–28	On money matters
30:1–25	On training children
31:1–11	On health and riches
31:12–32:13	On table etiquette
32:14–33:18	On keeping the commandments
33:19–31	On the treatment of servants
34:1–35:20	On the cult and the occult
36:1–17	"Have mercy upon us, O Lord"
36:18–38:23	On choosing wives, friends, counselors, physicians
38:24–34	On the trades
39:1–11	"He who devotes himself to the study of the law" (in praise of the scribe)
39:12–35	"Listen to me, O you holy sons" (in praise of the works of the Lord)
40:1–41:13	On human miseries, including death, calamity, trouble, and begging
41:14–42:14	On shameful things
42:15–43:33	"I WILL NOW CALL TO MIND THE WORKS OF THE LORD"
44:1–50:24	"LET US NOW PRAISE FAMOUS MEN"
50:27–29	Subscript
51:1–12	"I will give thanks"
51:13–22	"While I was still young . . . I sought wisdom"
51:23–30	"Draw near to me, you who are untaught"

codes, and etiologies; and (3) Hellenism. Since these were the very forces that determined the times in general, Ben Sira's work was not done in a corner. The patterns of response to these cultural impingements were, naturally, many and diverse among Ben Sira's contemporaries. Hellenism could be accommodated in a variety of ways. The Second Temple experiment (constructing a society on the model of the ancient Near Eastern temple-state without the benefit of royal power) could be rationalized in decidedly different ways. And the indications are that those who cherished the traditions of wisdom were not at all in agreement about how to apply the accumulated proverbial lore to new social circumstances. Putting the three streams of tradition together in any combination whatsoever would therefore have been quite a task. That being the case, Ben Sira's own particular construction will define his intellectual achievement.

In the Tradition of Wisdom

Ben Sira's place in the tradition of wisdom has been a major topic of scholarly investigation. Ever since Coert Rylaarsdam's book on the wisdom tradition in 1946, biblical scholars have arranged the books of Hebrew wisdom in a particular sequence, imagined a certain development of wisdom thought, and positioned Ben Sira at a precise place within the scheme. The sequence of texts documenting this development is as follows: (1) Proverbs 10–31; (2) Proverbs 1–9; (3) Job and Qohelet; (4) Sirach; and (5) Wisdom of Solomon. The corresponding stages of the development have frequently been described as (1) the ancient cultivation of practical wisdom; (2) the discovery of "theological wisdom," a development some explain as a response to the crisis created by the end of the monarchies in Israel and Judaea; (3) the period of skepticism, an intellectual attitude that some explain as a response to postexilic circumstances; (4) the "nationalization" of wisdom that Ben Sira achieved by "identifying" wisdom and *torah* (teaching, law); and (5) the use of wisdom mythology to express the notion of "revelation."

Within this framework, scholars have undertaken specialized studies on Ben Sira's theology of piety (Haspecker), his understanding of the law (Marböck;

Schnabel), his conservative theology (Di Lella, "Conservative and Progressive Theology"), his system of theodicy (Crenshaw, "The Problem of Theodicy"), his own analysis of the logical limits of proverbial thinking (Rad), and his solution to the crisis of wisdom thought by developing the concept of the "right time" (Rad). These studies have clearly demonstrated Ben Sira's place in the history of ideas, and most have emphasized his contributions to that history. When compared with Job and Qohelet, however, Ben Sira has frequently been thought a less penetrating analyst of his times and of the problem of the continuing validity of traditional wisdom. This assessment derives, no doubt, from the fact that most of these studies have been pursued without relating his intellectual achievements to the social-historical circumstances of his work.

Recent studies have found it helpful to ask about that relationship, especially as it may impinge both upon Ben Sira's view of Second Temple society and upon the nature of his intellectual achievements. His book is marked not only by a strong affirmation of living in accordance with proverbial wisdom but also by a very positive attitude toward the laws and codes that patterned practice in Second Temple Judaism. The two attitudes make a pair, and thus should be studied together. Both are constructive, and each works in support of the other. If Ben Sira's presentation of proverbial wisdom is studied in isolation from his advocacy of Second Temple sense and piety, his views appear naive when compared with Qohelet, shallow when compared with Job, and weak when confronted with the intellectual challenge occasioned by the "absence" of wisdom from Israel since the exiles.

If, on the other hand, Ben Sira's instruction in wisdom is related to a critical assessment of the social history of Second Temple Judaism, his intellectual labor can be judged much differently. Ben Sira was certainly not naive about the crisis of wisdom thought, nor unaware that proverbial wisdom had lost its authority. He was a sage who, in spite of the skeptical mood of the times, appropriated traditional wisdom for a constructive program. Courage, imagination, and intellectual creativity mark his novel proposal. It does not detract from Ben Sira's intellectual achievement to see that its purpose was to affirm the possibility of human well-being in a time of uncertainty. According to Ben Sira, the structures of social life in Second Temple society not only made sense, they were more than conducive to human flourishing. But he had to work out his proposal in the context of the crisis of wisdom thought.

The crisis of wisdom thought had been occasioned by the social crises of the times of exile and restoration. One response to the social crises had been to acknowledge the "absence" of wisdom from the world and explore the sense to be made of life in a world where traditional wisdom did not work (Job, Qohelet). Some sages wondered what it would take to restore patterns of sane behavior and discourse (Prov 1–9; scribal additions to Jeremiah). The connection was made between uncertainty about the validity of proverbial wisdom and uncertainty about the cult (and the efficacy of its systems of rectification). There were fundamental disagreements about what to think and do.

Ben Sira found it possible to give his blessing to the society Jews had succeeded in constructing during the fourth and third centuries B.C.E. His position was that the cult was efficacious and that the society structured by the cult fostered life in accordance with wisdom. In order to make the connection, the common sense of proverbs had to support the Second Temple codes, and the Second Temple codes had to make common sense. At one level, he achieved that merger simply by combining themes from proverbial wisdom with Jewish ethical principles in his elaborations. At another level, however, he produced a mythology in order to imagine how the first-level combinations could seriously be argued in view of both the crisis of wisdom thinking and the novelties encountered in the construction of the Second Temple state. The merger between cultic code and proverbial wisdom at the level of practice was matched at the level of imaginative abstraction.

Earlier sages personified Wisdom in order to conceptualize what had been lost when societies came apart during the fifth and fourth centuries. They imagined her as a mythic figure who, though absent now from the world of human intercourse, was known to the Creator and thus could be thought of in relation to the orderliness of the natural world. The notion of Wisdom's presence at the Creation did not alleviate the problem of her recognition in the world (Prov 8:22–31, Job 28). Ben Sira started with the figure of Wisdom at the Creation and turned the logic of its conception on its head. Instead of imagining Wisdom at the Creation merely in order to affirm her existence while accounting for her absence from human society, Ben Sira linked her with the Creator's activities in order to reaffirm her presence with humankind. He did accept the notion of the hiddenness of Wisdom, a notion that belonged to the older mythology. He did so, however, without allowing the figure of Wisdom to represent the notion of absence, but in order to account for the difference in perception between the foolish and the wise, or between the nations and Israel.

Two imaginative devices were used to "relocate" Wisdom in the world. One was the narrative device of moving Wisdom from one place to another. Thus Ben Sira wrote that the Lord "poured her out upon all his works" (Sir 1:9), and he had Wisdom sing that she "sought in whose territory [she] might lodge" (Sir 24:7). The other was to interpret the creation story in Genesis as the account of those events in which God imparted Wisdom to humankind. The narrative imagery of the quest for a dwelling was derived from Egyptian mythology of Maat (goddess of justice and order) and Isis (guarantor of leadership and rule). By using motifs from this popular mythology to enhance the narrative logic of the well-known stories in Genesis, Ben Sira created an extremely powerful imagery. This imagery could then be used to read the entire Hebrew epic as the story of Wisdom's sojourn on the way to residence in the Temple in Ben Sira's time.

Ben Sira's reading of the epic was correct from a priest's point of view. Two kinds of moment in the scriptural accounts received accentuation: those in which enlightenment occurred, and those in which covenants were established or at stake. Thus one perceives the slight hint of the Garden in the first wisdom poem ("He rained down knowledge and discerning comprehension" [Sir 1:19]), as well as the subtle allusion to the covenants ("She made among men an eternal foundation" [Sir 1:15]). In the creation poetry in Sirach 16:26–18:14, the allusions have been sharpened, but still no distinction has been made between the enlightenment in Eden and at

Sinai: "He . . . made them in his own image"; "He filled them with knowledge . . . and showed them good and evil"; "He . . . allotted to them the law of life"; "He established with them an eternal covenant"; "Their eyes saw his glorious majesty"; "And he gave commandment" (Sir 17:3–14). In the wisdom poem in Sirach 24, however, the distinction between the nations and Israel is emphasized, and the moments of significance are now said to be the establishment of wisdom in Jerusalem (narrated, Sir 24:8–12) and the fact that Israel has the "book of the covenant" in its possession (appended in discourse, Sir 24:23). The book contains both "the covenant of the Most High God" and "the law which Moses commanded us," thus combining the function of Second Temple charter with that of the "statutes and commandments" fundamental to Second Temple piety. It is this book as epic, charter, and commandment that "fills men with wisdom" and "makes instruction shine forth like light" (Sir 24:25, 27).

It is now possible to explain how the epic poetry in Sirach 44–50 relates to the wisdom poetry in Sirach 1–24. Ben Sira's solution to the question of how to imagine the "presence of wisdom" in Second Temple society was answered at the level of symbol by conflating a myth of Wisdom's quest for a resting place with the Hebrew epic as the story of the Creator's covenants with Israel. Beginning with the notion that Wisdom was known only to the Creator, Ben Sira devised a set of poems that relocated her imaginatively in all of the major moments of the epic: the Creation, covenants, law, entrance into the land, history of the prophets and kings, construction of the Temple at Jerusalem, and possession of the books of Moses. In the wisdom poem in Sirach 24, the story is told from the perspective of Wisdom's quest. In the epic poetry in Sirach 44–50, the story is told from the people's point of view.

Structurally, the pattern for both poems is the same. The wisdom poem unfolds in three strophes, but contains four narrative scenes. The first strophe tells of Wisdom at the Creation, and her quest for a place to dwell (Sir 24:3–7). The second strophe builds upon the first by having the Lord create Wisdom, and command a dwelling in Israel. The second strophe also adds the notice that she took root there and ministered in the Temple (Sir 24:8–12).

The third strophe continues the story by describing the glories of Wisdom's exaltation as she grew up and flourished in Jerusalem. This pattern matches the four-part structure of the epic poem in Sirach 44–50: after the establishment of the covenants (Sir 44:17–45:26), the conquest takes place and the quest begins to establish the covenantal order in Israel (Sir 46:1–12, 47:1–49:10). At last the order of the covenants is actualized in the restoration (Sir 49:11–13), and Simon is exalted as he ministers in the Temple at Jerusalem (Sir 50:1–21). The rehearsal leads the reader to imagine Second Temple society as the flowering of the Lord's intentions for Israel, founded upon the system of covenants established in primeval time, and reflecting the very order of creation, which is the glorious manifestation of the Lord's power and wisdom.

This intellectual achievement made it possible to integrate within a single imaginative frame disparate aspects of Ben Sira's social world. The most important aspects were matters of observance that belonged to the cult and its institutions on the one hand, and patterns of behavior and practice that belonged to the everyday world on the other. The single imaginative frame was that of "wisdom" in creation and in Israel's epic history. From the epic a set of covenants gave charter to the system of Second Temple institutions. The epic was also used to establish the priestly offices and provide divine legitimacy for the "statutes and commandments" derived from Moses. From the tradition of wisdom came the accumulation of proverbs, the distinction between wise and foolish behavior, and the rudiments of a logic for making judgments about specific cases of human encounter. Ben Sira gathered it up, selecting proverbial wisdom heavy with admonition and ethical consequence, and paying close attention to the need to correlate proverbial wisdom of the general kind with specifically Jewish values. Then he eroded the boundaries between the wisdom of the proverbs and the circumspection of the codes. He did so simply by equating "wise" with pious, and foolish with "sinful."

The proof of this procedure is the frequent reference throughout the book, in the context of the poetry of theological wisdom and proverbial units, to the keeping of the law as the way to be wise. The intention to merge the two is confirmed, moreover, when it is seen that "the law" was not limited to matters that correlate easily with the self-evident principles of proverbial wisdom, but was obviously taken to include the full range of observances that belonged to the Temple cult. Thus there is mention of alms (Sir 3:30, 7:10, 17:22, 29:12–13), prayers (Sir 7:10; 17:25–26; 21:1, 5; 35:12–20; 38:9–10), vows (Sir 18:22–23), honoring the priests (Sir 4:14, 7:29–30), offerings and sacrifices (Sir 7:31, 18:11, 34:18–35:11), hymns (Sir 15:9–10, 17:27–28), warnings against taking the name of God in vain (Sir 23:7–11), warnings against the occult (Sir 34:1–8), and other matters of concern specifically related to observance. By including them among his admonitions and instructions of wisdom, Ben Sira revealed his practical stance and motivation. He wanted to see life as an integrated whole, and he thought that life within the bounds of the Second Temple structure made wonderful human sense. In the last analysis, his imaginative poetry was conceived and written just to make that clear.

At the Scholar's Desk

Ben Sira's intellectual achievement was accomplished in the office of the scribe. The poetry he wrote was imaginative and richly nuanced because the books he read were many and varied. It would be wrong to think of Ben Sira as a philosopher without books, or in the stereotype of a romantic or religious poet who worked strictly from personal experience. He was a scholar, widely read and deeply learned. His work betrays an impressive research, not only in the Hebrew scriptures but in the literature of the *ecumene* available at his time.

Ben Sira's many texts included much of the corpus of the Hebrew scriptures that later became known as the Law and the Prophets (Middendorp, *Die Stellung*; Sheppard; Stadelmann), some wisdom writings (Middendorp, *Die Stellung*), a book of psalms (Middendorp, *Die Stellung*), an Isis aretalogy (from which the mythic imagery of Sirach 24 was taken; Conzelmann, "The Mother of Wisdom"), examples of Greek gnomological literature (e.g., Theognis; Middendorp, *Die Stellung*), examples of Greek historiography and biography (Mack, *Wisdom*), some form of Greek encomiastic literature (Mack, *Wisdom*; Lee), probably a handbook for teachers in the Hellen-istic system of *paideia*, possibly some snippets of popular philosophical tracts, and perhaps some handbook for instruction in rhetoric.

Nevertheless, Ben Sira's indebtedness to a cosmopolitan scholarship is not acknowledged and is far from obvious. Scholars have found it necessary to work out very detailed demonstrations of probable influences. That is because Ben Sira's writings are creative compositions that do not obviously reflect dependence upon precursors. Even in the case of the epic poetry—a poetry fully dependent upon the language and description of the scriptural accounts and obviously intended to evoke in the reader familiar lines and scenes—nothing is merely copied out. Clever nuances and novel constructions abound that diffuse the reader's orientation to the scriptural texts as soon as attention has been called to them. This penchant for putting his own constructions upon the writings to which he obviously referred makes it difficult to trace all of the lines of dependence and allusion. Those who have studied Ben Sira's use of the Hebrew scriptures have nevertheless been able to show that he worked his way through an immensely detailed observation of these writings in order to find just the right points of departure for his poetry.

Ben Sira's reading and use of Hellenistic texts is more difficult to trace. The clues must be found in his use of motifs, terminology, patterns of thought, studied clichés, standard metaphors, and themes characteristic of Hellenistic literature. He was acquainted with the encomium, for instance (Lee), and the terminology of succession, which he used in his chronicle of the series of leaders (Hengel, *Judaism* 1, 136; Mack, *Wisdom*, 44–47, 125–126). In the case of his composition of proverbs, some seem hauntingly reminiscent of Greek maxims, just as others remind the reader of traditional Hebrew wisdom. Some formulations seem designed to point in both directions, as if Ben Sira wanted to merge cross-cultural sensibilities or delighted in the moment of comparison and contrast (Middendorp, *Die Stellung*, 13–14, 72–75).

His genius was to know the limits beyond which he dared not go without endangering his purposes. He was a conservative theologian, after all, and chose to write in Hebrew. Moses' book was the text of privilege for him, and Ben Sira treated it as the source of his own inspiration. All other literature was read in its light as an exercise in cultural domestication. Ben Sira's scribe "will seek out the wisdom of all the ancients" but "devote himself to the study of the law of the Most High" (Sir 39:1). Just so with Ben Sira. He stood in the office of Moses as teacher (Sir 45:5), an office that Moses delegated to Aaron, with "authority in statutes and judgments, to teach Jacob the testimonies, and to enlighten Israel with his law" (Sir 45:17).

Scholars have emphasized the "identification" of "wisdom" and "law" in Ben Sira's program (Schnabel). Neither of the two notions was a simple construct, and their correlation was hardly a matter of intellectual sleight of hand. *Torah* referred to covenants in all their mythic, symbolic, genealogical, and legal meanings, but also to the stories about them and to the books that contained the stories. It was the same with "commandments," "statutes," "judgments," and "testimonies." Moses' books were not "law" apart from their function as epic or constitutional charter. Ben Sira understood that and, when devising a poetry "to enlighten Israel with its law," read the law primarily as Israel's national epic. According to Ben Sira, wisdom was first and foremost the insight that Israel's epic history laid the firm foundations for Second Temple institutions, and that Second Temple institutions fostered well-being. All of the wisdom poetry in Ben Sira's book is therefore hermeneutical with respect to the law as epic. Within the context of that large imaginative frame, a frame created by the scholar working with his texts, the thought was possible that "keeping the law" (as observance) was the same as being wise.

In the Context of Hellenization

Openness to the wisdom of the Hellenistic world does not seem to fit with Ben Sira's conservative commitments. Many scholars have therefore found it convenient to disallow the evidence for his insatiable curiosity and wide-ranging investigation of Hellenistic life and thought. It has been possible to take this reading because the evidence for his accommodation of Hellenistic learning is not as obvious as that for his support of Second Temple piety. Nevertheless, denial of Hellenistic influence does not further an understanding of Ben Sira's work.

A combination of Hellenistic learning and Jewish piety in Ben Sira's time seems strange to modern readers for several reasons. One reason that is frequently articulated draws upon the ideological split that surfaced soon after Ben Sira's time in Jerusalem, in the Maccabean revolt against Antiochus IV Epiphanes. Traditionally, the split has been understood as the sign of the incompatibility of conservative Judaism and Hellenistic culture. According to the Maccabean historians, that was the way the issue was put. The Maccabees were on the side of the "traditions of the fathers" and "the law of God," fighting against the influence of Hellenism and the designs of the "Hellenists" to convert Jerusalem into a Hellenistic polis. But the issues were both more simple and more complex than that. To accept the Maccabean reconstruction of that history does not do justice to the social problems and political interests involved, or to the fact that Hellenistic influence came in different packages and did not divide along party lines. Ben Sira is a clear example of an intellectual who was committed to Second Temple Judaism without being hostile to Hellenistic learning. He was, in fact, actively engaged in exploring the relations between the two cultures.

The evidence of Ben Sira's education in Hellenistic literature and culture includes not only the traces of his reading indicated above but also his consciousness of authorship. Patterns of thought were given with the learning, such as the penchant for correlating cosmic, historical, and anthropological orders of "wisdom," and the persuasion that a conceptual system might be used to rationalize conventions. To find support for such a reasonable view of the world in the proverbial wisdom at hand, and to choose to elaborate its logic according to the rules of rhetoric, were also strategies most probably learned from the Greeks. The power of the epic as a chronicle of praise to celebrate a local institution was not a discovery made in isolation from the rest of the Hellenistic world of thought. It does not detract from Ben Sira's poetic and intellectual achievements to say that they could not have happened without a profound education in the culture of Hellenism.

The scribal office is therefore suspiciously Hellenistic in design. Ben Sira's kind of wisdom and the modes of its transmission are very close to those found in Hellenistic educational practice. Greek *paideia* was also aimed at the cultivation of conventional values and based upon conventional wisdom. Conventional wisdom found its expressions, moreover, not only in the collections of maxims and sayings attributed to the sages but also in the works of the poets and the chronicles, histories, encomia, odes, and hymns that celebrated the learning and glory of the cultural tradition. Teachers and students in the Hellenistic system of education were charged with duties in preparation for the round of public festivals. Religious celebrations were not holidays from school, but simply different occasions for participating in the educational enterprise. The contents of Ben Sira's book of wisdom match perfectly the range of materials appropriate to the Hellenistic teacher's duties, and the educational aim was the same, namely, the inculcation of cultural values.

If one reads Ben Sira's book in the context of the tradition of Hebrew wisdom, the conceptual issue finally comes to focus on the relation between wisdom and *torah*. If one reads Ben Sira's book in the context of Hellenism, however, the conceptual issue finally comes to focus on the equation of Hebrew wisdom and Greek *paideia*. Ben Sira's openness to Hellenism was probably based upon his recognition of the fundamental similarities between the two functions. Building an educational enterprise on the foundation of proverbial wisdom would not have seemed strange at all. Nor would it have occurred to him that the integration of proverbial wisdom and religious convention was a novel order of the day. At the level of logic, pedagogy, persuasion, and the composition of literary forms in which a culture might conserve and inculcate its conventional wisdom, Ben Sira found it easy to accommodate the wisdom of the Greeks. It was at the level of *torah* and *paideia* as distinct systems of cultural values that Ben Sira drew the line. Jewish experience, sensibility, and culture were precious treasures, according to Ben Sira. The scribal office was clearly culture specific, as he understood it. And cultural differences set boundaries that Ben Sira did not intend to erase.

Nevertheless, the limits set for cultural accommodation are very difficult to determine in Ben Sira's book. It simply does not address many critical issues of practical or ideological significance for Jews during this time. There is no polemic against mixed mar-

riage, for instance, no caution about the importance of circumcision, no threat to those who do not keep the law, no instruction about good and bad kingship. In their place, however, there is an obvious preoccupation with the institution of the family and the need constantly to guard its integrity. One notes also a clear endorsement of Jewish particularity in the way in which reference is made to Jewish institutions and traditions. And the high priesthood is eulogized in terms of royal functions as if, were the opportunity given, Jerusalem could get along quite well without a king. So perhaps Ben Sira was just being cautious, even as his wisdom warned his students to be. And yet, the lack of polemical tone agrees with the lack of fear one discerns in Ben Sira's pursuit of the wisdom of the Greeks. Perhaps the limits he set for himself were not grounded in a fear of going too far, but in a confidence about the toughness and sanity of his own Jewish view of the world.

A careful reading from this perspective turns up several interesting observations. For one thing, Ben Sira's heroes are described by using the pattern of the Greek encomium, but they are not described in terms of Greek values. They do not manifest Greek virtues, do not accomplish Greek achievements, and are not praised as great individuals. They are praised as obedient and effective performers of divine offices in the service of the people, and priests and prophets are numbered among them.

As for the notion of *paideia*, the path to virtue through practice, and the notion of virtue as the excellence of character to be achieved by this means, there is little trace. The Greek schema of the two stages of *paideia*—first discipline, then reward—is used to describe the path of Wisdom (Sir 4:17–19, 6:18–31). But her yoke is easy (Sir 51:23–27) and the one "who holds to the law will obtain wisdom" (Sir 15:1). At the "end" of the way, moreover, there will be a visitation that recognizes faithful service and grants assurance that one will not be forgotten. It is the same with Ben Sira's play on "glory," view of death, attitude toward mystification, and definition of righteousness. What matters is not the Greek notion of virtue, heroics, and fantasies of immortality. What finally matters for Ben Sira is observance, "keeping the law," and the recognition that paying attention to simple wonders and basic human relationships can provide one with more than enough opportunity to live life to the full.

Ben Sira's position was conservative, but his piety was not mean. His loyalty to Judaism was not rationalized in terms of hostility to other parties or peoples, or of a polemic against other ways of thinking. His wisdom was won, ultimately, not in the exchange with Greek culture, which was real and significant for conceptualizing his program, but from his sense of what was important, a sense of the social small enough to be managed and large enough to be filled with the "light of the Lord" (Sir 50:29). For Ben Sira, true wisdom was the gift to know that life within the bounds of his own religious tradition could be glorious.

Bibliography

General Introductions

Box, G. H., and W. O. E. Oesterley. "The Book of Sirach." In *The Apocrypha and Pseudepigrapha of the Old Testament*, vol. 1, edited by R. H. Charles. Oxford, 1913. Reprinted 1971. Pp. 268–314.

Crenshaw, James. *Old Testament Wisdom: An Introduction*. Atlanta, 1981. Pp. 149–173.

Hengel, Martin. *Judaism and Hellenism*. Philadelphia, 1974. Pp. 131–162.

Mack, Burton L., and Roland Murphy. "Wisdom Literature." In *Early Judaism and Its Modern Interpreters*, edited by Robert A. Kraft and George W. E. Nickelsburg. Philadelphia, 1986. Pp. 373–377.

Nickelsburg, George W. E., *Jewish Literature Between the Bible and the Mishnah*. Philadelphia, 1981. Pp. 55–69.

Rad, Gerhard von. *Wisdom in Israel*. Nashville, Tenn., 1978. Pp. 240–262.

Greek Text

Ziegler, Joseph, ed. *Septuaginta, XII/2: Sapientia, Iesu Filii Sirach*. Göttingen, 1965. The Greek text is reconstructed with critical apparatus.

Hebrew Text

The Hebrew texts from the Cairo Genizah and Masada are available in several publications with critical introductions, studies, variant readings, and notes.

Barthélemy, Jean Dominique, and Otto Rickenbacher. *Konkordanz zum hebräischen Sirach mit syrisch-hebräischem Index*. Göttingen, 1973.

The Book of Ben Sira: Text, Concordance, and an Analysis of the Vocabulary. Jerusalem, 1973. In Hebrew with an introduction in English.

Di Lella, Alexander A. *The Hebrew Text of Sirach: A Text Critical and Historical Study*. London, 1966.

Rüger, Hans Peter. *Text und Textform im hebräischen Sirach*. Berlin, 1970.

Segal, Moshe Zevi. *Sepher Ben Sira ha-Shalem*. Jerusalem, 1958.

Vattioni, Francesco. *Ecclesiastico: Testo ebraico con apparato critico e versioni greca, latina, e siriaca*. Naples, 1968.

Yadin, Yigael. *The Ben Sira Scroll from Masada with Introduction, Emendations, and Commentary*. Jerusalem, 1965.

Major Studies

Haspecker, Josef. *Gottesfurcht bei Jesus Sirach*. Rome, 1976.

Marböck, Johann. *Weisheit im Wandel: Untersuchungen zur Weisheitstheologie bei Ben Sira*. Bonn, 1971.

Middendorp, Theophil. *Die Stellung Jesu Ben Siras zwischen Judentum und Hellenismus*. Leiden, 1973.

Rickenbacher, Otto. *Weisheitsperikopen bei Ben Sira*. Freiburg, 1973.

Stadelmann, Helge. *Ben Sira als Schriftgelehrter*. Tübingen, 1980.

Hellenistic Influence

Conzelmann, Hans. "The Mother of Wisdom." In *The Future of Our Religious Past*, edited by James M. Robinson. Philadelphia, 1971. Pp. 230–243.

Hengel, Martin. *Judaism and Hellenism*. Philadelphia, 1974. Pp. 149–173.

Lee, Thomas Robert. *Studies in the Form of Sirach 44–50*. Atlanta, 1986.

Mack, Burton L. *Wisdom and the Hebrew Epic: Ben Sira's Hymn in Praise of the Fathers*. Chicago, 1985.

Special Studies

Bauckmann, E. G. "Die Proverbien und die Sprüche des Jesus Sirach." *Zeitschrift für die alttestamentliche Wissenschaft* 72 (1960): 33–63.

Baumgartner, Walter. "Die literarischen Gattungen in der Weisheit des Jesus Sirach." *Zeitschrift für die alttestamentliche Wissenschaft* 34 (1914): 161–198.

Crenshaw, James L. "The Problem of Theodicy in Sirach: On Human Bondage." *Journal of Biblical Literature* 94 (1975): 47–64.

Di Lella, Alexander A. "Conservative and Progressive Theology: Sirach and Wisdom." *Catholic Biblical Quarterly* 28 (1966): 139–154.

Gilbert, Maurice. "L'éloge de la Sagesse (Siracide 24)." *Revue Théologique de Louvain* 5 (1974): 326–348.

Harrington, Daniel J. "The Wisdom of the Scribe According to Ben Sira." In *Ideal Figures in Ancient Judaism*, edited by George W. E. Nickelsburg and John J. Collins. Chico, Calif., 1980. Pp. 181–188.

Perdue, Leo G. *Wisdom and Cult.* Missoula, 1977. Pp. 188–211.

Roth, Wolfgang. "On the Gnomic-Discursive Wisdom of Jesus ben Sirach." *Semeia* 17 (1980): 59–79.

Rylaarsdam, J. Coert. *Revelation in Jewish Wisdom Literature.* Chicago, 1946.

Sanders, Jack T. *Ben Sira and Demotic Wisdom.* Chico, Calif., 1983.

Sanders, James A. "The Psalter at the Time of Christ." *The Bible Today* 22 (1966): 1462–1469.

Schnabel, Eckhard J. *Law and Wisdom from Ben Sira to Paul.* Tübingen, 1985.

Sheppard, Gerald T. *Wisdom as a Hermeneutical Construct.* New York, 1980.

Skehan, Patrick W. "Structures in Poems on Wisdom: Proverbs 8 and Sirach 24." *Catholic Biblical Quarterly* 41 (1979): 365–379.

Trenchard, Warren C. *Ben Sira's View of Women.* Chico, Calif., 1982.

BURTON L. MACK

Baruch
The Letter of Jeremiah
The Prayer of Manasseh

THE BOOK OF BARUCH, The Letter of Jeremiah, and The Prayer of Manasseh are pseudepigraphic works. They are set in the sixth and fifth centuries B.C.E., but they did not receive their final forms until much later. Greatly varied in theology, form, and purpose, all three deal in some way with the problem of foreign nations or their gods.

Baruch

The Book of Baruch is a theodicy. It defends God against the charge of unjust governance of history by asserting that it is not God's cruelty but the people's sin that is responsible for their captivity by foreign overlords. To escape that suffering, the book advises, they must repent and regain, relationship with God, who alone can rescue them. In teaching these things the book aims to provide "strength" and "light" (1:12) so that the prisoners will survive their ordeal. (All translations are from the Revised Standard Version, *New Oxford Annotated Bible*.)

The book professes to be the work of Jeremiah's companion Baruch (1:1), writing to Israel's exiles in Babylon in the sixth century B.C.E. (1:2). It is, however, a collection of literary pieces written by different authors at different times. The date of the final redaction of Baruch is uncertain. Historical inaccuracies in the introduction, similarities to the Book of Daniel, and the derivation of the wisdom poem (3:9–4:4) from Sirach 24 preclude a date earlier than the second century. Though the book fits nicely into that period of Hellenist hegemony, it may come from as late a time as the Roman period at the end of the first century C.E. (Rost 1976).

The author's adoption both of an exilic setting and of Baruchan authorship carries important theological implications. The setting provides the book with a historical parallel to the actual situation of its audience, while Baruch's authorship indirectly claims for the book the authority of one of the great interpreters of the exile, the prophet Jeremiah.

Efforts to divide the book into literary units reveal the composite nature of the work. From a form-critical point of view it divides easily into two main parts, prose (1:1–3:8) and poetry (3:9–5:6), but these two sections subdivide into smaller literary units: introduction (1:1–14); a confession of sin and an appeal for mercy (1:5–3:8); a poem in praise of Wisdom (3:9–4:4); and a poem of comfort and restoration (4:5–5:9).

The variations in styles, traditions, and points of view in Baruch at first appear restricted to the two main divisions. For example, the prose half of the book addresses God by the title "Lord," "Lord our God," or "Lord Almighty." The poetry drops that term and substitutes "God" or other titles. Similarly, the prose units express a conciliatory attitude toward

Israel's captors, but the poetry looks less favorably upon them.

The literary and theological differences among the parts are still more complicated. For instance, one prose unit (1:15–3:8) and one poetic unit (4:5–5:9) are prophetic in style, but the former unit draws upon Jeremianic and Deuteronomic traditions, while the later relies heavily on Second Isaiah. Furthermore, the poem falling between these two (3:9–4:4) is not prophetic at all but derives from the wisdom tradition. The book, therefore, is only loosely unified.

The introduction (1:1–14) reports that Baruch's reading of "this book" to the entire community of exiles wrought two things: the repentance of all the captives and a collection to be sent to the Temple in Jerusalem for prayers on their behalf (1:5–6). Besides expressing hope for accommodation with their rulers, these prayers introduce the themes to follow. Through them the captives ask to receive "strength" and "light for their eyes" (1:12) and for help because they are sinners who suffer from God's wrath "to this day" (1:12–13).

The following division, the confession of sin and call to repentance (1:15–3:8), develops the double-edged theme begun in the introduction and explicitly stated in the refrain, "Righteousness belongs to the Lord our God, but confusion of face . . . to us . . . because we have sinned" (1:15–16; 2:6). Lest the point be missed, a litany of Israel's sins (1:19–2:5) illustrates the refrain. From the day God rescued them from Egypt "until today," they disobeyed, would not listen, and refused to walk in the statutes of their God (1:19). In the formulaic language of Jeremiah (11:1–4), Deuteronomy (28), and Daniel (9:7–10), Baruch portrays the past as a history of idolatry (1:21), of heinous crimes (2:2–3), and of willful deafness to God's word (1:18–21, 2:5). Consequently, God is merely being faithful to past promises in bringing the current calamities upon them (1:20).

Today, argues Baruch, the people remain intransigent. Despite the fulfillment of the promise of punishment (2:7, 9), they have not refrained from sin (2:8, 10), nor entreated God for mercy (2:8). Clearly the responsibility to initiate a restored relationship rests with them; and Baruch provides that opportunity in the prayer that follows (2:11–3:8). In the corporate "we" of the people he speaks to God directly for the

first time, not as judge but in the formula of divine mercy. God, who rescued us from Egypt "with a mighty hand and with signs and wonders" (2:11), may perhaps do so again. Motivated by memories of God's compassion, the people confess that they are sinners (2:12, 2:24, 3:2) and beg for a cessation of divine anger (2:13–17, 3:4), not for their sake, but for God's own sake (2:14–15, 18).

Though Baruch's prayer proclaims that God is not responsible for their troubles (2:20–26), there is still hope that God may show them kindness (2:27). Even at the time of Moses, God foresaw their sin and its consequences (2:30). In language that echoes Jeremiah (32:38–40) and Ezekiel (36:26–28), God promises that their captivity will benefit them. There "they will come to themselves, and they will know that I am the Lord their God" (2:30–31). They will come again to their land to praise their God (3:32–35).

The wisdom poem that follows is sharply different from the prose. Nonetheless, it also addresses the problem of foreign domination (3:10), and it, too, blames the people for forsaking their tradition (3:10) and for failing to walk in the way of God (3:13). However, even as it acknowledges the people's sin, this poem does not dwell on it but urges them to seek a solution to their difficulties. Pursue Wisdom, learn Wisdom, for with her is precisely what captives need: strength, understanding, "length of days and life," "light for the eyes," and peace (3:14; cf. 1:12).

Wisdom, however, is inaccessible. She cannot be found by human effort. Search though they might, great peoples of the world have not succeeded in gaining her (3:15–23). There is a long history of failed searches that felled even the fabled giants of old (3:24–28). Finally the text announces, "No one knows the way to her," but the one "who knows all things knows her" (3:31–32). The creator of the universe, "our God," gave her to Israel, and "she appeared upon earth" to live among humans (3:35–37). Like Sirach, the author of this poem makes Wisdom's location unmistakable. She can be found only in Israel: "She is the book of the commandments of God" (4:1). By embracing her, by keeping the law, Israel will live. Therefore, they should not turn toward "alien peoples," for Israel alone knows what is pleasing to God (4:1–4).

Baruch's final poem of comfort and restoration (4:5–5:9) brings the book to a pitch of expectation and hopefulness for the imminent release of the captives and their return to Jerusalem. The poetic figure of personified Jerusalem dominates the poem. It is her voice that exhorts her children to "take courage" (4:5, 21, 27) and interprets their captivity for them (4:5–29). A grieving mother scolding her children, she tells them their exile is their own fault: "You forgot the everlasting God" (4:8). Then she addresses her neighbors, describing her own sorrow, desolation, and shame caused by her children's delinquency (4:9–16). She, too, believes that the suffering of Israel is just punishment for its infidelity.

Now, however, the captors are not to be prayed for. They are a "shameless nation" with no respect for the old nor pity for the child (4:15). Because Jerusalem is powerless to help her children, she dons her mourning garb and cries out to the Everlasting (4:20). Then, with a great change of heart, as if time had passed and circumstances changed, she urges her children to cry to God because "he will deliver you" (4:21). For the first time, joy enters the poem and the book because of the wonderful reversal of circumstances about to occur. Soon, she reports, you will see the enemies' destruction and "tread upon their necks" (4:25).

In the second part of this poem (4:30–5:9), the speaker addresses Jerusalem. Jerusalem is to take courage, for the enemy will exchange places with her, and the captor will be grieved at its own desolation (4:31–36). Expectancy increases as the speaker urges Jerusalem to look east for her returning children. "Joy is coming to you from your God" (4:36–37). The joyous mother is to exchange her sackcloth for the splendid attire of God's exalted (5:1–4) and then to rush to the heights to await her children whom God is leading home (5:5–9).

This beautiful poem reverses the gloom and desolation not only of Jerusalem but of the Book of Baruch. It assures the captives that their relationship with God, albeit harmed, is not irrevocably severed, and it promises them a future of unmerited and unexpected joy. Though derivative in form and content, the Book of Baruch is nonetheless a treasure of Jewish faith.

Baruch is extant only in Greek translation; most of it, however, is translated from a Hebrew or Aramaic original. Though it is excluded from the Hebrew and Protestant canons, Roman Catholic and Greek Orthodox canons include Baruch, perhaps because of early Christian interest in 3:36–37, thought to refer to the incarnation of Christ.

The Letter of Jeremiah

The Letter of Jeremiah is a comical satire of pagan gods and of the worship offered them by their devotees. Its purpose is to convince the Jewish community that it is Yahweh alone whom they must serve (v. 6). Rather than arguing for the exclusive worship of Yahweh, however, the letter achieves its goals by belittling pagan gods and everything associated with their cult.

Fashioned after Jeremiah's letter to the Babylonian exiles (Jer 29), this pseudepigraphic work claims to be the second letter of Jeremiah to the same community (vv. 1–4). Were it by Jeremiah, however, it would require a date in the early sixth century B.C.E. Instead, a reference to a captivity lasting seven generations (v. 3), an expansion of the seventy years Jeremiah prophesied (Jer 29:10), suggests a date closer to 300 B.C.E., the time of the Hellenists' rule. Foreign cults with their richly decorated idols and comparatively lush liturgies were a perennial temptation to the Jews, whose only lawful images of God were verbal. This attraction to foreign deities was particularly strong during the early Hellenist era.

The Vulgate attaches the letter to the Book of Baruch; other ancient sources place it as a separate book. Though there are superficial resemblances between the letter and Baruch, such as supposed exilic settings and connections with the Jeremianic traditions, the letter is a distinct work with its own title (v. 1), introduction (vv. 1–7), literary form, and theological argument. It is likely that it was originally written in Hebrew and later translated into rather poor Greek. In fact, the letter is actually not a letter but a homily, a lengthy embellishment of Jeremiah 10:2–15. In addition to its origins in the Jeremianic traditions, it also borrows language and arguments from a long biblical tradition of polemics against the false gods (Isa 40:19–20, 41:7, 44:9–20; Ps 115:4–8).

Many scholars speak disparagingly of the Letter

of Jeremiah, describing it as florid in style, lacking in order, organization, and literary merit (Moore 1977). However, although it is repetitive and does skip from idea to idea without apparent order, these features may be deliberate satirical tactics of the homilist-author. Furthermore, the letter's argument is cumulative rather than linear. Each paragraph contributes evidence against the gods that is summarized by a refrain or its variation, "Therefore they are evidently not gods; so do not fear them" (v. 16). Repeated nine more times (vv. 23, 29, 30, 40, 44, 52, 56, 65, 69) this refrain is an integrating thread, holding together the diffuse comments of the author and separating the paragraphs from one another. Like a collection of photographs that randomly capture the details and events of cultic worship, the paragraphs accumulate "proof" that the whole enterprise of worshiping false gods is ridiculous. Each paragraph focuses on details of the worship that evoke awe and "fear," and then exposes the chicanery of the priests or the foolishness of their practices. For instance, the worshipers make gold crowns for the gods (v. 9), but secretly the priests steal the gold to use it for themselves, even for such unworthy pleasures as the services of harlots (vv. 10–11). In this case, the glamour of the gold crowns cloaks a sordid reality.

In other instances, the details of the worship merely conceal the emptiness of their beliefs. For example, the worshipers dress their gods in royal clothing, but then they have to wipe off the dust from the divine faces (vv. 12–13). The priests lock the temples to keep out robbers, but in the process they also imprison the gods (v. 18). Though the gods are made of wood and precious metals (vv. 4, 8, 24, 50, 57), and though they hold scepters and daggers (vv. 14–15), they are powerless to protect themselves from robbery, plunder, or war (vv. 56–59).

At the heart of the letter is the claim that the whole system of pagan worship is a huge deception. Its gods are absurd and effete creations of human beings. Though priests rant and rave in liturgical frenzies before their gods (vv. 31–32), the deities can do none of the things expected of divine beings. They cannot depose or establish a king, nor require the fulfillment of a vow, nor dispense wealth, nor save from death, nor give sight to the blind, nor rescue the widow and orphan (vv. 34–38). Indirectly, therefore, the letter reminds its readers of the one God who can do these things.

In the course of its argument the letter deliberately insults the foreign gods by making banal observations and unflattering comparisons: "Just as one's dish is useless when it is broken, so are the gods" (v. 17). "Bats, swallows, and birds light on their bodies and heads; and so do cats" (v. 22). "By the purple and linen that rot upon them you will know that they are not gods" (v. 72). Even the ordinary objects of daily living have more value than these gods. It is better to be "a household utensil that serves its owner's need, than to be these false gods; better even the door of a house that protects its contents, than these false gods" (v. 59). These lowly objects at least are useful to humans.

Observations of this sort need not be made in a systematic way. They are more outrageous as casual observations, as the comments made by piercing common sense, and they produce their desired effects —laughter and scorn. The Letter of Jeremiah does not oppose pagan worship on moral grounds. The issue is not sin but sense. The false gods do nothing helpful for humans. Though the wealth and pomp of their cult may be attractive to people whose God is not imaged in artifact, the glory and beauty of that worship is a sham. From the viewpoint of the Letter of Jeremiah, to worship them is to demean oneself. Not only are the pagan gods not to be feared, they are to be laughed at and their followers pitied. Better therefore the just who have no idols, for they will be far from reproach (v. 73).

The Prayer of Manasseh

The Prayer of Manasseh is a penitential psalm of fifteen verses. It expresses a sinner's remorse and desperate yearning for forgiveness and restored relationship. The freshness with which it reveals the human experience of desolation, mediated by faith in a compassionate God, makes it a classic of liturgical literature.

The precise origins of the prayer are unclear. Whether its original language was Greek, Hebrew, or Aramaic is disputed, and even the date is difficult to know with certainty. Parallels with other Jewish apocrypha suggest a date in the last two centuries B.C.E., despite the absence of manuscripts remaining from that time. However, some interpreters place it in the first or second century C.E. The earliest version of the prayer appeared in the *Didascalia*, a Syrian Christian work of the third century that was later incorporated into the *Apostolic Constitutions*. The fifth-century Codex Alexandrinus attaches the Prayer of Manasseh to the Psalter, but the prayer does not appear in any ancient manuscripts of the Septuagint.

Manasseh, whose name was pseudonymously ascribed to the work, is the Deuteronomistic prototype of the great sinner. According to 2 Kings 21:1–18, he was Judah's most wicked king, more sinful even than the Amorites, who inhabited the land before Israel (2 Kgs 21:11). His crimes included idolatrous worship, the erection of an idol in the Temple, the burning of his child as a sacrifice, consultations with sorcerers, the seduction of the people to commit great evil, and the shedding of innocent blood "till he had filled Jerusalem from one end to another" (2 Kgs 21:16). In the view of the Deuteronomistic historian, Jerusalem fell, in part, because of the sins of this unrepentant king (2 Kgs 21:13).

The Chronicler provides a somewhat different account of the life of Manasseh. In 2 Chronicles 33:1–20, the wicked king commits the same sins as those related in Kings, but after the Assyrians take him captive to Babylon, he repents of his sins and prays for forgiveness. By including this unsubstantiated account of captivity and repentance, the Chronicler transforms Manasseh from a prototype of wickedness into a model recipient of God's forgiving mercy. Though Chronicles does not record the king's prayer, it refers the reader to two other sources, no longer extant, where that prayer could be found. The Prayer of Manasseh purports to be this missing prayer.

Constructed in the form of a psalm of individual lament, the prayer contains four main divisions: direct address to God in praise of divine power and mercy (vv. 1–8); cry of distress and confession of sin (vv. 9–12); request for forgiveness (vv. 13–14); promise of praise (v. 15).

The purpose of the first division of the prayer (vv. 1–8) is to make God receptive to the speaker's petition for forgiveness and to assure the reader that God is both powerful and merciful. The opening verse sets up a tension that develops throughout the following verses. It addresses God, who is both distant and nearby. The One who is "Lord Almighty" is, at the same time, closely related to Israel's ancestors and their righteous offspring (v. 1). Employing creation motifs, verses 2–5 expand the theme of God's transcendent power. Whereas creation themes usually show God's benevolence, here they illustrate God's awful might. The divine word of the creator "shackles the sea" (v. 3), and before the divine name "all things shudder" (v. 4). The effect of this splendor upon humans is unbearable and upon the sinner, unendurable (v. 5).

However, the divine promise of "immeasurable and unsearchable" mercy (v. 6) contrasts with and counterbalances God's formidable power. The One who is the "Most High" is equally the One who reaches toward sinners (vv. 7–8), who is compassionate and long-suffering and who regrets human evils (v. 7a). Because divine mercy is overflowing and multitudinous, God's distance from humans does not form a barrier to divine compassion for sinners. The speaker reminds God of God's promise of repentance and forgiveness (v. 7) and then shrewdly claims that this general promise applies to him (v. 8). What is extraordinary in his claim is that this "grace," as Charlesworth translates it (1985), is not for the righteous ancestors, who have no need of it, but specifically for the sinner, for Manasseh. How, then, can the almighty and merciful God refuse the petition for forgiveness to which the psalm is building? It is in God's own character, revealed in the promises of Israel's history, to intervene most particularly to save sinners. Even as heinous a sinner as Manasseh can dare to come forward and hope for forgiveness.

In its first-person description of the speaker's predicament and confession of sin (vv. 9–12), the prayer becomes most moving and eloquent. Just as the children of Abraham and Sarah were to grow as numerous as the sands of the sea, so Manasseh's sins are beyond counting (v. 9). Vaguely summarized as the "setting up of abominations and multiplying offenses," the speaker's sins weigh him down and isolate him from the community (v. 10). In the depths of guilt and self-loathing, he expresses the most humble prostration of his spirit, "I bend the knee of my heart, beseeching thee for kindness" (v. 11). Like David in another penitential psalm (Ps 51:3), he knows his transgressions; he acknowledges his guilt (v. 12).

In the dramatic climax of the poem he petitions God to rescue him (vv. 13–14): "Forgive me, O Lord, forgive me." In three clauses he begs God not to choose alternative ways to deal with him: "Do not destroy me"; "do not be angry with me and lay up evil for me; do not condemn me to the depths of the earth." The reason God should forgive instead of punish is God's own character, "for thou art the God of those who repent." It is God's nature to forgive, and the psalmist provides God with an opportunity to exercise that nature: "In me thou will manifest thy mercy." The prayer closes in the typical lament form, with the speaker promising to praise God "all the days of my life." God's forgiveness of the sinner would restore him to the community of Israel's praise and join him to the praises of "all the host of heaven" (v. 15).

The Prayer of Manasseh expresses faith in the midst of guilt, alienation, and self-hatred: faith that God is always ready to bring home the sinner, to restore relationship, to create life anew. All that is required is for the sinner to accept responsibility and "bend the knee of the heart." Because the sins of the psalmist are described generally as "setting up abominations and multiplying offenses," they extend beyond the specific sins of Manasseh to cover a wide range of transgressions. This prayer probably functioned during periods of idolatry to restore apostates to the community. It was preserved because it captures a common experience of believers.

Bibliography

Charles, R. H. *The Apocrypha and Pseudepigrapha of the Old Testament,* vol. 1. Oxford, 1913. Pp. 569–595, 596–611, 612–624. This old classic still contains fresh insights to all three works.

Charlesworth, J. H. "The Prayer of Manasseh," in *The Old Testament Pseudepigrapha,* vol. 2. Garden City, N.Y., 1985. Pp. 602–624. This essay contains the most complete survey of scholarship to date. It even includes two translations, one literal and the other idiomatic. See also the "Introduction for the General Reader," pp. xxi–xxxiv, for a thorough scholarly introduction to pseudepigrapha in general.

Dancy, J. C. *The Shorter Books of the Apocrypha.* Cambridge Bible Commentary. Cambridge, 1972. Pp. 169–196, 197–209, 242–248. Contains brief but thorough introduction, translation, and critical notes.

Fitzgerald, Aloysius. "Baruch." In *The Jerome Biblical Commentary,* edited by Raymond E. Brown, Joseph A. Fitzmyer, and Ronald E. Murphy. Englewood Cliffs, N.J., 1968. Pp. 614–619. This commentary pays close attention to the various versions of Baruch and explains details not considered elsewhere. It also includes the Letter of Jeremiah in the discussion, following the Vulgate's linking of the two.

McNamara, Martin. *Intertestamental Literature.* Wilmington, Del., 1983. Despite a very brief discussion of the Prayer of Manasseh, the contribution of this work is to place the prayer with other prayers and hymns of the same period.

Metzger, Bruce. *Introduction to the Apocrypha.* New York, 1957. Pp. 89–94, 95–98, 123–128. In addition to providing an appealing discussion of the books and their critical problems, this study also addresses their subsequent use by the believing community.

Moore, Carey A. *Daniel, Esther, and Jeremiah: The Additions.* Anchor Bible, vol. 44. Garden City, N.Y., 1977. Contains translations, text-critical notes, balanced comment, and extensive bibliography for Baruch and the Letter of Jeremiah.

Rost, Leonhard. *Judaism Outside the Hebrew Canon: An Introduction to the Documents.* Translated by David E. Green. Nashville, Tenn., 1976. Provides good bibliography and helpful discussions of text, contents, and historical problems.

KATHLEEN M. O'CONNOR

I and II Maccabees

THE MACCABEAN REVOLT, named for the famous leader Judas Maccabeus, is described by two authors in the books entitled 1 Maccabees and 2 Maccabees. The authors differ in their language, their style, the part of the revolt they choose to cover, and their attitude toward the dynasty that was spawned by the revolt. We have no information as to who the authors were, or when or where they wrote, other than what we can deduce from the books themselves. It is therefore very important to gain insight into the literary goals and purposes of each separate work. First Maccabees is favorably inclined toward the Hasmonean dynasty in Israel, which sprang up as a result of the Maccabean revolt. The Hasmoneans ruled as high priests and kings from 142 to 63 B.C.E. and then, with the advent of the Romans, were gradually replaced by the Idumean Antipater and his son Herod. Second Maccabees is more critical of the family of Judas Maccabeus. Second-century Judaism was by no means monolithic.

Revolutions fracture societies, and the process by which the pieces are rearranged to form new societal patterns is often long and difficult. In order to better understand the mid-second-century revolt of the province of Judaea against its Seleucid overlords in Syria, it is necessary to consider its broader context.

The beginning of the second century B.C.E. saw shifts of power throughout the Mediterranean world. After the conquests of Alexander the Great, the area around the eastern Mediterranean experienced three major powers—the Macedonian empire, the Ptolemaic empire based in Egypt, and the Seleucid empire, which originally had extended from Asia Minor to Afghanistan. At the beginning of the second century a new player entered the field. However hesitatingly and clumsily, Rome was rapidly emerging as the dominant force in the eastern Mediterranean. Rome's victories first over Philip V of Macedonia at Cynoscephalae in Greece in 197, then over his son Perseus at Pydna in Macedonia in 168, and the defeat of the Greek leagues by 146 left Rome in complete control of Macedonia and Greece. Antiochus III had been rebuilding the Seleucid empire in Asia Minor and extending his control eastward, but he too was defeated by Rome at Magnesia in Asia Minor in 188. The subsequent treaty of Apamea took away many of his possessions in Asia Minor. When Antiochus IV tried to extend his influence into Egypt, the Roman envoy C. Popillius Laenas told him of the Senate's order that he leave Egypt, drew a circle around him in the sand, and demanded that he decide before he stepped out of the circle. Antiochus withdrew. Lurking in the background of any discussion of power shifts in the eastern Mediterranean during the second century lies Rome. The weaker party in any political dispute could appeal to Rome, and representatives of Rome were constantly traveling to the east to investigate conflicts and advise the Senate on solutions.

Closer to the foreground of the revolt in Judaea lay the dispute between the Ptolemaic and Seleucid empires over southern Syria. The Seleucids had claimed sovereignty over the area since Antigonus Monopthalmos was defeated at Ipsus in Asia Minor in 301 B.C.E., but the Ptolemies had ruled it. It was not until 198 that Antiochus III subdued all of southern Syria, including Palestine for the Seleucids. With the death of Antiochus IV (in 164) the Seleucid empire was rent by rival claimants to the throne, and the Ptolemaic kings encouraged and supported various claimants in an effort to keep the Seleucid empire weak. This bickering between the two declining empires took place while Rome was to a certain extent out of the picture—engaged first in the war with the Greek leagues, then in the last war with Carthage, and finally in the upheaval of the social reforms of the Gracchi in Rome itself. The dissensions between empires helped the rising power of Parthia in the east and also separatist movements such as that in Judaea. It is noteworthy that Judaea could not stand against the Seleucids under the strong leadership of Antiochus VII Sidetes (159–129), but his capture and death by the Parthians in 129 assured Judaea its independence. As centuries earlier the Davidic kingdom gained independence because Egypt did not interfere and Assyria was weak, so too the Maccabees succeeded when the Ptolemaic and Seleucid empires were on the wane, and when Roman might was not yet fully extended.

I Maccabees

Style

First Maccabees is written in a straightforward narrative style, interspersed with some poetic passages as, for example, at 1:36–40, 3:3–9, and 14:4–15. The use of a simple succession of clauses connected by "and" heightens the sense of an objective narrative of events—for example, "and he made war on Ptolemy king of Egypt, and Ptolemy turned and fled before him, and many fell wounded, and they captured the walled cities in the land of Egypt, and he plundered the land of Egypt, and Antiochus turned back after subduing Egypt" (1:18–20). The style is highly reminiscent of the historical books of the Bible, and, although 1 Maccabees is extant only in Greek, most scholars hold that it was composed in Hebrew. That the author chose as his stylistic model the historical books of the Bible is a significant clue as to his intentions in writing the work.

The author has used the biblical narratives as a model in more than style. The opening act of rebellion by Mattathias, the venerable ancestor of the Hasmoneans, is explicitly modeled on that of Phinehas in Numbers 25:6–13. As Mattathias refuses to offer sacrifice in transgression of the Law,

> a Jew went up in the sight of all to offer sacrifice on the altar in Modin in accordance with the king's command. Mattathias saw him and was filled with zeal, his heart trembled, and he rightly roused his anger; he ran up and slaughtered him on the altar. At the same time he killed the king's officer who was trying to compel them to sacrifice, and he broke down the altar. He showed his zeal for the Torah, just as Phinehas did to Zemri, the son of Salom. Then Mattathias cried out in a loud voice in the town and said, "Let everyone who is zealous for the Torah and upholds the covenant follow after me." (1 Macc 2:23–27)

When one compares this passage with the story of Phinehas in Numbers 25:6–13, the correspondence is clear:

> And behold, one of the people of Israel came and brought a Midianite woman to his family, in the sight of Moses and in the sight of the whole congregation of the people of Israel, while they were weeping at the door of the tent of meeting. When Phinehas the son of Eleazar, son of Aaron the priest, saw it, he rose and left the congregation, and took a spear in his hand and went after the man of Israel into the inner room, and pierced both of them, the man of Israel and the woman, through her body. Thus the plague was stayed from the people of Israel. Nevertheless those that died by the plague were twenty-four thousand. And the Lord said to Moses, "Phinehas the son of Eleazar, son of Aaron the priest, has turned back my wrath from the people of Israel, in that he was jealous with my jealousy among them, so that I did not consume the people of Israel in my jealousy. Therefore say, 'Behold, I give to him my covenant of peace; and it shall be to him, and to his descendants after him, the covenant of a perpetual priesthood, because he was jealous for his God, and made atonement for the people of Israel.'" (RSV)

As Phinehas killed an apostate Jew and his seducing foreign woman, so Mattathias in zeal kills the Jew and the one leading him to apostasy. The language also recalls other biblical passages. Mattathias breaks down the altar as commanded at Exodus 34:13 and Deuteronomy 7:5, and as carried out by Josiah, who also established the words of the Law (2 Kgs 23:20, 24). The thrust of the comparison with Phinehas is clear —just as Phinehas, the Hasmoneans' forefather (1 Macc 2:54), by his zeal gained for his descendants the priesthood, so did Mattathias.

This use of the biblical narrative appears also in the way the Hasmoneans are depicted through descriptions used of the Judges of ancient Israel. Jonathan is said to begin "to judge the people," a clear echo of the Book of Judges (1 Macc 9:73; *cf.* Judg 10:1–3, 12:7–13). The narrative of Jonathan's election to succeed Judas (1 Macc 9:28–31) shows resemblances to the election of Jephthah (Judg 10:18, 11:6–11). As a time-marker in his narrative the author has also used the cyclic structural principle found repeatedly in Judges: the Israelites did what was wrong in the eyes of the Lord, he became angry and punished them; they cried to the Lord for help; he raised up a man or woman to deliver them; and the land was at peace while that person lived (see Judg 2:16–18, 3:7–11). So also in 1 Maccabees. When a set of renegades tries to lead Israel astray (1 Macc 1:11) and tribulation follows, Mattathias and his sons begin to bring deliverance. In this time of "disaster and fierce anger" (1 Macc 2:49), Mattathias commissions his sons Judas and Simon (2:49–70) just as Moses invested Joshua (Deut 31:7, 23; Josh 1:6–9) and David did Solomon (1 Chr 22:13, 28:20). Judas, by his zeal against the wicked, turns away God's anger (1 Macc 3:8) and becomes the savior of Israel (9:21) under whom the land of Judah is at peace, if only for a time (7:50). The enemies press again, and Judas falls. Then a terrible oppression begins in Israel such as had not been seen since the disappearance of prophecy (9:27), and Jonathan is chosen as was Jephthah, and during his time the sword no longer hangs over Israel. Jonathan settles in Michmash, where he begins to judge the people and to rid Israel of the godless (9:73). When oppression reappears, Jonathan is captured treacherously. A large army of the surrounding nations is ready to invade, and the people are afraid, but Simon steps forward and soon the country is at peace again (14:4).

Finally, in this discussion of style mention must be made of the characterization of the enemies of the Hasmoneans. They are the lawless men (2:44; 3:5–6; 7:5; 9:23, 58, 69), the workers of lawlessness (1:23) as well as sinners (2:44, 48, 62) and impious men (3:8, 6:21; 7:5, 9; 9:73). Perhaps more significant, however, is their description as "base fellows" (*huioi paranomoi* 1:11, 10:61, 11:21).

> In those days base fellows went out from Israel and led many astray saying, "Let us go and make a covenant with the nations round about us, because since we separated ourselves from them many evils have overtaken us."

The phrasing of this first depiction of those against whom the Hasmoneans fought echoes Deuteronomy 13:12–15, which describes "certain base fellows" who say, "Let us go and serve other gods." The civil war against the Benjaminites began because "base fellows" attacked the concubine of a Levite (Judg 19:22). The split between Judah and Israel is said to have occurred because Jeroboam, king of Israel, was surrounded by "base fellows" (2 Chr 13:7). The phrase thus has many resonances, and the author of 1 Maccabees plays on these echoes.

Throughout 1 Maccabees, therefore, the author uses biblical imagery to characterize his heroes and villains. His heroes have been raised up by God to defend the people just as the judges before them; his villains are destroyers of the social fabric like others before them. Through his use of such biblical overtones, the author portrays the Hasmoneans as upholding the ancestral faith and skillfully sets up a dichotomy between the Hasmoneans and all others.

The Narrative

First Maccabees covers events from the actions by these "base fellows" sometime after the accession of the Seleucid king Antiochus IV Epiphanes in 175 B.C.E. until the death of Simon, the last of the sons of Mattathias, in 134.

Prologue (1:1–10). The history is introduced by a prologue, which provides a setting for events both historically and thematically. Of these ten verses, seven are devoted to Alexander the Great, two verses to his successors and their dynasties, and one to Antiochus IV Epiphanes. In the midst of the narrative of Alexander's victories comes the editorial comment that "he was exalted and his heart was lifted up"

(1:3). His domination reached its climax when provinces, nations, and rulers paid tribute to him (1:4). The motifs of arrogance and the payment of tribute will recur throughout the narrative. Perhaps the notice of the death of Alexander at the height of his power after a reign of only twelve years also hints at what will happen to Alexander's successor in arrogance, Antiochus IV.

Apostasy and Punishment (1:11–64). The detailed narrative opens with an account of apostasy (1:11–15). The apostates are portrayed negatively through biblical allusions (as already noted with the phrase "base fellows" in 1:11). The central theme of being like the nations is also associated in biblical narrative, with wrongdoing (1 Sam 8:4–8; Exod 34:15; Deut 7:2–4), particularly at 2 Kings 17:7–18, a long reflection on the downfall of Samaria. There it is stressed how Israel "had feared other gods and walked in the customs of the nations," and "they went after false idols and became false, and they followed the nations that were round about them" (2 Kgs 17:7–8, 15). First Maccabees 1:14 further states that the apostates built a gymnasium, a statement again colored by the negative phrase "according to the customs of the gentiles." Biblical imagery also abounds in 1:15. The opponents are said to distance themselves from the holy covenant. The verb used is found frequently with this sense of apostasy (Deut 13:10, 13; 32:15; Josh 22:18, 19, 23, 29). The image of yoking themselves to the nations echoes the phrase of Numbers 25:3 and Psalm 106:28 when Israel yoked itself to Baal of Peor. Similarly, biblical narratives say that the Israelites "sold themselves to do evil" (2 Kgs 17:17) as also did the exceedingly wicked King Ahab (1 Kgs 21:20, 25). At 1:15, the author states that the apostates "made for themselves foreskins," in this way rejecting God's covenant as expressed, for example, at Genesis 17:14. Through his description the author has created a new metaphor that mocks both Greek pride in uncircumcision and the aping of Greek ways in general.

This image-packed description of the originators of Israel's woes contains only one hard piece of information—they sought to build a gymnasium. It does not mention the infighting and bickering among these leaders, which is detailed in 2 Maccabees. Some commentators have suggested that this may be a case

of *damnatio memoriae*, a deliberate omission of the very names of the apostate leaders. It may be, however, that the author's main interest is the story of the Hasmoneans, and so he provides just enough description to show that his heroes were fighting disrupters of Jewish society. He is not so much concerned with detailing the exact economic, political, and social causes of the revolt as with writing an encomium.

The apostasy brings punishment in its wake. As Antiochus becomes powerful, he enters Jerusalem in arrogance and robs the Temple, and the people mourn (1:16–28). Then he sends another officer, who plunders the city again and builds a citadel in Jerusalem, and the people lament (1:29–40). Finally, Antiochus outlaws Jewish worship, defiles and pollutes the Temple, and has those who follow the Law persecuted (1:41–64). In 1:41–42, the author uses hyperbole in claiming an imperial decree to have all the king's subjects abandon their own laws and religion and so emphasizes the separation between loyal Jews and all others. Loyal Jews maintain their ancestral customs against attempts to set up a monolithic entity, "one people." The exaggeration here is reminiscent of that found in Daniel 3 and Judith 3:8, where Nebuchadrezzar is accused of setting up a worship for all peoples. In all these texts the distinction between Jews and non-Jews is being stressed.

Although many are said to have followed Antiochus' decrees, many others determined to die rather than break the Torah. The description of the condition of Israel is summed up, however, in dark terms: "Indeed, very great wrath was upon Israel" (1:64). The anger of God against the apostasy of the people waxed strong.

The Saving of Israel (2:1–70). In response to the persecution of Antiochus arise Mattathias and his five sons. The lament of Mattathias over the state of Israel continues the earlier laments of the people. Between the narrative of the Phinehas-like zeal of Mattathias (2:15–28) and the account of the first successes of the revolt (2:42–48), in which the Torah obedience of Mattathias and his followers is stressed (*cf.* Exod 34:13, Deut 7:5, Gen 17:10–14, Josh 5:2–4), there appears the story of the slaughter of innocent Jews who were "seeking after righteousness" and who refused to defend themselves on the Sabbath (2:29–41). The death of these Torah observers poses a major problem to Mattathias and his followers, who are also zealous for the Torah. Does observance of the Sabbath entail no self-defense on the Sabbath? The slaughtered innocents in 2:29–38 answered affirmatively— the covenant lawsuit language of 2:37 implies their confidence that God will defend them. The result was complete annihilation, and even their cattle were destroyed. In the face of such obliteration, Mattathias and his friends deliberate whether they should defend themselves on the Sabbath and they decide they must.

Commentators have stressed the contrast between the way these Sabbath observers act and the way Mattathias and his followers behave. One should, however, also note how the author has emphasized the bond and sympathy between the two groups. Mattathias and his friends grieve over the deaths of Sabbath observers (2:39), just as Mattathias and his sons grieved over what had happened to Jerusalem (2:14). The incidents at Modin and in the wilderness both emphasize the unrelenting persecution. Mattathias left Jerusalem to live at Modin outside the territory of Judaea; the "seekers after righteousness" left for the wilderness, but neither could escape the demands of the king. The action of Mattathias and his followers is thus a purely defensive reaction to offenses against them. Even the decision to fight on the Sabbath is couched in defensive terms, as a last attempt to preserve the nation. The campaign of Mattathias and his followers is limited by the borders of Israel (2:46); they are not engaged in an offensive war against the king but only seek to follow their ancestral laws and customs.

The final scene in the life of Mattathias is the obligatory death scene in which Mattathias exhorts his sons. Noteworthy in the list of ancestors is Phinehas, whom Mattathias calls "our father." Singled out among the sons are Simon and Judas. Simon is to be a surrogate father, taking the place of Mattathias. Judas is to be the military leader. This division of roles anticipates the portrayals of Judas and Simon in the rest of the narrative. The eldest son, John, is mentioned by name only at his death (2:2, 9:35–38); the heroic death of Eleazar is narrated at 6:43–47. The omission in the testament of Mattathias of any mention of Jonathan, who preceded Simon as ruler and high priest, is surprising, but will perhaps be less so when we have looked at the whole narrative.

The continued campaign under Judas (3:1–9:27). The career of Judas opens with a hymn of praise telling how his mighty deeds turn away the anger of God against Israel (3:8). His early rebellious actions reflected the size of his forces. They were small-scale operations in the countryside but enough of a nuisance to cause Apollonius, a Syrian official, to lead a detachment of troops from Samaria. Judas' force, however, defeated them (3:10–12). Seron, a Syrian general, came with a larger force, but Judas successfully ambushed them at Beth-Horon (3:13–26). The next force sent against Judas was more formidable, but again Judas outmaneuvered the enemy by attacking their camp. This trick caused confusion and the flight of the enemy (3:27–4:25). By this point Judas was said to have a force of 3,000 men (4:6). By the following campaign against Lysias, a Seleucid commander, Judas had 10,000 men (4:29). While figures like these are not always reliable, it is clear that success had brought success. What had started as an uprising of malcontents had grown rapidly with each victory. Judas was now ready to move from the countryside to the city of Jerusalem. Once there, he had the Temple purified and the sacrificial cult was resumed on the twenty-fifth of the month of Kislev (4:36–61). The profanation of Antiochus had been removed, and the irony is heightened since the king's birthday was celebrated on the same date. Judas, however, was not able to do away with the citadel of Syrian troops Antiochus had placed in Jerusalem.

Judas now had effective control over Judaea. The author of 1 Maccabees next shows how the neighboring cities reacted to Judas' seizure of control. He describes reactions at Jamnia to the west along the coastal plain, in Galilee to the north, in Idumea to the south, and in Gilead to the east. In many of these areas, Judas is depicted as coming to the aid of fellow Jews who were being harassed—presumably this refers to Jews sympathetic to the Hasmoneans. Judas and his brother Simon are always shown as victorious, in striking contrast to other leaders in the movement, such as Joseph son of Zechariah and Azariah, who are defeated (5:55–62). The author states, "They did not belong to the family to whom it had been granted to save Israel" (5:62). The pro-Hasmonean stance of 1 Maccabees is thus made explicit.

The ethnocentric bias of the author appears in

his account of the grief-stricken death of Antiochus Epiphanes. According to the Greek historian Polybius, some authors said that the cause of Antiochus' death was his robbery of the temple at Elymais, but the author of 1 Maccabees places it squarely on his plunder of the Jerusalem Temple (6:5–13).

Antiochus' death, whether caused by divine retribution or not, had serious consequences for the rebellion. At the urging of Jews hostile to the Hasmoneans, a proper Seleucid army invaded Judaea. For all the bravery the author attributes to Judas' forces, it is clear that they were no match for the full force of the Seleucid army. The king's forces made short work of the fortified Beth-Zur, and Jerusalem also had to capitulate. The author shifts the blame for this to the shortage of food resulting from the observance of the sabbatical year (6:48–54), but one suspects that proper provisions would only have prolonged the siege, not changed the outcome. Only an external cause kept the revolt from being completely crushed —Lysias had to beat off a rival general, Philip, for control of the Seleucid kingdom. From this time on, the infighting for control of the Seleucid empire would have important consequences for the outcome of the Hasmonean revolt. At the time of Lysias' return to Antioch in early 162, however, other movements were afoot that threatened the Hasmoneans. Judas does not seem to have been in Jerusalem during the siege; if he had been, the author would probably have mentioned it. Antiochus V made an agreement not only with the besieged city but with the whole nation: "Let us allow them to follow their own laws as formerly. Because we abolished these laws, they were enraged and did all this" (6:59). The author of 1 Maccabees hastens to point out that one should not trust any such agreement; for him, the Seleucids were deceitful oppressors. Lysias and Antiochus V broke faith (6:62); later, a group of Jews called Hasideans died because of their trust (7:10–17), and Nicanor, another Seleucid commander, also deceitfully tried to trick Judas with peaceful words (7:27–30). From the author's standpoint, the Jews had to be always on guard against the Seleucids. The fact remains, however, that the persecution begun by Antiochus IV had ended; the Jews could now follow their own laws.

What was to happen to Judas and his followers in this changed situation? Would all those who had joined in the fight against the abrogation of Judaism, as, for example, the various groups mentioned at 2:42–43, remain united with Judas? Not all remained by his side, and the author of 1 Maccabees is at pains to show that they were duped by the Seleucids. Judas continued his guerrilla campaign, but he was forced to the border country (7:24); he made the countryside unsafe, but could not attempt to enter Jerusalem. The very mention of the high priest Alcimus by name suggests that an attempt to normalize the situation took place under him, but failed because of Judas' intransigence. Judas and his followers won a great victory over Nicanor, who is portrayed as consistently hostile to Judas, but they still could not enter Jerusalem (7:39–50). At this point in the narrative, the author shows Judas seeking outside help. In an attempt to offset the might of the Seleucids, Judas is said to have turned to the Romans. The idealized portrait of the Romans shows that the author clearly prefers an alliance of friendship with them to the state of subordination to the Seleucids, which is epitomized by the need to pay tribute (8:1–32).

The defeat of Nicanor only brought back the Seleucid commander Bacchides with a larger army from the Seleucids. Judas could not count on large numbers now. Greatly outnumbered, he fought bravely but died. What had Judas achieved? He had purified the Temple and restored worship there, and the original cause of the revolt, the outlawing of the Jewish religion, had been removed. However, his forming an alliance with Rome and his refusal to lay down arms after the revocation of the persecution indicated that he finally wanted not just the freedom from persecution, but independence.

Judas was lamented just as Saul was lamented (2 Sam 1:19–27), and one notes how the author insists that *all Israel* observed deep mourning for him, again emphasizing the importance of Judas. Of particular interest is 1 Maccabees 9:22: "The rest of the history of Judas, his wars, his heroic exploits and his greatness, they are not written down for they were very numerous." Almost unanimously commentators have seen in this verse an imitation of a formula found in the Books of Kings. For example, at the death of Solomon it was written: "Now the rest of the acts of Solomon, and all that he did, and his wisdom, are they not written in the book of the acts of Solomon?"

(1 Kgs 11:41). There is, however, a significant difference between the formula in 1 Maccabees and that in
the Books of Kings: the acts of the various kings *are*
written down, but Judas' exploits are so numerous that
they can *not* be written down. Such an expression of
the inability to enumerate all the deeds was traditional in encomiums of heroes; it appeared, for instance,
in Plato's encomium of the men of Athens:

> These men I recall to your memory, and you it becomes
> to join in praising and celebrating men such as these.
> And now we have related many of the noble deeds done
> by the men who are lying here, and by all the others who
> have died in defence of their city; yet far more numerous
> and more noble are those that remain unmentioned, for
> many days and nights would not suffice were one to relate
> them all in full. (*Menexenus* 246A)

Lucian in his encomium on Demonax stated that he
was only writing a little out of much, as did Eunapius
in his life of Iamblichus. The two endings of the
Gospel of John (20:30–31, 21:25) stress how Jesus did
much more than is written in the Gospel, and the
phrase became a commonplace in hagiography. The
author of 1 Maccabees at 9:22 is thus not referring to
ancient records as is the case in the Books of Kings.
Rather, he is glorifying his hero and his exploits,
emphasizing the importance of this guerrilla chieftain
in the struggle against religious persecution by the
Seleucids.

Jonathan (9:28–12:53). The treatment of Jonathan in 1 Maccabees is intriguing. Unlike Judas and
later Simon, Jonathan receives no poem to laud or
lament him. Much of the narrative about Jonathan
deals with his foreign policy, and contains quotes
from many documents of correspondence between the
Jews and the Seleucid kings and pretenders to the
Seleucid throne as well as to the Spartans. As one
scholar has noted, there was a tendency in later
Jewish literature to quote documents (Momigliano
1975). Scholars have raised questions about the
authenticity of these letters, as well as those between
Judas and the Romans at 1 Maccabees 8:20–32.
Trying to decide whether a document is wholly or
partly genuine is a very tricky matter. Do the texts use
the correct style for chancery documents, do they
have the proper greetings and wishes? Do they contain
any glaring historical mistakes that show them to be

anachronistic? These are some of the questions one
has to ask. Further, one might well ask what archival
procedures were available to Judas and to Jonathan in
his early years. If none of these stylistic and external
criteria are decisive in affirming or denying the genu-
ineness of the documents, one may then ask how
connected the documents are to the narrative. For
example, the fact that the letter of Demetrius I
(Seleucid king from 162 to 150) at 1 Maccabees
10:25–45 is addressed to the Jewish nation and no
mention is made of Jonathan—although the letter is
found in a section extolling Jonathan and both
Jonathan and the people are said to have heard the
terms of the letter (1 Macc 10:46)—argues for the
authenticity of the document. It is not completely at
home in its narrative context whereas, for example,
the correspondence between the Egyptian king Ptolemy and Alexander Balas (who defeated Demetrius I
and ruled during 150–145) at 10:52–56 is.

Whatever one's final decision as to the authenticity of these letters, one must still ask how the
author has used them in his narrative. In 1 Maccabees, three themes are repeated in the handling of the
documents:

1. The author emphasizes the untrustworthiness
of most of the Seleucids and Ptolemies. The offers of
Demetrius I are described as purely pragmatic, designed to win away Jonathan from his adversary
(10:3–5, 22–25). In contrast, the author describes
how Alexander Balas, with whom Jonathan finally
allied himself, admired Jonathan: "Can we ever find
another such man? Let us straightway make him our
friend and ally" (10:16). Alexander, of all the
Seleucids, was faithful to Jonathan (10:62–65, 88–
89) but was betrayed by his treacherous father-in-law,
Ptolemy of Egypt (11:1–3). The author describes
Ptolemy as acting deceitfully (11:1), lying in order to
blame Alexander, and coveting Alexander's kingdom
(11:11). Ptolemy's letter at 11:9–10 reverses that at
10:55–56. Demetrius II, who succeeded Alexander
Balas, in turn "lied in all that he had said" and did not
reciprocate the favors Jonathan had done for him
(11:53) even though he is said to have promised to do
so in two documents (11:32–37, 42–43). Trypho (a
usurper to the Seleucid throne of Antiochus VI) also
wrote treacherously to Simon at 13:15–16. The
documents thus provide us with first hand evi-

dence for the treachery of the Seleucids and Ptolemies.

2. Many of these documents serve as evidence that the Hasmoneans were legally appointed high priests. By letter, Alexander appointed Jonathan to this post (10:18–20) and Antiochus confirmed him in it (11:57).

3. The lessening of tribute and the control of the citadel in Jerusalem are two common subjects in the documents. They are found in the first, second, and third letters of Demetrius I (10:29–32; 11:34–36, 41–42), and the acquisition by Judaea of three districts (Apherema, Lydda, and Ramathaim) is also mentioned. Alexander the Great's reign had been characterized by the taking of tribute and later Antiochus IV had installed a garrison in the Jerusalem citadel. These concerns in the letters point toward the final removal from the Jewish nation of the tribute and the foreign troops in Jerusalem.

Finally, the correspondence between Jonathan and the Romans and Spartans evidences a different aspect of Hasmonean foreign policy. Jonathan Goldstein may be right in his suggestion that the treaty of friendship with the Spartans was initiated because the Spartans could intercede for the Jews with the Romans (Goldstein 1976, 448). In the context of the narrative, moreover, the Roman alliances of friendship and equality stand in stark contrast to the Seleucid and Ptolemaic policies of subjugation and treachery. The Hasmoneans are not portrayed as hostile to all foreigners, only to those who would impose on them. In fact, kinship is claimed with the Spartans, a fiction that was often part of a quest for an alliance, but which nevertheless signified a desire for a very close relationship (12:5–23).

The documents also attest to the prominence that Jonathan had attained, a prominence hardly to be dreamed of at the death of Judas. Although the author tries to put a brave face on it, Jonathan and his hard-core band were at that time being hounded out of the country. Most of the people had settled down under the high priest Alcimus and the governor Bacchides. The author reports that "the country went over to their side" (9:24) although he hints that it was through economic necessity, a suggestion that may be partly true since the country desired normalcy. Supporters of Jonathan were punished, and Jonathan himself was driven out of the normal base of operations of the Hasmoneans in southern Samaria into the wild country of southern Judaea. To Bacchides, he was no more than a criminal. The only bright spot the author can claim for this period of Jonathan's life was a successful ambush of a wedding party (9:37–42)! Otherwise Jonathan has to retreat before Bacchides, who also instituted a policy of placing troops throughout the country to deal effectively with any last support for Jonathan. The strength of the Hasmoneans had been in the countryside, and Bacchides' garrisons plus the taking of hostages from the families of the principal men of the country effectively squelched opposition.

Relief came from an unexpected quarter—Alcimus died. The author portrays his death as divine retribution for making alterations to the sanctuary (9:54–57). For the Hasmoneans, it was a heaven-sent opportunity. Bacchides returned to the king, possibly to consult on the successor to Alcimus in the high priesthood, but he also seems to have thought that the country was now pacified and could be left in the hands of local leaders. That proved wrong. During Bacchides' absence Jonathan and his forces seem to have regrouped, and when Bacchides returned he saw that he had seriously underestimated Jonathan's strength. Bacchides could not both besiege Jonathan's fortified retreat at Bethbasi and control the countryside (9:62–69), so that at last the two adversaries came to terms. One would love to know what the full terms were. Judging by Jonathan's behavior in the next few years, one suspects that Jonathan agreed not to cause any trouble. The years between Bacchides' leaving Judaea a second time in 157 and the attempt of Alexander to win power in 152 are crucial to the Hasmonean revolt and yet we know nothing of them. The author simply states, in language from the Book of Judges, that Jonathan lived in Michmash, the traditionally strong area of Hasmonean support, that he began to judge the people, and that he destroyed the ungodly of Israel (9:73).

It was during these years that Jonathan consolidated his hold over the people at the expense of other groups in Judaea at the time, groups who had supported Alcimus and been aligned with Bacchides. By 152 Jonathan had so strengthened his forces that his previous enemy King Demetrius I was forced to concede that Jonathan was the strongest power in Judaea and tried to win him to his side. His concessions, however, only further strengthened Jonathan's position, so that Jonathan now lived in Jerusalem (since 152), won the hearts of the leaders of the countryside by having their hostage sons released, and fortified Mount Zion. With the removal of Bacchides' troops from the garrison towns, Jonathan ruled both Jerusalem and the countryside. His strength was such that he could now indulge in foreign affairs. When captured by Trypho in 143, Jonathan is said to have had at least 40,000 men under his command. To be able to send off 3,000 men at a moment's notice (11:44) implies that he had a standing army. His official appointment as high priest and the appointment of his brother Simon as commander from the Ladder of Tyre to the Egyptian frontier (11:58) must have allowed him to set up a complete administrative bureaucracy to run Judaea. The author concentrates on the external policies and battles of Jonathan, but during the nine years that Jonathan was in charge, his supporters must have been placed in important positions and the Hasmonean power base consolidated. The letter to the Spartans was sent by "Jonathan and the council of the nation and the priests and the rest of the Jewish people" (12:6). Jonathan also consulted with the elders of the people about his plans to build fortresses in Judaea and to strengthen the walls of Jerusalem (12:35–37). We do not know the composition of the groups—"the council" and "the priests"—but Jonathan had clearly built a working relationship with them. Some elders accompanied him on his visit to Demetrius to answer charges brought against him (11:23).

This last reference alerts us to the fact that there was opposition to the Hasmoneans. Even this laudatory narrative cannot quite conceal that reality. As noted above, Jonathan was not able to gain control of the citadel, the Akra. The garrison in Jerusalem must have had contacts and supporters in the surrounding community to keep them supplied with provisions. It was only when Simon, Jonathan's successor, was able to institute a full blockade of the citadel that he could control it (13:49–50). When Jonathan besieged the Akra in early 145, fully seven years after his appointment as high priest, opponents of the Hasmoneans objected to the king and Jonathan won the case only

by bribery (11:20–26). It was only in that same year that Simon could capture the important city of Beth-Zur, where opponents had taken refuge.

The attitude of the priests toward the Hasmoneans is difficult to assess. Some recognized Jonathan's authority as they accompanied him when he answered charges brought against him (11:23). However, commentators have noted the offhand way in which the author reports Jonathan's investiture as high priest: "So Jonathan put on the sacred vestments in the seventh month of the year 160 [152] on the festival of Tabernacles, and he mustered troops and manufactured many arms" (10:21). The reader is almost left to wonder which is the more important, the investiture or the provisioning and mustering of an army. Whether Jonathan's efficacious prayer at 11:71 can be considered a high-priestly act is doubtful, and apart from that incident Jonathan is not shown participating in any specifically religious event. The lack of emphasis on Jonathan as high priest may be due to the fact that he was a Seleucid appointee. It may also be that the author was aware of opposition to Jonathan's being high priest. Several scholars have suggested that the "Wicked Priest" mentioned in the Qumran documents refers to Jonathan. Although such specificity is difficult to maintain in view of the extremely indirect quality of the allusion in the Qumran documents and their highly symbolic character, these texts at least alert us to priestly circles of opposition to the Hasmoneans.

Despite this opposition, it was Jonathan who firmly secured the Hasmoneans in power. He not only controlled Judaea but had expanded his territorial base to include the districts of Aphairema, Lydda, Ramathaim (11:34) as well as Akkaron (10:89), and perhaps Akrabattene. He had achieved all this through skillfully exploiting the dynastic rivalries of the Seleucids, but in the end he fell victim to those same rivalries in Trypho's bid to assume the crown (12:39, 46–48).

Simon (13:1–16:24). Throughout Jonathan's rule Simon had been his right-hand man. He it was who helped resist Bacchides at a crucial time (9:67–68); he besieged Beth-Zur and settled his own supporters there (11:65–66); he secured Joppa (12:33–34) and fortified Adida (12:38). He was the logical successor to Jonathan. His swift grasp of power forestalled attempts by neighboring cities to invade Judaea, possibly in revenge for Jonathan's attacks on cities such as Joppa and Azotus (10:74–84). There is some murkiness over Simon's rise, however, as can be seen from the elaborate way the author shields Simon from any blame attaching to Jonathan's execution (13:17–19). One wonders if the two sons sent as hostages were Jonathan's only sons. The author passes over their fate, but it is more than likely that they too were executed. Certainly their being sent to Trypho removed any center of dissent against Simon's assuming power.

Simon immediately showed himself to be an efficient commander. He first hastily built the fortifications around Jerusalem. Tagging along abreast of Trypho's forces (13:20), Simon made it difficult for Trypho to attempt to use the main roads leading up to Jerusalem. After Trypho's retreat, Simon fortified the strongholds of Judaea (13:33). Earlier, Simon had secured Joppa, expelled some of the residents, and put his own forces in possession of the town (13:11). Joppa was important strategically and it provided a port for landlocked Judaea (14:5). One notes here how Simon follows a pattern of replacing residents of a town with people loyal to him. He would do this also at Gazara (13:43–48) and the Akra in Jerusalem (13:49–53). He himself with loyal forces lived in the Akra and his son John in Gazara (13:53). Simon thus continued Jonathan's policy of expanding his territorial base and consolidating power so that, when he died, the dynasty continued in his son.

Not again that it was without opposition. The author takes care to note the important inscription set up in honor of Simon (14:25–45). It was written on bronze tablets and set up on pillars on Mount Zion. Yet that inscription perhaps reveals more than the author intended. The accuracy of this report has been questioned, although most scholars agree that some text was set up on Mount Zion. The author would hardly have stated that such a record existed in Jerusalem in plain sight if he could easily be contradicted. Again, the account of events in the document at times is at odds with the sequence found in the surrounding narrative. For example, in the narrative, Demetrius II's letter to Simon preceded the embassy to Rome, but in the document it followed. The great assembly of priests and people and leaders of the

nation and elders of the country took place in the third year of Simon, the high priest. There is thus a gap of some three years between Simon's acclamation by the people, mentioned at 13:7–8, 42 and echoed at 14:35, and the recognition at the assembly by the temple priests and other leaders. In between, Demetrius II had confirmed Simon in the position (13:36–40, 14:38), and Simon had gained possession of the Akra. It was only after this consolidation of power that the temple priests and lay leaders also consented to Simon's power. The decree thus reflects the last stage, when all segments of society, the populace, priests, and other leaders, assembled and formally recorded the provisions of Simon's power. Simon too had won his way from small beginnings to high honors against opposition from the ruling classes. A hint of the compromise reached by Simon and the hierocracy may be seen in the qualifying phrase in 14:41—Simon should be their leader and high priest "until a true prophet should arise." Simon's hold on power was not unconditional or unchecked.

It is also said at 14:41 that Simon would be their leader "for ever"—whether this assured dynastic succession for Simon's heirs or applied only to Simon's life is uncertain. What is certain is that Simon was given quite wide-ranging powers. Simon was to be distinguished from all other Jews by his dress—he alone could wear purple and gold (14:43–44)—which symbolized the unique position he now occupied. Perhaps the explicit granting to Simon of complete authority in the Temple and power to appoint deputies in charge of the countryside, the armaments, and the fortifications suggests that hitherto Simon's authority in these areas had not been fully recognized. Now Simon by his power of appointment could place his own supporters in important positions. The power to control public gatherings was also an important political instrument, as was the fact that all contracts had to be drawn up in Simon's name. One economic implication of this last provision is presumably that all contracts not so drawn up were invalid. But, perhaps more significantly, the provision was a means whereby Simon pervaded all spheres of life. He had become, in short, a Hellenistic tyrant.

The legal decree that spelled out in brutal clarity Simon's power—"Whoever acts against these provisions or annuls any of them shall be liable to punishment" (14:45)—stands in sharp contrast in the narrative to the earlier hymn to Simon at 14:4–15:

⁴The land had peace as long as Simon lived.
He sought the good of his people.
They welcomed his rule
　　and his glory as long as he lived.

. . . .

⁷He eliminated the unclean things from the Akra
　　and there was none to oppose him.
⁸The people farmed their land in peace
　　and the land gave forth its produce
　　and the trees of the fields their fruit.
⁹The old people sat in the town squares,
　　all chatting about their blessings,
　　while the young men put on the glorious raiment
　　　　of war.
¹⁰Simon supplied the towns with food
　　and equipped them with weapons for defence,
　　so that his glorious renown reached the end
　　　　of the earth.
¹¹He established peace in the land
　　and Israel rejoiced exceedingly.
¹²Everyone sat under his own vine and fig trees
　　with none to make him afraid.
¹³No longer was there anyone on earth waging
　　war against them.
　　The kings had been defeated in those days.
¹⁴Simon supported all the poor of his people.
He sought to fulfill the Torah
　　and wiped out all the impious and wicked
¹⁵He glorified the temple
　　and added to its furnishings.

(Anchor Bible)

The reign of Simon is described in almost messianic terms and abounds in allusions to Hebrew scriptures. Verse 8 echoes Ezekiel 34:27 ("And the trees of the field shall yield their fruit, and the earth shall yield its increase, and they shall be secure in their land," RSV) and Zechariah 8:12 ("For there shall be a sowing of peace; the vine shall yield its fruit, and the ground its increase, and the heavens shall give their dew." Verse 9 alludes to Zechariah 8:4 ("Old men and women shall again sit in the streets of Jerusalem, each with staff in hand for very age"), and verse 12 to Micah 4:4 ("But they shall sit every man under his vine and under his fig-tree, and none shall make them afraid"). The emphasis on Simon's concern for the poor, on his providing food for the people, on his

faithfulness to the Torah, which recalls that of the good king Josiah, places Simon in a perspective different from that of the decree on bronze tablets. No power plays are evident here as the positive benefits of Simon's rule are highlighted. He had brought peace.

In many ways this hymn to Simon would have been a fitting end to the story of 1 Maccabees. The praise of Simon in this hymn echoes the praise of Judas in the hymn at 1 Maccabees 3:3–9. The connection between the two brothers is further stressed in the narrative similarities found between Judas' cleansing of the Temple and Simon's capture of the Akra. Just as Judas cleansed the Temple and removed the stones of defilement (4:41–43), so Simon cleansed the Akra from its defilements (13:50). Both celebrated with songs and music (4:52–54, 13:51), and it was decreed that every year the event should be celebrated (4:59, 13:52). By the capture of the citadel, the wrongdoing of Antiochus IV was revoked. He had polluted the Temple, outlawed Jewish worship, and built a citadel in Jerusalem (1:29–40). The first two had been righted by Judas (4:41–59, 6:59), the last by Simon. The testamentary hymn of Mattathias (2:49–68) presaged the preeminence of these two as Mattathias mentioned only Judas and Simon by name.

Why then does the narrative continue beyond 14:15, which would have been a fitting dramatic climax to the war of liberation? Important information is found in the text after 14:15, including the decree honoring and empowering Simon, the results of the embassy to Rome (15:15–24), and the continued friendship with the Spartans (14:16–23). The continuing narrative also shows how the relationship with the Seleucids remained constant in its inconstancy. Antiochus VII Sidetes first promised great things to Simon (15:2–9), but then reneged on his commitments (15:27–31). Simon and his sons fought a battle reminiscent of earlier Maccabean campaigns and routed one of Antiochus' generals. The last scene narrated describes the attempt of Ptolemy the son of Abubus, Simon's son-in-law, to gain the rule, his treacherous murder of Simon, and the hazardous rise to power of John Hyrcanus, son of Simon.

In one sense, then, the narrative ends with the dynastic transfer of power from father to son. Of the five sons of Mattathias, it was Simon who founded the Hasmonean dynasty. The last words of 1 Maccabees speak of John Hyrcanus, "from the time he became high priest after his father." In some ways, that note is a fitting end to the story, but as a narrative, many loose ends are left. How will Antiochus Sidetes react to the defeat of his general? Will he let the matter rest, or will he invade with a larger force? What will happen to the treacherous son-in-law? Will he remain as a thorn throughout the reign of John Hyrcanus?

The abruptness of the ending becomes even more evident when we realize from Josephus (*Antiquities* 13:236–248) that Antiochus VII Sidetes invaded Judaea in the first year of John Hyrcanus' reign (135/134). He devastated Judaea and besieged Jerusalem. Hyrcanus had to sue for a peace in which the Jews had to surrender their arms, pay tribute for Joppa and other towns, give hostages, and pay an indemnity of 500 talents. The walls of Jerusalem were also demolished. Only after the death of Antiochus Sidetes in a campaign against Parthia in 129 was Hyrcanus able to exert his own power. Once again, the independence of Judaea depended on Seleucid weakness.

As for Ptolemy Abubus, we know from the narrative that he was rich and married into the high priest's family. He did not agree with Simon's desire for independence from Antiochus VII Sidetes and he wished to do away with the Hasmoneans' policy of expanding control to territory outside Judaea. Perhaps one can infer that he wished Judaea once again to be a client state of the Seleucids. The expression "his heart was lifted up" (1 Macc 16:12) takes the reader back to the beginning of the narrative, where Alexander the Great is so described (1:3). Ptolemy's desire to accommodate the wishes of Antiochus VII reminds the reader that the start of the troubles was the attempt of some lawless men to make a treaty with the nations round about and to introduce non-Jewish practices (1:11–15).

The ending at 16:23–24 suggests that John had a successful reign, so Ptolemy's rebellion did not last long. But the very formulaic quality of the ending raises only more questions. In contrast to the encomiastic description of Judas, John is described like all the rulers, both good and bad, mentioned in the books of Kings. Whereas Judas and Jonathan were mourned by the people (9:20, 12:52, 13:26), nothing is said of any mourning for Simon. Simon in fact died an ignominious death—he was assassinated while drunk. His death was like that of Elah, son of Baasha, narrated at 1 Kings 16:9–10, and like that of so many other rulers. Why does the author mention this fact? Josephus passes it over, stating simply that Simon died while at a banquet (*Antiquities* 13.228). Why does not the author of 1 Maccabees similarly gloss over the details? Perhaps the author is hinting that the Hasmoneans had become like any other kingdom, and that the idealized picture of the hymn at 1 Maccabees 14:4–15 has been replaced by a more pragmatic one. Certainly the sweeping powers of Simon as outlined in the decree of 14:27–45 and the indications of great wealth that had accrued to Simon and his family (14:24, 32; 15:32; 16:11–12) all point to the growing institutionalization of the Hasmonean reign. Judaea had a new master, but at least he was Jewish.

The Author

When the author of 1 Maccabees wrote is still debated. The friendly attitude toward the Romans would seem to preclude a date of composition after 63 B.C.E., when the Romans under Pompey the Great invaded Jerusalem; the concluding reference to a chronicle of the acts of John Hyrcanus would suggest that his rule is over or nearly so. The author probably finished his work late in the reign of John Hyrcanus I (135/134–104) or early in the reign of Alexander Jannaeus (103–76).

The fact that the work was originally written in Hebrew and that its style is modeled on the classics of the Hebrew scriptures leads one to infer that the author was steeped in his tradition. His enthusiasm for the war of liberation reinforces the sense that he is a nationalist. He clearly supported the Hasmoneans—they were the family chosen to save Israel (5:62)—as the encomium for Judas and Simon in the narrative through 14:15 shows. He may have felt that there were problems with Hasmonean rule, but it was better than subjugation to foreigners.

II Maccabees

The Second Book of Maccabees as now found is a composite work—two letters are prefixed to an epitome of a five-volume history by an otherwise unknown Jason of Cyrene.

The First Letter (1:1–9)

The first letter is a festal letter addressed by the Jews of Judaea to the Jews in Egypt in 124 B.C.E. After a long prayer for the well-being of the addressees (1:2–5), the senders then refer to a previous letter of the year 143 before inviting the Egyptian Jews to celebrate the days of Tabernacles in the month of Kislev.

This short document raises several questions. Are the prayers (in the Greek optative tense) to be viewed as general wishes for well-being, or are they to be construed as aimed at a particular problem, namely, the rival Jewish temple built by the high priest Onias IV at Leontopolis in Egypt? Are they seeking to win back Egyptian Jewry to Jerusalem while chiding them? This interpretation assumes that all Egyptian Jews, including those in Alexandria, were followers of Onias IV and his remote temple and military colony. Such an assumption, even given the military prominence that Jewish successors of Onias IV attained under Cleopatra II and III (Josephus, *Antiquities* 13.348–355), seems unwarranted in our present ignorance about Egyptian Jewry in the second century B.C.E.

Major difficulties also occur concerning the body of the letter. It is unusual for the main part of a letter, about the same length as the introductory prayers for well-being, to be simply a citation of a previous letter with no surrounding comment. Was this a subtle hint that the Temple in Jerusalem was protected by God and that the Oniad temple should be abandoned, or has the letter been abridged in some way? Why are Jason and his followers singled out, but no reference made to Antiochus IV, either his desecration of the Temple or his persecution, or to Judas? The body of the letter is cryptic in its brevity.

That the letters date from 143 and 124 seems best explained by political events in Egypt. Ptolemy VIII Euergetes came to power in Egypt through peace negotiations with Cleopatra II in spring 144 and, after a revolt by Cleopatra, which began in 132, reclaimed power in 124. It has been suggested that the loss of power by Cleopatra, who had been backed by Jewish generals and successors of Onias IV, may have provid-

ed the opportunity for the letters, but one is still puzzled by a twenty-year hiatus between festal letters, which should be annual.

The first letter, therefore, is an intriguing document but a difficult one to interpret.

The Second Letter (1:10–2:18)

The second letter also bristles with difficulties. It bears no date, but having Judas as one of the senders would date it, if authentic, to 164. It is unlikely that it is authentic.

The contents of the letter are fascinating. First is given an account of Antiochus IV's death, which differs from that in 2 Maccabees 9 as well as from the other versions of the king's death (1 Macc 6:5–13; Polybius 31:9; Appian, *Syriaca* 66). What one can say is that behind all these tellings of the king's death lies the belief that Temple robbery brings punishment. The account in 2 Maccabees 1:13–17 has the thief die at the very spot he wished to despoil, a very satisfactory moral.

After the transitional verse 18, a verse difficult to interpret because of its elliptical Greek, begins a series of narratives grouped around the theme of fire. First comes a story of the fire at the time of Nehemiah (1:19–36). In 1:18b, Nehemiah is described as the builder of the Temple and the altar, that is, he is identified with Zerubbabel as in the Babylonian Talmud (Sanhedrin 38b). The narrative stresses the continuity between the First Temple and the Second: the sacred fire of the First was hidden at the time of exile but then recovered in liquid form at the renewal of sacrifices in Jerusalem. Nehemiah is portrayed as the discoverer and inventor of naphtha, that fiery liquid known to Hellenistic scientists and geographers as pertaining to Babylonia (Eratosthenes as quoted by Strabo, *Geography* 16.1.15; Dioscorides 1.73). This emphasis on fire continues in the following narrative, and thus the festival in Kislev is interpreted as a festival of fire, as in Josephus (*Antiquities* 12.325), but nowhere else in 1 or 2 Maccabees.

The second story specifies that it was the prophet Jeremiah who ordered the fire from the First Temple to be hidden (2:1). In other ways, however, this narrative argues against the continuity of the First and Second Temples, for sacred vessels of the First are to remain hidden until God will ingather his people. At this final time, the glory of the Lord and the cloud will be seen again as in the time of Moses and Solomon. This reference leads back to the theme of fire and how both Moses and Solomon brought down fire from heaven (2:10). The proof-text for Moses' action is given at 2:11.

All these stories are said to be in the official records of Nehemiah, and alongside his activity of collecting the books of Judaism is placed Judas' similar activity. Thus the reader has been led from the mention of Judas in the address of the letter to Nehemiah to Jeremiah to Moses and Solomon and then back to Nehemiah and Judas. Placing all these traditions side by side enhances the traditional character of the festival in Kislev, which is conceived as a festival of fire. It would have been important to stress how this newly introduced festival was in accord with previous tradition.

Second Maccabees 2:16 picks up the request of 1:18 to celebrate the purification of the Temple. This second letter ends with the hope that God will gather his people together, a motif already mentioned at 2:7. In this letter, then, the purification of the Temple is seen as an important event, but not the climactic end of history.

The Epitome of Jason's History (2:19–15:39)

The bulk of 2 Maccabees is an epitome of a five-volume history of the period by an otherwise unknown Jason of Cyrene. The author of the epitome is also unknown but is explicit in his aim: to make Jason's work more accessible and easier reading by reducing it in size. Before going further, one must emphasize that, as we do not possess even fragments of Jason's composition, we have no idea how faithful or careful the epitomist was in relation to the original work. We do not know what he has left out, whether he has retained the same outline and emphases, or whether he ended where Jason ended. Given this fact, one must be aware that one can only speak of the epitomist's concerns, not Jason's.

Style. At several points it is clear that the narrative is condensed, as, for example, in the pile-up of verbs at 13:23–26 describing Antiochus V's retreat to Antioch; or the description of Judas' return to ordinary life at 14:25, where three verbs are placed side by side. One might also note how certain characters are mentioned in the narrative without any introduction. For example, 8:30–33 not only interrupts the narrative of Nicanor's defeat but also mentions a Timotheus, Bacchides, and Callisthenes as though the reader should be aware of who they are.

Most of the narrative, however, shows an author at home in the stylistic conventions of Hellenistic Greek literature. He loves to play with words, as, for example, at 4:26, describing "Jason, who had supplanted his brother's office, was now supplanted in his turn." He also employs a wide range of unusual or infrequent words, normally found among the poets, as well as words not attested elsewhere in Greek. It is a style intended to stir the emotions, as can be seen in the story of Heliodorus when the author describes the pain of the Jews as Heliodorus attempts to enter the Temple:

> The high priest's looks pierced every beholder to the heart, for his face and its changing color betrayed the anguish of his soul. Alarm and shuddering gripped him, and the pain he felt was clearly apparent to the onlookers. The people rushed pell-mell from their houses to join together in supplication because of the dishonor which threatened the holy place. Women in sackcloth, their breasts bare, filled the streets; unmarried girls who were kept in seclusion ran to the gates or walls of their houses, while others leaned out from the windows; all with outstretched hands made solemn entreaty to heaven. It was pitiful to see the crowd all lying prostrate in utter confusion, and the high priest in an agony of apprehension. (3:16–21; NEB)

Here the author has pulled out all the stops to gain the sympathy of his audience. The same is true of his spending so much time over the martyrdoms of particular figures: Eleazar, Rhazis, and the story of the mother and her seven sons who are tortured and die rather than renounce their faith (2 Macc 7). Such a story by its very nature engages the audience. The epitomist has also placed it in a strategic position, at the height of the persecution just before the Lord's anger turned to mercy (8:5), as the last and youngest of the sons to die predicted (7:33). Thus the story functions as a turning point, depicting the final outrage that brings about a change in Israel's condition. Such a story is found elsewhere not only in Jewish literature (e.g., the *Assumption of Moses* 9), but also in Polybius' description of the end of the tyrant Philip V of Macedonia. He too persecutes a mother and her children, and after their death comes his downfall (Polybius 23.10–17).

This incident points to another aspect of the epitomist's style—his awareness of Greek historiography. The prologue itself (2:19–32) is full of conventional phrases from Greek historiography: that the history should be both for pleasure and profit (2:25); that the epitomist has undertaken this labor for the benefit of others willingly (2:26–27); and even the image of the architect and the painter is used to describe, respectively, the work of the original author and that of the epitomist (2:29). Noteworthy also are the descriptions of the divine helpers of the Maccabean forces: they are drawn from Greek literature. The golden accoutrements of the men who appear in 2 Maccabees 3:25 and 11:8 are typical in Greek epiphanies, as are the prodigies recounted in 2 Maccabees 5:2–4; the supernatural protectors of Judas at 2 Maccabees 10:29–31 recall the miraculous defenders of Delphi against the Persians as told by Herodotus (8.36–39) and against the Gauls in Pausanias (10.23.1–6). Finally, the author makes use of digressions in which he explicitly comments on the events narrated, as at 5:17–20 or more especially at 6:12–17, where the first person singular is present. Such digressions are common in Greek historiography.

Stylistically, then, the epitomist has much in common with contemporary Greek historiographers. He follows their style, not that of the Hebrew scriptures.

Structure of the narrative. The narrative of 2 Maccabees spans the period from some time during the reign of Seleucus IV (187–175) to the defeat of Nicanor in 161. It stops before the death of Judas, and gives much more attention to the events leading to the Maccabean revolt than does 1 Maccabees. The author, in fact, has structured his narrative in three acts, all concerned with a threat to the Jerusalem Temple and its miraculous deliverance: 3:1–40, 4:1–10:9, 10:10–15:37. The story in 3:1–40 exhibits a pattern found in many narratives in which a deity defends his or her temple from attack. The other two acts of this narrative both end with a decree that a festival be celebrated every year to commemorate the deliverance wrought by God. One should note the almost formulaic similarity of the language recounting the decree passed for the feasts of Purification (10:8) and Nicanor (15:36) as well as those passages that close the three acts (3:40, 10:9, 15:37). Many inscriptions attest the celebrations by cities of the epiphanies of their patron deity, and so here too the author has followed the conventions of contemporary Greek writing.

Political feuds in Jerusalem. The specific form of the threat against the Temple is exceedingly interesting since it reveals the politics of power in a small temple state. At first the reader sees a high Temple official, Simon of Bilgah, quarreling with the high priest Onias III (3:4–6). Onias was later supplanted by his own brother Jason through bribery (4:7–9), while Jason in turn was supplanted by Menelaus, brother of Simon (4:23–26), and another brother of Menelaus, Lysimachus, is Menelaus' right-hand man (4:29). It is clear that Jerusalem was divided into feuding families, and the feud at times erupted into murder (4:3). As with the feuds of the Guelphs and the Ghibellines in medieval times, the original cause of the feud is unknown, but at stake was control of the Temple and the power that control represented.

The issues mentioned in the text are money (3:4–6) and education (4:9), but because of our limited knowledge of this period and because 2 Maccabees is a piece of propaganda against the likes of Simon, Jason, and Menelaus, it is hard to be precise as to what actually took place. The lack of knowledge has not led to a lack of theories, however, and I shall discuss the main approaches here.

The first suggestion is that there were pro-Seleucid and pro-Ptolemaic parties in Jerusalem. Support for this thesis is the mention of a Hyrcanus, son of Tobias, at 2 Maccabees 3:11 having deposits in the Jerusalem Temple. This Hyrcanus is identified with the Hyrcanus, son of Joseph son of Tobias, known from the Tobiad romance recounted by Josephus (*Antiquities* 12:154–236). In this romance, Hyrcanus is portrayed as an opportunistic tax gatherer for the Ptolemies, who settled east of the Jordan after being exiled from Jerusalem by his brothers and who committed suicide rather than be punished by Antiochus IV for warring against Arab tribesmen. From this it is deduced that Hyrcanus was pro-Ptolemaic and anti-Seleucid and, since Onias III allowed him to deposit funds in the Jerusalem Temple, Onias too must be seen as pro-Ptolemaic. A passage from Josephus (*Jewish War* 1.31–35), long notorious for its inaccuracies, has also been used to support the division into pro-Ptolemaic and pro-Seleucid forces, but the passage mainly proves that there were rival groups competing for power in Jerusalem. The use of 2 Maccabees 3:11 to validate a pro-Ptolemaic, pro-Seleucid feud is problematic. Not only does one have to emend the text but also, in a passage where the high priest is pleading for the Seleucid minister not to confiscate Temple funds, one would have him divulging that the funds of a known anti-Seleucid leader were in the Temple. This would not be a good defense. Doubtless different factions may have looked to one or another of the major regional powers for support, just as later the Maccabeans looked to Rome, but such a polarization was more likely the consequence of factional rivalries than the cause. The split was brought about by causes peculiar to the city-state of Jerusalem.

The second characterization of the parties is that of hellenizers versus those faithful to Jewish tradition. This view finds support in such passages as 2 Maccabees 2:21, which describes those who fought manfully for Judaism against barbarians; 4:10, where Jason is said to bring his fellow Jews over to the Greek style of life; 4:13–14, which tells how, under Jason, Hellenism reached a peak and priests no longer valued hereditary dignities but only Hellenistic honors. The epitomist clearly differentiates two ways of life—Judaism and Hellenism. One must not forget, however, that the author of 2 Maccabees is not an unbiased reporter; he is a skilled rhetorician pleading a case against a group whom he considers enemies, and he labels them so. He is the first author we know of to use the term "Judaism" and the first we know of to use the term "Hellenism" in the extended meaning of "Greek culture" rather than its earlier sense of using a pure Greek style or idiom in speaking and writing. He is therefore, as he writes in Greek, setting up an opposition by means of the language of the very culture he says is harmful. Interestingly enough, Rome is not seen as Hellenistic, inasmuch as Judas corresponded with the Romans (11:34–38). Onias III had also accepted the money from Seleucus IV to pay

for the expenses of the sacrificial worship (3:3); there are non-Jews who bear goodwill toward the Jews (12:30–31). Hellenism, for the epitomist, is used to characterize any attempt to change the Jewish ancestral customs as they are perceived by the author.

Such a dichotomy into hellenizers versus Torah-followers has been accepted by scholars and used to supply motives for the actions of certain key persons. The Simon who quarreled with Onias III over finances has been pictured as someone who wanted to introduce Greek trading and business practices and so do away with restrictions such as doing business on the Sabbath. Comparisons have been drawn with Nehemiah 13:15–22, where men trod wine-presses and sold food in Jerusalem on the Sabbath, where Tyrians also sold fish and all kinds of merchandise on the Sabbath, and Nehemiah prohibited it. The text of 2 Maccabees 3:4–6, however, does not suggest any such analogy. Perhaps Onias III was introducing new, more restrictive monopolistic practices of trading in line with the purity requirements of the Temple Scroll found at Qumran. We simply do not know.

Similarly, the plans of Jason for the full-scale hellenization of Jerusalem have also been detected behind the last words of 2 Maccabees 4:9, "to draw up the list of Antiochenes in Jerusalem." Jason is portrayed by some scholars as changing the constitution of Jerusalem into that of a Greek polis and renaming it Antioch, and so giving citizens of this new city the power to abrogate the Mosaic laws in favor of more liberal, "Hellenistic" ways. Citizenship would eventually be restricted, in this view, to those who had passed through the newly founded educational facilities, the *gymnasion* and the *ephebeion* (4:9). This interpretation also hangs on small textual evidence. That the epitomist, who knew how to berate roundly his opponents and to complain loudly at a later name change in Jerusalem (6:2), should have passed over so lightly such a radical constitutional reorganization and name change seems out of character. This interpretation also wrongly assumes that education at a *gymnasion* and *ephebeion* was a prerequisite for citizenship. Such was not the case in the second century B.C.E. What the text tells us is that Jason did build a *gymnasion* and an *ephebeion* but not what its curriculum was, and that some group in Jerusalem was called after Antiochus.

These theories have flourished because so little is known of this period of Jewish history, but one must be cautious of an uncritical acceptance of the viewpoint of the author of 2 Maccabees. What one can say from the text is that there were factions jockeying for power in pre-Hasmonean Jerusalem, and that Jason used the devious stratagem of buying the high priesthood from the Seleucids. Jason knew that his power depended on the favor of Antiochus, and so he flattered him by naming some group, connected with a *gymnasion,* after the king. He wanted to participate thoroughly in games sponsored by Antiochus (4:18–20), and lavishly welcomed the king on his visit to Jerusalem (4:22). Jason is said to have had no scruples about the fact that the entrance fee for participants in the Tyrian games would be used to offer a sacrifice to Heracles, whereas the Jewish delegates were more strict in not wanting to give any appearance of being involved in sacrifice to pagan deities. However, the games were by their very nature religious, and it is hard to see how some scholars can say that participation in the games was "widely viewed as a nonreligious activity" (Goldstein 1983, 233). Second Maccabees reports that the pious Onias III did not hesitate to take asylum in a pagan shrine, using the sanctions of Greek religion to save his life (4:33). Thus one wonders at the precise view Jewish leaders had toward non-Jewish religions at this time.

Although in order to gain power in Jerusalem Jason had sided with Menelaus and Simon, the enemies of his brother Onias, Jason in his turn was supplanted by Menelaus. Menelaus increased the amount to be paid to Antiochus IV, and thus the taxes the people of Judaea had to pay more than doubled over four years. In fact, one of the main charges brought against Menelaus was that he appropriated the Temple gold for himself and that he and his brother Lysimachus were in reality Temple robbers (4:32, 39, 42). Here again surfaces the problem posed by Simon in the first act of 2 Maccabees—to whom does the Temple money belong? Simon had suggested that it belonged to the high priest and could be confiscated (3:6), whereas Onias III spoke only of deposits in the Temple bank (3:10) and thereby excluded from discussion any of the gold plate and vessels Menelaus subsequently appropriated.

This problem was an old one: when the Assyrian king Sennacherib imposed a heavy penalty on King Hezekiah, it is reported that "Hezekiah gave him all the silver that was found in the house of the Lord and in the treasuries of the king's house. At that time Hezekiah stripped the gold from the doors of the Temple of the Lord, and from the doorposts which Hezekiah king of Judah had overlaid and gave it to the king of Assyria" (2 Kgs 18:15–16). This was the good and pious Hezekiah, who was said to put his trust in the Lord (2 Kgs 18:5–7). In the corresponding section of 2 Chronicles this incident is not mentioned, and one finds instead an elaborate description earlier of how Hezekiah had reformed the Temple service (2 Chr 29–31). In the account in 2 Kings, Hezekiah clearly believed that the money could be used in a national emergency and was not completely sacrosanct. Was Menelaus acting in the same way, using the gold plate to pay the heavy taxes on Judaea? The author of 2 Maccabees, as had the author of 2 Chronicles, rejected the idea that the gold of the Temple could be used in this way and portrayed its appropriation in the worst light.

The intervention of Antiochus IV. The fate of Judaea was now to be intertwined with the foreign policy of Antiochus IV. Toward the end of 170, Antiochus saw the chance to gain effective control of Egypt. His first invasion in 170/169 was successful since he used his young nephew Ptolemy VI Philometer as puppet, but his second incursion, in 168, ended in humiliation before a Roman envoy. The condensed narrative of the events leading up to the Maccabean uprising in 2 Maccabees 5 provides the fullest account of this period, but also presents several chronological problems. The date for Antiochus' plunder of Jerusalem is given as 169 by 1 Maccabees 1:20, whereas the wording of 2 Maccabees 5:1, "the second departure against Egypt," would seem to indicate 168. The problem is further complicated by the cryptic pronouncements of Daniel 11:28–31. The main outline of events would seem to be that, after his successful campaign against Egypt in 169, Antiochus ruthlessly put down an attempt by Jason to regain control of Jerusalem. Some scholars have posited a popular uprising against both Jason and Menelaus that Antiochus suppressed, but it is more likely that Antiochus' return forced Jason to flee. Antiochus then plundered the Temple with the help, according to 2 Maccabees, of Menelaus. The precise sequence of events is hard to reconstruct, as the author of 2 Maccabees is concerned only to throw blame on those of whom he disapproves. The king treated Jerusalem as conquered territory, and placed a Phrygian in charge of Jerusalem. In 167 Antiochus sent another punitive expedition against Jerusalem. The reason for the expedition given in 5:23 is Antiochus' hateful disposition toward the Jews, but the reader wonders what could have caused such an attitude. In 1 Maccabees 1:29 the leader of this punitive expedition is called a tax gatherer, and his orders in 2 Maccabees 5:24 are to sell all the women and children as slaves. Was a failure to pay taxes behind this second spoliation of Jerusalem? Had some armed opposition to the new regime imposed in 169 already surfaced and caused disruption? One may surmise so, but the author only narrates that Judas now appeared on the scene as one of a band of ten. No mention is made of Mattathias and his zeal for the Torah.

Some time later Antiochus IV forbade the Jews in Judaea and Samaria to practice their ancestral religion—Sabbath observance and traditional festivals were outlawed, as was circumcision. This persecution of a religion seems to be at variance with normal practice in the Hellenistic world, and numerous attempts have been made to explain it. Tacitus (*Histories* 5.8.2) argued that Antiochus was trying to drag the Jews out of superstition to the more enlightened ways of the Greeks, and many scholars have followed him in seeing Antiochus as trying to unify and stabilize his kingdom through the imposition of a unified religion. There is nothing to support this view. Many other indigenous religions flourished at the time, nor were the Jews forced to venerate Olympian Zeus but rather the Syrian-Phoenician god of heaven, Baal Shamin.

Other scholars, notably E. Bickermann, have suggested that Antiochus was motivated by renegade Jews such as Menelaus who wanted to change Judaism in line with their enlightened notions. Besides the fact that the Temple cult practiced at Jerusalem during this "reform" was not terribly enlightened, one also finds that 2 Maccabees states that it was precisely Menelaus who caused Antiochus IV in 164 to call off the persecution and allow the Jews to follow their customs as previously (2 Macc 11:27–33). Within the

historical context, the edict of persecution may be more understandable. The rebellion by Jason and the second punitive expedition against Jerusalem must be seen in conjunction with the fact that the Romans repulsed Antiochus from Egypt. The disturbances in Jerusalem may have forced Antiochus to take drastic steps to maintain the security of his southern border by resettling Jerusalem with a colony of soldiers loyal to him. These non-Jews set up their own cult practices. Such a hypothesis still does not explain why the former inhabitants of Jerusalem were prohibited from practicing their own religion.

The prohibition must be seen as punishment for rebelliousness, perhaps involving personal spleen, rather than an attempt to introduce an enlightened religion, a purified Judaism. Antiochus seems to have been ready to lift this punishment three years later, when it was clear that this punitive policy had only brought more disturbance. The role of Menelaus in this policy is obscure. Was he a willing collaborator, indeed the instigator of the policy, or was he an unwilling participant, forced to go along with the policy because of his desire to remain in power at any cost but using the first opportunity he had to change the policy? He seems to have had a hand in stopping it, but his role at the beginning is unknown.

The epitomist works skillfully on the reader's emotions as he describes the persecution of individuals—the noble Eleazar and the seven brothers and their mother. Particularly interesting is the way the author uses the latter. He contrasts the supposedly weak woman with the powerful male monarch, the apparent choice of death by mother and sons with their real choice for life in resurrection, and the present victory of the king in their deaths with the future victory of the Jews. The author, through the scriptural theme of the vindication of the righteous, thus depicted the double defeat of the wicked Antiochus.

The beginning of the revolt (8:1–10:9). The concentration on the individual continues in 2 Maccabees 8 and 9. Whereas the author of 1 Maccabees details four battles before the reentry to Jerusalem (1 Macc 3:10–35), the author of 2 Maccabees chooses only one. In describing that one battle, 1 Maccabees speaks of three commanders, Ptolemaeus, Nicanor, and Gorgias (1 Macc 3:38); 2 Maccabees concentrates on Nicanor, which allows the author to indulge in the irony that Nicanor, who had wanted to make the Jews slaves, escaped like a runaway slave (2 Macc 8:10–11, 34–36).

That humiliation is then followed by the narrative of Antiochus' own death. He was struck down still threatening the Jews, but then repented of his crimes against them. The author follows a common narrative practice by having Antiochus pen a letter in the last moments of his life (9:19–27). The letter is not authentic, but the author has used realistic chancery formulas. The letter praises the Jews as good citizens and ends by requesting them to maintain their good will toward him and his son. These are formulas, to be sure, but by placing this fictional text after the description of Antiochus' hateful disposition toward the Jews, the epitomist alerts the reader to one of his important concerns, namely, to portray the Jews as good citizens who did not instigate rebellion.

It is only appropriate that the death of Antiochus, the arch-villain, preceded the purification of the Temple, with the added twist that the purification took place on the same day as the desecration, perhaps the king's birthday. Whether the death did in fact precede the Temple's purification is still disputed, but it makes a good story.

The reign of Antiochus V (10:10–13:26). The events of the reign of Antiochus V Eupator have been arranged by the epitomist in an interesting pattern. Victories by Judas over neighboring Seleucid officials in 10:14–38 and 12 are followed by campaigns of major Seleucid armies in 11 and 13 respectively. It is a pattern determined by the epitomist's misreading of the letters found in 11:16–33. The author has set all these letters after his introduction of the reign of Antiochus V and so placed the campaign of Lysias referred to in the first letter during this monarch's reign. Scholars agree, however, that Lysias' campaign should be dated during the latter part of Antiochus IV's reign, as it is in 1 Maccabees 4:28–35. One must therefore question which King Antiochus is referred to in these letters. The Antiochus of the second letter (2 Macc 11:22–26) refers to the death of his father. The sender therefore is Antiochus V, and the letter seems to be the usual grant of amnesty at the beginning of a reign. The third letter (11:27–33)

speaks of an amnesty on the initiative of Menelaus. Such an amnesty probably preceded that of the second letter. Here therefore the sender would be Antiochus IV. The majority of scholars would thus rearrange the chronology of this correspondence, although sharp scholarly divisions still remain as to the precise dating of each letter. What is interesting is that the epitomist has thought it important to quote fully these documents in his abridged account and so expressly attest by these witnesses, including Rome, that the Jews were to be allowed to follow their own laws. The epitomist's decision that all this correspondence is to be dated to the reign of Antiochus V may stem from his belief that the arch-villain Antiochus IV could not have granted amnesty—it did not fit with his artistic rendering of Antiochus' death.

The reign of Demetrius I (14:1–15:39). The last two chapters dealing with events in the reign of Demetrius incorporate many of the themes found earlier in the book. The high priest Alcimus is the antithesis of the pious Onias III, who truly was a protector of his fellow Jews (2 Macc 4:2). Alcimus, in the view of the epitomist, only feigned such sentiments (14:8–9). Alcimus accused the "Hasideans" under the leadership of Judas of being disturbers of the peace (14:6, 10), whereas the previous narrative had shown that hostilities were always initiated by non-Jews (10:14–15, 12:2). When non-Jews had shown good will to their Jewish neighbors, as at Scythopolis, Judas and his men had thanked them (12:29–31). Alcimus' speech thus betrays him as a traitor to his country, one who by his ambition would bring ruin to Jerusalem, as had Simon of Bilgah's disclosures against Onias III. The peaceful nature of the Jews is shown by Judas' initially harmonious relations with Nicanor (14:22–25). Judas married, settled down, and took part in the communal life. Here Judas is portrayed not as seeking independence for Judaea, but as willing to accept Seleucid authority; Nicanor even appointed Judas to an official position as his deputy (14:26).

The change in the behavior of Nicanor was instigated by Alcimus, and it was a complete change. Nicanor is portrayed as uttering threats against the Temple (14:33) and boldly challenging the authority of God (15:3–5). The threat of Nicanor fell on his own head when the prayer of the priests after the threat (14:35–36) was answered and Nicanor's head was hung from the citadel, as God answered the challenge to his authority (15:28–35). The outcome had already been decided in a dream portent, in which Judas dreamed that he received God's sword of power from the prophet Jeremiah (15:12–16). Within the account of Nicanor's attack, one also finds the story of the martyrdom of Rhazis. In gruesome detail it tells how he poured out his life rather than be captured, and how he prayed, just as had the seven brothers and their mother, that God bring him to life again (14:37–46). The fact that one person named Nicanor is highlighted as the commander in 2 Maccabees 8 and that another person with the same name plays a role in the final epiphanic victory may not be coincidence since the author seeks to play the events leading to this second festival (15:36) against those that lead to the first (10:8).

With this final epiphany (15:27) the epitomist ends his work. He claims that since the defeat of Nicanor, Jerusalem has remained in the possession of the Hebrews (15:37). This statement is hard to reconcile with the fact that just a year later the forces of Demetrius I under Bacchides routed Judas' army, and Judas himself was killed and Alcimus installed as high priest in Jerusalem (1 Macc 9:1–21). The epitomist's unflattering description of Alcimus and his characterization of Alcimus' plans to return to the high priesthood as "mad designs" (14:3–5) would seem to argue against the author's willingness to number Alcimus among those Hebrews. The epitomist's concern, however, seems centered on threats to Jerusalem itself, not on whether the Seleucids were in control or not. He sees the two festivals of this time as representing threats against the Temple that were repulsed. Since there were no more festivals instituted after that of Nicanor, the Temple must not have been threatened. This suggestion as to why the author ended where he did shows how central the epitomist considered the epiphanic deliverance of the Temple. Just as at the end of 1 Maccabees the author gave no hint that John Hyrcanus would soon be defeated but showed how the dynasty continued and so ended his story, so also in 2 Maccabees the author saw no further threat to the Temple and so ended his narrative.

A COMPARISON OF 1 AND 2 MACCABEES

The reader of the two books of Maccabees can readily see how they complement each other and yet offer very different pictures of the Hasmonean revolt. Without 2 Maccabees we would know next to nothing of the prehistory of the revolt; without 1 Maccabees the continuation of the revolt under Judas' brothers would be obscure. Yet the works differ profoundly in style and outlook.

One central problem in both books is chronology. The dates provided in 1 Maccabees present inconsistencies and contradict some of the dates found in 2 Maccabees. The most striking difference is the dating of the death of Antiochus IV. Was it in 164, before the purification of the Temple, as 2 Maccabees 9–10 indicates, or after the purification, in 163, as 1 Maccabees 6:16 dates it? The dispute has not even been settled by the discovery of a cuneiform tablet providing a list of Seleucid kings and their dates. The tablet indicates that Antiochus IV died in the year 148 according to the Babylonian reckoning of the Seleucid era and that news of his death reached Babylon in the ninth month of that year, that is, November/December 164 (and so Antiochus died shortly before that time). Many of the chronological problems and divergences between the two works were thought to have been resolved by the brilliant suggestion of E. Bickermann that two dating systems were at play in 1 Maccabees. Bickermann argued that, in 1 Maccabees, events of Seleucid history were dated according to a Macedonian calendar, which placed the beginning of the Seleucid era in the fall of 312, while events of local Jewish history were dated according to a Babylonian calendar, which placed the beginning of the Seleucid era in the spring of 311. Thus 1 Maccabees 6:16 places the death of Antiochus IV just after the beginning of the year 149 of the Macedonian Seleucid era, which began in October 164, while the Babylonian king list dates his death to 148 of the Babylonian Seleucid era, since year 149 according to this calendar did not begin until the spring of 163. This hypothesis of two calendrical systems operating in 1 Maccabees has been challenged by K. Bringmann, and the complex matter of reconstructing the chronological details of the revolt remains unsettled.

The calendrical theory of Bickermann gave rise to a theory of sources behind 1 Maccabees. One source, a Seleucid chronicle, would have been responsible for events using the Macedonian calendar, while another source would have been responsible for those events dated by the Babylonian calendar. This latter source was thought to be common to both books of the Maccabees. The two books do narrate names and places in basically the same order, although often the events associated with each place are different in the two narratives. Perhaps the strongest argument for a common source is that both 1 and 2 Maccabees relate nothing about events between the departure of Antiochus V from Jerusalem early in 162 and the complaint of Alcimus to Demetrius after the latter came to power later that year or early in the next. This omission is, of course, an argument from silence. Attempts have been made to reconstruct this common source, and it has been characterized by Schunck as a "Life of Judas" and by Goldstein as a Jewish history of an age of wonders. The task of finding such sources embedded in or presupposed by any narrative is extremely difficult, however, and such highly speculative reconstructions should be approached with great caution.

The list of differences between the two works is extensive. Where 2 Maccabees abounds in epiphanies and prodigies, 1 Maccabees does not. Where 2 Maccabees emphasizes the role of martyrs and the coming resurrection of those who die for the Lord, 1 Maccabees does not. While 1 Maccabees extols all the Hasmonean brothers and states that only to that family had it been granted to bring deliverance to Israel (1 Macc 5:62), 2 Maccabees portrays Judas' brother Simon as an unsuccessful leader on two occasions (2 Macc 10:20, 14:17). Most interesting, however, is the difference in style between the two works. First Maccabees is a conscious imitation of the Hebrew scriptures, and the style itself appears to be a weapon in the author's attempt to glorify the Hasmonean dynasty. In contrast, the author of 2 Maccabees used contemporary Greek style while attacking the Seleucids. His style may be a strategy in his attempt to show that the Jews are not hostile to foreigners, only to those who try to forbid them to follow their ancestral customs.

First Maccabees was composed in Judaea sometime during or shortly after the reign of John Hyrcanus (130–104), but it is hard to be more precise. As for 2 Maccabees, the situation is more complex. When were the two letters that open the book prefixed to the epitome? Were they added to an already existing epitome, which should then be dated before 124, the date of the first letter (1:9)? Was the epitome written to go with the first letter? Did the letters and the epitome all exist independently and at some later date come to be joined together? Such uncertainties mean that one has to rely on internal evidence to ferret out the purposes and scope of the works.

THE CONTINUING TRADITION

A narrative about Jews suffering at the hands of a cruel tyrant is also found in the book entitled 3 Maccabees. The book has nothing to do with the Maccabean revolt, and most probably received its title from its position in the manuscripts after 1 and 2 Maccabees. The story is set during the reign of Ptolemy V Philopator (221–205), half a century before the Maccabean revolt. There are two main acts to the narrative. First Ptolemy, visiting Jerusalem after his victory over Antiochus the Great at Raphia in 217, wanted to enter the Holy of Holies of the Temple and, on being told that it was not allowed, tried to force his way in. As the Jewish bystanders prayed, Ptolemy fell to the ground stunned. Enraged, he returned to Egypt bent on revenge. He stripped Alexandrian Jews of their civil rights and had all the rural Jews of Egypt brought in chains to Alexandria. His first and second attempts to have them massacred were foiled. At the third try, angels appeared and Ptolemy's own forces were destroyed. Ptolemy then recalled what good citizens the Jews had previously been and freed them. The Jews celebrated their deliverance with a festival. Even in this brief sketch one can sense the resonances with 2 Maccabees in the epiphanic deliverance and the resulting festival. The style of 3 Maccabees is also emotional and dramatic. Although some scholars have considered 3 Maccabees to be historically accurate, more likely it is a work of fiction composed during the first half of the first century in Alexandria, Egypt.

The last of the books of Maccabees, 4 Maccabees, is more intimately connected with 2 Maccabees. Written in the form of a discourse, 4 Maccabees retells in vivid detail the martyrdoms of Eleazar and the seven brothers found in 2 Maccabees 6 and 7. The author stresses the philosophical courage of the martyrs as they are guided by devout reason and keep control of their passions. The work evidences some knowledge of the eclectic philosophy, especially Stoicism, of the turn of the eras and was most likely written in the mid first century C.E.

Bibliography

Abel, Felix Marie. *Les livres des Maccabées.* Paris, 1949.

Arenhoevel, Diego. *Die Theokratie nach dem 1. und 2. Makkabäerbuch.* Mainz, 1967.

Bickermann, Elias. *Der Gott der Makkabäer.* Berlin, 1937. Translated by Horst R. Moehring as *The God of the Maccabees.* Leiden, 1979.

Bringmann, Klaus. "Die Verfolgung der jüdischen Religion durch Antiochus IV: Ein Konflikt zwischen Judentum und Hellenismus?" *Antike und Abendland* 26 (1980): 176–190.

———. *Hellenistische Reform und Religionsverfolgung in Judäa.* Göttingen, 1983.

Bunge, Jochen Gabriel. "Zur Geschichte und Chronologie des Untergangs der Oniaden und des Aufstiegs der Hasmonäer." *Journal for the Study of Judaism* 6 (1975): 1–46.

———. *Untersuchungen zum 2. Makkabäerbuch.* Bonn, 1971.

Davies, Philip. "Hasidim in the Maccabean Period." *Journal of Jewish Studies* 28 (1977): 127–140.

Doran, Robert. *Temple Propaganda: The Purpose and Character of 2 Maccabees.* Washington, 1981.

Fischer, Thomas. *Seleukiden und Makkabaer.* Bochum, 1980.

Goldstein, Jonathan A. *I Maccabees.* Garden City, N.Y., 1976.

———. *II Maccabees.* Garden City, N.Y., 1983.

Habicht, Christian. *2. Makkabäerbuch.* Gütersloh, 1976.

———. "Royal Documents in Maccabees II." *Harvard Studies in Classical Philology* 80 (1976): 1–18.

Hengel, Martin. *Judaism and Hellenism.* 2 vols. Philadelphia, 1974.

Kampen, J. *The Hasideans and the Origin of Pharisaism: A Study in 1 and 2 Maccabees.* Atlanta, 1988.

Kreissig, K. "Der Makkabäeraufstand: Zur Frage seiner sozial-ökonomischen Zusammenhänge und Wirkungen." *Studi Classici* 4 (1962): 143–172.

Martola, Nils. *Capture and Liberation: A Study in the Composition of the First Book of Maccabees.* Turku (Åbo), Finland, 1984.

Millar, Fergus. "The Background of the Maccabean Revolution: Reflections on Martin Hengel's *Judaism and Hellenism.*" *Journal of Jewish Studies* 29 (1978): 1–21.

Mørkholm, Otto. *Antiochus IV of Syria.* Copenhagen, 1966.

Momigliano, Arnaldo. *Alien Wisdom: The Limits of Hellenization.* Cambridge, 1975.

———. "The Second Book of Maccabees." *Classical Philology* 70 (1975): 81–88.

Neuhaus, Günter O. *Studien zu den poetischen Stücken im 1. Makkabäerbuch.* Würzburg, 1974.

———. "Quellen im 1. Makkabäerbuch?" *Journal for the Study of Judaism* 5 (1974): 162–175.

Nickelsburg, George W. E. "1 and 2 Maccabees: Same Story, Different Meanings." *Concordia Theological Monthly* (1971): 515–526.

Schunck, Klaus Dietrich. *Die Quellen des I. und II. Makkabäerbuches.* Halle (Saale), East Germany, 1954.

———. *1. Makkabäerbuch.* Gütersloh, 1980.

Sievers, Joseph. "The Hasmoneans and Their Supporters from Mattathias to John Hyrcanus I." Ph.D. diss., Columbia University, 1981.

Tcherikover, Avigdor. *Hellenistic Civilization and the Jews.* Philadelphia, 1959.

Wacholder, Ben Zion. "The Letter from Judah Maccabee to Aristobulos: Is 2 Maccabees 1:10b–2:18 Authentic?" *Hebrew Union College Annual* 49 (1978): 89–133.

ROBERT DORAN

The New Testament

Introduction to the New Testament

THE ESSAYS THAT follow concern the twenty-seven books of the New Testament. While information is given on the background and source material that influenced the authors, the main focus of these essays is on the final written form of Scripture—the contents and the authors' message, to the extent that they are knowable after so many centuries. This introduction discusses a further issue not treated in the individual essays; namely, after the individual books were written, how were they brought together into collections, ultimately to become the New Testament? How does their existence side-by-side in the collected New Testament affect the meaning of the individual books? To answer these questions an overall view of the role of Scripture, or sacred writings, in Christianity is needed.

HOW DID CHRISTIANS COME TO WRITE BOOKS?

Perhaps we need to start with an admission that may seem strange in a work entitled *The Books of the Bible.* Although Islam classified Judaism and Christianity with itself as "religions of the Book," that designation is not precise. There were people who honored the God of Abraham, of Isaac, and of Jacob long before a word of Genesis was written. So also Jesus was believed in and proclaimed for several decades before there was even one New Testament writing. Israelite religion and Christianity may be said to have been first religions of the people of God rather than religions of the Book. Of course, by the time of Jesus, Israel had become very conscious of sacred writings: the Law, the Prophets, and the other books, constituting much of what is now known as the Old Testament. Consequently, for the first 100 years when Jesus' followers referred to Scripture, they were referring to those books, not to the writings of fellow Christians.

Why were the first Christians somewhat slow in writing their own books? What changed the situation? A major retarding factor was that Jesus, unlike Moses and Moḥammed, was not remembered as a writer. Accordingly, the proclamation of the kingdom of God made present in Jesus scarcely depended on writing. Moreover, the early generations of Christians were strongly eschatological: for them the "last times" were at hand, and undoubtedly Jesus would return soon—"Maranatha" (1 Cor 16:22), "Our Lord, come" (also Rev 22:20). Such anticipation of the end of the world did not encourage Christians to write compositions for future generations (who would not be around to read them). It is no accident, then, that the first Christian literature of which we know consisted of letters—that is, documents whose immediate task was to answer pressing problems. This form of writing was consistent with an urgent eschatology.

When one notices that these letters were written

by Paul, another factor pertinent to the appearance of Christian literature becomes clear. Paul was a traveling apostle who planted knowledge of Jesus in one town and then moved on to another. Letters became his means of communication with converts who lived at a distance from him. Thus in the fifties of the first century Paul produced the earliest surviving Christian documents: 1 Thessalonians, Galatians, 1 and 2 Corinthians, Philippians, Philemon, and Romans. There is a somewhat different tone and emphasis to each, corresponding to what Paul perceived as the needs of the particular community at a particular time. This fact should make us cautious about generalizations in reference to Pauline theology. Paul was not a systematic theologian but an evangelistic preacher, giving strong emphasis at one moment to one aspect of faith in Jesus, at another moment to another aspect, even to a degree that may seem somewhat inconsistent. Very dangerous is the tendency to make assumptions about Paul's views based on the fact that he does not mention an idea or practice. For example, the Eucharist is mentioned only once in the Pauline writings, and that was because there were abuses at the eucharistic meal in Corinth. Except for that fortuitous incident, scholars might be misled to assume that there was no Eucharist in the Pauline churches, reasoning that Paul could scarcely have written so much without mentioning such an important aspect of Christian life.

If the geographical spread of Christianity produced Christian letters, it is probably no accident that we do not have any letters of the twelve apostles to the Jewish-Christian community of Jerusalem. The Twelve lived in Jerusalem, and if we may judge from the silence of the New Testament, most of them seem to have traveled little, Peter excepted. They could communicate verbally, and this seems to have remained the privileged or expected form of proclamation even after there were written accounts (see Rom. 10:14–15). Attestation to this is given by Papias, a Christian writer, as late as 125 (see Eusebius, *Church History* 3.39.4).

Nevertheless, the need for Christian writings grew as chronological distance became a factor. The passing of the first generation of Christians contributed to the production of works of a more permanent nature. By the mid sixties, the most famous among those who had known Jesus or who had seen the risen Lord (1 Cor 15:3–8) had died: Peter, Paul, and James, "the brother of the Lord." The chronological distance between Jesus and the Christian believers of the last third of the first century was bridged in part by writings that preserved the witness of the first generation. Letters, or epistles, remained an important means of Christian communication even if they were no longer actually written by Paul but instead written in his name and, in a sense, to preserve his spirit and authority. Many scholars classify Colossians, Ephesians, the Pastoral Letters (1 and 2 Timothy and Titus), and 2 Thessalonians in this category of "deutero-Pauline" writings, composed in the period 70–100 or even later. A plausible explanation is that disciples or admirers of Paul were dealing with new problems of the post-70 era by giving the advice they thought faithful to Paul's mind. But while still dealing with immediate problems such as false teachers or counterfeit Pauline letters, the deutero-Pauline letters often have a tone that is more universal (Colossians and Ephesians theologize about the church rather than about local churches) or more permanent. For instance, the structure advocated by the Pastorals, consisting of presbyters/bishops and deacons, is meant to help the church survive for future generations. The idea of the second coming of Jesus was not lost but it became less emphatic. Indeed, 2 Thessalonians warns against those who overemphasize its immediacy.

According to many scholars, to this post-70 period also belong the epistles attributed by name to Peter, James, and Jude—letters attempting in the name of the great apostles or members of Jesus' family to speak to problems of later Christian generations. Once again, beyond treating immediate problems, these letters often had a universal or permanent tone. Indeed (along with 1, 2, and 3 John) they eventually became known as Catholic (or "universal") Epistles, a term that in Eastern Christianity was seen as appropriate to works addressed to the church universal.

Literary genres other than letters also appeared. Just about 70, according to a common scholarly view, the Gospel according to Mark was written, preserving a memory of Jesus' deeds and words remarkably absent from the letters discussed above. Of course, this memory was colored by experiences from the decades that separated Jesus from the evangelist and his sources. Selection of what was preserved from the Jesus tradition was determined in part by its relevance to the Christian problems of the period 30–70. For example, the emphasis on the necessity of suffering and the cross in Mark may reflect the persecution of Christians by Nero, if Mark was truly written in Rome as tradition claims. Expansion or explication of the Jesus tradition was demanded because the hearers and readers were now no longer the Palestinian Jews of Jesus' lifetime but gentiles to whom Jewish customs and ideas were strange (see Mk 7:3–4).

The Gospels according to Matthew and Luke, probably written ten or twenty years after Mark, preserved much more of the Jesus tradition, especially by way of sayings (thought to be drawn from a lost collection of sayings known as Q). This wider tradition betrays experiences different from those of Mark's church background. Still another form of the Jesus tradition was given by the Fourth Gospel (John), written around 90–100—a form so different that scholars have labored extensively to reconstruct the peculiar community history behind this composition. Despite the local colorings of all four canonical Gospels, their overall import was to preserve for late-first-century readers (and indeed for those of all time) a memory of Jesus that did not perish when the eyewitnesses died. It is quite possible that none of the Gospels, which never mention their authors' names, was actually written by the one whose name has become attached to it in traditions stemming from the end of the second century (John Mark, companion of Paul and then of Peter; Matthew, one of the Twelve; Luke, companion of Paul; John, one of the Twelve). Nevertheless, those names constitute a claim that Jesus was being interpreted in a way faithful to the first and second generation of witnesses and preachers.

Another form of early Christian literature of a more permanent nature than letters is exemplified in the Acts of the Apostles. Intended by the author to constitute the second part of a work that commenced with the Gospel according to Luke (which began and ended in Jerusalem), this book moved the story of Christianity beyond Jerusalem and Judaea to Samaria and even to the ends of the earth. The atmosphere in which the work was written is suggested by Acts

1:6–11: knowledge of the time of the second coming has not been given to the disciples of Jesus, and more important than looking to heaven in expectation of that coming is the spread of Christianity. This is symbolized by beginning the story in Jerusalem with the Twelve and ending it in Rome with Paul, whose last words proclaim that the future of Christianity lies with the gentile world (Acts 28:25–28). Such a work clearly envisions an enduring Christianity that needs to know of its continuity with Jesus, Peter, and Paul, and to be certain that its development has not been haphazard, but under the guidance of the Spirit given by Jesus.

The Book of Revelation (often called the Apocalypse) represents still another genre in the Christian writing activity of the post-70 period. With roots in Ezekiel and Zechariah, this book represents "apocalyptic" literature, a designation derived from a Greek noun meaning "disclosure" or "revelation." Such apocalyptic literature was well known in Judaism, as exemplified by Daniel and by two books written after the destruction of the Jerusalem Temple in 70 C.E., namely, 2 Esdras (4 Ezra) and 2 Baruch. The latter two would have been contemporary with Revelation. Persecution of God's people by the great world empires has raised the question of the extent to which history is under God's control. Apocalyptic literature answers this question by visions that see what is going on in heaven and on earth at the same time— visions that can be expressed only in luxuriant symbols. The parallelism of heaven and earth assures the reader that what happens below is under the control of God above, and that earthly persecution reflects struggles between God and the evil spirits. The Book of Revelation, by expressing the attributes of God in a symbolism that goes beyond rational description, reminded the Christians of the late first century that the kingdom of God was larger than the history they were experiencing. It gave them hope, nay assurance, that despite (or even because of) the setbacks they suffered, God would make them victorious. Unfortunately, ignorance of this type of literature and of the plasticity of its images and time symbols (so prevalent in the Jewish apocalypses cited above) has led some to think of Revelation as an exact prediction of the future. Rather, the grandeur of "the Alpha and Omega, the first and the last" (Rev 22:13), lies beyond chronology and human calculation.

Still other forms of early Christian literature exist, concealed under the designation "letter" or "epistle." Precisely because letters were the dominant literary production of the first Christians, later works that were not really letters were classified as such. (First Peter and James are borderline cases: they have elements of a letter format, but the content is closer to a homily [1 Peter] or a type of oratorical debate known as a diatribe [James].) The "Epistle" to the Hebrews has the conclusion of a letter but no epistolary address, so that the destination "to the Hebrews" refers to an early analysis of its contents. The polished style is that of Hellenistic or Alexandrian oratory. Although the work envisions a particular problem (seemingly backsliding from aspects of Christian adherence because of the attractions of Judaism), it elaborates a profound Christology of God's Son, who is like us in everything except sin—one who is superior to the angels (who gave the Law) and to Moses, and who replaced by his death the Israelite cult and priesthood. The distance of style and development between this "epistle" and the early Pauline letters is striking. The First "Epistle" of John (which has *no* letter format and never mentions John) is extremely difficult to classify. In many ways it is the application of themes of the Fourth Gospel to a situation in which the Johannine community is no longer wracked by expulsion from the synagogue but by internal disagreement and schism.

Thus in various literary genres, Christians of the era after 70 continued to wrestle with problems and threats, but the phrasing of their answers created works that could easily speak to other Christian situations in both time and space—to the point that often it is no longer possible to analyze the particular problem the author had in mind. Accordingly, while the earlier Christian literature (the "proto-Pauline" letters written during Paul's lifetime) can be dated with accuracy, allowing a variance of only a few years or even a few months, one almost always has to allow a margin of several decades for suggested dating of the post-Pauline works. Indeed, in the instance of one or two New Testament writings (Mark, Acts, 2 Peter) the different dates suggested by well-informed scholars have a range of fifty to one hundred years.

WHY CERTAIN WRITINGS WERE PRESERVED AND ACCEPTED

The Christian compositions we have been discussing, written between the years 50 and 150, were not only preserved but eventually deemed uniquely sacred and authoritative; they were placed on the same level as the Jewish Scriptures (the Law, Prophets, and other Writings), and evaluated as a New Testament alongside them (so that the Jewish Scriptures became the Old Testament). How did this come about? I shall consider here the first step, consisting of preservation and acceptance; we do not know the process fully, but several factors played a role.

First, apostolic origin, real or putative, was considered important. I have already discussed how letters not physically written by Paul, Peter, and James could become very important because they were written in the name, spirit, and authority of the apostles. The Gospels were eventually attributed either to apostles (Matthew, John) or to "apostolic men" (Mark, a companion of Peter; Luke, a companion of Paul). The Book of Revelation, containing the visions of a prophet named John (1:1–2, 22:8), won acceptance in the West in part because he was assumed to be the apostle John. When Dionysius of Alexandria perceptively argued around 250 that Revelation could not have been written by the author of the Fourth Gospel and of the Johannine Epistles (who was also assumed to have been John the Apostle), the acceptance of the book waned in the East (see Eusebius, *Church History* 7.25.6–27). Hebrews had the opposite fate: although cited early at Rome, it was not accepted in Western lists of sacred writings; in the third century, however, it was accepted in the East as written by Paul, an attribution that the Roman church judiciously denied.

Nevertheless, apostolic origin was not an absolute criterion for either preservation or acceptance. Letters written by Paul or in his name to the Corinthians (2 Cor 2:4) and to Laodicea (Col 4:16) have not survived. Moreover, some letters purporting to be by Paul were to be discounted, according to 2 Thessalonians 2:2, even if scholars today have no idea how such letters were distinct from the deutero-Pauline letters. In the late second century the *Gospel of Peter* was rejected by a bishop because of its content, without any debate as to whether or not it came from Peter. Many apocryphal works rejected by later church authorities as spurious or false bore the names of apostles. One must look, then, for other criteria of preservation and acceptance.

Second, the Christian communities for whom the writings were intended had a role in preserving them and winning acceptance for them. Apparently no work addressed to the Jerusalem or Palestinian communities has survived, although some of the sources of the Gospels and of Acts may have been Palestinian. The disruption of that area by the Jewish-Roman War of 66–70 probably contributed to such a hiatus. Plausibly, Antioch or another community in Syria received James and the Gospel according to Matthew, with the latter becoming extremely influential. Seemingly, the churches of Greece and of Asia Minor (e.g., Ephesus) preserved the largest parts of the New Testament: the Pauline and the Johannine writings, and perhaps Luke-Acts as well. (Some scholars, however, locate the Johannine writings in Syria.) The church of Rome is thought to have preserved Romans, Mark, and perhaps Hebrews; it is another candidate for the locus of Luke-Acts. When, circa 170, Irenaeus rejected the gnostics' claims to apostolic origins for their writings (*Against Heresies* 3.3), the traceable connections of apostles to major churches in Asia Minor, Greece, and, above all, Rome were important arguments for the inclusion of works he considered part of the canonical New Testament. This ecclesiastical factor (perhaps through the influence of some personality mentioned in a New Testament book who later was prominent in a particular church) may explain the preservation of works like Philemon and Jude, which are not lengthy or significant enough to be explained easily otherwise.

Third, conformity with the rule of faith was a factor in the acceptance of Christian writings as sacred or canonical. Indeed, the term "canon" or norm may first have referred to the standard beliefs of the Christian communities before it referred to the collection of writings that became standard. The importance of such conformity may be illustrated by a story told by Eusebius (*Church History* 6.12.1) of Serapion, the bishop of Antioch (*ca.* 190), who found the people in nearby Rhossus reading in church from the *Gospel of Peter*, a work with which he was

unfamiliar. At first hearing he found it a bit strange, but he was inclined to tolerate it. Serapion learned later that this gospel was being used to support the teaching of Docetists, who held that Jesus was not truly human (the Docetists may have appealed to the passage in the *Gospel of Peter* 4:10 that has Jesus silent, as if he felt no pain when crucified), and so he forbade further church use of the work. Some gnostic writings reflected the idea that Jesus did not truly die on the cross, a view that consequently led to disparagement of Christian martyrdom. By comparison, the four Gospels and the letters of Paul, which highlight the centrality of the cross and the death of Jesus, along with the Acts of the Apostles, with its description of the death of Stephen and the suffering of Peter and Paul, would be clearly preferred by the many Christian communities in which the blood of the martyrs had proved to be the seed of the church. The reason for the uneasiness of Dionysius of Alexandria about Revelation and what caused him to submit the book to a fine examination as to authorship was that it described Christ reigning on earth for 1000 years (Rev 20:4–5): a millenarian or chiliastic doctrine that he denied.

Although contributing to the preservation and importance of certain writings, these three factors scarcely do justice to what seems to have been an intuitive process and to what was thought of as Spirit-guided. Let us now turn to the collection of some of the important works and their ultimate shaping into the New Testament.

HOW EARLY CHRISTIAN WRITINGS BECAME A COLLECTION

The various literary genres had different histories of preliminary collection, and these histories throw light on the attitudes that shaped the final collection of the New Testament.

Collection of Paul's Letters

As we have seen, Paul's name appears on thirteen New Testament letters written to separate communities over a period of some fifty years (or even longer if the Pastorals were written after 100). If one audaciously posits that Paul himself and the (approximately) four authors of the deutero-Pauline letters kept copies, we still do not know how these copies were gathered. If copies were not kept by the senders, receiving communities not too distant from each other may have exchanged letters (Col 4:16), thus gradually amassing collections. However, some letters seem to have been edited after being sent, and such a literary process would require more than community interchange. A plausible suggestion is that after Acts was written and the career of Paul more widely known there was a systematic attempt to collect his letters. Such an attempt has been attributed to Onesimus (Phlm 10), to Timothy, or to a Pauline school of writers (perhaps some of the authors of the deutero-Pauline letters); but the attempt would have had to continue after the first post-Pauline generation. While writers about the year 100 (such as Ignatius of Antioch, the authors of *1 Clement* and 2 Peter) betray knowledge of several Pauline letters, the first clear evidence of a large collection comes later, with Polycarp and Marcion. The latter's acceptance of ten letters did not include the Pastorals (also absent from P[46], a third-century manuscript of the letters). By the end of the second century, thirteen were accepted in the Western church, with a fourteenth (Hebrews) soon being added in the East; only by the fourth century did this last book come into general use in the West.

The Collection of the Gospels

The church eventually accepted four Gospels composed in the period 65–100. Why four? Although Paul does not refer to a written account, his warning in Galatians 1:8–9 against "a gospel contrary to what we have preached to you" suggests that the idea of only one gospel may have been axiomatic (*cf.* 1 Cor 15:11). The Gospel according to Mark, which most scholars consider to have been written earliest, calls itself majestically "the gospel of Jesus Christ, the Son of God," without suggesting that the readers would have access to another gospel. When the author of Matthew wrote several decades after Mark, he incorporated other material, especially from the sayings-collection that scholars call Q, into a reshaped Mark, seemingly supposing that now there would be no need for readers to consult either of these two major sources. The author of Luke knows of "many" previous narratives, but has set out to produce his "orderly

account" with the idea that Theophilus (and other readers) should know the truth more effectively (Lk 1:1–4). The fact that there is never a citation from Mark, Matthew, or Luke in the Johannine Epistles, even where the Synoptic themes could have served the author well, suggests that for the Johannine community "the message we have heard" (1 Jn 1:5; *cf.* 3:11) was the Fourth Gospel alone. Bishop Papias (*ca.* 125) knew of several Gospels, but before 150 there is no clear example of more than one Gospel being read as authoritative in a given church.

Indeed the practice of using one Gospel had a disturbing exclusivity. The Jewish Christians preferred Matthew (or another gospel of their own composition) because of the Jewishness of that Gospel and its insistence on every jot and tittle of the Law (5:18). They did this, presumably, as a polemic against gentile Christians, who used other writings to support nonobservance of the Law. Marcion used a truncated form of Luke alone for the opposite reason of rejecting the Jewish heritage. Gnostic commentaries on John appeared early, for that Gospel supplied ammunition for a gnostic rejection of this world as evil. (See the Johannine Jesus' statements that he had come from above, that neither he nor his believing followers were of this world [17:16], and that he would take them with him to another world [14:2–3].) Thus, concentration on one Gospel could sometimes be used to support a theology rejected by the larger number of Christians. By reaction, the acceptance of more than one Gospel became the practice in "the great church" (a term used by the nonbeliever Celsus: Origen, *Against Celsus* 5.59). Four Gospels received ever-widening acceptance after 150. Tatian attempted a compromise between the one and the four by composing a single harmonized account out of the four (the Diatessaron)—a compromise that was accepted for several centuries by the Syriac-speaking churches in the East but rejected by the Greek- and Latin-speaking churches. Irenaeus in the West and Origen in the East were influential in establishing the view that God wanted four separate Gospels for the church.

The Influence of Marcion

A brilliant theologian, Marcion came from the East to Rome in the 140s proclaiming that the God revealed by Jesus was not the creator attested in the

Old Testament, who was a demiurge. This total rejection of the Jewish heritage, while not surprising given the increasing separation from the Law, the cult, and the synagogue attested in Paul, Hebrews, and John, was decried as heresy by the church of Rome. Part of the struggle centered around the collection of Luke (*euangelion*) and ten Pauline letters (*apostolikon*) that Marcion used to show support for his theology. One should not exaggerate; opposition to Marcion was not the only factor that led the church to a notion of canon and, indeed, to a wider canon of authoritative Scripture. Many factors led to a canonical Christian collection: opposition to Jewish Christians and to gnostics, liturgical usage, a sense of loyalty to tradition, the need for reassurance in face of martyrdom, among other factors. Nevertheless, the format of an enlarged *euangelion* (four Gospels rather than Luke alone) and enlarged *apostolikon* (at least thirteen Pauline letters rather than ten) may have been directly influenced by opposition to Marcion. The expansion of the apostolic section may also account for the inclusion of the second half of the Lucan work, the Acts of the Apostles. Since Acts prefaces a narrative of the work of the Twelve (represented by Peter) to its account of the work of Paul, it stands fittingly in an intermediate position between the Gospels and the Pauline letters. The same instinct for favoring the Twelve probably explains the inclusion of 1 Peter and 1 John. In any case, church writers in Greek and in Latin in the decades just before and after 200 attest to a wide acceptance of an expanded collection of twenty works as a New Testament alongside the Jewish Old Testament.

Completing the Collection

The remaining seven works (Hebrews, Revelation, James, 2 and 3 John, Jude, 2 Peter) were cited in the third and early fourth centuries and accepted as Scripture in some churches but not in all. By the late fourth century in the Greek East and the Latin West there was a wide (but not absolute) accord on a canon of twenty-seven works. The Syriac-speaking communities eventually replaced the Diatessaron with the four Gospels, but did not include the minor Catholic Epistles and Revelation. The Ethiopian church used a larger canon often estimated at thirty-five books. Standardization at a twenty-seven-book canon in-

volved churches accepting from other churches books about which they had had some doubts, and such "ecumenism" reflected an increasing contact and communion between the East and the West. Origen went to Rome and learned the biblical views of the church where Peter and Paul had been martyred and which had struggled against Marcion. On the other hand, Western thinkers like Ambrose and Augustine became familiar with the works of Origen and through him with the biblical views of the highly literate Alexandrian Christianity. The most learned Latin church father, Jerome, spent much of his life in Palestine and Syria. Thus, in a sense, the larger canon in the fourth century, like the shorter collection in the late second century, testified to the experience of what Ignatius had earlier called "the catholic church" (*Smyrnaeans* 8:2).

THE IMPORT OF THE COLLECTED NEW TESTAMENT

No New Testament writer knew that what he wrote would be included in a collection of twenty-seven books and read as an enduring message centuries or even millennia later. Indeed, given their strong emphases, some writers might not have been happy about having works of a different cast set alongside their own with similar authority. In view of what he wrote in Galatians 2:11–14 about Cephas (Peter) and the men from James, one might imagine the initial annoyance of Paul on finding his letter in a volume with Matthew 5:18–19, 16:17–18, 23:2–3 (passages that stress Law observance and the authority of Peter), and James 2:22–24 (with this letter's emphasis on the importance of human works). Yet Paul's testimony in 1 Corinthian 15:5–11 to a common preaching and faith with Cephas and James might mean that his final attitude would be more inclusive.

An honest treatment of the New Testament must recognize a true diversity of views among its writers. Whether this diversity was pressed to the point of contradiction is another issue. We have no clear evidence that any New Testament writer had broken communion (*koinōnia*) with another. Even John, which can be quite critical of other followers of Jesus, recognizes a wider flock than the Johannine fold (10:16) and prays for oneness (17:20–21).

Undoubtedly, the essays in this volume will clarify the diverse emphases of the individual books of the New Testament. But appropriate attention should also be given to the modification of those emphases caused by inclusion in the collection. In a certain sense, a book is not biblical until enclosed in the Bible, or the whole collection. In studying the Jewish Scriptures one should concentrate on what the authors meant and be clear that those authors were dealing with issues of their own times and not predictions about Jesus. But scholars who have done this carefully have also insisted that once the Jewish Scriptures were placed alongside the Christian Scriptures in the same Bible, a significant relationship between the two Testaments was introduced into interpretation.

Similarly, a complementary shading of meaning occurred when once-independent Christian writings were placed in the same New Testament. For example, from frequency of use one may surmise that Paul coined or at least made thematic the idea of "gospel" (*euangelion*, or "good news"); but for Paul the news seems to have been centered in the death and resurrection of Christ as God's means of justifying all from sin. The church has placed Mark, a work that calls itself preemptively "the gospel of Jesus Christ," ahead of Paul in the canon. It begins with the baptism, giving more pages to the preaching and miracles of Jesus (absent from Paul) than to the crucifixion and resurrection. And then the church has chosen further to place ahead of Mark and to give the title "gospel" to Matthew, which begins with a genealogy and the story of Jesus' conception. The result? When one mentions "gospel" to Christians, virtually all think of the whole life of Jesus rather than simply the Pauline emphasis.

Some scholars would reject the hermeneutics of church usage illustrated by the canon. Through contemporary historical criticism scholarship can go back beyond the collections of the fourth or second century to the individual authors of the first century, and for some this means a liberation from the "tyranny of church control and distortion" of the Scriptures. Others of equally scholarly stature argue that the books were originally written for churches, and that church life remained and remains the appropriate and beneficial hermeneutical "place" for interpretation—that the pulpit would be closer to the original author's context than the scholar's desk. Of course, the perceptive adherents of the latter approach recognize that there were changes in church context from the first to the second to the fourth century, and so on to today; but they argue that rejecting these church contexts does more violence to the text than does a nuanced recognition of continuity.

Part of the current reaction against the church context of the canon is a preference for "apocryphal" Christian writings. A large body of these was discovered in the 1940s at Nag Hammadi in Egypt. What right did the larger church have to reject these from the canonical collection? Was that narrow prejudice, or can one appeal to divine guidance for the church in decisions pertaining to documents composed by believers for believers? Although the present author thinks that the evidence favors the latter answer, such a debate should encourage readers to plunge ahead to investigate the individual biblical books, knowing that the study of the New Testament has profound import for the course of Christianity and that all questions are far from settled.

Yet among the uncertainties about details in our knowledge of the New Testament, readers should not overlook one massive certainty. However they were written, preserved, collected, and selected, these twenty-seven books have brought untold millions of people from different times and places into contact with Jesus of Nazareth. Through the pages of the New Testament he has been able to present ever anew the challenge of the kingdom of God. Those who gain from the essays in this volume factual knowledge and basic interpretative guidance may well be enticed to read the New Testament carefully for themselves. If they do, they may discover a coherent meaning that makes scholarly disputes but a minor distraction. Jesus was said to have taught with authority, unlike the scribes; the New Testament, like its Master, has more authority than the scholars who interpret it.

RAYMOND E. BROWN S.S.

124

Matthew

THE GOSPEL ACCORDING to Matthew stands at the head of the New Testament canon by reason of historical convention. Beginning with the nineteenth century, most scholars have held that Mark was the first Gospel to be written. St. Augustine (354–430), however, believed that the canonical Gospels arose in the order in which they appear in the various versions of the Bible. His is the view that has been perpetuated throughout the centuries.

NATURE AND PURPOSE

From the literary point of view, Matthew's Gospel compares more favorably to ancient biography than to any other genre. It is a story that tells of the life and ministry of Jesus of Nazareth from conception and birth (1:18–25) to death and resurrection (chaps. 26–28). The purpose of this story is to proclaim "the gospel of the kingdom" (4:23, 9:35, 24:14, 26:13).

What the phrase "the gospel of the kingdom" means comes to light in Matthew's use of the terms "gospel" and "kingdom." The term "gospel" denotes "good news," and Jesus himself is portrayed, in proffering salvation to Israel, as proclaiming the gospel of the kingdom (4:23, 9:35). In the time following Easter, the disciples will be the ones who proclaim the gospel of the kingdom, as they proffer salvation to the gentiles (24:14, 26:13). Included in their proclamation, says the Matthean Jesus, will also be mention of the fact that, shortly before his death, an unnamed woman anointed his head with costly ointment and thus prepared his body in advance for burial (26:7, 12–13). Together, what these several passages indicate is that the "gospel" in Matthean perspective encompasses traditions both of words of Jesus and of accounts about him. In sum, therefore, the term "gospel" in the phrase "the gospel of the kingdom" may be defined as the good news about the kingdom that is revealed in and through Jesus and that announces salvation first to Israel and then to the gentiles.

To consider the term "kingdom," the first thing to note is that it stands as an abbreviation for the fuller expression "the kingdom of heaven." Although Matthew prefers the latter to "the kingdom of God" and uses it more often, the two expressions are synonymous. Because the genitive "(of) heaven" is a metonym for "God," the purpose of the expression "the kingdom of heaven" is to assert the truth that "God rules (reigns)." Hence, "the rule of God," or "the reign of God," is a proper paraphrase of it.

Matthew presents John the Baptist, Jesus, and the disciples of the earthly Jesus as all announcing in Israel that "the kingdom of heaven is at hand" (3:2, 4:17, 10:7). The Greek word that underlies "to be at hand" in these passages denotes a "coming near," or "approaching," that is both spatial and temporal in character. Hence, for John the Baptist, Jesus, and

Jesus' disciples to announce that the kingdom of heaven is at hand is for them to announce that God has drawn near with his end-time rule.

How does Matthew conceive of God as having drawn near? Matthew associates the nearness of God with the person of Jesus, who is the Messiah, the Son of God. At 1:23, Matthew says in words drawn from the Old Testament that it is in the son conceived by the Holy Spirit (1:20) and born of the virgin that God at the last draws near to dwell with people. And in 12:28, Jesus himself declares: "But if it is by the Spirit of God that I cast out demons, then the kingdom of God has come upon you" (RSV).

To pull the strands of this argument together, it is apparent that in the phrase "the gospel of the kingdom," the focus of the term "gospel" is on Jesus, who is the Messiah, the Son of God. Similarly, the focus of the term "kingdom" is on God. Still, because Jesus is the one in whom God draws near with his end-time rule, the term "kingdom" may properly be said to have a double focus. But be that as it may, the way in which Matthew would have the reader define the phrase "the gospel of the kingdom" is clear: it is the good news revealed in and through Jesus Messiah (*Christos*, or "Anointed One"), the Son of God, which is proclaimed first to Israel and then to the gentiles to the effect that in him God has drawn near with his end-time rule to humankind, thus inaugurating the age of salvation.

The stress of my discussion thus far has been on God's kingdom as a present reality. As Matthew describes it, however, the kingdom is also both a hidden reality and a reality yet to be consummated. The circumstance that the kingdom is a hidden reality is attested to by the reaction Jesus' activity elicits from the crowds and the Jewish leaders. Although the crowds follow Jesus (4:25) and even acclaim him for his ministry of word and deed (7:28; 9:8, 33; 15:30–31), they do not perceive him to be the bearer of God's kingdom. On the contrary, they see in him only a prophet (16:13–14; 21:11, 46), and he in turn censures them as "this [evil] generation" that repudiates both him and John the Baptist, his forerunner (11:16–19). For their part, the Jewish leaders, too, witness Jesus' ministry, but far from discerning in him the presence of God, they take him to be an errorist, or false messiah (27:63), who owes his astonishing

authority to the prince of demons (9:34, 12:24). God's kingdom is present in Jesus, but as a hidden reality.

God's kingdom is furthermore a reality that will be consummated only in the future. Not until the end of the age, when the exalted Jesus shall return with his angels in power and great splendor to preside over the final judgment, will the rule of God encompass the world and be acknowledged by all people everywhere (13:36–43, 25:31–46).

STRUCTURE AND VIEW OF SALVATION HISTORY

In nature and purpose, then, Matthew's Gospel is a story about Jesus of Nazareth that sets forth the gospel of the kingdom. The two chief structural features of the Gospel are (1) the topical outline by which Matthew has arranged its contents, and (2) the view of the history of salvation he has incorporated in it. A look at these two structural features corroborates what has been said of the Gospel's nature and purpose.

The key indicator of the topical outline Matthew has fashioned is the formula that appears at 4:17 and 16:21: "From that time on Jesus began to proclaim [show his disciples] . . ." (Au. trans.). The very wording of this formula reveals its function: to alert the reader to the beginning of a new phase in the life and ministry of Jesus. The function in each case of the rest of the verse this formula introduces is to inform the reader of the tenor of the new phase that follows: Jesus' public ministry in the one instance and his suffering and death in the other. Hence, if one construes 4:17 and 16:21, and 1:1 as well, as "headings" and presses them thematically, the following topical outline readily emerges: (1) the person of Jesus Messiah (1:1–4:16); (2) the public ministry of Jesus Messiah (4:17–16:20); and (3) the journey of Jesus Messiah to Jerusalem and his suffering, death, and resurrection (16:21–28:20).

This topical outline corroborates what I have said of the nature and purpose of Matthew's Gospel in two ways. To begin with, it underscores the point that Matthew's Gospel assumes the contours of a story about Jesus. In its first part, this story presents Jesus to the reader (1:1–4:16). In its second part, it tells of

Jesus' ministry to Israel of teaching, preaching, and healing, and of Israel's repudiation of him (4:17–16:20). And in its third part, it tells of Jesus' journey to Jerusalem, of his clash with the Jewish leaders in the Temple, and of his suffering, death, and resurrection (16:21–28:20).

The second way the topical outline corroborates what I have said of the nature and purpose of Matthew's Gospel is by prominently depicting Jesus Messiah, in the culminating pericope of each main part, as the Son of God, that is, as the one in whom God is uniquely present with his end-time rule. In its first part (1:1–4:16), Matthew's story culminates in the pericope on the baptism of Jesus (3:13–17). In the climactic scene of this pericope, God himself is portrayed as entering the world of the story to declare over Jesus (and in the hearing of the world of transcendent beings such as Satan) that Jesus is God's beloved Son, whom he has chosen for end-time ministry (3:17; 4:3, 6). In its second part (4:17–16:20), Matthew's story culminates in Peter's confession of Jesus in the regions of Caesarea Philippi (16:13–20). Though proffered salvation by Jesus, the Jewish public considers him to be no more than a prophet and repudiates him (11:16–19, 16:14); by contrast, Peter confesses him, on behalf of all the disciples, to be the one God said he is, the Son of God (16:16). And in its third part (16:21–28:20), Matthew's story culminates in the scene of the Great Commission (28:16–20). Here Jesus, whom the Roman soldiers had affirmed upon his death to be the Son of God (27:54), appears as the resurrected Son whom God has exalted to lordship over heaven and earth, and he commissions his disciples to their worldwide mission (28:18–20). In Matthew's story, Jesus is preeminently the Son of God, and the topical outline I have advanced highlights this understanding of him.

Matthew's view of the history of salvation also corroborates what I have proposed concerning the nature and purpose of his Gospel. The history of salvation has to do with God's dealings in history, especially with Israel but also with the gentiles. The span of time Matthew envisages extends from Abraham (1:1–17) to the consummation of the age (28:20). As the so-called formula quotations show (cf. 1:22–23; 2:15, 17–18, 23), Matthew fundamentally distinguishes between two epochs: "the time of Israel" (the Old Testament), which is the time of prophecy, and "the time of Jesus," which is the time of fulfillment. For its part, "the time of Jesus" extends from his birth to his return at the end of the age (1:22–23, 28:20). Within the time of Jesus, Matthew further distinguishes among several ministries: There are the ministries to Israel of John the Baptist (3:1–2), of Jesus (4:17, 15:24), and of the twelve disciples (10:5–7); and there is the ministry to the nations of the post-Easter church (24:14, 28:18–20). Central to all these ministries, however, is the ministry of Jesus, for John's ministry prepares the way for that of Jesus (3:3) and the ministries of the twelve disciples and the post-Easter church are an extension of his (10:1; 28:19). Because Jesus' ministry is thus central, it is he and his activity that prove to be of decisive significance for the salvation of all humankind, Jew and gentile alike. This claim that Matthew makes of Jesus is fundamentally the same as the claim I have made of Matthew's Gospel: that it is a story that sets forth the gospel of the kingdom through which salvation is proffered to both Israel and the gentiles. The fundamental sameness of these two claims, therefore, shows that Matthew's view of the history of salvation does in fact corroborate what I have said about this Gospel's nature and purpose.

To recapitulate: Matthew's Gospel is a story that tells of Jesus of Nazareth and in so doing proclaims the gospel of the kingdom. The gospel of the kingdom is the good news that God, in the person of Jesus Messiah, his Son, has drawn near with his end-time rule to humankind, thus inaugurating the age of salvation. Matthew has arranged the contents of his story about Jesus according to a topical outline that treats, in turn, of the person of Jesus (1:1–4:16), of his public ministry in Israel (4:17–16:20), and of his suffering, death, and resurrection (16:21–28:20). Through the use of this outline, Matthew focuses on Jesus as being the one in whom God is uniquely present to save. By the same token, Matthew also situates his story about Jesus within the broad context of the history of salvation. By so doing, he raises the claim that, for the salvation of Israel and the gentiles alike, Jesus is of decisive significance.

AUTHOR AND DATE

The first person to cite the name of a written Gospel appears to have been Papias, who was bishop of Hierapolis in Asia Minor (*d. ca.* 130). Seemingly, Papias had at his disposal the canonical Gospels of Mark, Matthew, and John. On the origin of Matthew's Gospel he comments: "Matthew wrote [collected] the oracles [accounts] in the Hebrew language and every one interpreted them as he was able." This notice, preserved around 323 by Eusebius in his *Church History* (3.39.16), is at the root of the traditional view that the author of the First Gospel was the apostle Matthew. In support of this view, reference has also been made to the Gospel itself. Allegedly, to place his "signature" on the Gospel he wrote, the apostle Matthew has deftly recast the Marcan text on the call of Levi/Matthew so as to point to himself by recounting his call from Jesus to abandon the toll collector's booth and to become one of the Twelve (Mark 2:14; Matt 9:9, 10:3).

In all likelihood, however, one errs if one identifies Matthew the author with Matthew the apostle. For one thing, most scholars believe that Matthew the author, in writing his Gospel, took over virtually the whole of Mark's Gospel together with a source containing sayings of Jesus, called Q. But if Matthew the author was Matthew the apostle, how is it to be explained that one who was an eye- and ear-witness to the words and deeds of the earthly Jesus should lay at the basis of his Gospel the work of one like Mark, who no one has ever claimed knew the earthly Jesus? For another thing, if it is true that Matthew the author wrote, as is commonly believed, about 85, the question must also be raised whether it is even reasonable to suppose that Matthew the apostle could be expected to have lived long enough to write the First Gospel. And as for the "signature" Matthew the author has allegedly left behind, one might more plausibly conjecture that Matthew the apostle was in some way instrumental in the founding or life of the Christian community in which the First Gospel arose and that the scene telling of the call of Matthew the toll collector is Matthew the author's way of paying tribute to the "patron saint" of the church of which he was a member.

Although Matthew the author is unknown to history, examination of the First Gospel suggests that he was probably a Greek-speaking Jewish Christian of the second generation after Christ who possessed a universal missionary outlook and may have enjoyed some measure of scribal training. That Matthew spoke Greek is apparent from the quality of the language he wrote. His is not "translation Greek," the secondary rendering, for example, of a Hebrew or Aramaic original. On the contrary, although he exhibits, as one scholar points out in a test of his language, a feeling for "Semitic atmosphere" and has at times taken over Semitisms from his sources or even given a phrase a Semitic twist himself (e.g., 7:28: "*And it happened* when Jesus finished"; Au. trans.), he can be seen on the whole to have been "an educated person commanding sound Greek with a considerable vocabulary" (Moule 1962). Whether Matthew also had, beyond his knowledge of Greek, some mastery of Aramaic or Hebrew is disputed but seems likely, judging from the many indications that he had in fact been trained as a scribe.

In background, Matthew is generally regarded by scholars as being of Jewish extraction, although some few contend he was a gentile. Those who assert the latter base their case by and large on Matthew's alleged "distance" from Judaism (he is reputed to have lived in a gentile environment and to have had no firsthand knowledge of Judaism); on his misrepresentation of peculiarly Jewish matters (e.g., he is said to have shown that he was unaware that the Pharisees and the Sadducees were not one party during the time of Jesus but rival parties [16:12], and to have misconstrued Hebraic parallelism so that Jesus is made to enter Jerusalem on two animals instead of on one [21:5, 7]); on his preference for the Greek Septuagint in quoting from the Old Testament; and on his tendency to decrease, in comparison with Mark, the fund of Semitic loanwords he inherited from the tradition (Strecker 1962; Meier 1979). Whatever the merit of each of these allegations, the thing to note is that the contention that Matthew was gentile in origin can be sustained only on the supposition that the interpreter can distinguish with certainty between "tradition" (materials in the Gospel inherited by Matthew) and "redaction" (materials in the Gospel stemming from Matthew's own hand), and that whereas the tradition is Jewish-Christian in tenor, the redaction is gentile-Christian. Because this presupposition is problematic in the extreme, the proposition that Matthew was a gentile remains suspect and has never enjoyed more than limited acceptance among scholars.

Reasons for believing that Matthew was a Jewish Christian are strong. First of all, the portrait of Jesus he sketches is thoroughly Jewish in tone. To be sure, the portrait of Jesus he inherited was already Jewish. Nevertheless, he has enhanced this particular feature considerably. Thus, Jesus is the "Son of Abraham," the one in whom the entire history of Israel reaches its culmination (1:1–17). As the "Messiah" (1:1, 16, 17, 18), or "Coming One" (11:2–3), he has been sent specifically to "the lost sheep from the house of Israel" (15:24). As the "Son of David," he carries out an extensive ministry of healing in Israel (9:27–31, 12:22–23, 15:21–28, 20:29–34, 21:14–15) and is also hailed as such upon his entry into Jerusalem (21:9). While still an infant, he is worshiped by the Magi as the "King of the Jews" (2:1–12). In that he is given the name "Emmanuel" (Isa 7:14), the essential feature of his being the "Son of God" is expressly stated: in him, "God is with us" (Matt 1:23). And the fact that as "this (Son of) man" he can be expected to return for judgment is an especially characteristic feature of the First Gospel (cf. 10:23, 13:41, 16:28, 19:28, 24:30, 25:31).

The Jewishness of Matthew is also reflected in the way in which he portrays the ministry of Jesus. Matthew is at pains to show that Jesus' ministry takes place almost exclusively within the confines of Israel (10:6, 15:24). Except for the fateful journey to Jerusalem (16:21, 19:1), Galilee is the place of Jesus' activity (4:12, 18, 23), particularly the environs of Capernaum (chaps. 8–9, 11:23, 17:24). Indeed, Capernaum is Jesus' "own city" (9:1), where he "dwells" (4:13) and apparently has a "house" (9:10, 28; 12:46; 13:1, 36; 17:25). The upshot is that it is *from* Galilee that the news of Jesus spreads throughout all Syria (4:24), and it is *to* Galilee that the crowds from the Decapolis, Jerusalem, Judaea, and across the Jordan come to be with him (4:25). When Jesus leaves Galilee, it is only briefly (3:13–4:12, 8:23–9:1, 16:13–20). In fact, on one occasion when he withdraws into the regions of Tyre and Sidon (Phoenicia), it appears that he merely crosses the border, for the Canaanite woman is depicted as "coming out" toward Jesus (15:21–28).

Still another way in which Matthew attests to his Jewish origin is the description he gives of the piety disciples of Jesus are to practice. In his teaching, Jesus enunciates the will of God in terms of its original intention (7:21; 15:4; 19:4, 8). Far from overthrowing the Mosaic law, he fulfills it and gives it abiding validity (5:17–18). The piety his disciples are to practice in their life together is that of the greater righteousness (5:20). Before God, disciples practice this righteousness by worshipfully giving alms, praying, and fasting (6:1–18), the three acts that also, notably, distinguish the piety of contemporary Judaism. Toward the neighbor, disciples practice the greater righteousness when they do unto others as they would have others do unto them (7:12; cf. 5:21–48). Fundamental to practicing the greater righteousness, whether before God or toward the neighbor, is that disciples be "perfect" (5:48), that is, that they be "whole-hearted," or single-hearted, in their devotion to God (as in Deut 18:13; NEB). Disciples are perfect in their devotion to God when they love God with heart, soul, and mind, and love the neighbor as the self (Matt 22:36–40). On balance, then, at the root of practicing the greater righteousness is the practice of love. However "Christian" this ethic has become, it breathes the air of a heritage that is profoundly Israelite and Jewish.

Though Jewish-Christian, Matthew is nevertheless universal in his missionary outlook. His openness to gentiles suggests, in fact, that his is the second, not the first, generation of Christians following the earthly Jesus. One searches the First Gospel in vain for traces of the fierce controversy surrounding the gentile mission, which are so prominent in Paul (Gal 2) and Acts (chap. 15). On the contrary, one can detect in the First Gospel from beginning to end a "gentile bias." Already in the genealogy of Jesus (1:3, 5–6), four non-Israelite women are listed as the ancestors of Jesus: Tamar, Rahab, Ruth, and "the wife of Uriah" (Bathsheba). In chapter 2, the "Magi from the East" are pictured as "worshiping" Jesus and presenting him gifts. Jesus' settling in "Galilee of the gentiles" to begin his ministry to Israel prefigures the post-Easter return of the disciples to Galilee, from where they will undertake their mission to the nations (4:12, 15;

28:7, 16–20). As the second of a series of ten miracles, Jesus heals the servant of a centurion, and attendant to this he declares: "Truly, I say to you, not even in Israel have I found such faith. I tell you, many will come from east and west and sit at table with Abraham, Isaac, and Jacob in the kingdom of heaven" (8:10–11; RSV). At 12:21, Matthew quotes from the Old Testament in order to proclaim Jesus as the one in whom "the gentiles will hope," and at 13:38 he writes that it is in the "world" that "sons of the kingdom" will be raised up. In the very pericope in which Jesus at first refuses to heal the daughter of a Canaanite woman on the grounds that his mission is exclusively to Israel, he relinquishes at the last and exclaims, "O woman, great is your faith! Be it done for you as you desire" (15:28; RSV). In the parables of the wicked husbandmen (21:33–46) and of the great supper (22:1–14), Matthew employs figurative speech to depict the influx of the gentiles into the church (21:41, 22:9–10); and, more directly, he has Jesus announce in 24:14 and 26:13 that it is throughout the entire world that the gospel of the kingdom will be proclaimed. Last, the circumstance that Matthew (in a saying of Jesus) can also designate the church as a "nation" (21:43) further goes to prove that he, and his community as well, has surmounted the problem of the mission to the nations.

Indications are that Matthew had furthermore been trained as a scribe. While some scholars are prepared to regard Matthew as a converted rabbi (e.g., von Dobschütz 1928), others think of him more modestly as having been on the order of a provincial schoolmaster whose scribal training evinces itself in numerous ways (e.g., Goulder 1974). For one thing, Matthew appears to have been conversant with rabbinic methods of interpretation and techniques of writing: he makes use of such rabbinic principles as "light and heavy" (7:11, 12:12), "principle and cases" (5:20, 21–48; 6:1, 2–18), and the "summary" (7:12; 22:37–40). He can also be found to "gloss interpretations" (5:32, 19:9), to use parables to illustrate particular teachings (chaps. 13, 21–22, 24–25), to begin discourses of Jesus with a formal proem (5:3–12 [13–16], 23:2–12) or to close them with a peroration (7:13–27, 23:37–39, 25:31–46), to group materials according to topic (chaps. 5–7, 8–9, 10, 13, 18, 23, 24–25), and to make use of such rhetorical devices as

"inclusion" (4:23 and 9:35; 7:16 and 7:20) or "chiasm" (10:28, 13:15, 19:30, 20:16).

For another thing, the attitude Matthew takes toward the Law and the tradition of the elders is also scribal in nature. True, Matthew does distinguish between "lighter" and "heavier" in such fashion as to establish the exercise of love as the deepest intention of the Law and therefore as grounds for setting aside precepts of the Law (5:31–42, 9:13, 12:7, 22:37–40, 23:23). But this notwithstanding, Matthew presents Jesus not as abolishing the Mosaic law but as fulfilling it (5:17–18), and Matthew furthermore appears to uphold the keeping of the tradition of the elders where it does not conflict with some precept of the Law itself (15:6) or with love as the weightiest matter of the Law (23:23; cf. 23:2–3). And third, besides making reference to scribes who are Jewish, Matthew likewise refers to "Christian scribes" (23:34), above all in 13:52, where he holds up the scribe who has been instructed about the kingdom of heaven as a model every disciple is to emulate. It is not farfetched to look upon 13:52 as the verse in which Matthew makes allusion to himself and his own work.

The description I have pieced together of Matthew the author is that he was a Greek-speaking Jewish Christian of the second generation after Christ who was universal in his missionary outlook and had been trained as a scribe. Approximately when did he write his Gospel? In the parable of the great supper (22:1–14), Matthew sketches, through the mouth of Jesus, the history of salvation from the time of Jesus' earthly ministry (22:2) to his own time (22:11–14). Verse 7 of the parable reads: "The king was angry, and he sent his troops and destroyed those murderers and burned their city" (RSV). If this verse refers obliquely to the destruction of Jerusalem (66–70) as an event lying behind Matthew, one has reason to fix the writing of the Gospel at about 85. This date would also square with the widespread belief that Matthew made use of Mark's Gospel, for if Mark was written, as scholars maintain, about the year 70, fifteen years would allow ample time for it to circulate and gain acceptance in the community of Matthew. Finally, the fact that by the time Matthew took pen to hand his community had already resolved to missionize the gentiles would likewise point to a date around 85.

PLACE AND READERS

Should it be correct that Matthew was a Jewish Christian whose language was Greek and whose missionary outlook was universal, it would follow that the members of the community for whom he wrote were Greek-speaking Christians of both Jewish and gentile origin. Where these Christians lived is a matter of conjecture. Locations as diverse as Palestine, Alexandria, and Phoenicia have been suggested, but Antioch of Syria is the choice of most scholars. The reason is that the social conditions obtaining in Antioch about 85 seem congruent with what can be known of the situation of Matthew's church.

Evidence both direct and indirect indicates that the church of Matthew was urban, well-to-do, and organizationally autonomous, but also subject to persecution from without and afflicted with dissension from within. The judgment that Matthew's church was both urban and well-to-do is based on a comparison of Matthew's Gospel with the Gospels of Mark and Luke. Whereas Mark, for example, uses the word "city" eight times and the word "village" seven times, Matthew uses the word "village" only four times but the word "city" no fewer than twenty-six times. The latter statistic is all the more revealing when one observes that several occurrences of the word "city" seem to relate to circumstances in Matthew's own time (10:11, 14, 15, 23; 23:34; cf. 5:14). Perhaps, then, the Matthean church was a "city church."

Indicators that this church was also well-to-do are numerous. The Lucan Jesus, for instance, pronounces a blessing on "the poor" (Luke 6:20) but the Matthean Jesus on "the poor in spirit" (Matt 5:3). The Marcan Jesus commands the disciples in conjunction with their missionary journey to take with them no "copper coin," that is, small change (Mark 6:8), but the Matthean Jesus commands them to take no "gold, nor silver, nor copper coin" (Matt 10:9). The Lucan Jesus tells a parable about "minas" (Luke 19:11–27) but the Matthean Jesus about "talents" (Matt 25:14–30), one of the latter being worth approximately fifty times as much as one of the former. The Lucan Jesus says, in the words of the householder in the parable of the great supper, "Go out quickly to the streets and lanes of the city, and bring in the poor and maimed and blind and lame"

(Luke 14:21; RSV); by contrast, the Matthean Jesus makes no special mention of the disadvantaged but simply says, "Go therefore to the thoroughfares, and invite to the marriage feast as many as you find" (Matt 22:9; RSV). And in the Gospels of Mark (15:43) and Luke (23:50–51), Joseph of Arimathea is a member of the council who is looking for the kingdom of God, but in Matthew's Gospel he is a "rich man . . . who also was a disciple of Jesus" (27:57; RSV).

Urban and prosperous, Matthew's church furthermore seems to have been organizationally autonomous in the sense that it had severed its ties to Judaism and was no longer a member of the Jewish league of synagogues. Three factors suggest this: Matthew's use of the expression "their [your] synagogue(s)," the polemic he wages against Israel as an institution, and the internal organization his church had seemingly developed.

To take the first two points together, Matthew attests idiomatically to the disassociation of his church from Judaism. By making frequent reference to synagogues that are "theirs" or "yours," he repeatedly calls attention to the "distance" that had opened up between "those Jews" and "us Christians" (4:23, 9:35, 10:17, 12:9, 13:54, 23:34). In addition, except to acknowledge that the "scribes and the Pharisees are seated on the chair of Moses" (23:2; Au. trans.), Matthew has virtually nothing good to say about Israel as a religious institution. Typically, there is no "friendly scribe" in his Gospel as there is in Mark's, of whom it is written, "And when Jesus saw that he answered wisely, he said to him, 'You are not far from the kingdom of God'" (Mark 12:34; RSV). On the contrary, the one scribe who requests of Jesus that he become his disciple is turned away with the words "Foxes have holes, and birds of the air have nests, but the Son of man has nowhere to lay his head" (Matt 8:20, RSV; see Kingsbury 1988). Indeed, far from evincing affinity for contemporary Israel, Matthew has Jesus summarily condemn it in the words: "Every plant which my heavenly Father has not planted will be rooted up" (15:13; RSV).

Having broken with Judaism, Matthew's church developed its own structures for governing its affairs. In principle, it defined itself, as will be recalled, as a "brotherhood" of the "sons of God" and of the "disciples of Jesus." Within this brotherhood, two or three groups can be distinguished. The one group is that of the "prophets" (10:41, 23:34). These appear to have been itinerant missionaries who proclaimed the gospel of the kingdom to Jews (cf. 10:41 to 10:6, 17, 23, and 23:34) but especially to gentiles (cf. 10:41 to 10:18, 24:14, 26:13, 28:19). The second group, whatever its relation to the first group, is the "false prophets." These Matthew denounces as those "who come to you in sheep's clothing, but inwardly are ravenous wolves" (7:15; RSV). Invoking the name of Christ, they prophesied, cast out demons, and performed many miracles (7:22). In truth, however, their works contravened their profession of the name of Christ (7:16–20). As a result, Matthew decries them as being "workers of lawlessness" whom the exalted Jesus will at the latter day banish from his presence (7:23). Last, the third group one can isolate is those who functioned as teachers. They are designated variously. Thus, the term "righteous man" (10:41) denotes a teacher of righteousness, and the terms "rabbi" (23:8), "scribe" (23:34), and "wise man" (23:34) most likely refer without distinction to those who were expert in matters pertaining to the Scriptures and the Law. The verses 10:41 and 23:34, in which three of these four terms occur, show that Christian teachers, too, served as missionaries to the Jews.

From Matthew's portrait of Peter and the disciples one can infer how his church governed its affairs. In the scene in which Jesus elicits from Peter the climactic confession that he is the Son of the living God, Peter receives from Jesus the promise of the power of the "keys of the kingdom of heaven" (16:19). In receiving this promise, Peter stands out as the first of the disciples to have been called (4:18–20; 10:2; 16:16) and consequently as the one who is their spokesman and who is typical of them in their moments of both great and little faith. Peter's "primacy," therefore, is not that of being elevated to a station above the other disciples but is "salvation-historical" in nature: the first disciple called by Jesus, he is the first among equals (Kingsbury 1979). Accordingly, the power of the keys Jesus promises Peter is none other than the power of "binding and loosing," which the other disciples exercise as well as he (16:19, 18:18). The power of binding and loosing, in turn, pertains to the regulation of church doctrine and discipline. Consequently, in the group to which Matthew belonged the governance of the church fell to the entire assembly of Christians. As the passage 18:18–20 indicates, this church made such governing decisions gathered together in the name and hence in the presence and on the authority of the exalted Son of God. Moreover, as it did so, it was conscious of the fact that the touchstone of whatever it decided was that it must be in keeping with the injunction given by Jesus to "observe all that I have commanded you" (28:20).

Purposely, then, the church of Matthew was without a peculiar "teaching office" such as contemporary Judaism was in the process of developing. Indeed, with an eye toward those engaged in teaching, Matthew is explicit about the problem of position and status. These persons were forbidden by words of Jesus to arrogate to themselves a station that would set them above others in the church. They were not, for example, to assume the titles of "rabbi" or "teacher," for these are the prerogatives of Jesus Messiah, the Son of God (23:8, 10). Neither were they to assume the title of "father," for this is the prerogative of God himself (23:9). On the contrary, in the church "all are brothers" (23:8), and the end-time maxim applies that "whoever exalts himself will be humbled, and whoever humbles himself will be exalted" (23:12; RSV).

Though urban, well-to-do, and organizationally autonomous, Matthew's church was nonetheless subject to persecution from without and afflicted with dissension from within. From without, Matthew's church suffered at the hands of its vastly more populous Jewish and gentile neighbors (Hare 1967). In describing Jewish persecution, Matthew reports that disciples of Jesus, particularly "missionaries," were made to submit to such ill-treatment as verbal abuse (5:11), arraignment for disturbing the peace (10:17), perjured testimony in court (5:11), flogging in the local synagogue (10:17, 23:34), stoning (21:35), pursuit from city to city (10:23, 23:34), and even death (10:28, 21:35, 23:34). On the topic of gentile persecution, Matthew tells of disciples being hauled into court by the authorities (10:18), judicially harassed ("handed over to tribulation," 13:21, 24:9), hated "by all" (10:22; 24:9), and even put to death (24:9). What can be surmised is that it was in large measure the "mission to the nations" that provoked such ill-treatment.

But Matthew's church was also rife with internal dissension. There were, as noted, the "false prophets" who led other disciples astray (7:15–23, 24:11). In addition, there were such other communal difficulties as the following: There were members who did "not understand" the word of the kingdom and consequently were without true faith (13:19), or who surrendered their faith because they could not endure persecution or tribulation (13:21, 24:9–10), or whose lives as disciples remained sterile because their faith had succumbed to the cares of the world or to the seduction of wealth (13:22), or who denied Jesus Son of God (10:33), or who despised others in the community (18:10) or betrayed fellow-disciples to gentile opponents (24:10) or caused other disciples to lose their faith (18:6). And there was the threat of status-seeking in the church (23:8–12), hatred among members (24:10), rampant "lawlessness" (Au. trans.) resulting in lovelessness (24:12, cf. 20:15), lukewarmness toward Christian duty (25:26), an unwillingness to forgive the neighbor (18:35), and other evil that endangered the spiritual welfare of the church (15:19). In the face of all such discord, Matthew directs the attention of his church in his Gospel squarely to the consummation of the age and the inauguration of the future kingdom by the exalted Jesus (chaps. 13, 24, 25). Matthew reminds disciples that the God who will miraculously establish his rule "then" is even "now" at work in his Son to motivate disciples ethically to do his will.

STORY OF JESUS
Presentation of Jesus

The aim of Matthew in the first part of his gospel story (1:1–4:16) is to present Jesus to the reader. This part culminates in the scene following Jesus' baptism (3:16–17), where God himself enters the world of the story and declares Jesus to be his beloved Son (3:17). This understanding of Jesus expressed by God, that Jesus is his Son (i.e., the "Son of God"), is the norm against which all other understandings of Jesus are to be measured.

Matthew begins his story with the genealogy of Jesus (1:1–17), whose purpose is dual: to inform the reader that Jesus is "Christ," "Son of David," and "Son of Abraham" (1:1); and to affirm that the whole of Israel's history has been so guided by God that the promises that were made to Abraham and to King David, which ostensibly had come to naught in the Babylonian captivity, have attained their fulfillment in the coming of this Jesus who is the Christ (1:17).

The titles Matthew ascribes to Jesus explain who he is and what he is about. "Christ" means "Anointed One" or "Messiah." Characteristic of Matthew's use of this title are the diverse ways in which he both employs and defines it. Thus, Matthew employs "Christ" in 1:1 as a personal name ("Jesus Christ") that is also a title ("Jesus [who is] Messiah"). In the last verses of the genealogy, however, he employs it only as a title ("Messiah," 1:16–17). In further defining "Christ," Matthew interprets the title in terms of "Son of David" and "Son of Abraham" (as in 1:1), and also by employing it alternately with the titles "Coming One" (11:2–3) or "King of the Jews" (2:2, 4) or "Son of God" (16:16, 20; 26:63, 68). "Christ" therefore proves to be a general title for Jesus in Matthew's story, and one must look to the immediate or wider context to know how to construe it.

In addition to "Christ," Matthew also designates Jesus in the genealogy, as I have noted, as the "Son of Abraham" (1:1, 2, 17). In light of both the genealogy and a passage such as 8:11, what this title connotes is that in Jesus, who is the Messiah, the entire history of Israel, which began with "father Abraham," reaches its culmination, and that in Jesus the gentiles, too, will find blessing (cf. Gen 12:1–3).

With the final link (1:16), Matthew breaks his genealogy. He does not write that Joseph fathered Jesus but that Joseph is "the husband of Mary, from whom Jesus was born" (Au. trans). This break raises the question: How can Jesus legitimately be called "Son of David" (1:1) if Joseph son of David (1:20) is not his father? Matthew's answer is that Joseph, as instructed by the angel of the Lord, gives Jesus his name and hence adopts him into the line of David (1:20–21, 24–25).

Matthew shows later in his story that Jesus, in the line of David, fulfills the end-time expectations associated with David. Jesus does this mainly by healing (9:27–31, 12:22–23, 15:21–28, 20:29–34, 21:14), but also by "taking possession" of Jerusalem and the Temple (21:1–11, 12–17). A striking feature is the attitude that people assume toward Jesus as the Son of David. The Jewish leaders refuse even to entertain the idea that he could be the Son of David (12:23–24, 21:15). The Jewish crowds, while they toy with the thought, nevertheless dismiss it in favor of the notion that Jesus is a prophet (12:23, 21:9–11). For certain persons, however, "Son of David" constitutes their understanding of Jesus. Cases in point are the blind men whom Jesus heals (9:29, 20:30–31), the gentile woman who appeals to him (15:22), and the children in the Temple who acclaim him (21:15). Noteworthy is the fact that, relative to their societal status, these persons are all "no-accounts." By contrasting them with the crowds and their leaders (who comprise Israel), Matthew invites his readers to identify with these people and to distance themselves from Israel: these no-accounts "see" and "confess" the truth to which Israel is "blind," namely, that Jesus is indeed its Davidic Messiah (Kingsbury 1975).

Following the birth of Jesus, the Magi arrive in Jerusalem and inquire after him: "Where," they ask, "is he who has been born king of the Jews?" (2:1–2; RSV). "King of the Jews," therefore, constitutes the understanding the Magi have of Jesus, and because they have come to offer him their sincere "worship" (2:2, 11), Matthew urges the reader to accept this title, too, as correctly applying to Jesus.

Unlike the Magi, Herod and all Jerusalem react with fear to the news that the Messiah, the King of the Jews, has been born (2:2–4). Indeed, Herod hatches a plot calculated to find the child and have him killed (2:7–8, 13, 16). In Herod's eyes, the one who is the King of the Jews is in effect a pretender to the throne of Israel: an insurrectionist. Later, this understanding of Jesus will also be the one that Pilate officially adopts, even though he will likewise show that, personally, he regards it as fabricated and baseless (27:11–44). Where Matthew reveals the true meaning of the title "King of the Jews" is in those scenes in which he depicts the Roman and Jewish mockery of Jesus during his passion: Jesus is in fact the King of the Jews, yet not as a national-political figure laying claim to the throne of Israel but, ironically, as the one who "saves others" by "not saving himself" and hence by enduring, in obedience to God, suffering that leads to death (27:27–31, 41–42).

God himself foils the plot of King Herod, by directing the Magi through a dream not to return to Herod (2:12) and by dispatching an angel to Joseph to instruct him in a dream to flee to Egypt and to remain there until Herod dies (2:13–14). After Herod's death, the angel of the Lord again comes to Joseph in a dream and commands him to return to Israel (2:19–21), and, warned by God through still another dream, Joseph settles in Nazareth (2:22–23).

In the next segment of his story, Matthew focuses on John the Baptist (3:1–12). John is Elijah revivified (11:14, 17:10–13), and he fulfills the prophecy associated with Elijah by summoning Israel to baptism and to repentance in view of the imminent inbreaking of the kingdom of heaven. Knowing himself to be the forerunner of another, John prophesies that the "Coming One," who is mightier than he and who will execute judgment to salvation and to condemnation, is about to appear (3:11–12). The title "Coming One," then, constitutes John's understanding of Jesus.

There follows the pericope on the baptism of Jesus (3:13–17). In accord with John's prophecy, Jesus suddenly arrives at the Jordan River to be baptized by John (3:13). At first John resists this, on the grounds that the greater is to baptize the lesser, not the reverse (3:14). Jesus, however, impels John to baptize him, not because he, like sinful Israel (3:1–10), has need of baptism, but because God has willed it (3:15). Once baptized, Jesus goes up from the water, and, thus removed from John (3:16a), he becomes the recipient of two revelatory events. In the first event, the heavens open and Jesus sees the Spirit of God descend upon him, empowering him (3:16). In the second event, a voice from heaven announces in words heard by Jesus and apparently by such transcendent beings as Satan as well (4:3, 6): "This is my beloved Son, in whom I take delight!" (3:17; Au. trans.).

God's empowerment of Jesus with his Spirit and especially his announcement from heaven bring the entire first part of Matthew's story to its culmination. With these events, God personally enters the world of Matthew's story as "actor" and marks Jesus out to be God's supreme agent. In this announcement, God sets forth (in phraseology drawn from Gen 22:2, Ps 2:7, and Isa 42:1) his own understanding of Jesus:

Jesus is his only, or unique, Son ("my beloved Son"), whom he has chosen for end-time ministry. To get at the meaning of the key designation "my Son," a look at Psalm 2 is of benefit. Here it is the king-designate from the house of David who on the day of his coronation is termed God's "anointed" ("christ") and God's "son" (Ps 2:2, 6–7). What, then, does "my Son" in the words of Matthew 3:17 connote? It connotes that Jesus, the Messiah-King from the line of David and of Abraham (1:2–6), is the royal Son of God.

Scrutiny of the designation "my Son" ("Son of God") reveals that it overlaps in meaning with the other designations encountered thus far. Anointed by God with the Spirit (3:16), Jesus Son of God is the Messiah, or Coming One (3:11, 17). Standing in the line of David and of Abraham, he is likewise the Son of Abraham (1:2, 16), the Son of David (1:18–25), and the King of the Jews (27:37, 54). On the other hand, "my Son" also transcends these other designations in significance. It does so because Matthew imbues it with a quality these others do not possess in like measure. This quality is that "my Son" attests to the unique filial relationship that Jesus has with God: Jesus is conceived by God's Spirit (1:18, 20) and empowered by God's Spirit (3:16) so that he is Emmanuel, or "God with us" (1:23), the one who reveals God (11:27) and is God's agent of salvation (26:28, 27:54). In Matthew's story, God himself dictates that Jesus is preeminently the Son of God.

The occurrence of God's baptismal announcement does not come as a complete surprise to the reader. Not only has Matthew alluded to the truth that Jesus is God's Son (1:18, 20), but twice he has stated it in the Old Testament quotations of 1:22–23 ("they shall call his name Emmanuel . . . God with us"; Au. trans.) and of 2:15 ("Out of Egypt have I called my son"; RSV). The thing to observe, however, is that these quotations are of the nature of a comment that Matthew directs to the reader alone. The reason God's baptismal announcement of Jesus' divine sonship is climactic is because it is central to the action of Matthew's story and is not merely a part of its frame.

Empowered by the Spirit at the baptism, Jesus Son of God is led by the Spirit into the desert to be tested by Satan (4:1–11). Three times Satan entices Jesus to break faith with God and hence disavow his divine sonship. But Jesus resists Satan's temptations and demonstrates that he, the Son, both knows and does the Father's will.

To conclude the first part of his story (1:1–4:16), Matthew tells of Jesus' return to Galilee and the completion of his "preliminary" travels. If Joseph had settled in Nazareth after the return from Egypt (2:22b–23), Jesus now leaves Nazareth and moves to Capernaum (4:12–13), which becomes "his own city" (9:1). He is therefore poised to begin his public ministry (4:12–16).

Ministry and Repudiation

In the second part of his story (4:17–16:20), Matthew depicts Jesus' ministry to Israel (4:23, 9:35, 11:1) and Israel's repudiation of him (11:6, 13:57). If in the first part Matthew presents Jesus to the reader and arranges for the narrative to culminate in God's baptismal announcement that Jesus is his Son, he so shapes the second part that it reaches its culmination in the confession of Peter on behalf of the disciples that, again, Jesus is God's Son (16:13–20). In the first part, God himself enters the world of Matthew's story as "actor" and declares his understanding of Jesus. In the second part, Peter shows by virtue of the confession he makes near Caesarea Philippi that the disciples' understanding of Jesus is in alignment with that of God.

The major summary passages (4:23, 9:35, and 11:1) indicate how Matthew would have the reader construe Jesus' public ministry in Israel: it is one of teaching, preaching, and healing. Jesus commences his ministry by proclaiming, "Repent, for the kingdom of heaven is at hand" (4:17; RSV). He next calls his first disciples (4:18–22), and in so doing surrounds himself with eye- and ear-witnesses. Followed by the disciples and attracting huge crowds (4:23–25), he ascends a mountain and there programmatically teaches the will of God (5:1–7:29). Then, wandering in the area of Capernaum and traveling across the sea of Galilee and back, he performs ten mighty acts of deliverance, at the same time setting forth the nature and cost of discipleship (8:1–9:34). At the height of his activity, he commissions the twelve disciples to a ministry in Israel modeled on his own, one of preaching and healing though not of teaching, since teaching is exclusively his prerogative (9:35–10:42).

The last of Matthew's three major summaries of Jesus' public ministry occurs at 11:1. In the section 11:2–16:20, which comprises the latter half of the second part of Matthew's story (4:17–16:20), the tenor of the plot changes. No longer does the motif of Jesus' teaching, preaching, and healing dominate the flow of events. Instead, it is the motif of repudiation, which is coupled in turn with the motif of wonderment and speculation about the identity of Jesus. The two pericopes that call attention to these twin motifs are John the Baptist's question and Jesus' answer (11:2–6) and Jesus' rejection at Nazareth (13:53–58). These two pericopes stand out for two reasons: they are strategically located as far as the latter half of the second part of Matthew's story is concerned (11:2–16:20); and each one contains both a question having to do with Jesus' identity (11:3, 13:55) and a prominent reference to "taking offense" at him (11:6, 13:57).

To trace the flow of Matthew's story in the section 11:2–16:20, Jesus' widespread activity of teaching, preaching, and healing results in the spread of his fame throughout Palestine and even Syria (4:24–25; 9:31, 11:2, 4; 14:1). Still, the spread of his fame and the thronging to him of the crowds do not signify that Israel has "accepted" him. Quite the contrary, Israel repudiates him (11:2–12:50), a circumstance of which Matthew has forewarned the reader (2:13, 3:7–12, 10:24–25). Jesus' response to his repudiation is to declare Israel to be obdurate and to give public demonstration of this by addressing the crowds "in parables," that is, in speech they cannot understand (13:1–35; see Kingsbury 1969). By contrast, he pronounces the disciples "blessed" (13:16–17) and explains to them the mysteries of the kingdom of heaven (13:11, 36–52). Nor does Jesus fare any better in his home town of Nazareth. When the people hear him teach in the synagogue, they take offense at him (13:53–58). Even more ominously, news reaches Jesus that John the Baptist has been beheaded (14:1–12), and this prompts him to embark on a series of journeys that take him to deserted places, back and forth across the sea, and into gentile lands (14:13, 22, 34; 15:21, 29, 33, 39; 16:4–5, 13).

I remarked earlier that people in Israel also react

to Jesus' public ministry in 11:2–16:20 by wondering or speculating about his identity. Thus, John the Baptist, expecting Jesus to execute final judgment (3:7–12), asks by way of the disciples he sends to Jesus, "Are you the Coming One [Messiah], or do we await another?" (11:2–3; Au. trans.). The crowds, having witnessed a healing by Jesus, query one another, though in a manner that anticipates a negative reply, "This man cannot be the Son of David, can he?" (12:23; Au. trans.). The hometown people of Nazareth, hearing Jesus teach in their synagogue, wonder in astonishment even as they take offense at him, "Is not this the carpenter's son?" (13:55; RSV). Herod Antipas, taking notice of the reports about Jesus, speculates, "This is John the Baptist; he has been raised from the dead, and therefore these miraculous powers are at work in him!" (14:2; Au. trans.). And the disciples, having watched Jesus walk on the water, calm the wind, and rescue Peter from drowning, worship Jesus and affirm, "Truly you are the Son of God" (14:33; RSV). In so doing, they in effect give answer to the earlier question they themselves had raised in an equally perilous situation at sea, "What sort of man is this, that even winds and sea obey him?" (8:27; RSV).

All of these conflicting thoughts about Jesus Matthew combines into two contrasting positions, which he juxtaposes in the climactic pericope of the second part of his story, namely, that of the confession of Peter at Caesarea Philippi (16:13–20). To begin with, Jesus asks the disciples who the public imagines him to be, and they reply, "Some say John the Baptist, others say Elijah, and others Jeremiah or one of the prophets" (16:13–14; RSV). In other words, the understanding of Jesus which the public has come to share is that he is a prophet of some stature or another (21:11, 26, 46). This understanding of Jesus, however, is false, on three counts: (1) Jesus cannot be John the Baptist, Elijah, Jeremiah, or one of the prophets because John, who is himself "Elijah," is the forerunner of Jesus (11:10, 14), and the task of Jeremiah and the prophets is to "foretell" of Jesus (2:17, 11:13, 13:17); (2) the answer that Jesus is a prophet evokes no "blessing" from him (16:17); and (3) what is most important, to understand Jesus as a prophet does not square with God's understanding of him (3:17).

In antithesis to his first question, Jesus next asks the disciples who they take him to be, and Peter replies on behalf of all, "You are the Messiah, the Son of the living God!" (16:16; Au. trans.). This answer of course is correct for two of the same reasons the other answer is wrong: (1) it evokes from Jesus a "blessing" (16:17); and (2) it squares with God's understanding of Jesus (3:17, 16:17). Accordingly, Matthew brings the second part of his story, in which he tells of Jesus' ministry to Israel and of Israel's repudiation of Jesus (4:17–16:20), to its culmination by showing that whereas the public in Israel does not receive Jesus and falsely thinks of him as being a prophet, the disciples confess him aright to be the Son of God and so reveal that their understanding of Jesus' identity is in alignment with God's.

Journey to Jerusalem and Passion

Matthew devotes the third part of his story (16:21–28:20) to Jesus' journey to Jerusalem and to his suffering, death, and resurrection. To alert the reader to this, Matthew makes prominent use of three passion-predictions (16:21, 17:22–23, 20:17–19), which are the counterpart to the three summary-passages he employs in the second part of his story (4:23, 9:35, 11:1). Of interest is the way Matthew lends cohesion to this third part. His initial act as narrator is to present the first of the three passion-predictions (16:21), in which he states that Jesus "goes" to Jerusalem. This reference to "going" is no idle comment, for with it Matthew signals the reader that Jesus will continue the travels he has already begun, at first within Galilee (16:21–18:35) and then away from there into the regions of Judaea beyond the Jordan (19:1–20:16) and finally on to Jerusalem (20:17–28:15 [16–20]). Consequently, Jesus' journey to Jerusalem and his presence there and in its environs serve as the "framework" by means of which Matthew binds together the materials that make up the third part of his story, and punctuating this framework are the three passion-predictions that sound the theme of this part.

If Matthew so guides his story that it culminates in its first and second parts in the related announcements by God (3:17) and Peter (16:16) of their understanding of Jesus, he so guides it in its third part that it culminates, first, in the declaration the Roman soldiers make of their understanding of Jesus (27:54) and, second, in the meeting Jesus has with the eleven disciples in Galilee and the commission he gives them (28:16–20). A brief review of Matthew's story will elucidate this.

Following Peter's confession of Jesus near Caesarea Philippi, Matthew has Jesus charge the disciples to tell no one that he is the Messiah Son of God (16:16, 20). Why this prohibition? Because although the disciples know who Jesus is, they are as yet in no position to "make disciples of all nations," for they are ignorant of the central purpose of his mission.

The central purpose of Jesus' mission is his suffering, and this is the first thing he tells the disciples in the section 16:21–28:20. Peter's response to Jesus' word is to reject out of hand the notion that he must suffer (16:22), and Jesus, in turn, reprimands Peter for this (16:23). Still, six days later Jesus leads Peter, James, and John atop a high mountain. There he is suddenly transfigured before them, and from a cloud that overshadows them a voice exclaims, "This is my beloved Son in whom I take delight; hear him!" (17:5; Au. trans.). As at the baptism, this voice is that of God, and within the context of Matthew's story it confirms the validity of Peter's recent confession by showing that it was in fact in alignment with God's understanding of Jesus (16:16, 17:5). Of still greater significance, however, is the circumstance that God does not simply repeat his baptismal proclamation but expands it, through the injunction to "hear him" (17:5). The stress, then, lies on this injunction, and necessarily so, for what the disciples must grasp in 16:21–28:20 is the truth of the very word of Jesus which Peter has repudiated, namely, that about his passion (16:21–23). At what point the disciples will finally grasp this truth the reader learns in the command to silence Jesus gives the disciples: not until after he has been raised from the dead are the three to tell anyone about their experience atop the mountain (17:9).

As Jesus is outside Jericho on his way to Jerusalem, Matthew portrays him as healing, in the presence of a great crowd, two blind men who appeal to him as the "Son of David" to open their eyes (20:29–34). Like the previous two blind men (9:27–31) and the gentile woman (15:22), these "no-accounts" "see" what the Jewish crowds and their leaders cannot: that Jesus is Israel's Davidic Messiah. The understanding of these no-accounts underlines the guilt that Israel incurs because of its "blindness."

The "blindness" of the Jewish crowds and their leaders also manifests itself in the pericopes on Jesus' entry into Jerusalem (21:1–11) and on his cleansing the Temple (21:12–17). As Jesus approaches Jerusalem, the crowds surround him and hail him as the "Son of David" (21:9). But despite this, when the people of Jerusalem ask the crowds who this man entering the city is, they reply, "This is the prophet Jesus, from Nazareth of Galilee" (21:10–11). Just as the disciples had said when questioned by Jesus at Caesarea Philippi, the crowds' understanding of Jesus is that he is merely a prophet (16:13–14). In a related vein, when Jesus cleanses the Temple and the children there acclaim him as the "Son of David," the leaders of the Jews become incensed at this (21:15). Like the crowds, they, too, are blind to Jesus' Davidic Messiahship. Unlike the crowds, however, they will not even countenance the thought that he could be so much as a prophet, for they adjudge him to be in league with Satan (9:34, 12:22–29).

But however valid it may be to look upon Jesus as being the Son of David, of itself this understanding of him proves to be insufficient. This is the point of Matthew's pericope on the question about David's son (22:41–46). In debate with the Pharisees, Jesus confounds them with a problem of antinomy. The question he puts to them is: How is it possible for the Messiah to be both the "son" of David and the "lord" of David when these two views are ostensibly contradictory? Although Jesus leaves the answer to be inferred, the reader of Matthew's story can well supply it: The Messiah is the "son" of David because he stands in the line of David (1:1, 6, 25); at the same time, the Messiah is also the "lord" of David because he is, as God's understanding of him reveals (3:17, 17:5), the Son of God and therefore of higher station and authority than David.

Matthew places Jesus, during his stay in Jerusalem prior to his passion, in the Temple, teaching, debating, and speaking in parables (21:12–23:39). The parables Jesus tells bespeak judgment against Israel because of its repudiation of John the Baptist (21:28–32) and of himself (21:33–46, 22:1–10). They also warn the reader against comporting himself

or herself in a manner which is contrary to the norms that befit life in the sphere of God's rule (22:11–14; also 21:42–44). Of particular interest is the second of these parables, that of the wicked husbandmen (21:33–46).

Jesus addresses this parable to the "chief priests and the elders of the people," that is, to Jewish officialdom associated with the Sanhedrin (21:23, 28, 33). In it Jesus sketches God's dealings with Israel in the history of salvation. He portrays God as the "owner of the vineyard" and himself as "the son" whom the owner calls "my son" and whom the wicked tenant farmers kill (21:37–39). Quoting from the Hebrew Scriptures, Jesus likewise predicts that it is this "son," the "stone" that the "builders" reject, whom God will place "at the head of the corner," that is, vindicate through the miraculous act of the resurrection (21:42).

Noteworthy is the fact that by having the "owner of the vineyard" designate "the son" as "my son," Jesus adopts for himself in this parable that understanding of his person and mission that God had enunciated at both the baptism and the transfiguration (3:17, 17:5). Accordingly, Jesus is making himself out to be the Son of God, even while he is making the Jewish leaders out to be the murderous tenant farmers. Because these identifications are by no means lost on the Jewish leaders and they reject them (21:45), they want to arrest Jesus (21:46). Ironically, however, in wanting to arrest Jesus, which is tantamount to denying the truth-claim of his parable, the Jewish leaders are unwittingly disavowing God's understanding of Jesus. Without doubt they have grasped Jesus' parable intellectually, but they remain blind as to who he is since they will not, and cannot, accept his claim of being the Son of God.

The parable of the wicked husbandmen points ahead to the pericope on Jesus' trial before the Sanhedrin (26:57–68). At his trial Jesus again faces the chief priests and the elders of the Jews (26:57, 59). As the presiding officer of the Sanhedrin, the high priest is privy to the claim to be the Son of God that Jesus had advanced in allegorical form in his parable. When, therefore, the high priest asks Jesus, "Are you the Messiah, the Son of God?" (26:63; Au. trans.), he is at once reformulating Jesus' claim in nonallegorical terms and aiming to turn it against him in order to destroy him. Moreover, from his own standpoint the high priest succeeds, for Jesus' reply is affirmative ("[So] you have said"; 26:64 [Au. trans.]; 27:43). In consequence of Jesus' reply, the Sanhedrin, at the instigation of the high priest, condemns Jesus to death for blasphemy (26:65–66). And therein lies the irony of Jesus' fate. In the case of Jesus, the irony is that although he is made to die for committing blasphemy against God, his "crime" has been to dare to "think" about himself as God has revealed (at Jesus' baptism and transfiguration) that he does in truth "think" about Jesus (3:17, 17:5, 21:37, 26:63–64). In the case of the high priest and the Sanhedrin, the irony is that in condemning Jesus to death for blaspheming God, they are alleging that they know the "thinking" of God; yet even while alleging that they have such knowledge, they are effectively disavowing it.

Bent on having Jesus put to death, the Jewish leaders deliver him to Pilate (27:1–2). At issue in the hearing before Pilate is whether Jesus is the "King of the Jews [Israel]" (27:11, 29, 37, 42). Matthew has Jesus affirm that he is (27:11). In the ears of Pilate, this means that Jesus is an insurrectionist (27:37), a charge that the Jewish leaders support (27:12) but that Pilate discounts completely even though he accedes to it (27:18, 23–24, 26). Wherein the truth of Jesus' affirmation lies is shown by Matthew in the two scenes of Roman and Jewish mockery: Jesus is indeed the King of the Jews (Israel), yet not as an insurrectionist but, ironically, as the one who "saves others" by himself submitting to suffering and death in obedience to God (27:27–31, 42).

Upon the death of Jesus, Matthew tells of the occurrence of supernatural portents (27:51–53), in response to which the Roman soldiers guarding Jesus exclaim, "Truly this man was the Son of God!" (27:54; Au. trans.). As characters who appear on the scene only briefly, it is not for the soldiers to grasp the full import of their words. That is for the reader. In this regard, three things stand out.

First, this acclamation of the Roman soldiers constitutes a vindication of Jesus' claim to be the Son of God (21:37, 26:63–64). In condemning Jesus to death at his trial and in blaspheming and mocking him as he hangs upon the cross, the Sanhedrin in the one instance and the passersby and the Jewish leaders

in the other repudiate Jesus' claim to be the Son of God (26:63–66, 27:39–43). Against the backdrop of this repudiation, the soldiers' acclamation becomes a counterassertion, evoked by God himself through the supernatural portents he causes to occur, that, on the contrary, Jesus "truly" was the "Son of God" (27:51–54).

The second thing that stands out is that the verb in this acclamation is in the past tense ("was," 27:54). In that the Roman soldiers say that Jesus was the Son of God, their acclamation calls attention to the fact that the cross marks the end of Jesus' earthly ministry. The end, however, is at the same time the culmination, for the cross is the place where Jesus "pours out" his blood for the forgiveness of sins (26:28) and thus "saves" his people from their sins (1:21). On the cross, Jesus atones for sins (20:28) and supersedes the Temple and the Jewish cult (27:51) as the "place" of salvation.

Finally, with this acclamation of the Roman soldiers, Matthew brings the entire third part of his story (16:21–28:20) to its initial climax. In attesting Jesus to be the Son of God, the Roman soldiers "think" about Jesus as God "thinks" about him (3:17, 17:5, 16:23), so that their understanding of Jesus can be seen to be in alignment with that of God. Moreover, in contrast, for example, to Peter's confession on behalf of the disciples, no comment of any kind, narrative or otherwise, that can function as a command to silence follows the soldiers' acclamation (but see 16:16, 20; 17:5, 9). The reason is apparent: Whereas Peter and the disciples at Caesarea Philippi correctly understood who Jesus is but were as yet ignorant of his passion, the Roman soldiers acclaim Jesus to be the Son of God at that juncture where he has completed his passion and, in fact, the whole of his earthly ministry. Because Jesus' earthly ministry is now over, the way is, in principle, at last open for the task of "going and making disciples of all nations" (see 20:19). And since the soldiers are themselves gentiles, they attest in this way, too, that the time for embarking upon this universal mission is at hand.

Matthew's concluding pericope (28:16–20) is the major climax not only of the third part of his story (16:21–28:20), but also of his entire story. The Jesus who meets the eleven disciples atop the mountain in Galilee stands forth as the crucified but resurrected Son of God. Thus, he is the resurrected Son of God whose end-time glory God revealed proleptically to Peter, James, and John on the mountain of the transfiguration (17:2, 5). Still, even as the resurrected Son of God, he remains the crucified Son of God ("the one who has been, and remains, the crucified," 28:5; Au. trans.). Indeed, he is the rejected "stone" and "son" whom God has placed "at the head of the corner," that is, raised from the dead and exalted to universal lordship (21:37, 42; 28:18). He is, in fact, Emmanuel, or "God with us," the Son conceived of the Spirit in whom God will abide with the disciples until the consummation of the age (1:20, 23; 28:20).

The disciples, in seeing Jesus Son of God as the resurrected one who nevertheless bears on his person the marks of his crucifixion (28:6–7, 10, 17), see him in new perspective. In the boat at sea and in the regions of Caesarea Philippi, the disciples confessed Jesus to be the Son of God and therefore confessed aright "who he is" (14:33, 16:16), but they did not as yet know of the central purpose of his mission, which was his passion. Atop the mountain of the transfiguration, God confirmed to Peter, James, and John that the disciples' confession of Jesus was indeed valid (i.e., in alignment with his own understanding), but he also enjoined them to "hear" Jesus (17:5), that is, he called upon them to pay heed to the very word of Jesus concerning his passion to which Peter had taken umbrage (16:21–22; see 17:10–13). Here on the mountain in Galilee, it is the crucified, albeit also resurrected, Son of God who appears to the eleven disciples (28:6, 16). Seeing Jesus as such, the disciples now comprehend not only what they had earlier perceived as well, namely, that he is the Son of God, but also the central purpose of his mission, which was his death on the cross and the salvation from sins he thereby accomplished. Still, this insight does not of itself guarantee that a post-Easter disciple is as a matter of course immune to the affliction of doubt or little faith (28:17; see 14:28–33). Nonetheless, equipped with this insight, the disciples are not again commanded by Jesus, as previously, to silence concerning him (16:20, 17:9), but are instead commissioned to go and make of all nations his disciples (28:19). In pursuit of this commission, the disciples move from Easter into the world Jesus described for them in his discourse concerning the last times presented in chapters 24–25.

Response of the Reader

Why does Matthew tell his story about Jesus along these lines? The answer lies in the effect this story is calculated to have upon the reader.

In the first part (1:1–4:16), the reader looks on as Matthew guides events to that point where God enters the story-world as "actor" in order to announce his understanding of Jesus: Jesus is his royal Son, whom he has chosen and empowered for messianic ministry (3:17). In the second part (4:17–16:20), Matthew describes for the reader the ministry of Jesus to Israel and Israel's repudiation of Jesus. Whereas the Jewish leaders think of Jesus as being in league with Satan and do not so much as raise the question of his identity, the Jewish public concludes that he is a prophet (16:14). By contrast, the disciples confess him to be the Son of God (16:16). The confession of the disciples thus constitutes the climax of this part of the story, for they give expression to an understanding of Jesus that is in alignment with that of God.

In the third part of the story (16:21–28:20), the reader follows along as Matthew tells of Jesus' journey to Jerusalem and of his suffering, death, and resurrection. At the moment Jesus dies, God causes a series of supernatural portents to occur, in response to which the Roman soldiers guarding Jesus acclaim him as truly having been the Son of God (27:54). This acclamation marks the initial culmination of this part of the story, for against the background of Israel's abject repudiation of Jesus, gentiles give expression to an understanding of Jesus that is also in alignment with God's.

Still, the ultimate culmination both of this part and of the whole of the story comes in the final scene. Here the disciples see Jesus Son of God as the resurrected one who nonetheless bears on his person the marks of the crucifixion. Although the disciples had earlier correctly confessed Jesus to be the Son of God, insight into the central purpose of his ministry (death on the cross accomplishing salvation from sins) had eluded them. In seeing Jesus Son of God as the crucified and resurrected one, the disciples now comprehend not only who he is, but also what he was (and is) about. In consequence of this, Jesus does not, as previously, command them to silence concerning his identity (16:20, 17:9), but commissions them to go and make of all nations his disciples (28:19).

The reader finds himself or herself at the end of Matthew's story "standing in the shoes" of the disciples. He or she views Jesus and his ministry as they do, that is, in alignment with the "thinking" of God (16:23). The commission Jesus gives the disciples assumes the form of direct address. Hence, as the disciples receive this commission, the reader, too, receives it. Accordingly, one reason Matthew tells his story along the lines he does is to bring the reader's "thinking" about Jesus into alignment with God's "thinking" about him and to invite the reader to become a disciple of Jesus and to regard the commission Jesus addresses to the disciples as also being addressed to him or her: "Go therefore and make disciples of all nations." This accent on discipleship at the end of the story reveals that the Gospel according to Matthew was not originally written to be distributed among "outsiders" but to meet the needs of "insiders." In this document, Matthew tells his story about Jesus as one member of a Christian community who recounts in narrative form and for the benefit of the other members the events they all recognize to be foundational to the faith they confess and live.

SERMON ON THE MOUNT

Within his gospel story, Matthew has embedded five great discourses of Jesus. Together, these discourses constitute the bulk of Jesus' teaching. Teaching, in turn, is one activity Matthew reserves for Jesus alone, which is testimony to its importance. The five discourses are known, respectively, as the Sermon on the Mount (chaps. 5–7), the Missionary Discourse (chap. 10), the Discourse in Parables (chap. 13), the Discourse on the Church (chap. 18), and the Discourse on the Last Times (chaps. 24–25). The most famous of these discourses is doubtless the Sermon on the Mount. An extraordinarily imposing composition, it is, except perhaps for the Ten Commandments, more familiar to more people than any other part of the Christian Bible. The purpose of what follows is to examine the Sermon on the Mount as one section of Matthew's Gospel. To guide this examination, questions such as the following will be explored: What is the structure of the Sermon on the Mount? What is its central theme and message, and how would Matthew have the reader regard it: as an impossible ethic, or as an ethic actually to be lived?

Structure and Message

The structure of the Sermon on the Mount is easily discerned. The narrative frame that encloses it describes Jesus as ascending the mountain to teach (5:1–2) and, after finishing, as descending again (7:28–8:1). Apart from this, the Sermon on the Mount divides itself into five parts: (1) Introduction: On Those Who Practice the Greater Righteousness (5:3–16); (2) On Practicing the Greater Righteousness Toward the Neighbor (5:17–48); (3) On Practicing the Greater Righteousness Before God (6:1–18); (4) On Practicing the Greater Righteousness in Other Areas of Life (6:19–7:12); and (5) Conclusion: Injunctions on Practicing the Greater Righteousness (7:13–27).

As this outline reveals, the theme of the Sermon on the Mount is the "greater righteousness." Perhaps the passage in which this theme finds expression most clearly is the pronouncement Jesus makes at 5:20: "For I tell you, unless *your righteousness exceeds* that of the scribes and Pharisees, you will never enter the kingdom of heaven" (RSV; emphasis added). What is the reader to understand by the "greater righteousness"?

The "greater righteousness" is that style of life intended to be the mark of disciples of Jesus. As noted above, Jesus in Matthew's story is preeminently the Son of God (1:18, 20; 3:16–17). As God's Son, he calls persons to follow him, which is to say that he summons them to enter and to live in the sphere of God's end-time kingdom, or rule. Those who hear Jesus' summons become his disciples (4:18–22, 9:9) and "sons of God" (5:9); they, too, know God as Father (5:45). In fact, they form a new "family" (12:48–50), described as a "brotherhood" of the sons of God and of the disciples of Jesus, which is the "church" (16:18, 23:8, 28:10). The greater righteousness, then, is the quality of life that is indicative of disciples who make up the church. It is behavior that comports itself with living in the sphere of God's kingdom (5:20, 6:33).

But yet more can be said of the greater righteousness. At 5:48, Jesus instructs disciples: "You, therefore, must be perfect, as your heavenly Father is perfect" (RSV). What "being perfect" means here is not, for example, being flawless, but "being wholehearted," as this is set forth in an injunction like Deuteronomy 18:13: "You shall be whole-hearted in your service of the Lord your God" (NEB). Accordingly, to be perfect is to be wholehearted in one's devotion to God, and disciples are wholehearted in Matthean perspective when they do God's will as this is taught by Jesus (7:21). In Jesus' teaching, however, to do God's will is, at its core, to exercise love (22:34–40). Hence, loving as God loves is the essence of the greater righteousness (5:44–45). When disciples love as God loves, this reflects itself further in the fact that they also love the neighbor (7:12). In sum, therefore, it is love toward God and love toward neighbor that constitute the heart of the greater righteousness.

If the greater righteousness is the theme of the Sermon on the Mount, Jesus specifies in the introduction (5:3–16) the types of persons disciples are who practice the greater righteousness. The introduction falls into two sections: the Beatitudes (5:3–12), and Jesus' words on salt and light (5:13–16).

The Beatitudes number nine (5:3–12). In pronouncing them, the Matthean Jesus confers end-time "blessings" upon disciples who are characterized by what they are (e.g., the poor) or do (e.g., the peacemakers). These blessings assure disciples of the vindication and reward that attend the salvation of God's consummated kingdom and thus provide encouragement in time of persecution and difficulty.

To take each beatitude in turn, "the poor in spirit" are disciples who not only are economically deprived but also stand before God with no illusions of self-righteousness or self-sufficiency (5:3). "Those who mourn" are disciples who grieve over sin and evil in the world. "The meek" are disciples who are lowly and powerless, whose only hope is God. "Those who hunger and thirst for righteousness" are disciples who yearn for the final salvation that only God can effect. "The merciful" are disciples who eschew judgment and forgive. "The pure in heart" are disciples who are undivided in their allegiance to God. "The peacemakers" are disciples who work for the wholeness and well-being that God wills for a broken world. "Those who are persecuted for righteousness' sake" are disciples who incur tribulation because they serve God. What Jesus promises all these disciples is fundamentally the same benefit, the end-time salvation that attends God's kingdom (5:3, 10).

Jesus pronounces his beatitudes upon disciples who, together, form the new community of God's end-time people, said above to be the church. In 5:13–16, Jesus affirms that this community both is, and is called to be, the "salt of the earth" and the "light of the world." As it pursues the life of the greater righteousness, this community summons others to glorify God, that is, to live in the sphere of his end-time rule by themselves becoming disciples of Jesus.

If in the introduction of the Sermon on the Mount Jesus focuses on the types of persons disciples are who practice the greater righteousness, in the second, third, and fourth parts he explicates what it is to practice this righteousness. At the head of the second part, which treats of practicing righteousness toward the neighbor (5:17–48), Jesus utters a series of programmatic statements that have to do with his end-time mission, the abiding validity of the Law, and the necessity of doing God's commandments and of leading the life of the greater righteousness (5:17–20). In 5:17, Jesus roundly declares that it is not the purpose of his mission to abolish the Law or the prophets but—by virtue of who he is, God's Son, in whom God's end-time kingdom is a present though hidden reality, and through what he says and does—to fulfill them. In 5:18, he flatly asserts that the Law will never pass away and that all that it requires will be done. In 5:19, he utters "sentences" that pledge to disciples higher and lower degrees of end-time reward so as to warn in the one instance against breaking even the most insignificant of the commandments and to urge in the other the observance of them all. And in 5:20, he similarly enjoins disciples to practice the greater righteousness "now" on pain of otherwise not entering the consummated kingdom of heaven "then." On balance, Jesus Son of God asserts in 5:17–20 that in his coming, whereby God's kingdom has become a present though hidden reality, he accomplishes the fulfillment of the Law, giving it abiding validity, and that to do the Law (or will of God) is to do the greater righteousness, at the heart

142

of which is, one will recall, love toward God and neighbor.

Jesus continues the second part of the Sermon on the Mount by proclaiming the six antitheses (5:21–48). Each "antithesis" overrides in some respect a "thesis" of the Mosaic law. Since the Law as Jesus teaches it has abiding validity, the antithesis intensifies, or radicalizes, the thesis. Introducing each thesis is a formula that may be longer or shorter in length. Always intended, however, is the formula in its entirety, which reads: "You have heard that it was said to the people of old" (5:21, 33; Au. trans.). This formula divides itself into three parts: The first part ("You have heard") reminds disciples of the traditional custom (e.g., in the Jewish synagogue) of hearing the Law read and expounded in services of worship. The second part ("it was said") features the use of the "divine passive" and is a circumlocution for "God said." And the third part ("to the people of old") envisages the Israelites at Sinai who received the Law but includes as well the generations subsequent to them who have likewise received it. In its totality, therefore, the formula introducing each thesis reminds disciples that it has been taught to them that God, at Sinai, delivered to Israel his Law.

In stark contrast to this introductory formula stands the formula with which Jesus introduces each of his antitheses. It reads: "But I say to you . . ." (see, e.g., 5:22). The force of this formula is unparalleled, for Jesus, in uttering it, is in effect pitting his word against the word God spoke at Sinai, that is to say, against the Law as known through Moses. In the last analysis, therefore, the astonishing thing about the antitheses is that in them Jesus Son of God dares to place his word and his authority above those of Moses.

To turn now to the antitheses: Jesus commands, variously, that disciples are not only not to kill, but not even to become enraged (5:21–26); not only not to commit adultery, but not even to lust (5:27–30); not merely to comply with the Law in obtaining a divorce, but not to divorce at all except in the case of the incestuous marriage (5:31–32; cf. Lev 18:6–18); not merely to obey the Law and not swear falsely, but not to swear at all (5:33–37); not merely to adhere to the Law in securing retribution, but to offer no resistance at all to one who would harm or exploit them (5:38–42); and not merely to love the neighbor while hating the enemy, but not to hate the enemy at all but instead to love him (5:43–48).

As Jesus takes up the third part of the Sermon on the Mount (6:1–18), he has arrived at its center. This is true both formally and materially. Formally, the third part constitutes the center because it is preceded by the introduction and the second part and followed by the fourth part and the conclusion. By the same token, the third part itself contains three parts: it treats of almsgiving, prayer, and fasting. What is more, at the center of the middle part, on prayer, is the Lord's Prayer. Formally, therefore, the Lord's Prayer can be seen to lie at the very heart of the Sermon on the Mount.

Materially, too, the third part constitutes the center of the Sermon on the Mount. Thus far, Jesus has delivered the introduction and addressed the topic of practicing the greater righteousness toward the neighbor. Upon completion of this third part, he will speak on practicing the greater righteousness in other areas of life and conclude the Sermon. Here in this part, he concerns himself with the fundamental issue of practicing the greater righteousness before God (6:1–18). In the Lord's Prayer, the centerpiece of the Sermon, Jesus highlights the essential element on which all such practice is predicated: that disciples know God as "Father" (6:9). Through Jesus Son of God, disciples are invited to live in the sphere of God's end-time rule, where they, as sons of God, are rightly related to God and hence know him as Father. Consequently, as Jesus instructs disciples on how they are to give alms, pray, and fast, he is instructing them on how to give expression to their right relationship to God.

To give alms is to perform charitable deeds, to pray is to approach God in petition as Father, and to fast is to show contrition. In contemporary Judaism, as well as for disciples of Jesus, these were the three cardinal acts of piety. As Jesus describes the doing of these acts, he contrasts the practice of such acts "to be seen by men" (6:1) with piety "in secret" (6:4, 6, 18). This contrast is manifestly not one between "public" and "private" per se, as though Jesus were denying legitimacy to all public expression of charitable activity, prayer, and fasting. No, "to be seen by men" expresses intent, and the contrast Jesus draws is between "ostentation" and "proper motivation." The hypocrites who practice their acts of piety ostentatiously do so in order to win public acclaim for themselves. Such acclaim is all the reward they shall receive (6:2, 5, 16). Disciples are to practice their acts of piety "in secret," that is, out of heartfelt devotion to God. Such practice God acquits with the promise of eternal reward at the latter day (6:4, 6, 17–18).

The Lord's Prayer (6:7–15) is recited by Jesus to provide disciples with an example of how they are to pray (6:9a). It divides itself, including the doxology, into four parts. The "address" (6:9b) shows that the prayer is directed to God as Father. The "thou petitions" (6:9c–10) focus on God and the advent of his kingdom as a consummated reality. The "we petitions" (6:11–13) focus on the suppliants and their physical and spiritual needs. The "doxology," a later addition to verse 13, closes the prayer on a strong note of praise.

In the fourth part of the Sermon on the Mount (6:19–7:12), Jesus deals with the practice of the greater righteousness in areas of life he has not already touched on. The prohibitions and imperatives he employs mark the subunits: "Do not store up" (6:19–24); "Do not be anxious" (6:25–34); "Judge not" (7:1–5); "Do not give" (7:6); and "Ask . . . seek . . . knock" (7:7–11). The Golden Rule (7:12) serves as both the conclusion and culmination of this fourth part.

In each of these subunits, a climactic utterance of Jesus occurs that captures the unit's intention. In 6:19–24, Jesus enjoins disciples not to store up for themselves treasures on earth, for "no one can serve two masters . . . . You cannot serve God and mammon" (6:24; RSV). In 6:25–34, Jesus commands disciples not to be anxious about food, drink, or clothing but to "seek first [God's] kingdom and his righteousness, and all these things shall be yours as well" (6:33; RSV). In 7:1–5, Jesus forbids disciples to judge others, on pain that "with the judgment you pronounce you will be judged" (7:2; RSV). In 7:6, Jesus warns disciples against giving what they hold to be sacred and precious to persons who are undeserving, lest they, like swine, "trample [what is precious] underfoot and turn to attack you" (RSV). In 7:7–11, Jesus suddenly shifts from the negative to the positive and exhorts disciples to constant and fervent prayer ("Ask . . . seek . . . knock"), for they can rest as-

sured that "your Father who is in heaven [will] give good things to those who ask him" (7:11; RSV). And with the Golden Rule, Jesus ends this part of the Sermon on the Mount by reminding disciples of what he has stressed earlier as well: Doing the greater righteousness is always, finally, an exercise in love (7:12).

In the fifth part of the Sermon on the Mount (7:13–27), Jesus concludes his teaching. The point he drives home to disciples is unmistakable: It is not only the hearing of his words but also the doing of them that counts. Disciples who both hear and do are like the "wise man who built his house upon the rock" (7:24; RSV). They, unlike the false prophets (who will prove themselves to have been workers of lawlessness), will at the latter day "enter the kingdom of heaven," for they shall have done "the will of my Father who is in heaven" (7:15–16, 20–23; RSV).

This survey of the five parts of Jesus' Sermon on the Mount still leaves one question unanswered. How would Matthew have disciples regard the Sermon on the Mount: as an impossible ethic, or as an ethic actually to be lived?

A Radical Ethic

Matthew holds up Jesus' teaching in the Sermon on the Mount as an ethic disciples are to live. Disciples have been called by Jesus to enter the sphere of God's end-time kingdom, the sphere in which God rules as Father. The ethic of the Sermon on the Mount describes life in this sphere. Disciples of Jesus are summoned to lead this life, which is to say that they are summoned to lead the life of the greater righteousness. They are to love God with heart, soul, and mind, and to love the neighbor as the self.

Does this mean, then, that Matthew is, in his understanding of human nature, completely unrealistic? Not as Matthew sees it. His Gospel shows that he is fully aware of the reality of sin and of little faith. In the Lord's Prayer, disciples are invited to pray:

And forgive us our debts,
  As we also have forgiven our debtors;
And lead us not into temptation,
  But deliver us from the evil one.
        (6:12–13; RSV)

Matthew is aware that disciples experience failure as they lead the life of the greater righteousness and that they are continually in need of forgiveness from both God and neighbor.

The thing to observe, however, is that what Matthew does not do is make the reality of sin and of little faith the determining factor in his ethic. Instead, the determining factor for him is the reality of God's end-time kingdom, or rule, which is present even now in the earthly and risen Jesus Son of God. For disciples who live in the sphere where God rules through the risen Jesus, doing the greater righteousness is the normal order of things. Until the consummation, disciples will, to be sure, have to contend with the shadows that invade this normal order, with sin and little faith. But this notwithstanding, they are indeed summoned to be the kind of person Jesus describes in the Sermon on the Mount, the kind of person who loves God perfectly and loves the neighbor as the self.

Summoned as disciples are to lead the life of the greater righteousness yet being unable to realize this summons, are they therefore left without example? Again, not as Matthew sees it. Disciples are also bidden to pray:

> Our Father who art in heaven,
> Hallowed be thy name. Thy kingdom come.
> Thy will be done,
> On earth as it is in heaven.
>
> (6:9–10, RSV)

The only human being in Matthew's Gospel who is whole in his relationship to the Father, in whom God's kingdom is a present reality, and who does God's will perfectly is of course Jesus Son of God. He it is who stands before disciples as the one who realizes in his life the ethic of the greater righteousness. Accordingly, bound to him in trust and assured of his forgiveness, disciples "follow after him" as they hear his call and lead the life of the greater righteousness.

Bibliography

Bauer, David R. *The Structure of Matthew's Gospel*. Sheffield, England, 1988. Reviews current hypotheses on the structure of Matthew's Gospel and analyzes this structure afresh by drawing on recognizable and definable principles of rhetorical criticism.

Betz, Hans Dieter. *Essays on the Sermon on the Mount.* Translations by L. L. Welborn. Philadelphia, 1985. Reconstructs the Sermon on the Mount as a pre-Matthean source dating from around 50 and sees it as an epitome of the theology of Jesus written from the perspective of early Jewish Christianity.

Bornkamm, Günther, Gerhard Barth, and Heinz Joachim Held. *Tradition and Interpretation in Matthew.* Translated by Percy Scott. Philadelphia, 1963. A collection of three studies: The first stresses that the orientation of the church in Matthean perspective is toward the future coming of Jesus as the judge of all; the second deals with Matthew's understanding of the Mosaic law; and the third discusses how Matthew interprets the miracle stories of Jesus.

Brown, Raymond E. *The Birth of the Messiah.* Garden City, N.Y., 1977. A commentary on the infancy narratives of Matthew and Luke that also probes the role these narratives played in the early Christian understanding of Jesus and contends that each one constitutes the essential gospel story in miniature.

Burnett, Fred W. *The Testament of Jesus-Sophia.* Washington, D.C., 1979. Argues that the "apocalyptic discourse" of Matthew (24:3–31) functions within the Gospel as a farewell speech that Jesus delivers in his capacity as Wisdom and as the (soon to be exalted) Son of man.

Cope, O. Lamar. *Matthew: A Scribe Trained for the Kingdom of Heaven.* Washington, D.C., 1976. Attempts to determine by a minute literary analysis of selected passages how Matthew has arranged and edited his Gospel.

Davies, W. D. *The Setting of the Sermon on the Mount.* Cambridge, 1964. Considers first-century influences, within both Judaism and the church, that led to the compilation and presentation of the moral teaching that is commonly known as the Sermon on the Mount.

Dobschütz, Ernst von. "Matthäus als Rabbi und Katechet," *Zeitschrift für die neutestamentliche Wissenschaft* 27 (1928). Contends that the evangelist Matthew was a converted Jewish rabbi who, in composing his Gospel, made obvious use of the considerable catechetical skill he had acquired.

Garland, David E. *The Intention of Matthew 23.* Leiden, 1979. Proposes to uncover the intention Matthew pursued in writing chapter 23 by attending to the compositional makeup of the chapter and its place within the structure of the Gospel.

Gerhardsson, Birger. *The Mighty Acts of Jesus According to Matthew.* Lund, Sweden, 1979. Interprets the miracles, or "mighty acts," that Matthew depicts Jesus, or his followers, as performing in his Gospel.

Goulder, M. D. *Midrash and Lection in Matthew.* London, 1974. Maintains that Matthew's Gospel is an adaptation and expansion of Mark's Gospel by means of *midrash* and was written to be read in the setting of Christian worship.

Guelich, Robert A. *The Sermon on the Mount*. Waco, Tex., 1982. A commentary on the Sermon on the Mount that views God's personal covenant through Jesus as a vantage point from which to understand the Sermon within the context of Matthew's Gospel as a whole.

Gundry, Robert Horton. *The Use of the Old Testament in St. Matthew's Gospel*. Leiden, 1967. Investigates the Old Testament quotations in Matthew's Gospel with special reference to the theme of the fulfillment of messianic prophecy.

Hare, Douglas R. A. *The Theme of Jewish Persecution of Christians in the Gospel According to St. Matthew*. Cambridge, 1967. Discusses the theme of Jewish persecution of Christians at the time of Matthew and aims both to show how such persecution has influenced the theology of Matthew and to argue that it was directed primarily against Christian missionaries.

Hill, David. *The Gospel of Matthew*. London, 1972. A concise commentary on Matthew's Gospel from the perspective of an evangelical scholar.

Johnson, Marshall D. *The Purpose of the Biblical Genealogies*. Cambridge, 1969. Analyzes the genealogies of Matthew and Luke and understands them to be a form of literary expression that is used to articulate the conviction that Jesus is the fulfillment of the hope of Israel.

Kingsbury, Jack Dean. *The Parables of Jesus in Matthew 13*. Richmond, Va., 1969. Investigates the eight parables that make up Jesus' Discourse in Parables so as to ascertain the role this discourse plays within Matthew's Gospel and what it reveals both of Matthew's theology and of the situation of his church.

———. *Matthew: Structure, Christology, Kingdom*. Philadelphia, 1975. Examines the structure of Matthew's Gospel and his view of the history of salvation, the titles of majesty that together constitute Matthew's portrait of Jesus, and his concept of the kingdom of heaven, in the interest of explicating the theology Matthew espouses.

———. "The Figure of Peter in Matthew's Gospel as a Theological Problem." *Journal of Biblical Literature* 98 (1979): 67–83. Examines Matthew's portrait of Peter and the role Peter plays within the circle of the twelve disciples.

———. *Matthew as Story*. 2d ed. Philadelphia, 1988. Treats the gospel story of Matthew by explaining literary-critical method, describing the major characters, and tracing the development of the story in terms of both Jesus' conflict with his Jewish opponents and his interaction with the disciples.

Luz, Ulrich. *Das Evangelium nach Matthäus*. Zürich, 1985–. A detailed commentary on Matthew's Gospel, with two volumes still in preparation.

Meier, John P. *The Vision of Matthew*. New York, 1979. A study of Matthew's Gospel in three parts: Part I introduces the reader to Matthew and his situation; Part II argues that the special characteristic of the Gospel is the nexus between Christ and church; and Part III examines the relation of Christ to the Law in Matthew 5:17–20.

———. *Matthew*. Wilmington, Del., 1980. A concise commentary on Matthew's Gospel from the perspective of a Roman Catholic scholar.

Mohrlang, Roger. *Matthew and Paul: A Comparison of Ethical Perspectives*. New York, 1984. Compares the basic structures of Matthew's and Paul's ethics, concluding that while the elements of law and grace are found in both, Matthew's emphasis is on an ethical system based on law and submission to authority.

Moule, C. F. D. *The Birth of the New Testament*. London, 1962. Deals with the subject of New Testament introduction by focusing attention not on the New Testament documents themselves, but on the life of the early church as reflected in them.

Schweizer, Eduard. *The Good News According to Matthew*. Translated by David E. Green. Atlanta, 1975. A commentary on Matthew's Gospel from the perspective of a Protestant scholar.

Senior, Donald. *The Passion of Jesus in the Gospel of Matthew*. Wilmington, Del., 1985. Focuses on the theological perspective Matthew has adopted in reinterpreting Mark's passion story and presenting Jesus' death and resurrection as the climax of his mission.

Shuler, Philip L. *A Genre for the Gospels: The Biographical Character of Matthew*. Philadelphia, 1982. Advances the thesis that Matthew's Gospel belongs to the genre of ancient literature called encomium or laudatory biography.

Stanton, Graham, ed. *The Interpretation of Matthew*. Translated by Robert Morgan et al. Philadelphia, 1983. A collection of eight articles on Matthew's Gospel, introduced by the editor.

Stendahl, Krister. *The School of St. Matthew and Its Use of the Old Testament*. Lund, Sweden, 1954; Philadelphia, 1968. Discusses the Old Testament quotations in Matthew's Gospel and compares certain of the Gospel's literary features with the Habakkuk Commentary from Qumran with a view to advancing the thesis that Matthew's Gospel was used as a manual for teaching and administration within the church.

Strecker, Georg. *Der Weg der Gerechtigkeit*. Göttingen, 1962. Understands Matthew as presenting the "time of Jesus" as the midpoint of salvation history in which Jesus proclaims and practices the "way of righteousness" and thus stands forth as a "model" to be emulated by the Christians of Matthew's church.

Suggs, M. Jack. *Wisdom, Christology, and Law in Matthew's Gospel*. Cambridge, Mass., 1970. Investigates the figure of Wisdom in Matthew's Gospel and aims to show that Wisdom constitutes a fundamental part of Matthew's theology and that Matthew has identified Wisdom with Christ.

Thompson, William G. *Matthew's Advice to a Divided Community: Mt. 17.22–18.35.* Rome, 1970. Analyzes the structure and theology of the Discourse on the Church and pays special attention to the many literary techniques Matthew has employed in composing this section.

Tilborg, Sjef Van. *The Jewish Leaders in Matthew.* Leiden, 1972. Studies the texts in Matthew's Gospel dealing with the Jewish leaders as an index of Matthew's relation to contemporary Judaism and concludes that Matthew regards all the Jewish leaders equally as the representatives of the one Israel his church must face.

Waetjen, Herman C. *The Origin and Destiny of Humanness.* Corte Madera, Calif., 1976. Construes Matthew's Gospel as a "Book of Origin" written for the purpose of conveying to upper-class Christian Jews at home in Syrian Antioch the self-understanding that they constitute the community of Jesus, the new Human Being, who has inaugurated the new humankind.

JACK DEAN KINGSBURY

Mark

MARK'S STORY OF JESUS

Prologue (1:1)

THE UNNAMED WRITER begins his Gospel with a brief introductory statement in which he tells his readers how the events that he describes as "good news" (i.e., "gospel") were launched and through whom God launched this work: Jesus Christ, whom the author then identifies as God's son (1:1). Through his account of Jesus' words and actions, the author shows what God has begun to do through Jesus, and what Jesus' role is in the purpose of God.

Launching the Good News of God's New Work (1:2–3:35)

John the Baptist is the human instrument through whom Jesus is sent forth on God's mission. The continuity with what God has done in the past is implied by the quotations from the prophets that describe John's task to prepare the way for Jesus (1:2–8). Like God's agents of old, Jesus is divinely commissioned (1:9–11) and tested (1:12–13) before his work of preparing for the inbreaking of God's rule begins (1:14–15). After calling his co-workers (1:16–20), he launches his mission, which includes both the overcoming of the evil powers that warp human lives (1:21–34) and the challenge to the religious requirements that Jewish law claimed to be binding on God's

people (1:40–3:12). As a consequence of these activities and claims, Jesus rouses the hostility of the religious leaders and evokes misunderstanding from his own family (3:19–35).

God's Rule in Word and Act (4:1–5:43)

Jesus' claim that God's rule has begun to manifest itself in the present begins with a series of parables, in which the evidence of new, developing life in such familiar phenomena as sprouting, growing seeds and plants are compared to the vital work of God in the world (4:1–32). Yet only the followers of Jesus understand what is happening (4:33–34). Similarly, his extraordinary powers in calming a storm on the lake (4:35–41), in expelling demons from a wretched man living in a tomb (5:1–20), and in performing cures (5:21–43) evoke amazement and puzzlement rather than understanding as to the source of Jesus' authority.

Jesus Confronts Mounting Opposition (6:1–8:26)

Even though they know of his "mighty works," the people of his hometown reject him (6:1–6). This comes to the attention of Herod Antipas, the local puppet ruler, who, as Mark reports (6:14–29), had executed John the Baptist. The miracles continue, including the feeding of the five thousand and Jesus' walking on the water, as well as extensive healing activity in the vicinity of the Sea of Galilee (6:30–56). Jesus' basic challenge to the Pharisees on the issue of ritual separation as a primary factor in the identity of God's people is presented by Mark as a watershed in his narrative (7:1–23). From this point on, Jesus turns to the needs of non-Jews, in healing (7:24–37) and feeding (8:1–10) those who are outside of Judaism. Meanwhile, the Pharisees demand that Jesus display some form of divine approval (8:11–13), which he refuses to do, responding instead with a warning against their influence (8:14–21). By way of contrast with their lack of perception, there follows a story of a blind man who is enabled to see (8:22–26).

Suffering, Death, and Deliverance for Jesus (8:27–9:50)

Once the opposition to Jesus is clearly identified, he begins to tell his followers that his suffering and death are a part of the divine purpose to be accomplished through him. His disciples, who think of messiahship in terms of power and triumph, cannot accept this, although they are told three times (8:27–33, 9:30–32, 10:32–34). Each time they respond with a bid for power and must be warned of the cost of following Jesus (8:34–9:1, 9:33–37, 10:35–45). Meanwhile, Jesus is granted divine confirmation of his special place in God's purpose through a transforming vision that his followers share in but do not understand (9:2–8). He links this experience with the prophetic promise of the coming of Elijah before the final achievement of God's purpose in the creation (9:9–13). Once more a symbolic healing occurs, in which a helpless child is brought to a life of wholeness (9:14–29). The disciples are further warned about those who will use the name of Jesus as a tool (9:38–41), and about the presence of God among them (symbolized by salt) in conflict and in peace (9:49–50).

Confronting Issues Between Jesus and Judaism (10:1–13:37)

Leaving Galilee for Judaea and Jerusalem (10:1), Jesus is depicted by Mark as engaging in a series of debates and confrontations with Jewish authorities over issues central to their understanding of covenantal identity and purity. The first of these is divorce and remarriage (10:2–12). Others deal with the place of little children in God's purpose (10:13–16), with wealth as a factor in one's relationship to God (10:17–31), with the proper response to foreign political domination (12:13–17), and with the relationship to the Davidic royal line of one who claims to be God's agent in behalf of his people (12:35–37). More explicitly religious issues include belief in the resurrection (12:18–27) and priority among the commandments (12:28–34). Direct challenge to Jewish assumptions is offered in the story of Jesus entering Jerusalem as a king in humility rather than in triumph (11:1–10), in his unauthorized actions in the Temple (11:11, 15–19), in the prediction of its destruction (13:1–4), which is followed by a transformed version of the prophet Daniel's vision of the giving of the kingdom to the Son of Man (13:5–37), and by the denunciation of the Pharisees (12:38–40). Most controversial are the portrayals of the cursing of historic Israel under the traditional images of the fig tree (11:12–14, 20–25) and the vineyard of Isaiah 5 (Mark 12:1–12). Once more Mark includes in this section a symbolic story of a blind man who is enabled to see (10:46–52), in contrast to the unseeing religious leaders.

The Coalition to Destroy Jesus (14:1–15:47)

The plot to seize Jesus has been indicated earlier (as in 12:12), but it is now given in detail (14:1–2). Following the symbolic action of his being anointed for death (14:3–9), the roles of Jesus' betrayer (14:10–11, 17–21) and his denier (14:26–31) are foretold. The significance of Jesus' death as the basis of the new covenant is given in the bread and wine of the last meal (14:12–25). Jesus' own preparation for suffering and death are depicted in the Gethsemane scene (14:32–42), followed by the arrest (14:43–52) and hearings before the religious (14:53–72) and the political authorities (15:1–5). This results in his arbitrary condemnation on the grounds of political aspirations to be king of Israel (15:6–15), for which he is derided by the soldiers (15:16–20) and executed (15:22–41). The effects of his death are noted: on the Temple (15:38), on a pagan observer (15:39), and on the core of faithful women followers (15:40–41). The burial is accomplished by Joseph of Arimathea and noted by the women (15:42–47).

Epilogue (16:1–8)

The tomb is found empty of Jesus' body, and the promise is recalled that his followers will see him again in Galilee. The Gospel ends on a note of mingled awe and expectancy. Later on, endings were attached to Mark that describe appearances of Jesus, but the oldest and best manuscripts of Mark end at 16:8, with a characteristically apocalyptic attitude of waiting for God to fulfill his promise.

THE ORIGINS

According to an old tradition, reported by the fourth-century church historian Eusebius of Caesarea, someone named Mark had been an interpreter of Peter and had written down from memory what he had heard Peter tell of the words and acts of Jesus. The person whom Eusebius is quoting here, Papias, probably wrote down this report in the early part of the second century. This claim was, of course, linked by those who read Papias with the mention of Mark in Acts 12:12 (where his mother is said to have provided the place of prayer for the young church) and especially with 1 Peter 5:13, where the author refers to Mark as his son. Early medieval manuscripts of Mark's Gospel picture him copying down the Gospel while Peter is dictating to him, as other ancient illustrations portray each of the other evangelists dictating his Gospel to a younger aide. Clearly these traditions are part of the concern of the church from the second century onward to guarantee the reliability of the accounts of Jesus' life and teachings by linking them with one of the apostles.

Careful analysis of the original Greek text of Mark (as well as the other Gospels) shows, however, that the origins of the Gospels are more complex. The canonical texts almost certainly developed to their current form in stages, moving from an oral to the present written form over a period of some decades. Further, there can be no question but that Mark was written originally in Greek. Thus it is not likely that Peter would have dictated or even have reported the Jesus traditions to Mark in that language. There is evidence that groups of sayings of Jesus and collections of stories about him circulated in the early church, first in oral and then probably in written form, be-fore the first complete Gospel—Mark—was written down. Although we have no certain knowledge about the author of this Gospel, for convenience I shall refer to him by the traditional name, Mark.

The first question to be asked is: Why did Mark write the brief work we know as a Gospel? It does not seem likely that in the manner of a modern reporter someone simply wrote down the full story as a "gospel" (which comes from the Greek word *euangellion,* and means "good news") for purposes of general public information. Some scholars have suggested that the first consecutive account of Jesus was limited to his arrest, trial, and death in order to explain more fully what was involved in Jesus' atoning death, and that "Mark" subsequently wrote an extended introduction to the story of Jesus' passion. But as we shall see, there is a weaving together of a pattern of sayings and narratives into a developed structure that takes in the whole of Jesus' public activity, even though it is true that the trial and death scenes are the most detailed features.

Others have suggested that Mark was attempting to write a biography of Jesus, comparable to those of Socrates or the Roman emperors. But the biographical style of the first and second centuries always included an account of the birth, the family background, and the chain of circumstances connected with upbringing or assumption of authority that brought the hero to the position of power or renown in which he eventually appears. Some of that kind of material is present in Luke and Matthew, but none in Mark. There we read nothing of Jesus' birth or education, and his move into his mission of word and work in preparation for the coming of God's rule (or "kingdom") is based on the purely private disclosure by the voice from heaven (Mark 1:10–11).

The most appropriate model for Mark's literary undertaking is what is called by anthropologists a "foundation document." This term refers to a writing that describes how a social or religious movement began. It depicts the circumstances of the founder of the group, including what he was critical of in his time or culture, and how he went about offering a new approach to God and the world, or an escape into some other realm of existence. For Judaism of the first century we have two documents that fit this description, both of them found among the Dead Sea Scrolls:

the Damascus Document and the Scroll of the Rule (sometimes known as the Manual of Discipline). Both these writings include reports of the disillusionment of the man known as the Teacher of Righteousness with the religious establishment of his time, and how he urged his followers to withdraw from the corrupted circumstances of Jerusalem and its Temple in order to become pure in the desert community that he founded in the hills overlooking the Dead Sea. Strict rules were laid down about how that purity was to be gained and maintained, and clear promises were given about how God would soon intervene in behalf of this faithful remnant of Israel. God would defeat their enemies and establish them as the true and faithful guides of restored Israel in a new age that was soon to come.

As we shall see, many comparable features are to be found in Mark, although the specifics with which the community of the faithful is defined by the author of this Gospel stand in the sharpest contrast to that of the Dead Sea community, which was rigidly exclusive in its attitude toward gentiles or toward other Jews who did not obey the Law as their Teacher interpreted it. Jesus, on the other hand, included among his followers persons who on ritual, social, ethnic, or political grounds would have been excluded from fellowship by both Pharisees and members of the Dead Sea community: the blind, lepers, tax collectors, and gentiles. In the analysis of Mark that follows we shall see how important just these kinds of people are for the covenant community as Jesus defines it.

Before turning to some further considerations of the way Mark wrote his Gospel and why he wrote it, we must ask the question whether Mark, which is the briefest of the Gospels, was copied from one of the others. On the basis of length alone, one might come to the conclusion that Mark was an abridged edition of Matthew. But careful comparison of the three Gospels that so closely resemble each other in content and style—Matthew, Mark, and Luke—shows that Mark is the common source for the other two Gospels. Matthew and Luke are completely independent of each other in those sections of their Gospels which are not found in Mark, as is evident in their wholly different accounts of Jesus' birth and of the appearances following the resurrection. Yet where they have the Marcan account as their source—from the report of

John's baptism to the burial of Jesus in the tomb— they follow Mark closely on the whole, although one or the other will vary at times in the interests of his own basic aims or structure. Where Matthew and Luke agree with each other but differ from Mark in detail, the most plausible explanation is that either they have modified Mark for their own special purposes, or they are drawing on a common source not used by Mark. This hypothetical source, which is designated by scholars as Q (from *Quelle,* the German word for "source"), consists almost wholly of sayings rather than narrative, and so its material is more easily shifted in position than is the case with narrative. Mark, therefore, is not only the oldest existing Gospel but also the basic source used by Matthew and Luke.

LITERARY STYLE

Mark is written in simple style, mostly in simple sentences. Much of its narrative proceeds in childlike fashion: "And he did this; and he did this." There is nothing comparable in Mark to the formal literary introductions that Luke has placed at the beginning of his Gospel and Acts. Nor is there any attempt to organize the material in blocks, with special phrases to mark the transitions, as in Matthew's five times repeated, "When Jesus had finished . . ." (Matt 7:28, 11:1, 13:53, 19:1, 26:1), which gives to the central section of his Gospel a fivefold structure like that of the Mosaic law (Genesis to Deuteronomy). In his Gospel, Luke makes an important point of the movement of Jesus back and forth between Jerusalem and Galilee, since for Luke Jerusalem is the central place where God began and will continue his work with his covenant people (note, e.g., Luke 2:41, 9:53, 21:24, 24:47, Acts 1:8). But for Mark, the story simply begins in the Jordan Valley, shifts to Galilee, moving through the cities of the Decapolis to the east of Galilee, and ends in Jerusalem, where Jesus confronts the political and religious leaders. The closest to a recurrent theme in Mark is the threefold prediction of Jesus' death and resurrection (8:31, 9:31, 10:33), which I shall consider below. In contrast to Luke and Matthew, where Jesus is depicted as uttering extended speeches, in Mark the prediction of the destruction of the Temple and the related events is the only chapter-length report of Jesus' public statements.

The result is that in detail and in overall structure, Mark is simple and direct in literary style. Some scholars have suggested that it was intended to be conveyed orally to hearers rather than read as a literary document. The writer's use of the present tense and the uncomplicated nature of his sentences make it an effective medium of oral communication, which is the way most of the members of the Christian group for whom Mark was written would have come to know its contents. Presumably it would be read in whole or in part to the members of the community and thereby would have served its intended function as a foundation document, telling the group of its origins through the ministry of Jesus and explaining what its hopes and responsibilities are—all this in vivid, simple language.

Although there is evidence in Mark of the Semitic background of Jesus and his followers, it is clear that the Gospel was written in Greek. A few phrases from Aramaic (the language akin to Hebrew that was dominant in Palestine and Syria in the four or five centuries before and after the birth of Jesus) appear in the Gospels. An example is *ephphatha*, in Mark 7:34, where it is immediately translated, "Be opened." Although the transliterated Semitic term *amēn* (meaning "surely") appears frequently in Mark (fourteen times), it is found thirty-two times in Matthew, which is an expansion of Greek sources, as I have noted. It is evident, therefore, that the Christian communities for which the Gospels—including Mark —were written used Greek as their mode of communication. But they seem to have liked to recall the native language of Jesus by repeating an occasional term in Aramaic, which had to be transliterated into Greek if the readers or hearers of the Gospel were to understand it.

This conclusion about Greek as the original language of the Gospel of Mark is confirmed when one looks closely at the many quotations from and allusions to Scripture. Rather than being direct translations from the Hebrew original, Mark's biblical references are to the ancient Greek translation of the Bible. Most of them match closely the Greek version known as the Septuagint, which in its original form was probably made in the second century B.C.E. Since by the third century B.C.E. most Jews lived outside of Palestine, and since Greek had become the dominant language of the eastern Mediterranean world and the Middle East, it was essential and inevitable that Jews would come to know and to communicate in Greek. For Mark to be written in Greek was a guarantee of the work's potential to convey the story of Jesus to both Jews and gentiles living in the wider Roman world.

Certain patterns are evident in the narrative components that Mark has woven into his Gospel. Some of the healing stories, for example, are extremely brief, concentrating on the characters involved, the problem, and the solution. Examples of the compact story type include the expulsion of the unclean spirit (1:23–26) and the cure of Peter's mother-in-law (1:29–31). Other stories include considerable detail, as in the cure of the demoniac in the cave near Gerasa (5:1–20) or the combined accounts of the healing of Jairus' daughter and the hemorrhaging woman (5:21–43), or the healing of the epileptic boy (9:14–29).

Some of the narratives included in Mark reach their climax in a saying of Jesus. Two examples of this type occur in Mark 2: (1) the call of Levi the tax collector to be a follower of Jesus, which concludes with the saying that it is those who are sick who need the physician (2:17); (2) Jesus' defense of allowing his disciples to pick grain on the Sabbath, which ends with, "The Son of man is lord even of the Sabbath" (2:28; RSV). Scholars have come to classify this type of narrative as a pronouncement by Jesus of his authority or his reinterpretation of the will of God for his people.

Other stories are notable for the symbolic significance that is given along with the narrative detail itself. These elements are common in the narratives of the Gospel of John, where an explanation by Jesus often follows the story itself, but are already apparent in Mark's story of the feeding of the five thousand (6:30–44). There the location of the incident in a desert place, with a hungry throng to whom the agent of God provides miraculous food, recalls the story of Moses and the bread from heaven in Exodus 16. John makes the link explicit (John 6:25–51), but Mark's version is content to suggest the connections with the experience of God's covenant people. In the details of Mark 6:41, however, the crucial words, "he took, he blessed, he broke, he gave," recall the traditional terms of the Christian Eucharist, which is the celebration of God's new covenant with his new people, as we shall see in 14:22–25. Elsewhere Mark is content to report the activities of Jesus in compressed form, as in the summary of 6:53–56 of Jesus' power of healing and the growing response of the populace.

Unlike the Q tradition, in which the sayings of Jesus seem to have circulated in a loosely collected form, the Marcan method is to include the sayings in narrative contexts. Thus, for example, Jesus' teaching about divorce is set in a narrative about some Pharisees who call on him to raise the issue of the circumstances under which divorce and remarriage are permissible in keeping with Mosaic law (10:2–12). His teaching about wealth is given in response to an inquiry from a rich man (10:17–27), which in turn provides the occasion for Jesus to tell his followers that their break with home and family as a result of their becoming his disciples will be amply rewarded in the age to come (10:28–31). Even the longest discourse section in Mark (13:5–37) is presented by Mark as a response from Jesus to remarks of his disciples about the splendor of the Temple in Jerusalem.

More important than the specific setting in which Mark has placed the report of Jesus' teaching about the end of the present age are the form and content of this discourse, which takes up the whole of Mark 13. From the literary standpoint, it is an example of an apocalyptic pronouncement. An "apocalypse" (which comes from a Greek word meaning "revelation") is a special type of prophecy that began to appear in the later stages of the Jewish prophetic writings. It differs from the more classical prophecy in that the apocalyptic seer makes a radical distinction between the good God of Israel and the evil powers that have seized control of God's creation. Also different from prophecy is the prediction of a break between the present age, which is characterized by conflict and the dominance of evil over God's people, and the near future, in which God's purpose will triumph and his faithful will be rewarded. In Mark, Jesus is linked with the prophets (6:4, 15; 8:28), but it is the apocalyptic outlook that is dominant.

The earliest and perhaps the best example of an apocalyptic writing is the Book of Daniel. In Jewish literature of the period following the reestablishment in 164–163 B.C.E. of the Jewish monarchy under Judah of the Hasmonean family (also known by his nickname, "Maccabee," or "hammer"), there is evidence of growing disillusionment with the Hasmonean rulers. They had become as repressive and secular in their values as the Hellenistic kings whom they had replaced. Although Daniel describes the conflict between the pagan ruler and God's people as though it were taking place while Israel was still in Babylon, the symbolic meaning of the stories of the struggles of the faithful and of Daniel's visions refers to the experience of the Jews who had returned to Palestine and were living under the Hellenistic rulers (specifically, Antiochus IV Epiphanes around 168) when the Maccabees revolted and established the independent Jewish state. The pagan empires that had dominated this part of the world in preceding centuries are depicted as horrendous beasts—all of whom are slain by divine action. At the end of the age, however, the rule over creation is given by God to one who resembles a human being—or as Daniel phrases it, "one like a son of man" (Dan 7:13–14)—and who is then identified as a figure of the true and faithful people of God. These are then said to be "the people of the saints of the Most High" (Dan 7:27; RSV). Unlike most of the oracles of the prophets, the revelations in the apocalyptic tradition are reserved for the members of an inner group, to whom divine wisdom has been granted.

I will show in my analysis of Mark how radically different from Daniel's definition of the people of God is the definition attributed to Jesus in Mark's Gospel. But what is shared by Mark and Daniel is a set of convictions and expectations: that knowledge of God's purpose for the world, and especially for his people, has been revealed to them through visions and insights of his chosen agent; that the faithful must be willing to accept suffering or even death in the face of fierce opposition from the religious and political powers that are presently in control; that beyond the present time of testing and martyrdom lies a new age, in which God's purpose in and for the creation will be achieved and in which his people will be fully and eternally vindicated. The link between Daniel and Mark is explicit, however. Both writings include predictions of the desecration of the Temple, and do so using the term usually translated as "abomination of desolation" or "desolating sacrilege" (*cf.* Dan 9:27,

12:11 with Mark 13:14). The historical reference for Mark may be the (unfulfilled) proposal of the Roman emperor Caligula (ruled 37–41 C.E.) to have a statue of himself erected in the Jerusalem Temple. But the possibility of this idolatrous pollution of the house of Israel's God was a continuing threat to the integrity of the nation's special relationship with God. In contrast to Daniel, Jesus is reported by Mark as announcing only the destruction of the Temple, not its restoration (Mark 13:2). In both writings, however, the term that is used to designate the one(s) through whom God's rule is finally and forever established is "son of man" (Mark 13:26–27).

Thus the apocalyptic perspective is important for Mark, not only in terms of the discourse about the destruction of the Temple and the fulfillment of God's purpose for his people, but also with respect to the basic apocalyptic view of history and of God's way of accomplishing his purpose in the world through his chosen agent and in behalf of his chosen people. In both form and substance, this literary and conceptual aspect of Judaism underlies the Gospel of Mark, even though Mark pictures Jesus as radically altering that perspective as it relates to God's people and purpose. As is the case with the literary and conceptual patterns in use in his own time, Mark has freely adopted some and has modified others to serve his own distinctive purposes.

THE BASIC PURPOSE OF MARK

Viewed as a foundation document for a religious community, the chief aim of Mark is to convey to his readers an understanding of who Jesus is and what his role is in the purpose of God. To achieve this goal, Mark describes the public career of Jesus from its beginning in association with John the Baptist to the discovery by a nucleus of his followers that the tomb in which he had been buried is now empty—which is the ground for the belief of his followers that God has vindicated him by raising him from the dead. Between these two events Mark sketches in concise, vivid style how Jesus began to announce the inbreaking of God's rule by his words and actions. The defeat of the God-opposing powers is already evident in the healings and exorcisms that Jesus performs. And the final triumph of God's grace in the midst of an evil world is signified by Jesus' announcing God's forgiveness of sins.

The challenges that Jesus offered to the then-current Jewish understanding of covenant participation are sketched in detail by Mark, as reports are given of his setting aside such basic requirements of the Jewish law as Sabbath observance, avoidance of contact with unclean substances, and the refusal to make social contact with those who stand outside the community that seeks to obey the Law given through Moses. The prediction of the destruction of the Temple—which is not followed by any announcement of a sanctuary to replace it as the meeting place between God and his people—is in sharp conflict with the central importance of the holy place for those in Daniel who identify themselves as "the saints of the Most High."

Jesus' claim that he speaks in God's behalf is seen by his Jewish contemporaries on the whole as incompatible with the Law's demands on Israel as the requirements for gaining and maintaining identity as the covenant people. By the use of two biblical terms with reference to himself—Son of God and Son of man—Jesus is pictured as claiming to be the leader of God's people and the one through whom God's rule is to be reestablished on the earth (Ps 2:6–7, Dan 7:13–14). Clearly, claims as audacious as these, publicly declared, cannot be and are not ignored by the political and religious authorities, as Mark tells his readers throughout his Gospel, with the conflict coming to a climax in the closing chapters. Jesus' special relationship to God is further confirmed by the second vision and voice from heaven at the transfiguration scene in Mark 9. Jesus is now acclaimed as God's son, and the disciples are instructed to listen to what he has to say. Further confirming the authority of his role and its place in the overall divine purpose is the presence in this vision of two persons who exemplify the legal and prophetic traditions of Israel: Moses and Elijah. What is at stake is not merely Jesus' being accepted as one among the cast of characters of the ongoing biblical drama, but his being represented in Mark as the one through whom the climax of that drama is to be achieved. The astonishing acts he performs, his radical reinterpretation of the Law, and especially his redefining of covenant participation confront Mark's reader with an understanding of the issues that are raised by the claims associated with Jesus. These actions of Jesus and his radical redefinitions highlight what those who reject him see as being at stake in the claims made by and for him. At the same time, these claims and redefinitions demonstrate for the people of faith the basis of the Marcan community's confidence that he is God's agent to establish God's new people and bring in the new age.

Since those who trust in Jesus are convinced that Jesus is God's agent to establish this new people, they must give careful attention to what God, through Jesus, requires of them in their personal, social, and political activities. In short, what does obedience mean for the new covenant community? The other side of that question is: How does the new mode of obedience stand in relationship to the modes prevailing in Judaism of the first century, and especially to the modes of the group within Judaism that had survived the crisis of 66–70—which had resulted in the crushing of the nationalistic revolt, the destruction of the Temple, the end of the functioning of the priesthood, and the annihilation of the Dead Sea community? That group was the Pharisees, who were encouraged by the Roman authorities to organize into an established religious system what had begun informally as voluntary meetings in houses and small public rooms for the purpose of prayer and study of the Scriptures. Although, as we shall see, many of the features of the movement launched by Jesus resembled the emergent Pharisaic movement, his insistence on the inclusion in his fellowship of those who were ritually or legally excluded from the Jewish community created severe tensions. These conflicts were present during the lifetime of Jesus, and seem to have intensified in the decades after his death (as is especially apparent in Matthew 23, where, in a large group of sayings, the Pharisees are bitterly denounced while being contrasted with the community of Jesus). The issues on which the followers of Jesus must make decisions include divorce, payment of taxes to Rome, attitudes toward nationalistic hopes, and how non-Israelites may join the covenant people.

In light of the mounting conflict between Judaism and the Jesus movement, as well as the growing suspicion that the Christian movement—with its constant use of such political terms as "king" and "kingdom"—is secretly anti-Roman, Mark seeks to forewarn Christians in the latter third of the first century about official opposition, which would take the form of trial, imprisonment, or execution. It is likely that the followers of Jesus were persecuted from the earliest times, even though the only firm evidence we have of the active persecution of Christians by Roman authorities before the early second century is the story reported in Tacitus' *Annals* (15.44). There the historian, writing probably about the turn of the second century, alludes to the crucifixion of Jesus under Pontius Pilate and the spread of the movement associated with him to Rome itself. Tacitus relates how Nero (who reigned from 54 to 68) had set fire to parts of Rome in order to rebuild it more splendidly, and was surprised when the populace did not admire his urban renewal efforts. In order to divert the blame to a group that could be despised by the citizenry at large, he accused the Christians of having started the fires, and then punished them publicly in the Circus. The death of Peter came to be linked with this persecution at Rome, so that the claim arose that he had been the leader of the church there, and later tradition asserted that Mark had written his gospel there as well.

What is historically probable is that Christians in every part of the Roman world, including Palestine and Syria, repeatedly ran into conflict with the Roman authorities, were imprisoned, and often were executed. One area of potentially deadly conflict was within the very households of those who became followers of the Jesus movement. Mark 13:12 speaks of this as a prediction, but it probably describes what was actually occurring among the Christians in the second half of the first century. Thus the role model of Jesus as the one who was faithful unto death on the cross, as well as the solemn warnings about hostility and persecution that awaits those who serve the Gospel, were wholly appropriate for these earliest Christians, who shared an apocalyptic view of the world and who were already experiencing official hostility and facing the possibility of martyrdom.

One of the major functions of Mark's Gospel, therefore, was to enable the members of the community to remain faithful in spite of opposition and the threat of death. Since they were convinced that the present age was soon to come to an end—indeed, within the lifetime of some of them (9:1)—the important thing was that they be encouraged and enabled to endure (13:13). The rewards that would be theirs in the new age were described (10:29–30). But there are also details of the persecutions they are to experience (13:9–10), as well as of the divine assistance that will be given them during the times of their testing (13:11). Meanwhile, however, the followers of Jesus are to accept roles as humble servants, rather than vying in advance for positions of special honor in the age to come (10:35–45). Here again, it is the death of Jesus that is to serve as the paradigm for his followers as they look beyond suffering and death to divine vindication in the new age.

ANALYSIS

Launching the Good News of God's New Work (1:2–3:35)

Jesus' identity (1:1). Jesus as God's agent to establish his rule in the world is identified by Mark in three ways: (1) *Jesus*, which means "Jehovah [or Yahweh] saves," carries the implicit claims that God is at work through Jesus, and that the task to be completed through Jesus is the deliverance of God's people from sin and death, and their renewal. (2) *Christ*, which is the Greek equivalent of the Semitic term Messiah, means "anointed"; that is, chosen and empowered by God for a specific role in the fulfillment of his purpose for his people. It is used of the king (Ps 2:2–6) but also of the anointed priest, as in the Dead Sea Scrolls and in Psalm 133:2 and Zechariah 4:14. (3) *Son of God*, which is used in the Old Testament for the whole people of God (Hos 11:1), as well as for their royal leader (Ps 2:7).

Throughout the Old Testament and the post-biblical writings there is an abundance of titles and roles that are foreseen for various persons who are expected to be agents of God for the transformation and renewal of his covenant people. Often the roles are described without the assignment of a specific title.

The role of John the Baptist (1:4–8). John's call to repentance and the public act of washing in the Jordan imply that the present condition of God's people is so clearly at odds with God's purpose for them that they must make a radical shift, acknowledging their disobedience in word and action. His task as challenger of Israel recalls that of Elijah, whom the prophet Malachi had said God would send at the end of the age to call his people to penitence (Mal 4:5). Even John's garb is like that of Elijah (2 Kgs 1:8), whose task it was to call to account a disobedient people. John looks forward to the renewal of God's people, which will be signified by an outpouring of the Spirit of God—an event that was foretold in Joel 2:28–29. John sees this new manifestation of God's Spirit occurring through someone who is to come after his own work is completed.

Jesus' commission (1:9–13). By accepting baptism, Jesus makes a public identification of himself with the movement toward renewal of Israel that John had inaugurated. As he emerges from the water, Jesus has two related experiences that bring into focus his mission under God: (1) he sees the Spirit come upon him, in anticipation of the new age, wherein God's power will be poured out, potentially, on all humanity (note Joel 2:28, "on all flesh"); (2) he hears God's voice affirming Jesus' unique relationship to and role in the divine purpose for the creation ("You are my Son"). The struggles involved in fulfilling these roles are dramatized in Mark's account of the story of Jesus' being tempted and tested by Satan, God's adversary. The incident recalls the times of testing that both Moses and Elijah passed through in preparation for the fulfillment of their respective modes of divine call, as lawgiver and as prophet (Exod 34:28; 1 Kgs 19:8).

Jesus' announcement: God's rule is coming (1:14–15). As Jesus begins his public mission, he proclaims the essence of God's good news in word and act: the time has come when God is going to achieve his purpose for the creation and for the human race. The new freedom for men and women from the powers of evil and from humanly imposed religious restrictions is being experienced through Jesus' preaching and healing. The response appropriate to these new realities is to turn from one's old ways—that is, to repent—and to place one's trust in the news that is being brought by Jesus.

Jesus chooses his co-workers and empowers them (1:16–20). For God's work to be done, Jesus must have followers, chosen and commissioned by him, to extend his words and works. They are referred to as "learners," which is the literal meaning of the word *mathētai*, regularly translated as "disciples." From

Jesus they learn the message of God's new work in their midst and receive the power to extend it. Leaving wives, family, and business in order to engage in this urgent undertaking, the disciples set out empowered by him and his example.

Jesus' healings and exorcisms attract attention (1:21–31). The larger significance of Jesus' work is quickly apparent when he performs an exorcism in the midst of the meeting (i.e., the "synagogue") of pious Jews gathered for prayer and study of the Bible in Capernaum. The demons themselves recognize in Jesus the agent of their defeat. But the onlookers are alerted as well to Jesus' extraordinary authority, both in his teaching and in his actions. The huge question posed is: What is the source of his authority? The members of the families of his followers share in the benefits of his healing and liberating actions, as the story of the healing of Peter's mother-in-law attests.

Widening interest in Jesus' power (1:32–45). Mark tells his readers what enormous popular interest was aroused by Jesus' activities. Throngs crowd to see him, to be healed or to have their demons exorcised, or to hear his message of the coming of God's rule in their midst. Nowhere is the newness of the situation clearer than in the story of Jesus' healing the leper. According to Mosaic law, lepers were to live in solitary isolation in order to avoid defiling others by physical contact. They were even to warn others who might come near them, by loud crying, of the ritual impurity that would result from touching them (Lev 13:45–46). The Dead Sea writings from this period are especially stern in warning against contact with lepers. Yet Jesus not only reaches out and touches the leper but also pronounces him clean—a responsibility assigned in the Law to the priests. Jesus tells the man to go to the priest not to gain purity, but to have his purity confirmed (Lev 13:49, 14:2). Thus his assumption of authority goes beyond what was anticipated in the Mosaic law. It is Jesus' word and touch that bring about transformation in the new age, which he has been chosen and empowered by God to inaugurate.

Jesus assumes authority to forgive sins (2:1–12). In 2:1 there is an implication that Jesus moved his place of residence from Nazareth to Capernaum. The house was apparently a one-room structure, with a roof of mixed sticks and mud—quite serviceable in this part of the world, where it rarely rains from February to late November. So determined are the friends of a paralytic to bring him to Jesus for healing that they dig through the roof and lower him on a pallet into the midst of the gathering in Jesus' house. Some scholars think that the earlier version of the story went from the first words of 2:5 to 2:11, so that the action of Jesus is central: the man is cured. But in its present form the story implies that sickness is a sign of human failing and therefore requires forgiveness, if the person is to be healed. As it stands, the crucial feature of the story is not the healing, but the bold claim of Jesus to pronounce the man's sins to be forgiven. His critics claim that God alone has that right; Jesus claims that as God's agent to bring in the new age—that is, as Son of man—he has been given that authority. And the healing that he has accomplished confirms his authorization.

Jesus' challenge to the requirements of the old covenant (2:13–3:35). Among those whom Jesus chose and commissioned to carry forward God's new work was Levi, a tax collector (2:13–17). This office was established when the Roman authorities contracted with local individuals to collect taxes to be paid to the Roman treasury. The candidate for the job bid for the assignment, with the understanding that he could keep what he collected beyond what he contracted for. A major source of tax revenue was a duty placed on items in transit through the province where the tax collector was assigned. In addition to the basic unpopularity of such persons who contracted with the hated pagan power, the collectors had to handle items that were ritually impure by Jewish standards. These factors, combined with envy of their wealth, made tax collectors a despised group. Yet Jesus not only had social contact with them but invited one of their number to join the inner group of his followers. Jesus did not condone Levi's actions or overlook his violations of the Jewish law, but rather pictured him as a prime example of those who were "sick," who knew it, and who were willing to accept the healing, restoring power that was at work through Jesus.

Various groups within Judaism in this period had insisted that their members fast periodically. In the Old Testament law, the only time a fast is required of Israel is at the time of the Day of Atonement (Lev 16:29–34). When fasting was practiced after the return of Israel from the Babylonian exile, the prophets made the point that works of justice and mercy were more significant than the practice of fasting, which had become a form of religious showing off (Isa 58, Zech 7). Jesus' response to the question why his followers do not fast is even more revolutionary, but is in keeping with his message as a whole: God has already begun the process of renewal of his people and of the creation, and fasting is wholly inappropriate. Using the familiar image of the wedding feast as a symbol of the consummation of God's purpose, Jesus calls instead for rejoicing in the new reality that is in their midst. Further, this new reality cannot be forced into old, inflexible molds or traditional containers. Instead there must be new patterns and models for Jesus' followers (2:21–22).

Unlike the practice of fasting, which was a voluntary act of piety, obedience to the Sabbath law was demanded in the Ten Commandments (Exod 20:8, Lev 19:3, Deut 5:12–15). Yet Jesus not only refused to rebuke his followers for violating the Sabbath law by helping themselves to a snack as they passed through a grain field, but he also went to the extreme of declaring himself to have authority over the Sabbath law. As in the case of his right to pronounce the forgiveness of sins, he does so under the title of Son of man (2:27). There is understandable interest on the part of the opposition to Jesus in whether or not he will himself violate the Sabbath law—which he promptly does, in Mark's narrative. In doing so he insists that works of mercy and the saving of life are not in violation of the Sabbath law (3:4). It is wholly understandable, therefore, that an unlikely coalition now forms to "destroy" Jesus (3:6), since he is viewed as a threat to the integrity of Israel's covenantal existence, whether from the standpoint of the importance of political collaboration with the Romans (as the Herodians viewed it) or from the conviction that ritual purity is the essence of Jewish identity (as the Pharisees were persuaded).

The reasonableness of this concern about the long-range import of Jesus' message and work is apparent in the report of Mark that those who respond to Jesus as God's agent preparing for the new age include many from outside Israel: from Tyre and Sidon to the north of Palestine, and from Idumea to the east (modern Jordan). Ironically, the demons acknowledge what the leaders of Israel will not: that

he is God's anointed and empowered agent, "the Son of God" (3:11).

Leaders for the new Israel (3:13–19). The symbolic significance of the choice of the number twelve as the central core of followers of Jesus is obvious: they are the equivalent of the twelve sons of historic Israel. Even though the other Gospels do not exactly match Mark in the list of names of those appointed to accompany him, to go out and proclaim the good news, and to have authority to bring the evil powers under control, the sources all agree on their number: twelve. They are the central figures around whom will grow the new covenant people of God.

What is the source of Jesus' authority? (3:19–35). Jesus' words and deeds, which challenged the basis for Jewish identity as the elect people of God who are under obligation to maintain the boundaries between themselves and the rest of the human race, demanded a response. Essential to that response was an assessment of the basis of his authoritative acts and claims. This section of Mark describes three such assessments: (1) His family assumes that he is mad and seeks to remove him from public view (3:19–21, 31–32). It is surprising, therefore, that his mother and brothers were later to assume roles in the emerging Jesus movement, with his brother James taking over as leader of the Jerusalem-based apostles (Gal 1:19). Apparently the earlier doubts of Jesus' family about him were overcome by the climactic events of his confrontation with the authorities in Jerusalem, his death, and the conviction shared by his followers that God had vindicated him by raising him from the dead. In 1 Corinthians 15:7, Paul notes specifically that the risen Jesus appeared to James, the brother of Jesus. (2) The interpreters of the Law who have come from Jerusalem to Galilee to assess what Jesus is doing have their own explanation: he is in league with the demons and their leader and thus is able to manipulate them for his own purposes. (3) His answer to this charge is that he is Satan's conqueror, not his ally. Jesus will bind him and take from him what he has seized (3:27). And Jesus adds that to mistake his triumph over Satan for an alliance with him is to sin against the Spirit of God, which came upon Jesus and which is being poured out in preparation for the coming of the new age (2:28–29).

This section of Mark culminates in a redefinition

of the family of God (3:33–35). It is no longer to be defined as those with genetic or family links, but as those who do the will of God. It is important to note here that, unlike historic Judaism, which defined itself in terms of the twelve sons of Jacob, Jesus specifies that not only the males, but also the sisters and mothers, have central places among the new people of God.

God's Rule in Word and Act (4:1–5:43)

In this section of Mark a paradox is evident: what Jesus says and does are matters of public knowledge, but an understanding of his words and deeds is reserved for those to whom God chooses to disclose his purpose through Jesus. This attitude is in keeping with the apocalyptic worldview that I considered in my survey of the Gospel. Now the story of Jesus and the report of his deeds are specifically declared to be understood only by those who stand within the community of his followers. In addition, the point of each of Jesus' parables here involves a contrast between the small, seemingly insignificant beginnings and the astounding results. Stated another way, what God is doing through Jesus is contrary to ordinary human assumptions about power and significant change.

The parable of the sower and its interpretation (4:1–9, 13–20). Mark begins his report of the first of Jesus' parables with a description of the great crowds that have gathered to hear him. This stands in contrast to the note in 4:10, which says that the explanation of the parable is limited to the inner circle. One may define a parable as an extended metaphor or comparison in the form of a story, usually quite brief. The story here is a simple account of the standard pattern of grain-growing in Palestine: The seed is sown without what we might call adequate preparation of the soil, and the results are accordingly mixed. Some seed is snatched away by the birds; some is dried up by the sun; some is crowded out by weeds. But the seeds that do germinate and grow produce huge harvests, ranging from thirty to one hundred times what was sown. The parable concludes with the invitation to those who "have ears to hear" to do so. That is, those privileged by God to perceive his purpose through Jesus are urged to get the point of the parable.

Some scholars think that a sharp distinction should be made between a parable, which is supposed to have one main point, and an allegory, in which each detail has some symbolic significance. That distinction is probably an exaggeration, but it seems clear that Mark has included in his account of Jesus' teaching an allegorical expansion of the parable of the sower (4:13–20). The explanation of the parable is vivid, even though it is not always self-consistent. The sower, who must represent the preacher, sows the word (v. 14). The birds that snatch away the word represent Satan (v. 15). The seed that sprouts rapidly and then withers symbolizes those who receive the good news, but then under pressure from persecution fall away from the faithful community (vv. 16–17). Others fail to sustain the growth of the word as a result of their preoccupation with ordinary human concerns and values (vv. 18–19). The good soil consists of the enduring, faithful, productive members of the community, whose work for the gospel produces astounding results (v. 20). Here we have a symbolic picture not so much of the time of Jesus, but of the situation of the Marcan community, from which outside pressures and attractions have caused former members to lapse. Instead of being primarily an encouragement to preach ("sow the word"), the allegorical interpretation is a warning against unproductive or lapsed membership.

The parable of the seed growing secretly (4:26–29). The capacity of the seed to grow and produce is beyond human calculation ("he knows not how"), but is certain to produce results. And those results will be fully known and appreciated only at the time of the harvest, which in the biblical tradition is a symbol of the time when God's plan for his people will be fulfilled (as in Ps 126), though it is also used by the prophets to refer to the time when God calls his people to account (Jer 8). The parable here makes the point that the accomplishment of the divine purpose can be neither fully understood nor precisely calculated by human beings, apart from divine disclosure.

The parable of the mustard seed (4:30–32). Here again Jesus contrasts the small and unpromising beginnings of God's work ("the smallest of all the seeds on earth") and the astounding results ("the greatest of all shrubs"). The work of God's coming rule is not subject to human scheming or comprehension, nor does it come about by the operation of ordinary human values and virtues. It is God's work, accomplished in his own way and in his own time.

Jesus' reason for speaking in parables (4:10–12, 21–25, 33–34). In this series of brief sayings the point, mentioned above, is made explicit: parables are not a mode of simple, direct communication, but a symbolic means by which God's purpose through Jesus is disclosed to the community of faith. What has been granted to them is insight into the divine "mystery of the kingdom of God" (v. 11), while for those outside the community there is only a puzzle or enigma (which is the root meaning of the Semitic word *mashal,* often translated as "parable"). Forgiveness is announced to all, but is effective only for those who recognize Jesus to be God's agent for renewal of his people (v. 12). The information is available: the lamp is on the stand and nothing is hidden. But only the one to whom insight has been granted ("whoever has ears") will grasp the good news. There is a sharp division between those who have—that is, the God-given insight into who Jesus is—and those who do not (4:9, 24–25). This method of speaking in parables in public and then offering explanations to his followers in private characterizes Jesus' teaching as Mark reports it (4:33–34).

Jesus' power over the wind and waters (4:35–41). One of the important images in the Hebrew Scriptures for depicting God's establishment of his authority over the creation is his control of the waters. The image appears in the story of creation, where God divides the waters (Gen 1), and it is affirmed in Psalms 24 and Job 38. His control of the waters likewise figures importantly in the Exodus stories, including the crossing of the sea (Exod 14–15), the supply of water to Israel in the desert (Exod 17), and the crossing of the Jordan into the Promised Land (Josh 3–4). This image for God's controlling power should be viewed against the background of older Semitic mythology, in which the personification of the chaotic waters of the sea, Yam, is brought under control by the deity.

It is the word of Jesus, addressed to the stormy wind, that brings the waves of the sea under control (4:39). The peace and calm that result are surely symbolic of what Mark sees God as accomplishing through Jesus in behalf of his new people as they undergo the stresses and testings of their faith.

Overstepping the bounds of Judaism (5:1–42). Concurrent with the growing questions of Jewish leaders about Jesus and the source of his authority is the portrayal in Mark of Jesus' reaching outside of and across the boundaries of traditional Jewish covenantal identity to make God's renewing power available to all who respond to Jesus in faith, from whatever ethnic, moral, or ritual situation. This point is made in the two longest miracle stories that Mark has included. The first takes place outside Jewish territory in the vicinity of one of the cities of the Decapolis, Gerasa. These ten cities (which is what "Decapolis" means) had been developed by the Hellenistic rulers of Syria and Palestine in the third and second centuries as exemplars of Greek culture, complete with theaters, racecourses, temples to the Greek deities, and gymnasia, where Greek-style recreation was practiced. Obviously, the population of these cities was predominantly non-Jewish, although some Jews adopted and enjoyed this way of life.

As though it were not sufficiently questionable for Jesus to venture into such a pagan territory, he allows himself to become involved there with a man who is possessed of demons and is living in a tomb—which would have made him ritually untouchable for a pious Jew, since any contact with the dead was strictly prohibited. The gentile atmosphere of that area is confirmed by the detail that there were herds of swine nearby—which would also be wholly unacceptable to Law-observant Jews. The man recognizes (or the demons who possess the man recognize) that in Jesus they have met their master, and ask to be transferred by his authority to the pigs. Jesus complies with their request. The man is cured and fully restored to his place in the pagan society in which he lived (5:13–15). His request to become a follower of Jesus is denied, but he is urged to bear testimony to what happened to him through Jesus, and to do so "in the Decapolis"—that is, to a potentially non-Jewish audience (5:20).

Although the next pair of interlocked stories both concern Jews, the issue of violation of ritual purity is central to each (5:21–43). In the case of the daughter of Jairus, the head of the local synagogue, Jesus on his belated arrival at the house reaches out and touches the dead child—once more in violation of ritual purity. Similarly, the woman with the flow of blood who came and touched Jesus (5:27) could have been denounced by him for having defiled him ritually (Lev 15:25–30). Instead, she is healed by him, commended for her faith, and sent on her way in peace (5:34). The issues between Jesus and his ritually observant Jewish contemporaries are now sharply drawn, though for the most part implicitly. In the next section, the conflicting understanding of who God's people are and how one maintains standing in that community are made more explicit.

Jesus Confronts Mounting Opposition (6:1–8:26)

Jesus rejected in his hometown (6:1–6). Returning to his own district after this mission of preaching and healing in a wider territory, Jesus is teaching in the synagogue in Nazareth. The reaction is one of astonishment— at the wisdom that comes through in his words and at the power that is evident in his works. What especially puzzles Jesus' hearers is that the other members of his family, who presumably stayed at home and were well known to all in the synagogue, have done nothing of comparable power. He is known to them as a local builder, who may have worked in wood or stone, or both. Matthew, who has given his version of the story of the birth of Jesus to the virgin Mary, identifies Jesus as "the son of the builder" (Matt 13:55). Luke places the story of Jesus' rejection in Nazareth at the opening of his public career, and omits mention of Jesus' trade or that of his father (Luke 4:16–30). In any case, there is in Mark only astonishment that one with such a simple background and upbringing would embark on such a spectacular undertaking as Jesus' role of announcing and demonstrating the coming of God's rule. The ultimate local reaction to him, however, is one of bitter rejection, to which he responds by identifying himself as standing in the line of the prophets. As such, he receives honor from neither his neighbors nor his family. So great is the local distrust of him that his powers to heal are limited (Mark 6:5). It is worth noting that here, in one of the relatively few passages in which Jesus is reported as depicting his own role in the purpose of God, he does so by designating himself not as messianic king or priest but as a prophet.

The twelve extend Jesus' mission (6:6–13). Un-deterred by the negative local and family response, Jesus dispatches the twelve disciples to carry forward the work of preparing for the coming of the kingdom of God. The instructions for equipment to be taken and for living arrangements on the road resemble those from that period that were adopted by itinerant teacher-preachers of the Cynic school of philosophy. These traveling philosophers went barefoot from place to place, seeking to gather an audience in public places, denouncing the vain values of the age, and calling their hearers to renounce the present age and its search for material security. The philosophers took with them only a minimum of necessities for their life on the road and were dependent on contributions for which they begged in public. Jesus' followers are given an even more extreme set of guidelines for their itinerant life: they are to take neither food nor money nor a begging bag, but are to carry a staff for minimal protection and sandals for their feet. For food and shelter they are to be dependent on the hospitality of their hearers (6:10). If a village spurns them and their message, they are quickly to move on to the next (6:11). The result of their efforts, in addition to their preaching role, is that many exorcisms and healings are performed (6:13).

A politician's reaction to the Jesus movement (6:14–29). Although Herod Antipas, who served as Roman governor of Galilee and the region to the east, was confused as to the specific identity of Jesus, he correctly linked him with the prophetic movement represented by John the Baptist and to the expectation of Elijah's return at the end of the age. Herod thinks Jesus is John raised from the dead, which provides Mark the occasion for telling in vivid detail the horrible circumstances of John's death. The report of this serves Mark's scheme well, since it alerts the reader to the possibility of gross miscarriage of Roman justice and to the consequences for the messengers of God. The details of the story even give the reader a hint about Jesus' being raised from the dead, in spite of Herod's misinformation, as well as an anticipation of Jesus' being laid in a tomb by his few faithful followers.

God's provision for his new people (6:30–44). As I have noted above, the details of this story clearly correspond to the experience of Israel in the desert of Sinai, when they lacked food (Exod 16:13–21). That the aim of the story is to highlight the reconstitution of the people of God is made clear in the saying of Jesus' (Mark 6:34) about the lack of a leader (shepherd) for the covenant people—an image that is used in Numbers 27:17 in connection with the choice of Joshua to succeed Moses as the leader of the people, and in 1 Kings 22:17 as an indication of the corrupt leadership and consequent doom of the northern kingdom of Israel. The ordering of the five thousand, as they prepare to be miraculously fed, to divide themselves into one hundred groups consisting of fifty people each (Mark 6:40) gives the impression that this is more than merely a chance gathering of those interested in following Jesus—or in a free meal! The deeper symbolic significance of the meal becomes clear in the four verbs that are used to describe the central act of feeding: took, blessed, broke, gave. Obviously these words are also found in the Last Supper scene (14:22) and in one of the few sayings of Jesus reported by Paul (1 Cor 11:23–24). The Gospel of John makes these parallels explicit in its version of the miraculous-feeding story (John 6), but there can be no mistaking that this scene is a symbolic portrayal of the constitution of the new covenant people. When we come to the Last Supper scene we shall see that the sacrifice which ratifies the new covenant is Jesus' own death.

Jesus' power over the chaotic waters (6:45–52). As in the earlier account of Jesus stilling the storm, the story of Jesus walking on the water reminds the reader of the cosmic dimensions of his authority. Mark's editorial comment in 6:51–52, however, shows the reader that at this point Jesus' followers, who have witnessed his extraordinary powers, do not yet understand who he is.

Popular response to Jesus (6:53–56). In ironic contrast, the report of the lack of perception on the part of the disciples is followed by a summary account of the arrival of throngs from throughout the surrounding area who seek Jesus out in order to be healed.

Confronting the purity issue (7:1–13). In the first century, as the Pharisaic movement began to flourish, with its primary emphasis on applying the purity laws of the Temple to voluntary gatherings in the home, the demands for ritual purity multiplied and the Pharisaic determination to see that they were observed intensified. Jesus is described by Mark as meeting this issue head on. In addition to his rejection of the Pharisees' modification of the Law (such as their justification for avoiding the responsibility of honoring one's parents as reported in 7:8–10), Jesus is recorded as rejecting the very notion that purity is a matter of ritual observance. Instead, purity concerns human social behavior, with evil attitudes and actions coming out of the human heart and corrupting relationships with other human beings (7:21–23). On such a basis, there could be no compromise between the Jesus movement and the Pharisees, for whom ritual purity was the central concern.

Reaching out to the outsiders (7:24–8:10). Both the story of the expelling of the demon from the daughter of the gentile Syrian woman and the account of the healing of the deaf man from the region of the Decapolis show that the benefits of the new age are already available to those whose ethnic origins and ritual status exclude them from covenantal participation as perceived in the Jewish tradition. The implications of this new openness to non-Israelites is confirmed symbolically by Mark in the story of the feeding of the four thousand (8:1–10). This takes place on gentile soil, and the significant number of baskets of remaining fragments is not twelve (as in the feeding of the five thousand), but seven, which number was linked in early Christian tradition with the outreach to the gentiles, as the Jerusalem church's choice of seven to serve the needs of the Greek converts attests (Acts 6:1–3).

The coalition against Jesus takes shape (8:11–21). The demand of the Pharisees that Jesus perform a miracle in order to prove that God is with him corresponds to the stories preserved in the later rabbinic tradition, but stemming from the first century, according to which a rabbi's interpretation of the Law was often confirmed by a miracle. Jesus insists that his actions are performed to serve the needs of others and must stand on their own. Accordingly, he refuses to invoke some form of divine attestation in his own behalf. Instead, he warns his hearers against the evil influences of the Pharisees and the Herodians, who are plotting to destroy him. Even at this point, however, Mark makes it clear that the disciples do not understand either who Jesus is or the divine significance of what he has done (8:17–21).

The blind can see (8:22–26). Once more Mark

reports a miracle of Jesus' which the discerning reader can recognize as occurring in fulfillment of the prophecy in Isaiah 35:5, but which points up at the same time that Jesus' closest followers are still blind to God's purpose through him. Jesus acts here to restore both the blind man's sight and his comprehension; it is through such insight that the disciples will come fully to understand Jesus and his role under God.

Suffering, Death, and Deliverance for Jesus (8:27–9:50)

What Jesus' messianic role involves: suffering (8:27–33). Jesus' task of enabling the disciples to see that his suffering and death are essential to the fulfillment of his God-given role is depicted in stages in this section, which begins with Jesus asking the disciples who other people say he is. Their answers all point to his role in preparing for the coming of the new age: John the Baptist, Elijah, or one of the prophets. We know from the Dead Sea Scrolls that the promise to Moses (in Deut 18:18) of a prophet like him who would come to Israel in the future was believed to have been fulfilled by the Teacher of Righteousness, who founded that group. Peter speaks for the disciples in acclaiming Jesus not as prophet, but as Messiah or Christ (Mark 8:29). But when Jesus explains that his role involves his rejection by the Jewish leaders, his suffering and death, Peter not only does not understand this, but also rejects the basic notion of a suffering messiah. Jesus, in turn, rejects Peter's mistaken notion of how God will achieve his purpose for his people. What Peter assumes, in his refusal to accept the notion of suffering as a means to divine fulfillment, is a human misconception and is linked with the forces that oppose God (8:33).

The conditions for discipleship (8:34–9:1). The experience of Jesus' disciples will match his own: they must be prepared for persecution and suffering, and hence to take up the cross—the symbol of rejection, humiliation, and death at the hands of the earthly powers (8:34). If they accept this role and the suffering it involves, they will be vindicated by the Son of man at his coming (8:38). Indeed, Mark reports Jesus as declaring that they can expect the fulfillment of God's promised kingdom within the lifetime of some of his disciples (9:1). It may be noted that Paul also expected to be alive at the time of

Christ's appearance in triumph (1 Thess 4:15). So powerful is the launching of the process of establishing God's rule through the words and acts of Jesus that the first generation of his followers clearly expected the task to be completed within their own lifetime. This lent a greater sense of urgency to their tasks as messengers and agents of the gospel.

Divine confirmation of Jesus (9:2–8). Further confirmation of the hope of fulfillment is offered by the transfiguration event (9:2–8). As in the case of Daniel, who is transformed in a radiant vision of the presence of God and given words of assurance that the visions that have been granted him will come to pass (Dan 10), Jesus' own appearance is for the moment changed in anticipation of the new age of triumph of God's purpose. It serves to strengthen him for the arrest, suffering, and death that he is about to experience.

The rejection of God's messengers (9:9–13). Once more, Jesus' disciples do not grasp the divine plan for the renewal of the creation, though they do associate these experiences with the coming of Elijah at the end of the age (Mark 9:11). Even so, they seem unable to accept the notion that God's agents must suffer before the final victory is achieved. The reference in verse 13 to a text that predicts Elijah's suffering is to an unknown source, but even in Daniel, the faithful are warned to be ready to accept suffering and even martyrdom, as such stories as the "starvation diet" and the fiery furnace in Daniel 1–3 attest.

Life from the dead (9:14–29). The vivid story of the autistic, epileptic child serves a symbolic purpose, since it shows how the power of Jesus can transform death (v. 26, "the boy was like a corpse"; "he is dead") into the resurrected life. The Greek words in verse 27 for the phrases "he lifted him up," and "he arose," are the technical terms for the resurrection used elsewhere in the New Testament.

The second and third predictions of Jesus' death and resurrection (9:30–32, 10:32–34). The repeated predictions of Jesus' arrest and death in Jerusalem continue to provide further details concerning these events. In addition to the rejection by the religious leaders noted in 8:31, in the second prediction the reader learns that Jesus will be handed over to "men"—presumably the Roman authorities—who "will kill him" (9:31). The third prediction makes this explicit: gentiles will mock and scourge him, and kill him (10:33–34). In each case, the resurrection after three days is specifically mentioned as well. The lack of comprehension by the disciples is apparent from their subsequent vying for power.

The disciples' bid for power (9:33–37, 10:35–45). In the first of these exchanges, the disciples will not acknowledge that they have been arguing about which of them was the greatest. In response, Jesus sets a child before them as an example. Elsewhere in the gospel tradition, the presence of the child is the occasion for a statement about humility (Matt 18:3) or the simplicity with which a child receives a gift—that is, the kingdom of God (Mark 10:15, Luke 18:17). Here (at Mark 9:33–37), however, there may be an implied pun on the Greek word *pais* (or *paidion*), which can mean either "child" or "servant." Yet the mode of service that Jesus here describes (the term for servant in 10:43 is *diakonos*) is that of caring for the needs of others, not simply bondage to another (as the word *doulos* might be taken to imply at 10:44).

The second power play is led by the sons of Zebedee, who in anticipation of Jesus' future exaltation as Son of man ask for the places of special favor at his left and right hand (10:37). Now Jesus tells them explicitly of the necessity for them to accept martyrdom, as symbolized by the cup and baptism (10:38). Though they claim to be ready, they will in fact soon abandon him in his hour of suffering. Then Jesus shifts to another understanding of the servant role—this time in apparent link with the redemptive suffering of the servant in Isaiah 53—in that he as both Servant and Son of man will suffer to effect the release of many from their sins (10:45).

Authority and responsibility in the new community (9:38–50). The authority inherent in the name of Jesus is so great that the disciples are not to forbid its use by outsiders, who might through appeal to his name become followers (9:38–41). On the other hand, those who offer support for the disciples because of their link with the name of Jesus will be rewarded by God (9:41). Members of the community are to take care that they do not discourage or drive away those less strong in the faith, and are to practice strict discipline so that they can overcome unworthy impulses that could hinder their entering the new age (9:42–48). Meanwhile, God's presence among his

people is symbolized by salt, either for judgment ("salted with fire") or for peace (9:50).

Issues Between Jesus and Judaism (10:1–13:37)

When is divorce permissible? (10:1–12). From the rabbinic sources it seems that some interpreters of Deuteronomy 24:1 understood the prescribed condition for divorce—"if [the husband] finds some indecency in [his wife]"—to mean her infidelity, while others interpreted it to mean any act that her husband found disgusting. Jesus sets aside the law entirely, appealing rather to the male-female pattern that God established in creation (Gen 1:27, 2:24) as the basis for an enduring marital relationship. In the private subsequent explanation to the disciples (Mark 10:10–12), Jesus states flatly that divorce and remarriage result in adultery for both man and woman. Unique to Jewish debate on this subject is Jesus' placing men and women on terms of equal responsibility, in contrast to the Mosaic law's leaving the initiative entirely in the hands of the man. Matthew fundamentally alters this saying by introducing unchastity as an adequate basis for divorce (Matt 5:32). Mark's version is far more radical.

Children's place within the community (10:13–16). Although boys were circumcised in ancient Israel, it seems that only by the time of the exile did the rite become central to covenantal identity. Much later the practice was introduced of having adolescent boys inducted as "sons of the covenant." Here, however, Jesus is claiming even small children for the people of God. It is significant that reports of conversion in Acts and the letters of Paul constantly refer not to individuals but to households—that is, including the children. They, like the poor and the ailing, were excluded from significant covenant participation by the Jewish standards of the day. In contrast to the view expressed in Mark, the *Gospel of Thomas*, a later product of gnostics, understood "becoming as a child" to mean divesting oneself of sexual practice or even of sexual identity through castration.

The ultimate value of wealth (10:17–31). The easy human assumption that the possession of wealth is a sign of divine favor or at least a guarantee of a secure existence is rejected by Jesus. What one owns is a hindrance to entering the kingdom of God, Jesus declares, since admission is dependent on what God has done, not on one's own achievements. That as awkward a beast as a camel, which complains fiercely if it has to get up or down, could crawl through a needle's eye is an intentionally absurd statement. But the point is clear: discipleship demands renunciation of reliance on what one possesses. The passage ends with a promise, however: in the common life of God's new people, the disciples will have all they need, and in the age to come, they will be showered with rewards (10:28–30).

Blind Bartimaeus receives his sight (10:46–52). In yet another miracle story with symbolic import for Mark's reader (although even the disciples in the story cannot grasp Jesus' meaning), a poor blind man cries out to Jesus for healing, and, having received it, becomes a follower.

In the rest of this section of Mark there are a series of sharp challenges by Jesus to the religious institutions and norms of Judaism in his time. They are grouped here by subject:

The national identity (11:1–10, 12:13–17, 12:35–37). Jesus' seemingly conscious choice of a donkey to ride into Jerusalem is an obvious enactment of the prophecy of Zechariah 9:9 that Israel's king will come to Zion not in triumph on a charger, but in humility on the colt of an ass—on which no rider could look triumphant. Despite that, he is greeted by his followers with a quote from Psalm 118:25–26, which was understood to be a messianic prediction and linked with the king of the line of David. And yet, not only is there no attempt on Jesus' part to seize power, but when pressed about paying taxes to Rome (12:13–17), he states that Caesar should receive what is due him. When the question is raised about the relation of Messiah to David's royal descendant, Jesus gives an ambiguous answer (12:35–37).

The religious issues (12:18–27, 28–34, 37–40). Since, among the Hebrew Scriptures, the resurrection of the dead is taught only in the Book of Daniel, the Sadducees (who acknowledged only the Pentateuch as authoritative) rejected it. The Pharisees affirmed it, on the other hand. Jesus, on being questioned, seeks to prove that the doctrine of the resurrection has justification within the Law of Moses by showing that God continues to be spoken of as the God of the patriarchs, even though they have died. As God of the living, he was, is, and will be their God on the day of resurrection (12:26–27).

On the issue, much discussed by the rabbis, as to which is the greatest commandment (12:28–34), Jesus commends the linking of love of God and love of neighbor. The implication is that love of God enables one to love the neighbor, and love of neighbor is the outward expression of one's love of God. To the Pharisees' insistence that maintaining ritual purity is the essential feature of covenant existence Jesus gives a flat rejection. Their pious practices do nothing but draw attention to themselves.

Mark portrays Jesus as announcing that the Temple will be destroyed and implying that it is not fulfilling its intended function as "a house of prayer for all the nations" (11:17; RSV) and therefore is dispensable. The details of its destruction are given in the characteristic language of apocalyptic literature (13:1–37). Prior to this catastrophe there will be civil and cosmic disturbances, with mounting hostility toward Jesus' followers from the side of the religious and political leaders (13:5–13). The mission of the Gospel is to go forward on a worldwide basis, however (13:10). The final sign of the impending destruction will be the desecration of the Temple, to be followed by unprecedented suffering for the faithful followers of Jesus (13:14–20). Then the triumphant Son of man will appear (13:24–27), accompanied by heavenly armies. No one can predict the exact time of this cosmic event, but the faithful are to be ever watchful (13:30–37).

Equally as repugnant to his contemporaries as his prediction of the destruction of the Temple must have been the use by Jesus of Old Testament images for Israel, which Jesus now interprets to point to the replacement of historic Israel as the people of God. The first of these images is the fig tree, which is cursed and has already begun to wither away (11:12–14, 20–25). The second is the vineyard (12:1–12), which in Isaiah 5 represents the unfruitful nation Israel. In a parable that begins by recalling phrases from Isaiah, Jesus goes on to describe how the tenants who are occupying the vineyard mistreat the messengers sent by the owner (presumably the prophets) and finally expel and kill the owner's son (i.e., Jesus). The main point of the parable is the declaration by Jesus that the owner will "destroy the tenants and give the vineyard to others" (12:9). The justice of this is confirmed by a quotation from a favorite psalm of the early Christians, which affirms that the rejected stone has become the foundation for the new structure—that is, the covenant people—which God is bringing into being (Ps 118:22–23).

The Coalition to Destroy Jesus (14:1–15:47)

The conspiracy of the Jewish leaders (14:1–2). Mark now reports that the priestly and scribal leaders pool their efforts to be rid of Jesus, and to do so before the great Passover feast, which is only a few days ahead. Apparently the Passover fell on the Sabbath that year, so the effort is to have Jesus executed during the day, before the holy day began at sundown. That dating fits with the information in John 13:1, and explains why only bread and wine are mentioned at the Last Supper, rather than the sacrificial animal required for the Passover celebration (Deut 16). For the readers of Mark, Jesus' death was itself the sacrifice for the people of the new covenant, which is the body of Christians.

The symbolic anointing of Jesus (14:3–9). It is significant that Jesus is in the home of a leper and is anointed by a woman, not a priest, since both these features point to the inclusiveness of his community and his departure from the dominant ritual obligations of his fellow Jews. His followers wanted him to be the anointed (Messiah) king: Jesus understands that God's role for him first demands his death.

Judas the betrayer (14:10–11, 17–21, 43–52). The leaders knew who Jesus was, of course, but they sought to "arrest him by stealth," which required that one of his intimates guarantee that the guards seize the right person. Judas, apparently disillusioned by Jesus' criticisms of Judaism or his failure to seize power, agrees to assist in his secret arrest. The fact that Judas, one of the inner circle of the Twelve, has planned to do this is represented as known to Jesus, who alludes to it at the Last Supper. The plot is carried out when the guards arrive in the darkness of Gethsemane to take Jesus away to the authorities (14:43–52). Jesus' question why they take him by stealth when they might have arrested him in one of his public acts goes unanswered.

Peter the denier (14:29–31, 66–72). The empti-ness of Peter's protests of fidelity to Jesus is seen and noted by Jesus, even though the other disciples echo Peter's sentiments. As the hearing before the Jewish council is in process, however, Peter disclaims knowledge of or association with Jesus. In anticipation of this abandonment by his followers, Jesus quotes from Zechariah 13:7 (Mark 14:27) about the scattering of the sheep when the leader has been struck. But Jesus also promises that the shattered community will be restored when he appears to them in Galilee after his crucifixion (14:28).

The Last Supper: covenantal meal (14:12–16, 22–25). By careful planning or by divine arrangement, the room and the table are set for Jesus' final meal with his followers. The broken bread and the poured-out wine symbolize Jesus' sacrifice of his own life, which ratifies the new covenant. The meal not only focuses on that death (soon to occur), but it also looks forward to the time when God's purpose through Jesus will be fully accomplished, "in the kingdom of God" (14:25). Ironically, this celebration of the new community is followed immediately by the agony of Jesus and the shattering of the inner circle of his followers, as the details of the Gethsemane scene show (14:32–42). In spite of misguided efforts to attack the guards (14:47), and Jesus' protests at their capturing him like a robber or an insurrectionist (14:48), he yields to his captors.

The hearings before the religious and civil powers (14:53–15:15). Roman policy allowed local councils to deal with issues that arose out of violations of local law, so the Jewish council could have found Jesus guilty under their law and executed him. But they can come to no consensus about the charge or the nature of his guilt. The one item they do extract from the hearing is Jesus' acknowledgment of the claim to be Messiah, Son of God, though it is not clear from the statement itself what the council or Jesus understood by that title. In any case, they turn him over to the local Roman governor for a hearing on civil charges. Pilate's question follows up one possible significance of Jesus' messianic claim: that he considers himself a candidate for the kingship of Israel. But his response to Pilate's question is not an answer (15:2). After trying without success to find some way to release Jesus, Pilate accedes to the demand of the religious leaders and sentences Jesus to death as a pretender to the throne of Israel, on the ground that such an ambition was an act of insurrection.

The execution and burial of Jesus (15:16–47). The soldiers who perform the crucifixion pick up on the idea of Jesus as king, as is evident from their mocking acclaim of him, the crown of thorns (the spikes of which are a caricature of the sun-like rays extending outward from the crown of the divinized emperor), the robe of royal purple, and the sign affixed to the cross: "The King of the Jews." Similar scornful questioning of his claim to be king is uttered by both priests and scribes (15:31). Finally, in his moment of death, he cries out in an Aramaic paraphrase of a line from Psalm 22:1 about being forsaken by God, thereby showing the depth and reality of his suffering, and his personal struggle in his obedience to the point of death (15:34). His crying out to God is mistaken by the crowd for a call to Elijah to deliver him. But mention of Elijah serves to remind the reader of Mark about Jesus' central role in the turn of the ages, in preparation for the coming of God's rule.

The responses to Jesus' death are significant for Mark (15:38–40). The veil of the Temple, which separated the Holy of Holies from the rest of the sanctuary, marking it off as the actual dwelling place of God, is torn from the top down. God has acted through the death of Jesus to provide everyone access to his presence. The Roman military officer acclaims Jesus as God's son, and becomes one of the forerunners of the gentiles who will turn to God through Jesus. The women alone from among all his followers remain faithful to the end. As they ministered to his needs during his public activity, so they will seek to take care of his body in death (15:47–16:2). One of the members of the council, Joseph of Arimathea, is permitted to remove the body of Jesus for burial in his private tomb, where it is enclosed by a stone across the opening. Mark tells us only that Joseph was looking for the kingdom of God, but gives no hint that he was a follower of Jesus. Perhaps we can infer that he had heard and was attracted by Jesus' message. The body had to be entombed quickly, since its exposure on the Sabbath—and especially on a feast day such as Passover—would defile the land and the day.

Epilogue (16:1–8). The first opportunity that came for the women to return to the tomb in order to properly prepare the hastily buried body was at dawn on Sunday. It would not have been safe for women to venture outside the city after dark, and the Sabbath ended on Saturday at sunset. They are debating how they will roll back the stone from the tomb entrance, but are astounded to find it rolled back and the tomb empty, except for an unidentified young man. This man recalls the promise of Jesus (14:28) that the disciples will be met by Jesus when they reassemble in Galilee. Just as the Book of Daniel ends on a note of expectancy, rather than with the promises fulfilled, so Mark notes that mingled fear and astonishment filled the women. Yet the prediction of Jesus' resurrection and the prophecies about his role in the coming of the end of the age have been laid out in detail earlier by Mark. It is in keeping with the strategy of apocalypticism that the young man puts the responsibility on the informed members of the community to recognize what God has already disclosed and accomplished, as well as the consummation that is awaited in the near future. From this viewpoint, the ending of Mark is wholly appropriate.

Later readers of Mark, including those who made much later copies of his Gospel, were not satisfied with this ending. Other, "happier endings" were invented, and found their way into ancient manuscripts and some modern translations. The supplements to Mark are derived mostly from Matthew, with some other new features introduced, but the oldest and best manuscripts of Mark end at 16:8, which serves well the aims of Mark as I have sketched them.

Bibliography

General Studies

Kee, Howard Clark. *Community of the New Age: Studies in Mark's Gospel.* Philadelphia, 1977. A study of the aims and method of Mark.

———. *Jesus in History: An Approach to the Study of the Gospels.* New York, 1977. A comparison of Mark with the other Gospels.

Kümmel, Werner Georg. *Introduction to the New Testament.* Translated by Howard Clark Kee. Nashville, Tenn., 1975. The section on Mark includes the best survey of bibliography and technical issues related to the aims and methods of Mark.

Commentary

Achtemeier, Paul J. *Mark.* Philadelphia, 1975. Fine analysis, as an aid for preaching.

Lane, William L. *Commentary on Mark*. New International Commentary on the New Testament, vol. 2. Grand Rapids, 1974. The most complete recent analysis of the Greek text.

Nineham, Dennis Eric. *The Gospel of Saint Mark*. Pelican Gospel Commentary. Baltimore, 1963.

Schweizer, Eduard. *The Good News According to Mark*. Translated by Donald H. Madvig. Richmond, Va., 1970.

Taylor, Vincent. *The Gospel According to Saint Mark*. London, 1952. Old but valuable detailed analysis of the Greek text.

HOWARD CLARK KEE

Luke and Acts

PERHAPS THE MOST important thing to know about the Gospel according to St. Luke and the Acts of the Apostles is that they belong together. Both works were dedicated to someone named Theophilus; both bear the stamp of the same author, who remains anonymous throughout. The question naturally arises why the two are separated in the present canon of the New Testament and why they have been read independently of one another throughout most of the history of the church. Reasons for the separation must lie in the process by which biblical works were collected and approved for public reading in the church. Individual books were read and circulated independently before they were assembled to form a collection. When they were collected, categories had to be created to form some organizing principles. Such categories were "gospels" and "epistles." There was no such literary category as "gospel" in the ancient world; the word means "good message" and is used in Paul's letters and in Acts as a technical term for the message of salvation in Jesus. The church actually invented a literary category as a way of describing four accounts of Jesus' ministry. Some compositions, like the Revelation to John (the Apocalypse), which already corresponded to known types of literature, had to be fitted into the category of "epistle." Acts was neither a "gospel" nor an "epistle." The first volume of Luke's work was included in the New Testament as a "gospel," and Acts as something of an

exception. Acknowledgment by modern scholarship that the two works belong together as part of one literary project thus represents a departure from a tradition that can be traced to the second-century church.

Christian writings can only with qualification be classified as "literature" as measured by ancient standards. As I have already noted, there was no such category as "gospel." Luke-Acts comes closest, however, to known categories of literature. The four-verse preface to the first volume, rather elegantly composed in decent Greek, suggests literary ambition. Whether the parallels are to be found in biographies of philosophers or in the writings of historians, we can learn something about Luke-Acts by locating the work in its cultural setting. There is good reason to use categories like "historiography" as opposed to "gospel" to speak about the two-volume work.

It is equally important to locate Luke-Acts, as well as the rest of the New Testament, within the religious culture of Greek-speaking Judaism in the first century. Christianity began as a Jewish sect. The word "Christian" is used only three times in the New Testament: twice in Acts, where it is used by pagans to describe the strange Jewish sect that seemed preoccupied with Jesus "Christ" (i.e., "Messiah"), and once in 1 Peter 4:16. Acts views the Jesus movement as a Jewish sect, using such terms as "the Way" to speak about it. The imagery used to speak about Jesus is furnished by the Jewish scriptures. Even the style of Luke-Acts (particularly Acts) is reminiscent of the historical books in the Greek Old Testament (the Septuagint). If it is helpful to locate Luke-Acts within the tradition of Hellenistic history writing, it is also necessary to acknowledge its place within Jewish tradition. That would suggest that comparison with the writings of a Jewish historian like Josephus, who wrote during the same period, should be instructive.

Perhaps the major difficulty in writing on Luke-Acts is the size of the work. Enormous commentaries have been written on each book of the New Testament, of which Luke-Acts encompasses one-fourth. The massive two-volume commentary on Luke written by Joseph A. Fitzmyer (1981–1985), the equally impressive volume produced by Ernst Haenchen on Acts (1971), and the five-volume work on Acts published by Foakes Jackson and Lake (1920–1933) are symptomatic of the problem. If the distinctive feature of Luke's Gospel is its continuation in Acts, and if Acts cannot be understood apart from preparation made in the Gospel, there must be some compromise with respect to material covered in studies of the two-part work. I begin this study with the sense that interpreting literary works has to do with large patterns and themes as well as small details. We cannot lose sight of individual trees, but some glimpse of the forest is what this essay intends.

Luke

THE PREFACE

Determining appropriate rules for reading the New Testament must begin with an acknowledgment that rules have already been provided by both sacred and secular tradition. The Bible is a public book, part of church tradition but also very much part of Western culture. Popular culture often provides as much information about the authors of biblical works as either the Bible itself or the traditions of the church. Who wrote Luke-Acts? Some readers might think immediately of Taylor Caldwell's *Dear and Glorious Physician* (1959), an imaginative novel with tiny bits of genuine ecclesiastical tradition woven into a fabric of artificial fibers. Those who know something about the Bible will likely agree that Luke-Acts was written by a

physician who traveled with the Apostle Paul. Such information provides from the outset definite expectations about the story that follows. It is possible that some of the traditional views of Luke-Acts and its author are correct; some are undoubtedly wrong. If we are to learn anything from the books, we should train ourselves to test our hunches; some of them may prove to be fruitful, yet others may obscure the words in front of us.

Alone among the Gospel writers, the author of Luke-Acts steps briefly from the shadows to make a personal statement about his work. That he chooses to preface his work with such a statement is as important as what is said. The short preface in Luke 1:1–4 places Luke-Acts among known works like the writings of the Jewish historian Josephus. It may suggest that the author has some desire to imitate known literary models, uncommon among the Gospel writers, who seem unaware of or unconcerned with literary tradition in their cultures. The preface discloses little about the writer, however, apart from his status as a "third generation" Christian: the author knew not only the testimony of "eyewitnesses," but also "ministers of the word" and written narratives (1:1), among which the Gospel of Mark may be included. The narrator of Luke's Gospel remains steadfastly anonymous apart from the preface. The enigmatic "we sections" in Acts seem to break the anonymity, but even in Acts there is no clue as to the identity of the author, and the "we" weaves in and out of the story with little apparent change in style or outlook.

A few brief comments about the four-verse preface are necessary. The author tells us, first of all, that he is not an eyewitness. He writes, in fact, knowing that "many" have undertaken the task of telling Jesus' story. Probably the most important sentence in the preface is the last (v. 4), where the author states his purpose for offering his own version of the events that have been "accomplished in our midst" (v. 1). Luke has himself undertaken the task of composing a narrative, he tells the mysterious "Theophilus," "so that you may learn how well-founded the teaching is that you have received" (JB). A glance at several different translations of the New Testament shows how differently the short Greek phrase can be read. The New English Bible says Luke intends to provide "authentic knowledge about the matters of which you have been informed." According to this rendering, Theophilus is someone who has been misinformed and needs clarification. According to the Jerusalem Bible (and NIV), Theophilus is someone who has been "instructed" and who needs confidence about what he has been taught. Translations of this crucial phrase will determine how readers approach the two-volume enterprise, and the considerable disagreement among translators about how to render the words presents readers with an important decision from the outset.

The translation I prefer is that of the Jerusalem Bible and the New International Version. The rendering is more literal, and it is a more adequate introduction to Luke's work (a view, of course, that must be defended). At this point interpretation and translation cannot be separated. According to the translation I will follow, Luke writes to provide confidence for someone who has already been instructed—thus probably for believers. Whether "Theophilus" is a symbolic name for all "friends of God" who have been instructed in the faith or an actual person, the old theory that "Theophilus" was a Roman official and a nonbeliever seems unlikely: it founders on the solid ground of translation. Luke writes for the faithful, for those who have "been taught" and who need something more.

THE STORY OPENS

The Gospel moves immediately from the carefully crafted introduction to the story, which opens with two unlikely characters, a country priest and his wife. They are in Jerusalem because Zechariah's division is on duty. (The priesthood was divided into twenty-four divisions; country priests would come to Jerusalem twice a year for a one-week term to preside at the various Temple ceremonies.) As the story begins, Zechariah has been given the privilege of presiding at the incense offering in the Temple and has just entered the holy place. We are told two things about the aging couple: first, they are both righteous as measured by the Law ("blameless"); second, they have no child. The situation is not new, at least for those who know the Old Testament. The story of Abra-

ham and Sarah (Gen 16–18, 21), as well as of Hannah and her husband (1 Sam 1–2), begin with the common plight: the future holds no promise because the woman in each story has been unable to bear a child. As in the Book of Genesis, the action begins in Luke's Gospel with an extraordinary promise from God: "Do not be afraid, Zechariah, for your prayer is heard, and your wife Elizabeth will bear you a son, and you shall call his name John" (1:13; RSV).

Striking is the concentration of images drawn from Israel's religious heritage. The story opens in Jerusalem, in the Temple. The characters are priests. The story begins with the promise of a child to people who have no reason to expect one, a familiar theme from Israel's past. The more we know about Israel's scriptures and traditions, the more we see and hear in Luke. In the message of the heavenly emissary to Zechariah, more imagery appears. Zechariah and Elizabeth's son, John, will play the role of Elijah in his career; that is important to people who knew the prophecy that Elijah would appear "before the great and terrible day of the Lord" (Mal 4:5–6). John's role will consist in turning "the hearts of the fathers to the children . . . to make ready for the Lord a people prepared" (Luke 1:17; RSV).

In the subsequent visit by the same heavenly messenger to Mary, we learn for what John's career will prepare. Mary, an unmarried, unlikely young woman with no apparent pedigree, is told that she has been chosen to bear the Messiah, the promised king from the line of David, a figure who had occupied a prominent place in the dreams of Jewish people in the preceding centuries:

> He will be great, and will be called the Son
> of the Most High;
> and the Lord God will give to him the throne
> of his father David,
> and he will reign over the house of Jacob
> for ever;
> and of his kingdom there will be no end.
> (1:32–33; RSV)

At every juncture in these opening two chapters, the careers of the principal characters are described in imagery from Israel's scriptural heritage, and the extraordinary course of events initiated by God's intervention is linked to oracles and promises drawn from the scriptures:

> He has helped his servant Israel,
> in remembrance of his mercy,
> as he spoke to our fathers,
> to Abraham and to his posterity for ever.
> (1:54–55)

> Blessed be the Lord God of Israel,
> for he has visited and redeemed his people,
>
> .   .   .   .
>
> as he spoke by the mouth of his
> holy prophets from of old,
>
> .   .   .   .
>
> to perform the mercy promised to our fathers,
> and to remember his holy covenant,
> the oath which he swore to our father Abraham.
> (1:68, 70, 72–73; RSV)

Whatever we shall learn about the author, audience, occasion, and purpose of Luke-Acts from our study of the two-part work, it seems prudent to begin with what we have. The narrator of this story presumes his audience knows about the hopes and dreams of God's people, Israel; he is familiar with Israel's scriptures and their promises. The story he will tell must be understood within the framework of that larger history. The day to which Malachi, the last of the prophets, points (according to Luke-Acts) begins to dawn with Zechariah's vision in the Temple and the announcement of the birth of John. The long-awaited birth of the Messiah, the savior who will sit on David's throne and reign over the house of Jacob, has now taken place. The author's desire to demonstrate how "well founded are the things you have been taught" must in some way be related to matters close to the hearts of Jews and the family of Israel, for it is their language he speaks, and it is from their hopes and dreams that he draws in introducing the story of Jesus.

The opening chapters likewise anticipate far-reaching changes that will occur when God fulfills his ancient promises. The tone is nicely summarized in Mary's song, the Magnificat:

> My soul magnifies the Lord,
> and my spirit rejoices in God my Savior,
> for he has regarded the low estate of his handmaiden.

> For behold, henceforth all generations will call me
> blessed;
> for he who is mighty has done great things
> for me, and holy is his name.
>
> .   .   .   .
>
> He has shown strength with his arm,
> he has scattered the proud in the imagination
> of their hearts,
> he has put down the mighty from their thrones,
> and exalted those of low degree;
> he has filled the hungry with good things,
> and the rich he has sent empty away.
> (1:46–49, 51–53; RSV)

Like Hannah, Samuel's mother, Mary sees in her conception of a child the action of a God who regularly vindicates the oppressed and downtrodden. The theme is introduced within these initial chapters: Jesus' career will bring about reversals. Women had little status or power in Jewish society. Yet it is a woman who serves as the example of obedience in Luke. While Zechariah the priest cannot believe the angel's news (1:18–20), Mary does (1:38). Though without any obvious credentials, she is chosen to bear the world's savior. Her son is born in humble circumstances, the birth of the king is attended only by crude shepherds, and all this signals changes to come. God will bring down the mighty and exalt the humble. Jesus will devote his career principally to the poor and the outcast, who will find in him a champion.

If the opening chapters of Luke echo ancient promises and anticipate a new era of deliverance, they also foreshadow opposition and trouble. The fulfillment of God's promises to his people will involve some drama. The sense is clearest, perhaps, in the last of the oracles in the opening chapters, attributed to Simeon:

[Simeon blesses God:]

Lord, now let your servant depart in peace,
according to your word;
for my eyes have seen your salvation
which you have prepared before the face of all peoples,
a light for revelation to the Gentiles,
and for glory to your people Israel.
(2:29–32; RSV, revised)

[Simeon blesses Jesus' parents:]

Behold, this child is set for the fall and rising of many
    in Israel,
and for a sign that is spoken against
(and a sword will pierce through your own soul also),
that thoughts out of many hearts may be revealed.

(2:34–35; RSV)

The words of Simeon play a crucial role in Luke's composition. In his double blessing of God and of Jesus' parents, new items are introduced into the story. For the first time gentiles are mentioned: Mary's child, the king-to-be, will be a "light" for the gentiles and glory for Israel. The words, reminiscent of Isaiah, extend the boundaries of the story to the ends of the earth—to use the words of Jesus addressed to his followers in Acts 1. The parallel blessing of Jesus' parents offers some comment on the optimistic promise of salvation: there will be opposition. Jesus is set for the "fall and rising of many in Israel." He will be a "sign to be spoken against." If salvation for both Israel and the nations may be spoken of as a major theme in Luke's writing, it must be added that opposition is also a major theme. Jesus' work will not go unopposed. And it is opposition within Israel that is the critical matter. In bringing about the salvation promised by Israel's prophets, Jesus will bring about division in Israel. There will be controversy, even about the manner of including non-Jews within the circle of God's people.

One might well say it is the tension between the promise of salvation in Simeon's blessing of God and the promise of opposition in his blessing of Jesus' parents that makes the story go—and that makes the story one worth telling, indeed one that must be told. It is not the simple fact that Jesus is the promised savior which motivates the writing of two volumes. The promised savior stirs up opposition and is finally executed by Roman officials. His followers announce that he has been raised from the dead and offer salvation in his name. They stir up controversy as well: some of them are persecuted, even killed, by members of their own Jewish family. Those Jews who confess Jesus as Messiah are soon overwhelmed by a flood of gentiles who also believe Jesus to be savior and join in his worship, finding a place at the same table as those who observe the Law of Moses. That is what makes the story of the savior worth telling: it is the remarkable manner in which God has chosen to fulfill

his promises of redemption that requires someone to write—perhaps to demonstrate to the confused that the story is indeed "well-founded," that God's word has not failed whatever may appear to be the case.

THE PLOT

Stories generally have something that drives them, some goal toward which everything moves, in light of which individual episodes make sense. That is certainly true of histories. Many people think of historians as people who are interested in facts. People who write history are of course interested in the details, but only insofar as they fit into some story (the root of the word "history"). Particularly in the ancient world, historians were people who believed the world made sense, that events were related to one another in some meaningful way. The purpose for writing may be to point out that events fit together in some pattern; or perhaps an author may write to show that things make sense in a way different from what most people believe. Josephus, for example, wrote his history of the Jewish wars against Rome to refute what he regarded as false interpretations. It is quite common today for a historian to write about an event like the war in Viet-Nam to show that the real causes of American involvement have not been fully understood by earlier writers.

What is it that drives the story Luke tells? The question can be answered at several levels. We might ask first about the goal of the work as expressed in the proem: "that you may know how well-founded are the things you have been taught" (1:4). We may read the story as a lengthy argument in narrative form, in which case our task would be to identify the position being argued and the means by which it is advanced. Or, we might choose to set aside for the present questions about the author's intention and ask about the plot of the story itself. One answer might be that promises provide direction in the story.

Promises and Opposition

The action in Luke-Acts begins with heavenly intervention in various forms. The first, and most frequent, form is that of a vision. Zechariah the priest is in the Temple, presiding over the incense offering. He is visited by a divine messenger who makes a promise: you and your wife shall have a son. The message says more, providing detailed information about the ministry of John in terms of traditional language about Elijah. Zechariah's disbelief does not deter the promise; what the angel foretells comes to pass. Mary is likewise introduced as someone chosen to be the recipient of divine gifts: she is to bear a son who will be known as "Son of the Most High." Unlike Zechariah, however, Mary believes. Promises abound in the story. Simeon makes promises about what is to happen to Jesus and his mother. In his initial appearance in the synagogue in his hometown, Jesus speaks of what will come in his own ministry, borrowing language from Isaiah 61:1–2, which speaks about preaching good news to the poor and opening the eyes of the blind (Luke 4:16–30). In his ministry, God's promises from Isaiah are fulfilled. In Acts, the intervention of the Spirit at Pentecost, interpreted in terms of Joel 2:28–29, points forward to the mission of the apostles—fulfilling Jesus' promise about carrying the message to the end of the earth. Despite opposition from a variety of religious and political groups, the promises are fulfilled.

Opposition to the promises is as much an element in the plot, however, as is the promise itself. What provides drama and adds depth to the story is that most of the characters do not understand the promises of God to be embodied in Jesus; some even take offense at the suggestion that Jesus has anything to do with God's promises. Pharisees accuse Jesus of impiety; religious leaders accuse him of blasphemy and sedition; Roman imperial forces put him to death as a threat to law and order. Promise and opposition together make up a tension that drives the story onward.

The same tension is present in Acts, while the players are different. In Acts, it is the apostles who, empowered by the Holy Spirit, are bearers of the promise that the message of repentance and forgiveness shall be carried to the end of the earth. Religious leaders in Jerusalem oppose them as they opposed Jesus, imprisoning Peter and John and executing Stephen. Imperial forces again play a role, though it is surprisingly minor. The procurators Felix and Festus have a hand in Paul's arrest and eventual journey to Rome as a prisoner of the Roman state. Yet at almost every turn, the Roman leaders confess their bewilderment at the charges made against Paul, even suggesting finally that if Paul had not appealed to the emperor, he would have been set free (Acts 26:30–32).

The opposition that drives virtually the whole of Paul's story in Acts, which comprises almost half the book, arises from within the Jewish community. Paul's detractors attack him as an apostate Jew, one whose preaching seems calculated to undermine confidence in the Law of Moses and the tradition. Repeated accusations from within the Jewish community drive Paul from city to city, often for his safety. Rumors about Paul that have reached Jerusalem require an elaborate demonstration of Paul's fidelity to the Law. After his arrest, accusations from within the Jewish community provide an occasion for apologetic speeches, in which Paul argues his continuing fidelity to the scriptures and tradition of Israel, and which cast opposition to Paul in terms of inner-Jewish struggles of long standing between Pharisees and Sadducees.

The patterns of opposition in both the Gospel and Acts, as Norman Petersen has pointed out, focus on religious centers (synagogue and Temple) and have to do with religious issues (Petersen 1978). If we are to understand Luke-Acts, one major feature of the narrative that must be interpreted is the opposition to Jesus and his followers from within the Jewish community.

Opposition needs to be balanced by support. Many have argued that the role of "the Jews" both in the Gospel and in Acts is negative: they are the enemy. The reality is far more complex. Opposition to Jesus in Luke's Gospel is varied. Some Pharisees complain about Jesus' lack of attention to matters of purity and his willingness to eat with sinners and tax collectors, while other Pharisees regularly invite him to dinner. Scribes, chief priests, and elders, on the other hand, feel obliged to hand him over to the Romans for execution as a threat to the peace. The common people support him throughout, at least up to his arrest and execution. The disciples, obviously Jews, can hardly be classified as enemies.

The same complexity is present in Acts. Those who seek to silence the apostolic preaching in Jerusalem are identified as Sadducees—members of the priestly aristocracy and defenders of a particular understanding of scripture and tradition (Acts 4:1–2). While the Pharisee Gamaliel can hardly be classified as a supporter, he at least gives a speech that lays out the principle on the basis of which the new movement will be evaluated: if it is of God, it will succeed (Acts 5:33–39). Pharisees are identified as incipient supporters of Paul, believing as he does in the Spirit, the resurrection, and angels (contrary to the Sadducees: Acts 23:6–8). And while there is opposition to the apostolic preaching, there is also remarkable success. Peter succeeds in convincing thousands in Jerusalem that salvation is in Jesus' name (Acts 2 and 3). By the time Paul returns to Jerusalem at the end of his ministry, there are tens of thousands of Jews who believe in Jesus (Acts 21:20–21). Even Paul, while evoking intense hostility from his countrymen, succeeds in convincing some Jews that Jesus is indeed the Messiah. The last scene in Acts is set in a synagogue in Rome, where Paul's preaching once more results in some believing and others disbelieving (Acts 28:24).

Opposition to Jesus and his apostles is a major ingredient in the plot of Luke-Acts, and it would not be an overstatement to suggest that interpreting this opposition is one of the major tasks of the narrative. If God's intervention sets the whole story in motion, and if his involvement in the story is understood as consistent with his ancient promises, what does opposition to his actions mean, particularly when it comes principally from within God's own people? Does the narrative recount a tragedy, ending with the demise of Israel as the people of God? Or is tragedy a category ill-suited to elucidate what Luke's history sets out to accomplish? The question may be posed in theological terms: If the promises of God are a major ingredient in the story, does the narrative recount the failure of those promises or their fulfillment? Answering such a question was obviously difficult: the Jewish people were violently divided over the question of Jesus. Yet that is precisely why the story was necessary. Understanding Luke's story should provide some answer to the question about the promises of God.

JESUS AND THE GUARDIANS OF THE BOUNDARIES

The opening chapters of the Gospel sketch Jesus with features familiar from the tradition. He is the child born to be king—"Son of the Most High," destined to sit "on the throne of his father David and reign over the house of Jacob forever." John will go before to prepare his way, playing the role of Elijah. There are some surprises. The young king is born of remarkably humble parents in the most abject of circumstances. There are nevertheless signs of what is to come. A heavenly chorus sings at his birth, even if the only audience is a group of shepherds. When the infant is brought to Jerusalem, the pious Simeon recognizes the young king and sings of what is to come. If Jesus' youth is too unimportant to recount, it is at least clear from his first visit to Jerusalem that he has "his Father's business" to attend to and that he will show considerable interest in religious matters (Luke 2:41–51).

A real surprise comes with Jesus' first appearance as an adult (thirty years of age, we are told, at 3:23), where without explanation he comes to be baptized by John. John, the fearless preacher of a baptism of repentance for the forgiveness of sins, baptizes Jesus, who, we are told, will himself baptize "with the Holy Spirit and with fire" (3:16). Why should the king-to-be submit to such a baptism? Why should he identify with the multitudes come to John for repentance and washing? We are not told. We learn only that the heaven was opened, the Holy Spirit descended, and God spoke words of confirmation, using familiar cadences from special biblical verses: "Thou art my beloved Son . . . " (3:22, quoting Psalms 2:7, among other passages). Jesus is apparently where he should be. God approves. Yet measured by all conventional standards the setting and the occasion for such a royal pronouncement by God are wrong.

In Jesus' first appearance in a synagogue, in Nazareth, there is that same tension between fulfilled promises and surprise. Jesus reads from Isaiah about the ministry of the one "anointed to preach good news to the poor" (4:18, quoting Isa 61:1–2). There is no difficulty with the notion that God's anointed one will deliver the poor and the oppressed. Yet Jesus interprets the verses by referring to Elijah and Elisha, both of whose ministry was in some sense extended to foreigners at the expense of their own people. Jesus' words so enrage his countrymen that they nearly throw him off a cliff. He escapes—but only for a time. Jesus' ministry is depicted in terms borrowed from tradition, but it is not confined by them. There is something surprising, unexpected, even scandalous about his preaching that anticipates the whole of his ministry.

In what follows Jesus' inaugural sermon, we observe that the ancient promises of Isaiah are indeed fulfilled. His first act is to confront an "unclean spirit" in a synagogue. He casts the unclean spirit out, thus cleansing the holy place. The authority by which he commands even the spirits goes beyond traditional bounds. People are amazed, and his fame soon spreads (4:36–37). The sick flock to him and are healed. Even lepers, the untouchables of Jewish society, whose ritual uncleanliness rendered anyone they touched unclean, come to Jesus, and he touches them. Yet he is not made unclean; they are cleansed. He raises the dead and gives sight to the blind. He dares to forgive the sins of a paralytic, speaking as if in God's place—and sends him home with his pallet.

Jesus' place is with the sick and the outcast, as Mary's song and Isaiah anticipated. He brings deliverance as the agent of God's kingdom. His special concern for the poor is reminiscent of Israel's prophets. "Blessed are you poor," he preaches, "for yours is the kingdom of God. Blessed are you that hunger now, for you shall be satisfied" (6:20–21; RSV). There can be no doubt that Jesus is the promised deliverer. When the imprisoned John sends messengers to asks Jesus if he is the one to come, Jesus replies: "Go and tell John what you have seen and heard: the blind receive their sight, the lame walk, lepers are cleansed, and the deaf hear, the dead are raised up, the poor have good news preached to them. And blessed is he who takes no offense at me" (7:22–23; RSV).

Jesus has power, and he does good works. Yet there are some who take offense. He does not fit conventional categories. His authority verges on blasphemy. He associates with sinners and tax collectors, does not observe fasts as do other religious people, and seems lax about Sabbath observance (5:17–6:11). He does not respect traditional boundaries, and therein lies the problem for his contemporaries. The Pharisees, who appear frequently as Jesus' critics, were the religious people of their age. They were a small group of Jews who took their heritage seriously. Their conception of religion involved constructing and maintaining boundaries between the pure and impure, the responsible and irresponsible, the observant and the nonobservant. By so doing they were able to keep observance of the Law of Moses as a viable alternative to their contemporaries at a time when the "civilized" ways of the Greek-speaking world convinced many Jews that their traditions were provincial and embarrassing. Jesus threatened all those boundaries. His willingness to eat with sinners and tax collectors suggested moral irresponsibility. Not only did he risk contamination, but he also risked destroying any motivation for ethical seriousness. Was he not blessing the very ones whose lives threatened to obliterate the Jewish alternative to paganism? If the boundaries were destroyed, what would become of a way of life that alone seemed concerned to acknowledge God's election of a people and his gift of the Law?

Jesus was "high-risk," the more because he had power. His success only made him more dangerous if, as some of his contemporaries feared, his ministry was undermining the tradition. Jesus denied that he was out to destroy the Law. He claimed that his behavior had a very different result—that it served not to destroy the family but to welcome back strays, to cleanse the unclean. Religious Jews, however, recognized in Jesus a threat to their way of life. From the very beginning of Luke's story, narrative patterns feature conflicts that have to do with breaking barriers and transgressing boundaries. Jesus came, he tells his followers, to give not peace "but rather division" (12:51). Not even the family will provide a secure refuge, for "they will be divided, father against son and son against father" (12:53). Boundaries drawn to provide a secure sphere for daily life were transgressed. People were confronted by one who claimed authority himself, who claimed to speak and act for God. There was no neutral zone from which to evaluate Jesus. He forced people to make decisions about him. When pressed, religious and political leaders decide in favor of their traditions and codes and put Jesus to death.

Conflicts involve religious centers—first the synagogue, then the Temple. They have to do with the function of the tradition as a whole. Jesus comes into the world with the promise of salvation; he is the "savior who is Christ the Lord" (2:11). The deliverance he offers, however, threatens structures erected to offer protection and meaning in an otherwise threatening and confusing world. Where does the promise lie? That is the question that runs through the narrative.

The Protest of a Responsible Child

The question about Jesus' strange affinity for the outcast and the irresponsible is addressed directly in chapter 15 in a series of three parables. The protest of the Pharisees introduces the chapter: "Now the tax collectors and sinners were all drawing near to hear him. And the Pharisees and the scribes murmured, saying, 'This man receives sinners and eats with them'" (15:1–2).

As a response, Jesus told parables, one of the characteristic teaching forms he uses in Luke. Though they have been read throughout the history of the church as allegories concealing deep mysteries, Jesus' parables are usually rather simple stories using imagery drawn from everyday life that were effective precisely because they were not difficult to understand (Jeremias 1963; Funk 1966). His parables served often as a form of argument. Part of the difficulty in the history of parable interpretation has been determining to what issues or questions Jesus' parables were directed. That is not a problem in Luke 15, where we are informed that Jesus tells these parables in response to criticism of the company he keeps.

In the first two of the parables, Jesus compares his action to that of a shepherd who discovers that one of his sheep is lost (15:3–7), and to a woman who finds that she has lost one of ten coins (15:8–10). In both cases, all that matters is finding what has been lost. All the energies of the shepherd and the housekeeper are directed toward that end. They are overwhelmingly preoccupied with the lost precisely because they are lost and need to be found. That same preoccupation typifies God, Jesus comments, for "there will be more joy in heaven over one sinner who repents than over ninety-nine righteous persons who need no repentance" (15:7; RSV).

The longest of the parables is about a family—or at least about the males in the family. In the case of this parable (15:11–32), the males are the only important characters because the issue is property ownership and inheritance, and in Jewish society women had rights to neither. The parable is commonly known as the "parable of the prodigal son," which suggests that the main focus of the story is the younger son, who, restless to break free from family constraints, demands his share of the family property and heads off into the world for adventure. Not surprisingly, the young man is not ready for the cruel world, and he wastes his property "in loose living." The story provides little insight into his character. We learn only that when he hit bottom he "came to himself" and decided to throw himself on his father's mercy and at least find a place among the hired hands. Though moralists have described this decision to return as an act of repentance and have used it to urge repentance on others, there is nothing to suggest that the young man's resolve to return home is anything more than common sense. Perhaps he knows that his father is an easy mark and will take him back. The absence of any psychological probing of the younger son makes it difficult to regard him as an attractive character worthy of respect.

At least one scholar has chosen to entitle the story the "parable of the waiting father," suggesting that the real focus is the father. It is not the younger son, in fact, who brings about any reconciliation. It is the father who is willing to accept him back into the family when his son has abandoned any legal right to claim a place in the household. In the story, the father has obviously been watching and waiting for precisely this moment. While the son is still far off, his father sees him and has compassion. He embraces his son, virtually ignoring the carefully rehearsed speech. His command to bring a robe and a ring have little to do with any demonstrated contrition. The father is more ready to forgive than his son is to ask. When the prodigal returns, the party can begin.

The neglected member of the family—and perhaps the most interesting—is the older brother. He is introduced as the only responsible member of the family: "Now his elder son was in the field" (15:25). On a farm, there is work to be done, and it is the older and responsible son who does it. A party has begun, yet no one has gone to the field to inform the older brother. He finds out only after he has done his chores—and then he must ask one of the servants. It is hardly surprising that he is angered and refuses to attend the party. His protest is serious, and will ring true to generations of older, responsible children: I have faithfully done what is expected of me, he protests, keeping the farm together, obeying your commands. Yet you never so much as said thank you. You never offered me a goat to serve at a party for my friends. Yet your son, whose contribution to the family has been to waste half our estate on a way of life that is a disgrace to all we stand for, now suddenly deserves a lavish party with a fatted calf! What have I done wrong? Perhaps my fault is that I have never wasted your money, never disobeyed your commands, never failed to do my chores. Perhaps if I had disobeyed, you would care for me as much as for the wastrel!

The protest of the Pharisees comes through eloquently. They require only justice, only what is fair. And Jesus is not fair. He invests his time with those who do not deserve it, even welcoming them to the intimacy of his table. Will that not encourage irresponsibility? Why not reward those who hold the world together, who do their chores and keep food on the table? Is it conceivable that God is more concerned about the wastrels and the irresponsible than with the righteous? Their protest is a serious one, and it rings true with responsible children, who know that those who get the most attention from parents are most often the children who are the most trouble to the family.

The story does not end with the protest of the elder son, but with the invitation of the father. Again, I paraphrase: Can you not share my joy? he asks. My son is also your brother. He was lost and is found, was dead and is now alive. Is that not something even you can appreciate?

The story uses family experience to shed light on how things are with God. Parental love cannot be reduced to justice. What is required to get the young man back into the family is a willingness to go beyond fairness, for what matters most is that the family be whole. The terrible irony is that what makes it difficult for the elder son to welcome his brother back is his virtue, beyond which he cannot see. His protest is accurate, but shortsighted. Fairness cannot reunite broken families and mend fractured lives. And if there is a priority with God, it is a commitment to reunite and mend. Those who turn out to be in the greatest bondage are the most virtuous and responsible. They sense only the unfairness of Jesus' love and not its possibilities.

The parable does not resolve the family crisis. It ends with an appeal. To the degree the parable sheds light on Jesus' ministry, we would have to say that the "older brothers" in the story of Jesus' life give their answer. Jesus will be put to death. And yet it is perhaps here that the possibilities of his message will finally begin to break through, for even their final rejection will not be the last word. Jesus' followers will preach a message of "repentance and forgiveness" for the responsible and irresponsible alike in the name of the one who was rejected but whom God raised up.

JERUSALEM

> When the days drew near for him to be received up, he set his face to go to Jerusalem. (Luke 9:51; RSV)

Considering that the whole Jerusalem phase in Jesus' ministry lasts no more than a few days, it occupies a prominent place in the narrative. On the one hand, Jerusalem is the Holy City, the place where the Temple is located. Jesus' parents take their child to be dedicated at the Temple and offer a sacrifice for Mary's purification, as prescribed in the Law (2:22–24). His parents are in Jerusalem at the time of Passover, as would be expected (2:41). Jesus finds himself at home in the city, in the Temple—"my Father's house" (2:46–49). Luke's story, in fact, begins and ends in the Temple, where the disciples return after Jesus departs from them (24:52–53).

Yet Jerusalem is also the place of Jesus' rejection. Early in his ministry, he announces to his followers that he must "be rejected by the elders and chief priests and scribes, and be killed, and on the third day be raised" (9:22). The fateful confrontation will take place in Jerusalem, a city that has a less favorable place in tradition as the site of numerous confrontations between Israel and God's emissaries. Jesus' resolve to go there is announced early:

> For it cannot be that a prophet should perish away from Jerusalem. O Jerusalem, Jerusalem, killing the prophets and stoning those who are sent to you! How often would I have gathered your children together as a hen gathers her brood under her wings, and you would not! Behold, your house is forsaken. And I tell you, you will not see me until you say, "Blessed is he who comes in the name of the Lord!" (13:33–35; RSV)

The importance of that final week in Jerusalem is reflected in the structure of the story. A large body of instructional material is grouped together in the so-called travel section in the Gospel. In 9:51, and again in 13:22, the narrative emphasizes that Jesus is on his way to Jerusalem, although he does not arrive in the city until chapter 19. The intervening chapters, made up largely of instructional material, give little impression of geographical movement. The actual journey is little more than a framing device. The very artificiality of the framework attests its importance (Fitzmyer 1981, 823–832). Somehow everything Jesus does and says must be understood in light of the confrontation to come. The shadow of his cross is cast over the whole story.

If Jesus' arrival in Jerusalem will have enormous consequences for his ministry, it will likewise be decisive for the future of the city. There is a sense in which Jesus' rejection brings to a climax some ancient pattern, sealing the city's fate:

> Woe to you! for you build the tombs of the prophets whom your fathers killed. So you are witnesses and consent to the deeds of your fathers; for they killed them, and you build their tombs. Therefore also the Wisdom of God said, "I will send them prophets and apostles, some of whom they will kill and persecute," that the blood of all the prophets shed from the foundation of the world may be required of this generation. . . . Yes, I tell you, it shall be required of this generation. (11:47–51; RSV)

The city, Jesus promises, shall be destroyed: "For the days shall come upon you, when your enemies will cast up a bank about you and surround you, and hem you in on every side, and dash you to the ground, you and your children within you, and they will not leave one stone upon another in you; because you did not know the time of your visitation" (19:43–44).

If opposition is an important feature of the plot, Jerusalem is the place where that opposition is focused. It is the leaders of the Temple who hand Jesus over to the Romans. Those same leaders persecute Peter and John, execute Stephen and James, and have Paul arrested. Simeon promises that Jesus is "set for the rise and fall of many within Israel." Jerusalem itself will fall because of its opposition to the one who "comes in the name of the Lord."

The Fate of the King

While Jesus' ministry is cast in images familiar from stories about prophets and holy men, the last phase of his ministry is reminiscent of royal tradition. Jesus rides into Jerusalem on a donkey, a familiar feature of coronation ritual, and is hailed by the crowds as "the King who comes in the name of the Lord!" (19:38). The leaders, convinced that Jesus must go, seek a way to arrest him so as not to stir up the crowds, who "hang upon his words." They are aware of the danger. Passover was a festival commemorating deliverance from foreign bondage; as one of the pilgrim festivals, it attracted thousands of people to Jerusalem, so that the city swelled to twice its size. Revolution was in the air, and the last thing the leaders wanted was for some spark to set off outright revolt. The Romans were just as concerned to head off trouble. At Passover and Tabernacles, the governor came to the city to supervise public order personally from the fortress Antonia, located adjacent to the Temple.

The crowd's acclamation of Jesus as king forced the hand of the religious and political leaders. In Caesar's realm there could be only one king: Caesar tolerated no competitors. And for the religious leaders charged with the responsibility of keeping the peace, the fervor of the crowds could only mean that Jesus was too great a risk.

The Arrest. The precise circumstances of Jesus' arrest are shrouded in mystery. Luke, like the other Gospel writers, is remarkably vague about the circumstances. Judas, one of the twelve disciples, betrays Jesus. No real motivation for the betrayal is offered, only the comment that Judas' actions were motivated by the devil:

> Then Satan entered into Judas, called Iscariot, who was of the number of the twelve; he went away and conferred with the chief priests and captains how he might betray him to them. And they were glad, and engaged to give him money. So he agreed, and sought an opportunity to betray him to them in the absence of the multitude. (22:3–6)

Though Satan's role in Luke's story is a small one, it is nevertheless decisive. At the beginning of his ministry, Jesus is tempted by the devil to employ spectacular means to achieve his ends. When Jesus refuses to bow to Satan, to whom belong "all the kingdoms of the world" (4:5–6), he sets himself in opposition to established powers. The comment that the devil departed "until an opportune time" (4:13) anticipates his return. Opposition from both Israel and Rome suggests not so subtly that for Luke, Satan's dominion extends to the leaders of the civilized world—and even to God's own people.

With Jesus' arrest, his circle of disciples is broken. Despite their rather elaborate training, Jesus' explicit predictions of what was to come, and his promise of places for them on thrones from which they will judge the twelve tribes of Israel (22:30), the disciples collapse under pressure. Only Peter follows as far as the home of the high priest, showing signs of courage. Yet he too disintegrates, and in a way his fall is greater, for he denies Jesus three times. The disintegration of Jesus' movement seems complete. He is brought before the Jewish leaders, where he is interrogated and mocked. He is then led to Pilate, where he is accused of crimes against the state. Mocked by King Herod and his soldiers, by rulers of the Jews, and by Roman soldiers, he is hung on a cross with two other criminals. The angel Gabriel promised Mary that Jesus would "sit on the throne of his father David and reign over the house of Jacob forever." Yet when Jesus is finally hailed as king, it is in mockery as he hangs on a cross with the inscription, "The King of the Jews."

"The Christ must suffer." There is little in the story to play down the scandal of Jesus' death. Though Israel's prophets encountered rejection and (at least according to tradition) were even martyred, the same was not expected of God's Christ. The "shoot from the stump of Jesse," the coming king from David's line, would "slay the wicked with the breath of his mouth" (Isa 11:1–4). Yet Jesus was destroyed by the wicked. The only acclamation he received was from taunters: "He saved others; let him save himself, if he is the Christ of God, his Chosen One!" (23:35; RSV).

The Jewish rulers, the Roman soldiers, and one of those executed with Jesus all speak for common sense. Jesus does not fit the role of deliverer. He associated with the wrong sorts and made promises he could not keep. Judged by tradition and by the Law and by common sense, he was a pretender, another would-be savior whose ambition finally did him in. The prominent place accorded Jesus' rejection and

death is reminiscent of tragedies, where the seeds of the hero's undoing, sown earlier in the story, finally bear their bitter fruit.

Yet there is a world of difference between Jesus' story and tragedies. His story does not end with his death. Another stunning reversal will occur when God raises him from the dead. Contrary to appearances, Jesus will keep his word. God will install him at his right hand, and the message about God's reign will be carried to the ends of the earth. What appears as tragic is in fact ironic. The events mean something very different from what the actors in the story assume.

Clues are not hard to find. When Jesus gives his followers final instructions after he is raised from the dead, he explains to them the scriptures: "Thus it is written, that the Christ should suffer and on the third day rise from the dead" (24:46). Words are borrowed from those sacred scriptures to tell the story. The comment that soldiers cast lots for Jesus' garments (23:34), for example, comes from Psalm 22:18. The offer of vinegar to Jesus (23:36) probably alludes to Psalm 69:21. Jesus' last words (23:46) are taken from Psalm 31:5. To those who know the scriptures Luke offers a glimpse of a deeper level of reality.

Some of the constructions are more elaborate. Herod has a prominent place in Luke's account of Jesus' passion, though he ends up playing virtually no role. The account of Jesus' visit to Herod ends with a strange comment: "And Herod and Pilate became friends with each other that very day, for before this they had been at enmity with each other" (23:12; RSV).

The significance of the comment—and of the whole story of Herod's involvement—becomes apparent only in Acts 4, when a prayer of thanks offers an interpretation of a scriptural passage taken from Psalm 2:

> Why did the Gentiles rage,
> and the peoples imagine vain things?
> The kings of the earth set themselves in array,
> and the rulers were gathered together,
> against the Lord and against his Anointed—
> (Acts 4:25–26)

The prayer offers this interpretation: "For truly in

this city there were gathered together against thy holy servant Jesus, whom thou didst anoint, both Herod and Pontius Pilate, with the Gentiles and the people of Israel, to do whatever thy hand and thy plan had predestined to take place" (Acts 4:27–28).

Herod is a "king"; Pilate is a "ruler." The story of Herod's involvement is worth telling because it fulfills the scriptures. Jesus' story, in other words, has "been written." We have not understood the story unless we have discovered those deeper dimensions. According to Luke, it is only here that the truth of the story becomes visible.

And it is in light of that deeper truth that the ironies become visible. Those who condemn Jesus become—quite contrary to their intentions—agents of God's will to save the world by the death of his Christ. Their mockery serves only to testify to the truth. It is Pilate, after all, who formulates the inscription, "The King of the Jews." He is correct. Herod and his soldiers invest Jesus as King, though they have no idea what they are doing. Even through the actions of Jesus' enemies, the scriptures are fulfilled and God's will is done.

Their actions reveal another terrible irony: those who pretend to know the truth—the guardians of tradition, the custodians of law and order—are farthest from it. Their condemnation of Jesus only reveals how profound is their bondage to appearance and custom. Judged by conventional standards, Jesus cannot pretend to be the King sent from God to deliver the world. But he is. From his exalted place at God's right hand he will reign until his return at the end of days (Acts 2 and 3). And in their rejection of him, the religious leaders reveal their own blindness and seal their own fate. Jerusalem will no longer be the center of the earth and the seat of God's throne. The great city and its Temple will be destroyed.

"And on the third day rise." Though Jesus' resurrection is not a surprise to the reader of Luke—Jesus has predicted it on numerous occasions—it is to his followers. His crucifixion left his movement in shambles. The disciples were in hiding. Only the women were left to tend to the business of providing Jesus with a proper burial. Since Jesus died on Sabbath eve, they had to wait until the end of Sabbath before preparing the body. These faithful women are thus the first to hear the glorious news that Jesus is not "among the dead." They run to report the joyous news to the disciples, only to be greeted with skepticism.

Luke is consistent to the end of the story. Just as Mary, an ordinary Jewish girl, gives birth to the Lord's Christ and serves as a model of obedience, so ordinary women become the first evangelists. The standards of society are not those of the movement reborn at the empty tomb. Jesus is concerned with the poor and the outcast; he does God's will, which is to "put down the mighty from their thrones," and exalt "those of low degree" (Luke 1:52). Courageous women, not frightened and disbelieving men, are the first to serve as witnesses to the good news.

Among the Gospel writers Luke alone tells the story of Jesus' appearance to two travelers on the road to Emmaus, a story that draws together major themes in the narrative. Jesus walks with the two travelers yet is not recognized. The dialogue focuses on crushed hopes. "We had hoped that he was the one to redeem Israel," they tell the stranger (24:21). Jesus counters their apparent disappointment with a brief lesson in scriptural interpretation: "'O foolish men, and slow of heart to believe all that the prophets have spoken! Was it not necessary that the Christ should suffer these things and enter into his glory?' And beginning with Moses and all the prophets, he interpreted to them in all the scriptures the things concerning himself" (24:25–27; RSV).

The travelers still do not recognize Jesus. The disclosure comes only when Jesus sits down at a meal with them, takes bread, gives thanks, and breaks it. The table scene reminds us of others in Luke, particularly the meal Jesus shared with his followers the night before his death, when he "took bread, gave thanks, broke, and gave to them" (22:19). Whether Luke's readers understood "the breaking of the bread" (24:35) as a reference to the Lord's Supper or to simple table fellowship in Christian homes or to both, the image anticipates the regular practice of "breaking bread in their homes" that was to become a feature of Christian fellowship in Acts (2:46). Just as Jesus shared himself with all sorts of people in the intimacy of meals during his ministry, so it is in the intimacy of table fellowship that his presence continues among his followers.

Jesus' appearance to the whole circle of the disciples serves to prepare for the next stage in the story. He offers another lesson in scriptural interpretation, emphasizing again the scriptural necessity of his death and resurrection. Also included in this scriptural program is a mission: "Thus it is written . . . that repentance and forgiveness of sins should be preached in his name to all nations, beginning from Jerusalem" (Luke 24:46–47).

Acts picks up the story of those chosen preachers, and it will offer detailed arguments from the scriptures to convince those who have doubts. The arguments are basic to Luke's whole literary enterprise, which intends to speak about the things "accomplished in our midst" (Luke 1:1) in such a way as to demonstrate "how well-founded are the things you have been taught" (1:4). Jesus' brief summary is a reminder that to be properly understood, his story must be read within the context of Israel's history as detailed in the scriptures. His words establish an agenda for part 2, the Acts of the Apostles (Schubert 1954).

Luke's Gospel concludes, as it began, in the Temple. We know that the story will not end here, however. The Temple will be destroyed; there will not be left in Jerusalem one stone on another. Preparations have been made for a campaign that will take followers of Jesus "to the end of the earth," and Jesus promises to empower them for that task. But for that part of the story we must turn to Acts.

The Acts of The Apostles

INTRODUCTION

The differences between the Gospel and Acts are striking. In Acts the narrative is not as choppy, nor broken so often into small episodes, as it is in Luke. There are long sections in which one consistent theme is pursued—as in the accounts of Paul's travels in the second half of the volume. In the Gospel, Jesus' so-called Journey to Jerusalem is a journey only in intent. Luke does not follow one consistent geographical path through Galilee to Jerusalem. On the other hand, we do follow Paul on three actual journeys: he sets out from Antioch and heads for Asia Minor; later he sets out for Greece, and we accompany him from Philippi to Thessalonica, to Borea, to Athens, and to Corinth. The stories are marked by attention to local color and detail.

Speeches in Acts are of a different sort than in Luke. There are no parables or aphorisms or short stories featuring a pronouncement by Jesus that settled some disputed interpretation of the Law. Instead, there are genuine speeches by Peter, Stephen, and Paul—speeches that feature learned interpretation of the scriptures, careful thematic development, and even a sense of rhetorical movement and structure. Though Luke's prose may not measure up to that of his contemporaries, it is considerably more impressive in Acts than in the Gospel.

Most scholars account for much of the difference between the Gospel and Acts in terms of theories about sources. Luke had clearly defined sources for his account of Jesus' ministry, one of which was Mark's Gospel. The same does not appear to be true for Acts. Accounts of the exploits of Jesus' followers are confined to later literature that belongs far more to the realm of legend. Though there is good reason to suppose that stories about the great pillars of the Christian movement circulated among believers and even served preachers with arguments for the faith, Acts is a far more unified composition than the Gospel probably because the author had a freer hand (Jervell 1979, 19–39).

That is not to suggest that Acts is any more "Lucan" than the Gospel. The introduction to Acts refers back to the "first volume" that has been prepared for Theophilus; the two obviously belong together. And whatever the limits provided by sources, Luke did fashion his own account of Jesus' ministry. Still, the stylistic and thematic consistency of Acts ought to serve as warrant for taking the second volume seriously as part of a unified conception, to which we refer as Luke-Acts.

There are significant interpretive questions that must be acknowledged and addressed at some point. For most, Acts has served chiefly as a history book. Its importance lies in the facts it reports. Such historical interests can hardly be ruled out. We know very little about the early days of the Jesus movement, and what we know comes almost exclusively from Acts. As in the case of all historical resources, the material must be subjected to principles of historical investigation if its information is to be used to construct a picture of the early Christian movement. The importance of the volume cannot be reduced to its value as a repository of information, however. As with other ancient histories, Luke-Acts seeks to commend some view of things to its readers. As I noted earlier, Luke's work may usefully be classified as religious propaganda. History is enlisted as an argument for confidence, to demonstrate "how well-founded are the things you have been taught." "Well-founded" may have something to do with historical accuracy, but that hardly exhausts the point of the story. To appreciate the contribution of Acts to the larger argument undertaken by its author, we shall have to pay attention to the theme of the work. What story does it tell? What case does it argue? In what sense does it contribute to a sense of confidence that what Luke's audience had been taught was "well-founded?"

"TO THE END OF THE EARTH"

Links between the Gospel and Acts provide a starting point for interpretation. The somewhat awkward transition from the end of Luke's Gospel to the beginning of Acts belies the intimate connection between the two parts of the story. The last scene in the Gospel, Jesus' conversation with the eleven disciples, introduces the theme:

> Thus it is written, that the Christ should suffer and on the third day rise from the dead, and that repentance and forgiveness of sins should be preached in his name to all nations, beginning from Jerusalem. You are witnesses of these things. And behold, I send the promise of my Father upon you; but stay in the city, until you are clothed with power from on high. (Luke 24:46–49; RSV)

That theme is picked up in Acts 1:8: "But you shall receive power when the Holy Spirit has come upon you; and you shall be my witnesses in Jerusalem and in all Judea and Samaria and to the end of the earth."

The story of Pentecost, which recounts the heavenly empowerment of these emissaries, harks back to the very opening of Luke's Gospel, where John the Baptist spoke of Jesus as one who would "baptize you with the Holy Spirit and with fire" (Luke 3:16; alluded to in Acts 1:5). Promises are fulfilled when the Spirit is poured out, distributed in "tongues as of fire." The point of that empowerment is that

Jesus' disciples are equipped for their mission. The gift of the Spirit will enable them to speak boldly (Luke 12:12, 21:10–19). That divinely inspired and impelled mission is perhaps the major theme of Acts.

The remainder of Jesus' comments to his followers in the initial verses of Acts cannot be overlooked, however. "Lord, will you at this time restore the kingdom to Israel?" they ask. "He said to them, 'It is not for you to know times or seasons which the Father has fixed by his own authority. But you shall receive power'" (Acts 1:6–8; RSV). The mission of the apostles has often been regarded as a substitute for the coming of the kingdom or perhaps as a promise that Israel will now be replaced by a new movement headed by the Twelve. That is not the point of Jesus' statement at all. There is no denial that the kingdom will be restored to Israel; it is only the timing that cannot be revealed. The ministry of the apostles in Acts cannot be divorced from the promises to Israel, noted here, in the opening chapters of Luke's Gospel, and repeated in the speeches of Acts. What is occurring in Jerusalem, according to Luke, is nothing less than the restoration of the kingdom to Israel.

A final comment: Regarding the spread of the message from Jerusalem to the end of the earth as the major unifying theme in Acts is not quite satisfying. From chapter 21 to the end of Acts—a significant portion of the volume—the story tells not of the spread of the gospel but of Paul's arrest, imprisonment, and eventual arrival in Rome (hardly the "end of the earth" in the conception of the ancients). One of the major interpretive questions must be how these chapters fit into the overall conception of Acts—unless one simply assumes they do not fit and are included as some kind of addendum (Jervell 1979, 153–184).

SPEECHES

Perhaps the most striking feature of Acts is the presence of extended, rather formal speeches by major characters (especially Peter, Stephen, and Paul). There is a considerable body of scholarship on these speeches, ranging from a comparison with speeches in the works of ancient historiographers (Dibelius 1956; Henry J. Cadbury, "The Speeches in Acts," in Foakes

Jackson and Lake 1933, vol. 5, 402–427) to an assessment of the speeches as historical reports. Analysis of the speeches yields results for a number of different quests.

C. H. Dodd, for example, read the speeches as remnants of early Christian preaching, constructing from them a framework of the earliest sermons (Dodd 1964). Several other British scholars have built on his work (e.g., Lindars 1961), finding in these speeches remnants of the earliest approaches to the Christian interpretation of the Old Testament, remnants of the most ancient Christology, and the beginning points of Christian theologizing.

Others, notably German scholars, have expressed doubts about the antiquity of these speeches and have suggested rather that they be read as evidence of Christian preaching at the time of Luke. The speeches, they have argued, are part of a literary composition. They seem to follow established patterns: Dibelius calls them "missionary speeches" (1956, 138–185). With a few exceptions, the vocabulary remains rather consistent whether the speeches are attributed to Peter, Stephen, or Paul. Formal analysis suggests that the patterns should be studied first of all within their setting in early Christian groups rather than as naive historical accounts of actual speeches.

Two of the important—and influential—studies on the speeches are those of Martin Dibelius and Henry Cadbury. Both scholars were students of antiquity as well as of the New Testament. They suggested Luke's works ought to be studied within their historical setting in the Greco-Roman world in which history writing was a craft for which people were trained in schools. Study of various rhetorical handbooks and of other ancient histories can provide helpful insight into the process of history writing and the function of speeches in historical works. The point of their studies is that the speeches should first be examined within the context provided by the author. They are part of a narrative, and they play an important role in the story. Only after questions about their function in Acts have been examined is it legitimate to ask further about their value as sources of information about Christian preaching contemporary with Luke or about the actual historical scenes they depict. When questions about history come to domi-

nate study of the speeches, the most important questions about their place in Luke-Acts can be obscured. That is unfortunate, since it is the literary questions about the role of the speeches in the work as a whole that are most capable of analysis and resolution.

A simple question to ask is what difference a particular speech makes in the narrative. What action is motivated? What do we learn about particular characters? What interpretation is offered that is critical to our view of the action?

In Acts we learn least about the character of the speakers. A certain stereotyping takes place in the speeches. There is not a great deal of difference between Peter's speeches and Paul's, or between Paul's and Stephen's. Differences have more to do with the particular situation than with distinctive modes of speech or outlook. On the other hand, speeches are important to action. Peter's first two speeches result in the repentance and baptism of thousands—and in his arrest. Stephen's speech, offered in his defense, ensures his execution—and the spread of "Hellenists" to cities in the Roman Empire where for the first time the Gospel message is preached to non-Jews. Paul's speeches usually succeed in stirring up opposition, which leads to his eventual arrest, trial, and journey to Rome—though they also result in some important conversions. Speeches, in other words, are significant moments in the development of action.

Still more important however, is the contribution the speeches make to an understanding of Acts as a whole. A brief analysis of a few crucial speeches is the most useful way to make the point.

Pentecost

Peter's speech to the crowd of Jews from all over the world, in Jerusalem to celebrate the festival of Weeks (Pentecost), is given as a response to the confusion occasioned by the strange behavior of the Spirit-filled disciples. The crowds attracted by the commotion have no idea what to make of the scene: "What does this mean?" Some offer an appraisal: "They are filled with new wine" (Acts 2:12–13). Peter offers his own explanation, drawing first of all on the prophet Joel: "These men are not drunk, as you suppose, since it is only the third hour of the day; but this is what was spoken by the prophet Joel: 'And in the last days, it shall be, God declares, that I will pour out my Spirit upon all flesh'" (Acts 2:15–17; RSV).

The strange behavior, typified by speaking in other tongues, is identified as prophetic speech in light of the scriptural citation. The remarkable events are likewise to be understood as signs that "the last days" are at hand, again appealing to imagery from Joel. The speech goes on to describe what the arrival of these last days means, again using scriptural words: "And it shall be that whoever calls on the name of the Lord shall be saved" (Acts 2:21, quoting Joel 2:32).

Peter goes on to argue, using learned methods of interpretation practiced by Jewish sages, that Jesus is the "Lord" spoken of in Joel (Juel 1981). The proof is summarized in Acts 2:36: "Let all the house of Israel therefore know assuredly that God has made him both Lord and Christ, this Jesus whom you crucified."

Once the proof has been offered, Peter can invite his audience, which he has now indicted, to "repent, and be baptized every one of you in the name of Jesus Christ for the forgiveness of your sins; and you shall receive the gift of the Holy Spirit" (2:38). The speech is rounded off with a reference back to the concluding verse of the oracle in Joel 2, which speaks of those "whom the Lord our God calls to him" (Acts 2:39).

The speech begins constructing a framework not only within which the events of Pentecost are to be understood but within which the whole narrative must be read. The movement of repentance and forgiveness that traces its origin to the crucified and risen Messiah, Jesus, is portrayed with the help of biblical imagery as Israel's promised restoration. The Jews from all over the world, to whom Peter preaches, represent the gathering of God's people, who are now given an opportunity to repent and be saved—in the name of the Lord Jesus. Peter's speech makes an argument, using Israel's scriptures and Jewish forms of interpretation, that will echo throughout the Book of Acts.

Peter's Speech at the Temple (Acts 3)

Peter's second speech likewise provides a way of understanding what has occurred. When Peter and John heal the cripple at the Beautiful Gate of the Temple, the witnesses are astounded. Peter's speech heads off any suggestion that the healing has occurred because he and John have supernatural powers. It is the name of Jesus that heals (3:12–16). The speech, as in the previous scene, issues a call to repentance and an offer of forgiveness (3:17–21). Toward the end of the speech, Peter again cites the scriptures, this time a passage from Deuteronomy: "Moses said, 'The Lord God will raise up for you a prophet from your brethren as he raised me up. You shall listen to him in whatever he tells you. And it shall be that every soul that does not listen to that prophet shall be destroyed from the people'" (Acts 3:22; RSV).

In the interpretation that follows, Peter argues that the figure to whom the scriptures refer is none other than Jesus. As the "prophet like Moses," he spoke on God's behalf. Those who heed his words—and repent—will be saved, as promised by Joel. Those who do not "shall be destroyed from the people," that is, excluded from Israel. Peter makes the bold claim that only those who believe in Jesus can regard themselves as true Jews, members of God's people. It is those who accept Jesus as Messiah who are "sons of the prophets and of the covenant which God gave to your fathers" (Acts 3:25). There is no suggestion here that a "new Israel" is being constructed on the ruins of the old. Rather, the preaching movement in Jerusalem is depicted as a reform, a purge, the establishment of a holy remnant.

The interpretation of what is taking place contributes to the framework whose construction began in Peter's first speech, and here as there the raw material from which the edifice is built comes from Israel's scriptures. The two speeches offer a way of reading the whole story as the account of Israel's restoration rather than as the account of Israel's demise and the birth of a new people of God.

Stephen's Speech (Acts 7)

Stephen's speech is of a different sort. It is a recital of Israel's history, a form familiar from the Old Testament. Scholars have noted the apparent inappropriateness of the lengthy speech as a defense before the Jewish court, with some like Dibelius insisting that most of the speech is irrelevant to the setting (Dibelius 1956, 167). In terms of the action, the speech does not win Stephen's acquittal; on the contrary, it assures his execution. Yet viewed in terms of the overall program of Luke-Acts, the long recital offers one more important piece in the construction of the interpretive framework (see Dahl 1976, 66–86).

A brief summary cannot do justice to the speech, but it will have to suffice. From the events and characters in Israel's past selected for review, several emphases can be inferred:

1. The history of God's people began, as it has continued, with God's promises. God took the initiative in calling Abraham with a purpose in mind. The promise that seems to set the history of Abraham's family in motion is in verse 7: "'But I will judge the nation which they serve,' said God, 'and after that they shall come out and worship me in this place.'" The question that lurks behind the story is at what point the promise of that "place" of worship is fulfilled. Stephen is on trial for speaking words against "this holy place" (i.e., the Temple; 6:13). His speech argues that the Temple is not the fulfillment of God's promise to Abraham. Solomon's building of the Temple, the act with which Stephen's recital ends, is not the end of the story. The "place" where God is worshiped is more like the ancient tent that Moses built and the Israelites carried with them through the wilderness (7:44–45), a place that has more to do with God's gathered people than with a particular building in Jerusalem. Those who prefer to defend the Temple—and in light of their concerns hand Jesus over to Pilate, persecute the apostles, execute Stephen, and have Paul arrested—have revealed their misunderstanding of their own history and will themselves be punished.

2. Jacob's (Israel's) family has always been at war with itself. Eleven brothers conspired against Joseph; Israelites resisted Moses and all the prophets. Their descendants have rejected Jesus and his emissaries, thus betraying their descent from the majority within Israel that has consistently resisted those sent by God. Stephen, and with him other believers in Jerusalem, are shown to be descended from the faithful within Israel, notably the prophets, who spoke the truth even when it meant persecution and death (7:51–53). Persecution of Jesus' followers by Jerusalem leaders is thus no argument against the truth of the followers' claim to represent the true Israel. The holy remnant, Stephen argues, has always been in the minority.

3. Israel has been sustained throughout by the God who called Abraham and has kept his word. Israel's history is one of promise, fulfillment, new promises, and new expectations of fulfillment. With terrible irony, the death of Stephen and the persecution of other "Hellenists" (Greek-speaking Jewish Christians?) succeeds only in driving missionaries out of Jerusalem to carry the message of repentance and forgiveness to Jews outside the city—and eventually to gentiles, thus fulfilling Jesus' initial injunction to his disciples (Acts 1:8) and the promise by Gamaliel that if the Jesus movement is of God, there is nothing that can be done to stop it (Acts 5:35–39).

These three speeches provide a decisive interpretation of the story as a whole. They are invaluable to the story not just in terms of action or as revelations of character, but as insight into the logic that makes a coherent whole of the disparate parts. Luke's story is about salvation and deliverance; it is also about "the rise and fall of many in Israel" (Luke 2:34), about a terrible division within the people of God occasioned by the ministry of Jesus and his emissaries—a division foreseen in the scriptures and thus a necessary but terrible component in the fulfillment of God's promised deliverance of his people.

The Speeches of Paul

It is unnecessary to say much about Paul's first speech in Pidisian Antioch. In form it is reminiscent both of Peter's speech at Pentecost and of Stephen's recital. Some of the scriptural arguments employed by Peter recur in Paul's oration. Though his summary of Israel's history offers a different selection and a different focus, the goal is much the same: God has kept his promises by raising Jesus from the dead, thus showing that he is the Messiah-King, the descendant of King David expected to sit on his throne forever. The only special addition is a short quotation from Habakkuk: "Beware, therefore, lest there come upon you what is said in the prophets, 'Behold, you scoffers, and wonder, and perish; for I do a deed in your days, a deed you will never believe, if one declares it to you'" (Acts 13:40–41). The scriptural verses promise that Paul will encounter opposition. Scripture had foreseen that some would not believe even when the truth was spoken to them. As in Acts 3 and 7, scriptural arguments are employed here to explain opposition to Jesus and his emissaries—and Paul's career will be characterized above all by opposition, resulting in his eventual arrest and trial.

Paul's speech to the Athenians on the Areopagus (17:22–31) represents a departure from the norm. It is the first speech addressed strictly to gentiles. The idiom is quite distinct. The speech draws on Greek tradition as well as Jewish, perhaps offering a glimpse of how Christian missionaries spoke to a non-Jewish audience (Dibelius 1956, 26–83). The importance of those non-Jews to the story is evident in several places, to which I shall turn presently.

The other exceptional speeches in Acts are Paul's speeches in his defense in chapters 22–26. Unlike Stephen's apology, Paul's orations focus on his situation and argue issues that arise from charges leveled against him. They are not missionary speeches, and they are not "typical." Since these speeches represent a special case, I will examine them below in the discussion of Paul's role in Acts.

THE GENTILES

There can be no surprise that the message of repentance and forgiveness should reach gentiles (non-Jews). Simeon spoke at the very beginning about "the salvation which you have prepared before all peoples, a light for the enlightenment of gentiles and glory for your people Israel" (Luke 2:30–32; Au. trans.); at his initial appearance at the synagogue in Nazareth Jesus spoke of Elijah's and Elisha's concern for foreigners (Luke 4:25–28). After his resurrection, Jesus spoke about the scriptural necessity of bringing the message of repentance for the forgiveness of sins "to all the nations [gentiles]" (Luke 24:47). Though at Pentecost the Spirit is poured out on Jews from all over the world, there can be little doubt that gentiles will finally be included among "all flesh" to whom God promised to give a share of the prophetic Spirit (Acts 2:17, quoting Joel). It is striking, rather, how long it takes for the matter to be raised in Acts and for the first gentile convert to be brought into the fold.

With Stephen's death and the persecution of the Hellenists, a new epoch begins as these Jerusalem believers find their way to distant cities, where they begin the work of evangelizing. Philip begins a successful ministry in Samaria (Acts 8). Some of the missionaries, we learn, find their way to Antioch and for the first time preach the Lord Jesus to Greeks

(11:20). Rather than destroying the messianists by executing Stephen and taking action against his group, persecution by Jerusalem only succeeds in spreading the fire—as Gamaliel had predicted (Acts 5:34–39).

It is not these Hellenists who have pride of place in preaching to non-Jews, however. It is not even Paul, whose conversion in Acts 9 prepares the way for a major program of evangelizing among gentiles and Jews in Asia Minor and Greece. It is rather Peter who is the first to preach to and convert a gentile—a Roman soldier named Cornelius (Acts 10).

The story is told with considerable solemnity. Peter is prepared for this encounter with a non-Jew by a vision, repeated three times, about eating unclean animals (Acts 10:9–16). When in his vision Peter protests that he would never eat such unclean food, he is told that "what God has cleansed you must not regard as common." At the same time, Cornelius, a Roman soldier, though he is uncircumcised, is in all other respects like a pious Jew, "a devout man who feared God with all his household, gave alms liberally to the people [i.e., Israel], and prayed constantly to God" (10:2; RSV). This pious gentile likewise has a vision in which he is told to invite Peter to his home. Peter has one final vision as Cornelius' messengers arrive, instructing him to accompany them to visit Cornelius (10:19–20). He has no choice but to do as he is bidden. The heavenly visions and portents signal some important change about to occur, as elsewhere in Luke-Acts.

Peter enters the home of the Roman and preaches, though with considerable reluctance. "You yourselves know how unlawful it is for a Jew to associate with or to visit any one of another nation," he protests (Acts 10:28). But he must do as God has instructed. To his amazement—and to the amazement of his companions—the Spirit is poured out on the group of gentiles and they speak in tongues, as at Pentecost. Like those among the Jews who repented, Cornelius and his household are baptized in the name of Jesus Christ (10:47–48). Despite his protests and quite contrary to his expectations, Peter becomes the first to convert a gentile.

The importance of the event becomes obvious in what follows. Twice Peter must recount his experience to fellow believers in Jerusalem. The issue is not whether gentiles will hear the good news, but whether they must be circumcised so that Jews can eat with them. Peter is criticized not for speaking to Cornelius but for risking ritual defilement by eating with him: "Why did you go to uncircumcised men and eat with them?" (11:3). The question has to do with ritual purity as defined by the Law of Moses. According to Acts, a significant group among the messianists take a hard line on matters of purity, insisting that Jews are not permitted to eat with gentiles. Jewish laws of purity, they argue, are as valid for believers in Jesus as for other Jews. The issue has very practical implications: Will these new converts be invited to the table with others baptized in the name of Jesus? The dispute about circumcision assumes the form of a discussion of table fellowship, familiar from Jesus' ministry. There the question was whether the impure and outcasts within Israel would be included at table; here the issue has to do with non-Jews. Here, as there, the table fellowship is extended—but not without considerable debate.

What is at stake in this formal opening of a mission to non-Jews is the unity of the church. Acts does not deny the priority of Israel even within the church: salvation is from the Jews. Peter preaches "to you first"—that is, to his countrymen (3:26). The question has to do with how that priority is to be expressed. Luke must deal with a problem familiar within the New Testament. From earliest times, non-Jews came to be included within the fellowship of Jews who believed Jesus to be Israel's Messiah. Practice preceded theory, and some explanation of the state of affairs had to be offered after the fact. Luke offers his own justification.

The matter is settled at the so-called Apostolic Conference reported in chapter 15 of Acts. Paul's version of this meeting in his letter to the Galatians offers a rather different perspective. In Paul's version, he has the major part to play in the discussions and the eventual agreement (Gal 2:1–10). According to Luke, Paul plays a rather minor role in the conference. Because of the remarkable success in evangelizing gentiles, some decision must be made about table fellowship. The question is whether gentile converts will have to become full Jews. The council decides they will not. Circumcision will not be required of

non-Jewish males. But then the issue of table fellowship must be settled. Laws of purity must be taken seriously, since there is no suggestion in Acts that the Law of Moses has been suspended. A compromise is proposed by James:

> Therefore my judgment is that we should not trouble those of the Gentiles who turn to God, but should write to them to abstain from the pollutions of idols and from unchastity and from what is strangled and from blood. For from early generations Moses has had in every city those who preach him, for he is read every sabbath in the synagogues. (Acts 15:19–21; RSV)

The so-called Apostolic Decree draws on ancient traditions regarding "sojourners" in Israel—non-Jews who lived with Jews without themselves accepting circumcision. Discussions of such questions among Jews usually made reference to the covenant God made with Noah (Gen 9:1–7), a covenant binding on all human beings that forbids consumption of blood. The letter sent out by the Jerusalem church urges gentile believers to abstain from idols, unchastity, and non-kosher food so that there can be table fellowship. The solution to the problem of table fellowship is found within Israel's own tradition, backed with scriptural quotations, so that the coexistence of Jew and non-Jew within the church cannot be taken as a sign that believers in Jesus have deserted their heritage. The agreement about gentiles will continue the testimony to Moses which James insists has been taking place in every city. The inclusion of gentiles is dealt with at length and with great care so as to head off any suggestion that the preaching movement headed by Peter and Paul could be accused of apostasy from Moses. The difference from Paul's approach, which he argues at length in Galatians and Romans, is striking.

With the decisive question of gentile admission settled, the narrative now turns its attention completely to Paul.

PAUL

Paul is the most important character in Acts. Though Peter gives foundational speeches and Stephen the longest speech, Paul's orations are more varied and more numerous. He addresses a group of Jews at Pisidian Antioch and of Greeks in Athens; his farewell remarks to the elders from Ephesus are recorded as well as speeches in his defense delivered before Roman officials and Jewish accusers. Paul's final words to the Jewish community in Rome bring the story to an end, with the comment that he continued to preach unhindered in the imperial capital. Paul's career takes up more than half of Acts.

Paul's apparent preeminence seems extraordinary. He was not one of Jesus' followers. He is introduced in Acts 7 as a Jew who was involved in the execution of Stephen, and he appears in chapter 9 as a quasi-official opponent of the new sect, with special interest in its progress in Syria. Measured by Luke's standards of an apostle as given in Acts 1, Paul cannot be included within the classification. And with the exception of Acts 14:4 and 14, Paul is not called an apostle. The designation is reserved for the specific group in Jerusalem. Half the Book of Acts is devoted to an "outsider."

On the other hand, interest in Paul's career is perhaps not so extraordinary. The theme of Acts is the spread of the gospel "to the end of the earth" (1:8). Though others, like Peter, Philip, the Hellenists, Barnabas, and unnamed missionaries, also had a share in bringing the message of repentance and forgiveness to those outside Palestine, none was more active than Paul. If Acts tells the story of the birth and growth of the church, its most prominent missionary ought to play a major role.

Interest in Paul's career as a missionary, however, cannot provide the only reason for Luke's interest. More than half of Paul's story is devoted to his trial. Beginning with his arrest in Jerusalem in chapter 21, we follow the course of his career as a prisoner first under Felix, then Festus, and finally as one destined to place his case before Caesar himself. In these chapters Paul delivers several speeches about his views, defending himself from charges aimed at him by leaders in the Jewish community. The theme of these chapters cannot be viewed as the expansion of the church, despite a few surprising conversions. For this reason they demand particular attention, since they seem to require some modification of the traditional view of Acts as a story that tells of the missionary expansion of the church.

The Trials of Paul

There can be no doubt in Acts that Paul (formerly Saul) was a major figure in the spread of the movement known as "the Way." His conversion (and call) is told with particular solemnity and, like the conversion of Cornelius, is repeated twice in subsequent chapters (22 and 26). Paul's experience is described using visionary language, though there is confusion among the accounts regarding who saw or heard what. Jesus' appearance to Paul in chapter 9 takes the form of a confrontation: "Why are you persecuting me?" (9:4). The encounter leaves Paul blind and confused. His call to preach comes only later, when he is visited by a "disciple," a pious Jew named Ananias. The Lord's words to Ananias provide a thematic introduction to Paul's career: "Go, for he is a chosen instrument of mine to carry my name before the Gentiles and kings and the sons of Israel; for I will show him how much he must suffer for the sake of my name" (Acts 9:15–16; RSV).

Of interest is the last clause: Paul is chosen to be a suffering emissary. The same might be said about others in Acts. Peter and John are arrested; Stephen is stoned and the Hellenists driven out of Jerusalem. Later James the brother of John is killed. Still, in Acts, Paul is the clearest example of the suffering preacher. His mission is colored by conflict from the very first. After his initial preaching in Damascus, Jews plot to kill him; in Jerusalem, his preaching achieves the same results (9:23–24, 29). Though Paul achieves remarkable success in speaking in synagogues at Antioch of Pisidia and at Iconium, some Jews begin to see in Paul a dangerous enemy and follow him from city to city, stirring up opposition. He meets particular hostility at Thessalonica, and Jewish opponents follow him through Greece. Opposition from Asia eventually finds its way to Jerusalem, and it is these Asian Jews who convince the Jerusalem authorities that Paul is guilty of defiling the Temple (21:27–29).

Paul's opposition is not restricted to Jews, of course. When Paul casts an evil spirit out of a young slave girl in Philippi, he incurs the wrath of her owners, who have made a profit from her soothsaying, and they have him arrested (16:16–24). Citizens in Thessalonica are convinced that Paul is a threat to Caesar, proclaiming another king, Jesus, in his place (17:7). In Corinth, Paul is accused of teaching worship contrary to the Law (18:13)—though the event has the earmarks of a pogrom directed against all Jews, since the crowd beats up Sosthenes, the head of the Jewish synagogue. Artisans who benefit from Artemis-worship in Ephesus come to regard Paul and his entourage as a threat to their business as well as their religion (19:21–41).

It is opposition from within the Jewish family, however, that is at the center of the story. Although Paul's preaching to gentiles is mentioned, and though he states several times that his rejection at the hands of Jews means he will preach to gentiles, he returns again and again to synagogues, to the end of the story, and his preaching and teaching remain focused on matters of importance to Jews.

Paul's career is an extraordinary triumph. He succeeds in planting churches across the face of the Roman world. Acts is interested in the trials of Paul, however, and in an important sense his career, like that of Jesus, is one of consistent opposition. Why that should be the case, and what importance that opposition has for understanding Paul (and the Christian movement), are major themes in the second section of Acts.

The Trial of Paul

Acts 20 is a major turning point. Paul meets with elders from Ephesus and bids them farewell. His speech is a familiar form in ancient literature. It is Paul's testament. He reviews his work among the Ephesians and speaks about his legacy, warning them to hold fast to the truth as he taught it to them. His speech looks forward as well, offering a preview of what is to come:

> And now, behold, I am going to Jerusalem, bound in the Spirit, not knowing what shall befall me there; except that the Holy Spirit testifies to me in every city that imprisonment and afflictions await me. But I do not account my life of any value nor as precious to myself, if only I may accomplish my course and the ministry which I received from the Lord Jesus, to testify to the gospel of the grace of God. (Acts 20:22–24; RSV)

It is clear that Paul's work as a missionary in Asia and Greece is over. All attention turns to Jerusalem.

There is every reason to expect trouble when Paul travels to Jerusalem. Ananias' words from the Lord are supplemented by those of the prophet Agabus, whose symbolic binding of himself and whose oracle warn explicitly that Paul will be arrested and bound over to gentiles (21:10–11). Of greatest importance is the reason for Paul's troubles. The amount of space Luke devotes to Paul's trial indicates the significance of the matter.

The introduction to Paul's arrest and trial is provided by elders in the Jerusalem church, who welcome Paul with some troubled words about his reputation: "You see, brother, how many thousands there are among the Jews of those who have believed; they are all zealous for the Law, and they have been told about you that you teach all the Jews who are among the Gentiles to forsake Moses, telling them not to circumcise their children or observe the customs" (21:20–21).

The issue, according to the elders, is not what Paul taught gentiles but what he taught Jews. The church in Acts has already acknowledged that gentiles will become believers and has decided on what basis they will be allowed to eat with Jewish believers. The concern of the Jerusalem elders is what implications are to be drawn from Paul's preaching regarding Jewish observance of the Law. It is necessary to keep questions straight here. With the exception of his letter to Christians in Rome, Paul never wrote to Jewish believers. He wrote to gentile Christian congregations he had established. His discussions of the Law of Moses occur in Galatians and Romans, where his concern is the implication of faith in Christ for gentile observance of the Law. The focus in Acts is different. The elders are concerned about Paul as a potential teacher of Israel (Jervell 1979, 153–184). According to substantial rumor (21:21; the Greek says believers have been "taught" about Paul), Paul is an apostate who seeks to dissuade Jews from living as Jews.

The elders do not believe the rumors for a moment, but they are concerned enough to propose a graphic demonstration of Paul's continuing fidelity to the Law—which he readily accepts. He pays for a vow undertaken by four men, purifying himself and attending the Temple with them. There is not the slightest hint that Paul is insincere. Those who so interpret Acts do so on the basis of unsupported psychologizing and of alleged knowledge of what Paul really thought about the Law. The relationship between Acts and Paul's letters is a matter of some difficulty, but that is not the issue here. We are interested in Acts, and the author of Acts has no doubt about the matter. Paul readily agrees to demonstrate his fidelity to the Law of Moses. It is thus highly ironic that Paul is arrested for alleged defilement of the Temple at the very moment he is ritually the most pure. The incident that marks his arrest contains the elements that will provide a focal point for all that follows: Paul is accused of apostasy, of deserting the Law; in fact, he is a pious Jew who would do nothing contrary to the Law and would never teach Jews to abandon Moses and their way of life.

The numerous speeches Paul delivers in the course of his ill-fated trial make the point over and over. In his first address in Jerusalem, he recounts the story of his own call after listing his impeccable credentials as a Pharisee (22:3–5). The crowd listens with sympathy until he comes to the matter of his call to preach to gentiles: "And he said to me, 'Depart; for I will send you far away to the Gentiles'" (22:21). The violent reaction from the crowd signals the sensitive nature of this issue (compare with Jesus' mention of Elijah and Elisha in his opening visit to the synagogue in Luke 4). The reason for their reaction is only apparent from the ensuing narrative, however. The problem is not Paul's interest in gentiles per se but the implications for his status as an observant Jew and as a teacher of Jews. Paul is repeatedly accused of crimes against the Jewish Law. Tertullus, his accuser before the governor Felix, speaks of Paul as "a pestilent fellow, an agitator among all the Jews throughout the world, and a ringleader of the sect of the Nazarenes," and he accuses Paul of trying to profane the Temple (24:2–8).

Many commentators have identified the political element in the accusations as central. Paul is accused of sedition: he is an agitator. In that accusation, they insist, we can overhear charges leveled against Christians in Luke's day, charges he hopes to diffuse by writing Acts. According to this interpretation, Luke writes to argue for the political innocence of Christianity: it poses no threat to the empire. Paul's consistent efforts to demonstrate in his apologetic speeches that he is still a faithful Jew are taken as evidence of Luke's strategy. Since Judaism was accorded freedom of religion by the emperor, Luke sought to argue

that because Jesus' followers were Jews, the new "Christian" movement should come under the general provisions for Jews within the empire (thus Conzelmann 1963 and Haenchen 1971).

The difficulty with this interpretation is that it does not take the historical audience seriously. The verdict of all the Roman officials who examine Paul is that he has committed no crime against the state. They also confess, however, that they do not understand what the charges against Paul involve, since they have to do with religious matters internal to the Jewish community:

Claudius Lysias to Felix: "I found that he was accused about questions of their law, but charged with nothing deserving death or imprisonment." (Acts 23:29; RSV)

Festus to Agrippa: "When the accusers stood up, they brought no charge in his case of such evils as I supposed; but they had certain points of dispute with him about their own superstition." (25:18–19)

Festus: "King Agrippa and all who are present with us, you see this man about whom the whole Jewish people petitioned me, both at Jerusalem and here, shouting that he ought not to live any longer. But I found that he had done nothing deserving death; and as he himself appealed to the emperor, I decided to send him. But I have nothing definite to write to my lord about him. . . . It seems to me unreasonable, in sending a prisoner, not to indicate the charges against him." (25:24–27)

Festus and King Agrippa agree, after hearing Paul: "This man is doing nothing deserving death or imprisonment." (26:31)

Roman officials testify to Paul's innocence in matters of Roman law, but only by identifying the issues as matters of Jewish law—from their vantage point, "superstition." Paul's speeches defend against not political but religious accusations, about which the Roman officials understand nothing and about which they are not concerned. The alleged Roman audience for Luke's political apologetic would have made no sense at all of Paul's arguments about his fidelity to Jewish tradition, as C. H. Barrett pointed out some years ago (Barrett 1961, 63). Roman officials in the story speak for that historical audience. It is not for their benefit that Paul delivers his speeches. The "apologetic" element in his speeches has to do with the accusations featured already in the Jerusalem elders' statement to Paul about his reputation among Jewish believers (Acts 21:20–21). Paul is accused of apostasy from Judaism, and it is against such charges he defends himself at his trial.

> I am a Jew, born at Tarsus in Cilicia, but brought up in this city at the feet of Gamaliel, educated according to the strict manner of the law of our fathers, being zealous for God as you all are this day. (22:3; RSV)

> Brethren, I am a Pharisee, a son of Pharisees; with respect to the hope and the resurrection of the dead I am on trial. (23:6)

> But this I admit to you, that according to the Way, which they call a sect, I worship the God of our fathers, believing everything laid down by the law or written in the prophets, having a hope in God which these themselves accept, that there will be a resurrection of both the just and the unjust. (24:14–15)

> To this day I have had the help that comes from God, and so I stand here testifying both to small and great, saying nothing but what the prophets and Moses said would come to pass. (26:22)

There is no point at which Roman officials believe Paul to be guilty of crimes against Roman law. That such a view can be historical is not at issue here. Luke has chosen the trial as a forum to argue matters important to his audience. The question is not the political innocence of Christianity, but the status of Paul in respect to the Law of Moses. Could Paul have taught that "Christ is the end of the law" (Rom 10:4)? From Luke's perspective, certainly not! There are good reasons to ask to what degree Luke understood Paul and has represented the views of the great missionary adequately. There can be little doubt about the view of Acts, however. Paul appears as a faithful Jew who accepts Jesus as Messiah. The charges that he taught Jews to abandon the Law and defiled the Temple are without foundation.

The question that must be answered before a conclusive interpretation of Luke's whole enterprise can be established is what place this elaborate defense of Paul has. Why is Paul of such importance, and why is it essential to defend his Jewishness? Answering this question will involve an appraisal of the overall literary enterprise in which Luke is engaged.

THE PURPOSE OF LUKE-ACTS

One difficulty in dealing with Luke-Acts is the sheer bulk of material. It would require considerable space to show how all the chapters and verses fit into any particular thematic structure (assuming that is even possible). Simplification is a necessity in making any statement about the thematic unity of the two volumes and their overall purpose. I have suggested that there is a controlling purpose: Luke wrote to offer an argument calculated to provide confidence to the faithful.

It is quite likely there are secondary themes and subsidiary motivations in the composition. Some of Luke's material, for example, intends to inculcate a particular piety. Luke's Gospel shows a particular interest in wealth and its use (Juel 1983, 90–93; Johnson 1977). Jesus sides with the poor, blessing them and warning against the dangers of riches. Yet many of the stories about possessions are intended for those with property (e.g., Luke 10:29–37, 12:16–21, 16:19–31, 19:11–27); while they warn against the dangers of possessions, they also speak about possibilities for their proper use. Zacchaeus, a notorious tax collector, serves as an example of someone who learns how to do good with his wealth (Luke 19). In Acts, there are others who, like Zacchaeus, have property and know how to use it—people like Barnabas and Lydia and Paul. The stories about wealth and property are intended to shape proper attitudes toward stewardship and do not seem immediately derivable from the major argument the narrative makes.

It is nevertheless proper to ask about organizing themes and major emphases in the story. Luke writes, he says, "so that you may know how well-founded are the things you have been taught." That confidence about what has been taught is intimately tied to the identity of Jesus' followers as the people of God. Many have understood that Luke writes a history in which he ties the story of Jesus into the story of the mission of his followers. Equally important—and less appreciated by interpreters—is Luke's argument that both parts of the story must be read as chapters in the history of Israel.

I have already noted that Luke's story is narrated against the background of objections. Jesus' ministry was marked by opposition from various groups within the Jewish family. His followers encountered similar opposition. One function of the story is to clarify and deal with those objections. Jesus, and later his followers, turn to Israel's scriptures for precedent. Peter, Stephen, and Paul offer an appraisal of events by means of learned biblical interpretation that portrays their preaching as part of the promised restoration of Israel. Those who refuse to accept their preaching forfeit their right to be called children of Israel, like their ancestors who resisted the warnings of Moses and the prophets. The argument Luke offers is one directed to Jewish Christians.

There are obvious sensitive points that required attention. One has to do with table fellowship with gentiles. Acts takes great pains to show how gentiles came to be included within the fellowship of God's people. Visions and heavenly apparitions attend the conversion of Cornelius; the agent of his conversion is Peter, probably the major figure within the Jerusalem church, who offers the decisive testimony for including these "cleansed" gentiles at the table. James, another prominent Jewish believer with impeccable Jewish credentials, finds a way to accommodate them at the table by citing precedent from scripture and from Jewish tradition (Acts 15; see Jervell 1979, 185–207).

Table fellowship was an issue for the church prior to and long after Luke-Acts was written. A comparison between Acts and Paul's letters on the one hand, and Acts and Justin Martyr's *Dialogue with Trypho the Jew* (written in the middle of the second century) on the other, helps to clarify the distinctive perspective of Acts. Justin mentions that there are Christians who continue to observe Jewish dietary laws. By his day, they are a tiny minority in a predominantly gentile church. He notes there is some question whether such Law-observant Christians have any place in the church. Though Justin believes they do, he admits that he does not represent the opinion of the majority. In Acts, the question is asked from the other side. One group of Jewish believers, the "circumcision party" (Acts 11:1–3, 15:1), insists that gentiles may not be allowed at the table without complete observance of the Law of Moses, including circumcision. The arguments offered by Peter and James—which include reference to visions and the outpouring of the

Spirit, to scripture and tradition—are for the benefit of this "party" and those sympathetic to their respect for purity. The concern about gentiles in Acts reflects a commonsense knowledge of Judaism and a clear awareness of what questions needed to be answered for Jewish Christians in an increasingly non-Jewish church (Jervell 1979, 133–152).

Paul's own approach to the matter of table fellowship in his letters is far more radical (Gal 1–2), which is perhaps why he is a problem for Luke and his audience (see, among others, Sanders 1983). Some have suggested that Acts was written largely as a defense of the great apostle. Though that may be an exaggeration, the author expends considerable energy defending Paul against the charge that he was an apostate Jew who taught his countrymen to abandon the Law of Moses. Paul himself admits that he was a controversial figure and that many opposed him for a variety of reasons. In Acts, however, Luke is concerned with Paul's reputation among Jewish audiences (Jervell 1979, 153–184). Their worries about Paul's attitude toward the Law are dealt with and their fears allayed. Paul was obviously someone who could not be ignored. The numerous churches he established claimed to be part of the one people of God. For believers with a Jewish past, there might have been some question about the legitimacy of such churches if they were founded by an apostate who had abandoned the Law and urged others to do the same. If Luke sets out to demonstrate how firmly rooted the "Christian" movement is in the scriptures; if the "certainty" he seeks to instill is tied to the claim that Jesus' followers represent the true Israel among whom God's promised deliverance is being accomplished, there is little wonder that Paul receives as much attention as he does. Paul—at least the public figure whose teaching was the subject of rumors and fears among Jewish Christians—could well have represented a major counterargument to Luke's proposal. Thus Luke must demonstrate that Paul remained a Law-observant Jew throughout his life and taught only what he found in Moses and the prophets.

The certainty Luke seeks to provide for his readers is theological: it has to do with God. The doubts to which his story is directed may be summarized in a theological question: Have the promises of God failed? The opening chapters of Luke's Gospel hark back to promises made to Abraham and "our fathers." They refer repeatedly to the deliverance God promised Israel. If the story of Jesus and his followers is really about the fulfillment of those promises, what about opposition to Jesus from within Israel? What about continued opposition to his followers? If Jesus' death and vindication represent God's merciful dealing with Israel, if the outpouring of the Spirit and the preaching of repentance and forgiveness of sins in Jesus' name represent the promised restoration of God's chosen, what about all the gentiles who find their way into the family? It is in response to such questions that Luke tells his story, seeking to demonstrate that even if Jesus brings about a division within Israel, his ministry and the testimony of his emissaries represent salvation and deliverance for the faithful remnant within Israel (according to Acts, the remnant includes tens of thousands in Jerusalem alone!). God has been true to his word and can be expected to act faithfully in the future as well.

Historical Setting

Though the data for interpreting Luke-Acts must come from the works themselves, interpretations can be tested by relating the literature to the historical period in which it was composed. There were reasons why Luke wrote his two volumes; the certainty he sought to provide was a response to some lack of confidence among a specific group of believers in the first century. We may ask if a particular reading of Luke-Acts is conceivable in light of what we know of the period. This presumes that we have some idea when Luke-Acts was written and some grasp of what was occurring at that time.

The data on the basis of which first-century writings are dated are slim. It is reasonable to argue that Luke antedates Mark. There is enough evidence that both halves of Luke-Acts were written after the destruction of the Temple in 70, though there is still some question. An occasional scholar will express amazement that the destruction of Jerusalem has not left a clearer stamp on Christian literature. To some degree such expectations are unrealistic. Luke writes about events that predate 70. The story in Acts breaks off with Paul in Rome, probably around 58–62. Speaking directly about the coming war in a story set decades prior would violate the integrity of the story.

There are, on the other hand, clear indications that the Temple had been destroyed by the time Luke wrote, and that the event required some interpretation (Fitzmyer 1981, 53–57). Jesus' predictions of its demise (Luke 13:34–35, 19:41–44), the alterations made in Mark's version of Jesus' warnings about the future (compare Luke 21:5–36 with Mark 13), and the speech of Stephen (Acts 7) represent places where such an interpretation is offered. Luke does for his readers what the rabbis would have to do for theirs— offer some way of coming to grips with the demise of Jerusalem and the Temple while still remaining within the tradition of Israel.

Since Albert Schweitzer, interpreters of early Christian history have identified Jesus' failure to return as the dominant feature in the development of the first-century church. The experience of his delay is cited as one of the major reasons Luke wrote (thus Conzelmann 1960 and Haenchen 1971). When it finally became clear Jesus was not about to return, so the argument runs, Luke set out to equip the Christian movement for the future by giving it a sense of its place in history and providing the trappings of an institution (bureaucratic structures, etc.). Such explanations, which depend upon a particular reading of early Christian history, have dominated biblical scholarship since the time of Schweitzer. Yet expectations about Jesus' immediate return were not uniform among Christians, and there was no gradual, decades-long decline in that belief. Paul could speak of the end as imminent or as distant within a brief span of time in his ministry; Mark could write, after Paul, that with the Temple's destruction the last chain of events had begun—while also insisting that "the end is not yet" (Mark 13:7–8). In some respects Matthew, written after Mark, looks as eagerly for the close of the age as Mark, while for John, written not much later, the end of the age is an image rarely used and certainly not something that dominates the story.

More promising as a way of understanding the composition of Luke-Acts is a glimpse of the external historical setting, to the degree it can be reconstructed. The period between 80 and 120 witnessed an enormous literary outburst from within the Jewish community, only some of which work has been preserved. Such writings include the impressive corpus of Josephus, apocalyptic works like *2 Baruch*, the

Ascension of Isaiah, etc. Though targumic traditions (Aramaic translations and interpretations of Hebrew scriptures) were edited in final form only centuries later, it seems clear that creative developments in popular paraphrases of the Old Testament likewise received a boost during this period. Within the Christian community, the Gospels of Matthew, Luke, and John, together with epistolary writings (the three letters of John, for example) and Revelation, were all composed during these decades. At least one impetus for the literary outburst was the destruction of the Temple and the implications of this event for Jewish identity.

Though the importance of the Temple for diaspora Judaism is difficult to document, the Temple and its sacrifices provided at least for Palestine and its environment a symbol of Jewish identity. Some, like the Essenes who lived on the shores of the Dead Sea at Qumran, defined themselves over against the Temple, believing the priestly authorities in power to be the embodiment of evil. Even for the disenfranchised and separatist Essenes, however, the Temple provided the central symbol of identity as God's people. Barred from the cult by priests who disagreed fundamentally with their interpretation of the Law, they could only bide their time until the day they were returned to power by the intervention of God. Their rather distinctive piety was merely an interim arrangement, until the time of the great battle should come.

The situation changed fundamentally after the war with Rome, when the Temple was destroyed (66–70). The situation even in Palestine became more like that in the diaspora; identity came to focus almost exclusively on a way of life. In such a setting, diversity became far more dangerous to the survival of Israel. What distinguished Jew from non-Jew was a way of life epitomized by such externals as circumcision and dietary and Sabbath observance. Marginal Jewish groups came to be viewed as a risk, since they threatened to blur the distinction between God's people and gentiles. A process of sorting out began that would end in the creation of "orthodoxy": a religion defined by sages, with a particular conception of Jewish identity reflected in the traditions written in the Mishnah and the Talmuds. (On the birth of rabbinic Judaism, see the numerous works by Jacob Neusner and his students; see also Segal 1986.)

All parties in the ensuing family battles required some basic self-conception from which to operate. What does it mean to be the people of God? Competing views led to divisions within the family, sometimes bitter. Those who found themselves outside the mainstream—Jewish Christians, for example, as well as groups that later came to be known as "gnostic"—required not only some means of understanding the fundamental changes that had occurred (Why did God allow Jerusalem and the Temple to be destroyed?) but also a way to deal with hostility and opposition from others within the family. The crisis was of such magnitude as to require new traditions and even new books. Scholars have come to appreciate the impact this family battle had on Matthew and John (Davies 1964, Martyn 1979, Brown 1966–1970). More recently, scholars have examined its impact on Luke-Acts (Dahl 1976, Jervell 1979, Tiede 1980, Juel 1983).

While matters internal to the Jewish community demanded some written expression, so did affairs in the wider world. Roman historians had to offer some appraisal of the collapse of Augustus' famed Pax Romana and the ensuing chaos within Rome in the middle decades of the first century, when assassinations prevented any stable governmental policy. Questions of history and fate demanded response from Roman as well as other historians, as we can observe in the writings of Tacitus (Tiede 1980).

It is during such a period of instability that a work like Luke-Acts best fits. The two volumes are themselves an argument for stability, for a belief in the providence of God encountered in Jesus the Messiah, a providence that offers a basis for confidence in the future based on a sense of what God has accomplished in the past and present. Luke had to deal with a question on the minds of many of his contemporaries: Have the promises of God failed? For Jewish Christians, reasons for so believing were only too apparent. Jerusalem, the city where God promised to dwell forever (Psalm 132), had been destroyed; the Jewish family had turned in on itself and divided on the question of Jesus' messiahship as well as on other matters; meanwhile, gentiles—non-Jews—continued to flood into the church, threatening to overwhelm the core of circumcised children of Abraham who represented the continuity in God's history of blessing. There were doubtless many who upon surveying the scene felt the story of Israel was ending in tragedy. God had apparently abandoned his people Israel and had withdrawn—or perhaps was now establishing a new people from among the nations. In either case, it would have seemed that God's promises of deliverance to his people Israel were indeed failing. And a God who abandoned his chosen people could hardly be trusted with the destiny of anyone else.

Luke seeks to counter such a view by telling how God's promises to his people were fulfilled in Jesus, how a faithful remnant from Israel was gathered and had been preserved, and how because of this gentiles were offered a place among God's elect. If that is his argument, if those who learn "how well-founded are the things you have been taught" manifest concerns typical of Christian Jews after the destruction of the Temple, it seems most likely to locate the composition of Luke-Acts during the decades following the war against Rome. A plausible date would be 80–90. The relative stability of the era of Domitian may well provide a time for consolidation and review.

Author

There is an obvious relationship between identifying the author and interpreting his work. Church tradition, deriving from the early centuries of the Christian movement, attributes the two volumes to Luke, a gentile companion of Paul's (Fitzmyer 1981, 35–53). Viewing Luke as a "Paulinist" among the Gospel writers and reading his work as an account of Christianity's spread to the gentiles has depended upon this identification. Tracing the ancient tradition to its roots poses considerable problems, however. It was not the practice of authors to affix names to their works at the beginning. The designation "according to Luke" derives from the church; the regularized titles of all four Gospels ("according to Mark," "according to Matthew," etc.) presume a period of interpretation the early stages of which are unknown to us. And apart from its occurrence in the title, the name "Luke" appears nowhere else.

There is at least some evidence that portions of Acts derive from an acquaintance of Paul's. Beginning with Acts 16:10, a mysterious "we" enters the narrative: "And when he had seen the vision, immediately we sought to go on into Macedonia, concluding that God had called us to preach the gospel to them" (RSV). From here on, the enigmatic first-person plural weaves in and out of the story, giving the impression that at least part of the narrative derives from an eyewitness.

Interpretations of this "travel narrative" move in various directions. It is possible, on the one hand, to identify the final author of Acts (and thus of the Gospel as well) as the person who traveled with Paul during at least a portion of Paul's mission. The rest of the information would presumably have been gathered from Paul and his companions by the unknown author. Another possibility is that the author of Acts made use of a source, perhaps written, by someone who journeyed with the famous missionary. Since there is no obvious stylistic difference between the "we" passages and the rest of the narrative, we would have to assume that the final editor reworked the source in his own style (or that the traveler and the author are the same person). Dibelius even tried to argue that the "we" was added by the author for purely stylistic reasons (a view that has not found wide support; for a review, see Haenchen 1971).

There are difficulties with the view that the author of Luke-Acts traveled with Paul. One is the considerable tension between Paul's own reports of his travels in his letters and the account in Acts (see Jewett 1979). Another is the rather striking difference in theological perspective. There is no reason why one of Paul's entourage could not have had views different from those of the apostle, particularly when we take into account the situational nature of Paul's correspondence. We may well have a one-sided view of Paul from the few letters that have been preserved. Still, it is difficult to harmonize Luke's Paul, so willing to compromise on matters of the Law of Moses, with the Paul of Galatians and Romans. One of the most striking differences lies in the view of the Apostolic Conference in Jerusalem. Paul's view is at such variance with that of Acts that it is difficult to imagine they were both speaking of the same event. Paul never mentions the letter reputed to have been sent to all the churches by James and the elders (Acts 15)—though such a letter may well have been composed after the conference. Finally, the author of Acts seems to have no knowledge of Paul's letters. The kind of information reported about Paul—particularly his alleged teaching about the Law—sounds more like rumor and legend than like firsthand or even second-hand opinion (Jervell 1979, 153–184).

Even if it could be argued convincingly that the author of Luke-Acts traveled with Paul, that still does not tell us about his identity. Attempts to identify the author as "Luke the physician" about whom Paul speaks in Colossians 4:14 carry weight only if we assume the two volumes were written by "Luke." Henry Cadbury proved long ago that the alleged medical expertise reflected in Luke's writings shows little more than that the author was careful to use specialized language in his narrative—like other historians of his time (Cadbury 1920).

Why the name "Luke"? Perhaps the ascription rests on fact. If so, it is not necessary to assume the author is the same "Luke" about whom Paul writes. And in any case, there is little evidence on the basis of which to argue the case. The numerous opinions expressed about the author of Luke-Acts are inversely proportional to the amount of hard data available on the basis of which to make a decision.

More useful is the information the author provides about himself in the preface to the Gospel. Like his contemporary Josephus, Luke wrote history, and in the preface he offers some glimpse of the reason. He speaks of himself as "third generation"—having access not only to eyewitnesses, but also to "ministers of the word" and even written accounts of Jesus' ministry. He writes aware that others have preceded him. As I have noted, he writes to demonstrate how "well-founded are the things you have been taught."

Whether the author was a Jew or a gentile prior to his becoming a follower of Christ is perhaps impossible to say. There are at least as many reasons to view him as a Jew or a proselyte to Judaism as to view him, as has traditionally been the case, as a gentile. Here, authorship will depend upon an assessment of the whole. From whose perspective and for whose benefit is the story told? Preoccupation with Jewish matters from beginning to end, detailed knowledge of Jewish practice, concern to justify table fellowship among Jewish and gentile Christians, and some need to argue for Paul's "orthodoxy" as measured by Jewish standards may suggest the author was writing from within the Jewish family. Though this is not a necessary inference, it seems to have more solid basis

in his writing than the traditional interpretation. The presumed link between "Luke" and Paul may in the history of interpretation have been more decisive for reading Luke-Acts than the literary facts themselves.

The link between identification of the author and interpretation of the two-volume work is apparent. It is not impossible to understand why a gentile, writing to a non-Jewish audience, might wish to offer an accurate portrait of the movement's early days in Jerusalem. Claim for the antiquity of an apparently new religious movement was standard in a world where novelty was viewed with suspicion. It is conceivable that Luke-Acts was written to offer some sense of roots to a movement that required a sense of its identity and of its past. The author certainly knew something about the writing of history and its conventions.

Yet perhaps the closest parallels to Luke-Acts can be found in the writings of Jewish historians—notably in the books called 1 and 2 Chronicles. Luke's style is imitative of such biblical histories, and his program seems very similar. Like the chronicler, Luke wrote for a generation of God's people who faced new crises that threatened faith in the God of Abraham, Isaac, and Jacob. The crises were different—Temple destruction, disillusionment with savior figures, hostility and division within the Jewish family—but the needs were much the same. Luke wrote to update the history of Israel, to offer a new glimpse of crucial moments in the story of God's dealing with his people in order to argue a case—to use his own words, "to show how well-founded are the things you have been taught." The story he tells demonstrates that the history of Jesus and the early movement he began represents the fulfillment of ancient prophecies; the events that provide the basis for a movement of repentance and forgiveness show God's faithfulness to his people; and the whole story demonstrates that there is promise in history, reason to be confident about the future because it is in the hands of the God who called Abraham, raised Jesus from the dead, empowered the mission of the apostles, and will one day complete what he began.

There is no ending to the story in Acts. The narrator leaves us with a picture of Paul preaching in Rome. The reason is perhaps that Luke could no more conclude his story than the author of 1 and 2

Chronicles could conclude his. Chronicles ends with the edict of Cyrus of Persia that the Temple will be built in Jerusalem, and with the words, "Whoever is among you of all his people, may the Lord his God be with him. Let him go up [to Jerusalem]" (2 Chr 36:23). Luke's history points beyond itself; it ends with Paul in Rome, on the verge of the next chapter, when the message of repentance and forgiveness in Jesus' name would be carried by a new generation "to the end of the earth."

EPILOGUE: ANTI-SEMITISM

Since the Holocaust, no literature on the New Testament can avoid the question of anti-Semitism. What has so emblazoned the experience of the concentration camps on the imaginations of our age is not the sheer numbers or the horrors of the camps. There are other atrocities that are equally unimaginable—for example, the numbers of those executed by Stalin during his time in office. The special horror of the Holocaust for Christians is that a "Christian" society perpetrated such atrocities on a people designated as God's elect in the Bible. For some, Jesus' experience at the hands of his people was cited as justification for such persecution. In view of such recent history, certain features of the Bible take on a different aspect. The New Testament certainly paints at least some Jews in an unfavorable light. Ought we brand these features of the narratives "anti-Semitic," and if so, what do we make of them in a society committed never to allow another Holocaust?

Answering that question depends upon an analysis of the narrative and upon historical judgments regarding its placement. One question might be asked in this way: Does the narrator of Luke-Acts assume a position outside the Jewish family? Conflict within the family of Israel is a major—perhaps the major—feature of the narrative plot. Gentiles play a minor role, both in Luke's Gospel and in Acts. The few exceptions, like the Roman centurion in Luke 7 and Cornelius in Acts 10, are portrayed as lovers of Israel at the very least. Gentiles—as a group and in terms of individual characters—are largely colorless. The story attributes importance to them, but largely in terms of what is to come. Acts ends on the verge of the "time of the gentiles."

From what perspective is the story told, and to what end? It is difficult to believe the vantage point is outside Israel. Who, after all, are those who follow Jesus? The term "Christian" (more appropriately from a Jewish point of view, "messianist") is used only twice in Acts, both times in the Greek-speaking world by outsiders who seek to characterize a group of Jews (a sect) with special loyalty to Jesus the Messiah. Terms like "the way" belong more to the vocabulary of the narrator and, we might presume, the implied audience. The confusion about various parties in disputes (i.e., Is Paul opposed by Jewish Christians in Jerusalem or non-Christian Jews? Are the rumors spread about Paul carried by supporters of Jesus or opponents?) may indicate that there are no hard and fast categories by which to distinguish between Jews who accept Jesus as Messiah and those who do not. One might argue, in fact, that one function of the narrative is to offer some way of identifying the various factions. The speeches in Acts suggest that the way this enterprise is carried out is by going to the tradition and scriptures of Israel for assistance. The particular argument is that only those who associate themselves with the messianists deserve the name "Jew" and can claim the rights to Abraham's heritage.

If the vantage point of the narrator is outside Israel, his story might well be classified as anti-Semitic. The "church" is born on the ruins of the Temple and the leadership of the Jewish community. If, as seems more likely, the vantage point is somewhere within Israel, the story tells of the destruction of a family—but neither to discredit Israel nor to undermine confidence in the promises of God. On the contrary, the narrative, much in the manner of Chronicles, seeks to tell the story of Jesus and his followers in such a way as to offer an argument for regarding the movement established by Peter, John, Stephen, James, and Paul as the only true Israel, heirs of the scriptures and its promises. The story makes the remarkable claim that even the flood of gentiles who have joined the people of God at the table does not jeopardize the heritage. Someone as radical as Paul still has a place within that family as a faithful defender of Moses.

If that is true, Luke-Acts still belongs on the other side of a great divide, marked by the opening decades of the second century, when the children of

Abraham went in separate directions and came to use labels to mark their difference. The argument of Luke-Acts, if we may call it that, worked differently for that generation than for later ones. New Testament writings, produced largely for Jewish believers in Jesus, came to be the scriptures of a predominantly gentile Christianity. Those who have read the Gospels and Acts in the ensuing centuries are an important step removed from the audience the story projects. Luke-Acts does not answer the decisive question that history has now thrust upon the Christian movement (in which circumcised Jewish "messianists" committed to Jesus the Messiah, who embody the continuity of God's promises, represent a definite minority within the church). In referring to the church as a "new Israel" (a term not used in the New Testament), interpreters have transformed Luke-Acts into an anti-Semitic or a tragic piece. The interpretive question, which is also a theological matter of considerable consequence, is how properly to acknowledge the distance between the present audience and the audience projected by the narrative. By transforming Luke-Acts into a story about the demise of Israel, interpreters have done what Luke could not possibly have done: allowing the division within Israel to be used as an argument that God's promises have failed. It is not difficult in this regard to understand how Luke's work could have become the favorite of Marcion, the radical disciple of Paul who concluded that the Old Testament and its God were to be rejected by followers of Jesus. For Luke, the future offered promise because the God who raised Jesus from the dead was Israel's God. The roots of the Christian story are buried deep in the tradition of Israel. For Luke, at least, this rootedness is what certifies to Theophilus that the teaching he has received is indeed well-founded.

Bibliography

Barrett, C. K. *Luke the Historian in Recent Study.* London, 1961; new ed., Philadelphia, 1970.

Brown, Raymond E. *The Gospel According to John.* Anchor Bible, vols. 29 and 29a. Garden City, N.Y., 1966–1970.

Cadbury, Henry J. *The Style and Literary Method of Luke.* Cambridge, Mass., 1920.

———. *The Making of Luke-Acts.* New York, 1927.

Conzelmann, Hans. *The Theology of St. Luke.* Translated by Geoffrey Buswell. New York, 1960.

———. *Die Apostelgeschichte.* Tübingen, 1963.

Dahl, Nils Alstrup. "The Story of Abraham in Luke-Acts" and "The Purpose of Luke-Acts." In Dahl's *Jesus in the Memory of the Early Church.* Minneapolis, 1976.

Davies, W. D. *The Setting of the Sermon on the Mount.* Cambridge, 1964.

Dibelius, Martin. *Studies in the Acts of the Apostles.* Edited by Heinrich Greeven and translated by Mary Ling. New York, 1956.

Dodd, C. H. *The Apostolic Preaching and Its Developments.* New York, 1964.

Fitzmyer, Joseph A. *The Gospel According to Luke.* Anchor Bible, vols. 28 and 28a. Garden City, N.Y., 1981–1985.

Foakes Jackson, F. J., and Kirsopp Lake, eds. *The Beginnings of Christianity.* 5 vols. London, 1920–1933.

Funk, Robert W. *Language, Hermeneutic, and Word of God.* New York, 1966.

Haenchen, Ernst. *The Acts of the Apostles.* Translated by Bernard Noble and Gerald Shinn. Philadelphia, 1971.

Jeremias, Joachim. *The Parables of Jesus.* Translated by S. H. Hooke. Rev. ed. New York, 1963.

Jervell, Jacob. *Luke and the People of God.* Minneapolis, 1979.

———. *The Unknown Paul: Essays on Luke-Acts and Early Christian History.* Minneapolis, 1984.

Jewett, Robert. *A Chronology of Paul's Life.* Philadelphia, 1979.

Johnson, Luke Timothy. *The Literary Function of Possessions in Luke-Acts.* Missoula, 1977.

Juel, Donald. "Social Dimensions of Exegesis: The Use of Psalm 16 in Acts 2." *Catholic Biblical Quarterly* 43 (1981): 543–556.

———. *Luke-Acts: The Promise of History.* Atlanta, 1983.

Keck, Leander E., and J. Louis Martyn, eds. *Studies in Luke-Acts.* Nashville, Tenn., 1966.

Lindars, Barnabas. *New Testament Apologetic.* Philadelphia, 1961.

Marshall, I. Howard. *The Gospel of Luke: A Commentary on the Greek Text.* Grand Rapids, 1978.

Martyn, J. Louis. *History and Theology in the Fourth Gospel.* 2d ed., rev. and enl. Nashville, Tenn., 1979.

Petersen, Norman R. *Literary Criticism for New Testament Critics.* Philadelphia, 1978.

Sanders, E. P., ed. *Jewish and Christian Self-Definition.* 3 vols. Philadelphia, 1980–1983.

Sanders, E. P. *Paul, the Law, and the Jewish People.* Philadelphia, 1983.

Schubert, Paul. "The Structure and Significance of Luke 24." In *Neutestamentliche Studien für Rudolf Bultmann.* Berlin, 1954.

Segal, Alan F. *Rebecca's Children: Judaism and Christianity in the Roman World.* Cambridge, Mass., 1986.

Talbert, Charles H. *Literary Patterns, Theological Themes, and the Genre of Luke-Acts.* Missoula, 1974.

Tiede, David Lenz. *Prophecy and History in Luke-Acts.* Philadelphia, 1980.

DONALD JUEL

John

THE GOSPEL OF John is at once the most sublime and the most enigmatic of the four Gospels. Its language is simple and eloquent, its symbols—especially light, darkness, bread, and water—are universal and timeless. Yet, its message is profound and strikingly original, and its narrative texture is rich and intricate.

Entry into the fascinating world of the Gospel of John requires at least three keys: understanding and appreciation for (1) the life setting of the Gospel, (2) the narrative style of the Gospel, and (3) the principal themes of the Gospel. The following pages will provide an overview of each of these areas.

LIFE SETTING

Insight into the life setting of the Gospel developed first as a by-product of interest in its authorship. From the second century until the modern era its apostolic authorship was seldom questioned. The testimony of Papias, Polycarp, and Irenaeus seemed sufficient to establish the Gospel's claim to apostolic authorship. The prevailing view, therefore, was that the Gospel was written by the apostle John in Ephesus toward the end of his life.

In 1792 Edward Evanston, in a work entitled *The Dissonance of the Four Generally Received Evangelists and the Evidence of Their Authenticity Examined*, concluded that the differences among the four Gospels and the peculiar character of the Gospel of John indicated that it was written in the middle of the second century by a Platonist, not by the apostle. This bold challenge to the orthodox view subsequently received support from K. G. Bretschneider and D. F. Strauss. By the end of the nineteenth century the battle lines were clearly drawn, and the authority of the Gospel was tied to the question of authorship.

During the early 1800s, L. A. Dieffenbach and H. E. G. Paulus suggested that the Gospel was written by a disciple of the apostle, and E. Renan and J. B. Lightfoot were early champions of the view that there was a "school of St. John," some of whose members took the teachings of the apostle and completed the writing of the Gospel. This position was again articulated by C. K. Barrett (1978, 133–134). The thesis that disciples of the apostle John completed the Gospel served as a mediating position between those who affirmed and those who denied apostolic authorship. It also provided a basis for explaining both the similarities and the differences among the Gospel, the Johannine Epistles, and Revelation, all of which had been attributed to the apostle.

A Developmental Approach

The Gospel of John itself provides both explicit evidence and further hints that it was not composed by a single hand in a brief period of time. The closing verses of the Gospel identify (1) the Beloved Disciple, who bore witness and wrote material contained in the Gospel, (2) the community—"we"—who know that his testimony is true, and (3) the final editor, or redactor, the "I" who finally speaks in the first person.

Further evidence that the Gospel of John is the final product of a long process of composition can be drawn from the following observations. First, the Gospel offers a distinctive, unique interpretation of the life and significance of Jesus. It does not depend primarily upon the synoptic Gospels for its tradition. Instead, it gives evidence of an independent line of tradition, which in turn requires that there was a traditioning community. Second, the Gospel makes extensive use of in-group language, metaphors, symbols, and irony (Meeks 1972; Duke 1985). This language may not be impenetrable by outsiders, but it clearly points to a community that cultivated, polished, and enjoyed the nuances of this idiom. Third, the multiplicity of genres or types of material in the Gospel (signs, discourses, passion narrative) may indicate earlier settings in which each form of the gospel tradition had its own functions. Fourth, the Gospel itself gives evidence of several sources. Poetic sections of the prologue to the Gospel (1:1–18) are stylistically distinct, and disjunctions (or *aporia*) later in the Gospel (e.g., 14:31) can be used to identify a narrative source (Fortna 1970). Finally, theological tensions within the Gospel suggest that it preserves theological emphases that developed and changed over a period of time. For example, in its present form the Gospel both emphasizes and minimizes the significance of the sacraments. Both signs and faith apart from signs are emphasized. Both the glory of Jesus and the word "in flesh" are emphasized; and while the Gospel contains elements of a more traditional understanding that God's redemptive work will be fulfilled in the future, "in the last day" (6:39, 40, 44, 54), it also presents a distinctive "realized eschatology" which contends that all that was hoped for in the future has already been realized in the person of Jesus. The community behind the Gospel of John, therefore, clung to traditional views while creatively formulating new understandings and interpretations of the core elements of its faith. Taken together, these factors provide significant evidence for the existence of a "Johannine community" within which the Gospel and the epistles attributed to John were written.

From the 1960s through the 1980s Johannine scholarship has given a great deal of attention to attempts to uncover the history of the Johannine community and theories of the stages in the composition of the Gospel of John. This effort has been significant for both historical and exegetical concerns. We are gaining insight into the peculiar history of one early Christian community, and we are establishing a historical setting for the interpretation of the Gospel. More than any other single work, J. Louis Martyn's *History and Theology in the Fourth Gospel* (1979) has influenced current American interpretations of the life setting of the Gospel of John, and much of the following history of the community depends on his work, and on the enduring contributions of Raymond E. Brown (in such works as *The Community of the Beloved Disciple*, 1979) and others.

Before making any attempt to sketch a history of the community and the composition of the Gospel, we must remind ourselves that this venture is speculative and that the evidence, such as it is, is open to alternative interpretations. No developmental hypothesis as to the origin of the Gospel can be established conclusively in the absence of additional archaeological or literary evidence. A developmental hypothesis can nevertheless be very useful, providing a basis for reaching further insights into the Gospel. Alternative hypotheses can only be evaluated by their coherence, correspondence with the data, utility, plausibility or probability, and to a lesser extent, by their simplicity. Nevertheless, there is always the danger of offering a logical explanation for historical and literary data that may not be the result of orderly, predictable processes. Even where there is evidence of different strata or stages in the composition of the Gospel, it is difficult to determine the sequence of development (whether from A to B or B to A). When dealing with multiple issues, moreover, it is difficult to know which events may have occurred at the same stage in the history of the community, and links between theological developments and developments in the history of the community (or between elements of the Gospel narrative and events in the life of the community) are difficult to establish. In fact, awareness of the nature of the Gospel as narrative has rendered the move from textual, literary features of the Gospel to observations about the community history all the more difficult. The characters in the Gospel, for example, do not necessarily represent groups related to the Johannine community.

A History of the Johannine Community

The history of the Johannine community can be divided into five periods. Although little can be known about the first two periods, events in the latter three can be reconstructed with more confidence. The description of the first four periods is based solely on inferences from the Gospel itself. The final period is reconstructed from evidence provided by the Johannine Epistles.

Origins. The Gospel begins with an account of Jesus calling his earliest disciples from among the followers of John the Baptist (1:19–51). At other points the Gospel takes pains to show the superiority of Jesus over the Baptist (1:6–8, 15; 3:23–30; 5:33–36; 10:40–42). It is possible that the Beloved Disciple was Andrew's unidentified companion in 1:35–40, one of the disciples who had been a follower of John the Baptist (Bultmann 1971, 18). Parallels between the language of the Gospel of John and the scrolls that come from the Essene community at Qumran may stem from this earliest period (Charlesworth 1972). Whether the Beloved Disciple was one of the twelve disciples or not, he was an actual person and an eyewitness of at least part of Jesus' ministry. The Gospel's familiarity with the geography of Judaea and the Jewish festivals celebrated in Jerusalem may also point to individuals or a group that came from this area. The simple, Semitic, paratactic style of the Gospel may also derive from Aramaic influence. Whether any link can be established between the Johannine Christians and the Hellenists in the early church in Jerusalem, as Cullmann proposed (1976, 39–53), seems more problematic. If the Johannine Christians were associated with the Hellenists, then they were probably forced out of Judaea following the stoning of Stephen. At this time they may have moved to Antioch or the surrounding area, following other Christian Jews (Acts 8:1, 11:19–21).

Early period: within the synagogue. Following J. Louis Martyn's thesis, the history of the Johannine community from its earliest days as an identifiable group can be divided into an early, middle, and late period, though I will define the contours of each

period in ways that extend Martyn's work (1978, 1979).

The specific data of locations and dates are the most tentative and problematic parts of this history. Once the earliest Johannine Christians were forced to leave Judaea, they may have gone to Antioch, or directly to Ephesus. Those who see a close connection between the Gospel of John and early gnostic thought champion Syria as a more probable location (Koester 1982). Recently Klaus Wengst (1981) has offered another possibility—the area of Gamla in upper Galilee. If one is disposed to use the Book of Acts in the absence of other data, the hypothesis that the community spent a period of time in the area of Antioch receives a measure of support. We know that early Christians from Judaea settled there, and later, when Acts describes Paul's ministry in Ephesus, there is no mention of a group of Johannine Christians. Linguistic and conceptual parallels between the Gospel of John, the *Odes of Solomon,* and the letters of Ignatius of Antioch can also be explained more easily if Johannine Christians spent some time in this area.

At this point one must also raise the troubling question regarding the role of Samaritans among the Johannine Christians. The Gospel of John clearly devotes unusual attention to the Samaritans. Interestingly enough, the last reference to the apostle John in the Book of Acts leaves him in Samaria (Acts 8:14, 25). Were the Johannine Christians in or on the border of Samaria at this time? Were the Johannine Christians engaged in mission work among the Samaritans? Did Samaritan converts join them in such numbers that they influenced the development of Johannine Christology? An affirmative answer to one or more of these questions seems called for, but it is difficult to define the specific nature of the contact with Samaritans.

During this early period, Johannine Christians functioned more or less comfortably within the Jewish synagogue. They lived as Jews and thought of themselves as Jews who had found the Messiah. As John 1:35–49 suggests, they regarded Jesus as the fulfillment of messianic expectations drawn from the Hebrew scriptures. For them, Jesus was the prophet like Moses (but one greater than Moses), the returning Elijah (the fulfillment of the prophets), the king of Israel, and the coming Son of man. Because of the heavy influence of the Elijah-Elisha materials on their Christology (Martyn 1978), the proclamation of signs was an appropriate way to proclaim Jesus to fellow Jews. Jesus' signs also served a polemical function, establishing the superiority of Jesus over John the Baptist, "who did no signs" (10:41).

The passion narrative in John makes extensive use of references and allusions to the Hebrew scriptures. Moreover, it is difficult to see how the proclamation of signs could have continued long without some interpretation of Jesus' death. The passion narrative, therefore, may have been shaped during this period also. The signs were collected in a written "signs source" (Smith 1965), and eventually the passion narrative was attached to the collection of signs, forming a "gospel of signs" (Fortna 1970).

Middle period: formation of the Johannine community. The middle period begins with the exclusion of the Johannine Christians from the synagogue. The factors that precipitated this break in relations with the Jewish community are probably multiple. R. E. Brown has suggested that the exclusion of Christians came as the result of the development of a new, higher Christology that was not based on the Davidic pattern (Brown 1979, 43–47). On the other hand, the development of a higher Christology, based on the wisdom tradition of the Old Testament and Apocrypha, and resulting in John's distinctive Logos Christology, which characterized Jesus as the incarnation of the divine word of God, could just as well have occurred after the exodus from the synagogue. It is difficult to establish a causal relationship between a theological development and a social crisis. Either may have provoked the other. The Acts of the Apostles and 2 Corinthians 11:24–25 show that Paul experienced conflict in synagogues on more than one occasion. The relaxation of the Law in ritual and cultic matters by Johannine Christians may have eventually led to their exclusion from the synagogue. Differences between Christian Jews and non-Christian Jews over the war of 66–70 may also have hardened relations between the two groups.

J. Louis Martyn provided the single most important datum for reconstructing the history of the community when he stated the case for seeing the threat of being put out of the synagogue (9:22, 12:42, 16:2) as an action that was related to the *Birkath ha-Minim* adopted by the Pharisees led by Gamaliel II at Jamnia. This blessing contained a prayer for the destruction of heretics (the *Minim*), who probably included the early Christians. The action in view in John may not have been the enforcement of the *Birkath ha-Minim* (Martyn 1979, 50–55), but it probably reflects the kind of situation that led to the adoption of this blessing.

Caught in this traumatic development, some Johannine Christians elected to stay within the synagogue rather than confess their faith in Jesus as the Christ openly. The Gospel brands such persons as "secret believers" (12:42, 19:38). Others confessed their faith openly and were separated from the Jewish community. Undoubtedly, some families were divided, with various members responding to the crisis differently.

Those who were excluded from the synagogue gathered around the Beloved Disciple as the center of their new community, their living link with Jesus. He was the source of their teaching. The middle period, therefore, marks the emergence of the Johannine community. Under the leadership of their founder, the Beloved Disciple, members of the community began to establish their identity as the true children of God who had responded faithfully to the revelation received through Jesus. By observing the role of the Beloved Disciple within the community, they also began to formulate their understanding of the work of the Paraclete or Holy Spirit among them. The teachings of the Beloved Disciple became the normative guide to the interpretation of Scripture and the words of Jesus. Those closest to the Beloved Disciple gathered his sermons and discourses. The Beloved Disciple and his own disciples shaped the emerging Gospel tradition in light of the liturgical, polemical, apologetic, and catechetical needs of the community. Baptism, the sacramental meal, and foot washing were probably practiced by the community.

The discourses now contained in the Gospel were developed in the context of these diverse aspects of the community's life. Some of the discourse material evolved from reflection on various aphorisms and *logia* ("sayings") received from Jesus. Other discourses developed through preaching and teaching the "signs source" (as in John 5, 6, 9, and 11 especially). Other parts of the discourse material may reflect the activity of Christian prophets among the Johannine Christians, who declared words they had received from the risen Lord. Eventually the community found it necessary to test prophetic utterances against the norm of the tradition received from the Beloved Disciple. Throughout this process the Beloved Disciple and the school that was developing around him reflected on their situation in light of Jesus' conflict with the religious authorities in his day. Once formulated, some of this discourse material was inserted into the early "signs gospel." The new gospel gave more attention to the radical demand for obedience and confession of one's faith, the conflict between Jesus and "the Jews," and examples of individuals caught between Jesus' demands for faith and "the Jews'" rejections of his claims.

The community now used more dualistic language to describe its faith and its relationship to the world around it. From a "greater than Moses" Christology, the community heightened the authority of its Lord by Christianizing the high claims that were made for Wisdom, which had been personified as the divine agent of creation (e.g., Proverbs 8:22ff.). They had a higher revelation than that given to Moses. Jesus was the preexistent Logos who had become flesh and whose revelation gave them "grace and truth" (1:17), a revelation that supplanted the authority of the Law of Moses.

The community was persecuted by the Pharisaic authorities from the synagogue (15:18–16:2). The writing of the Gospel (on the basis of the earlier signs gospel) was in part a response to this persecution. If the community had been located in Antioch during this period, it may have been forced by the persecution to move to Ephesus at this time. The Revelation of John, which is somehow related to the Gospel and the Johannine Epistles, came from this area, and the early patristic evidence locates the writing of John in Ephesus. When, why, and how the community came to Ephesus remain matters of conjecture.

Middle period: the second generation. Sometime during the middle period the community was shaken by the death of the Beloved Disciple. Evidence for his death is furnished by John 21:23. Many in the community believed that the Beloved Disciple would not die until the Lord returned. The need to correct that misunderstanding is most easily explained on the assumption that the Beloved Disciple had in fact died.

The death of the Beloved Disciple provoked further reflection on the role of the Spirit in the community. This reflection resulted in an affirmation of the role of the Paraclete (or Counselor), who would be with them always (14:16; see Culpepper 1975, 267–270). Because of this reaffirmation of the role of the Spirit within the community, no hierarchy or structure of authority developed. The community retained its egalitarian character since all possessed the Spirit. The chief concern for the emerging second generation, referred to in 17:20, was that it preserve the unity of the community—with one another and with the risen Lord (17:21–23). It was crucial to the survival of the community that they love one another (13:34) and that they "abide" in the risen Lord and his words as they had received them through the tradition coming from the Beloved Disciple (15:1–12). These emphases are reflected in discourse material that was added to the Gospel during this period, especially chapters 15–17.

The relationship between the Johannine community and other Christian groups was becoming an issue. The expulsion of Christians from the synagogues created several groups of Jewish Christians. These other groups were "other sheep . . . not of this fold" (10:16), and the Johannine Christians sought unity with these other groups of Jewish Christians in their area. Evidence of the relationship between these communities can be gleaned from the letters 2 and 3 John (Brown 1982, 107–108, 728–739; Brown 1979, 97–103; Culpepper 1985, 1–5, 116–139). The presbyter—the author of the three epistles of John—sought to maintain a position of leadership with these communities by sending emissaries like Demetrius (3 John, vv. 5–6, 12) and by sending letters like 2 and 3 John. This network of churches may also be related in some way to the seven churches addressed in Revelation, chapters 2–3.

At this point we may identify an inner group closely related to the Beloved Disciple that participated in the leadership of the community, led in worship, and produced the community's written materials. This group can be called the "Johannine school." The "Johannine community" was the center of the network of churches that can be called "Johannine Christianity." The cultural, philosophical, and geographical environment of Johannine Christianity is designated by the term "Johannine milieu."

Johannine Christianity also faced rival claims that came from churches that regarded Peter as their apostolic authority. The Johannine Christians recognized Peter's pastoral role in the church but defended the authority of their tradition by telling stories that maintained the superiority of the Beloved Disciple (13:23–26; 18:15–16; 19:26–27, 35; 20:3–10; 21:2–14, 20–22). Eventually, however, internal schism so destroyed the community that its members were absorbed by other Christian groups.

Late period: schism. New Testament scholars are now generally agreed that the Johannine Epistles come from a period after the composition of the Gospel (or at least late in the process of its composition). This period is characterized by the emergence of a group advocating a "higher" Christology that emphasized the divinity of the Christ while minimizing the humanity of Jesus (see 1 John 2:19, 4:2). This group also taught that believers had been delivered from sin and had already crossed from death into life (1 John 1:8, 10; 3:14). Such a heavy emphasis on realized eschatology led in turn to a disregard for the necessity to continue to resist sin. Dissension resulted in schism, and the presbyter charged that those who had left the community were false prophets and teachers who had gone out into the world, thereby violating the community ethic of love for one another (1 John 2:19, 3:10, 4:1–6). In response to this crisis, the presbyter wrote 1 John to warn the community of the dangers of this false teaching and to encourage those who remained to continue in their faithfulness. Second John was written to warn a sister community of the dangers that were posed by this group (Culpepper 1975, 279–286). R. E. Brown has written the definitive statement of the later history of the community in *The Community of the Beloved Disciple* (1979) and *The Epistles of John* (1982).

The relationship between the final redaction of the Gospel and the composition of the epistles is still open to debate. The prologue to John's Gospel, John 6:51–58, the references to the Beloved Disciple, and chapter 21 were probably among the last passages added to the Gospel. These passages are the work of one who, like the presbyter, was a member of the Johannine school; but the final redactor was probably not the author of the epistles.

The last we see of the Johannine community, it is wrecked by dissension and struggling for survival. The presbyter's group was probably absorbed by the dominant Christian groups of the early second century. The presbyter's opponents, on the other hand, probably found their way into the gnostic communities of the second century. The community's legacy was its story—the Gospel that tells the story of Jesus in such a way that it had become their story also.

Implications:
New Perspectives on Introductory Issues

If this reconstruction of the origin and life setting of the Gospel is at all accurate, the implications for the interpretation of the Gospel are significant. The answers to standard introductory questions must be modified. The earlier debate over authorship has been radically altered. We must talk about the school or community in which the Gospel was composed. Recognizing that the Gospel is the product of several hands does not mean, of course, that we cannot recognize the prevailing genius of the evangelist, who was probably a disciple of the Beloved Disciple, and who shaped the Gospel from written and oral sources in the community. We can also recognize in places the material that comes from the early sources, and we can identify at least some of the work of the final redactor.

Rather than speaking of the date of the Gospel, as though it were written in one short period of time, we must now say that the Gospel was composed over a period of probably five decades (the years 50–100), reaching its final form in the 90s. Since all of the material comes from the tradition of the Johannine community, the sections that were added late in the process are of no less historical or theological value than the earlier material.

Finally, the Gospel must be read as the foundational story that gave the Johannine community its identity. The authoritative tradition shaped the community's beliefs, its ethic, its worship, and its self-understanding. In turn, each of these aspects of the community's life shaped the way in which it told its story. The community, moreover, told and retold its story in order to encourage its members to higher levels of commitment and discipleship, to defend themselves against external groups, and to encourage others to join with them and claim the Gospel story as theirs also.

NARRATIVE STYLE

Complementing investigation of the life setting of the Gospel of John, recent work applying contemporary work in narratology to the study of the Gospel of John has helped interpreters to appreciate the artistry and effects of the Gospel as narrative. Because the Gospel is a narrative rather than a psalm, prayer, or epistle, it conveys meaning in the same way as other narratives—by drawing the reader into the narrative world to hear, watch, and interact with the characters, settings, and events that compose that world. Then, the reader must reexamine his or her perceptions, beliefs, and commitments in the light of that reading experience. To read the Gospel of John perceptively, therefore, one must be sensitive to the narrative style of the Gospel as well as its historical setting.

Outline of the Gospel of John

Prologue (1:1–18)
Part 1: Jesus before the world (1:19–12:50)
1. Calling disciples (1:19–2:11)
2. The Temple and Nicodemus (2:12–3:21)
3. An interlude in Judaea (3:22–36)
4. The Samaritan woman and the nobleman (4:1–54)
5. The man at the pool of Bethesda (5:1–47)
6. Feeding the multitude (6:1–71)
7. Confrontation in Jerusalem (7:1–8:59)
8. The blind man and the shepherd's sheep (9:1–10:42)
9. The raising of Lazarus (11:1–54)
10. Preparations for the Passover (11:55–12:50)
Part 2: Jesus with his own (13:1–20:31)
1. The farewell discourse (13:1–17:26)
   The footwashing (13:1–30)
   The farewell discourse:
      Part 1 (13:31–14:31)
      Part 2 (15:1–16:4)
      Part 3 (16:5–33)
   The prayer of consecration (17:1–26)

2. The trial of Jesus (18:1–19:16a)
3. The death of Jesus (19:16b–42)
4. The resurrection of Jesus (20:1–29)
5. Conclusion (20:30–31)
Epilogue (21:1–25)

The Gospel as Narrative

When one begins to read the Gospel of John, one enters a strange and fascinating world. The reader is introduced to this narrative world by the voice of a narrator who is able to tell the reader about events in the past, even the prehistoric past, and events that have not yet occurred. This narrator knows the main characters of the story and is able to interpret what they think and the meaning of what they say. The narrator tells the story retrospectively, explaining events from a higher vantage point than any of the characters around Jesus.

Within this narrative the reader finds a world created by God through the Logos, the preexistent Word of God. The Logos enters the world in the person of Jesus and through his words and actions begins to reveal God, the Father, to those around him. The sequence in which the reader gains information is controlled by the narrator. From the narrative the reader is usually able to reconstruct the sequence of events in the story, but the narrative may range back and forth through the story reminding the reader of past events and foreshadowing events that have not yet been narrated. In this way events take on new meaning, gaps in the story are created and filled, and the narrative is able to evoke surprise, curiosity, and suspense from the reader.

Through the reading experience one is introduced to a wide range of interpretations and responses to Jesus. One is invited to view the world from the perspective of faith in Jesus as the Christ, the Son of God, and to explore various types of faith and various misunderstandings that plague those who seek to respond in faith. The Gospel, therefore, does not have a "message" that can be distilled from the narrative. Instead, the Gospel, because it is a narrative, is a textual strategy or means of evoking an intricate series of responses from the reader. In the case of the Gospel of John, as we read we are invited to view the ministry of Jesus from the point of view of the narrator and to rehearse various responses to Jesus' call for faith. By studying its narrative structures and rhetoric, we are better able to appreciate the Gospel for what it is, not just what it is about, and to read it sensitively and perceptively.

The Episodic Plot

As with all literature, understanding the structure of the Gospel of John—its plot, its various parts or movements, and the narrative structures that it employs to create sense and unity—is an important task for the interpreter. The Gospel of John, moreover, uses numerous different structures, and at times a section of the Gospel functions within multiple structures. The following paragraphs will examine the plot of the Gospel, its macrostructure, and the structuring principles and devices used in specific passages.

The fundamental conflict. Sequence, causality, unity, and affective power are all significant aspects of a narrative's plot (Culpepper 1983, 79–84). Jesus' mission is announced in the prologue and first chapter of the Gospel. He will reveal the Father, take away the sin of the world, and authorize the children of God (1:12, 18, 29). These three facets are interrelated: sin is taken away when one responds to Jesus' revelation with faith, and such a response identifies and empowers that person as one of the children of God.

The plot of the Gospel concerns the way Jesus' identity as the Logos, the Christ, the Son of God is revealed. Will those around Jesus see who he is? How will they respond to that revelation? Will they see and believe, or will they refuse to see and turn away in unbelief? The plot of the Gospel of John, therefore, revolves around the axis of revelation and faith. In seeking to reveal the Father, Jesus battles cosmic forces of evil that are evident in the human inclination toward darkness, evil, and unbelief. The more clearly Jesus demonstrates and speaks of his identity, the more intense the hostility toward him becomes. This hostile opposition leads eventually to the cross, where in an apparent triumph of evil over good Jesus dies. Jesus' death and resurrection, however, are ironically the ultimate revelation of the Father's glory. It is Jesus' "lifting up" (3:14, 8:28, 12:32), his enthronement as king, the first step in his exaltation to the Father (20:17).

In the prologue we as readers learn who Jesus is, where he is from, and what his mission is. From this privileged position, we watch as the various characters are confronted by Jesus and struggle to discern his identity. The Gospel of John is not tightly plotted in a unified sequence of action. Instead, it is episodic. In episode after episode one character after another is placed in relationship to Jesus, hears his words or sees his signs, and then chooses a response that moves either toward faith or toward unbelief. Will Nicodemus, the Samaritan woman, the man at the pool of Bethesda, the blind man, Martha, the disciples, the Jews, or Pilate see who Jesus is? How will they respond to him? As the same basic pattern is rehearsed in scene after scene, the Gospel develops rich thematic complexity and the reader is allowed to examine a whole range of alternative responses to Jesus. The characters around Jesus are like a prism that breaks up the pure light of his revelation into a range of colors. After reading the Gospel, however, the reader must make some response to its claims; and in doing so identify with a certain set of characters in the Gospel.

The Structure of the Gospel

Commentators have regularly recognized four principal sections of the Gospel: the prologue (1:1–18), Jesus' public ministry (1:19–12:50), Jesus' ministry to his own (13:1–20:31), and the epilogue (21:1–25).

The prologue introduces Jesus as the Logos, but it also introduces the primary themes of the Gospel, images such as light and darkness, the relationship of Jesus to John the Baptist, and the juxtaposition of Jesus and Moses. Since the response of faith is connected with the identity of the children of God, verses 11–12 of the first chapter of John serve as a summary of the entire Gospel.

Ten episodes can be identified in John 1:19–12:50. These are generally identified by a reference to time, a change of location, a transitional phrase like "after these things," or the introduction of a new setting or new characters:

1. Calling disciples (1:19–2:11)
2. The Temple and Nicodemus (2:12–3:21)
3. An interlude in Judaea (3:22–36)
4. The Samaritan woman and the nobleman (4:1–54)
5. The man at the pool of Bethesda (5:1–47)
6. Feeding the multitude (6:1–71)

7. Confrontation in Jerusalem (7:1–8:59)
8. The blind man and the shepherd's sheep (9:1–10:42)
9. The raising of Lazarus (11:1–54)
10. Preparations for the Passover (11:55–12:50)

Some of these episodes are in turn composed of a series of related scenes. Jesus meets with very little opposition through the first four chapters of the Gospel. The reader's acceptance of the narrator's reliability is thereby established before the introduction of "the Jews'" opposition to Jesus in John 5:16, 18. Throughout John 5–12 the action centers around the Jewish festivals. Jesus shows himself to be the fulfillment of all that these festivals celebrate and all they point to. As Jesus declares himself openly, however, hostility mounts. One can detect both the rising hostility within episodes and the escalation of hostility from one episode to the next.

Within these ten episodes the Gospel presents a series of seven signs—six if the walking on the water is not counted separately:

1. The wedding at Cana (2:1–11)
2. The healing of the nobleman's son (4:46–54)
3. The healing at the pool of Bethesda (5:1–9)
4. The feeding of the five thousand (6:1–15)
5. The walking on the water (6:16–21)
6. The healing of the blind man (9:1–7)
7. The raising of Lazarus (11:1–46)

If the walking on the water—which is sandwiched between the feeding of the five thousand and the discourse on bread from heaven—is not counted as a separate sign (and assuming that sequences of seven are important in John), it is possible that either the resurrection of Jesus or the catch of fish in John 21 originally filled out the number to seven signs.

The Jewish festivals and Jesus' trips to Jerusalem may also be significant clues to the structure of John 2–12, as shown in the accompanying table. From these temporal references one can see that the Gospel of John covers a span of time that includes three Passovers (2:13, 6:4, 12:1ff.) and that Jesus makes four journeys to Jerusalem (2:13, 5:1, 7:10, 12:12). The public ministry of Jesus, therefore, might also be outlined around these four journeys.

At the end of John 12, Jesus closes his public ministry with a soliloquy. The rest of the Gospel describes Jesus' ministry to "his own" (13:1), who are now not Israel but his disciples. John 13 introduces the second half of the Gospel with the foot washing. There are no "words of institution," or giving of the bread and the wine at this Last Supper as there are in the other Gospels. Instead, Jesus washes the disciples' feet and gives them the new command: that they love one another as he loved them. Jesus' farewell discourse seems to have at least two parts. The first begins just after Judas' departure from the room and continues to

JESUS' JOURNEYS IN THE GOSPEL OF JOHN

Chapter	Jewish Festivals	Jesus' Travels
John 2:1		Cana of Galilee
John 2:12		to Capernaum
John 2:13	Passover	to Jerusalem
John 3:22–23		in Judaea, to Aenon, near Salim
John 4:3–4		to Galilee, through Samaria, to the city of Sychar
John 4:43, 46		to Galilee, to Cana
John 5:1	"a feast of the Jews"	to Jerusalem
John 6:1, 4	Passover	to the other side of the Sea of Galilee
John 7:1		in Galilee
John 7:10	Tabernacles	to Jerusalem
John 10:22	Dedication	(in Jerusalem)
John 10:40		across the Jordan
John 11:17		to Bethany
John 11:54		to a town called Ephraim
John 12:1	six days before Passover	to Bethany
John 12:12		to Jerusalem

John 14:31. The second encompasses John 15–16. In both parts Jesus speaks of his departure, his return to the Father, and the coming of the Paraclete (or Counselor). The persecution of the disciples after Jesus' exaltation is a major concern of the second part of the discourse (esp. 15:18–16:4). Some commentators have suggested that the discourse in chapters 15 and 16 should be divided, so that the Farewell Discourse falls into three parts: 13:31–14:31, 15:1–16:4a, 16:4b–33 (Painter 1981). John 17 contains Jesus' prayer for the glorification of the Father, for the disciples, and for those who would believe as a result of their testimony (the second generation of believers).

Jesus' arrest and trial are clearly set off in John 18:1–19:16. The crucifixion of Jesus in John 19:17–37 contains five scenes: the title "the King of the Jews" (19:17–22); dividing the garments (19:23–24); Jesus' mother and the Beloved Disciple (1:25–27); Jesus' last words (19:28–30); and the piercing of Jesus' side (19:31–37). Jesus is then given a kingly burial by Joseph of Arimathea and Nicodemus (19:38–42).

John 20 can be divided between the discovery of the empty tomb (20:1–18) and the appearances to the disciples (20:19–29). Verses 30–31 state the purpose for the writing of the Gospel and seem to form an appropriate conclusion for it. John 21 is therefore generally regarded as an appendix or epilogue to the Gospel (although there is no manuscript evidence that the Gospel ever circulated without it). The risen Lord has appeared to the disciples, commissioned them, and breathed Holy Spirit into them. He has overcome Thomas' doubt and pronounced a final beatitude for those who would come later, and the editor has drawn the chapter to a conclusion by recognizing that Jesus performed other signs and stating the purpose for which these were recorded. John 21 then reopens the narrative and tells of a further appearance of the risen Lord before again framing a conclusion for the Gospel. The material in this epilogue was probably drawn from the traditions that circulated in the Johannine community, so even though it was added to the Gospel late in the process of composition it is not necessarily late or secondary in its origin. The redactor, who added the chapter without disturbing the original conclusion, apparently felt it necessary to attach this additional appearance

account and clarify the respective roles of Peter and the Beloved Disciple.

Narrative Structures

In addition to the macrostructure of the Gospel discussed in the previous section, one finds various structures and narrative devices that give passages in the Gospel order, unity, completeness, or significance in relation to other parts of the Gospel. By recognizing these structures, the reader is able to appreciate the artistry of the Gospel more fully.

Sequences. Sequence is a common device for structuring narrative. Events are placed in chronological relation to one another, and at times the number of the events is specified. One finds this device early in John. The phrase "the next day" is repeated in 1:29, 35, and 43; and 2:1 specifies "on the third day." The first two signs are numbered also (see 2:11, 4:54).

Sequences are more interesting when they are discovered than when they are made explicit. The author trusts the reader's ability to find the design, and the reader who sees it joins in an intellectual dance with the author. The sequence of seven scenes is evident both in John 9 and in the trial before Pilate (18:28–19:16). John 9 is a complete narrative unity. Beginning with the healing and moving to the reversal of sight and blindness at the end of the chapter, it contains seven scenes that are distinguishable by change in setting or dialogue partners.

1. The healing of the blind man (9:1–7)
2. Neighbors question the man (9:8–12)
3. Pharisees question the man (9:13–17)
4. Pharisees question the parents (9:18–23)
5. Pharisees question the man again (9:24–34)
6. Jesus questions the man (9:35–38)
7. Pharisees question Jesus (9:39–41)

The seven scenes in the trial narrative are signaled by Pilate's alternating movement out of and into the praetorium.

1. *Outside:* Accusations against Jesus (18:28–32)
2. *Inside:* Pilate interrogates Jesus (18:33–38a)
3. *Outside:* Declaration of innocence (18:38b–40)
4. *Inside:* Scourging and mockery— "Hail, King of the Jews" (19:1–3)
5. *Outside:* Declaration of innocence (19:4–7)
6. *Inside:* Pilate interrogates Jesus (19:8–12)
7. *Outside:* Jesus delivered to be crucified (19:13–16)

Within this sequence of seven scenes, one can also see another structure that appears frequently in the Gospel of John: a concentric structure or chiasm.

Concentric structures. A common literary device is to bring the ending back to the beginning, thereby creating a sense of wholeness or completion. The two Cana miracles (2:11; 4:46, 54) frame chapters 2–4, just as references to John the Baptist (1:19ff., 10:40–41) and the Transjordan (1:28, 10:40) bracket chapters 1–10. This device is called *inclusio.*

A *chiasm* or concentric structure follows an *abba* or *abcba* pattern. Simple, small concentric structures are easily identified, as for example: "I came from the *Father* and have come into the *world,* again, I am leaving the *world* and going to the *Father*" (16:28; RSV). More extensive and more intricate concentric structures are not so easily recognized. Many interpreters, following the lead of M. E. Boismard's *St. John's Prologue* (1957), have found a chiasm in the prologue (see Culpepper 1980; Giblin 1985). Raymond E. Brown (1966, 1970) found chiastic structures in 6:36–40, 13:31–17:26, 15:7–17, 16:16–33, 18:28–19:16a, and 19:16b–19:42. Some interpreters have suggested that major sections—or even the entire Gospel—are arranged in an elaborate chiastic structure (Talbert 1970; Ellis 1984; Staley 1988), but these theories have not been widely accepted.

Parallelism. Hebrew poetry used the device of parallelism. The second line of a couplet could repeat the first line in different words, state its antithesis, or move the thought ahead. The Gospel of John uses each of these poetic structures:

1. Synonymous parallelism:

> We speak of what we know,
> and bear witness to what we have seen.
> (3:11)

2. Antithetic parallelism:

> He who believes in him is not condemned;
> he who does not believe is condemned already.
> (3:18)

3. Synthetic parallelism.

> In him was life,
> and the life was the light of men.

> The light shines in the darkness,
> and the darkness has not overcome it.
> (1:4–5)

These structures are also used on a larger scale. In 3:20–21, for example, the second sentence states the antithesis of the first. Parallel statements can be separated, as with 3:3 and 3:5. Parallelism between paragraphs can also be noted (e.g., 1:19–23 and 1:24–28, or 1:29–34 and 1:35–42), and doublets of the same traditions are occasionally recorded, as in John 13:31–14:31 and John 15–16.

Equally striking is the Gospel's use of parallel scenes and parallel characters. Jesus performs two signs in Cana (2:1–11 and 4:46–54) and heals two men in Jerusalem (John 5 and 9). A pool is mentioned in both of the healings, both occur on the Sabbath, and both lead to a confrontation with the authorities. Such parallelism invites the reader to compare the scenes and the responses of the characters involved in each.

Foreshadowing and echoing. At points in the narrative the narrator or Jesus may point ahead to an event that has not yet occurred (Jesus' hour, the lifting up of the Son of man, Judas' betrayal, Peter's denial). This technique, called "foreshadowing," opens a gap in the narrative. The reader knows something is coming but may not understand just what that event is or how it will occur. Foreshadowing, therefore, can create curiosity or suspense. How is the reader to understand Jesus' statement, repeated to both the Jews and the disciples, that he is going away and they will not be able to come where he is going (7:33–35, 8:21–22, 13:33)?

At other points the narrator recalls or "echoes" events that happened earlier. The narrator occasionally reintroduces characters who appeared in earlier scenes (Nicodemus, 7:50; Caiaphas, 18:14; the Beloved Disciple, 21:20). On two occasions the narrator introduces characters in light of their role later in the narrative (Mary, 11:2 [12:3]; and Judas, 6:71). Some of the echoes are not explicit. The narrator trusts the reader to make the connection to the earlier scene and make the proper inferences. For example, Jesus challenges his mother, "O woman, what have you to do with me? My hour has not yet come" (2:4). Jesus' mother does not reappear in the narrative until his hour has come. Compare, then, John 19:25–27, which is the only other passage in which Jesus' mother appears, at the cross, the hour of his death: "and from that hour the disciple took her to his own home" (19:27). Read in isolation, this verse would not carry much meaning; but in context it resonates with the earlier references to Jesus' hour and heightens the impact of the scene on the reader.

Implicit Commentary

One of the most distinctive and effective ways in which the Gospel achieves its effects is through its use of implicit commentary. This term covers the narrative devices by which the implied author communicates with the reader without explicitly commenting on the story. At various points the narrator makes explicit comments or asides to the reader (see Tenney 1960; O'Rourke 1979; Hedrick 1985). The quotations from the Old Testament are also a form of explicit commentary. Through implicit commentary, however, author and reader join in an intellectual dance in which the reader is trusted to detect and understand more or less subtle signals—winks, nods, and scowls—that direct the reader to a superior understanding of what is taking place in the story.

Misunderstanding. A common technique in the Gospel of John exposes the misunderstanding of the characters in dialogue with Jesus. Misunderstandings abound in the Gospel, but in their most distinct form Jesus voices a statement that contains an ambiguity, a metaphor, or a double entendre. In many instances the statement functions like a Hebrew *mashal*: it is a riddle. The question in John is whether the characters have seen who Jesus is, so that they may then understand his words. Normally, the dialogue partner seizes upon the literal or superficial meaning of what Jesus has said, showing that the higher meaning has been missed. At times Jesus or the narrator supplies the higher meaning. At other times the narrative moves on, trusting that the informed reader has seen through the misunderstanding. The Gospel uses this technique in such varied ways that strict criteria of content or form cannot be imposed on the material. The following examples are illustrative:

"Destroy this temple, and in three days I will raise it up." The Jews then said, "It has taken forty-six years to build this temple, and will you raise it up in three days?" But he spoke of the temple of his body. (2:19–21)

"Truly, truly, I say to you, unless one is born anew [or "from above"] he cannot see the kingdom of God." Nicodemus said to him, "How can a man be born when he is old? Can he enter a second time into his mother's womb and be born?" (3:3–4)

". . . and he would have given you living water." The woman said to him, "Sir, you have nothing to draw with, and the well is deep; where do you get that living water?" (4:10–11)

Other examples of this device can be found in 4:31–34; 6:32–35, 51–53; 7:33–36; 8:21–22, 31–35, 51–53, 56–58, 11:11–15, 23–25; 12:32–34; 13:36–38; 14:4–6, 7–9; 16:16–19. Such misunderstandings draw the reader to the informed or privileged perspective of the narrator. The reader watches and listens while the characters mistake Jesus' meaning, thereby reinforcing the understanding of Jesus that the reader shares with the narrator. The misunderstandings also serve to teach the reader how to read the Gospel and how to interpret Jesus' words. The result is that the reader can then make sense of the Gospel's use of irony and symbolism.

Irony. The varieties of irony are so numerous and subtle that the term almost eludes definition. Nevertheless, the standard works on irony, by D. C. Muecke (1969, 1970) and Wayne Booth (1974), show that irony involves a contrast between appearance and reality that requires the reader to reject the confidence that the appearance is the only possible meaning, recognize alternative meanings, and then choose the new or higher meaning that is in harmony with the position of the speaker or narrator. Two recent monographs will help readers of the Fourth Gospel to detect and enjoy the varied ways this Gospel uses irony (Duke 1985; O'Day 1986).

The prologue foreshadows the irony of the Gospel story: "He came to his own home, and his own people received him not" (1:11). Foundational to the irony of the Gospel is the inability of the Messiah's own people to recognize his identity. Who will recognize the Logos in human form? Like a comedy of mistaken identities the Gospel shows character after character exposing their ignorance while the reader, from a secure and informed vantage point, watches the comedy of errors. Jesus is "from above," while the others cannot understand his "whence" or his "whither" (or what he says) because they are of this world, "from below" (8:23; *cf.* 3:12, 31).

Most of the irony in the Gospel arises from misperceptions of Jesus' origin, identity, and death. Nathanael asks, "Can anything good come out of Nazareth?" (1:46), and we smile with the implied author because we know that Jesus is not really from Nazareth. Perhaps we are to know that Jesus was born in Bethlehem, but ultimately, of course, Jesus is "from above," from the Father. Later the people in Jerusalem confidently assert, "We know where this man comes from; and when the Christ appears, no one will know where he comes from" (7:27), and again we smile knowingly. The Samaritan woman asks incredulously, "Are you greater than our father Jacob?" (4:12). The Jews ask, mocking Jesus, "Are you greater than our father Abraham?" (8:53). The officers report, "No man ever spoke like this man" (7:46). Caiaphas prophesies without knowing it: "You know nothing at all; you do not understand that it is expedient for you that one man should die for the people, and that the whole nation should not perish" (11:49–50; RSV). Extended or sustained irony is especially prominent as an element of characterization in three episodes: the Samaritan woman (John 4), the man born blind (John 9), and Pilate (John 18–19). In each case the reader recognizes the ironic contradiction between what the characters perceive and what the implied author intends.

As readers responding to the Gospel's repeated use of irony, we rehearse time after time the climb from appearances to that perception of Jesus that is informed by the response of faith. To make any other response places us alongside the victims of irony, over whom the Gospel allows its readers to assume a superior, privileged position.

Symbolism. John's symbolism is as subtle and varied as its irony, but it has a more universal, less exclusive appeal. Through such universally recognizable symbols as light and darkness, water, and bread, the Gospel invites its readers to recognize the higher realities to which they point. Through the Gospel's use of misunderstanding and irony, the reader is trained to suspect that these physical realities mean something more or something other than the obvious.

The "more" or "other" that is symbolized may be implied by the context, suggested by the narrator, or assumed from the shared background of author and reader.

Light is introduced in the prologue, where it is associated with the Logos and life: "In him was life, and the life was the light of men" (1:4). John the Baptist came to bear witness to the light; he was not the light, but a burning and shining lamp (5:35). The nature of judgment is stated in the following terms: "that the light has come into the world, and men loved darkness rather than the light" (3:19). The reader remembers that Nicodemus came to Jesus "at night" (3:2), and thereby understands why Nicodemus could not understand what Jesus said to him. Being from below, from the world, Nicodemus was still in darkness.

Jesus then explicitly identifies himself as "the light of the world" (8:12), and in the next chapter he gives sight to a man born blind. John 9 is a delightfully constructed story. The man born blind is an everyman sort of character. Everyone is born blind and must be given sight. Sin, therefore, does not come from being born blind but from refusing to see when light has been given. Those in darkness cannot work the works of God (9:4). Instead, they stumble, so we understand what John means when it says that Judas went out, "and it was night" (13:30). By the end of the Gospel the symbolic significance of light and darkness has been so clearly established that it does not need to be underlined or explained. In the night those who reject the light of the world must carry torches and lanterns (18:3) and huddle around a charcoal fire (18:18). We also sense symbolic significance when we read that Mary Magdalene came to the tomb "while it was still dark" (20:1), and we know why the disciples who fished at night caught nothing (21:3).

Water appears in various contexts. John baptizes in water while pointing to another who would baptize with the Holy Spirit (1:26, 31, 33). Jesus changes water to wine (2:1–11) in the context of a wedding feast. Cleansing thereby gives way to the joy and celebration that was expected at the great eschatological banquet in the messianic age. The children of God, moreover, are born of "water and spirit" (3:5). In John 4, therefore, Jesus offers the Samaritan woman living water as he teaches her that those who worship God must worship "in spirit and in truth" (4:10, 14, 24). Having received the living water Jesus offered, the woman no longer needed her bucket (4:28). The man at the pool of Bethesda learns that while the water in the pool was thought to have healing power, healing comes from Jesus. Moses led the people of Israel through the sea, but Jesus walks on the water (6:19; *cf.* Job 9:8; Ps 77:16, 19). Jesus washes the disciples' feet, but they are cleansed by his word (15:3). In the end, with irony that provokes meditation, the one who gives living water thirsts as he dies (19:28), thereby joining the fellowship of those who thirst.

Jesus himself is the **bread** of life, true food and drink for the children of God. He has food to eat that they do not know of (4:32), and in the economy of John's Gospel bread is not bought and sold (6:5), it is given and received. Just as food is necessary to nourish and sustain physical life, so Jesus (his revelation, or the Spirit) is vital for sustaining the life that he promises to those who believe in him. Some who eat Jesus' bread, however, lift their heel against him (13:18; *cf.* Ps. 41:9): the crowds forsake him, Judas betrays him, and Peter denies him. In the end, however, the risen Lord asks the unsuccessful fishermen if they have anything to eat and then provides them with fish and bread (21:9, 13).

The images that abound in the Gospel of John vibrate with a "surplus of meaning." The settings often function as metaphorical interpretations of the character of Jesus. The signs Jesus performs point beyond themselves, just as his words carry overtones that are sometimes obvious and sometimes subtle. Doves, sheep, and the lamb appear. Garments, sandals, the robe, the towel, and even a fisherman's net all take on fresh meaning for those who recognize how the Gospel's symbols point beyond themselves to higher realities. With remarkable effect, therefore, they invite the reader to see beyond appearances and grasp the reality to which they point.

Representative Characters

In a sense the primary task for the reader of the Gospel is to determine the identity of the characters, especially Jesus. At the end of the Gospel, the narrator states that the Gospel was written in order that the reader might believe that Jesus is "the Christ, the Son of God" (20:31). Along the way, however, the reader must also determine the identities of each of the other main characters and groups in the Gospel. Actually, the identities of the characters are not left unclear; the narrator introduces and identifies each one clearly. The real question is whether the narrator can convince the reader that each of the players has been identified correctly.

Characters are defined for the reader by what the narrator says about them, by what they say, by what they do, and by what other characters say about them. Characters may be either simple (having only one or two traits) or complex (having many traits). They may be static, or they may change and develop. Characterization is also affected by the degree to which the narrator is allowed to give the reader "inside views" of the character's thoughts, feelings, and motives.

In the Gospel of John there are two competing norms: God's and that which is opposed to it. Every character eventually lines up on one side or the other. Every action and every statement is judged by these norms, so every character who encounters Jesus is moving either toward or away from God's evaluative point of view (which is the truth). In turn, the truth is revealed through Jesus. All of the other characters serve to clarify the identity of Jesus and illustrate the ways in which the reader may respond to the revelation that comes through him.

Jesus. Jesus is carefully and repeatedly introduced to the reader before he appears in the narrative. His identity is then confirmed by what he does before opposing interpretations of who he is are introduced. Perhaps because the claims on Jesus' behalf are so lofty, he is first introduced in metaphorical and abstract terms. The reader is first introduced to "the Word" that was with God and that was God (1:1). In him was life and light (1:4). John was sent to bear witness to the light (1:6–8), which was coming into the world (1:9). Although the world did not recognize the light, Jesus authorized those who believed in his name, that they might become "children of God" (1:12). The Word became flesh (1:14), and John bore witness to him. From his fullness we have received grace (1:16), and he is even greater than Moses, through whom the Law was given (1:17). Finally, in verse 17 of the prologue, Jesus is named for the first time. The reader quickly associates Jesus with all that has been said about the Word, life, light, the role of John, the children of God, glory, Moses, the Law, and grace and truth. Jesus is the only one who has seen God and made him known (1:18).

The narrative begins with the testimony of John. The reader is left to suppose that Jesus is the fulfillment of all of the roles John denies: the Christ, Elijah, the prophet (1:20–21). John then testifies that Jesus is "the Lamb of God who takes away the sin of the world" (1:29), and that the Spirit is abiding in him (1:32). He is the one who will baptize with Holy Spirit (1:33); he is the Son of God (1:34).

The first disciples then attribute to Jesus other lofty titles: "rabbi" (teacher, 1:38), "the Messiah" (the Christ, 1:41), "the one of whom Moses and the prophets wrote" (1:45), "the Son of God" (1:49), and "the king of Israel" (1:49). At the end of the chapter, Jesus himself introduces the term "the Son of man" (1:51).

Before Jesus actually does anything in the Gospel, therefore, he is fully introduced by the narrator and by John, a man sent from God to bear witness to Jesus. One can scarcely think of a more definitive or a more authoritative introduction to the main character. Later in the Gospel the narrator shows the reader the signs that Jesus does, which serve further to confirm Jesus' identity as "the Christ, the Son of God."

Jesus describes his mission in metaphorical terms, referring to his "hour" (2:4), raising the Temple in three days (2:19), the lifting up of the Son of man (3:14), God's giving his only son (3:16), the coming of the light (3:19), and the giving of living water (4:10; cf. 4:14, "welling up to eternal life"). Jesus also speaks of his own identity, both in veiled terms and explicit claims: "the one who comes from heaven" (3:31), "the son" (3:16, 35), "I am he [the Messiah]" (4:26). Jesus' clearest words on his relationship to the Father come later: "the Father loves the Son, and has given all things into his hand" (3:35); "the Son can do nothing of his own accord, but only what he sees the Father doing" (5:19). The narrator explains that Jesus made himself equal with God (5:18), and Jesus later claims: "I and the Father are one" (10:30), and "He who has seen me has seen the Father" (14:9). In John, therefore, Jesus does *not* pray "not my will but thine" (as in the Gethsemane scenes of the three Synoptic Gospels).

At the same time, Jesus maintains his absolute dependence on the Father: his "food" is to do "the will of the one who sent me" (4:34); the "works" that he does have been given to him by the Father (5:36); and all who come to him have been given (6:37, 65; 10:29; 17:2) or drawn (6:44) by the Father. Jesus does nothing on his own authority, therefore, and says only what the Father has taught him (8:28). At one point Jesus says, "The Father is greater than I" (14:28). The Son, therefore, is glorified by the Father so that the Son may glorify the Father (17:1).

As the one who is "from above," Jesus remains an enigmatic figure throughout the Gospel. He does not change or develop—in a sense, he is what he always has been. Because he is the preexistent Word, Jesus knows all things. He knows what is in the hearts of others, so he has no need that anyone should tell him (2:24–25). Before Philip brought Nathanael to him, he saw Nathanael under the fig tree (1:48). He does not need to ask for information from others (see 6:5–6). Just as the Word was active in creation, so Jesus can change water to wine or give sight to a man born blind. Those who are "from below" (i.e., earthly) cannot understand him. For this reason, the dialogues in the Gospel of John are often fractured and disjointed. Jesus' responses do not answer the questions addressed to him. Indeed, Jesus seems almost incapable of giving a straight answer.

Those who have been guided by the narrator, however, are able to see and hear Jesus from a more enlightened perspective. Like those "born from above," they are given to understand the true meanings of Jesus' words and works. They understand that Jesus is "the Christ, the Son of God," while characters in the Gospel mistake his identity and reveal their own ignorance. Through this narrative strategy, the reader is subtly drawn to "the truth" revealed by Jesus and conveyed by the Beloved Disciple—"and we know that his testimony is true" (21:24).

The Jews. The term *Ioudaios* (Gr., "Jew" or "Judean") or *hoi Ioudaioi* ("the Jews" or "Judeans") occurs seventy times in the Gospel of John. Studies devoted specifically to identifying the referents of the plural, *hoi Ioudaioi,* have typically proposed four or five categories that have either neutral or hostile overtones

217

(Grässer 1964–1965; Bratcher 1975; Fuller 1977; von Wahlde 1982).

First, *hoi Ioudaioi* is used to designate Jews or Judeans in contrast to Samaritans or gentiles. Such phrases as "feast of the Jews" (5:1, 6:4, 7:2), "Passover of the Jews" (2:13, 11:55), and "King of the Jews" (18:33, 39; 19:3, 19, 21 [twice]) may be placed in this category. Most notable (and problematic) among the neutral references is John 4:22—"Salvation is from the Jews."

Of more particular concern is the hostile or "typically Johannine" use of *hoi Ioudaioi* to refer to those who rejected Jesus and eventually demanded his death. The Gospel's use of *hoi Ioudaioi* to characterize the willful rejection of Jesus received its classic definition from Rudolf Bultmann: "The term *hoi Ioudaioi*, characteristic of the Evangelist, gives an overall portrayal of the Jews, viewed from the standpoint of Christian faith, as the representatives of unbelief (and thereby, as will appear, of the unbelieving 'world' in general)" (Bultmann 1971, 86).

Gathering data from ancient, Jewish, Christian, and pagan writings, Malcolm Lowe has argued that while among "gentiles and Diaspora Jews the word had already a secondary religious meaning . . . the primary meaning of *Ioudaioi* was geographical" (Lowe 1976, 106–107). Lowe contends that the term *Ioudaioi* designated "Judeans" as opposed to people living in other areas. While others recognize that *Ioudaioi* refers to Judeans in 11:19, 31, 33, 36, 45, 54; 12:9, 11; 19:20, and possibly also 3:25 and 11:8, Lowe concludes that all the references to *Ioudaioi* in John denote Judeans, with exception of the instances in Samaria (in John 4), where "Jews" has "the correct denotation, but lacks the connotation of Judea" (Lowe 1976, 126). The phrase *basileus tōn Ioudaiōn* means "King of the Judeans." In the hostile instances, therefore, the *Ioudaioi* are Judeans, "either in references to the Judean population in general or (less frequently except after Jesus' arrest) to the Judean authorities" (Lowe 1976, 128).

In a study on the subject, John Ashton responds to Lowe's work by first distinguishing three related questions: (1) Who are the *Ioudaioi*? (2) What role or function do they fulfill in John? and (3) Why did the evangelist regard them with such hostility? (Ashton 1985, 40). Ashton reviews Lowe's thesis sympatheti-cally, defending its plausibility but withholding final judgment until more historical evidence is adduced. Groups of people were commonly identified by their place of origin or their principal deity. The religious and geographical meanings, therefore, may not have been sharply distinguished. Granting the difficulty of the references in John 6, Ashton accepts that "wherever *Ioudaioi* is used . . . these are natives or inhabitants of Judea" (Ashton 1985, 55), but he also perceptively lodges the complaint that neither Lowe nor von Wahlde distinguished between "referent" and "sense." The "referent" of *Ioudaioi* would be "natives or inhabitants of Judea." By "sense" Ashton means the role the *Ioudaioi* play in the Gospel narrative. The distinction is essential. In the Gospel, historical persons become characters in a narrative in which they take on varying degrees of symbolic significance and characterize different responses to Jesus.

Distinguishing hostile from neutral instances and limiting the referent to Judeans or authorities, or even Judean authorities, does not address the issue of John's characterization of the *Ioudaioi*, their function in the Gospel, or the effect of using the same term to refer to both the hostile authorities and the (neutral) Jews or Judeans. Rather than describe Jesus' opponents as Pharisees, rulers, scribes, or chief priests (as the Synoptics do), John characterizes the opponents with the more general term *Ioudaioi*, thereby coloring all occurrences of the term in the Gospel (at least in retrospect) with the hostile sense. Parenthetically, it is important to observe that John's characterization of the *Ioudaioi* is no less shaped by theology and historical circumstances than is its characterization of Jesus, which has long been recognized as the product of Johannine theology.

The *Ioudaioi* characterize the response of unbelief in the Gospel of John. The reasons for their unbelief, however, are related not to their being Jewish but to universal qualities. Through the *Ioudaioi* the Gospel explores the causes for unbelief. The *Ioudaioi* do not accept the revelation Jesus brings because they are from "below," from a different world order than Jesus: "You are from below, I am from above; you are of the world, I am not of this world" (8:23). They have never seen or heard the Father (5:37). They do not have the love of God in themselves (5:42). Instead, their love is misdirected: they love darkness rather than light

(3:19–21), and human glory rather than the glory of God (5:41–44, 12:43). The *Ioudaioi*, therefore, are associated with all of the negative categories and images in the Gospel: the world, sin, the devil, darkness, blindness, and death. They represent the human condition apart from God. The pathos is heightened, of course, because they are "his own" people (1:11); yet they do not recognize the Word incarnate.

By not having seen or heard the Father, the *Ioudaioi* are Jesus' opposite. In their response to Jesus, they are the opposite of the disciples (Culpepper 1983, 125–131).

The Disciples. "The Twelve" are mentioned only four times in the Gospel, and they are never called apostles. Instead, the Gospel of John calls Jesus' followers "disciples" (seventy-eight times). Through the disciples the Gospel explores a variety of believing responses to Jesus. The disciples are models of faith, but they misinterpret Jesus at times and show that they still have not grasped the full meaning of his revelation. In this mix of faithfulness and failure in the context of belief and following, the disciples offer models with which the readers can identify. Through the disciples, believing readers can explore the meaning of discipleship, learn from the failures of the disciples, and be moved toward the model of the Beloved Disciple.

The role of the disciples is shaped first in the prologue. John the Baptist, though he is not a disciple, bears witness to the light. The reader is then told that those who "receive" Jesus, who "believe in his name," will be given authority to become "children of God." The narrator also identifies with the community of believers by confessing, "The Word became flesh and dwelt among us, full of grace and truth; we beheld his glory" (1:14; RSV).

The first few disciples come to Jesus as a result of the testimony of John the Baptist. They offer lofty confessions of Jesus in the first chapter, but they have hardly begun to discover his identity. They see the sign in the wine at Cana and believe in him (2:11), but the Gospel is intent on showing that there is more to faith than a response to what can be seen. They will not fully understand what they were seeing and hearing until after the resurrection, when they will remember what Jesus has said and interpret it in the light of Scripture (2:22, 12:16).

Early in the Gospel the disciples assume the role of disciples of a rabbi, using the term "rabbi" frequently when they address Jesus, securing food for him, traveling with him, listening to his teaching, and baptizing others (4:2, though this verse may be a gloss). A crisis occurs following Jesus' words about the "bread of life" in John 6. Jesus' works do not precipitate the crisis; it is his words that scandalize his followers. The Jews murmur and dispute among themselves (6:41, 52) following the first "I am" sayings and Jesus' implicit claim to superiority over Moses (6:32–35). The disciples then begin to murmur also (6:61), and many of them turn away from Jesus (6:66). Only the Twelve are left, and one of them will betray Jesus. In John, therefore, the Twelve seem to be the remnant of disciples who stay with Jesus following the collapse of his ministry in Galilee.

Although the disciples are scarcely mentioned in John 7–10, discipleship is defined in 8:31 by the statement, "If you continue in my word, you are truly my disciples." As the disciples continue to follow Jesus, they learn that Jesus' love for his friends and his obedience to the Father require him to return to Bethany, where he calls Lazarus out of the tomb and sets in motion the events that will lead to his arrest. All along it is evident that the disciples still understand very little of what Jesus has said or what he is doing. They will not understand these things until later.

Jesus washes the disciples' feet and gives them the command that they are to wash one another's feet. The ethic of love, as Jesus has loved them, will identify them as his disciples (13:35). Still, they do not understand where Jesus is going (13:36, 14:5); they do not understand the "way" to the Father or that they have seen the Father in Jesus (14:5–11). Neither do they understand what Jesus says about the "little while" (16:17–18). Only after Jesus has risen from the dead and breathed the Holy Spirit into them will they understand these things. When Jesus tells Mary Magdalene to go and tell his "brothers" that he is risen, she goes directly to tell the disciples. The Gospel may be subtly making the point that the disciples have now become "children of God" through their faith in the unique Son of God. They are now his "brothers." In the closing scenes in both John 20 and 21, Jesus comforts the disciples, commissions them, and consecrates them for their work as those who have been sent into the world just as the Father had sent him.

Seven disciples have individual roles in the Gospel: the Beloved Disciple, Peter, Andrew, Philip, Nathanael, Thomas, and Judas. Judas (not Iscariot) speaks once (14:22), and the sons of Zebedee are mentioned once (21:2). Through the **Beloved Disciple** the Gospel portrays the ideal of discipleship. Although the Gospel never identifies the Beloved Disciple by name, on the basis of internal evidence alone we might gather that the Beloved Disciple is Lazarus. After all, Lazarus is identified as "he whom you love" in John 11:3 (*cf.* 11:36), Jesus has called him "friend" (11:11; *cf.* 15:15), and Lazarus is at table with Jesus in John 12, just as the Beloved Disciple reclines on Jesus' breast in the next chapter. Certainly one can understand how the community thought the Beloved Disciple would not die until the Lord returned (21:23) if the Beloved Disciple had already been raised from the dead.

The Beloved Disciple is not introduced until the meal in John 13, but from then on he is the disciple closest to Jesus. Peter motions to the Beloved Disciple to find out who the betrayer is. When the Beloved Disciple asks Jesus, Jesus responds by telling him that it is the one to whom he will give the morsel (13:26). The Beloved Disciple is apparently privileged to share even this knowledge that is concealed from the other disciples. At the cross, Jesus gives his mother to the Beloved Disciple and the disciple to his mother (19:26–27). The Beloved Disciple arrives at the tomb before Peter and is the first to believe in the resurrection. In John 21 he is also the first to recognize the risen Lord. Although Peter is given a pastoral role, the Gospel makes clear that the Beloved Disciple does not take second place. He bears a true witness (19:34–35, 21:24). Indeed, one can argue that the Beloved Disciple does the very things that Jesus promised the Paraclete (Holy Spirit, Comforter) would do after his death: He bears witness, reminds others of what Jesus said, teaches all things, and bears witness to the world. The Beloved Disciple, therefore, is the model of ideal discipleship.

Next to Jesus, **Peter** is the most complex character in the Gospel. The Gospel of John denies to Peter the privilege of giving the confession "Thou art the Christ," for which he is known in each of the Synoptic Gospels. Instead, when Andrew finds Peter he tells him right off, " 'We have found the Messiah' (which means Christ)" (1:41). Peter does later make an important confession: "You have the words of eternal life; and we have believed, and have come to know that you are the Holy One of God" (6:68–69; RSV), but this confession is surpassed by Martha's response, "I believe that you are the Christ, the Son of God" (11:27), and by Thomas' climactic confession, "My Lord and my God" (20:28).

The Gospel subtly exploits the ironies of Peter's character. He is Cephas, but he is not a rock of faith. Peter at first refuses to let Jesus wash his feet, then he wants to be washed all over. He does not understand that he has been cleansed by Jesus' word (see 15:3) and needs only to have his feet washed. His misunderstanding concerns the necessity of Jesus' death, and he even takes the sword to prevent it from happening (18:10). At the time of Jesus' death Peter is not able to follow him. He denies three times that he is Jesus' disciple. He turns from the light of the world to the warmth of a charcoal fire (18:18, 25; *cf.* 21:9). While Jesus is inside with Caiaphas being questioned about his disciples and challenging the authorities to ask those who had heard him (18:19–21), Peter is busy denying that he is a follower of Jesus. Yet the disciple who resists Jesus' dying will follow Jesus in martyrdom (13:36–38, 21:15–19). Peter will be the shepherd of Jesus' sheep, and like the good shepherd he will lay down his life for the sheep (see 10:14–16).

Andrew brings others to Jesus (1:40, 6:8–9, 12:22). **Philip,** who is often linked with Andrew, repeatedly shows his lack of understanding (6:5–7, 12:21–22, 14:8); but at a minimum Philip can give encouragement to readers who attempt to follow but find that they fail repeatedly. Unlike Peter, **Thomas** sees clearly that Jesus is going to die (11:16) and commits himself to go and die with him. The problem for Thomas is believing that the one who died has risen and appeared to the other disciples. He does not know where Jesus is going (14:5); how can he know the way? Thomas, therefore, represents those who have accepted that Jesus came "in flesh" but have not seen his glory.

Judas is the defector, one of the disciples who

leaves the community (like those in 1 John 2:19) and betrays Jesus. From the beginning Jesus knows that Judas will betray him (6:64, 70). Whereas Jesus and the Father will make an abiding place in the disciples (14:20, 23), the devil enters into Judas (13:27). Although Judas is guilty of pilfering from the common purse (12:6), he does not betray Jesus for money. Jesus is not able to win over the "son of perdition" (17:12), not even by giving him the morsel (13:26). Leaving the circle of the children of God, Judas joins the children of the devil, who hate and kill (8:44; 1 John 3:8, 10). He goes out into the world, into the darkness (John 13:30), and that is punishment enough. Judas, therefore, models the response of those who join with the Christian community, but then go out from it and turn against it (see 1 John 2:19, 4:1).

The minor characters. Much of the distinctiveness of the Gospel of John is due to the minor characters in the story. Interacting with the Jews and the disciples, but most often with Jesus, one finds a series of characters who appear only briefly in the Gospel. Several of these minor characters do not appear in the Synoptic Gospels: Nicodemus, the royal official, the Samaritan woman, the man at the pool of Bethesda, the blind man, and Lazarus. All of these except Lazarus are confronted by Jesus as the revealer, and the Gospel describes their response to Jesus. Through these characters, therefore, the basic conflict of the Gospel's plot, the conflict between belief and unbelief in response to Jesus, is played out repeatedly.

Nicodemus appears three times (3:1–10, 7:50–52, 19:39–42), first at night (and darkness is always symbolic in John), then challenging the crowd to follow due process as stipulated by the Law, and finally at Jesus' burial. In the second passage he may be an example of one of the "authorities or the Pharisees" who believed in Jesus (see 7:48), but his association with Joseph of Arimathea identifies him as "a disciple of Jesus, but secretly, for fear of the Jews" (19:38). The faith of such "secret believers" is not acceptable, however, because "they loved the praise of men more than the praise of God" (12:42; *cf.* 5:44). Nicodemus is left at the tomb, therefore, and never meets the risen Lord.

The royal official (4:46–53) serves to turn the reader away from faith based on the signs Jesus does to faith in response to the words of Jesus. The repetition of the verb "to live" three times in these verses makes the point that life comes not through "signs and wonders" (4:48) but through faith.

The Samaritan woman (4:4–42) shows how the revelation in Jesus can break across all the barriers that destroy human community: racial, national, sexual, geographic, ethnic, and religious. The scene at the well moves from a provincial context ("a city of Samaria, called Sychar, near the field that Jacob gave") to a universal setting ("neither on this mountain nor in Jerusalem," "in spirit and truth," "the Savior of the world"). Through the carefully structured dialogue, the Samaritan woman moves step by step toward a clearer understanding of who Jesus is ("sir," "a prophet," "the Christ"), and the reader is allowed to rehearse once more the pilgrimage that leads to a believing response (O'Day 1986, 49–92; Duke 1985, 101–103).

The man at the pool of Bethesda (5:2–16) is an enigmatic character. The parallels in structure between John 5 and John 9—healing on the Sabbath followed by dialogue with the Pharisees—invite the reader to contrast the responses of the man at the pool and the blind man. The man at the pool makes excuses by blaming others. Jesus, who knows what is in the hearts of men (2:25), asks him whether he wants to be well, but the man evades the question. He is the way he is because he does not have anyone to put him into the pool when the waters are stirred. Even after he has been healed, when the Pharisees confront him for carrying his pallet on the Sabbath he blames his healer—whose name he does not even know—for his breach of Sabbath law. Then, when Jesus finds him and tells him to sin no more, he goes immediately to tell the authorities that it was Jesus who had healed him. This last action may be interpreted positively as a witness to Jesus, but the pattern of his evasive, self-excusing responses tilts the balance toward interpreting his action as reporting Jesus to those who had accused him of breaking the Law.

In contrast, **the blind man** (9:1–41) stands up to those who confront him over the same issue, Sabbath violation, and moves steadily toward his final response to Jesus: "Lord, I believe" (9:38). This chapter is artistically structured in seven scenes. With beautiful irony the Pharisees, who repeatedly claim to know, are exposed as ignorant; and the blind man, who repeatedly says he does not know, comes to understand who Jesus is. The conclusion underscores the reversal: "If you were blind, you would have no guilt; but now that you say, 'We see,' your guilt remains" (9:41; RSV). Guilt, therefore, does not reside in blindness but in willful, chosen blindness. The blind man is an everyman sort of character, for in John's world all are born blind and must receive the sight that is offered to them. Once more, the reader rehearses the response of faith, watching as the Pharisees trap themselves in their presumed knowledge and the blind man moves step by step toward true sight: "the man" (9:11), "a prophet" (9:17), "from God" (9:33), "the Son of man" (9:35), "Lord, I believe" (9:38). Again in this chapter we see that *how* the Gospel tells its story is just as important as *what* it says about Jesus (see Martyn 1979, 24–62; Duke 1985, 117–126).

Lazarus (11:1–46, 12:1–11) is the representative "friend" of Jesus, whom Jesus loves, and to whom Jesus gives life. Whereas in earlier chapters (John 5, 6, and 9) discourse follows the sign and develops themes from it, in John 11 dialogue precedes the raising of Lazarus, thereby delaying the sign itself, creating suspense, and developing its thematic significance in advance. The challenge to the reader, represented in the conversation with Martha, is to understand that Jesus offers eternal life not in some future resurrection and judgment but immediately. Hope for the future is already realized in the present through faith in Jesus.

The minor characters who also appear in the Synoptics are given distinctive roles in John: John the Baptist, Jesus' mother, the brothers of Jesus, Mary and Martha, Caiaphas and Annas, Pilate, Joseph of Arimathea, and Mary Magdalene.

John the Baptist (1:6–8, 15, 19–36; 3:23–30; 4:1; 5:33–36; 10:40–42) is introduced as a man sent from God who bears witness to Jesus. Throughout the narrative he fulfills this role. In contrast to the Synoptics, John is not a prophet calling for repentance, and even his baptizing is secondary to his function as a witness for Jesus. John denies that he is himself the Christ, Elijah, or the prophet. Apparently the fulfillment of all of these roles is reserved for Jesus. John is the bridegroom's friend, not the bridegroom, the lamp, not the light.

Jesus' mother appears in only two scenes (2:1–5, 12; 19:25–27). Like the Beloved Disciple, she is never named. Jesus' sharp retort in the first scene indicates that his mother's only significant role has to do with his "hour": "O woman, what have you to do with me? My hour has not yet come" (2:4; RSV). When that hour arrives, Jesus' mother stands at the cross with the Beloved Disciple. As he dies, Jesus gives each into the keeping of the other. Together these two symbolic figures constitute a new family for the "children of God."

The brothers of Jesus (7:2–10) appear only once, and then in the role of tempters. They are part of the unbelieving world, and their time is always. Like the devil in the Synoptic temptation accounts, the brothers, who do not believe in Jesus, tempt him to go up to Jerusalem and do something spectacular: "Show yourself to the world" (7:4), "that your disciples may see the works that you are doing" (7:3). Although the brothers of Jesus are included among the faithful in Acts (1:14), they are displaced in John. We are never told that they believed in Jesus, and when the risen Lord tells Mary Magdalene to go and tell his "brothers" that he is risen, she immediately goes to tell the disciples, who by implication are now Jesus' true brothers, those to whom he has given authority to become the children of God (1:12, 20:17–18).

Mary and Martha (11:1–46, 12:1–11), together with Lazarus, are Jesus' friends (11:11). Mary is best remembered for having wiped Jesus' feet with her hair (11:2, 12:3). As in the Lucan account, when they are at table Martha serves (12:2; *cf.* Luke 10:38–42). Each of the sisters challenges Jesus that if he had been there their brother would not have died. In response, Jesus challenges Martha to believe that he himself is the resurrection and that the hope of resurrection is already fulfilled in him. Then he asks Mary to take him to the tomb of Lazarus, where he calls Lazarus out. Through Martha and Mary, the Gospel of John illustrates the inadequacy of traditional, future-oriented hope. The hope for eternal life is already fulfilled in Jesus. Jesus' friends do not need to grieve as those who have no hope (*cf.* 1 Thess 4:13–18). Instead, they can affirm their faith in Jesus (as Martha does, 11:27) and worship him (as Mary does, 12:3).

Caiaphas and Annas (11:47–53; 18:13–14, 19–24, 28) are both identified as "the high priest"

(Caiaphas, 11:49, 51; 18:13, 24; Annas, 18:15, 16, 19). Annas was the father-in-law of Caiaphas, who was high priest that year. Apparently Annas retained the title "high priest" as an honorary title. Caiaphas prophesies unwittingly that it is better for one man (Jesus) to die than for the whole nation to perish (11:50, 18:14). As high priest he was to preside over the sacrifice of the Passover lamb. The Gospel, therefore, takes delight in his unwitting prophecy, explaining that he did not say this of his own accord but because he was high priest. Indeed, Jesus would die not for the nation alone but "to gather into one the children of God who are scattered abroad" (11:52).

The character of **Pilate** is more highly developed in John than in the other Gospels (18:29–19:16, 21–22, 31, 38). The trial is staged in seven scenes. Pilate is caught between the demands of "the Jews" outside the praetorium, who would not enter the praetorium, "so that they might not be defiled" (18:28), and Jesus on the inside. Yielding for a time to both, Pilate moves back and forth from one to the other. Jesus' accusers will not be satisfied with anything less than his death, and Jesus will not cease to press Pilate for a response of faith. Pilate refuses to make such a response, but the reader senses that Pilate knows more than he believes. In the end he takes vengeance on both the Jews and Jesus. He wrings from the Jews the denial of their heritage and faith ("We have no king but Caesar," 19:15), and he hands Jesus over to be crucified (19:16). Then Pilate lets the charge stand as written, "the King of the Jews." For him it is a bitter testimony. He has denied what he sensed to be the truth, and he has condemned to death one whom he knew to be innocent. Readers of the Gospel are thereby warned: those who refuse to believe because they seek to be friends of the world ("Caesar's friend," 19:12) cannot take their place among the friends of Jesus.

Joseph of Arimathea (19:38–42) was "a disciple of Jesus, but secretly, for fear of the Jews." With Nicodemus (who was also a secret believer) he buries the body of Jesus. It is a royal burial, with a hundred pounds of myrrh and aloes; but because they will not confess their faith openly, Joseph of Arimathea and Nicodemus remain grieving over the crucified Messiah. John's judgment on the secret believers is that they do not experience the joy of Jesus' resurrection and the giving of the Spirit.

Mary Magdalene (19:25; 20:1–2, 11–18) is the woman who discovers the empty tomb. Her difficulty is that she does not understand that the resurrection means the exaltation and glorification of Jesus: his return to the Father. She does not understand Jesus' "whither." She seeks for Jesus, but her repeated lament is "They have taken away my Lord" (20:2, 13, 15). In a striking fashion, Mary Magdalene is privileged to be at the cross and then at the empty tomb, to hear the angels and to see the risen Lord. Each of these is mentioned in the Pauline confession in 1 Corinthians 15:3–8, but none of these experiences leads her to faith in the risen Lord. It is only when the Lord calls her and she responds to his words that she is able to see and believe. In the context of the rest of the Gospel, therefore, Mary Magdalene focuses the light so that the reader can see the meaning of the resurrection and understand how one comes to faith in the risen Lord.

The plot of the Gospel is episodic. In scene after scene Jesus reveals his identity to new characters and challenges them to grasp the revelation from above. The characters serve, therefore, both to draw out new themes related to Jesus and the revelation and to represent alternative responses to Jesus (see Culpepper 1983, 145–148). In reading the Gospel, one is invited to study the consequences of these alternative responses, watch the characters grope and stumble from the higher vantage point supplied by the narrator, and rehearse the response of faith to which the Gospel leads. The Gospel, therefore, does not contain a message so much as it is a textual means of moving the reader to the response of faith in Jesus as "the Christ, the Son of God" (20:31).

Once we understand how the Gospel of John conveys meaning, we may begin to survey the primary themes that are conveyed by the Gospel narrative.

BASIC THEMES

In the first section of this essay, I situated the Gospel of John in the context of an early Christian community's emergence from the synagogue and its subsequent conflicts both with its parent community and within its own membership. In the second part, I explored the fascinating ways in which the Gospel tells its story and involves the reader in interpretation. This present section turns to the basic themes of the Gospel.

The Gospel states that its purpose is to lead the reader to believe that Jesus is "the Christ, the Son of God" and that "believing you may have life in his name" (20:31). The principal themes of the Gospel revolve around this central purpose. They involve the identity of Jesus, the condition of the world (humanity apart from God), the nature of faith, and the life of the children of God.

The Identity of Jesus

Earlier in this essay I examined the characterization of Jesus. Here the question is: What is conveyed through that characterization? Moving one step beyond characterization, we see that the Gospel of John casts Jesus in a role with three primary facets: he is the Logos, the revealer, and the redeemer.

Logos. Jesus is first introduced as the Logos ("the Word"; 1:1–4, 14). The roots of this concept reach deep into the Wisdom tradition. Wisdom was personified. She existed with God even before the earth was created, and she was God's agent in creation (Prov 8:22–23, Sir 24:9, Wis 6:22). Wisdom also descended from heaven to dwell among human beings and to teach them (Prov 8:31, Sir 24:8, Wis 9:10, 16–18). John also follows a well-established pattern when it connects the Logos, as wisdom, with light (Wis 7:10, 26, 29).

As the incarnation of Divine Wisdom, Jesus goes on doing what the Logos had done from the beginning. Jesus continues to have power over the creation. He changes water to wine, or, as an ancient poet wrote, "The water recognized its creator, and blushed" (*Epigrammata Sacra: Aquae in vinum versae,* translated by Richard Crashaw [1613–1649]). He multiplies bread and fish. Then he walks on water, which only God could do (Job 9:8; Ps 77:16, 19). He makes clay and fashions eyes that see for a man born blind. He calls forth the dead, and he breathes spirit into the disciples. In the Gospel of John, therefore, Jesus acts and speaks as the Logos who has descended from above, and he continues the creative, revelatory, and redemptive work of that Logos.

Revealer. Jesus' role as revealer is closely linked with his identity as the unique (Gr., *monogenēs*) Son of the Father. Only he has seen God (1:18, 5:37), and he was sent to make the Father known. He is one with the Father (10:30), but the Father is greater (14:28). He does what he sees the Father doing (5:19, 30), and he says just what the Father has taught him (8:28).

Jesus was sent by the Father, and as the one sent he represents the Father and acts on his authority. Through what Jesus does and says the Father is revealed. Jesus' words call for hearers to grasp their higher meaning, and his works point beyond themselves. They are the works of the one who sent Jesus. When one has seen Jesus, therefore, one has seen the Father (12:45, 14:9). He is in the Father, and the Father in him (14:10). The mission to reveal the Father, however, is not finished until Jesus dies on the cross.

Redeemer. Jesus' mission as the Logos revealing the Father is a redemptive one. The Gospel of John affirms both Jesus' redemptive work as revealer and his redemptive death on the cross. As readers, we are left to work out the relationship between these two aspects of his work. John neither omits the passion narrative nor denies the value of Jesus' redemptive death. Traditional sacrificial language is preserved: Jesus is the "Lamb of God that takes away the sin of the world" (1:29, 36). Nevertheless, John translates the traditional sacrificial imagery into an idiom more closely related to Jesus' role as revealer. The disciples are cleansed by the word that Jesus has spoken to them (15:3). And, even to the children of Abraham (who thought they were free already) he promises that if they will abide in his word they will know the truth and the truth will make them free (8:31–32).

As the redeemer, Jesus frees people from the "ruler of this world" (12:31, 14:30, 16:11), the devil (6:70, 8:44, 13:2), or Satan (13:27). Jesus redeems by bringing people to believe in him, for he is the revelation of the Father. Sin is the evidence of the power of the ruler of this world and consists basically in unbelief (16:8). Therefore, when one believes in Jesus, that person is freed from the tyranny of sin. In John, consequently, redemption takes place primarily through revelation. Those who respond to the revelation of God in Jesus Christ are brought into light and life; those who see the light and choose darkness instead will perish in their sin.

The World:
The Human Condition Apart from God

In the Gospel of John "the world" (Gr., *kosmos*) is used to represent the created order as a whole (1:9–10), but "the world" usually designates all that has fallen under the power of evil and is opposed to God (Cassem 1972). The world is now inherently evil; John affirms that it was created by the Logos. It is now under the power of "the ruler of this world" (12:31, 14:30, 16:11), and its natural condition is darkness (1:5, 3:19). Jesus comes as the light of the world (8:12, 9:5). He is the Lamb of God that takes away the world's sin (1:29, 36), and God sent him into the world that the world might be saved through him (3:16–17). Those who are under the dominion of the prince of this world, however, love darkness instead of light. They walk in darkness, stumble, and do not know where they are going (12:35). They claim to be free, but they are bound by sin (8:34) and death (8:21, 24). This condition is marked by a second false love; they love human glory rather than the glory of God (5:41, 44; 7:18; 12:43). The third false love is loving one's own life in this world rather than seeking eternal life (12:25; Painter 1986, 73).

Jesus is the savior of the world (4:42, 12:47), but his coming is a judgment on the world (9:39, 12:31) and on the children of darkness. Jesus' kingdom is not of this world (18:36–37). He has come to bear witness to the truth, but the world can neither understand nor accept Jesus. Neither can it accept the Spirit whom Jesus gives (14:17). It hates and persecutes both Jesus and his followers (7:7, 15:18–19). Through his death, his exaltation, and his return to the Father, Jesus has overcome the world and vanquished the ruler of this world (12:31, 16:33). Still, God's redemptive work goes on. Jesus sends his disciples into the world (17:18, 20:21), though they are not "of the world" (17:16). As those sent by Jesus, the disciples will lead others to believe that the Father sent him into the world (17:21) and that the Father loves them just as he has loved Jesus (17:23). Apart from faith, however, one remains bound in the world's sin, darkness, unrighteousness, false pursuits, and hatred.

The Nature of Faith

Much of the thematic development in John centers around the nature of the response of faith.

Jesus comes as the revealing and redeeming Logos, calling for belief. His coming brings a sifting among those who are confronted by the revelation. Some turn away in unbelief, but those who are given, called, or drawn by the Father respond in faith. Through various characters the Gospel explores this response, exposing a series of faith responses. In the process of reading the Gospel, therefore, the reader is invited to lay aside inadequate or lesser responses and move on to an authentic faith.

Signs. The lowest level of response comes from those who believe in Jesus because they see the signs that he does. Jesus manifested his glory in the first of his signs, at the wedding at Cana, "and his disciples believed in him" (2:11). Later in the same chapter readers learn that in Jerusalem "many believed in his name [*cf.* 1:12] when they saw the signs which he did; but Jesus did not trust himself to them" (2:23–24; RSV). Those whose faith is based on signs (or "works") are likely to turn away from Jesus when they are confronted by the demands of his words. This weakness of faith based on signs is illustrated pointedly in John 6, which begins with a multitude that "followed him, because they saw the signs which he did" (6:2), and ends with a mass defection both from the multitude and from his disciples, who said, "This is a hard saying, who can listen to it?" (6:60; *cf.* 6:66). Faith based on signs, therefore, is less than a believing response to the full revelation that comes through Jesus. Nevertheless, it is a beginning, and Jesus urges, "Even though you do not believe me, believe the works, that you may know and understand that the Father is in me and I am in the Father" (10:38; *cf.* 14:11).

Seeing. John uses six different verbal forms to express the activity of seeing (Painter 1986, 71). These verbs can indicate either physical sight (the general perception of events) or the seeing of faith, which sees beyond mere appearances. The man born blind receives both physical sight and the seeing of faith, while the spiritual blindness of the Pharisees, who have physical sight, is exposed (John 9). By the end of the Gospel, Jesus calls his disciples to a faith that is not based on sight: "Have you believed because you have seen me? Blessed are those who have not seen and yet believe" (20:29; RSV). With this final beatitude the Gospel opens the way for future generations of disciples who will believe even though they were not eyewitnesses.

Hearing. The next higher level of faith response is based on hearing. Jesus is the Logos, and those who receive his word are drawn to faith. Nicodemus judges from the signs that Jesus is "a teacher sent from God" (3:2), but when Jesus tells him even "earthly things" (3:12) he is unable to believe. Jesus does no sign for the Samaritan woman, but she believes; and when the Samaritans hear Jesus, they say to the woman, "It is no longer because of your words that we believe [*cf.* 4:39], for we have heard for ourselves, and we know that this is indeed the Savior of the world" (4:42). Similarly, the royal official whose son was dying believes and returns home because he hears Jesus' words (4:50, 53; contrast 4:48). The multitude Jesus fed followed him because of his signs, but they could not accept Jesus' words. Much of the double entendre and misunderstanding in the Gospel serves to reinforce the reader's self-understanding as one who can hear and understand Jesus' words, and can therefore move to a faith that is based on hearing rather than seeing. Jesus calls his sheep by name, and they hear his voice and follow him (10:4–5, 16, 25–26; *cf.* 11:43, 20:16).

Knowing. The highest level of faith involves knowing, love, and bearing witness. The goal of faith is a personal knowledge of God that brings a unity between believer and Deity like that between Jesus and the Father. The world did not know Jesus (1:10–11), for one cannot know him without knowing his origin from the Father (7:28). Through faith (even faith that begins with belief on account of the works of Jesus), the believer "may know and understand that the Father is in me and I am in the Father" (10:38). That knowledge which comes from abiding in Jesus' word, moreover, is a knowledge of the truth that makes one free (8:31–32). Full knowledge, however, is not possible until after Jesus has been glorified through his crucifixion, resurrection, and return to the Father. Then, the Spirit teaches all things. The result of this knowledge is eternal life, life lived in the knowledge of God that has come through Jesus Christ (17:3). The ultimate effect of Jesus' life, therefore, is that he has made God known in the world (1:18, 17:26).

Those who have received this knowledge of God in turn are commissioned to continue the mission of Jesus so that "the world may know that thou [i.e., God] has sent me" (17:23, 20:21). Like the Beloved Disciple, those who share this authentic faith will bear witness to the truth (19:35, 21:24). They will live "just as" Jesus lived (10:15, 17:18, 20:21), and they share in his peace (14:27), his joy (16:20, 22, 24), and his love (13:34, 15:12). Indeed, the world knows that they are his disciples because they love one another "just as" he loved them (13:35). That love, of course, also requires obedience to Jesus' word (14:15) and results in an abiding, or indwelling, that is like Jesus' relationship to the Father (14:23, 15:4).

The Children of God

The Gospel of John describes the new status of those who receive Jesus in faith by calling them "children of God" (1:12). Against the socio-historical background sketched earlier, one can imagine that the Gospel served to confirm the self-understanding of readers in the Johannine community by assuring them that they were the true children of God. Those who opposed faith in Jesus, on the other hand, were children of the devil (John 8:44, 1 John 3:10). By drawing readers to a full, authentic faith by means of the reading experience, the Gospel also gave them a secure identity in their conflict with "the world."

Birth. Once the theme of the "children of God" is introduced in John 1:12, it is developed in significant passages throughout the Gospel. First, the new birth required of the children of God is explained in the discourse with Nicodemus (3:3, 5). As a result of this new birth, the children of God already possess eternal life.

Life. Life is not something the children of God will receive only at the end of time, they already experience that quality of life which is marked by fellowship with God (17:3). Martha, for example, needed to learn that Jesus was already the resurrection and the life. Those who believe never die (11:26); they have already crossed from death into life (John 5:24, 1 John 3:14).

The life of the children of God is sustained by a sustenance the world cannot see. Like Jesus, they have food "of which you do not know" (4:32). They receive living water that wells up to eternal life (4:10, 14; 7:37–39), and they have the bread of life, bread from heaven, on which to feast (6:27, 33, 35, 51).

As the children of God, their life is to be marked by all of those characteristics of a full, authentic faith (an issue discussed earlier in this essay). The Spirit abides in them, and they keep the words of Jesus.

Community. As a community, the children of God practice the love that Jesus commanded. They are one, just as Jesus was one with the Father. They are the sheep of the Good Shepherd, so they know his voice and they follow him. They are the branches of the vine, and they bear fruit by their obedience to Jesus' commands. They are "friends" (John 11:11, 15:14–15; 3 John 15), so they are to lay down their lives for one another just as Jesus did for them (John 15:13). The children of God, therefore, live in a community that is very democratic and egalitarian. Women (such as Martha and Mary, the mother of Jesus, and Mary Magdalene) are received as persons of equal standing and faith. All have beheld Jesus' glory and possess the Spirit, so none is distinguished by virtue of greater authority. On the contrary, they are to wash one another's feet, just as Jesus washed the disciples' feet (13:14–15).

Vocation. The children of God are also called to a task. They are to continue the mission of Jesus, so that the world may know that he was sent by the Father. Integral to that mission are the roles of fishing and shepherding. In symbolic imagery the final chapter of the Gospel paints a picture of the disciples of Jesus fishing. By following his command (and fishing in light rather than darkness), they enclose a great catch of fish, one hundred fifty-three in all (a number that some think represented every known species). Still, the net is not torn (21:11). The unity of the community of believers is maintained, and the apostle Peter drags the net full of fish to the risen Lord, who has prepared a meal of fish and bread. Peter is then commissioned as a "good shepherd," who will feed the sheep and eventually lay down his life for them (21:15–19, *cf.* 10:11). The Beloved Disciple, likewise, has an authorized role, following Jesus and bearing witness to the truth (21:24).

Bibliography

Commentaries

Barrett, C. K. *The Gospel According to St. John.* 2d ed. Philadelphia, 1978.

Brown, Raymond E. *The Gospel According to John.* Anchor Bible, vols. 29 and 29a. Garden City, N.Y., 1966–1970.

————. *The Epistles of John.* Anchor Bible, vol. 30. Garden City, N.Y., 1982.

Bultmann, Rudolf. *The Gospel of John.* Translated by G. R. Beasley-Murray and edited by R. W. N. Hoare and J. K. Riches. Oxford, 1971.

Culpepper, R. Alan. *1 John, 2 John, 3 John.* Atlanta, 1985.

Ellis, Peter F. *The Genius of John: A Composition-Critical Commentary on the Fourth Gospel.* Collegeville, Minn., 1984.

The Life Setting of the Gospel of John

Brown, Raymond E. *The Community of the Beloved Disciple.* New York, 1979.

Charlesworth, James H., ed. *John and Qumran.* London, 1972.

Cullmann, Oscar. *The Johannine Circle.* Translated by John Bowden. London, 1976.

Culpepper, R. Alan. *The Johannine School.* Society of Biblical Literature Dissertation Series, 26. Missoula, 1975.

Fortna, Robert T. *The Gospel of Signs: A Reconstruction of the Narrative Source Underlying the Fourth Gospel.* Society for New Testament Studies Monograph Series, 11. London, 1970.

Koester, Helmut. *Introduction to the New Testament.* Vol. 2, *History and Literature of Early Christianity.* New York, 1982.

Martyn, J. Louis. *The Gospel of John in Christian History.* New York, 1978.

————. *History and Theology in the Fourth Gospel.* 2d ed., rev. and enl. Nashville, Tenn., 1979.

Meeks, Wayne A. "The Man from Heaven in Johannine Sectarianism." *Journal of Biblical Literature* 91 (1972). 44–72.

Painter, John. "The Farewell Discourses and the History of Johannine Christianity." *New Testament Studies* 27 (1981): 525–543.

Smith, Dwight Moody. *The Composition and Order of the Fourth Gospel: Bultmann's Literary Theory.* Yale Publications in Religion, 10. New Haven, 1965.

Wengst, Klaus. *Bedrängte Gemeinde und verherrlichter Christus: Der historische Ort des Johannesevangeliums als Schlüssel zu seiner Interpretation.* Biblische-Theologische Studien, 5. Neukirchen-Vluyn, 1981.

The Narrative Style of the Gospel of John

Boismard, Marie Émile. *St. John's Prologue.* Translated by Carisbrooke Dominicans. London, 1957.

Culpepper, R. Alan. "The Pivot of John's Prologue." *New Testament Studies* 27 (1980): 1–31.

———. *Anatomy of the Fourth Gospel: A Study in Literary Design.* Philadelphia, 1983.

Duke, Paul D. *Irony in the Fourth Gospel.* Atlanta, 1985.

Giblin, Charles H. "Two Complementary Literary Structures in John 1:1–18." *Journal of Biblical Literature* 104 (1985): 87–103.

O'Day, Gail R. *Revelation in the Fourth Gospel: Narrative Mode and Theological Claim.* Philadelphia, 1986.

Staley, Jeffrey. *The Print's First Kiss: A Rhetorical Investigation of the Implied Reader in the Fourth Gospel.* Society of Biblical Literature Dissertation Series. Missoula, 1988.

Talbert, Charles H. "Artistry and Theology: An Analysis of the Architecture of Jn 1, 19–5, 47." *Catholic Biblical Quarterly* 32 (1970): 341–366.

Implicit Commentary

Booth, Wayne. *A Rhetoric of Irony.* Chicago, 1974.

Hedrick, Charles W. "Authorial Presence and Narrator in John: *Hermeneia* and *Paradosis.*" Unpublished seminar paper submitted to the Johannine Seminar of the Society of Biblical Literature, 1985.

Muecke, D. C. *The Compass of Irony.* New York, 1969.

———. *Irony.* New York, 13 (1970).

O'Rourke, John J. "Asides in the Gospel of John." *Novum Testamentum* 21 (1979): 210–219.

Tenney, Merrill C. "The Footnotes of John's Gospel." *Bibliotheca Sacra* 117 (1960): 350–364.

Characterization

Ashton, John. "The Identity and Function of the *Ioudaioi* in the Fourth Gospel." *Novum Testamentum* 27 (1985): 40–75.

Bratcher, Robert G. "'The Jews' in the Gospel of John." *Bible Translator* 26 (1975): 401–409.

Fuller, Reginald. "The 'Jews' in the Fourth Gospel." *Dialog* 16 (1977): 31–37.

Grässer, Erich. "Die antijüdische Polemik im Johannesevangelium." *New Testament Studies* 11 (1964–1965): 74–90.

Lowe, Malcolm. "Who Were the *Ioudaioi?*" *Novum Testamentum* 18 (1976): 101–130.

Wahlde, Urban C. von. "The Johannine 'Jews': A Critical Survey." *New Testament Studies* 28 (1982): 33–60.

Basic Themes

Cassem, N. H. "A Grammatical and Contextual Inventory of the Use of *kosmos* in the Johannine Corpus, with Some Implications for a Johannine Cosmic Theology." *New Testament Studies* 19 (1972): 81–91.

Painter, John. *Reading John's Gospel Today.* 3d ed. Atlanta, 1986. First published in 1975 as *John: Witness and Theologian.*

R. ALAN CULPEPPER

Romans

INTRODUCTION:
HISTORY OF INTERPRETATION

Paul's Letter to the Romans has exercised an enormous influence on the history of Christianity, especially in the West. Although similar claims could be made for other books of the New Testament, such as the Gospels according to Matthew and John, Romans has made an even more significant contribution to the history of the development of Christian doctrine. One only has to recall some of the milestones of that history to discover the truth of this assertion. The literary influence of Romans on other letters in the New Testament attributed to Paul (such as Colossians, Ephesians, and the Pastoral Epistles) is remarkable. Then there is the position of Romans, Paul's longest and most important letter, either at the beginning (P⁴⁶) or at the end (Muratorian Canon) of the letter collection in the New Testament canon. In the early fifth century C.E., Augustine's conflict with Pelagius revolved around issues like the all-sufficient nature of grace, divine determinism, and human free will: issues involving Paul's interpretation in Romans of justification by grace alone. This letter again played a crucial role in the sixteenth-century Protestant Reformation and in John Wesley's break with Anglicanism in the eighteenth century. Martin Luther's reflection on Romans 1:17 testifies to its significance for his thought:

I greatly longed to understand Paul's Epistle to the Romans and nothing stood in the way but that one expression, "the justice of God," because I took it to mean that justice whereby God is just and deals justly in punishing the unjust. . . . Night and day I pondered until I saw the connection between the justice of God and the statement that "the just shall live by his faith." Then I grasped that the justice of God is that righteousness by which through grace and sheer mercy God justifies us through faith. Thereupon I felt myself to be reborn and to have gone through open doors to paradise. (Luther 1928; translation from Bainton 1950, 65)

Both Luther and John Calvin wrote commentaries on Romans. And while Luther concentrated on the contrast in Romans between Christ and the Law, and between faith and works, Calvin—although not abandoning this aspect—focused on the mystery of God's election and on the abiding validity of the Law as the structure of love, as inspired by Romans, chapters 9–11 and 12–15.

In the twentieth century, Karl Barth's commentary on Romans (1919) fell like a bombshell on the religious soil of Europe. The liberal consensus of nineteenth-century theology proved unable to meet the cultural crisis provoked by World War I. In this situation Barth pleaded for a new understanding of the message of Romans, which according to him depended on recognizing in the letter "the infinite qualitative distinction between God and humanity." Although

Barth's interpretation of Romans was subsequently criticized on historical-exegetical grounds, it generated new interest in Romans and produced a series of important new commentaries (see bibliography).

HISTORICAL CONTEXT

Christianity in Rome

The origin and circumstances of the Roman church prior to Paul's letter are not entirely clear. Our knowledge is limited to the following facts:

1. The church in Rome does not owe its foundation to a particular apostle. Although later tradition named Peter as the founder of the Roman church—a tradition probably arising from the martyrdom of both Peter and Paul in Rome (*ca.* 65)—Romans contains no reference to Peter, and it seems highly unlikely that he was present in Rome prior to the issuance of Paul's letter.

2. The Roman church owes its existence to the missionary activity of Jewish Christians who migrated there from the East.

3. The existence of numerous synagogues in Rome at the time of Paul's letter indicates the strength of the Jewish population in the city. It is not unlikely that the church drew a large number of its members from proselytes and God-fearers (gentiles loosely connected with the synagogue).

4. According to the Roman historian Suetonius (first–second century), Emperor Claudius (r. 41–54) expelled the Jews from Rome because of constant tumults "impulsore Chresto" (under the instigation of Chrestus), which is probably a reference to rioting in Rome over "Christus" (i.e., Christ). The Book of Acts supports Suetonius' report: it refers to two Jewish Christians, Aquila and his wife, Priscilla, who were expelled from Rome, "because Claudius had commanded all the Jews to leave Rome" (Acts 18:2). During the reign of Nero (54–68) Jews (and Jewish Christians) were permitted to return to Rome. Since Romans 16 is an integral part of Paul's letter to Rome (and not, as some commentators argue, an appendix originally sent to Ephesus), the presence in Rome of Prisca (i.e., Priscilla) and Aquila, "my fellow workers in Christ Jesus" (Rom 16:3), attests to the return of Jewish Christians.

5. The conflict in the Roman church between "the weak" and "the strong" as reported in Romans 14:1–15:13 is directly related to the imperial decrees of expulsion and return. Gentile Christians ("the strong"), who formed the majority in the church after the expulsion of the Jewish Christians ("the weak"), experienced tension and conflict with Jewish Christians upon the latter's return, especially with respect to the issue of the continuing validity of Jewish dietary laws.

6. Paul addresses the Roman Christians as "God's beloved in Rome" (1:7) but does not use his usual address: "to the church of God in . . ." (e.g., 1 Cor 1:2; 2 Cor 1:1; Gal 1:2 [plural, "churches"], 1 Thess 1:1). Moreover, he never uses the word "church" in this letter (except in chapter 16). This may indicate that the Roman church was not one body, but an aggregate of several house-churches.

The Purpose of the Letter

Paul wrote his letter to Rome around 60 during a three-month stay in Corinth at the conclusion of his so-called third missionary journey (Acts 20:1–3). His past career, present situation, and future plans, taken together, help to clarify the purpose of his letter to Rome.

When Paul writes Romans, he finds himself in a new situation. His missionary work in the East has been accomplished (15:19, 23–24). He now wants to use Rome both as a way station and as headquarters for a new mission in the West and in Spain (15:23–29). He is, therefore, eager to enlist the support of the Roman church for this purpose.

Before coming to Rome, however, Paul must visit Jerusalem with the collection gathered from the gentile churches (15:25–28a). In the letter he appeals for active intercession and support for his "collection-visit" to Jerusalem on the part of the most famous Christian community of the West ("your faith is proclaimed in all the world," 1:8). The collection-visit is the fulfillment of Paul's pledge of support to leaders of the Jerusalem church at the time of the Apostolic Council (Gal 2:10). Its meaning, however, transcends the pledge of economic support for the "poor among the saints at Jerusalem" (Rom 15:26) because it expresses symbolically the unity of the church of "Jews" and "gentiles" in the purpose of God as the fulfillment of Paul's apostolic mandate.

Paul's plea to the Roman church (15:30) shows his apprehension about the reception awaiting him from the pillars of the Jerusalem church (15:31) when he delivers the collection. It also reveals something about the purpose of his letter to the Romans: the letter outlines Paul's proclamation of the gospel, the gospel the Roman church must affirm in its support of Paul when he goes to Jerusalem (15:30–32). Thus, in some sense, Romans is a "hidden letter to Jerusalem" (Jervell 1971), in which Paul rehearses important elements of his impending dialogue with the leaders of the Jerusalem church.

Whereas these motives underlying the letter reveal Paul's momentary concerns (the collection-visit) and future plans (the mission to Spain), other motives stemming from his past career come into play as well in this letter. Just prior to the composition of Romans, Paul had not only written Galatians, but had probably lost his case with the Galatian churches. Therefore his anxiety about his collection-visit to Jerusalem is well founded. His radical response to the heretical desire of the Galatians to combine the gospel and the Law, and his insistence on the "either-or" of gospel or Law, may well have worsened his relations with the Jewish Christians at Jerusalem.

In Galatians, Paul had created the impression that the place of the Jews in salvation history was a purely negative one and that they had in fact outlived their purpose with the coming of Christ. In Romans, therefore, Paul seeks to correct the negative effects of his Galatian letter. He now discusses the "Jewish question" within the larger context of God's history of salvation (Rom 9–11). Indeed, a satisfactory treatment of the "Jewish question" is necessary not only to defuse the hostile reaction by the Jerusalem church to the Galatian letter and possibly in Rome and elsewhere, but also to resolve the conflict in Rome between Jewish Christians and gentile Christians.

Thus the attempt to solve the specific conflict between "the weak" and "the strong" in Rome is one more motive behind the letter. Paul was not as ignorant about Rome as many commentators suggest. Chapter 16 shows that Paul had many friends and associates in Rome who probably informed him about the situation there (for instance, Prisca and Aquila).

The issue is a serious one for Paul: the discord between Jewish Christians and gentile Christians threatens not only the success of his apostolic mandate to establish one church of Jews and gentiles but also his forthcoming mission to Spain. For how could Rome serve as his headquarters for that mission when its disunity might jeopardize the economic support for his mission and, what struck at the very heart of Paul's aims, his desire to see Jews and Greeks united in one church of God?

Thus, at least four motives undergird Paul's letter. They are, however, all controlled by one central concern: the challenge to the Roman Christians to adopt a stance vis-à-vis the gospel as preached by Paul. If he can win the Christians of Rome, they will support him in his mission to Spain as well as in his impending collection-visit to Jerusalem. They will also resolve the conflict between "the weak" and "the strong" in their midst and take his side in the conflict engendered by his Letter to the Galatians, believing, as he does, that there can be no compromise between the gospel and Jewish law.

OUTLINE OF THE LETTER

I. Introduction (1:1–7)

II. Thanksgiving and theme (1:8–17)

III. The revelation of the righteousness of God to faith alone: "the one who is righteous through faith" (1:18–4:25)
   A. Indictment of gentiles and Jews (1:18–3:20)
      1. Humanity under God's wrath (1:18–32)
      2. The Jews under God's wrath (2:1–3:8)
      3. The hopelessness of the human condition (3:9–20)
   B. The gift of God's righteousness to faith (3:21–4:25)
      1. The revelation of the righteousness of God (3:21–31)
      2. The argument from Scripture (4:1–25)

IV. The new life in Christ: the life of the one who is righteous through faith (5:1–8:39)
   A. Life in the new age (5:1–6:23)
      1. A new boasting (5:1–11)
      2. A new age (5:12–21)

DISCUSSION OF THE LETTER

Introduction (1:1–7)

Paul introduces himself to the members of the church in Rome in a manner that characterizes the letter as a whole. The tone of the letter is both authoritative and conciliatory. He emphasizes in verses 1–7 not only his apostolic authority but also the ecumenical bond that is the common heritage of all Christians. Thus, he begins with a reference to his apostolic authority. "Paul, a servant of Jesus Christ, a called apostle, set apart for the gospel of God . . . through whom [Jesus Christ] I received the grace of apostleship to bring about the obedience of faith among all the nations for his name's sake" (1:1, 4, 5; Au. trans.).

This authoritative tone is balanced by the citation of a traditional Christian confession that celebrates Christ as the Son of David on earth and as the Son of God in his resurrection life (1:3–4), which serves to unite Paul and the Roman church in a common cause. This mixture of authority and conciliation pervades the letter at crucial points (for instance, in 1:11, 12 and 15:14–16), demonstrating his desire to balance his assertion of apostolic authority with an acknowledgment of the church's own authority.

Thanksgiving and Theme (1:8–17)

The thanksgiving clause, which follows the salutation (1:7)—a common feature in Hellenistic-Roman letters—expresses Paul's fervent longing to visit the Roman church, not only because of its reputation among Christians everywhere (1:8) but also because of his apostolic call to missionize the gentile world, to which Rome belongs (1:11–15). His thought in verses 8–17 moves from the particular to the universal; that is, from his specific apostolic obligation to Rome to his universal apostolic commission ("I am under obligation both to Greeks and to barbarians, both to the wise and to the uneducated" [1:14; Au. trans.]). He then couples his apostolic commission with a definition of the gospel, as he preaches it: "For I am not ashamed of the gospel: it is the power of God for salvation to every one who has faith, to the Jew first and also to the Greek. For in it the righteousness of God is revealed through faith for faith; as it is written, 'He who through faith is righteous shall live'" (1:16–17; RSV).

The quotation from Scripture in verse 17b (Hab 2:4) serves to support his definition of the gospel as the righteousness of God for faith (1:16–17), and it provides the basic outline and theme for the first two main parts of the letter: (a) 1:18–4:25, "He who through faith is righteous"; and (b) 5:1–8:39, "He who through faith is righteous shall live." Verse 16b is an inherent part of Paul's definition of the gospel ("to the Jew first and also to the Greek"), and it foreshadows the theme of the third main part of the letter: Israel's destiny in God's plan of salvation (9:1–11:36).

Although most commentators mark 1:16–17 as a separate division that highlights the theme of the letter (e.g., Cranfield 1979, 87; *cf.* also the Greek text of Nestle and Aland 1981, 410), it is better to include these thematic verses within the thanksgiving clause (1:8–17), for both literary and theological reasons. Chapter 1:8–17 forms, on literary grounds, an indivisible thanksgiving clause. The close connection between the particularity of Paul's address to Rome (1:8–13) and the universality of his conception of the gospel (1:14–17) underscores the particularity of Paul's letter to the Romans. The interrelation of the universal and the particular in Romans deserves attention because the letter has all too often been treated as a "compendium doctrinae christianae," as the Protestant reformer Philip Melanchthon considered it; that is, as a timeless dogmatic treatise rather than as a letter addressed to a particular situation.

The Revelation of the Righteousness of God to Faith Alone (1:18–4:25)

Indictment of gentiles and Jews (1:18–3:20). Section 1:18–3:20 is the antithesis of the theme of the gospel (1:16–17) and serves as the negative foil necessary for the unfolding of the gospel's positive theme in 3:21–31. The unit 1:18–32 announces in prophetic language the wrath of God over human unrighteousness and idolatry and must be subdivided into two paragraphs (1:18–21, 22–32).

The first paragraph (1:18–21) demonstrates the justice of God's wrath and climaxes with the indictment that "people are without excuse" (1:20). Although God has made himself known to all people (1:19–20), they have rejected and perverted his revelation (1:20b–21). In other words, it is not the lack of *knowledge* that characterizes the human condition before God, but rather the lack of *acknowledgment*: the failure to acknowledge the majesty of God.

The second paragraph (1:22–32) reveals God's response to human idolatry. Paul argues that humanity's perverted ethical practices are the result of a prior cause: the perversion of the human heart and its consequent rebellion against God's sovereignty. Idolatry is the source of the disorientation of the human condition. It is the human desire to confuse the finite and the infinite and to endow the finite with infinite status (Tillich 1967, 13).

The paragraph is dominated by a threefold retribution clause (compare the threefold repetition of the verb "to give up" in 1:24, 26, and 28). In each case a human exchange of righteousness for sinfulness is met with a divine exchange of benevolence for neglect. Because human beings "exchange" God's glory for transient and finite glory (1:23), "exchange" God's truth for a lie (1:25), exchange the knowledge of God for their own idolatrous musings and actions (1:28), God responds each time with an exchange of his own, so that human bodies change from honor to dishonor (1:24); normal sexuality changes into homosexuality (1:26–27); and morality changes into immoral behavior (1:28–31). The frightening aspect of God's retribution is its permissive quality: God's wrath permits people to be what they desire to be, in accordance with their idolatrous inclinations.

The Jews under God's wrath (2:1–3:8). After the indictment of gentile idolatry (1:18–32), Paul directs his attention more specifically to the Jews. The two sections together (1:18–32, 2:1–3:8) constitute an indictment of all the people of Paul's world: gentiles and Jews. Although the second section (2:1–3:8) starts with an address to people in general (the "O man" of 2:1, 3), it is Paul's strategy to indict the Jews at first implicitly (2:1–16) in order to do so explicitly in the concluding section (2:17–29). After this indictment, he allows the Jews to voice their objections to his radical anti-Jewish argument, but only to refute them with angry impatience (3:1–8).

Whereas the indictment of the gentiles in 1:18–32 was a condemnation of the enslaving power of sin, the indictment of the Jews in chapter 2 occurs on different grounds. Paul accuses the Jews of hypocrisy; that is, a discrepancy between their words and their deeds (2:1–6, 12–27). In order to refute Jewish claims to special privilege, based on their election by God, Paul posits God's impartiality of judgment regarding the quality of a person's moral deeds (vv. 6–11, 12–16, 25–27).

The final paragraph (2:28–29) refers to theprophetic demand in the Old Testament for the circumcision of the heart ("Circumcise yourselves to the Lord, remove the foreskin of your hearts, O men of Judah and inhabitants of Jerusalem" [Jer 4:4, RSV; cf. Jer 9:25, Deut 30:6]) and foreshadows Paul's argument in chapter 5 on what constitutes true boasting as over and against what he regards as the false boasting of the Jews (2:17, 23; cf. 5:2–11).

A remarkable change in literary style occurs when we move from 1:18–32 to 2:1–3:8. After the discursive argument in 1:18–32, Paul uses in 2:1–3:8 a "diatribe" (an ancient rhetorical device introduced in order to enhance the liveliness of dialogue). Direct address and the second-person singular (2:1–6, 17–27) abound in this section, especially in 3:1–8, where Paul dismantles the Jewish claim to be a "special" people before God (3:1–2). Anticipating an extensive discussion of the matter in 6:1–23, Paul rejects out of hand as blasphemous the charge that his gospel is immoral: "And why not do evil that good may come?—as some people slanderously charge us with saying. Their condemnation is just" (3:8; RSV).

The hopelessness of the human condition (3:9–20). The climax of Paul's indictment of gentiles and

Jews is found in 3:9: "I have already charged that all men, both Jews and Greeks, are under the power of sin." He cites a chain of passages from Scripture in support of this statement (3:10b–18). The repeated occurrence of the phrase "there is not" (3:10, 11, 12, 18) confirms his view of the hopelessness of the human situation. A summary (3:19–20) concludes the section. The last clause (3:20), stated in negative terms prepares the way for the positive unfolding of the righteousness of God in the following section (3:21–31). Moreover, Paul's negative verdict in the clause "no human being will be justified in [God's] sight by works of the Law" (3:20a; RSV) cryptically anticipates an extensive discussion of the problem of the Law in chapter 7. (Similar anticipations, with respect to boasting and to the relation of sin and grace, occur in 2:28–29 [cf. 5:2–11] and in 3:6, 8 [cf. 6:1–24].)

The gift of God's righteousness to faith (3:21–4:25). In 3:21–31 Paul expounds the thesis in the gospel, already adumbrated in 1:17 against the foil of the discussion of 1:18–3:20. The foundation for the scriptural basis of the thesis is laid in 4:1–25. The phrase "But now" in the opening line (3:21) has a double significance: it not only denotes a new step in the argument but also points to the new age of righteousness that will succeed the old age of unrighteousness and condemnation. Humanity was in a "no exit" situation before God (i.e., the paraphrase of 3:9 in 3:23), but God himself then intervened through the redemptive death of Christ to grant righteousness to those who have faith in Jesus Christ. They are now "justified" before God ("set right with God"; 3:24, 26) and enjoy a new relation with him. The gift of righteousness has two aspects: it means not only the forgiveness of the sins of the past (3:25), but also a new and enduring relation with God (3:26). Paul explicates the gift of righteousness in brief, overloaded sentences (i.e., overuse of prepositional phrases in 3:22–26). Moreover, he employs a traditional Christian confession (3:24, 25), and reinterprets it (hence the twofold use of the noun "demonstration" in parallel formulations in 3:25, 26) so that it conforms to his own formulation of the gospel: "It was to demonstrate at the present time that he [God] himself is righteous and that he justifies him who has faith in Jesus" (3:26).

In the next paragraph (3:27–31) Paul discusses God's gift of righteousness to faith alone (3:21–26) and he does so in both a polemical and a positive way. Human boasting is excluded (3:27); the only authentic law is the law of faith (3:27b–28); and the true interpretation of the Shema (the Jewish confession of the oneness of God) confesses the justification by faith of Jews and gentiles alike (3:29–30).

The argument from Scripture (4:1–25). Paul's claim that the Law and the prophets are witness to the righteousness of God (3:21)—a claim he repeats in 3:31 ("We uphold the law")—requires an explanation. The Abraham story, especially the key text of Genesis 15:6, provides it: "Abraham believed God, and it was reckoned to him as righteousness" (Rom 4:3; RSV). Chapter 4 contains two argumentative units (4:1–12 and 13–22), and concludes the argument with a specific Christian application (4:23–25).

The first unit (4:1–12) revolves around a key term in the passage, "to reckon" (v. 3), derived from the citation of Genesis 15:6 (the term occurs eleven times in chapter 4 and eight times in 4:1–12 alone). The second unit (4:13–22) drops this term (except for the conclusion in v. 22); instead, its key term is the noun "the promise" (the term occurs five times in this unit). Paul argues in 4:1–12 that the "reckoning" by God to Abraham in Genesis 15:6 is not a reward for merit (4:4), but rather God's gift, bestowed by faith alone. In the course of the argument, Paul calls Abraham an "ungodly sinner" (4:5)—contrary to the Genesis story—in order to contrast Abraham's status before and after God's reckoning of righteousness.

Paul supports his reading of Genesis 15:6 with the help of a rabbinic-exegetical principle (the *geze-rah shavah*), according to which one passage in Scripture explains another passage. In this case, Psalm 32 must undergird Genesis 15:6 ("Blessed is the man against whom the Lord will not reckon his sin," Rom 4:8; RSV). Thus, "reckoning" in Genesis 15:6, according to Paul, actually means the forgiveness of sins.

Moreover, Paul argues against the Jewish tradition that Abraham was God's favorite and the object of God's special election, as symbolized by his circumcision. The "reckoning" of Genesis 15:6 took place *before* Abraham's circumcision, and therefore Abraham received God's righteousness while he was still a "gentile," which leads Paul to conclude that God's reckoning of righteousness by faith alone applies to Jews and gentiles alike (4:8–12).

In the second unit (4:13–22), Paul's interpretation of Genesis 15:6 (compare its recurrence in the conclusion of 4:22) centers on the key word "the promise." He argues that the promise and the Law are antithetical (4:13–16), not only because the Law provokes transgression and God's wrath (4:15) but especially because promise and faith are correlates and have nothing to do with the Law (4:13–14, 16). He then describes the nature of Abraham's faith in light of the promise of God. This description of the human disposition of faith is unique, found nowhere else in Paul's letters. Abraham's faith is characterized by unwavering trust in God's promise—a faith that was all the more remarkable since Abraham's and Sarah's advanced age seemed to render the promise of children ostensibly unfullfillable.

In the conclusion to the chapter (4:23–25), Paul applies God's justification of Abraham and his faith to the faithful in Christ who—like Abraham—believe with unwavering trust in Jesus' death and resurrection for their sake.

The New Life in Christ (5:1–8:39)

The next part of the letter, commencing with 5:1 and ending at 8:39, is characterized by several new elements of style and vocabulary. The phrase "Therefore, since we are justified by faith" (5:1) marks the completion of the preceding argument (1:18–4:25). From here on, Paul draws the consequences, and a shift in style becomes noticeable. The predominant descriptive third-person style of the previous part (1:8–4:25) is replaced by a confessional style through the use of the first-person plural. A whole new vocabulary is introduced in 5:1–11: "the Lord Jesus Christ" (5:1, 11); "glory" (5:2); "hope" (5:2–5); "love" (5:5); "the Spirit" (5:5); "death/to die" (5:6–8, 10); "peace" (5:1); "reconciliation" (5:10, 11); "to save" (5:9, 10); and "life" (5:10). This vocabulary is also evident in chapters 6–8, especially in the frequent use of the terms "the flesh" and "the Spirit" (see chap. 8); the participatory language of "being crucified with," "being raised with" (6:1–12); and so on. In fact, the language of Christ's "death and resurrection" does not figure earlier in the letter. Each

separate section of 5:1–8:39 concludes (or begins [5:1]) with the phrase "through/in our Lord Jesus Christ" (5:1, 11, 21; 6:23; 7:25; 8:39).

Notwithstanding the presence of clearly distinct units in this part of the letter (5:1–8:39), a logical sequence of thought and rational progression—such as exist in the first main part (1:18–4:25)—is difficult to trace, and an architectonic scheme characteristic of inductive or deductive reasoning seems absent. N. A. Dahl (1951) has clarified the structure of the passage. In his view the themes in section 5:1–11, "love of God" (5:5), "hope" (5:2–5), "peace," "reconciliation" (5:1, 10, 11) and "the Spirit" (5:5), find their recapitulation and explication in chapter 8, especially in 8:18–39. Dahl suggests that the intervening chapters (i.e., 6:1–23 and 7:1–25) are Paul's rebuttals to objections raised by his opponents, especially objections to his ostensibly outrageous statements in 5:20, 21, where he claims not only that it is the function of the Law to increase sin (5:20a) but also that "where sin increased, grace abounded all the more" (5:20b). Thus he advocates the apparently immoral conclusion that grace increases in proportion to our sinning.

Moreover, Dahl's solution to the problem of the order of the main part of 5:1–8:39 helps us to understand how and for what reason Paul wrote his letters. It thwarts the perennial attempts of scholars to impose an architectonic structure on the letters. In other words, rather than conforming to our Western way of logical induction/deduction or of composing a philosophical treatise, Paul's letters should be seen as real letters, as dialogues addressing specific situations. Thus the Pauline letter is not a systematic treatise, but rather the written deposit of the writer's oral missionary preaching—filled with elements of dialogue and audience responses.

Life in the new age (5:1–6:23). Section 5:1–11 celebrates in confessional manner a new boasting, the access Christians enjoy to God's grace in Christ (5:1–2a). Christian life, a new relation to God, opens new horizons (5:2b). This unit is imbued with hope for the coming glory of God and the end to the sufferings of the present age (5:2b–5a). The passage constitutes a remarkable literary composition; both its beginning and end (5:1–5, 9–11) celebrate the new life in Christ: "peace" (5:1), "reconciliation" (5:10,

11), and hope for the future (compare the future-passive tenses of 5:9 and 10). Moreover, the beginning and end of the passage have their literary and theological center in the very foundation of this new life and hope: Christ's atoning death (5:6–8).

And finally, the new life of Christians expresses itself in a new form of worship: over and against the "false boasting of the Jews" (2:17, 23; 3:27), Christians engage in authentic boasting (5:2, 3, 11) and thus, according to Paul, actualize what it is to be a "true Jew, whose praise is not from men but from God" (2:29).

In 5:12–21 Paul proclaims a new age. The location and meaning of this passage within the flow of the argument of Romans have caused much debate among scholars. Luther calls it in one place a "joyful outburst and excursion," and elsewhere he refers to it as one of the most superb texts in Scripture. The meaning of "therefore" in 5:12 is elusive and difficult to determine. Does it refer forward, implying "mark what follows" (Best 1967, 59; Robinson 1979, 60), or does it refer backward, suggesting "wherefore" (Cranfield 1975, 271), "therefore" (Wilckens 1978, 306), or "thus [it is true]" (Käsemann 1980, 139)? Interpreters have wondered why there is an anacoluthon (unfinished main clause) in 5:12, so that the main clause is not completed until 5:18. Why does Paul revert to a discursive style (third-person plural) between sections that exhibit a personal confessional style (5:1–11, 6:1–23; cf. also 4:24–25; 8:1–2, 9–17, 23–39)?

Several explanations suggest themselves. The "therefore" of 5:12 does not refer to the immediately preceding clause (5:11), or to the preceding passage as a whole (5:1–11), but rather to Paul's verdict in 3:23, where he breaks off the discussion of the universal power of sin ("all have sinned and fall short of the glory of God") in order to focus on a different issue: i.e., the gift of God's righteousness to the faithful (3:24–31). Having completed this train of thought, and having established the Christian hope of sharing the glory of God (5:2; cf. 2:23) Paul now resumes his earlier argument 3:23 in order to explicate it on a more comprehensive scale. He emphasizes the universal and cosmic consequences of God's action in Christ against the foil of the universal and cosmic power of sin in the world through a comparison between the archetypal figures of Adam and Christ, who each in their own way were responsible for the entrance of the universal powers of death (Adam) and eternal life (Christ) into the history of the world. The anacoluthon of 5:12 indicates Paul's desire to avoid a mythological-ahistorical comparison of Adam and Christ, and thus he places the comparison in a historical context. For instance, he stresses human responsibility for death's dominion in the world (5:12c) and points to the historical function of the Law (5:12–14, 20). Paul's comparison between Adam and Christ affirms the incomparable superiority of Christ over Adam (5:18), a superiority based on the gifts of the new age: grace, righteousness, and life (5:15–17). The passage concludes with a reiteration of the antithesis between Adam and Christ, and between death and life, showing how in Adam death has become the power that rules humankind, and in Christ new life for humankind has been made possible (5:18–19). However, whereas verses 18–19 round off the comparison between Adam and Christ with a simple equation ("thus . . . likewise" [5:18]; "just as . . . likewise" [5:19]), Paul establishes a causal relation not only between sin and grace but also between the Law and sin by inserting at this point the purpose clause "in order that," which asserts that sin is the presupposition of grace and that the Law stimulates sin rather than prevents it (5:20–21). The profoundly radical character of this assertion (blasphemous to Jewish ears) seems not only to demonize the Law but also to mock any moral conception of grace by suggesting that grace has no moral implications.

Paul's offensive assertions in 5:20–21 evoke a lively protest from an imagined interlocutor, to whom Paul responds in chapters 6 and 7 in a chiastic manner ("chiasmus" denotes a form of inverted ordering) and with phrases like "What shall we say then?" (6:1, 7:7; cf. 6:15).

In chapter 6, Paul elucidates further his statement in 5:20b that grace abounded as sin increased. In chapter 7, he explicates the statement made in 5:20a (chiasmus) on the relation between sin and the Law. First, Paul applies the issues of death and life (portrayed in 5:12–21 as the cosmic-universal determinants of history) directly to the human situation, climaxing with an existential description of life before and in Christ (6:1–7:6) through a depth analysis of the "I" (the "ego") in relation to the Law (7:7–25).

Paul opposes sin to Christ as two separate lordships. The Christian baptismal experience signifies, according to Paul, the "either-or" of life in Christ and life under the power of sin (6:2–5). Indeed "our old self was crucified with him [Christ] so that the sinful body might be destroyed, and we might no longer be enslaved to sin" (6:6; RSV). In light of this "either-or," the charge made by Paul's detractors that he establishes a causal relation between sin and grace (6:1; cf. 6:15) is false. This charge denies the existential character of Christian life (6:12–15; cf. 6:2a), which, because of the liberating lordship of Christ, has been freed from the lordship of sin (6:16–23; cf. the "freedom" language in 6:18–22). Paul concludes his argument with the climactic summary: "But now that you have been set free from sin and have become slaves of God, the return you get is sanctification and its end, eternal life" (6:22; RSV).

The old life under the Law (7:1–25). It seems strange that Paul in this part of the letter (5:1–8:39) with its theme of the new life in Christ (and which accordingly describes in 7:1–6 the Christian's freedom from the Law) should suddenly reintroduce the theme of the old life of sin under the Law (7:7–25). This switch is particularly offensive to interpreters who insist on a systematic ordering of the letter. For instance, Nygren (1967, 187 ff.) calls 5:1–8:39 "He who through faith is righteous shall live" and subdivides the part in this manner:

1. Free from wrath (5:1–11)
2. The two aeons: Adam and Christ (5:12–21)
3. Free from sin (6:1–23)
4. Free from the Law (7:1–25)
5. Free from death (8:1–39).

However, the clarity of this outline of freedoms is untenable, because the theme of 7:7–25 is not freedom from the Law, but rather enslavement under the Law.

Nygren is one of many interpreters who, in order to uphold the pervasive theme of "new life in Christ" in 5:1–8:39, interpret 7:7–25 erroneously in terms of a *Christian* struggle with the Law. However, the interpretation of 7:7–25 is determined by Paul's thematic preface in 7:5–6, which contrasts "the old age" of the Law and the flesh (7:5) with "the new age"

of Christ and the Spirit (7:6). Therefore it is erroneous to interpret 7:7–25 along the lines of Luther's expression *simul iustus et peccator* (the Christian as "both justified and a sinner"), as if Paul set up an unbearable tension in Christian life between freedom from sin and enslavement to sin. The truth of the matter is that Paul contrasts in temporal terms the bygone era of Law and sin with the present new era of life in Christ and the Spirit (7:5–6).

This contrast is evident in the composition of sections 7:1–6, 7:7–25, and 8:1–17. In 7:7–25, Paul expounds the thesis of 7:5 (concerning life under the Law and sin), whereas the thesis of 7:6 (concerning the new life of the Spirit) is explicated in 8:1–17 (by means of the word "now" in 7:6, which is taken up and developed at 8:1).

Paul's radical indictment of the Law (7:1–6, especially v. 5) necessitates a defense of the Law (7:7–25). The defense of the Law intends to show that the Law is not a demonic entity in itself, but is—as the Law of God—"holy, just, and good" (7:12). Thus the human situation of "wretchedness" (7:24) is not caused by the Law itself, but by the demonic and deceptive cunning of sin, which has managed to enlist the Law for its own destructive purposes (7:7–13).

Two stylistic elements mark the passage: (1) the introduction of the "I" (or "ego"; Gr., *egō*; 7:7–25); and (2) a shift from the past tense (7:7–13) to the present tense (7:14–25).

These stylistic features give rise to the following observations: (1) Paul employs the first-person singular (the "ego") and the present tense to convey the intimacy and liveliness of his analysis of Jewish life under the Law. (2) The argument of 7:7–11 (past tense) is largely based on a midrashic interpretation of the Genesis story of the Fall: it narrates the rise of sin, the deception of the serpent (sin), and his false promise of life. The argument refers as well to the giving of the Law at Sinai with its basic command: "You shall not covet" (7:7; see Exod 20:17, Deut 5:21). (3) After the apology of the Law (7:7–12) comes to a preliminary conclusion in 7:12, which establishes the sanctity of the Law, a transitional sentence (7:13) introduces the discussion of 7:14–25. In this section Paul analyzes the root of what he sees as the Jewish problem with the Law in a vivid existential style (present tense). After stating his thesis ("We know that the Law is spiritual; but I am carnal, sold under sin" 7:14), Paul argues that there is a complex triangular relation between the ego, sin, and the Law.

Rather than that the ego and the Law ally themselves in warding off the inroads of sin, sin forms a diabolical alliance with the Law against the ego and as a result the ego becomes enslaved to sin. Moreover, the ego's situation under the power of sin is made worse by the ego's inner plight: it is caught in a hopeless conflict between intention and action, between will and deed (7:15–16, 18b–19). Because of the fact that the ego is fully aware of its captivity to sin, it is torn between good and evil and also suffers from deep despair. And so the lament arises: "Wretched man that I am! Who will deliver me from this body of death?" (7:24; RSV). The lament is followed by a thanksgiving (7:25) that anticipates the description of Christian freedom from sin and the Law in chapter 8.

Life in the Spirit and in hope (8:1–39). Chapter 8 is a joyful celebration of Christian life in the Spirit and climaxes with a hymnic confession of the insuperable power of God's love (8:31–39). The theme of life in the Spirit (8:1–17) is all the more joyful because it occurs against the dark foil of people's past enslavement under sin and the Law, and because it depicts in sharply delineated contrasts life in the Spirit as against life in the flesh: "You are not in the flesh, you are in the Spirit" (8:9). The Spirit and the flesh are portrayed not only as personified powers that rule people but also as spatial domains that are starkly opposed to each other. ("Flesh" for Paul has the pejorative sense of "life in rebellion against God" or "life founded on one's own resources and strength.") Life in the Spirit (synonymous with life in Christ [8:10] and with owning the Spirit of Christ [8:9]) not only confers life, peace, and a new disposition (8:6); it also enables Christians to fulfill "the just requirement of the law" (8:4). Moreover—and here the text anticipates the following section (8:18–39)—life in the Spirit establishes Christian hope in the resurrection of the dead, and in victory over human mortality in this world (8:11, 13–14).

A transition within verse 8:17 posits the theme of life in the power of hope (8:18–39). The joyful celebration of Christian life in the Spirit that reaches a climax in 8:17ab ("If [we are] children, then [we are]

heirs, heirs of God and fellow heirs with Christ") is suddenly interrupted by an important proviso: "provided we suffer with him in order that we may also be glorified with him" (8:17c; RSV). The proviso opens up the windows of the church to the larger order of God's created world. The solidarity between the church and the world is based on the conviction that Christians cannot claim fullness of salvation apart from the salvation of the totality of God's creation, which is still "subjected to futility" (8:20). Therefore, Christian hope has a universal and cosmic scope. It demands redemptive suffering of Christians on behalf of the world (8:18–25) until the time comes when God will fully manifest his cosmic glory over his whole creation (8:18, 21, 30); i.e., when "the creation will be set free from its bondage to decay and obtain the freedom of the glory of the children of God" (8:21; Au. trans.). In the light of this expectation, the chapter climaxes with a celebration of Christian hope that is grounded in—and evoked by—the invincible nature of God's love in Christ (8:38–39).

Israel's Destiny in God's Plan of Salvation (9:1–11:36)

How do chapters 9–11 fit into the structure of Romans? This part of the letter is frequently considered to be an appendix or an afterthought. F. W. Beare is typical of many interpreters when he writes:

> We have left out of consideration three chapters (ix–xi) of this letter, chiefly because they do not form an integral part of the main argument. They are a kind of supplement, in which St. Paul struggles with the problem of the failure of his own nation. . . . We cannot feel that the apostle is at his best here, and we are inclined to ask if he has not got himself into inextricable (and needless) difficulties by attempting to salvage some remnant of racial privilege for the historical Israel—Israel "according to the flesh"—in spite of his own fundamental position that all men are in the same position before God." (Beare 1962, 103–104)

Even when interpreters propose more constructive approaches to this part of the letter, the tendency to universalize the whole letter as "dogmatics in outline," and a pervasive anti-Jewish element in much scholarship, combine to downgrade the importance of chapters 9–11. After all, what is the relevance of these reflections on historic first-century Israel for contemporary Christian dogmatics? Therefore, it has been common practice either to ascribe this part of the letter to Paul's ethnic bias or to transpose it into timeless categories (see, for instance, Karl Barth's equation of "Israel" with "the church, the world of religion" [Barth 1933, 327]). Notwithstanding such negative evaluations, chapters 9–11 occupy a crucial place within the structure of the letter. Indeed the understanding of the structure of the letter hinges on the correct interpretation of its twofold basic opening theme (1:16–17). Paul proclaims not only the universality of the gospel "to everyone who has faith" (1:16a), but also the preeminent role of the Jews in salvation history: "to the Jew first and also to the Greek" (1:16b).

What appears on the surface to be a contradiction between particularity and universality in the gospel itself is, on a deeper level (according to Paul), not a contradiction at all, but rather belongs to the very essence of the gospel. Thus, after the first two main parts of the letter (1:18–4:25, 5:1–8:39) have unfolded the universality of the gospel to Jew and Greek alike and their equal status in the church, the third main part (chapters 9–11) explicates the issue of the particularity of the Jew in the gospel: i.e., the priority of Israel. One must pay attention to two features in this part of the letter:

1. Although at least three subdivisions in these chapters can be discerned (9:1–29, 9:30–10:21, 11:1–36), this part of the letter forms a continuous whole and must be read as such. Paul's method of argumentation differs here considerably from the one he employs in 1:18–8:39. The argument of 9:1–11:36 is cumulative rather than synthetic (based on specific premises and warrants). Contrary to Paul's earlier arguments (e.g., 5:1–11, 12–21; 6:1–23; 7:1–6, 7–25; 8:1–17, 18–30, 31–39), his persuasive force here does not depend on the warrants and closures of each subunit. Rather, chapters 9–11 have, as it were, a narrative quality: they invite us to hear "the whole story" until the end; i.e., until at last Paul explicates God's revelation to him of "the mystery" of Israel's final salvation (11:25–36). In other words, more than anywhere else in his letters, Paul toys here with a variety of ideas and reflections.

2. Indeed, in this part of Romans, Paul struggles with one of the most vexing problems of his missionary career: the refusal of God's own people, Israel, to heed the gospel. That problem not only affects Paul, the former Pharisaic Jew, personally (9:1–5) but also impinges on the fundamental truth of the gospel. For how can gentiles, who are outsiders to the special covenant of God with Israel, rely on God's love for *them*, if in fact God has abandoned his own people? The basic theme of 9:1–29 is God's sovereign freedom. After expressing his profound grief over Israel's rejection of the gospel (9:1–5), Paul begins his discussion of Israel's relation to the gospel with these words: "It is not as though the word of God had failed" (9:6). The word of God (i.e., God's promise to Israel as recorded at 9:9), is valid because "the true Israel" refers, according to Scripture, not to the historic Israel, but rather to "the children of the promise" (9:8), who are chosen in agreement with "God's purpose of election" (9:11; cf. 11:5). In fact, God in his sovereign freedom determines not only the objects of his mercy (9:14–16), but also the objects of his wrath (9:17–21). Paul concludes the section with a celebration of God's call of a people (9:1–29), both Jews and gentiles (9:22–26), to which he adds a severe indictment against Israel along with the announcement that "only a remnant of them [the sons of Israel] will be saved" (9:27–29).

Israel's failure and fall are discussed in 9:30–10:21. The focus shifts from God's sovereign freedom to Israel's culpability and fall. Although Paul acknowledges Israel's religious zeal, he calls it "falsely oriented" (10:2): Israel desires to achieve by works of the Law what can only be obtained by faith, and it fails to understand that the "Christ-event" (i.e., the gift of God's righteousness) has brought about the "end of the law" (10:4; cf. 9:30–33).

Paul supports his argument with an appeal to Scripture (10:5–8; cf. Deut 30:12–14), which, since it refers, according to Paul, to the gospel of faith, invalidates "the righteousness based on the law" (10:5; cf. Lev 18:5). The chapter ends on a twofold note: the celebration of the equality of Jew and Greek in the gospel (10:12–15) coupled with an indictment of Israel for its refusal to heed the gospel (10:16–21; compare the similar emphasis in 9:27–29).

Paul foresees Israel's ultimate restoration (11:1–36). Whereas, in the earlier chapters of Romans, Paul usually refers to the people of the covenant as "Jews" (1:16; 2:9, 10; 2:17, 28, 29; 3:1, 9, 29) and addresses them at times directly (i.e., in the second person, as at 2:17, and implicitly at 2:28, 29; 3:1, 9, 29), in chapters 9–11, this term is almost absent and the predominant term becomes "Israel" (9:6 [twice], 27, 31; 10:19, 21; 11:2, 7, 25, 26) or "Israelite" (9:4, 11:1); "Jew(s)" occurs only in 9:24 and 10:12. Moreover, "Israel" is never directly addressed, rather, Paul's specific audience here is the gentile Christians in Rome (11:13, 17–31), and Israel is, as it were, only an outside party to the debate. Paul emphasizes the religious significance of the people of the covenant, with the explicit purpose of refuting the feeling of superiority among gentile Christians in Rome toward Jewish Christians. He not only asserts Israel's abiding role in God's salvation history, and its preeminence in the gospel, but he also reminds the gentile Christians of their spiritual dependence on Israel's election; i.e., that they (the gentiles) are "grafted, contrary to nature, into a cultivated olive tree [i.e., Israel]" (11:24; *cf.* 11:15–16, 28–29). Thus Paul highlights the two crucial moments in Israel's history of salvation that belong to the abiding truth of the gospel: Israel's election by God at the beginning of salvation history and its final redemption at the end of that history (11:25–36).

The tentative nature of Paul's reflections in these chapters reveals itself not only in the sharp turns of his thought—for instance, the major shift in the argument at 9:30, when he turns from the topic of God's freedom to Israel's failure—but also in a variety of definitions of "Israel." In 9:6–12, Israel is defined in spiritual terms, as "the children of the promise" (9:8) in contrast to the historic Israel. However, in 9:27–29 Paul adopts a different perspective: Israel is now defined in terms of an elect "remnant" (*cf.* also 11:5), in terms of a *part* of historic Israel. Again, in 11:26, still another perspective surfaces: Paul finally concludes that "*all* [historic] Israel will be saved" (11:26). These various definitions of "Israel" impinge as well on Paul's reflections concerning God's "hardening" of Israel: on the one hand he claims that God is free "to harden the heart of whomever he wills" (9:18)—a verdict that contains an implicit reference to Israel (9:22). On the other hand, he asserts that God has hardened a part of Israel forever (11:7–10; especially

at v. 10: "bend their backs forever"); but at last he comes to the insight that this hardening by God is only a temporary measure that will cease when "all Israel will be saved" (11:25–27).

The fluctuation in Paul's thought in chapters 9–11 may seem to us confusing and illogical, but it is preferable to view it as Paul's wrestling with a variety of insights until finally the special revelation by God of the "mystery" (11:25) gives him sudden clarity on the troublesome issue of Israel's place in the gospel (11:25–32).

The Righteousness of God in Daily Life; Conclusion and Greetings (12:1–16:27)

The final main part of the letter (12:1–15:13) draws from the gospel the ethical consequences of the righteousness of God as explicated in the preceding parts (1:16–11:36). The subdivisions deal with exhortations of both a general (12:1–13:14) and a specific (14:1–15:6) nature, and this part of the letter concludes with a joyful celebration of the one church of Jews and gentiles (15:7–13). Then follows an advisory to the Romans of his travel plans (15:14–32), and he concludes with an extensive list of greetings (16:1–23). A final doxology was added to the letter at a later time by a disciple of Paul (16:25–27).

Two opening paragraphs (12:1–2, 3–8) introduce the basic theme for the exhortations that follow (12:9–15:13), delineating the basic tenets of Christian moral life and its constitutive elements. The first paragraph (12:1–2) reminds the Roman Christians that their moral life is made possible "by the mercies of God" (12:1); that is, by the gift of the gospel of God's righteousness as outlined in the previous parts of the letter. Christian morality is characterized by an active "bodily" engagement of Christians in everyday life: "Present your *bodies* as a living sacrifice, holy and acceptable to God, which is your spiritual worship" (12:1, RSV; emphasis mine).

Finally, Paul uses the metaphor of "the body of Christ" (12:5) to teach the Roman church that the oneness of the body with its many members means that each member of the body has its own specific gift, so that unity in the church means neither uniformity nor the superiority of one member over another, but rather genuine "pluriformity" and heterogeneity (12:3–8).

In the following paragraphs these basic norms are applied, in brief staccato sentences, to the Christian life in general (12:9–13:14), and more specifically to the conflict between "the weak" and "the strong" in the Roman church itself (14:1–15:13), an issue discussed earlier in this essay.

Life in "the body of Christ" (12:3–8) must establish a "togetherness" (15:6) within diversity (14:1–11, 15:6–7), tolerance of others, and harmony and peace (14:17–19, 15:5), because this conforms to the behavior of Christ himself on behalf of all people (15:7–12). Therefore, the "welcoming one another" (15:7) amid conflicting opinions about food laws and calendar observances (14:5–6, 15–21) concretizes "spiritual worship" through the "bodily engagement" in everyday Christian life (12:1).

SUMMARY

After this brief journey through Romans it may be useful to underscore some significant features of the letter.

The length of Romans is remarkable. It is the longest letter not only in the Pauline letter collection but in the New Testament as well. Although quantity does not always mean quality, in the case of Romans its length is proportionate to its importance. Nowhere else does Paul unfold the components of his gospel in as extensive and orderly a way. The letter has a strong didactic quality, and it comes as no surprise that it has served as the model for many catechetical treatises, such as the Heidelberg Catechism (a sixteenth-century Protestant confession of faith) and Calvin's *Institutes of the Christian Religion*. The systematic and didactic nature of Romans has often led commentators to disregard its character as a "letter," addressed at a specific time in his life to a particular situation in Rome (cf. Melanchthon's description of Romans as a "compendium doctrinae Christianae"). Therefore it is important to recognize the balance in Romans between the universal and the particular, and the letter may appropriately be called a didactic letter or "letter-essay" (Donfried 1977, 144).

The style and sequence of Paul's argument demand attention. The style not only demonstrates Paul's argumentative skills (through such devices as

the diatribe, dialog, and the rhetorical combination of logic and emotional appeals as means of persuasion), but also reveals the unusual character of his relation to the Roman church. As I have shown in my earlier discussion of the motive underlying the letter, Paul is eager to claim apostolic authority in his own right, while at the same time he acknowledges the independent authority of the Roman church. Therefore the style of the letter is both authoritative and conciliatory. The flow of the argument shows this as well. In contrast to the polemical tone and the condensed argument of Galatians—a letter that parallels Romans in many ways—Romans exhibits a discursive and expansive flow of thought. After the statement of the thesis (1:16–17), Paul proceeds with the discussion in an orderly way: he outlines first the human situation before God (1:18–3:20), then the christological content of the gospel and its scriptural support (3:21–4:25). Subsequently, the consequences of God's act of justification in Christ are unfolded (5:1–8:39), interpolated by rebuttals to opponents (6:1–23, 7:1–6) and by an analysis of the human plight under the Law (7:7–25). Next (9:1–11:36) he clarifies the place of Jewish life in the gospel. The letter reaches its high point in Paul's outline of the nature of Christian ethical praxis (12:1–13:14) and its relevance for Rome (14:1–15:14). Finally he reminds the Roman Christians of his special apostolic authority and informs them about his travel plans (15:15–32), resuming the discussion of his relation to the Roman church begun in the opening section of the letter (1:1–15).

The issue of the center of the letter has been the subject of a lively debate, especially since the publication of Albert Schweitzer's classic work *The Mysticism of Paul the Apostle* (1931, 226). Schweitzer argues that Romans exhibits two theological "craters": the "main crater" (6:1–8:39) constitutes Paul's basic conviction of "being in Christ," whereas the "subsidiary crater" (1:18–5:21)—based on justification and the atoning character of Christ's death—is to be ascribed to a rabbinic argument that Paul employs against Jewish objections to the gospel, but that no longer represents the heart of the new Christian conviction. In other words, Schweitzer argues that the center of Romans is to be located not in "justification by faith"—as it had been commonly assumed since the days of the Reformation—but in Paul's eschatological mysticism of "being in Christ."

Schweitzer's position has some plausibility, because there seems to be a real break between the first main part (1:18–4:25) and the second main part of the letter (5:1–8:39). I noted this at the beginning of my discussion of 5:1, in the appearance of a new vocabulary, in the introduction of the "sacramental" and participatory language of dying and rising with Christ, and especially in the shift from a sociological discussion of the unity of Jew and Greek in the church (1:18–4:25) to the ontological topic of the cosmic and universal meaning of Christ's death and resurrection (5:1–8:39).

However, once one recognizes that it is an error to impose a logical architectonic structure on Romans (i.e., the error of confusing the letter with a philosophical treatise), the center of the letter within its compositional and dialogical fluidity becomes clear. As the theme (1:16–17) indicates, the center of Romans is indeed the righteousness of God in Christ to faith alone (3:21–31). However, this center unfolds itself in many directions. For instance, the righteousness of God in Christ entails the majesty and glory of God, in both his judgment (1:18–3:20) and grace (5:1–6:23); it entails (with its emphasis on the sovereign initiative of God's redemption in Christ [3:21–31, 6:1–23, 8:1–17]) the "no exit" plight of the human condition, whether enslaved by its own idolatry (1:18–3:20) or by the Law (7:1–25). Therefore, genuine human access to God can only be based on faith (3:21–4:25, 10:1–17), and on the gift of the Spirit (8:1–30) that negates both the works of the Law (3:27–31, 7:1–25, 10:1–21) and life in the flesh (8:1–17). Moreover, the righteousness of God evokes the vision of the coming glory of God (5:2–11).

Hope, based on God's saving action in Christ, not only enables Christians to be steadfast in the midst of suffering (5:2–11), but also demands of them to engage themselves in redemptive suffering for the sake of the whole world created by God, which, along with Israel (11:1–36), awaits its redemption by God (8:17–30).

And finally, the righteousness of God in Christ stimulates a way of life that embodies God's gift of righteousness in the everyday life of Christians, and which is made possible by the "pneumatic democracy"

within the "body of Christ"; that is, by the mutual give and take of its diverse members, all endowed by the Spirit with their unique individual gifts (12:1–15:13).

And so, Paul's letter to the Romans demonstrates in a most impressive way the special character of Christian religious sentiment: its conviction of the awe-inspiring togetherness in God of both his majesty and mercy, as revealed in Jesus Christ for the sake of the redemption of God's world.

Bibliography

Barrett, C. K. A *Commentary on the Epistle to the Romans.* New York, 1957. Clearly written commentary on individual units; provides his own translation; impressive theological perspective.

Barth, Karl. *The Epistle to the Romans.* Translated from the 6th German edition by Edwyn C. Hoskyns. London, 1933. A basic reworking of the 1st edition of 1919. A classic commentary; the work combines historical reflections and theological insights for the contemporary situation of the church in our culture.

———. *A Shorter Commentary on Romans.* Translated by D. H. van Daalen. Richmond, Va., 1959. A marvelous short version of Barth's commentary (see above). A lecture series delivered in Bonn (West Germany) after the end of World War II. The best work available for a concise understanding of the epistle as a whole.

Beare, Francis Wright. *St. Paul and His Letters.* London, 1962.

Beker, J. Christiaan. *Paul the Apostle.* Philadelphia, 1980; 2d ed., 1984. An overall perspective of Paul's thought with special attention to Romans.

Best, Ernest. *The Letter of Paul to the Romans.* Cambridge, 1967.

Cranfield, C. E. B. *A Critical and Exegetical Commentary on the Epistle to the Romans.* 2 vols. Edinburgh, 1975–1979. Detailed exegesis with numerous valuable supplemental essays on historical, grammatical, and theological issues. Excellent on grammar, syntax, and lexicography. Conservative perspective.

Dahl, N. A. "Two Notes on Romans 5." *Studia Theologica* 5 (1951): 37–48.

Donfried, Karl P., ed. *The Romans Debate.* Minneapolis, 1977.

Jervell, Jacob. "Der Brief nach Jerusalem: Über Veranlassung und Adresse des Römerbriefes." *Studia Theologica* 25 (1971): 61–73.

Käsemann, Ernst. *Commentary on Romans.* Translated and edited by Geoffrey W. Bromiley. Grand Rapids, 1980. A modern classic; written from a Lutheran point of view with a strong theological bent. Very good on bibliographies pertaining to individual sections. Worthwhile reference material on history of religion background. The English translation is not smooth (in part due to the difficult style of the German original).

Keck, Leander E. *Paul and His Letters*. Philadelphia, 1979. An excellent survey of the letters of Paul.

Luther, Martin. *D. Martin Luthers Werke (Weimar Ausgabe)*. Vol. 54, 185. Weimar, 1928. English translation quoted in this essay by Roland Herbert Bainton, in Bainton's *Here I Stand: A Life of Martin Luther*. New York, 1950.

Nestle, Eberhard, and Kurt Aland, eds. *Greek-English New Testament*. 26th rev. ed. Stuttgart, 1981.

Nygren, Anders. *Commentary on Romans*. Translated by Carl C. Rasmussen. Philadelphia, 1967.

Robinson, John A. T. *Wrestling with Romans*. Philadelphia, 1979. Very helpful: short and clear; a rapid journey through the letter, highlighting major theological issues.

Schweitzer, Albert. *The Mysticism of Paul the Apostle*. New York, 1931.

Tillich, Paul. *Systematic Theology*. 3 vols. in 1. Chicago, 1967. P. 13.

Wilckens, Ulrich. *Der Brief an die Römer*. 3 vols. Zurich, 1978–1982. Impressive exegesis. Incisive essays on theological issues and history of doctrine. The commentary is part of the series "E.K.K." ("Evangelical-Catholic Commentary"), which is an ecumenical venture. It opens up an important dialogue between Protestant and Roman Catholic interpreters.

J. CHRISTIAAN BEKER

I and II Corinthians

INTRODUCTION

THE APOSTLE PAUL was "called" (1 Cor 1:1) to proclaim the gospel to the gentiles. Paul was an itinerant preacher who concentrated his work among the major towns along the north and east of the Mediterranean Sea. When his churches needed him but he could not be present, he wrote letters to them.

Corinth, located about fifty-five miles southwest of Athens, was designated a Roman colony and situated in a prime place for trade. It was a bustling center in Paul's time (Furnish 1984). Paul probably first preached in Corinth in 50 or 51, and, with the aid of Silvanus and Timothy, established there a congregation of believers in Christ. Paul's correspondence with the Corinthian church spanned the rest of the decade of the 50s. The size of this community of believers cannot be determined; neither can one establish with certainty the type of place where they first met, though it was most likely in someone's home.

The Corinthian letters are extraordinary when compared with the other surviving Pauline letters. The sheer bulk of 1 and 2 Corinthians is noteworthy. Also, no other Pauline letters provide such a series of "windows" into different periods of an ongoing relationship between Paul and one of his congregations. Further, only in the Corinthian correspondence do we find reference to a letter that the recipients had sent to Paul.

Close examination reveals that in the Corinthian correspondence we have not two Pauline letters, as one might first suppose, but a series of messages that amount to "written conversations." These five "conversations" or letters may be outlined as follows:
1. The "Previous Letter" (now lost)
2. The present canonical 1 Corinthians
3. The "Painful Letter" (now lost)
4. The present canonical 2 Corinthians 1–9
5. The present canonical 2 Corinthians 10–13
Thus our first actual "hearing" of the ongoing written conversation between Paul and the Corinthians comes from a time probably four or five years after Paul's first preaching in Corinth. The New Testament letter 1 Corinthians was likely written in or near 54. In it we discover that the canonical 1 Corinthians is not in fact the first letter that Paul wrote them.

THE "PREVIOUS LETTER" (LETTER NO. 1)

Within the New Testament letter known as 2 Corinthians, Paul makes an unmistakable reference to a "previous letter": a letter written *before* 1 Corinthians ("I wrote to you in my letter. . . . But rather I wrote to you" [1 Cor 5:9, 11]). We learn about this letter and have a window opening onto Paul's earlier relationship with the Corinthians only because they have communicated to Paul some confusion concerning the previous letter. How many topics Paul's first letter covered cannot be known, but the one item Paul mentions from it is the issue of Christians associating with immoral people. Apparently (1 Cor 5:9ff.), some have asked how it is possible, in the course of one's life, to avoid immoral people, because (the assumption seems to be) they are everywhere. Paul does not dispute that. In fact, he reduces the Corinthian argument to the absurd: "I wrote to you in my letter not to associate with immoral men; not at all meaning the immoral of this world, or the greedy and robbers, or idolaters, since then you would need to go out of the world" (5:9–10; RSV). Instead, Paul entreats the Corinthian Christians to separate themselves from *other Christians* who live immorally. That was the purpose of the original letter; the incident of the man living with his father's wife (5:1ff.), probably his stepmother, shows that the Corinthians did not understand the previous letter and its message, or they would have driven out "the wicked person from among you" (5:13).

We know nothing else about the first instance in this succession of ongoing conversations that students of the New Testament call the "Corinthian correspondence." Did the Corinthians "drive out the wicked person"? It is difficult to know. Second Corinthians does note a person who has been expelled from the believing community (2:5–11). Whether it is the same individual mentioned in 1 Corinthians 5 is not clear. At least by the time of Paul's writing of 2 Corinthians, the recipients of the letter have adopted a principle like the one Paul urges in 1 Corinthians 5:9–13, and have excluded an immoral person "who bears the name of brother" (1 Cor 5:11).

THE PRESENT CANONICAL
1 CORINTHIANS (LETTER NO. 2)

The second "window" or vantage point we have upon Paul's exchanges with the Corinthian Christians is the New Testament document called 1 Corinthians.

Background

Paul had several reports about matters in Corinth. No doubt each source of information contribut-

ed to Paul's writing what I am calling Letter No. 2 (the canonical 1 Corinthians). Paul's own special representatives sometimes checked on a given church when Paul was too far away, or when he was imprisoned. Timothy and Titus are well-known examples. Timothy had only recently come from Corinth, where some people were already grumbling about Paul's absence (1 Cor 4:18). It is likely that Timothy's report was an important factor in eliciting 1 Corinthians from Paul.

Early in 1 Corinthians, Paul notes that "Chloe's people" have reported to him that "there is quarreling" among the Corinthians (1:11). We cannot know what every Corinthian knew; namely, the identity of Chloe and her representatives. One can only surmise that she was a woman of substance, probably engaged in commerce, and that she had (probably business) representatives who gave Paul an update on Corinthian matters while they were on a trip for her. At any rate, from these people Paul heard about difficulties and schisms among the Corinthian Christians.

Toward the end of 1 Corinthians, Paul also notes that three other Corinthians—Stephanas, Fortunatus, and Achaicus—have paid Paul a refreshing visit and in some sense "made up for your absence" (16:17).

Finally, Paul has received a letter from the Corinthian Christians, or at least from some among them. In 1 Corinthians, Paul specifically refers to a letter from them and takes up a series of issues that they have raised in it: "Now concerning the matters about which you wrote" (1 Cor 7:1). One may assume, then, that every "Now concerning" in the rest of 1 Corinthians also treats an issue from their letter to Paul (7:25, 8:1, 12:1, 16:1).

No wonder 1 Corinthians is such a lengthy letter. Not only are the Corinthians quarrelsome and divisive, but Paul has considerable individual and collective reporting about how things are going in the Corinthian church. Many items, including a letter from some of the Corinthians themselves, demand attention from the apostle in charge of their care.

The Structure of 1 Corinthians
The bulk of the letter—chapters 7 through 16—is framed around the issues raised in the letter from the Corinthians. In the chapters prior to that,

there are two matters of private and community practice: the man living with his father's wife (5:1ff.) and the Corinthians' propensity for taking one another to court (6:1ff.).

Chapters 1–4 function as context for the whole letter (Dahl 1967). They provide the frame of reference not only for understanding the basic issues that Paul identifies among the Corinthians but also for understanding the perspective out of which Paul supposes that the Corinthians ought to be living with one another.

There has been a long-standing debate among scholars as to whether 1 Corinthians is just a hodge-podge of problems variously and somewhat accidentally bound together by the eccentricities of the Corinthian congregation or whether the letter betrays a single malaise that manifests itself in a variety of symptoms. Increasingly, the latter argument seems to be prevailing (Conzelmann 1975).

The Corinthian Malaise

Paul says it directly and early on: the Corinthians are divisive; they are schismatic; they align themselves against each other (1:11ff.; *cf.* 11:18–19). But it is not just their taking sides that concerns Paul. At issue is the health of the Christian community, the body of Christ.

Some of the Corinthians—one may presume that it is not a majority—have come to view themselves as being superior to other Christians in their midst and as having a special freedom in Christ. For them, "all things are lawful" (6:12, 10:23). They get to the Lord's Supper early and they eat and drink to satiety. They have established that the showiest and most observable of all spiritual gifts (namely, speaking in tongues) is the sign of their preeminence. Not only do they think they have died with Christ; they believe they already share in the resurrection with Christ also. They conclude that they are, therefore, beyond normal moral constraints (Theissen 1982; Meeks 1983).

After the opening contextualizing chapters (1–4), Paul addresses two matters that bear directly upon these elitists. They have made the man who sleeps with his stepmother a person of some admiration: he lives out his new freedom in Christ fully. They freely go to court, knowing that the wealthy are

the ones most likely to gain a favorable verdict. It is these people whom Paul lashes with irony when he writes: "Already you are filled! Already you have become rich! Without us you have become kings!" (4:8; RSV). Even apostles do not have such status. Paul, as apostle, identifies with the ones who are thus excluded, that is, with the rest of the Corinthian congregation. To be ill-clad, dispossessed, buffeted, tossed aside as the refuse of the world—these are what characterize apostles, and indeed many other less prestigious Christians.

This same mighty minority among the Corinthian Christians has economic power behind it. These are the ones described by Paul as "not many" when he writes: "Not many of you were wise according to worldly standards, not many were powerful, not many were of noble birth" (1:26; RSV). But these people pride themselves on their wisdom. Unlike others less gifted, they claim special insight. That accounts for Paul's early contrast of the "wisdom of human beings" and the "power of God" (2:5). Likewise, a little later he emphasizes that the gospel message came not through "human wisdom" but "by the Spirit" (2:13). And in the next chapter he warns: "Let no one deceive himself. If any one among you thinks that he is wise in this age, let him become a fool that he may become wise. For the wisdom of this world is folly with God" (3:18–19; RSV).

A part of Paul's concern in writing 1 Corinthians is to restore perspective on what it means to belong to Christ, whether one is wealthy and has some eminence, or whether one is (as most of the Corinthian Christians are) neither highborn nor of any lofty social status. In sum, Paul seeks by various moves within the letter to show that the normal worldly distinctions people make and allow outside the Christian community will not work inside it.

Setting and Introduction (Chapters 1–4)

The letter opens with a salutation (1:1–3) in a form that was common in Paul's time: "person A to person B: greetings." Paul graces the form with special Christian trappings. Paul is called by God's will to be an apostle (1:1) and the Corinthians are called to be saints (1:2). He is sent to preach the gospel to the gentiles; the Corinthians are called to live as those "set apart for God"—that is what "saint" means.

Immediately following the salutation, Paul's letters usually have a thanksgiving that contains a hint of the central issue around which the letter is to focus, and 1 Corinthians is no exception in this regard: God's grace, given to the church at Corinth, provides them with everything they need, including every spiritual gift, so that they may be properly sustained till the end of time, when they may be found guiltless on the day of judgment (1:4–9).

Directly, Paul engages the central problem: the Corinthians are divided and their divisions contradict God's love for them and purposes with them. In chapters 1–4 Paul attacks their schismatic tendencies in two complementary ways. On the one hand, he attaches the two divisions to himself and Apollos. On the other, he tells them they have made the division falsely on the basis of a wisdom they claim to have. I will now look in more detail at each of these.

The keynote of chapters 1–4 is contained in the appeal: "I appeal to you, brethren, by the name of our Lord Jesus Christ, that all of you agree and that there be no dissensions among you, but that you be united in the same mind and the same judgment" (1:10; RSV). Chloe's people have reported quarreling among the Corinthians: some claim to belong to Paul, some to Apollos, some to Cephas (Paul's favorite name for Peter), and some to Christ. A few scholars have taken these four personages as indicative of four groups at Corinth, but I myself do not (*cf.* Hurd 1965). In his letters, Paul sometimes repudiates a position by carrying it to its logical extreme (e.g., 1 Cor 5:10). So here in the first notice of divisions among the Corinthian congregation, Paul adds the "some belong to Christ" as a means of showing how absurd all divisions in the church are. *Everyone* in the church belongs to Christ. In the rest of chapters 1–4 there is no further reference to a "Christ party" at Corinth because there was no such group within the church. It was mentioned in 1:12 as an indication of how absurd any divisions in Christian community are. This judgment is confirmed by Paul's other references to divisions in chapters 1–4.

In chapter 3, Paul chides the Corinthians for being retarded in their growth as Christians: they remain babies in the faith (3:1ff.); they are still behaving like regular people out in the world. What proof does Paul have of this? "For while there is jealousy and strife among you, are you not of the flesh, and behaving like ordinary men? For when one says, 'I belong to Paul,' and another, 'I belong to Apollos,' are you not merely men?" (3:3–4; RSV). No "Christ party" is mentioned. For that matter, there is no reference to Cephas either. It is just Paul and Apollos.

In verse 3:5 and following, the argument continues. What shall we make of Apollos, or of Paul, for that matter? The answer: nothing much. They are just servants doing the work that God gave them to do. One planted, another watered. But it is "God who gives the growth" (3:7). Behind any possible divisions represented by Paul and Apollos—or anyone else—is the power of God, which alone can provide life and growth.

This argument reaches its climax with Paul calling on the Corinthians, inclined as they are to divisions, to recognize that in Christ "all things are yours, whether Paul or Apollos or Cephas or the world or life or death or the present or the future, all are yours; and you are Christ's; and Christ is God's" (3:21–23; RSV). If the Corinthians understand even the most basic things, they will know that, having been claimed by God, they no longer need to secure any special place for themselves, because all things now belong to them in Christ.

Then Paul tries to limit the chances of being misunderstood. He tells the Corinthians exactly what he has been doing with these references to Apollos and himself: "I have applied all this to myself and Apollos for your benefit, brethren, that . . . none of you may be puffed up in favor of one against another" (4:6; RSV). There is no "Cephas party" in Corinth just as surely as there is no "Christ party" either. In fact, there probably are no groups allied simply to Apollos or to Paul. Apollos and Paul are in good standing with the Corinthians (see 16:12). The divisions within the community are not aligned around these pivotal characters. Instead, the division is the one I described earlier, where an elitist minority of socially and economically powerful people arrogate to themselves status and privilege, and reckon the majority of Christians as less privileged and of lower status (Theissen 1982). So Paul uses references to himself and Apollos as "illustrations" of the real divisions at Corinth. From this exercise, the Corinthians should see the silliness of the division they do have. The Paul-Apollos argument is designed by Paul to set the context for examining the real division in Corinth and the havoc that it has wrought.

Interwoven within this opening treatment of Paul and Apollos is a second way Paul strives to set the context for the Corinthians to overcome their divisiveness and for Paul to treat their particular problems. It has to do with the way he pits wisdom against foolishness, and power against weakness.

Paul signals early that his purpose was to "preach the gospel, and not with eloquent wisdom, lest the cross of Christ be emptied of its power" (1:17). Scripture (Isa 29:14) tells Paul that the "wisdom of the wise" will be destroyed and overturned by God (1:19). Paul separates himself from those who would boast of their wisdom: "We are fools for Christ's sake, but you are wise in Christ. We are weak, but you are strong" (4:10; RSV). The wisdom about which some Corinthians boast is indeed not wisdom at all, according to Paul. Though Greeks seek wisdom, and though the world values it, the Greeks and the world are blinded to the true wisdom because the "word of the cross" appears as folly or foolishness to them. Try as it might, the world has not known God through wisdom (1:21). Paul carries the argument a step further. God has turned things on their head, so Paul preaches not wisdom but folly (1:23). Besides, he argues, God's foolishness is wiser than people and God's weakness is stronger than folks (1:25). Furthermore, God has chosen a roundabout way to show power: in weakness, in the cross, in what might seem to be defeat and powerlessness. So, God chose what is foolish in the world's view to shame the wise (1:27); God chose what is weak in the world to shame the strong (1:27).

With such an assault on wisdom and power, Paul undercuts any boasting about status and wisdom. In fact, he directly warns the Corinthians not to deceive themselves: if some among you think that they are wise in this age, they would do better to "become a fool" so that they could become truly wise, with the wisdom that only God can grant (3:18). So much for boasting about one's wisdom, power, or standing. "So let no one boast of men" (3:21; *cf.* 1:29); rather, "Let him who boasts, boast of the Lord" (1:31).

Faced with a segment of the Corinthian Christians claiming that they were due special status and power, in part, because of their self-glorying wisdom,

Paul opens 1 Corinthians with a refocusing upon the cross of Christ, upon God's power shown in weakness, upon God's wisdom masked in the foolishness of the cross. By this, he calls all the Christians in Corinth back to their shared center: whether they have wealth, wisdom, or worldly status, they all share equally in the death of Christ. Their solidarity with Christ's death not only has been the way in which sin's power over them has been broken, but also is the ground for their unity and for their life together as believers.

In the opening chapters of 1 Corinthians Paul pursues a double course toward the single objective of bringing all the Corinthians back into harmony with one another in the body of Christ. The two courses are intricately interwoven by Paul: the one course features Paul's own life as a pattern that the Corinthians could and should follow; the other course seeks to set wisdom and status in perspective. Indeed, the latter effort is ultimately linked directly to the former because Paul describes his own preaching as centering not on wisdom but on the power of God revealed in the cross of Christ.

Beyond his own arguments expressed in chapters 1 through 4, Paul announces an imminent personal visit. Timothy has reported to Paul that "some are arrogant as though [Paul] were not coming" (4:18). Paul avers that he "will come to you soon," the Lord willing. Then he will be prepared to see if the "talk" of these arrogant people has any "power" to it. Having given that strong warning, Paul concludes the opening contextualizing section of his letter with a description of what he sees to be the Corinthians' options: they can "come around" or they can be defiant. "What do you wish? Shall I come to you with a rod, or with love in a spirit of gentleness?" (4:21; RSV). They can have it as they wish. If they continue divided and arrogant, then Paul will chastise them when he arrives. If they come to their senses, affirm their true unity in Christ, and thereby end their schism, then Paul will be with them lovingly and gently.

Now Paul turns to problems of which he has become aware; in his treatment of them we can see the detrimental results of the practices of the persons who claim wisdom and status in the Corinthian church. The elitist, power- and status-conscious Christians have left a trail of destruction across the church and across the letter—the way the path of a tornado is visible after it has wreaked its havoc. As we trace this trail, the fuller position of these schismatic Christians will be exposed.

Particular Problems at Corinth

A man and his father's wife (1 Cor 5:1ff.). Paul's reports indicate that "a man is living with his father's wife" (5:1), presumably his stepmother, a conduct that Paul brands as extraordinary even among gentiles. Paul laments the Corinthians' response: "And you are puffed up [arrogant]" (5:2). Mourning would have been more appropriate, he suggests. Paul directs no comment to the man in question. The other Christians at Corinth have let this man down by approving his action—and worse, they have taken pride in his accomplishment (5:6). As yeast pervades the whole lump of dough, so this man's immorality—perhaps masquerading as Christian freedom—endangers the entire Christian community.

To court: Christian vs. Christian (6:1ff.). Christians are taking one another to court in Corinth. Matters of what is right are being submitted to those who know nothing about righteousness or justice. It was a commonplace in the Greco-Roman world that the courts favored persons of status and wealth. Jews knew that as well as gentiles, and so must have the Corinthian elitists. One may suppose that it is they, accustomed to worldly power, who are the leaders in calling upon the civil court to resolve disputes. Paul decries the shamefulness of this move, asking with biting irony whether people who take pride in wisdom do not have someone "wise enough" to settle disputes among Christians.

Furthermore, believers who are destined to sit in judgment upon the angels (6:3)—presumably at the end of the age—should be able to decide "matters pertaining to this life" (6:3). Paul finds the Corinthians' actions out of joint with the gospel. "But you yourselves wrong and defraud, and that even your own brethren" (6:8). He warns that they will not inherit the kingdom of God (6:9–10) if they continue to behave toward one another in this way. He reminds all the Corinthian Christians that they were washed, they were sanctified, they were justified "in the name of the Lord Jesus Christ and in the Spirit of our God" (6:11). Accordingly, they cannot relate to one another divisively nor can they use their power and status to wrong one another.

Paul anticipates and evaluates a Corinthian rejoinder (6:12ff.). Paul voices their expected response: "All things are lawful for me." Paul does not reject it but qualifies it: "but not all things are helpful. . . . I will not be enslaved by anything" (6:12). Individual Christians may be convinced that "all things are lawful," but they are not thereby free to do whatever they wish. Paul introduces two other considerations. Christians should know that their bodies are temples of the Holy Spirit, which lives as a gift from God within them (6:19); their bodies were "not meant for immorality, but for the Lord, and the Lord for the body" (6:13). As a result, like slaves bought in the marketplace, "you are not your own; you were bought with a price" (6:19–20). So, though "all things" may be possible, God must be glorified "in your body" (6:20). That is half of Paul's argument.

Christians may affirm that "all things are lawful" but they must also reckon what is "helpful" (6:12), fitting, useful, or of advantage to others. At this juncture in the letter, Paul simply states this principle and drops it. It becomes a theme of primary importance as the letter unfolds, and it addresses directly those Corinthians who use their status and their wisdom—even their freedom in Christ—without regard for their weaker brothers and sisters in the faith.

Matters of human sexuality: The first question asked by the Corinthians in their own letter to Paul (7:1ff.). In all the unquestionably Pauline letters (Romans, 1 and 2 Corinthians, Galatians, Philippians, 1 Thessalonians, and Philemon), it is clear that Paul assumed that the end of the ages was coming very soon, in his own lifetime. In 7:26 Paul gives advice with the "present distress"—a sign of the impending end—as an explicit point of reckoning: "The form of this world is passing away" (7:31); "The appointed time has grown very short" (7:29). From that conviction Paul draws the conclusion that "it is well for a person to remain as he is" (7:26)—admittedly a conservative posture—and applies it across the board on the variety of sexual matters that he treats. The principle is developed in 7:17–24 and is boldly and universally stated in verse 24: "So, brethren, in whatever state each was called, there let him remain with God" (RSV). In most instances married people should stay married; single individuals should stay single if possible.

Paul recognizes that human sexual drives are formidable in power and he is convinced that sexual intercourse outside marriage is inappropriate, so he counsels single people who burn with passion to marry (7:9). The line of his reasoning goes like this: given the nearness of the end of the ages, it is better to remain single if you can; if you cannot, then get married; "if you marry, you do not sin" (7:28). Paul unambiguously expresses his wish "that all were as I myself am" (7:7), that is, celibate. But he recognizes that he has been given a special gift, a charism all his own, to remain single, and that God has not given that same charism to others (7:7).

Paul also recognizes that maintaining relations with other human beings takes energy that might be used for glorifying God. Given Paul's principle of maximizing devotion to God (7:35) and its corollary, minimizing worldly troubles (7:28; *cf.* 7:32), we can understand why he gives this counsel: to single people, stay single if you can; to those who burn with sexual desire, you will maximize devotion to God if you marry.

Dissolution of marriages is not called for (7:27); neither is abstention from sexual intercourse (7:5) among marriage partners. Maximum devotion to God—"how to please the Lord" (7:32)—while still maintaining the peace (7:15) is the goal (7:35).

Some lament that the unquestionably Pauline letters do not have a more lofty view of marriage (but compare Ephesians 5:21–33). It is fair to say that Paul, like most people of his time, does not harbor a romantic view of marriage. Neither does he identify procreation as one of its goals.

Such laments, however, overlook a noteworthy feature of Paul's advice to marriage partners: the reciprocity and parity he assumes between them. In form and in content, Paul calls for equal consideration of one another. As to form, almost every statement Paul makes about husbands is repeated word for word about wives, and vice versa. For example: "Each man should have his own wife and each woman her own husband" (7:3). Similarly, his counsel about mixed marriages between believers and unbelievers manifests the same form (7:13, 16; *cf.* 7:32 ff.).

The content of Paul's counsels also affirms a fundamental reciprocity between partners in marriage. Consider, for example, the advice that "the husband should give to his wife her conjugal rights, and likewise the wife to her husband" (7:3); note especially, in the next verse, the remarkable reasoning behind that counsel: "For the wife does not rule over her own body, but the husband does; likewise the husband does not rule over his own body, but the wife does" (7:4; RSV).

Paul's advice to the Corinthians concerning marriage puts into practice the pre-Pauline Christian formulation that Paul mentioned in the letter to the Galatians: "There is neither Jew nor Greek, there is neither slave nor free, there is neither male nor female; for you are all one in Christ Jesus" (Gal 3:28; RSV). He has taught this understanding earlier to the Corinthians, and can appeal to it as a point of reckoning (*cf.* 1 Cor 12:13). In chapter 7, Paul applies it to questions of marriage and human sexuality. In Christ, the normal societal differentiations that are made on the basis of sex are out of place. In Christ, equality and reciprocity must be realized—not just in worship but in all the levels of corporate life in community.

One final point must be noted here. The treatment of sexual matters shows for the second time that Paul did not expect Christians to withdraw from the world and engagement with it (the first treatment being in his recapitulation of the "previous letter"). Here Paul acknowledges that some Christians are married to unbelievers (7:12–18). He counsels Christians on how they should act toward unbelieving spouses, but does not advise them to separate from or divorce their unbelieving partners. He does countenance divorce from such marriages, but only when the unbelieving partner wishes it, and then on the principle that "God has called us to peace" (7:15).

Meat offered to idols: The second question from the Corinthians' letter to Paul. In Paul's time, Corinth had temples for most of the mystery cults, those religious associations grounded in great stories of gods and goddesses whose drama roughly paralleled the annual vegetation cycles. No doubt many of the congregation at Corinth had previously participated in the reenactment of those dramas and in the festive dinners that often accompanied them. The meat sold in Corinth would have been offered in sacrifice earlier to the deities of mystery cults. The letter asked: Can Christians eat that meat, or will the eating of it grant recognition to the deity to which it was sacrificed (Willis 1985)?

To the Corinthians' claim that "all of us possess knowledge" (8:1), Paul responds not in disagreement but in clarification. What matters is not just what one knows but how one loves, because "love builds up" (8:2). Like the Stoic philosophers of his time, Paul identifies certain matters as morally "indifferent": as not determinative for life. Here he draws on that pattern regarding food offered to idols: "Food will not commend us to God. We are no worse off if we do not eat, and no better off if we do" (8:8). Food and the eating of it—whether it has been offered to a deity or not—is morally neutral in and of itself. Just as Paul earlier did not stop with the Corinthians' slogan "All things are lawful" (6:12), but added, "not all things are helpful," so here the argument does not stop with the recognition or knowledge that food is an indifferent matter in one's standing before God.

Paul warns his readers: "Only take care lest this liberty of yours somehow become a stumbling block to the weak" (8:9). A pattern emerges in Pauline ethical counsel: consider not only whether the action in question will affect one's relation to God but also whether the action may cause someone else (especially someone weaker than oneself) to stumble. Either reckoning, without the other, is inadequate. Paul deals with the Corinthians' question on a practical level; I paraphrase his thought: "Suppose that you, as a Christian who knows that there is no God but one, go to the banquet of a mystery cult. As far as it bears on you, you could take part in that feast without any risk to your relation to God. So far so good. But suppose that there is another believer whose conscience is weaker, who does not understand as clearly as you do whether eating this food actually means that one recognizes the other deities. Might this weaker person be encouraged by your action to eat food offered to idols? 'And so by your knowledge this weak man is destroyed, the brother for whom Christ died' (8:10-11). To act on the basis of one's own knowledge without reckoning the effect it may have upon someone weaker—for whom Christ also died—is to sin. To sin against or wrong your brother in Christ is to 'sin against Christ'" (8:12).

Paul concludes the discussion by telling the Corinthians that he would "play it safe": "Therefore, if food is a cause of my brother's falling, I will never eat meat, lest I cause my brother to fall" (8:13; RSV). In sum, what one knows in Christ frees one with regard to certain actions such as what to eat or what to avoid eating, but that freedom cannot be exercised without regard for its impact on someone who might be weaker and not understand what one understands. One may be free and not find the exercise of that freedom helpful to another.

A Pauline digression for illumination by personal example, by Scripture, and by tradition. In chapters 9 through 11, Paul creatively leaves the questions raised by the Corinthians' letter, and attempts in three ways to illustrate and call for what he considers the proper balancing of personal freedom in Christ, and care for and consideration of others in the Christian commmunity. First, in chapter 9, he shows himself as a good model in his role as an apostle (9:1-18) and in his mode of evangelization (9:19ff.). Second, Scripture instructs and contains a warning that bears on the same issue (10:1-13). And last, tradition—in this case, regarding the Lord's Supper—should direct the Corinthians toward the unity and proper care of each other that Paul has been urging. When Paul has touched upon the matter in these three ways, he explicitly picks up the thread of the earlier argument by quoting the Corinthian reductionist slogan again: "All things are lawful" (10:23). Then (10:23-11:1) he sums up the matters that have been at the center of the discussion.

1. Paul as a personal example of the proper balance between individual freedom and community responsibility.

In two ways, Paul daringly establishes himself as a model of Christian freedom properly lived with an adaptive view to the capacities of those around him (9:1-27).

First, Paul offers himself as *apostolic model.* He opens this section with the question: "Am I not free?" (9:1). Having closed the previous point with a reference to how he would restrain his freedom (8:13) rather than "cause my brother to fall," Paul now asks the Corinthians, in effect, if they know anyone freer than Paul. At Corinth, there are some Christians who are boasting of their freedom and who seem—in Paul's view—to be abusing others by a misuse of their freedom. If they are free, then consider Paul, he suggests. By his own example and from their own knowledge of his actions when he has been with them, Paul's readers have had ample opportunity to see how freedom is properly bridled when the welfare of others is in danger. Paul has deftly shifted the discussion of freedom from the much-contested practices of the Corinthians to his own indisputable apostleship to them.

Apostles, as servants of the gospel, had certain rights (9:5): to food and drink (9:4) and to accompaniment by a wife (9:5), even though Paul's gift of celibacy made the last of no consequence to him. The fact that apostles had these rights was supported by secular practice (9:7) and religious custom (9:13), and confirmed by Scripture. (9:8–9). Even Jesus' own teaching supports the practice that "those who proclaim the gospel should get their living by the gospel" (9:14; *cf.* Luke 10:7). Not one of his rights has Paul claimed, however, nor is he now seeking to claim them. He insists that the rights are his, but pointedly eschews the exercise of them. Apart from making this point, what Paul normally does is pass over his rights in silence: "we endure anything" (9:12b), an expression he will later use (13:7) to describe the way love overlooks something that is displeasing in the other person.

Why does Paul not avail himself of the rights he is due as an apostle? Paul's answer: "We endure anything rather than put an obstacle in the way of the gospel of Christ" (9:12). The gospel, the free gift of God to those who believe, must be "free of charge," not with all sorts of appended rights (9:18). Accordingly, Paul concludes he does not have much choice in the matter. He must preach the gospel; that is his calling (9:16–17). And, properly, to make clear that grace (God's free gift) stands at the center of the preaching, Paul must not "make full use of my right in the gospel" (9:18). If Paul, as an apostle, can forgo the exercise of apostolic prerogatives, then the Corinthians can refrain from employment of their freedom if it places another person at risk. That is how Christian freedom is bound up inextricably with the expression of love for others.

Paul offers his *evangelistic practice* as a second

example of the balance between individual and community. He picks up the thread that runs through this section of the letter: "I am free from all people" (9:19). But now he turns the matter—and its attendant imagery—upside down, all the more to emphasize the proper use of freedom. Paul, although free from all, has enslaved himself to all, "that I might win the more" (9:19). By the exercise of his freedom, Paul has become a servant to all for the advancement of the gospel. For the sake of the gospel, Paul identifies with the limitations and possibilities of the people with whom he is associated (9:20ff.), whether they be Jews or gentiles, strong or weak. All of this is to advance the gospel. The message to the Corinthian Christians is that they, like Paul (their "father in the faith"), can place their freedom in service of the other Christians in the community. They can recognize the weakness of some believers, rather than be so insistent upon the exercise of their own full freedom and the claiming of all their rights.

Paul is not chary of "reward talk," despite some modern reticence in that regard. He knows that if his service to his call is faithfully carried out, he will "share in its blessings" (9:23). And the Corinthians, Paul says, can "run the race" so that they too will receive the prize (9:24) if they apply what they know from athletics: "Every athlete exercises self-control in all things" (9:25). Once again Paul speaks personally. Not only does he use self-control, as the Corinthians also ought to do, but he practices discipline. He pummels his body and subdues it "lest after preaching to others I myself should be disqualified" (9:27). Apostles—and all other Christians—employ self-control and discipline or face the possibility of disqualification.

2. Scripture and its warnings.

Paul's life pattern and his advice are not simply invented for this occasion: the Hebrew scriptures say the same thing. As wonderful as the Exodus from Egypt was, and as clearly as "our fathers" were baptized into Moses and ate and drank that spiritual food and water, "nevertheless, with most of them God was not pleased"; Paul deduces this divine displeasure "because they were overthrown in the wilderness" (10:5). "We must not put the Lord to the test, as some of them did and were destroyed by serpents" (10:9). The issue comes down to this warning: "I therefore let any one who thinks that he stands take heed lest he fall" (10:12). Specifically, the elitist, status-conscious Corinthians must not confuse their true situation.

In this section of warnings based on Scripture, Paul adds a veiled warning of his own. The Corinthian Christians must take individual responsibility for their comportment before God. They cannot blame their predicaments on God for having placed them in a situation of intolerable testing, thus turning human testing of God in 10:9 into a testing of the individual in 10:12–13. "No temptation has overtaken you that is not common to man. God is faithful, and he will not let you be tempted beyond your strength, but with the temptation will also provide the way of escape, that you may be able to endure it" (10:13; RSV).

As with the athlete (9:24ff.) and Scripture's Exodus story (10:1ff.), each Christian must take responsibility for the way he or she lives the life that God has given. No excuses can be made about not being warned (Scripture took care of that) or for being tested beyond your means by God (because God does not operate that way). With the baptism reference (10:1) and the mention of their eating and drinking supernatural food and drink (10:3–4), Paul may be giving the Corinthians a further warning that they must not presume on their baptism and access to the Lord's Supper as a guarantee that, no matter how they live, they will be assured of God's protection: as God was not pleased with the many in the Exodus and overthrew them (10:5), so the Corinthians had better watch how they live.

3. Christian eucharistic tradition and practice.

Beginning in 1 Corinthians 10:14, Paul returns to the most recent question of the Corinthians' letter to him: "Now concerning food offered to idols" (8:1). After so long an excursus, Paul has set the stage for his advice concerning whether he thinks it would be appropriate for the Christians to take part in the mystery-cult dinners and eat meat offered to idols. The understanding Paul wishes them to grasp takes this form (again, I paraphrase): "Knowing as we do that there is no God but one (8:1–6), we, like an apostle, who has the undisputed right to support (9:1ff.), could freely partake of food that had been sacrificed to idols and not defile our consciences. But freedom so exercised might cause 'the brother for whom Christ died' (8:11) to stumble, and thus we

would greatly displease God as our forebears did in the Exodus (10:1ff.). Rather than risk harm to another for whom Christ died, why should we exercise our freedom any more than Paul has demanded his rights as an apostle? Accordingly, we should 'shun the worship of idols' (10:14)."

With that conclusion Paul urges the Corinthians to "judge for yourselves what I say" (10:15), and, by reference to the Lord's Supper (10:16–17) and to the sacrifices of the people of Israel (10:18–19) and of gentiles (10:20), he calls for a clear demarcation between the Christians and all others by abstention from food offered to idols: "You cannot partake of the table of the Lord and the table of demons" (10:21). "Border talk" marking off the Christians from those around them is found in connection with the Lord's Supper, because it is here that the distinctiveness of Christian life is rehearsed and celebrated.

Paul knows the Corinthians well. "Judge for yourselves," he has told them (10:15). Then he has given them his own conclusion: it is too risky—when full consideration is given to the frailty of others—to eat food offered to idols. And now he knows that the Corinthian elitist chorus is about to chant once again their hallmark slogan: "All things are lawful!" (10:23). Indeed all things *are* permissible, when done from faith. But even then, Paul reflects, "not all things are helpful . . . not all things build up" (10:23). He enunciates a principle: let no one seek the thing that pertains to oneself; rather seek the thing that pertains to the other person (10:24). That is, after all, what Paul tries to do with his own life: "I try to please all people in everything I do, not seeking my own advantage, but that of many" (10:33).

So, as he has done from the earliest chapters, Paul urges the Corinthians to follow his lead because —and this is a new dimension to the argument— when Paul puts the concern of others ahead of his own he is modeling himself after Christ: "Be imitators of me, as I am of Christ" (11:1). Although he advises against their going to the public dinners of the mysteries, Paul counsels that in the privacy of their own homes they can "eat whatever is sold in the meat market without raising any question on the ground of conscience" (10:25). On what basis can they rightly do that? Because Scripture says, "The earth is the Lord's, and everything in it" (10:26). The same guideline works when an unbelieving neighbor invites you to dinner. Go and "eat whatever is set before you without raising any question on the ground of conscience" (10:27).

One can understand how Paul's quite different counsels here might have caused confusion at Corinth. On the one hand, in the privacy of their homes, he urges no restraint in the eating of meat offered to idols. On the other, though he affirms with the Corinthians that there is no other God, and therefore realizes that one would not personally be defiled by taking part in the mystery-cult dinners, Paul urges a conservative approach on this more public issue. To avoid the risk of causing someone for whom Christ died to stumble, to avoid encouraging another person to do something about which he or she has doubts, and therefore to avoid displeasing God, Paul calls on the Christians to avoid the mystery-cult dinners. And he urges them to draw a clear line between the worship of God and what he terms "the worship of demons."

One commendation (11:2–16) and one criticism (11:17–34) regarding their keeping of the traditions. Paul views the pre-Pauline Christian traditions as guidelines from which one can set the patterns of one's life. At this point in the letter Paul takes up two instances of the Corinthians' living according to the traditions, one of which is more favorably treated than the other. Both concern worship. In the first, the issue regards women, specifically whether they should have their heads covered when praying and prophesying. For a variety of reasons and arguments (from custom, 11:5 and 14–15; from Scripture, 11:7 and 12; and from the practice in the churches, 11:16) Paul says that women should have their heads covered when they pray or prophesy in church, whereas men should not. Basically, in 11:2–16 Paul sees that two traditions bear on the issue of women's comportment within worship. On the one hand is the tradition, explicitly referred to as such, that the "head of every man is Christ, the head of a woman is her husband, and the head of Christ is God" (11:3). On the other hand is the tradition that "in the Lord woman is not independent of man nor man of woman" (11:11). In light of those two traditions that stand in some degree of tension with one another, what counsel does Paul see for the question of women's head covering in

worship? Both traditions are of merit. Paul urges the Corinthians to "judge for yourselves" (11:13) and hopes that they will see the wisdom of women covering their heads.

Whatever one may make of the particular advice, two features of this passage should be noted. First, Paul assumes that Corinthian women are praying and prophesying in church. That practice is neither challenged nor questioned; at issue is simply whether they must cover their heads during worship. The second point has to do with the interpretation of 11:11–12: "Nevertheless, in the Lord woman is not independent of man nor man of woman; for as woman was made from man, so man is now born of woman. And all things are from God" (RSV). These verses parallel the claim of Galatians 3:28, which affirms that in Christ the normal distinctions between male and female do not pertain. Paul, in 11:11–12, reaffirms the fundamental reciprocity between men and women in Christ.

Beginning in 11:17, Paul does not view positively the Corinthians' handling of the traditions. Again, their schismatic tendencies show up in the way they treat the Lord's Supper. In fact, Paul declares that they abuse it so much that it is not the Lord's Supper that they eat (11:20). He condemns them for having no consideration of one another in their eating: are some eating early and getting the best food (Theissen 1982), so that others end up hungry? Not only that, but some actually get drunk at the supper (11:21). Paul has a practical suggestion: eat and drink at home (11:22). As it is, the conduct of some shows no respect for the "church of God" and it humiliates "those who have nothing" (11:22). No commendation can be accorded the Corinthians for that!

Paul rehearses the tradition he passed on to them regarding the Supper (11:23–26). From it he deduces that whoever "eats the bread or drinks the cup of the Lord in an unworthy manner"—as some of the Corinthians surely do—"will be guilty of profaning the body and blood of the Lord" (11:27). So the Corinthians had better take stock of themselves and adjust their actions or face judgment "by the Lord" (11:30–34; cf. 10:6–7).

Spiritual gifts and their proper use within the church: Another question from the Corinthians' letter to Paul (chapters 12–14). The argument in chapters

12–14 is sequential and can be seen as two related parts (chapter 12 and chapter 14) with a perspectival parenthesis (chapter 13, the great hymn in praise of love) in between. These chapters concern the nature of the church and the basis of its unity. At the heart of the issue is a relatively small group within the church who have the gift of speaking in tongues, or "glossolalia." It is likely that these persons are the same elitist, status-conscious ones whose presence in Corinth I have noted from the start of my discussion of 1 Corinthians. So Paul takes up the Corinthians' own question about spiritual gifts and declares that "there are varieties of gifts" (12:4), various ministries and different ways of working within the church (12:5–6), "but it is the same God who inspires them all in every one" (12:6). There is variety—and the working of the church must manifest it—but that differentiation must not cause anyone to lose sight of the fundamental unity that binds diverse people together in Christ.

As the passage unfolds, various gifts are twice listed. Both times, tongues and their interpretation are noted last (12:8–10, 28–30; *cf.* 13:8). In and around those lists, Paul tries to instruct the Corinthians about all gifts. Whatever gift one has, it is not one's own doing. Rather it is a "manifestation of the Spirit" that is to be used "for the common good" (12:7). The term "common good" is the same root word, translated as "helpful," that was used in Paul's critique of Corinthian freedom (10:23), where he followed their slogan "All things are lawful" with "But not all things are helpful." The two points parallel one another: one's actions are to be "helpful" to others; the Spirit's gift is to be used for the "common good." The Spirit allocates gifts as the Spirit wills (12:11; *cf.* 7:7). So Paul undercuts the grounds for boasting of possessing any particular gift. Gifts are not distributed on the basis of request or merit.

In order to explain how the various gifts work together for the common good, Paul employs the metaphor of the body and its members. It is ideal for his purposes. Everyone knows that "the body is one" (that makes clear the unity), and that it "has many members" (that makes room for the diversity). "So it is with Christ" (12:12), Paul declares: "We were all baptized into one body" (12:13).

How should the members of that body get along with one another? Paul pictures the parts of the body in strife with one another. And he pushes his point in two distinct ways. In the first, he attacks low self-evaluation. The foot laments that it is not a hand, and so considers itself not part of the body; but "that would not make it any less a part of the body" (12:15). The same is true if the ear should find it were not an eye. By logical extension, Paul reasons that if the whole body were an eye, then "where would be the sense of smell?" (12:17). In a restatement of 12:11, Paul declares that "God arranged the organs in the body" as God chose (12:18). After all, the body would be lost if every part were the same.

Then the metaphor is considered with regard to a second problem: low evaluation of others. One part of the body—for instance, the eye or the head—cannot say to another part that it is not needed (12:21). Having declared that, Paul embarks on a curious argument. Parts of the body may seem weaker and less honorable. Consider, he says, what we do about them. We give them greater honor and treat them with greater modesty (12:23) by clothing them. The result? "God has so composed the body, giving the greater honor to the inferior part, that there may be no discord in the body, but that the members may have the same care for one another" (12:24–25; RSV). Accordingly, Paul declares a principle that shows the interlinking of the various members of the body of Christ: "If one member suffers, all suffer together; if one member is honored, all rejoice together" (12:26; *cf.* Rom 12:15).

Chapter 14 shows how this interlinking and reciprocity of members works. There, the problem underlying chapter 12 (namely, how are the Spirit-given gifts, especially speaking in tongues, best put to use for the common good?) comes to the fore. Glossolalia is not to be treated differently from any other gift. It is to be used in love and will have edification as its goal.

There is nothing wrong with speaking in tongues. Tongues have a proper place in worship (14:26–27) as long as there is interpretation. The test that Paul insists upon throughout this chapter is whether one's efforts and gifts work to edify or build up other Christians. It is a familiar test by this point in the letter: whether things are helpful; whether they are for the common good; whether they are done out of love. Eagerness for "manifestations of the Spirit" is all right, but one must "strive to excel in building up the church" (14:12; *cf.* 14:5, 17). Further in the same chapter, he states his principle point-blank: "Let all things be done for edification" (14:26). Prophecy builds up the church, Paul says (14:3). By prophecy, Paul does not mean forecasting but speaking to people "for their upbuilding and encouragement and consolation" (14:3). Tongues plus interpretation equals prophecy, and prophecy "edifies the church" (14:4).

Somewhat like a "broken record," Paul once again applies a Corinthian problem to himself as a pattern they could emulate. He speaks in tongues "more than you all" (14:18) but he does not make use of that gift among the believers: "Nevertheless, in church I would rather speak five words with my mind, in order to instruct others, than ten thousand words in a tongue" (14:19; RSV). Also, like that same record, Paul plays back to the Corinthians the identical message that he has earlier given them about the proper use of their new freedom in Christ: do not use your freedom (or "gift of the Spirit") without regard for the well-being of others for whom Christ has died. Stated positively, the Corinthians should employ their gifts for the building up of the church. Paul wants them to grow up (14:20; *cf.* 3:1–2) from the childlike showing off of their gifts into a fuller realization of the disciplined use of those gifts in service of the community. Not only will other Christians be built up, but, Paul reckons, outsiders who wander into the worship services may be engaged (14:22–25). Paul brings it down to practical advice (14:26ff.). When they gather for worship, different people contribute different parts of the service (*cf.* 12:3, "There are varieties of gifts"), but, Paul advises, "Let all things be done for edification" (14:26; i.e., "for the common good," 12:7).

"Counsels of silence" follow. If there is no one to interpret the tongues, then the one gifted with tongues should remain silent (14:28). If a revelation comes to someone else, "let the first be silent" (14:30). And finally, in a passage (14:33b–36) that many consider a later editorial insertion into the letter (Conzelmann 1975), women are enjoined to keep silence (a stark contrast from 11:2ff.) in the churches.

[*Excursus: Women in the Pauline churches.* Across the Pauline corpus women play important leadership roles. Euodia and Syntyche are prominent in the

church at Philippi; Apphia is one of three addressees in Philemon; Prisca and other women are recognized as workers and greeted in Romans; Phoebe is identified as a deaconess of the Cenchreae church; and Chloe is known to the Corinthians. Further, as we have seen in 1 Corinthians 7, women are viewed as standing on equal footing with men in Christ. Finally, 1 Corinthians 11 shows clearly that women were praying and prophesying in the church; Paul knew it and raised absolutely no objection to it. The question might occur to someone: Why, out of all the undisputed Pauline letters, is it only the church at Corinth where any question is raised about full participation of women in the life and work of the church? Those who consider 1 Corinthians 14:33b–36 a later editorial insertion argue that this brings the Paul of the late 50s and early 60s into line with the more reactionary posture that the late-first-century churches seem to have adopted on this issue: "In this regulation we have a reflection of the bourgeois consolidation of the church, roughly on the level of the Pastoral Epistles: it binds itself to the general custom" (Conzelmann 1975).]

This section of the letter closes with an enforcement statement (14:37–40). Those who think of themselves as "spiritual"—the elite at Corinth—should recognize the truth of what he has written, Paul declares. If they do not, they are not to be recognized. Paul concludes these counsels by stating the premise from which many of his arguments have proceeded: "All things should be done decently and in order" (14:40; *cf.* 7:35). Why? Because "God is not a God of confusion but of peace" (14:33).

Directly in the middle of this lengthy discussion of spiritual gifts and their proper employment in the life of the church lies the deservedly famous "hymn of love" (chapter 13), the pivot point of Paul's reckoning not only about spiritual gifts but also about life before God in Christ. In 8:1, Paul had warned the "puffed-up" Corinthians that their wisdom was hazardous in the way they were employing it. In its place, he called for love because "love builds up." Chapter 13 portrays how love works. Whatever other gifts or powers or rights one has, they amount to nothing without love (13:1–3). Love "does not insist on its own way," but is patient and "rejoices in the right" (13:4–7). Although now, while we "see in a mirror dimly" as children, our knowledge and prophecy are imperfect, there will be a time when we shall "understand fully, even as I have been fully understood." From that vantage point, that is, when the perfect has come, we will see "face to face." Then we will be beyond our claims of knowledge and prophecy, as important as they are, but one thing will endure from here to there: love.

Though the term "love" has not occurred frequently in 1 Corinthians, it is in fact what Paul has been advocating right along. Love is the way that edification of fellow Christians is most directly accomplished. Love empowers a person—even Paul is not exempt—not to insist on one's rights if harm might result for another. Love guides the use of the gifts so that the common good is sought. Love orders the Christian life and the community of believers so that the weaker people are not trampled by the stronger ones and so that all Christians have their proper value and place in the body of Christ. Love fosters unity and wholeness without enforcing uniformity. Love allows for diversity and differentiation without establishing rank. It is for all these reasons that "love builds up" (8:1).

Questions regarding the resurrection. With chapter 15, Paul gives a lengthy treatment of the resurrection. He begins by rehearsing what he has already delivered to them as the received tradition of the church (15:3ff.). At the heart of that tradition is the death and resurrection of Jesus Christ, which Paul everywhere in his letters considers to be a completed fact of history and the heart of his gospel. Christ died and was raised from the dead (15:3ff.). It is in sharing Christ's death that believers emerge free from sin and become justified, that is, reconciled to God (*cf.* Rom 5:6ff.). All believers have in common the shared death with Christ. But Paul is usually careful to write that while believers already share Christ's death, their sharing of his resurrection or of a resurrection like his is a future expectation. Believers live toward that resurrection; they do not have it in the present. Their new life in Christ can be described as a "new creation" (2 Cor 5:17) or "newness of life" (Rom 6:4).

In this very long chapter (15), Paul tries to clarify what the resurrection is and what it means for the way the Corinthians live here and now. Various problems are addressed, and it is difficult for us to reconstruct just what questions about resurrection might have been raised by the Corinthians and what items Paul himself has introduced. In any case, when dealing with a problem, Paul typically rehearses "what we know" and then reasons from that. That practice continues in 15:3 through 15:58, where Paul reminds the Corinthians of the creedal formulation that stands at the center of his preaching: "So we preach and so you believed" (15:11). Of the items treated in this section, I single out the following for comment:

1. "How can some of you say that there is no resurrection of the dead?" (15:12). In 15:20, Paul recapitulates the creed and affirms that "in fact Christ has been raised from the dead." Significantly, he adds that the resurrected Christ is "the first fruits of those who have fallen asleep" (15:20), and that "in Christ shall all be made alive" (15:21). In two ways Paul carefully states that the resurrection of believers is a *future* event. Those who have died with Christ "*shall* all be made alive"; they do not yet have the resurrection. Second, Christ as raised from the dead is called the "first fruits," that part of the harvest which, by its dedication to God, sanctifies the remainder of the crop. That this sequence (Christ first, then others later) is at issue between Paul and the Corinthians becomes clear in 15:23: "But each in his own order: Christ the first fruits, then at his coming those who belong to Christ." I have previously noted that some Corinthians had claimed to be "already" filled, "already" rich and reigning (4:8). Perhaps these same people (the elitist minority in the Corinthian church that we have seen throughout 1 Corinthians) are the ones who also think that there is no future resurrection precisely because they have understood the resurrection to be a "spiritual" thing that has already taken place in their lives. Paul's corrective answer is "Christ has been raised from the dead" (15:20); so the tradition claims and so we all believe. But Christ is the first fruits; the rest of us have to wait our turn at Christ's end-time coming.

To hold otherwise—to claim that some spiritualized resurrection is already fully possible in this life and in this broken world—is to diminish the significance of mortality and of struggles in this life. Furthermore, it also confuses what God has already accomplished in believers with the ultimate glory of what will be God's finished work in them. Let us look at Paul's sequential arguments for both of these points.

2. "Why am I in peril every hour? . . . I die every day!" (15:30–31). Christ's resurrection and its promise of life that overcomes death transform the way believers live in the present. Furthermore, Christ's resurrection transforms the way they understand their struggles. "The form of this world is passing away" (1 Cor 7:31), so Christians live and struggle in the world as persons caught "in between": between the "already" of Christ's death (by which sin's power is broken), and the "not yet" of God's ultimate redemption of all creation (Rom 8). Though renewed and walking in "newness of life" (Rom 6:4), believers live in a world that "itself will be set free from its bondage to decay and obtain the glorious liberty of the children of God" (Rom 8:21). So God's work in individuals and in the world is begun, but not completed. Accordingly, the resurrection that believers confidently anticipate is in continuity with the new creation that God has already begun; but, at the same time (insofar as Christians still live in a world marked by brokenness and sin), the resurrection is in discontinuity with their present sufferings and struggles. In the meantime, short of sharing a resurrection like Christ's, Christians live in the world, but they live according to the new creation, not according to the standards of the world (cf Gal 6:14). Thus, in the world, Christians encounter perils (1 Cor 15:30). And any life of freedom (15:32–34) that does not incorporate care for others is shamefully inappropriate.

3. "But some one will ask, 'How are the dead raised? With what kind of body do they come?'" (15:35). Whatever God has already accomplished in believers—as great as that is, amounting as it does to a new life—pales by comparison with what God is yet to do. But the former provides analogs of the latter, a vista from which one can imagine the future of God's redemptive work already begun. Paul illuminates his comparison and contrast of the present and future life of the Christian by reference to a seed that produces new life only by being sown and dying. As the Spirit gives gifts to individuals as the Spirit chooses (12:11), so in the resurrection God gives the body God has chosen for the individual. What is perishable becomes imperishable (15:42), what is sown in dishonor and

weakness is raised in glory and power (15:43–44). As surely as there is a physical body in this life, so there will be a spiritual body (15:44) in the life to come. The perishable nature will put on the imperishable (15:53). This "in-between" world is the arena in which Christians live—until the end. On the one side, it is a world marked by finitude, suffering, and struggles—and Christians are in no wise protected from those tribulations; on the other side, Christians live in confidence and hope that "we shall all be changed" (15:51; restated in 15:52). God's work begun in believers as they shared Christ's death will come to full harvest in the end time when they share a resurrection like Christ's. Because of this confidence, Paul exhorts the Corinthians to "be steadfast, immovable, always abounding in the work of the Lord, knowing that in the Lord your labor is not in vain" (15:58; RSV). Christians labor to grow toward maturity in the faith; they work to build up other Christians. The Christian life is not just an ordeal that must be endured; Christians' labors take on added significance because by doing them believers coordinate with the great work that God has begun in Christ's death and resurrection and that God will complete at the end of this age. They do these works because God is at work in them and in the world "both to will and to work for [God's] good pleasure" (Phil 2:12–13).

The "contribution for the saints": the final item from the Corinthians' letter to Paul (16:1ff.). The Corinthians have asked Paul a question concerning the one-time collection that (at the Jerusalem conference [Gal 2:1–10]) Paul agreed to pull together from his churches to give to their fellow Christians at Jerusalem. Later, in 2 Corinthians (chapters 8 and 9), there will be further discussion of this matter. Other churches besides Corinth had questions about this collection (Gal 2:1ff.; cf. Rom 15:25ff.). In 1 Corinthians, however, Paul treats the collection on the level of logistics; that is, how they are to go about gathering the collection and how it will be delivered. Paul may or may not himself go with the offering to its Jerusalem destination (16:4). By the time he writes Romans, his last extant letter, he has definitely decided that he must deliver the collection, even at a certain risk to his life (Rom 15:30ff.).

Closing matters: Paul shares with the Corinthians his travel plans (16:5–9). At the writing of this present letter, he is in Ephesus (16:8) and is enjoying a good response to his work, so he will stay there until Pentecost. After that, he expects to travel through Macedonia and then arrive in the south for what he hopes may be a more protracted stay with the Corinthians. In the meantime, Timothy will make a shorter visit to them and he should be sped on his way back to Paul (16:10–11). Apollos did not see fit to visit the Corinthians now, even though Paul "strongly urged" him to do so (16:12). Paul's concluding admonitions are: "Be watchful, stand firm in your faith, be courageous, be strong. Let all that you do be done in love" (16:13–14). That this letter should end on a call for love in all things can be no surprise.

The commendation of three Corinthians (Stephanas, Fortunatus, and Achaicus) who may be the bearers of this letter (16:15–18) precedes greetings from other Christians (16:19–20) and Paul's own handwritten greeting (16:21). The letter closes with an enforcement formula ("If any one has no love for the Lord, let him be accursed" [16:22]), and with the traditional Pauline "grace" (or "benediction" [16:23]), to which, significantly, Paul appends one more affirmation of his love, this time love for "you all in Christ Jesus" (16:24).

THE "PAINFUL LETTER" (LETTER NO. 3)

Second Corinthians provides the next evidence for Paul's ongoing conversation with the Corinthians. Scholars generally concede that 2 Corinthians, as it stands in the New Testament, is composed of fragments of other letters that Paul wrote to the inhabitants of that city; but there is no consensus over the precise limits of those letter-fragments, nor is there agreement concerning their historical order (Furnish 1984). First, as to the composite character of 2 Corinthians, the most obvious evidence is the radical change of tone from the opening chapters (1–9) to the subsequent chapters (10–13). In the former, Paul declares that it had pained him greatly to write them a stern letter (2 Cor 2:4, 7:8), but he rejoices that the letter caused them to mend their ways (7:9ff.). By contrast the tone of 2 Corinthians 10–13 is one of anger, distress, self-defense, and thinly veiled threats.

The Corinthians have destroyed the confidence that Paul had in them (12:20, 13:10).

For the purposes of this essay, I will assume that 2 Corinthians 1–9 belongs to one letter and that 2 Corinthians 10–13 is a piece of a subsequent letter. We cannot determine in either case how much of each letter has been preserved in the canonical 2 Corinthians. Neither can we be sure how much time passed between Letter No. 2 (the canonical 1 Corinthians) and the letter reflected in 2 Corinthians 1–9. Similarly we are unable to be certain how much time elapsed between Paul's writing of 2 Corinthians 1–9 and 10–13.

One can, however, determine that important developments have affected both Paul and the Corinthians between the writing of 1 Corinthians and 2 Corinthians 1–9. Let us catalog some of these developments:

- Paul made a "painful visit" to the Corinthians during which things did not work out as he had hoped (2 Cor 1:23–2:1).
- Paul has written yet another letter (Letter No. 3), often referred to as his "tearful letter," or his "painful letter," to the Corinthians. Though some suggest that 2 Corinthians 10–13 is in fact a fragment of the "painful letter," it may be reasonable to suppose that letter is simply lost to us (Furnish 1984).
- Titus, Paul's trusted aide, has visited the Corinthians in an effort to see how they are doing. On returning to Paul, Titus confirmed that Paul's boasting about the Corinthians was appropriate (2 Cor 7:14) and that they longed for Paul and had great zeal for him (7:7).
- Outsiders have come into Corinth and insinuated themselves and their version of the gospel into the life of the church. As these outsiders have striven to establish their own credentials and thereby their authority, they have undercut Paul's standing. In 1 Corinthians, the problems were internal, namely how the Christian elitists and the rest of the church cared for and related to one another; by the time of the writing of 2 Corinthians, outsiders and the Corinthians' response to them are central.
- Paul's own well-being has been challenged by recent special difficulties, perhaps even a threat to his life (2 Cor 1:8ff.).

- Paul promised another visit to Corinth, but it did not take place (1:15ff.).
- Further questions have emerged among some Corinthians concerning the collection for the church at Jerusalem (2 Cor 8:1–9:15).

Like Letter No. 1, we learn of Letter No. 3 by Paul's reference to it in another letter, which I shall refer to as Letter No. 4 (2 Cor 1–9). As to the contents of the proposed Letter No. 3, one can deduce very little. After all, Paul does not need to rehearse the details of the letter because the Corinthians know exactly what it said, and it has already achieved its desired results. By the manner in which Paul describes Letter No. 3, we can tell that it dealt with "the one who did the wrong" and with "the one who suffered the wrong" (2 Cor 7:12). The Corinthians know what "the wrong" refers to and they also know the identity of the two people, though we can know neither.

One may assume that Paul also took care in that letter "to let you know the abundant love that I have for you" (2 Cor 2:4). Whatever other topics the letter might have addressed are unknown to us.

Something can be discerned, however, about Paul's disposition and purpose in sending Letter No. 3. It was no easier for Paul to write the letter than it was for the Corinthians to receive it: "I wrote you out of much affliction and anguish of heart and with many tears" (2 Cor 2:4; cf. 7:8).

THE PRESENT CANONICAL 2 CORINTHIANS 1–9 (LETTER NO. 4)

Between the writing of Letters 3 and 4, Titus returns to Paul. His report is good. The Corinthians have taken Letter No. 3—and indeed Paul himself—to heart (2 Cor 7:7). The Corinthians' "godly grief," their "indignation," their "alarm," and their "eagerness to clear" themselves (7:11) comfort Paul and restore his confidence in them. The Corinthians seem once again to have some confidence in Paul, even though a few issues continue to bother them.

Paul had "wanted to come" to them (1:15). Apparently, he failed to appear when they expected, and one can deduce from his apologetic answer that he has received some criticism for this failure. Does he speak out of both sides of his mouth (1:17)? No, he

declares. By God's faithfulness, Paul's whole life is offered as a grateful "Amen!" through Christ to God, to God's glory (1:20). As God is his witness, Paul purposefully decided not to "make you another painful visit" (2:1), but chose to write instead. The reason for writing was to straighten things out so that when Paul could visit them it might appropriately be a time marked by joy for all (2:3).

With 2:12–13 Paul continues to account for his travels, and (one might suppose), indirectly gives the reason why, though he did not come to Corinth, he was, nonetheless, greatly concerned about the Corinthians. Wherever he goes, whether to Corinth, or (in this case) to Troas, he goes "to preach the gospel of Christ" and, as usual, "a door was opened for me" (2:12). But Paul could gain no quietude because Titus (who would have a report about Corinth) could not be found in Troas (2:13). So Paul pressed on to Macedonia. What does Paul assume about his work and journeys? That God, in Christ, leads him (2:14); that God makes known "the fragrance of the knowledge [of God]" through Paul; and that Paul himself is the "sweet fragrance of Christ to God" in the midst of those who are being saved and those who are perishing (2:15). But there is no arrogance on account of his special role: "Who is sufficient for these things?" (2:16). The Corinthians themselves are proof enough that Paul is living through Christ toward God as he should. Paul's own comportment also witnesses to the propriety of Paul's life before God.

Paul's Opponents

Not only do some Corinthians have problems with Paul, but they also seem to have come under the influence of outsiders. Although Paul does not directly describe his rivals in Letter No. 4, one can reconstruct a profile of Paul's picture of them. They have come into town with "letters of recommendation" (3:1). Accordingly, Paul describes them by indirection as "those who pride themselves on a man's position and not on his heart" (5:12). Twice Paul casts aspersions on their sincerity (1:12, 2:17) and once he suggests they are "hucksters" (2:17). (Does 4:5 intimate that they preach not the gospel but themselves?)

Paul's Self-Defense

Paul's sense of Corinthian attraction to these outside authorities leads him on several occasions

261

throughout this letter-fragment to a self-defense (an apologia) for his ministry. His ministry is built on a life marked by "holiness and godly sincerity" (1:12). Excluded are "disgraceful, underhanded ways" and living cunningly (4:2), and making plans "like a worldly man" (1:17). Instead, "we work with you for your joy" (1:24). All Paul's work with and for his readers is grounded in a genuine caring for them (6:11–12, 7:2–3). The Corinthians themselves are the only letter of recommendation Paul has (3:2). The "proof" of Paul's ministry will be in the record that the Corinthians (and Paul) take into "the day of the Lord Jesus" (1:14), into the judgment. There Paul hopes "that you can be proud of us as we can be of you" (1:14).

In the meantime, Paul sees his role as a "persuader" (5:11). What he is comes from the heart and is not just a "front" put up for a good showing (5:12). Paul views himself as God's "servant" (*diakonos* is the term used in 6:4) whose ministry is documented in hardships (6:4–5) and by the way the world views and treats him (6:8–10). Paul's mark is "sincerity" (2:17; *cf.* 1:12). He speaks in Christ, before God, as one from God (2:17).

Comparisons and Contrasts in Letter No. 4

Developments at Corinth have had a profound effect upon the way Paul casts his thought in Letter No. 4. Particularly, a growing opposition from some Corinthians and the insurgency of rival religious leaders has brought out more clearly a basic Pauline tendency to see things in comparisons and contrasts.

Two groups of people: Unbelievers and believers. From 2:15 onward, Paul has entertained the notion that the gospel sorts people into two groups: those who are being saved and those who are perishing (2:16; *cf.* Rom 1:17–18). Realistically he recognizes that the gospel remains veiled to some whose minds are blinded so that they are kept from "seeing the light of the gospel of the glory of Christ, who is the likeness of God" (2 Cor 4:3–5).

As some scholars suggest, 6:14–7:1 may be a later, non-Pauline addition to the text (Thrall 1977). At best, it is in tension with the counsels about marriage between believers and unbelievers in 1 Corinthians 7:12–16. Indeed, 2 Corinthians 6:14–7:1 seeks to construct a wall of distinction between the insiders and unbelievers and supports it with Scripture (6:16–18). In 1 Corinthians (see 1 Cor 10:23ff.; 14:16, 23ff.), Paul draws few strictly defined borders between the believers and the rest of the people in Corinth. In 2 Corinthians 6:14–7:1, however, a separatist, holiness response is expected (7:1). On the other hand, 6:14–7:1 does fit the shift in perspective and situation of Letter No. 4, where outsiders are viewed as troublesome and to be avoided (Dahl 1977).

Two ministries, two covenants, and two glories. The encounter with rival ministers and charges against his own ministry, combined with his conviction that his work creates two distinct groups sharply delineated from one another, allow Paul to develop the idea of two very distinct ministries—his own and that of his opponents. His own ministry he associates with a new covenant linked with life and the spirit. His opponents' ministry is the "ministry [*diakonia*] of death, carved in letters on stone" (3:7), which is further identified as the "ministry of condemnation" (3:8). In contrast he calls his alternative the "ministry of Spirit" (3:8) or the "ministry of righteousness" (3:9).

There are even two glories associated with the two ministries. The ministry of condemnation is credited with a "glory" (Gr., *doxa*, Au. trans.; *cf.* RSV, "splendor"; 3:7, 9, 10, 11) but a glory that is "fading" (3:7, 11, 13), or, put differently, one that, though it had glory, can be said to have no glory in light of the surpassing glory now seen (3:10). By contrast, there is the glory (3:11) of the ministry of the Spirit (3:8) or ministry of righteousness (3:9). Its glory is greater (3:8, 9) and "permanent" (3:11); but the comparative, "greater glory," slips into the superlative, "surpassing glory" (3:10).

And with that Paul makes a clear identification of his opponents and their ministry with the glory that because it is so massively overshadowed by the "surpassing glory" may be said to have no glory at all (3:10). Like the minds of the Israelites in the presence of Moses, their minds are also hardened, their eyes are clouded, and they cannot read the scriptures with understanding (3:14–15). On the contrary, Paul's followers are identified with this "new covenant" and its surpassing glory because of the working of the Holy Spirit: "Written not with ink but with the Spirit of the living God, not on tablets of stone but on tablets of human hearts" (3:3; RSV). They are the ones who know that "the Spirit gives life" (3:6), and who have been given the Spirit "in our hearts as a guarantee" (1:22). Their hope is based on this gift, which enables them to be bold (3:12).

"New covenant" (3:6) is a rare expression in Paul's letters (elsewhere only in 1 Cor 11:25 in the pre-Pauline eucharistic words of Jesus), so it is difficult to be certain what it means for Paul. What follows in chapter 3 links the new covenant directly to the gift and working of the Spirit. Where the Spirit is (2 Cor 3:17) there is not only freedom, but there is also a clear, unhindered reading of the old covenant (i.e., Israel's scriptures; 3:14–16). Only through Christ are minds renewed (*cf.* Rom 12:2) and the veil lifted (2 Cor 3:16). The "old covenant," read without Christ, remains veiled "to this day" (3:15). When someone turns to the Lord "the veil is removed" (3:16).

One final matter regarding the two ministries and their two covenants deserves comment. The translation of *diakonia* in 3:7–9 as "dispensation" (RSV) has contributed to a consideration of this passage not as a contrast of two ministries as I have here suggested, but of two stages in history where the former is invalidated by the latter (in more modern categories, Judaism as invalidated by Christianity). But Paul credits the "old covenant" with a glory—a glory that only appears to be no glory in the dazzling light of the second, surpassing glory. With the surpassing glory and the new covenant available in Christ, the veil that used to cover the reading of the old covenant is removed (3:18). Paul does not say that the old covenant is removed. In fact, the old and new covenant comments in chapter 3 must be read with 1:20 in mind: "For all the promises of God [knowable through the scriptures of the old covenant] find their Yes in him [Christ]." After all, the minds (3:15–16) and the faces (3:18) of the beholders are veiled; not that there is some inherent inadequacy in the old covenant. Paul abandons neither his Jewish roots nor the former covenant; he simply sees them in a fresh new light (Stendahl 1976).

View to the future. In part, the freedom of believers is secured by the confidence with which they can look openly toward the future and what it holds for them. "And we all, with unveiled face, beholding

the glory of the Lord, are being changed into his likeness from one degree of glory to another; for this comes from the Lord who is the Spirit" (3:18; RSV). Believers are those who see clearly what is going on, whose eyes are fixed on the Lord's glory, and who "are being changed" from glory into glory (i.e., something is happening in their lives). And all of this, like Paul's own sufficiency (3:5–6), comes from the Lord; that is, it is a gift of the Spirit. Ministry of and in the new covenant is made possible only by the grace and mercy of God. The call to this ministry and the enabling mercy of God accompanying the call fill Paul with hope ("we do not lose heart," 4:1; *cf.* 4:16).

View of the present: Suffering and human frailty and the "walk of faith." All believers share and participate in Christ's suffering (1:5ff.). To become a believer is no guarantee of an uninterrupted string of victories; neither does it insulate one from suffering and tribulation. In fact, to die with Christ ensures that one will experience tribulation in the world. Furthermore, Paul recognizes the mortality and frailty of the earthly human body. Nevertheless, God has set the glory of God, the new creation, precisely within human frailty and misery, in the earthenware of daily life. Noteworthy at the other extreme is that Paul nowhere identifies suffering as punishment from God.

God's glory has been made present in unspectacular clay containers, symbolizing frailty, fragility, and finitude (4:7). A hardship list follows (4:8–9) as an illustration of the quality of life in Christ: suffering and difficulties will be present, but they cannot destroy or crush the believers (*cf.* Rom 8:38–39). In fact, believers have so fully identified with Christ by dying with him that they carry "in the body the death of Jesus" (2 Cor 4:10), and they live "always being given up to death for Jesus' sake" (4:11). These claims are very much like those Paul made exclusively about himself in 2 Corinthians 1:8–9. Whether 4:7–12 should be taken as strictly about Paul, or interpreted as I have here (as concerning all believers), is a difficult matter.

Paul's confidence toward the future is grounded in his conviction that, by dying with Christ and sharing his suffering, the believers have become part of the re-creative process that God has begun with the death of Christ. Believers can know that the God "who raised the Lord Jesus will raise us also with Jesus" and bring all believers ultimately into God's presence (4:14). Accordingly, this confident hope, itself a present reality, is the basis for thanksgiving, for glorifying God (4:15), and for not losing heart (4:16).

The whole story is not told by identifying humans with breakable clay pots (4:7). They are that, but there is more. The "outer nature" may be "wasting away" (4:16) and believers may be marked by suffering and death (4:9–12), but "our inner nature is being renewed day by day" (4:16) by God. That puts suffering and hardships in a different perspective: when viewed in light of the "eternal weight of glory beyond all comparison," believers' affliction is "momentary" and preparatory. (I must note here, that, as with the "two glories" discussion earlier, what began fundamentally as a comparison by Paul has moved to a contrast as a means of highlighting what the believers have in Christ.) To go by what is observable, to judge by externals, would be mistaken and could lead to despair. Faith attunes one to the eternal and hidden work that God has begun in Christ. That is what it means to "walk by faith, not by sight" (5:7). So, "we look not to the things that are seen but to the things that are unseen; for the things that are seen are transient, but the things that are unseen are eternal" (4:18; RSV).

How and why Christians can look to the future with hope. Here in this world "we groan" or sigh and are weighed down with burdens almost too much to bear (5:4; *cf.* 1:8). In this mortal life, believers "long to put on our heavenly dwelling" (Paul probably refers here to the heavenly body he wrote about in 1 Cor 15) and are buoyed by the hope that "what is mortal may be swallowed up by life" (2 Cor 5:4). How can believers have that confident hope? Not by observing their bodies or how things are going in the world, but only by recognizing that the one "who has prepared us for this very thing is God, who has given us the Spirit as a guarantee" (5:5).

Because it depends completely upon God, and because believers know that the Holy Spirit already given to them is a "down payment" guaranteeing the remainder of what is promised, "we are always of good courage" (5:6; repeated in v. 8). Then Paul puts worldly concerns and earthly things in perspective: it matters not whether believers live or die (*cf.* Rom 14:7–8); what matters is whether "we make it our aim to please" the Lord (2 Cor 5:9; *cf.* Rom 12:1), before whose judgment seat everyone must appear (2 Cor 5:10).

The love of Christ controls us (5:14). The Greek translated "love of Christ" can mean Christ's love for people or people's love for Christ, and there is probably no reason why both could not have been intended by Paul. The verb translated "controls" means to "hold within bounds" but it also means to "urge on, impel." Again, both translations suggest important ways in which the love of Christ functions in the life of the believers. In any case, the love of Christ works in that way because believers are convinced that Christ has died for all (5:15) so that the believers can live for Christ.

That makes all the difference in the way believers live in the world. "From now on, therefore, we regard no one from a human point of view" even though Christ was once understood in that way (5:16). Paul now no longer views anyone—it does not say just believers, but *anyone*—as if Christ had not died for them ("he died for all," 5:14–15). Whether anyone has responded to the grace of God in the death of Jesus Christ is not determinative of how Paul relates to them. For Paul it is sufficient to know that each one in the world is one for whom Christ died.

Those "in Christ" are "a new creation" (5:17). They were enemies of God (Rom 5:10), but now they are reconciled (2 Cor 5:18), and are thereby a part of the larger work of God, who, in Christ, is reconciling the world to God (5:19). Not only are the believers reconciled, but they are also entrusted with the "message" (5:19) and "ministry of reconciliation" (5:18). So Paul and other believers work together with God and "entreat you not to accept the grace of God in vain" (6:1). Paul, the "persuader," says "Behold, now is the acceptable time; behold, now is the day of salvation" (6:2).

The collection. In 1 Corinthians 16:1 and following, Paul responds to the Corinthians, who had written to him about the collection for the church at Jerusalem. There his treatment of the matter is cursory; Paul provides some logistical suggestions for how the collection might be gathered. But by the time of Letter No. 4 (2 Cor 1–9), either the proportions of the problem have changed or Paul has come to realize that he misjudged the degree of support earlier. In

Letter No. 4 two chapters are devoted to the collection (Betz 1985). Accordingly, the collection has to be considered one of the main reasons why Letter No. 4 was written. On a practical level, the restoration of mutual confidence established in 2 Corinthians 1–7 provides the context requisite for the protracted discussion of the collection.

Paul reports how the Macedonians—the two main churches in that area were at Philippi and Thessalonica—provided a model response. Though in "extreme poverty" and in great affliction, the Macedonians freely gave "beyond their means, . . . begging us earnestly for the favor of taking part in the relief of the saints" (8:2–4; RSV). Paul designates Titus to "complete among you [Corinthians] this gracious work" (8:6), and he calls upon the Corinthians, whom he dubs specialists in abundance "in faith, in utterance, in knowledge, in all earnestness, and in your love for us," to abound in "this gracious work also" (8:7).

Paul pictures the collection as a wonderful opportunity for the Corinthians to show others that their love is genuine (8:8). Paul's counsel is buttressed by a christological portrait: Christ, though rich, became poor for your sake, so that, by his poverty, you might become rich (8:9). Paul invokes a twofold principle of equality and of meeting the needs of those who have less from those who have more. His purpose is not to overburden anyone "but that as a matter of equality your abundance at the present time should supply their want" (8:14). Paul finds this in accord with Scripture (7:15; Exod 16:18).

Titus is commended as a pattern for the Corinthians. Not only did he accept Paul's appeal, but he is also eager to go to them in this matter (8:17). With him Paul sends two unnamed others, the "famous" brother (8:18) and the "tested" brother (8:22). All of this openness and cooperation shows Paul's blamelessness in his dealings on the issue (8:20). After all, he aims at what is "honorable not only in the Lord's sight but also in the sight" of others (8:21). When these people arrive at Corinth, the believers will have an opportunity to "give proof, before the churches, of your love and of our boasting about you to these men" (8:24).

Brethren are being sent, though their mission may be superfluous because of the Corinthians' eagerness, about which Paul has boasted to the Macedonians, saying, "Achaia [the area including Corinth] has been ready for a year" (9:2). Indeed, the Corinthians have become a pattern for the Macedonians. Lest Paul's confidence be misplaced, the brethren are being sent ahead of Paul and any Macedonians who may come with him to "arrange in advance for this gift you have promised" (9:5).

Paul continues to hope that what the Corinthians willingly began they will willingly complete (9:5). He piles up his arguments: Reluctance and compulsion are out of order (9:7); all must do as they have decided for themselves. They should know, however, not only that you reap as you sow, whether sparingly or bountifully (9:6), but also that "God loves a cheerful giver" (9:7). Stinginess is inappropriate because the God Paul knows can provide abundantly, and Scripture makes that clear (9:9; *cf.* Ps 112:9). Paul assures the Corinthians that they "will be enriched in every way for great generosity" (9:11), and besides, at issue is not just a gift for the saints, but "many thanksgivings to God" (9:12).

The appeal culminates in an affirmation of the fundamental unity and reciprocity of all Christians: the Corinthians will glorify God by their contribution for the saints in Jerusalem "while they long for you and pray for you" (9:13–14). And all of this is made possible because of God's grace at work. So Paul concludes with an exclamation: "Thanks be to God for his inexpressible gift!" (9:15).

That brings us to the end of what remains of Letter No. 4 from Paul to the Corinthians. It is difficult to find much evidence by which to assess what happened in response to that letter. One can tell from Paul's letter to the Romans (15:26), the last of the Pauline letters, that the Corinthians did in fact take part in the collection.

The other piece of evidence for assessing the results of Letter No. 4 is found in Letter No. 5 (2 Cor 10–13). In the latter there is no explicit mention of the former. But the tone and content of what is preserved of Letter No. 5 make it clear that, from Paul's perspective, things in Corinth have deteriorated markedly (Furnish 1984). Let us now turn to consider the last "window" we have into a Pauline communication with Corinth.

THE PRESENT CANONICAL
2 CORINTHIANS 10–13
(LETTER NO. 5)

There is no way to know how much time elapsed between the writing of Letters 4 and 5. Also, one cannot determine what percentage of Letter No. 5 is preserved in 2 Corinthians 10–13. We can be sure, however, that Paul writes Letter No. 5 in a spirit of distress, anger, and concern. Letter No. 4 showed that some outsiders had made inroads into the community of believers at Corinth and had begun to gain a following. Letter No. 5, by the amount of attention given to rival religious leaders and by the defense of his apostolic status, shows that Paul considers those people a real and present threat to his standing at Corinth and to the well-being of the Christians there (Sampley 1988).

The letter-fragment opens with an implicit reference to a claim that is going around Corinth about Paul: he is meek enough when he is with us, but he becomes very bold when he is sheltered by distance and writes another of his letters (10:1). Paul turns the charge back on the Corinthians, saying that he hopes that when he is next present in Corinth he will not have to "show boldness with such confidence as I count on showing against some who suspect us" of walking according to the values of the world (10:2). Paul warns them that he is not lacking in the power of God (10:4).

The Corinthians should look at what is clear: if it is a question of who has basis for confidence (*cf.* 2 Cor 3:4–6), they should not underestimate Paul (10:7). Paul's authority comes not from a comparative judgment regarding others (10:12); rather, his authority—for building them up, not for destroying them—was given directly to Paul by the Lord (10:8). Because of that, he can boast: "I shall not be put to shame" (10:8).

Paul assures the Corinthians that he will not boast beyond limits (10:13, 15) and certainly not of the labors of others (10:15). Nor does he boast (as perhaps some do) over work done in another's field (10:16). Like Jeremiah's, his boasting is focused on God, on the Lord (10:17; *cf.* Jer 9:24). Besides, whether one is found acceptable depends not on one's own self-commendation but on the commendation of the Lord (2 Cor 10:18). Paul feels himself driven to "a little foolishness" and hopes the Corinthians put up with him in it (11:1). He confesses to a great zeal for them, a zeal appropriate to God and to Paul's role as matchmaker in getting Christ and the church together as bridegroom and bride. But as the serpent deceived Eve, Paul fears that the church "will be led astray from a sincere and pure devotion to Christ" (11:3). Is not that exactly what is happening to the Corinthians? Paul accuses them of submitting "readily enough" to outsiders who have come among them preaching a different gospel and another Jesus (11:4). Paul admits that he may not be a great orator (11:6), but he insists that he does not have to take a back seat to "these superlative apostles" (11:5).

Paul asks, in effect, "Where did I go wrong with you people? Abasing myself and preaching a cost-free gospel to you is being treated as a sin" (11:7; my paraphrase). Then Paul reminds them that, even when he was in need, he never burdened them (11:9). The people from Macedonia took care of his needs. Some in Corinth may view this practice as "robbery" of other churches (11:8). But Paul is undaunted. He will continue to refrain from accepting support from the Corinthians (11:9). And it is not because he does not love them. "God knows I do!" (11:11).

This practice distinguishes Paul clearly from those intruding, masquerading preachers whom he characterizes as "false apostles, deceitful workmen, disguising themselves as apostles of Christ" (11:13). (Paul probably uses the term "apostle" here not as a designation of any of the Twelve. It may well have been the self-designation of these people, who, like Paul, were never members of the original group of disciples of the earthly Jesus.) As if those accusations were not negative enough, Paul links these "apostles," and their way of operating, with Satan. Just as surely as "Satan disguises himself as an angel of light" (11:14), "his servants also disguise themselves as servants of righteousness" (11:15). Paul declares that anyone can see the emptiness of their boast that "they work on the same terms as we do" (11:12).

If someone could boast, Paul thinks it would be he (11:18). And, though he knows the ridiculousness of it, he feels himself drawn into it like a fool. "I repeat, let no one think me foolish; but even if you do, accept me as a fool, so that I too may boast a little"

(11:16; RSV). Paul considers this is not too much to ask of the Corinthians because they show, by their fawning attention to the rival, false religious leaders, that they "gladly bear with fools" and put up with it if people make slaves of them and otherwise take advantage of them (11:19–20). With irony designed once again to highlight the differences between himself and the so-called apostles, Paul says: "To my shame, I must say, we were too weak for that [i.e., to take advantage of them]" (11:21a).

The fool's talk continues (11:21b) as Paul moves the contrast between himself and the rival apostles beyond one of how they fund their missions. Paul claims to be a better "servant of Christ" than they are, even though he knows that such talk can only be a sign of his being a "madman" (11:23). Nevertheless, he feels driven to catalog the evidence of his superior servanthood to Christ. And what is that evidence? A long list of hardships that he has endured as he has lived true to his call to preach the gospel to gentiles such as the Corinthians (11:23–27). These difficulties display his weakness: it must be remembered that, with the Corinthians, Paul has already established that weakness lets the power of the gospel work more fully and directly. Paul's own hardships identify him, and therefore his gospel, with those who are weak and who have stumbled in life (11:29). Then he offers a specific example of his weakness and deliverance: in Damascus he avoided yet another arrest and who knows what related punishment by a dramatic escape by basket through a window in the town wall (11:32–33).

These hardships only begin to tap Paul's resources for boasting. How about visions and revelations? Such an amazing story follows that Paul makes a thinly veiled effort to describe it as if it happened to someone other than himself (Baird 1985). Paul tells of a man—himself—who "was caught up to the third heaven . . . into Paradise" (12:2–3), and who received a revelation "of things that cannot be told, which man may not utter" (12:4). It is on behalf of that man that Paul boasts (12:5); if he were to boast on his own behalf, he would only boast of his weaknesses (12:5), just as he has done in 11:22–33. If he did wish to boast, Paul writes, he could do so because, as this story of his translation into heaven reveals, he would "be speaking the truth" (12:6). But,

like a cardplayer who purposefully drops an ace onto the table so that all the other players can know that he is holding a strong hand, Paul makes nothing more of this extraordinary vision. Instead he declares that he would rather have others' opinions of him based strictly on what he or she "sees in me or hears from me" (12:6).

As to what others can see in Paul, he turns to the opposite of ecstatic heavenly visions. He tells of his "thorn in the flesh" (12:7–9). The important matter here is not the identification of the problem—people have speculated from A to Z on that. The Corinthians probably knew exactly what it was. What is important to Paul is that, though he three times asked that it be removed from him, he was refused. The Lord reassured Paul that "my grace is sufficient for you, for my power is made perfect in weakness" (12:9). Paul has understood this paradox for some time and he has been trying to help the Corinthians understand it as well. That is why Paul can boast of his weaknesses, because through them "the power of Christ" rests upon him (12:9). That is why, for the sake of Christ, Paul is "content with weaknesses, insults, hardships, persecutions, and calamities; for when I am weak, then I am strong" (12:10; RSV).

Paul realizes that with these boastings he has indeed played the fool (12:11). If the Corinthians had been in their right minds, *they* would have commended *him* and he would not have felt forced to commend himself. Even though he is nothing—when viewed from the perspective of God's power—he is "not at all inferior to these superlative apostles" (12:11). And the Corinthians should acknowledge it because the "wonders and mighty works" that are "signs of a true apostle were performed among you in all patience" (12:12). With the exception of not burdening them with his needs Paul has treated the Corinthians on at least with a par with all the other churches, and (again with irony) he begs their pardon for this "injustice" (12:13).

Paul notifies the Corinthians that he is about to pay them an official visit (12:14). As has been his custom right along, he will not be a burden for them because his interest lies in them, not in what they have. Regarding cost, Paul assures them, "I will most gladly spend and be spent for your souls" (12:15). But their accusations against Paul continue to gnaw at him. They say that Paul was ready to do anything and got the better of them by guile or fraud, that he took advantage of them (12:16–17). Paul claims the evidence denies it. Could they possibly say that Paul took advantage of them through his representatives? Through Titus? Paul sent him. How about the unnamed brother whom Paul sent with Titus (12:18)? No, they all acted in the same spirit and took the same steps (12:18). Paul then asks the Corinthians if they have been thinking that he is merely engaged in an exercise of self-defense in what he has written. Is it only or even primarily Paul's reputation that is at stake? No, he declares, that would be to misunderstand what is at issue. In the balance is the Corinthians' well-being, whether they will be found to live according to the one and only gospel and whether they will not be experiencing the "upbuilding" (12:19) that Paul knows love brings about among Christians. Instead, Paul fears that when he comes to see them he will find them beset with "quarreling, jealousy, anger, selfishness, slander, gossip, conceit, and disorder" (12:20). If that fear proves right, then Paul expects that "my God may humble me before you" and that Paul will have to fall to mourning over those whose lives are marked by sin (12:21).

So, with such an awesome prospect attached to his projected visit, Paul takes care to lay down the guidelines by which he and they will have to operate when he arrives and they try to adjudicate the differences between Paul and them. In good biblical fashion, "Any charge must be sustained by the evidence of two or three witnesses" (13:1; *cf.* Deut 19:15). He warns them—as indeed he did on his last visit—that his patience (*cf.* 12:12) is wearing thin; that, in this upcoming visit, he will not spare the ones who sinned (13:2). Some at Corinth seem to want "proof that Christ is speaking in [Paul]" (13:3). Paul warns such people that as surely as Christ "is not weak in dealing with you" (13:3), so Paul, though weak in Christ, brings with himself the assurance that "in dealing with you we shall live with him by the power of God" (13:4). Paul tells those who are so eager to put him to the test that they had better examine themselves. Whether Paul meets the test or not, he hopes and prays that (even though he may seem to have failed) the Corinthians "may not do wrong" but may live as those who truly have Christ Jesus within

them (13:5–7). Paul has nothing to fear from their examination of him because he can do nothing "against the truth"; his only option is to work "for the truth" (13:8; *cf.* 1 Cor 4:3–5). It does not bother Paul if he is found to be "weak" and they are "strong." After all, *that* is what Paul prays for, their improvement (2 Cor 13:9). In fact, that is why he has gone to the trouble to write to them: so that when he comes to see them he will not have to "be severe in my use of the authority which the Lord has given me for building up and not for tearing down" (13:10; *cf.* 10:8). Only the Corinthians can determine, by their response to this letter, whether Paul will have to be severe when he arrives on the scene.

In the last of this letter-fragment, Paul expresses his goals for the Corinthians in little encapsulations, short sayings designed to focus the Corinthians' thinking. He bids them farewell and enjoins them: "Mend your ways, heed my appeal, agree with one another, live in peace, and the God of love and peace will be with you" (13:11; RSV). He calls for very much the opposite of what he thinks has been the divisive effect of the intruding, fake apostles and their gospel. Noteworthy in its absence from these pithy little appeals is any requested change of view regarding Paul and his status. That absence lends some credence to Paul's assertions beginning in 12:19 that he really has been using the claims about himself only to get them back on track in their Christian lives.

With his traditional greetings from the saints (13:13) and a rather fully faceted grace—"The grace of the Lord Jesus Christ and the love of God and the fellowship of the Holy Spirit be with you all" (13:14)—Paul concludes Letter No. 5.

And with it we hear the last of our record of Paul's rather lengthy and "on-again, off-again" conversations with the Corinthians. Whether he made his anticipated visit to Corinth, and if he did, what their response to him was, one simply cannot know. We do know that Paul's letter to the Romans, written probably not too long after our Letter No. 5 to the Corinthians, shows that he has definitely decided to accompany the delivery of the collection to Jerusalem and that he fears for his well-being in so doing (Rom 15:25–33). The Acts of the Apostles reports that Paul was arrested in Jerusalem (Acts 21:33), and thus his opportunity to return to Corinth was thereby terminated.

In retrospect, one must note that the apostle Paul's relation to Corinth over a period of years was marked by his great commitment to and care for the Christians there. Paul's first preaching of the gospel at Corinth had created a community of Christians from diverse social standings. All of them found themselves in a new situation, where in the midst of their day-to-day transactions they were called to begin living a new life on new terms. Paul's letters always show Paul engaged with real problems of everyday life. The agenda—and even the tone—of each letter is set not in some dispassionate, armchair fashion by someone who from transcendent heights deigns to share his thoughts with people less fortunate. Paul is nothing if not passionate, nothing if not engaged. Similarly, Paul's gospel is always directly tied to specific situations and problems, where people, attuned to what God is doing, are struggling to live in the world.

Bibliography

Books and Commentaries

Barrett, C. K. *A Commentary on the First Epistle to the Corinthians.* New York, 1968.

———. *A Commentary on the Second Epistle to the Corinthians.* New York, 1973.

Betz, Hans Dieter. *2 Corinthians 8 and 9.* Philadelphia, 1985.

Conzelmann, Hans. *1 Corinthians.* Translated by James W. Leitch. Philadelphia, 1975.

Dahl, Nils A., assisted by Paul Donahue. *Studies in Paul: Theology for the Early Christian Mission.* Minneapolis, 1977.

Furnish, Victor Paul. *II Corinthians.* Anchor Bible, vol. 32a. Garden City, N.Y. 1984.

Hurd, John Coolidge. *The Origin of I Corinthians.* New York, 1965.

Meeks, Wayne A. *The First Urban Christians: The Social World of the Apostle Paul.* New Haven, 1983.

Stendahl, Krister. *Paul Among Jews and Gentiles.* Philadelphia, 1976.

Theissen, Gerd. *The Social Setting of Pauline Christianity: Essays on Corinth.* Edited, translated, and with an introduction by John H. Schütz. Philadelphia, 1982.

Willis, Wendell Lee. *Idol Meat in Corinth: The Pauline Argument in 1 Corinthians 8 and 10.* Chico, Calif., 1985.

White, John Lee. *The Form and Function of the Body of the Greek Letter.* Missoula, 1972.

Articles

Baird, William. "Visions, Revelation, and Ministry: Reflections on 2 Cor 12:1–5 and Gal 1:11–17." *Journal of Biblical Literature* 104 (1985): 651–662.

Dahl, Nils A. "Paul and the Church at Corinth According to I Corinthians 1–4." In *Christian History and Interpretation,* edited by William Reuben Farmer et al. Cambridge, 1967.

Sampley, J. Paul. "Paul, His Opponents in 2 Cor. 10–13, and the Rhetorical Handbooks." In *The Social World of Formative Christianity and Judaism,* edited by Jacob Neusner et al. Philadelphia, 1988.

Thrall, Margaret E. "The Problem of II Cor. VI.14–VII.1 in Some Recent Discussion." *New Testament Studies* 24 (1977): 132–148.

J. PAUL SAMPLEY

Galatians

THE DOCUMENT WE know as the Epistle to the Galatians is a letter written by Paul to several churches linked to one another in three ways: they were all founded by Paul in a relatively brief span of time; they were all located in the same geographical area; and they had, finally, a common history. That shared history of the Galatian churches is the first of two major keys to the interpretation of the letter.

THE CHURCHES OF GALATIA

Prior to Paul's Arrival

We cannot be altogether certain of the locale of these churches. By Paul's time the Roman province called Galatia included not only the old Celtic kingdom in north-central Asia Minor, centered in the city of Ancyra (modern Ankara), but also the area stretching to the south, and including the cities of Iconium, Lystra, and Derbe. Most interpreters today are inclined to think of the northern region. What is important for understanding this letter is the fact that, whether in the north or in the south, the Galatians to whom Paul preached the gospel were gentiles, who worshiped gods that Jews identified as false and powerless (Gal 4:8–9).

The Arrival of Paul

For some period of time Paul was active in the mission to gentiles that was carried out from the church of Syrian Antioch, a congregation that included both Jews and gentiles. Paul was, in fact, one of the persons chosen by that church to represent it and its gentile mission at an important meeting with the church in Jerusalem, where a broad agreement was reached that the gospel would be preached to Jews in a way that left intact their observance of the Law, whereas to gentiles it would be preached without the requirement of circumcision (Gal 2:1–10). Not long after that concordant event, however, the Antioch church was shaken by a sharp debate in which Paul was a central actor.

One could have thought that the agreement reached at the Jerusalem meeting had solved the Jew-gentile issue in the church. Not so. It had been agreed not to require circumcision of gentiles. No one, however, seems to have brought up the question as to how the Jewish food laws were to be handled in a mixed congregation, such as the church of Antioch itself. A battle focused on the food laws developed in that church (see the more detailed discussion of 2:11–14 later in this essay), and in that battle Paul was politically the loser. Thereafter he withdrew from the church of Antioch.

Paul did not withdraw, however, from the task of preaching the Law-free gospel to gentiles. He merely turned to the west, peering over the horizon, as it were, to the cities of Macedonia, Thessaly, and Achaia, and intending eventually to go all the way to

Spain. Taking the overland route toward the west, he traveled from Syrian Antioch through Asia Minor, and, due to a sickness of some sort, he paused among the cities of Galatia. Here, surprised that, in spite of his illness, the preaching of the gospel bore fruit, Paul founded the Galatian churches (Gal 4:13–15). What precisely did he say to these hellenized, Greek-speaking gentiles?

The center of his message was a verbal picture of Jesus as he suffered the horrifying death of crucifixion, a death died on behalf of all people (3:1). Paul also spoke of God's having raised Jesus from the dead, giving him power over forces that threaten, intimidate, and dehumanize human beings (1:1). Thus, in the death and resurrection of Jesus Christ, God has already acted to change the world; moreover, at the future coming of Christ, God will overcome all enemies (5:5). Meanwhile, God is calling all human beings to their redemption, integrating them into the death and the life of this corporate Christ by baptism and by the receipt of Christ's Spirit. God is thus regrasping the whole world for himself, by establishing everywhere churches that are parts of his one church, the new community of persons who know themselves to be redeemed, being thereby made responsible for one another.

This message kindled a fire in the Galatians' hearts; it elicited their faith; the Spirit fell upon them; and they knew themselves to be God's outpost in their region (3:1–2, 4:6–7). They also attached themselves with great enthusiasm to Paul, who had brought them God's powerful good news of liberation from fear and superstition (4:12–15, 19). One imagines a tearful parting when Paul left Galatia to continue his westward mission; we know that at his departure Paul was confident that the Galatian churches were communities firmly established in the gospel of Christ (see Gal 1:6, where Paul says he is "amazed" that they have turned away from God).

The Arrival of the Teachers

Some time after Paul's departure, a group of traveling evangelists arrived with a gospel different from the one the Galatians had heard from Paul. We do not know exactly who these missionaries were; none of their writings—if they produced any—has come down to us. From Paul's letter, however, we gain some invaluable glimpses of them and a fairly well-defined outline of their message.

These missionaries were Jews who, without ceasing to be Jews, had come to believe Jesus to be the Messiah. They also believed that, as God's Messiah, Jesus had come to affirm God's Law. They did not think, however, that the message of this newly affirmed Law was for Jews alone. The Law of the Messiah, they believed, was for the whole of the world (it is probably from these missionaries that the Galatians first heard about "the Law of the Messiah," an expression that Paul also employed in his own way in 6:2). They knew themselves, therefore, to be called to take the Law to the gentiles precisely as "the gospel." It was perhaps by chance that in Galatia they crossed Paul's trail, for it seems that they had their own worldwide mission to bring to the gentiles the true interpretation and observance of the Law.

How, precisely, did the Teachers (a neutral term by which we can refer to these evangelists without prejudice) commend the Law of Moses to Law-less gentiles? As we have noted, we have none of their own writings, but from Paul's letter we can piece together a sermon that is probably quite similar to one the Galatians would have heard from them:

> Listen, now. It all began with Abraham. He was the first human being to discern that there is but one God. Because of that perception he turned from the service of dumb idols to the worship of the true God. Therefore God made him the father of our great nation; but that was only the beginning, for God spoke to Abraham a solemn, covenantal blessing, which through our mission has begun to find its fulfillment in the present time. Speaking through a glorious angel, God said to Abraham:
>
> > In you shall all nations of the world be blessed . . . for I shall multiply your descendants as the stars of heaven. . . . Come outside, and look toward heaven, and number the stars, if you are able. . . . So shall your descendants be . . . for I speak this blessing to you and to your descendants.
>
> What is the meaning of this blessing that God gave to Abraham? Pay attention to these things: Abraham was the first proselyte. As we have said, he discerned the one true God and turned to him. God therefore made an unshakable covenant with Abraham, and as a sign of this covenant he gave to Abraham the commandment of circumcision. He also revealed to Abraham the heavenly

calendar, so that in his own lifetime our father was in fact obedient to the Law, not only keeping the commandment of circumcision, but also observing the holy feasts on the correct days.

Later, when God actually handed down the Law at Sinai, he spoke once again in the mouths of his glorious angels, who passed the Law through the hand of the mediator, Moses (cf. Gal 3:19). And now the Messiah has come, confirming for eternity God's blessed Law, revealed to Abraham and spoken through Moses (cf. 6:2).

And what does this mean for you gentiles? We know from the Scriptures that Abraham had two sons, Isaac and Ishmael (4:22). On the day of the feast of the first fruits Isaac was born of Sarah the freewoman, and through him have come we Jews, who are descendants of Abraham. Ishmael was born of Hagar the slave girl, and through him have come you gentiles. Thus also you are descendants of the patriarch. We are in fact brothers!

We also know from the Scripture we have just quoted that God pronounced the covenantal blessing on both Abraham and his descendants, saying: "In you shall all the nations be blessed. The inheritance of salvation is to your children's children!" That fact faces us all with the crucial question: Who is it who are the true and therefore blessed descendants of Abraham (3:7, 29)? And the answer is equally clear from the Scriptures: Abraham himself turned from idols to the observance of the Law, circumcising himself and Isaac. As we have said, he even kept the holy feasts at their precisely appointed times. And not least, by keeping God's commandments, he avoided walking in the power of the Evil Impulse (5:16, cf. Gen 6:5). It follows that the true descendants are clearly those who are faithfully obedient to the Law with faithful Abraham (cf. Gal 3:6–9). At the present holy time God has been pleased to extend this line of true descent through the community in Jerusalem, the community that lives by the Law of Christ (6:2), the community of James, Cephas, and John, and the community of which we are the true representatives to the gentile nations (2:1–10).

What are you to do, therefore, as Abraham's descendants through Ishmael, the child of Hagar the slave girl? The gate of conversion stands open (4:17, 4:9)! You are to cast off your enslavement to the Evil Impulse by turning in repentance and conversion to God's righteous Law as it is confirmed by his Christ. Follow Abraham in the holy and liberating rite of circumcision (6:13); observe the feasts at their appointed times (4:10); keep the sacred dietary requirements (2:11–14); and abstain from idolatry and from the passions of the flesh (5:19–21). Then you will be true descendants of Abraham, heirs of salvation according to the blessed covenant that God made with Abraham and his descendants; you will be persons made right with God by observing God's holy Law (2:16; 3:5, 7, 8).

You say that you have already been converted by Paul? We say that you are still outside the covenant, living in a darkness entirely similar to the darkness in which not long ago you were serving the cosmic elements—earth, air, fire, water—supposing them, as Abraham once did, to be gods that rule the world (4:3, 9). In fact the fights and contentions in your communities show that you have not really been converted, that Paul did not give you God's holy guidance. Paul left you, a group of sailors on the treacherous high seas, in nothing more than a small and poorly equipped boat. He gave you no provisions for the trip, no map, no compass, no rudder, and no anchor. In a word, he failed to pass on to you God's greatest gift, the Law. But that is exactly the mission to which God has called us. Through our work the good news of God's covenantal Law is invading the world of gentile sin, turning that world to righteousness. We adjure you, therefore, to claim the inheritance of the blessing of Abraham, and thus to escape the curse of the Evil Impulse and sin (5:16). For, be assured, those who follow the path of the Evil Impulse and sin will not inherit the kingdom of God (5:21). It is entirely possible for you to be shut out (4:17). You will do well to consider this possibility and to tremble with fear. For you will certainly be shut out, unless you are truly incorporated into Abraham (3:29) by observing the glorious and angelic Law of the Messiah. Turn therefore in true repentance and come under the wings of the Divine Presence, so that with us you shall be saved as true descendants of our common father, Abraham.

With a message of this sort, offering to gentiles entrance into the Abrahamic covenant via the venerable religion of the Jewish Law, with its specific guidance and protective instruction, the Teachers had enormous success among the Galatians.

The Report to Paul

We do not know who carried a report to Paul about the Teachers' success among his Galatian churches; but the fact that the churches did not themselves write to him, making their own report, asking his assessment of the Teachers' message, or at least seeking his advice about this and that (as the Corinthian church would later do), indicates the gravity of the situation. After the Teachers' work among them, a number of the Galatians do not any longer view Paul as the trusted leader to whom they turn for advice. Indeed the Teachers have convinced a large number of them that Paul is actually their enemy, having withheld from them that which they most need: the guidance of God's eternal Law (Gal 4:16).

Informed of the Teachers' work, and of the degree to which the Galatians have already defected, Paul is genuinely anxious about his churches and intensely angry at the Teachers. In the midst of demanding labors elsewhere—probably in Macedonia or Greece, about 55 C.E.—he must now pause, somewhat impatient at being interrupted, in order to compose a letter to the wayward Galatians (6:17). Confident that the report he has received is accurate, Paul weighs his words, considering very carefully the way in which these words will fall on the ears of the Galatians. From the reports he has received, he knows some elements of the Teachers' sermons, their major themes, and even a number of their favorite expressions. He knows that the Galatians will have those themes and expressions fresh in their minds when they hear his letter. He therefore takes great pains to make contact with the Teachers' message at point after point as he composes his own.

Paul's Letter as a Linguistic Event

Just as we do not know who carried the disturbing report to Paul, so we do not know whom Paul sent as the messenger, who, in one Galatian city after another, would have read the letter aloud to the assembled churches. It may indeed be yet another indication of the degree to which the Galatians had already been led out of the orb of Paul and his coworkers that Paul does not name the messenger, indicating, for example, that he is known to the Galatians, at least by name, as a trustworthy minister (contrast Paul's references to Titus in 2 Cor 7:13–16). Neither does Paul build a bridge to the Galatians by naming, as known to them, those with whom he is currently working (1:2); nor does he mention by name anyone in Galatia to whom special greetings would be in order (contrast Rom 16:3–16). He may have empowered the messenger to interpret passages the Galatians found opaque, but essentially he was forced to allow the letter to do all of its own speaking. When Paul's messenger read the letter aloud, what did the Galatians hear?

They heard a letter that begins on a polemical tone (the third word is an emphatic "not"—Paul is an apostle *not* sent out on his mission by other human beings, such as the leaders of the Antioch or Jerusalem churches); and they would have noticed that the letter sustains that tone through its entirety. The messenger would scarcely have been able to conceal its highly affective character. At the point at which the Galatians might have expected to hear Paul giving thanks for them, they heard instead his initial tirade against their being attracted to the Teachers' gospel (1:6–9). Later in the letter, they are sure to have been stung to the quick when they heard Paul call them foolish, saying that they had allowed the newcomers to mesmerize them (3:1). Some of them would quickly have sided with the impressive Teachers when they heard Paul impugning the latter's motives (4:17, 6:12) and even coming close to the language of the gutter (5:12). We can be sure that, as Paul's emissary read the letter aloud, none of the Galatians nodded off to sleep.

They heard, however, far more than mere polemics. They noticed that Paul was using words and expressions now quite familiar to them, but doing so in ways that were new and astonishing. In order fully to hear Paul's letter, therefore, the Galatians had to acquire a new lexicon, as it were. The meanings of words and phrases, on which they have had a secure grip, seem in Paul's mouth to be shifting, sometimes subtly, sometimes dramatically. By attending to these shifts, we can imagine some of the thoughts that went through the Galatians' minds.

"The present evil age" (1:4). There are good reasons to think that in the first half of this verse Paul is quoting a sort of creed that he knows the Galatians to be regularly hearing from the Teachers: "Christ died as a sacrifice for our sins." The Galatians will then have noticed that in his letter Paul is interpreting this creed to mean that Christ has thereby snatched us from the fearsome grasp of "the present evil age." Christ is much more than the one who forgives sins we have ourselves committed. He is also the one who liberates us from malignant powers that have us in their grasp.

"Gospel"; "apocalypse"; "freedom"; "Jerusalem" (1:6–2:10). It was from Paul himself that the Galatians first heard the term "gospel" (good news) in the singular (as though it were "good new") and used to refer to the message about Jesus Christ. With

Paul's departure, they have seen the Teachers come and lay exclusive claim to this term, adding that while Paul originally learned the true gospel from the Jerusalem leaders, he has now deviated from it fundamentally. And what will Paul himself now say about the gospel?

He categorically denies having learned the gospel from any human being, but he also does more. Paul links the familiar word "gospel" to a word with which the Galatians may not have been very familiar, the word "apocalypse," insisting that God revealed (literally, "apocalypsed") the gospel to him directly. He also says that God is continuing actively and powerfully "to apocalypse" the gospel into the whole of the world, thus creating a new gospel-history, the narration of which is an apocalyptic matter (1:12, 16; 2:1; we will return in the second part of this essay to Paul's apocalyptic perspective). Moreover, as he has already hinted in 1:4, he now says explicitly that "the truth of the gospel" involves liberation from malignant powers and, therefore, "freedom." As part of his gospel narrative, Paul speaks of God's having revealed to him that he should fight for this freedom when, at the Jerusalem meeting, it was threatened by persons who only pretended to belong to God's church (2:4). He does not say that the "false brothers" in Jerusalem (who threatened the freedom of the gospel) are directly related to the Teachers who have now come to Galatia, but the Galatians will have sensed an implied connection, especially in light of their having heard the Teachers' claim to be closely related to the Jerusalem church. They will also have noticed that Paul's syntax suffers when he speaks of those false brothers (2:4–5 begins a sentence without completing it), and that the same thing happens when he refers to the leaders of the Jerusalem church (2:6). Paul cannot now pronounce the words "Jerusalem" and "leaders" (of the Jerusalem church) without experiencing a rise in blood pressure, for he knows that the Teachers are using those words to good advantage in their message. In the meeting of which he speaks, however, "the truth of the gospel" prevailed over the objections of the false brothers; and with that happy development, God's Law-free gospel continued its victorious march into the gentile world, thus coming into Galatia, as the Galatians themselves remember very well (2:5).

"Rectification"; "observance of the Law";

"Christ's faith" (2:11–21). Continuing his narrative of the history created by God's good news, Paul tells the Galatians of a second battle for the truth of the gospel, this time in the Antioch church. For reasons not stated, Peter, coming to Antioch from Jerusalem, had been resident for some time in the partly Jewish and partly gentile church of that city. Presumably he was carrying out an evangelistic mission of some sort. In any case, during this period he had regularly entered into the Antioch church's practice of holding common meals (including the Eucharist) without observing the Jewish food laws. Then some representatives of James came from Jerusalem; after their arrival Peter withdrew from the common meals, and the members of the Antioch church who were Jews by birth followed his example.

In this development Paul saw a new threat to the truth of the gospel; he therefore confronted Peter, speaking harshly to him about his compelling the gentile members of the church to live in a Jewish manner, observing the food laws. The narrative of this confrontation that Paul relates to the Galatians ends as he is quoting himself, citing the climactic remark he made on that earlier occasion to Peter (2:14). With considerable artistry, however, he extends that remark into a speech that is now directed to the Teachers in Galatia (2:15–21; the only point in the letter at which he addresses these persons themselves). As Paul once spoke fearlessly to Peter in the presence of the Antioch church, so he now speaks fearlessly to the Teachers in the presence of the Galatian churches.

In this speech the Galatians would have noticed the stress Paul places on the matter of God's "rectification" of human beings (the Greek noun is *dikaiosynē*, commonly translated as "justification" or "righteousness"). The term presupposes that something is wrong in the human scene and needs to be set right. It is altogether probable that the Teachers themselves have used this term, linking it firmly to the Law, by telling the gentile Galatians that they can become righteous in God's sight by observing the Law. Paul's response is sharp and uncompromising. In his mouth the term refers fundamentally to the powerful deed God has carried out in Christ, the deed by which God is making things right in the whole of the world, quite apart from the Law. Thus, in his sharp and uncompromising way, Paul speaks of a pair of opposites: Law observance and Christ's faith (the latter being, as 2:21 shows, Christ's faithful death). It is as though he had said:

> Let us indeed talk about a fundamental issue, God's making things right in the human scene; and speaking about that issue, let us stick to the way things are in the real world. How, in fact, are people being rectified by God? You Teachers are telling my Galatian churches that they are being made right by observing the Law. Wrong! God is rectifying human beings not by Law observance, but by Christ's faith, that is to say, by Christ's faithful death on our behalf. If the Law had the power to make things right, then Christ died in vain, something we all know to be false!

"Observance of the Law"; "the proclamation that kindles faith" (3:1–5). Extending his account of the history of the gospel into the period in which he brought that proclamation to the Galatians, Paul lays before them another pair of opposites. Knowing that when he was with them there was no talk about Law observance, Paul confidently asks them whether they received the Spirit as a result of their observing the Law or as a result of preaching in which he portrayed Christ suffering death by crucifixion, preaching that was so powerful as to elicit their faith.

"Descendants in the family of Abraham"; "children adopted into the family of God" (3:6–4:7). Paul knows that the Teachers are impressive exegetes of Scripture; he knows that, having spoken effectively of the blessing awaiting the true descendants of Abraham, they have shown from Scripture—if one is to believe them—that God is now passing Abraham's blessing to the gentiles who follow Abraham in the rite of circumcision (the sign of their observance of the Law). He therefore writes the first of his own exegetical sections, taking as his point of connection the Teachers' theme, descent from Abraham (3:7), but compelling that theme to serve one that is far more basic: descent from God (4:6–7). In the course of his exegesis, Paul uses some of the very texts employed by the Teachers (e.g., Gen 12:3 and 18:18 in Gal 3:8), and he introduces some of his own (e.g., Gen 15:6 in Gal 3:6; Hab 2:4 in Gal 3:11). Through the whole, however, he takes his own theological point of departure not in Scripture as such, but rather in God's deed in Christ.

What Paul sees is that in that deed God has changed the world by making its structure conform to new pairs of opposites. Long before the Law came into existence, God himself spoke his covenantal promise of a descendant directly to Abraham; and the descendant God promised has now arrived in the person of Christ. The Law is a mere parenthesis that entered in only for a limited period of time. It cannot even be truly identified as God's covenant. Seen in this light, the Law and the covenantal promise God spoke to Abraham are far from being the compatible pair the Teachers have claimed them to be. They are in fact a pair of opposites. God was not even personally present at the genesis of the Law (3:19–20)! The promise, by contrast, was the covenant spoken to Abraham by God himself; and that promise has now come to us in the Spirit of God's Son. If one longs to be a descendant of Abraham, well and good. By incorporation into Christ (Abraham's promised descendant) we have already become Abraham's children, heirs of the promise (3:29). More important, however, is the fact that in Christ God has freed us from enslavement to the malignant structures of the world, and has sent the Spirit of Christ into our hearts; so that delivered from superstition, and adopted into God's family, we cry out confidently to God as our Father (4:6–7).

"The weak and poverty-stricken elements of the world"; sacred times; friendship in the gospel (4:8–20). Paul has already drawn a close and astonishing connection between existence under the power of the Law and existence in slavery to the cosmic elements (4:3–5). Now, having said, in essence, that prior to the advent of Christ, the world was a monolith of enslavement (to the power of the Law in the Jewish orb, to the power of the world-elements in the gentile orb), he can compound the astonishment of the Galatian gentiles (not to mention that of the Jewish Teachers) by telling them that for gentiles to "convert" to the Law, observing certain days and periods as though there were sacred times, is tantamount to their returning to their pagan religion. How can those who have come to know God—or, as Paul corrects himself, to be known by God—return to the slavery of

any religion, he asks, not entirely certain that the Galatians will give the true answer. In any case, he can hope that they will ponder what he has earlier stated as a fact: in Christ the age-old distinction between Jew and gentile has been abolished (3:28).

From this solemn warning Paul turns to a warm reminder of those earlier days when he first preached to the Galatians, days marked by extraordinarily close friendship in the gospel. Knowing that the Teachers have greatly disturbed this friendship, he responds by impugning the sincerity of their apparent concern for the Galatians. His own anxious concern for the Galatians is, he says, analogous to the concern of a prospective mother for her child. What is at stake in that concern is the formation of Christ in the corporate life of their churches. Everything depends on that.

"The two sons of Abraham"; "two covenants"; "Jerusalem"; "freedom" (4:21–5:1). Here Paul returns abruptly to the style of the rhetorical question (*cf.* 3:2, 5), asking the Galatians whether—tutored by the Teachers—they have really heard the voice of that Law to which they are tempted to turn. The implication is clear (again, I give a paraphrastic summary): "The Teachers are not reliable interpreters of Scripture; and now, in a second exegetical section, I will show you that, correctly interpreted, the Law raises its voice, first, in order to controvert the claim that it itself has the power to beget children into the state of freedom and, second, in order to bear witness to the begetting of free children by the promised Spirit." In analyzing the first of Paul's exegetical efforts (3:6–4:7), I noted that he achieved his remarkable effect, in part, by taking the initial theme and some of the texts themselves from the Teachers. He does the same here, and with results equally impressive.

As we noted, when we reconstructed a typical sermon of the Teachers, these talented exegetes have laid before the Galatians their interpretation not only of God's pronouncement of a covenantal blessing upon Abraham (*cf.* 3:8), but also of the first step in God's fulfillment of that blessing: the birth of Isaac. They have, in fact, told the scriptural story of Abraham's two sons, presenting in the process a miniature table of opposites, arranged, as it were, under the names of the mothers of the two sons:

Hagar	Sarah
Slave	Free
Gentiles	Jews
The absence of a covenant	The realm of the covenant
The nations	The church of those who observe the covenantal Law of Sinai (i.e., the ruling powers of the Jerusalem church and the Law-observant mission sponsored by them)

The Teachers' message is clear. The Galatian gentiles are to transfer from the left column to the right one, entering the covenant by becoming Law-observant believers in the Law-confirming Messiah.

Paul's exegesis is designed to correct this table of opposites by several astonishing claims. First, having earlier announced a divorce between the terms "Law" and "covenant" (3:17), Paul now puts the two back together. The Law is indeed a covenant; but being firmly linked with Mount Sinai and thus with Hagar (!), this Law-covenant, like that slave woman, is presently bearing children into slavery. Thus the Sinai covenant is not in the Sarah/freedom column, but rather in the Hagar/slavery column. It follows that the Law-observant mission to gentiles sponsored by the Jerusalem church is an enterprise bringing about gentile enslavement.

As if that columnar rearrangement were not sufficiently astonishing, Paul forges ahead, completely without precedent, by speaking not of one covenant (the one from Mount Sinai), but rather of two. What he had accomplished in Galatians 3 by identifying God's promise and the Law as a pair of opposites, he now underscores and explicates by saying that opposite the Hagar/slavery covenant of Sinai (and of the present Jerusalem) stands the Sarah/freedom covenant of the Jerusalem above. This latter covenant is the mother who is presently bearing children in the Law-free mission among gentiles, children of the Spirit and of freedom from the Law. In Paul's view the true table of opposites is, then, the following:

Hagar	*Sarah*
Slave	Free
The covenant from Mount Sinai	The covenant of God's promise to Abraham (3:17)
The present Jerusalem (i.e., the False Brothers in the Jerusalem church, as sponsors of the Law-observant mission to gentiles)	The Jerusalem above, our mother (an apocalyptic expression in Rev 3:12, 21:2)
Children of the slave woman, born into slavery	Children of the free woman
One born in accordance with the Flesh (i.e., the Evil Impulse; see comment on 5:13–6:10 below)	One born in accordance with the Spirit (i.e., the promise of God)
The slave woman and her son (i.e., the Teachers, who are to be expelled)	The son of the free woman (i.e., the Galatians as those born of the promised Spirit)

By this exegesis Paul says to the Galatians, in effect,

> The Teachers have indeed shared with you the traditions, from the Law, about Abraham's two sons; and they are right to interpret these traditions allegorically, that is to say, by noting columnar correspondences. They have told you that Hagar is in the same column with slavery, and so she is. But they have not caused you really to hear the Law; for they have not told you the astonishing truth, that Hagar, the slave woman, is also in the same column with Mount Sinai, the locus of the genesis of the Law, *and* that Hagar, the slave woman, is in the same column with Jerusalem itself! Whoever sees the oppositional columns as they actually stand in the dawning of the New Creation of the Spirit will see that the present Jerusalem is connected with the Law of Mount Sinai by *being connected with slavery*, and that, being so connected, the present Jerusalem is even now bearing children into slavery. And how is the present Jerusalem doing that? Precisely by the support that the false brothers in the Jerusalem church are even now giving to the Teachers' Law-observant mission among gentiles like you.

The sharpness of Paul's comment is unmistakable. What is important for our present concern is the nature of his polemic. It is crucial to see that Paul focuses his critique quite specifically on the Law-observant mission that is currently "bearing children into slavery" among the gentiles (4:24). His polemic is, therefore, fundamentally and dangerously misconstrued when it is said to have to do with Judaism and Christianity, a widespread interpretation begun in the second century by Marcion, who incorrectly explicated Paul's reference to two covenants by speaking of the synagogue and the church. At no point in the passage we are considering does Paul mention Judaism, and Christianity as such had not yet come into existence. Paul's astonishing rearrangement of the Teachers' pairs of opposites and his unprecedented reference to two covenants is far, then, from constituting an attack on Judaism. On the contrary, it is specifically directed, as we have seen, against the Law-observant mission among gentiles; and by the same token it is a witness to the birth of gentile churches by the power of the Spirit.

In a word, the coming of the Spirit has brought into being a new set of oppositional columns, a new set of antinomies, so that these antinomies have in fact replaced the oppositional columns characteristic of the old one. The result is Paul's ringing proclamation of the freedom that Christ has already accomplished for his own. The Galatians are to stand firmly in that freedom, not submitting to the slavery preached by the Teachers.

"Circumcision"; "the scandal of the cross" (5:2–12). In a direct manner Paul again refers to the Galatians' temptation to find their security in observance of the Law. And again he interprets that temptation by viewing it in the framework of the new table of opposites, the major pair of opposites being an act that human beings can carry out (circumcision as the sign of Law observance) and the act that God has already carried out (the redemption of the world in the scandal of the cross). If the Teachers speak of something the Galatians ought to do—they ought to transfer from the Law-less state of gentile existence to the Law-observant state of Abraham's true children—Paul speaks of something God has already done: God has already freed the captives, invading the world of enslavement by the sending of his Son. It is, on the one hand, the language of human transfer, and, on the other hand, the language of divine invasion.

Life directed by the "fleshy Impulse"; life directed by "the Spirit" (5:13–6:10). Paul now brings the body of his letter to a close by responding forcefully to the Teachers' charge that in his Law-less preaching he inevitably leads his hearers into ethical chaos, since, by abandoning the divine Law, he abandons the only antidote to the Evil Impulse, and, in effect, makes Christ an advocate of sin (cf. 2:17; Paul refers to the Evil Impulse as a power to which human beings can be subjected when he speaks in 5:16 of "the desires of the flesh"; cf. the expression *yetser basar* in the Dead Sea Scrolls; for Jewish and early Christian traditions about the Evil Impulse, see Marcus 1982 and 1986). The Teachers have given the Galatians detailed instructions about the Impulse; and Paul is himself far from questioning its existence. He may, in fact, echo the Teachers when he points to strife in the Galatian churches as evidence of its power. The issue is not the existence of the Evil Impulse, but rather the identity of the antidote, and in this regard Paul is willing to formulate a promise: "I say to you, if in your churches you live under the guidance of the Spirit, your corporate life will not be characterized by conduct dictated by the fleshy Impulse" (my paraphrase of 5:16). In a word, says Paul,

> not the Law, but rather the Spirit is the power that defeats the Evil Impulse, for it is the Spirit that, being active in your communities, is bearing the fruit of love, joy, peace, and faith. Are there instances of transgression in your midst? Do not repair to the Law. You have the Spirit! And in the Spirit, by bearing the burden of the transgressor, and by knowing that you too are fallible, you are to restore the transgressor to the community. The fabric of our daily life is not a matter of indifference to God; and I have never implied that it was (5:21, 6:7–8a). Indeed, it is the gift of that daily, Spirit-led life that will become eternal life by the power of the Spirit that is already at work when you are doing good to everyone, and especially to those in the church.

"Crucified world"; "new creation"; "the Israel of God" (6:11–18). Having dictated the body of the letter to a scribe, Paul now takes the pen himself in order to summarize his message in a highly personal and emphatic way, thus doing his best to cause the epistle to serve as a substitute for his literal presence ("Notice the large letters I am using, as I now write to you with my own hand" [6:11; Au. trans.]). He makes a final attack on the Teachers (6:12–13), and he closes by preaching once again the gospel of the cross of Christ. In this encapsulated proclamation Paul uses three arresting expressions. First, by his participation

in Christ's death Paul found that the world in which he had been living—its structures, its values, its way of distinguishing order from disorder—*that world itself was crucified* (6:14). It is thus essentially dead and gone. Second, in its place there now stands the *new creation* (6:15), with its new structures, its new pairs of opposites, and its new alignments of powers. Christians thus live in an invaded world, so fundamentally changed by the powerful advent of Christ and of Christ's Spirit that one has to speak of it as nothing less than the new creation.

The third arresting expression is built on one the Galatians probably heard for the first time from the Teachers: *Israel.* If this is so, they will have been told that by becoming Law-observant they not only become true children of Abraham; they also enter into Israel. Paul, by contrast, says that the Israel *of God* (6:16) is those who live in God's new creation, where the distinction between circumcision and uncircumcision has been obliterated. Upon this Israel of God, made up of former Jews and former gentiles, Paul pronounces the blessing of peace and mercy.

PAUL'S APOCALYPTIC PERSPECTIVE

We have said above that the first of two major keys to the interpretation of Galatians is the shared history of the Galatian churches, from Paul's founding visit to the arrival of the Teachers. The analysis given in the first part of this essay has shown that Paul considers this Galatian history to be in fact part of the history that God is now creating by causing the powerful gospel to march from one victory to another through the world. By taking this history seriously into account, we have begun to hear the letter with the ears of the Galatians themselves, and thus to hear it, to some degree, as Paul intended it to be heard.

The other major key to the letter's interpretation is Paul's apocalyptic perspective. This may seem an odd claim, because Pauline apocalyptic is usually defined by reference to such motifs as the future Parousia of Christ, the archangel's cry, the blowing of the last trumpet, and the general resurrection of the dead (1 Thess 4:13–5:11 and 1 Cor 15:20–28, 51–58), motifs that Paul nowhere mentions in Galatians. In fact, however, Paul's apocalyptic perspective has two foci, Christ's future Parousia and Christ's past death and resurrection. As we have noted above, Christ's crucifixion in particular is seen by Paul as an event no less apocalyptic than Christ's resurrection, in the sense that in that event God has invaded the world in which human beings live, thereby fundamentally changing it: "New Creation!" (an expression at home in apocalyptic texts). The term "invasion" conveys, in fact, a large part of Paul's apocalyptic. One notes that in Galatians 3:23 and 3:25 Paul uses interchangeably the verbs "to be apocalypsed" and "to come," referring both times to the event of Christ's faith as the event of an invasion (not merely of an unveiling). It is a freeing invasion, for, after its occurrence, human beings are no longer slaves of the world's elemental structures and of the Law. Living in the invaded world, they are being liberated.

It follows that to carry on one's life as though that liberating invasion had not occurred is to fail to acknowledge what time it is and thus to fail to live in the real world. We now live *after* the crucifixion of Christ, the event that has caused the time to be what it is by snatching us out of the grasp of the present evil age (1:4). We now live *after* the advent of the Spirit, and therefore *in* the war that the Spirit is victoriously waging against the fleshy Impulse. Paul writes the letter, therefore, to shake the Galatians awake, to bring them back to life in the real (apocalyptic) world, and to put them back into the true battle for Christ's complete and completely liberating victory in the whole of creation.

EXEGETICAL HISTORY

Paul's letter to the Galatians has had a highly significant history of exegesis; we can mention two interpretations made in Paul's own time, two formulated in the second century, and one written in the sixteenth century.

In Paul's Own Time

Interpretation by the Galatians. The earliest interpretation of the letter was made, of course, by the Galatians themselves. We have no sources by which we can reconstruct the details of that interpretation, but we are not wholly in the dark. We can be sure that the Teachers were present when Paul's messenger read the letter aloud, and, as noted above, we can be equally sure they did not hesitate to share with the Galatians their own understanding of Paul's text. We also know that at one time the Galatians were energetically active in the collection Paul assembled from his gentile churches for delivery to the church in Jerusalem (1 Cor 16:1), whereas we note that at a later point they seem to have withdrawn from this project (Rom 15:26), perhaps indicating that most of them did not wish to be perceived in Jerusalem as belonging to the orb of Paul's Law-free mission. From these two considerations we can conclude with some probability that the Teachers were as successful in their negative interpretation of Paul's letter as they were in their initial mission among the Galatians. In a word, there are reasons for thinking that the Galatians' decision to withdraw from the collection was related to their having arrived at a highly critical interpretation of the letter they had received from Paul.

What points were the Galatians—tutored by the Teachers—likely to have accented in their sharply critical interpretation of Paul's letter? The question is not difficult to answer. Everyone reads selectively, and, as I have noted at length, everyone hears words against the background of what one has previously heard on the same subject. Given the Teachers' sermons, the Galatians' attention must have been seized in particular by two matters: Paul's comments about the Law and his less than satisfactory reference to Israel. Although they would have applauded Paul's insistence that the Law bears witness to the birth of children of the Spirit (4:21–5:1), and although they would have been pleased to hear him speaking with emphasis about fulfilling the Law (5:14), they would have found quite unacceptable Paul's charge that the Law is one of the powers in the world that enslave human beings (3:23, 4:5, etc.). Indeed that charge must have angered them considerably, leading them to interpret the letter quite harshly. These earliest interpreters would also have been less than pleased, as we have already noted, to encounter Paul's supra-Jewish reference to Israel (6:16). They would certainly have noticed that, whereas he made reference to Abraham, Sarah (the "free woman" of 4:22), and Isaac, he nowhere mentioned the long and crucially important history of God's dealings with Israel, the people they now knew to have been made special by God's election and continuous care, and the people into which the Galatians believed they were themselves now being incorporated by commencing observance of the Law. Thus, both with regard to the Law and with regard to Israel, Paul's letter almost certainly proved unacceptable to the majority of the Galatians, influenced, as they were, by the Teachers.

Paul's interpretation of his own letter. Was that earliest and ominous reception of the letter a matter that remained unknown to Paul? Quite the contrary. We are to imagine Paul receiving a discouraging report from the messenger whom he had trusted to deliver the letter (*cf. 1 Clement* 65). Indeed, there is reason to think that Paul not only learned of the harsh interpretations of his letter by the Galatians (and by the Teachers), but also that, after learning of such interpretations, he decided to correct them. He did not write another letter to the Galatians themselves (contrast 1 Cor 5:9), but in his letter to the Roman church he clearly made use of his letter to the Galatians, and part of his reason for doing so was to guard that earlier letter from interpretations he considered misleading.

And why would it be in a letter to the Roman church that Paul should be concerned to correct misinterpretations of his earlier letter to the Galatians? The reason is complex: As he wrote the Roman letter, Paul was surely thinking of several weighty matters. He was concerned to address problems faced by the mixed (Jewish and gentile) church in the great capital; he was thinking of the Spanish mission he planned to launch from that church; with that mission in mind, he was determined that the Roman church have a fully accurate grasp of his gospel. His thoughts also went, however, to the East, to the Jewish Christian church in Jerusalem, and specifically to the trip he had momentarily to make to that church, in order to deliver to it the collection that he saw as a crucial witness to the grand unity of the church of God in the whole of the world.

As we have already noted, there was in the Jerusalem church a group of persons who did not at all share Paul's conviction that the unified church included Law-free gentile congregations. These persons were members of the circumcision party, the false brothers with whom Paul had had to deal at the time

of the Jerusalem meeting. They were also, as we have suggested, theological allies of the Teachers. Paul's plan to journey to Jerusalem thus brought to him the prospect of a renewed confrontation with this circumcision party. It was as though he would shortly have to face the Teachers themselves, now functioning not as interlopers in what he considered to be his mission field, but as a constituent element within the Jerusalem church, intent once again on excluding from the church of God his Law-free gentile congregations. This prospect created in Paul a considerable amount of anxiety (see Rom 15:30–33; and recall Paul's earlier anxiety at having to deal with this same group [Gal 2:2–5]).

There is, moreover, good reason to think that Paul's anxiety was related both to the Galatians and to the letter Paul had written to them. The circumcision party in the Jerusalem church was almost certainly in touch with the Teachers, both before and after the latter's work in Paul's Galatian congregations. We have already noted the probability that, under the influence of the Teachers, the Galatians had ceased to participate in Paul's collection. Now we must add that this step had very serious consequences for Paul's trip to Jerusalem. For Paul had now to consider the possibility that, when the Jerusalem church debated within its own ranks whether to accept his collection, some of those in the circumcision party—already knowing the answer—would ask him whether any of the monies were coming from the Galatian churches. Should that question be posed, he knew he would have to admit that the Galatians had withdrawn from the circle of his churches. Paul may even have had to consider the possibility that Jewish Christians in the Jerusalem church who knew enough to ask that embarrassing question might also know something of his Galatian letter, such as its very negative words about the Law and its apparently un-Jewish reference to a newly formed Israel of God (*cf.* Acts 21:21).

We have no indication, to be sure, that Paul ever regretted writing the Galatian letter, but one can easily imagine that, on the eve of his last trip to Jerusalem, he regretted the harsh interpretations that had been placed upon the letter. Such regret, in any case, is consonant with the fact that in writing to the Romans Paul clarified, supplemented, and perhaps even modified things he had said to the Galatians.

Seen in this way, parts of Romans constitute the second interpretation of Galatians made in Paul's time, and, obviously, one made by Paul himself. Because Galatians has often seemed to give the Christian church permission to adopt a somewhat anti-Judaic stance, Paul's own interpretation of that letter is of great import. By attending briefly to the ways in which Paul spoke in Romans about the Law and about Israel, one may be able to see more clearly what he intended when he referred to the Law and to Israel in the earlier letter to the Galatians.

(1) The Law. Writing to the gentile Christians in Galatia and being concerned about their incipient adherence to the Law (their being under the conviction that Law-observance is salvific), Paul spoke in their letter about the Law being itself an enslaving tyrant, thus expressing a view of the Law completely foreign to all strains of Jewish thought known to us.

When he writes to the Romans, Paul does not reverse himself as regards there being a connection between the Law and tyranny; but his concern that he be accurately understood by Jewish Christians who are fully Law-observant does lead him to a carefully nuanced formulation of that connection. Thus in Romans he says that the Law itself is holy and even spiritual (Rom 7:12, 14), an affirmation that would surely have been misunderstood had he said it to the gentile Christians in Galatia. He still insists, however, that when this holy and spiritual Law is faced with the overwhelming and malignant power of Sin, it proves to be impotent to bring Sin under control (Gal 3:21, 5:16; Rom 8:3). That controlling task is accomplished by God's sending of his Son, not by the Law. In the light, then, of God's act in Christ, Paul sees that the Law, being impotent, has fallen into the hands of Sin, and Sin has been able to use the Law to kill human beings (Rom 7:7–11). From Galatians to Romans, therefore, Paul is entirely consistent in drawing a connection between the Law and tyranny, but in Romans he clarifies what he had said in Galatians. The Law is indeed connected with tyranny, but only by way of Sin; for the tyrant itself is Sin, the Law then being the instrument in Sin's hands, and, in that sense, Sin's effective power (*cf.* 1 Cor 15:56).

(2) Israel. Whereas in Galatians 6:16 Paul had referred in an apparently supra-Jewish way to "the Israel of God," in Romans he clarifies and supplements that reference by expanding it into three long and complex chapters on the subject of God's relationship to Israel (Rom 9–11). He is clearly aware that some have charged him with a callous apostasy from this special people of God, the people to whom the proper mission of the Jerusalem church was directed. Significantly he does not defend himself by speaking immediately of his high regard for Israel's lengthy history. He begins, rather, with the history of the gospel, referring to his deep pain and profound grief at one aspect of that history: most of Israel is now rejecting the gospel. Of course as a world traveler Paul knows of widespread disobedience. The disobedience of Israel, however, has about it something special. It is the great contradiction: the very people specially blessed by *God* is now largely disobeying *God's* gospel. This development is necessarily the great contradiction, because Paul can deny neither God's ancient election of Israel nor God's present utterance of the gospel. Squarely facing this paradox, Paul necessarily sees that Israel is now standing "between God and God" (a perceptive expression coined by Gerhard Ebeling; note its applicability to Rom 11:28). In the final analysis, the great contradiction, incomprehensible to human reason, points, then, to God's own mystery, about which Paul has to speak in parables (Rom 11:16–24) and in the mysterious language of apocalyptic (Rom 11:25–36), in order to affirm God's sovereign election, God's faithfulness to Israel, and God's invincible power.

There are elements of this discussion that clarify and explicate what Paul had said about Israel in Galatians. True enough, the author of Galatians surely believed when he wrote that letter that already in ancient times God had made Israel his special people, the people of the glory, the covenants, the giving of the Law, the patriarchs; he also believed that it was from this people that the Christ had come, as far as natural descendance is concerned (*cf.* Gal 4:4; Rom 9:4–5, 15:8). He believed these things when he wrote Galatians, but he did not mention them. Now, preparing for his trip to the Jewish Christian church in Jerusalem, he speaks explicitly of Abraham, Sarah, Isaac, Rebecca, and Jacob. He also makes clear that the patriarchs, being the first embodiment of God's gracious election, form the first fruits (Rom 11:16). Thus, by considering the patriarchal history, he demonstrates that God is true to his word of elective grace (Rom 9:6–13). Indeed, because God's word is both invincible and indelible, the ancient election of Israel remains the paradigm for God's dealing with all of humanity. We note again that these are things Paul did not say in Galatians.

The basis on which he says them is, however, precisely the basis of everything he did say in Galatians: the gospel. That God is true to his gospel-word of elective grace means, as Paul had said in Galatians, that the true Israel is the Israel *of God*. Far from rescinding this earlier reference, Paul now explicates it by speaking of a division within Israel: "not all who are descended from Israel belong to Israel" (Rom 9:6b; RSV). Genuine descent is solely by God's election. That is true today, Paul claims, as one sees in the history of the gospel; it was also true in every patriarchal generation (Rom 9:6–13).

In this elective gospel Paul also sees, however, the invincibility of God's graceful word; this word tells Paul that Israel stands not between God and Satan, but, as we have already said, between God and God. Thus, it is both true and of crucial importance that Paul now makes explicit the salvation of "all Israel" (Rom 11:26). It is equally important to notice the grounds for that eschatological confidence. All Israel will be saved because, being the God who rectifies the ungodly, God is also the one whose capacity to show mercy is more powerful than the capacity of human beings to be disobedient (Rom 11:30–31). In a word, reversing a classic view of Israel's eschatological relation to all other human beings (according to which at the End the gentiles will flow up to Jerusalem, being saved by being absorbed into Israel), Paul now knows of Israel's ultimate salvation because he knows of God's ultimate purpose for all human beings: "God has shut up *all* into disobedience, in order that he might have mercy on *all*" (Rom 11:32; an interpretation of Gal 3:22). One notes with surprise that in this climactic sentence of his discussion of Israel, Paul does not mention Israel! He speaks rather of God's powerful mercy being shown to all human beings, and he bases his argument on that mercy. It is clear, therefore, that in Romans Paul derives his theology of Israel from the universality of the gospel, about which he had already spoken in Galatians. Far from laying a foundation for the pernicious view that the church has replaced Israel, this theology is free of all anti-Judaic cant; it is a theology drawn from the gospel; fundamentally it is Paul's theology both in Galatians and in Romans.

In the Second Century

The Jewish Christians. The Jewish Christian groups of the second century were as hostile to Paul's theology, and especially to his Galatian letter, as were the Teachers in Galatia and the circumcision party in Jerusalem. Here the primary sources are the *Epistle of Peter to James* (where Paul is said to have preached a Law-less and therefore false gospel) and *Ascents of James* (where Paul's work is charged with having greatly hindered the growth of the church among Jews). Both of these documents are pseudonymous, being written in the latter part of the second century.

The gnostics and Marcion. If the Jewish Christians of the second century were hostile to Galatians, the Christian gnostics, and especially Marcion, more than compensated, by holding it in extraordinarily high regard. Marcion, in fact, developed the kernel of his theology from Paul's tendency to think in terms of pairs of opposites, and that tendency is nowhere more clearly and strongly in evidence than in Galatians. Marcion thus placed Galatians at the head of his collection of Paul's letters, in order to display clearly what he characterized as a series of ontological antitheses between the old and the new.

In the process, Marcion showed a keen sensitivity for Pauline passages that speak of polar opposites, but he failed utterly to note that for Paul those opposites were not wooden, ontological antitheses, but rather, as I have noted, lively, apocalyptic antinomies. The difference is monumental. Marcion's concern for inflexible, antithetical consistency led him finally to posit a distinctly un-Pauline antithesis between a creator God and a redeemer God. In this way, Marcion's antitheses, altogether unlike Paul's antinomies, became anti-Judaic, with disastrous results, extending into the anti-Judaism that is yet present in some corners of the church. Franz Overbeck put the matter in a memorable sentence: "Paul had only one student who understood him, Marcion—and this student misunderstood him."

In the Sixteenth Century

A few modern exegetes would be tempted to say something similar about Martin Luther, not least because of the reformer's pejorative and indefensible references to "Jews, Turks, papists, and sectarians." Most Christian interpreters, however, both Roman Catholic and Protestant, find help in Luther's passionate love affair with Galatians: the letter he dubbed his "Katherine von Bora" (the name of his betrothed, who later became his wife). In any case, both in his Roman Catholic period and after he became the unwilling founder of the Lutheran church, Luther was captivated by the message of free grace that he heard in Galatians. Wherever interpreters have recognized that the gospel Paul preached in Galatians is itself the powerful antidote to the virus of anti-Semitism among Christians, Luther's interpretation has happily influenced—to one degree or another—most readings of the letter since his time.

Bibliography

Beker, J. Christiaan. *Paul the Apostle.* Philadelphia, 1980; 2d ed., 1984.

Betz, Hans Dieter. *Galatians.* Philadelphia, 1979.

Brinsmead, Bernard Hunger. *Galatians: Dialogical Response to Opponents.* Chico, 1982.

Brown, Raymond E., and John P. Meier. *Antioch and Rome.* New York, 1983.

Bruce, F. F. *The Epistle to the Galatians.* Grand Rapids, 1982.

Burton, Ernest De Witt. *A Critical and Exegetical Commentary on the Epistle to the Galatians.* New York, 1920.

de Boer, Martinus C. "Images of Paul in the Post-Apostolic Period." *Catholic Biblical Quarterly* 42 (1980): 359–380.

Dunn, James D. G. "Works of the Law and the Curse of the Law." *New Testament Studies* 31 (1985): 523–542.

Gaventa, Beverly R. "Galatians 1 and 2: Autobiography as Paradigm." *Novum Testamentum* 28 (1986): 309–326.

Hays, Richard B. *The Faith of Jesus Christ: An Investigation into the Narrative Substructure of Galatians 3:1–4:11.* Chico, 1983.

Hoffmann, R. Joseph. *Marcion: On the Restitution of Christianity.* Chico, 1984.

Howard, George. *Paul: Crisis in Galatia.* New York, 1979.

Lull, David John. *The Spirit in Galatia: Paul's Interpretation of Pneuma as Divine Power.* Chico, 1980.

Luther, Martin. *Lectures on Galatians—1519 and 1535.* Vols. 26–27 of *Luther's Works,* edited by Jaroslav Pelikan and Walter A. Hansen. Saint Louis, 1963–1964.

Marcus, Joel. "The Evil Inclination in the Epistle of James." *Catholic Biblical Quarterly* 44 (1982): 606–621.

———. "The Evil Inclination in the Letters of Paul." *Irish Biblical Studies* 8 (1986): 8–21.

Martyn, J. Louis. "A Law-Observant Mission to Gentiles: The Background of Galatians." *Scottish Journal of Theology* 38 (1985): 307–324.

———. "Apocalyptic Antinomies in Paul's Letter to the Galatians." *New Testament Studies* 31 (1985): 410–424.

———. "Paul and His Jewish-Christian Interpreters." *Union Seminary Quarterly Review* 42 (1988): 1–15.

Meyer, Paul W. "Romans." In *Harper's Bible Commentary,* edited by James L. Mays. San Francisco, 1988. Pp. 1130–1167.

Sanders, E. P. *Paul, the Law, and the Jewish People.* Philadelphia, 1983.

Schoeps, Hans Joachim. *Jewish Christianity: Factional Disputes in the Early Church.* Translated by Douglas R. A. Hare. Philadelphia, 1969.

Schütz, John Howard. *Paul and the Anatomy of Apostolic Authority.* New York, 1975.

Strecker, Georg. "The Kerygmata Petrou." In *New Testament Apocrypha,* vol. 2, edited by Edgar Hennecke and Wilhelm Schneemelcher, English translation edited by R. McL. Wilson. Philadelphia, 1965. Pp. 102–127.

Williams, Sam K. "Again *Pistis Christou.*" *Catholic Biblical Quarterly* 49 (1987): 431–447.

J. LOUIS MARTYN

Ephesians

A VISIT TO the Turkish city of Selçuk, near the Aegean Sea below Izmir (formerly Smyrna) and adjacent to the ruins of Ephesus, opens two windows on the ancient world to the modern visitor. One provides a good view of the cult of Cybele, whom the Greeks took over as Artemis and the Romans as Diana. This goddess of fertility—many-breasted to the point of monstrosity, or perhaps displaying an apron of dates or the genitals of bulls, as some maintain—is represented a few dozen times in marble and alabaster in the well-kept municipal museum. The site of her temple, however, is a disappointment. The Artemision, which appears on ancient lists as one of the Seven Wonders of the World, survives only as a carefully manicured lawn of heroic proportions. A visit to the museum, however, helps a traveler visualize the commercial losses of the keepsake trade in silver occasioned by Paul's visit (see Acts 19:24–27). Miniature shrines (v. 24) and deities (v. 26) much like today's Statues of Liberty and Eiffel Towers in luminously painted lead would have been hawked throughout the ancient city.

The other view the traveler has is of an archaeological dig of very large proportions adjacent to the modern town. The ancient estuary has long been silted in, making the remains of the brothels "down by the docks" an exercise in imagination. Nowadays the Aegean harbor town of Kuşadasi is ten miles away. If Paul in fact was at Ephesus for any good part of the two years of discussions with which Acts credits him (19:10), he would have known the city's streets well. The reconstructed facade of the library of Celsus and the immense stone amphitheater are still there. A side benefit for Christians with a sense of theological tradition is the foundation of the double basilica (porch to porch) dedicated to Mary as "God-bearer" (*theotokos*). The council held in it in 431 accorded her that title. A mystery of Christ rather than of Mary was thereby enunciated against the Nestorian or "two-nature" party, which thought that "Christ-bearer" was the more accurate title; they had no problem with Christ's divinity. The twin churches were small, and the second of the two was not yet there in the fifth century. Across the narrow blacktop road from the basilica enclave the presence of a Club Mediterranée serves to remind the pious that incarnation was not a gnostic figment but a human reality.

It can be questioned whether this port city of the province of Asia should be featured in introducing the epistle that bears its name. The phrase "in Ephesus" is missing after "to the saints" in the first verse of the earliest manuscripts. Still, we can reasonably conclude that the epistle circulated from there, given its affinity in content to the letter addressed to the not far distant Colossae. Experts in ancient rhetoric testify that the orotund style of Ephesians is characteristic of literary products of the area.

The absence of a specific address says something

about the document's generalized contents. There is nothing personal about it, despite its claim to be from Paul in prison (3:1) and its concluding paragraph, which says that Tychicus (see Acts 20:4) has been sent as Paul's emissary to the recipients of the letter. Certainly it could not have been written to a community Paul knew well. Their faith is a matter of hearsay to him (1:15; *cf.* 3:2–4). Like Colossians, this text too fails the tests of vocabulary and style as a work of the apostle.

Some attribute the composition of the epistle to Tychicus, the most obvious candidate nearby (but not imprisoned) to be acquainted with Paul's current thinking. But the near identity of Ephesians (6:21–22) with Colossians (4:7–8) on the subject of Tychicus is a suspicious detail. In fact, the close literary affinity of this treatise—for it is that rather than a letter—with Colossians creates an interesting problem. Is either one directly dependent on the other and if so, which upon which? The commonest solution is that Ephesians was conceived as a second edition of Colossians for a wider audience, without its sharp polemical edges. This is a distinct possibility. That Colossians derives from Ephesians—as a few maintain—is barely credible, as a cursory comparison (Col 1:5 with Eph 1:13–14; Col 1:23 with Eph 3:7; and Col 4:24 with Eph 6:18–20) will show. The elaborations on the more succinct Colossians are evident throughout; an editing of the complex Ephesians down to the proportions of the shorter Colossians can scarcely have been the case. A second possibility is that both are derived from an earlier writing filled with catechetical teaching characteristic of the area.

Whatever the case, Ephesians is not merely more developed than Colossians but is a richer mosaic of seemingly traditional materials and is written in much better Greek. It seems to be a circular letter (to the churches of Asia?) presenting a summary of faith and conduct to gentile Christians. Its author knows a wider Pauline collection of letters, not just the ones Colossians incorporates. This has led to the theory that it was a cover letter accompanying the first assemblage of Paul's correspondence that was made. There is little evidence, however, to support this attractive theory.

The first half of Ephesians (chaps. 1–3) is largely doctrinal, while the second (chaps. 4–6) is ethical. The latter portion closely resembles the paraenesis, or counsel, of Colossians, but the former is a highly diffused version of that epistle. Overall, though, both concerns are present in both halves. It is not easy to say in which direction Ephesians mainly goes. As in Colossians, Jesus Christ sits "at [God's] right hand in the heavenly realms, far above all government and authority, all power and dominion" (1:20b–21; NEB). There is no indication, however, that the addressees have been tempted to venerate these dominions and powers. As former pagans, they were once beholden to "the prince of the power of the air" (2:2; RSV), a term that Jews would have understood to mean the devil. But that is described as behind them now. God has put "all things under the feet" of the risen Christ "and has made him the head of all things *for* the church, which is his body, the fullness of [the one] who fills all in all" (1:22–23; Au. trans.; unless otherwise noted, subsequent translations are the author's). Marked by a subtle shade of difference from the text of Colossians 1:17–18, Ephesians makes Christ the head of all "*for* the church . . . his body," thereby offering a direct challenge to any philosophy that would make a Platonic logos the head of creation. By this dative of reference (for the church) the narrower extension, "the church," falls within the wider "all things." Christ, being the head of the cosmos, is by that fact supreme over the church. In Colossians it had gone in reverse: his headship of the church was potentially dominion over all authority in the cosmos (2:10). In Ephesians, his supremacy over the redeemed community in history is at the heart of the epistle's demythologizing of the cosmos.

A second difference is that God, the Father of glory (Eph 1:17), has made the church, Christ's body, "the fullness of [God] who fills all in all" (v. 23; RSV). In Colossians the fullness of God dwells in Christ (Col 1:19), making him the reconciling agent of all things in heaven and on earth. Here the community is the repository of the divine fullness, and probably for two reasons. Ephesians has a major concern with ecclesiology—a theology of the community of "the saints" (1:1)—which is lacking in Colossians; and its author is far less concerned with incursions of pagan outlook and practice into Christian life than was its predecessor. The divine *plērōma* just below the All and above the cosmic powers is not an immediate concern for him. Ephesians wishes to situate the fullness of godhead in Christ as Colossians does but in Christ head and members, not in Christ alone. Such elements of cosmic myth as may underlie Ephesians run fairly thin. Only the evil spirits in the regions above remain (6:11–12; cf. 4:27). The emphasis is on an earthly community of Jews and non-Jews whose head is Christ (2:11–22). Their enemy is the devil, against whose wiles exercised through the world's rulers (kosmokratoras) they should arm themselves. The struggle is here, not in some distant skies.

God has already given the capacity not to yield to sin (4:26). Rich treasures of redemption through Christ's blood and the forgiveness of trespasses have been bestowed, all summed up as "grace" (1:7). The addressees are called in hope to a glorious inheritance (1:14, 18), but even now they are raised up in the heavenly places with Christ (2:6), as he has been raised up from the dead (1:20–21). Both inhabit the "heavenly places." The effect of grace is present, but at the same time it is not present. It can be imperiled by yielding, in sin, to the diabolical wiles.

The message of Ephesians is not by any means purely one of morality. There is a dream of cosmic reconciliation behind it that is at root a vision of peace on the plane of earth. The mystery of God's will and purpose that has been made known in Christ, set forth as a plan to be completed in the fullness of time, is the uniting in Christ of all elements of discord as between the heavens and the earth (1:9–10). Christ is God's peacemaker on earth through his headship of the church. If peace is to be achieved on earth, the world and then the cosmos must first take note of this headship of the church. The prince of the air cannot but capitulate.

Believers are destined to a life of the praise of God's glory (1:12). The gospel was preached to them, as Paul might have put it; they were then given the seal of the promised Spirit, as Ephesians did put it (1:13; cf. 2 Cor 1:22). What follows? As the gifts of wisdom and of revelation in the knowledge of God tumble out as from a cornucopia (1:17), the realization dawns that those dead in trespasses and sins have been made alive (2:1). Jarvis Lorry's message from the stage on the Dover Road in A Tale of Two Cities was:

"Recalled to life." Such was the message of newness after the former careers of the Christians of Asia—"children of wrath like the rest of humanity" (2:3). This is a clear touch of Pauline universalism in sin. The writer lumps himself in with the onetime offspring of disobedience (can he be an ethnic Jew? see 2:11–17) and attributes to God's love the rescue of all from death. It is a death of the spirit, the opposite of which is a rescue accomplished through faith (2:8). The whole affair was a gift of God; works had no part in it (2:4–9). But just when the author seems a well-schooled disciple of Paul on this point, it turns out that his major interest is in a single deed of God: the fashioning of this very company in Christ for the performance of good works long ago prepared for (2:10). The struggle over law observance as a necessary complement to faith in Christ is far from this author's mind. He knows Paul's vocabulary on the subject well enough, but puts it in the service of a different matter. Ephesians is interested in a body of Christ raised up from death in sin to do the works of peace (2:10, 14, 17).

Supporting the challenge "you gentiles in the flesh" (2:11; RSV) as an indication of the writer's Jewishness is his knowledge of the vocabulary of circumcision and its opposite, although he may be following Colossians 2:11. The term "uncircumcision" describes not merely not being circumcised but also the custom of surgery to reverse the process by those bent on assimilation to the Greeks. The far and the near who cry out for peace in Isaiah (57:19) are here interpreted to be gentiles and Jews. God's people are called "the near" in Psalm 148:14. The non-Jews alienated from the holy people have been brought close, according to this believer, by the blood of Christ, who "is our peace" (Eph 2:14). The dividing wall of hostility between the two could be the barrier assumed to separate the lower air from the upper air, if the epistle were using the imagery of ancient cosmology. But, again, there is not much evidence for this. Here the barrier seems in fact to be Mosaic Law: in figure, perhaps it is the wall in the Temple courtyard in Jerusalem that prohibited gentiles from coming any closer. Whatever the case, no barrier between Jew and gentile exists any longer for the author of Ephesians.

His is far from a legally observant community, but he knows the history of Jewish separatism, of which keeping the Law was the most evident symbol. Christ the peacemaker creates one new human out of two by "abolishing" (a word this author uses without a scruple) the Law. Paul would never say this. Nonobservance of the Law by gentiles who aspire to membership in Israel—which for Jews was the insurmountable dividing wall—is for the writer and those he addresses the elimination of a wall.

Ephesians sees the new body, the church, as one. The cross (2:16), earlier Christ's blood (2:13), has achieved the unification. This body as a nonfragmented humanity can now approach the Father in one spirit (2:18). The epistle claims no superiority for non-Jews, only an end to their traditional alienation from a Jewish standpoint. They are in the household of God now, as from time immemorial they were not. The patriarchs and Moses are not claimed as the foundation of this household, as might be expected, but the apostles and prophets, with Christ as the stone at the corner (2:20). He is both the peacemaker and the one into whose hands God has entrusted the terms of the peace. The Spirit dwells in the temple that rises on the new foundation (an entirely unlikely foundation for Paul to claim, by the way; the apostles are not a past generation distinct from him).

The temple is not a cosmic dwelling but an earthly habitation. It is the church. The assurance offered to Jews in the new community is that their primacy of election was never in doubt. That given to gentiles is other: their days as "strangers and sojourners," as biblical Israel viewed them, are over. Two quite different figures of speech describe the gentiles' new condition. In one they are fellow "citizens" with the saints (2:19) in the "commonwealth" of Israel (2:12), words that in Greek are formed from *polis*, the word for "city," and in the other they are "built into" the holy temple of the Lord (2:22), in a verb that derives from *oikos*, the word for "house" (see 2 Samuel 7:11). The biblical heritage is well remembered in this epistle. The ethnic Jews in the communities written to are not told as much as the gentiles are for their comfort, only that theirs was a glorious past, that they are the "saints," and that the gentiles had better put off their heathen ways completely and join themselves to them.

In Colossians the mystery concealed within godhead over long ages had the riches of its glory among the gentiles made known to the saints. This mystery, once identified, proves to be one concerned with the end-time but also with partial realization in the present: Christ in you, the hope of glory (Col 1:26–27). Given the probable gentile orientation of Colossians—although, again, there is testimony from historical sources to a large Jewish population at Colossae—the "you," estranged and hostile in mind (Col 1:21), are being told obliquely that the mystery includes God's design to share Israel's end-time hope with them. Ephesians unequivocally makes the "mystery of Christ" told to Paul by revelation (3:3–4; *cf.* Gal. 1:12) a matter of the gentiles' being co-inheritors of the promise with the Jews. Strangely, it is not "the promise made to Abraham." This author concentrates on the one whom Paul has called Abraham's singular "seed" or offspring, Christ (see Gal 3:16). The Spirit has revealed the plan of the mystery—that which Paul usually calls the gospel—as "the eternal purpose realized in Christ Jesus our Lord" (Eph 3:11). This comes close to the phrasing of Romans 16:25–26 and may even derive from it, a final doxology not universally supported by textual witness, in which Paul describes his gospel as the revelation of the mystery long kept secret. It is now disclosed and made known through the prophetic writings "to all the gentiles," as most translations put it. The preposition *eis* (into) is followed by the accusative rather than the dative, however, giving the sense of a disclosure to the gentiles that is lodged *within* them. The mystery is not only about them, it is fulfilled in them. The fulfillment is made known through the church, which must publish the manifold wisdom of God to principalities and powers (3:10). Their undoing as a cosmic force is almost understated by this author. Paramount is the realization of the eternal plan in a gentile-Jewish church that has Christ as its head.

Paul is a prisoner for the sake of "you gentiles" (3:1) in this epistle and a sufferer as well (3:13). He prays for strength for all of them in their inner being (*esō anthrōpon*, 3:16), a peculiarly Hellenistic expression, as the reference to Christ's dwelling in their hearts through trust (3:17) is peculiarly Hebraic. Cosmic concern has not departed utterly from Ephesians, since there is the concluding prayer (3:14–19, followed by a doxology, 3:20–21) that the recipients, along with other believers, may comprehend the cosmic dimensions of Christ's love. In its breadth, length, height, and depth this love reaches everywhere to overcome whatever powers there are. The love of Christ is "beyond knowledge" here (3:19), somewhat as his peace "surpasseth understanding," in the familiar phrase of the Authorized Version.

The hortatory portion of the epistle begins with a plea for humility, patience, and mutual forbearance so that the bond of peace may be maintained (4:1–4). Could it be that the gentiles, who are growing far more numerous in the communities addressed here, are being asked not to lord it over the Jews? Certainly they are being reminded of their religious origins in Israel (2:12, 19). The distinction between the way they were schooled in discipleship in Christ (4:20) and the way they have been both hearers and learners "in him, as the truth is in Jesus" (4:21; RSV), does not occur anywhere else in the New Testament. It also hints ironically at a flawed antinomian instruction centered on the heavenly Christ without reference to the Jewish teacher Jesus, the embodiment of God's truth.

In support of the contention that the author does not wish the Jewish background of the "one body" to escape his hearers, there is the rabbinic convention employed early in chapter 4 that underscores the oneness of God by presenting a list of three, five, or seven things that are also unique and testify to the divine uniqueness. In verses 4–6, six unique realities culminate in a seventh, which is God: one body, one Spirit, one hope, one Lord, one faith, one baptism.

Often the last three are quoted separately in Christian usage, giving a wrong impression of what is going on here. The one body at the head of the list is the prime analogue for God. It is the work of the one God through the Spirit; its head is the Lord; by adhering to it in the faith that led to baptism, believers can experience the fulfillment of end-time hope. These three verses contain mention of the Spirit, the Lord, and the God who is Father; hence they may have constituted a catechetical summary to be memorized by candidates for baptism.

As so often in this treatise on the church's faith, there is swift alternation from the sphere of humanity to that of deity and back. The initial exhortation is that believers live a life worthy of their calling, which is basically to maintain the bond of peace in the Spirit

(4:1–3). But their common life in the body is shortly caught up in the threefold mystery of a godhead that penetrates all (for 4:6, see 1 Cor 8:6). It does not stay on deity's plane, for God will give deity "to each of us" as grace in the measure of Christ's bestowal (4:7).

The immediately next move is one of ascent. The psalm verse (Ps 68:18) paraphrased by Colossians (2:15) is here given in full (4:8) but with an important alteration. The Judahite king of the psalm humiliated his enemies as he led them upward to Mount Zion. Here the verse is understood to refer to the exalted Christ who gives gifts rather than receives them, as the text has it. But God's enemies are no less humiliated in the Ephesians interpretation. The "captives" are the vanquished powers who are brought low. Jewish apocalyptic believed that the fallen angels of light were cast down to the earth (see Rev 12:7–9, Luke 10:15, Jude 6) and even to the depths of the underworld. Here, the claim is made for Christ that as victor over the powers he ascends to the heights and descends to the depths, filling all the reaches of space with his power and giving gifts on the earth. "Into the lower parts of [or: regions beneath] the earth" is the translation of *eis ta katōtera* (4:9) in most English Bibles. The last word is a substantival adjective meaning "those things that are below." Some later Greek manuscripts make this explicit by adding the noun for "places" or "regions," but even without it that is probably the meaning, and not "down to the earth." In 1 Peter 3:19 and Romans 10:7, echoes of the apocryphal 1 Enoch 9:10 and 10:11–15 led to the creedal phrase "descended into hell." This could mean simply Jesus' burial in the tomb, which for the Jews of his day was a going down into *sheol*, the netherworld; or it could mean (as it probably does here) a descent to the mythical realm of the dark powers to break their hold.

The gifts Christ gave to those on earth were the various ministries that Paul described (4:11–12; *cf.* 1 Cor 12:5, 28–30), calculated to build up the body of Christ until it reaches unity in faith and all in it achieve maturity to the stature of the fullness of Christ (4:13–14; *cf.* Col 1:19, 28). It is tempting from this point on in the epistle to point out its Colossians-like phrases or others seemingly derived from Paul's seven letters. That would both be tedious and give the impression, through a forest of citations, that there was nothing original or ingenious about the work. It is, in fact, a most remarkable catechetical summary of all that the third-generation church in a particular area did and taught about itself and hoped for at the consummation of all.

The danger might be to categorize Ephesians as a mere anthology of Pauline thought in which the directness and spontaneity of the apostle's letters are lacking. But since it is not a piece of correspondence, this might miss the point altogether. Ephesians is a carefully crafted exercise in persuasive rhetoric—largely but not exclusively Paul-inspired—that probably draws on an oral tradition of instruction rather than directly on written sources (with the probable exception of Colossians). Its author, far from being merely derivative, has produced an ingenious handbook that is breathtaking in its compass and completeness. Just when the text seems to descend to an excoriation of the sins of the pagans as horrible examples of a way of life to avoid (e.g., 4:17–32), it will be interspersed with appeals to a fresh way of thinking in the Spirit and a tenderheartedness and mutual forgiveness. The old human nature must yield to the new. The Holy Spirit must not be grieved by bitterness and anger and slander. Thieves in the communities must get out of the business of preying on others and into the productive labor that can relieve people's needs. When Ephesians is not soaring in the heights—or, more precisely, once having soared—it is a hardheaded manual of social ethics, the themes of which will not be unfamiliar to modern-day readers. "Deceitful lusts" (4:22; RSV) were part of that ancient world, just as seduction and date-rape are part of ours; and there was plenty of drunkenness, humanity's best-known addiction. The reminder that the right name for covetousness is idolatry (5:5) is a statement that summarizes the predominant religious cult of our age: "I want it all."

The gift Ephesians has for memorable expression has made it a sourcebook not only for doctrine and morality but for piety and liturgy. Like the student discovering what a "handbook of quotations" *Hamlet* is, the modern adult of literate habits is likely to exclaim at many points: "So that's where it comes from!" Here are just a few nuggets known—if they are known at all—in various half-remembered versions, often from an annual public reading in church: "Once you were darkness but now you are light in the Lord; walk then as children of light" (5:8). "Awake, O sleeper, and arise from the dead,/and Christ shall give you light" (5:14; RSV). "Look carefully then how you walk, not as fools but as wise, ransoming the time, because the days are evil" (5:15–16). "And walk in love, as Christ loved us and gave himself up for us, a fragrant offering and sacrifice to God" (5:2; RSV). "An ambassador in chains" (6:20; RSV). Often people who know these texts in a general way will grow confused as to where to look for them. The commonest question, for those capable of entertaining it, is whether a particular text is to be found in Colossians or Ephesians—or both? "Psalms and hymns and spiritual songs," to take a representative example (Col 3:16, Eph 5:19; RSV) should be sung in different circumstances in the two epistles; in the first, thankfully, as the context of mutual teaching and admonishing of the indwelling word of Christ; in the second as a mode of Spirit-filled address to God, again in gratitude but with the memorable "making melody to the Lord with all your heart."

It was said of Alfred Loisy earlier in this century that he not only had committed the four Gospels in Greek to memory but could solve problems of the interdependence of the first three without looking them up. Whoever can claim the same recall regarding these two epistles (and including the address and farewell of the Epistle to Philemon) is to be viewed with awe. Such feats of memory should not be put in the service of solving literary problems, however, but should be a means of praying the church's Scriptures.

Two considerations remain: the long section of the domestic duties of followers of Christ (5:21–6:9) and the extended image of military armory against the powers of evil (6:10–20). Ephesians begins its injunctions to the married by speaking of a mutual subjection (5:21) as part of the awe due to Christ. Colossians has failed to do this. But the immediate acceptability of the phrase to the modern ear may go unregistered because of the assumed order in the life of the family that follows: as Christ is to the church, namely Lord and head, so the husband is to the wife. Women of every generation have welcomed the lifetime support of their husbands, but making the husband a "savior" (5:23) after the manner of Christ takes little account of the female experience of male weakness, not to say sin.

The subjection of wives to husbands "in all things" (5:24) will have the warrant of rabbinical interpretation of the Genesis account of the first pair. The prevailing Greek culture probably thought the same way. It could have been an unquestioned male axiom at the time of the writing. In our day, these words can only be heard with modern ears, not ancient ones, whether they appear in a Sunday pulpit reading or in the marriage service. This is tragic, for the words tend to obliterate all the exhortations to male tenderness in marriage in verses 25–30 and 33a. The fact is, though, that these lines will not be heard by feminists of either sex who are still angered by verses 23–24. Nor will it give contemporaries any relief to say that Paul is not their enemy, as they had supposed, but a disciple of his; to point out that if, as seems likely, 1 Corinthians 14:33b–35 is a gloss imported from 1 Timothy 2:11–12 ("Women should keep silent in the assemblies . . . if there is anything they wish to know, let them ask their husbands at home"), Paul has a better record as a feminist than all who claimed his mantle (see, e.g., 1 Cor 11:11). It is gratuitous to suppose, however, that he would have conceived order in the family differently from his peers. The Christ:church::husband:wife analogy would have come as naturally to him as to the author of Ephesians.

Ephesians gets better marks for its development of a bridegroom's solicitude for his bride as an image of Christ's concern for the church. But, of course, neither Jewish nor pagan culture permitted the man intimate bridal preparation of the woman. Theology has clearly taken over from folk custom, but the treatment is gentle. It is even insightful, if unconsciously so. Male love for a spouse is reductively self-love (5:28b–29a). Every man wants a bride who reflects credit on *him* (5:27). One can only hope that Christ has better motives for cherishing the church than the image allows, namely that its membership of him makes the church lovable in and for itself (5:30). Genesis 2:24 is perhaps quoted because of the weight put on it in the tradition by a remembered word of Jesus'. The joining of two as one becomes a great symbol of Christ and the church (5:31–32), just as the later "mystery" symbolizes the older one.

The duty of children to obey their parents comes next after spouses in the household table (6:1). The New Testament term "children," along with the reminder that none of the other commandments carries a promise with it (6:2), tends to obliterate the Mosaic concern that adult sons and daughters should attend to their aged parents. Longevity for dutiful offspring had long ceased to be a literal hope of hellenized believers like the author, but concern for their children had to come first after that for spouses. Fathers provoking their children to anger (6:4; *cf.* Col 3:21, which used a similar verb) we would nowadays call nagging or "riding." It is a timeless counsel. "Bring them up in the *paideia* of the Lord," the injunction goes on. The Greek word came in time to mean "education," but here it means "nurture," the art of conveying what a good young human being should be.

As to slaves, the "fear and trembling" with which Paul proposed Christians work out their salvation is hardly the counsel we would give to these unfortunates, nor would we be likely to name their masters as surrogates for Christ (6:5). Granted, the ancient world was organized much differently from ours; even so, Americans familiar with the sermons delivered in slave quarters by white preachers on just this text are wary of saying a kind word for it. The command to masters not to threaten their slaves is an easier matter (6:9; *cf.* Col 4:4, where dealing with them justly and fairly is the only command).

Ephesians 6:10–17 has in common with 1 Thessalonians 5:8, but in a much more developed form, the allegory of the soldier in full panoply who can resist the wiles and wickedness of the devil, here made equivalent to the "powers" or hosts of wickedness in the regions above. Such military imagery, traceable to the Wisdom of Solomon 5:18–20a, was much favored in the past by preachers who accepted war and battle as a part of life. Those alerted to the horrors of modern war are far less likely to be attracted to military figures of speech. The sword of the Spirit as the word of God (6:17) has become a familiar phrase—so much so that one is tempted to forget that a sword's primary purpose is to decapitate or run a person through.

New Testament critics have taken Ephesians to task for its stylistic exuberance, but a careful examination reveals their main complaint: the letter is not Paul's. There is no expectation of the Parousia; "church" means the universal church, not an individual congregation; believers have to prove themselves worthy of membership in the body; and Christ and the church are yoked in a way that Paul would never do. In a word, with Ephesians (not Luke) "early Catholicism" has set in. This had to happen sometime, for preaching such as Paul's was saying less and less to the Christians, who barely remembered the first diaspora generation. God raised someone up for the important task of bringing a gospel that had been clothed in eschatological categories to a pagan world familiar with its own mythology. As is so often the case in regard to biblical authorship, we do not know the person's name.

Bibliography

Barth, Markus. *Ephesians: Introduction, Translation, and Commentary.* Anchor Bible, vols. 34–34a. Garden City, N.Y., 1974.

Caird, G. B. *Paul's Letters from Prison: Ephesians, Philippians, Colossians, Philemon.* Oxford, 1976.

Schillebeeckx, Edward. "The Peace of Christ Among the Gentiles: Ephesians." In his *Christ: The Experience of Jesus as Lord.* New York, 1980. Pp. 195–217.

Talbert, C. H. "The Myth of a Descending-Ascending Redeemer in Mediterranean Antiquity." *New Testament Studies* 22 (1976): 418–440.

GERARD S. SLOYAN

Philippians

HISTORICAL SETTING

IN PHILIPPIANS, PAUL addresses Christians of the renowned city of Philippi in the Roman province of Macedonia, Christians with whom he shared a remarkable affection. It has been long accepted that the imprisonment Paul mentions (Phil 1:7) was in Rome, since, according to Acts 28:16–31, he was under house arrest there. Several reasons for this opinion are usually given, especially Paul's final greetings from the "household of Caesar" (Phil 4:22), his apparent freedom of movement (which was characteristic of his Roman imprisonment), and his several allusions in the letter to facing death, together with the tradition that Paul died in Rome under Nero around the years 60–64. Further, it has been argued that Philippians belongs with the other "captivity letters" (i.e., Ephesians, Colossians, and Philemon) and that these were written from the same imprisonment, namely, in Rome near the end of his life, between 61 and 63.

In modern times, however, this opinion has been challenged, and Ephesus has been suggested as the place of Paul's imprisonment when writing Philippians. A primary argument for Ephesus is the facility and frequency of the visits between Paul and the members of the Philippian community that are indicated by the correspondence. Paul implies that exchanges of messages and gifts were possible on three or four occasions. Such exchanges would make the week-long journey between Philippi and Ephesus more reasonable than the month-long, arduous journey to Rome. Although Acts does not mention an imprisonment at Ephesus, Paul himself says that he faced death in Asia (1 Cor 15:30–32; 2 Cor 1:8–10), a circumstance that fits the situation he describes in Philippians. Inscriptions found at Ephesus show that the praetorian guard (Phil 1:13) was stationed there, a possible basis for Paul's reference to "Caesar's household."

Paul made converts at Philippi, especially among the gentiles. According to Acts 16:14–15 and 16:40, a woman named Lydia seems to have been the head of the house church there, and other women were also prominent, as Philippians 4:2–3 indicates. Nevertheless, in contrast to his close relationship with the Christians in that town, Paul experienced a great deal of trouble with the authorities and merchants of Philippi, according to Acts, because he had exorcised "a spirit of divination" from a slave-girl thereby eliminating a source of income for several people (Acts 16:16–24). After being jailed and beaten, Paul identified himself as a Roman citizen and was pressured to leave the city. This he was willing to do only after he had taken leave of the community at Lydia's house. Apparently Paul did not visit the community again before he wrote Philippians.

A COMPOSITE LETTER

This Epistle to the Philippians is probably a composite of letters or letter fragments. The impression of fragmentation is based on abrupt transitions and the independent character of several passages (e.g., 4:10–20), as well as on the non-Pauline language and poetic style of some verses (e.g., 2:6–11). The general tone is affectionate; nevertheless, the strident words about the Judaizers in 3:2–4:3 suggest that this was a separate note or fragment. Further, the farewell of 4:4–9 comes more naturally after 3:1. Interpreters therefore usually identify three basic fragments, which probably were united only when Philippians came to be used in liturgies. According to Joseph Fitzmyer, for example, there were originally three letters or fragments: Letter A (1:1–2, 4:10–20) is a thanksgiving for the Philippians' aid to Paul. Letter B (1:3–3:1, 4:4–9, 4:21–23) gives news regarding Paul in prison, greetings and news about Epaphroditus and Timothy, and instructions for the community. It incorporates a liturgical hymn in 2:6–11. Letter C (3:2–4:3) is a warning about the Judaizers.

As a composite letter, Philippians reflects the give and take of a close personal relationship between the writer and his community. Paul appreciates the support he has received from the Philippians (4:14–20). Even in prison his burden is significantly lightened by consistent signs of the community's concern for him. He in turn shows his affection for them, advising against anxiety for him and urging caution about the dangers of their internal divisions.

Several issues developed in Philippians suggest why this letter has been held in high esteem in the Christian tradition. These issues are the ecclesiology of the letter, the hymn of 2:6–11, and the warning about the Judaizers. In discussing these elements, it is important to remember the apocalyptic perspective that influences Paul's reflections on suffering and persecution.

PAUL'S APOCALYPTIC PERSPECTIVE

It is important to understand the impact of apocalyptic thinking on Paul. Jewish apocalyptic literature originated during the time of the Babylonian exile (587–538 B.C.E.), when the Israelites were experiencing great hardship and suffering and therefore confusion about the fidelity of God and their own expectations that God would save them. As the people of God, Israel had long professed a covenant relationship by which they celebrated God's favor to them in worship and practiced their belief that they would always be God's chosen ones. During the captivity, the Israelites were driven from their homeland and forced into slavery and exile in Babylon. There, bereft of the Temple and without freedom of religious expression, they sought meaning and solace in their faith, and they developed a manner of communicating through apocalyptic language and literature that promised reward for faithful suffering, including martyrdom, and punishment for their oppressors. They nourished the deep-rooted longing for the coming of God's reign over all, which involved the elimination of all suffering and all evil.

This apocalyptic thinking, which meant hope for the oppressed and the suffering, had a great impact on early Christian writers, especially Paul. We can see its impact in the Epistle to the Philippians. Some examples are Paul's undaunted hope even as he faces his own imprisonment and the possibility of death. Paul encourages the Philippians, who are experiencing harassment and suffering at the hands of outsiders and threats of division from within, to hold fast to their common faith and to stand firm and fearless against their opponents (1:28). He warns that the latter are destined to "perish," while the faithful will be saved (1:28–29, 3:19). For Paul the reign of God is effected in the resurrection and exaltation of Jesus. In the end "at Jesus' name every knee shall bend" (2:10). The ultimate victory of God in Jesus will be revealed on the "day of Christ" (1:6, 2:16; cf. 3:20–21). Paul's prayer for the Philippians is that they will remain blameless and innocent in the midst of a "crooked and perverse generation" (2:15; cf. Acts 2:40).

The apocalyptic perspective allows Paul to think in categorically exclusive terms, opposing "circumcision of the flesh" to "circumcision of the spirit" (3:3). Similarly Paul contrasts his former valuation of himself with the reevaluation of all things in Christ (3:8–11).

Paul reminds the Philippians to remain steadfast

and firm (1:27–28), to sustain their community in mutual love, sympathy, and encouragement (2:1–5) even while they resist judaizing efforts (3:2–11). Paul entrusts his own life and the lives of the Philippians to the assurance of the coming "day of Christ," when all will be revealed and when God "will bring to completion the good work he began in you" (1:6). Like an athlete, Paul strains forward (2:16, 3:13–14). He would even consider death a "gain," and he eagerly expects the coming of the Lord (1:20–21). Paul encourages the Philippians with the words "Rejoice . . . the Lord is at hand" (4:4–5). Yet the time of the Lord's coming is unknown to Paul, even as he serenely faces the possibility of death in the not distant future, or the uncertainty of remaining yet a longer time in prison.

ECCLESIOLOGY

Philippians' ecclesiology is developed primarily through Paul's reflections on the social relationships among Christians, the role of the liturgy, and the practice of Christian virtues.

Familial and Ministry Models of Relationships

One of the most fruitful avenues of biblical scholarship is the study of the sociological implications of early Christianity. In Philippians such study raises a variety of questions: What are the implications of baptism for church order? What was it like to be a woman in the early Christian communities? What do the letters tell us about the complexity of life in the urban societies, which both promoted and challenged the development of Pauline Christianity? Philippians offers insights about the social relationships developed through commitment to one baptism.

Philippians is one of Paul's more personal letters in the sense that he speaks from the heart about his own situation, his affection for the Philippians, and his fears and concerns. Yet Paul names Timothy as coauthor and identifies both himself and Timothy as "servants of Jesus Christ." The greeting and thanksgiving (1:1–11) reflect the mutuality Paul envisioned for Christians. He relies on the support and the fidelity of the Philippians, just as he knows that they are earnestly concerned about his welfare and that of Timothy (2:19–20) and Epaphroditus (2:25–30).

Paul addresses the Philippians as *adelphoi* ("brothers and sisters," 1:12; 3:1, 13, 17; 4:1, 8; cf. 4:21) since they have become members of the same family in faith. The Philippians are Paul's "beloved" (2:12, 4:1), "saints in Christ Jesus" (1:1; cf. 4:21). They are "partners" with Paul (1:5, 4:15), sharing in the work of spreading the gospel, sharing suffering (cf. 1:29) with unanimity of mind, heart, and spirit in Christ Jesus (2:1–5), and with joy (4:4, 10).

In the service of the gospel, Paul and Timothy have become father and son (2:22). Epaphroditus is Paul's beloved "brother and fellow worker," the Philippians' "messenger" (*apostolon*), and "minister" (*leitourgon*) to Paul's need (2:25). Epaphroditus deserves honor because he nearly died for the work of Christ (2:29–30). According to Paul, suffering is a credential qualifying a minister of the gospel (cf. 2 Cor 4:7–12, 10:1–13:4), and Paul often uses his own suffering as evidence of his authority to speak as an apostle of the gospel.

Paul identifies his own authority with the leadership of Euodia and Syntyche, as well as with Clement and the unnamed person to whom at least the fragment that contains 4:2–3 is addressed. The fact that they labored side by side with Paul indicates that the women enjoyed prestige and recognition in the community.

The freedom enjoyed by women in the Christian communities undoubtedly presented problems for the early church (e.g., 1 Cor 11:2–16, 14:34–36). In Galatians, Paul cited an early baptismal formula saying, "There is neither Jew nor Greek, there is neither slave nor free, there is neither male nor female; for you are all one in Christ" (Gal 3:28). Christianity professed, as Elisabeth Schüssler Fiorenza has stated, a "discipleship of equals." This idea, in the words of Wayne Meeks, signified a new "status inconsistency" with respect to the secular society of the day. Paul does not command Clement or the unnamed addressee to demand obedience from either or both of the women, although in society at large obedience probably could have been expected of women by men. Nor does Paul use his own authority to command a certain resolution of the problem. Rather, he recognizes the work of both women "side by side" with himself, and urges a peaceful resolution by all working together, concentrating on the "peace of God" (4:7) and believing that "the God of peace will be with you" (4:9).

The Role of the Liturgy

The function of the liturgy in the development of the New Testament can hardly be overestimated. Philippians, a composite of letter fragments, seems to have been preserved and eventually treated as a unity as a result of its liturgical use. As a letter, it serves as a kind of "apostolic representative," in the time of Paul's absence and imprisonment. Paul's authority is exercised when his words and advice are read, pondered, acted upon in the Christian assembly, and used as a means to unity.

The greeting "grace and peace" (1:2), the thanksgiving "in all my remembrance of you, always in every prayer of mine" (1:3–4), the doxology (4:20), and the stereotypic final greeting (4:21–23) all add a liturgical dimension to Paul's personal sentiments, his concern for the Philippians, and his strong warning against the judaizing agitators. At times the liturgy seems to have smoothed over the lack of clear transition between fragments. For example, the advice concerning the disagreement between Euodia and Syntyche (4:2–3) could relate to Paul's exhortation about striving for peace through imitation of him and through harmony (4:4–9), although this advice appeared originally as part of the strongly worded warning about agitators (3:2–4:3). The place of insertion of the letter fragment is eased more at the ending than at the beginning (*cf.* the abrupt change between 3:1 and 3:2). The liturgy seems to have provided a setting for the fragments of Paul's letters to be added between the stereotyped beginning and end, within the course of instruction to a praying community. Philippians, with its theme of community and its emphasis on the practice of Christian virtues in imitation of Paul and of Christ himself, is particularly appropriate as an example of the effect of liturgy on the everyday life of Christians.

EXHORTATIONS FOR THE PHILIPPIAN COMMUNITY

Faithful witness to the gospel is carried out in the midst of suffering, divisions, distress, opposition, and even persecution. Paul places before the Philippians the example of Christ and himself. He exhorts them to steadfastness, harmony, humility, obedience, joy, and courage. Paul urges the Philippians to "remain firm in one spirit" (1:27), whether he is with them or not, even in the midst of opposition (1:28) and agitation (3:2). Amid many trials, Christians in the world are "energized" by God to "work out their salvation in fear and trembling" (2:12–13). Paul appeals to the Philippians' desire to please him, speaking of "completing my joy" (2:2) and of the accord they are in the process of developing. He urges them to think with the "mind" of "one love, one heart."

Many of the virtues recommended by Paul were drawn from standard Greek philosophical lists. One remarkable exception is the inclusion of humility or meekness as worthy of Christian practice. This virtue is opposed to self-seeking (2:3; *cf.* Rom 2:8), the petty jealousies that scandalize the community (Phil 4:2), and rivalry born of base motives (1:17). A similar commendation can be seen in 4:8–9. Paul lists the virtues recommended by the Greek philosophers in 4:8 as worthy of the Christians' meditation and imitation. This list is followed by the startling inclusion of Paul's own example in 4:9. True humility, the opposite of arrogance, allows Paul to propose his own life as an example to be followed.

Paul often mentions obedience (*hypakoe*, from the Greek root *akoe*, "hearing") in his letters (*cf.* Phil 2:12; Rom 1:5, 15:18, 16:26; Gal 3:2, 5). Just as Jesus was obedient to God (Phil 2:6–11), the Philippians are urged to practice obedience, a further application of humility.

Whereas "grumbling" characterized the Israelites of old (*cf.* Num 14; 1 Cor 10:9–10), hopeful acceptance without complaint are Christian qualifications (Phil 2:14). This generation is "crooked and perverse" (2:15; *cf.* Matt 12:39; Luke 11:29) as opposed to the Christians, who are to be "innocent and blameless" (*cf.* Matt 10:16, 11:25; Luke 10:21), like lamps to the world (*cf.* Matt 5:14–16). One of the paradoxes of Philippians is that beside Paul's reflections on community, joy, and peace (*cf.* 1:19; 2:2, 18; 4:9) are indications of his own personal suffering and his awareness of the many afflictions endured by the Philippians. Paul enjoins joy and serenity as the hallmark of Christian community—as feelings reaching deeper than the confusion and suffering presently experienced (*cf.* Rom 8:18).

Paul in prison faces the possibility of his own death, perhaps imminently (1:20–22). His life is being "poured out like a libation," an image suggesting that the prospect of death does not lessen Paul's encouragement to the Philippians. He portrays the sacrifice of Christ (2:6–11), aware of the threat suffering poses for faith. Paul's description of the Christian virtue of courage is strengthened by its contrast to shame (1:19–20). In Romans 1:16–17, Paul says that he is not ashamed of the gospel; it is the power of God. God's power, Paul learned, is made perfect in weakness (2 Cor 11:9). The vulnerability of the Philippians is evidence that God will deliver them (Phil 1:6, 28–30).

THE CHRISTOLOGICAL HYMN

The hymn celebrating the example of Christ is all the more powerful within the context of Paul's exhortation to the Philippians to exercise perseverance, humility, and selflessness and to demonstrate the power of joy and peace even in the midst of trial. Paul quotes a christological hymn, adapting it to the needs of the Philippian community and thus adding Christ's own example to his admonitions about maintaining harmony within the community It is very possible that this hymn was already known to the Philippians, since Paul simply inserts it without introduction or explanation. It could be that the verses were part of the common liturgical repertoire that the Philippians shared with other Christian communities. The early church had developed a set of creedal formulas, such as "God raised Jesus from the dead," and confessional formulas, such as "Jesus is Lord" (see Rom 10:9). Similarly the celebrations of the Eucharist and Baptism included the singing of hymns, the recitation of creeds, and the proclaiming of acclamations—all of which helped to solidify and unify the basic Christian beliefs.

The rhythm, parallelism, and terminology of this hymn all tend to distinguish it from its context and from Pauline authorship. The hymn divides into two sentences, each containing three strophes. Christ is the subject of the first sentence (2:6–8), while God is the subject of the second (2:9–11). The first three

strophes speak of preexistence and descent (i.e., the humiliation of Jesus' incarnation and death). The last three refer to exaltation and ascent, in which God honored Christ by giving him a "name above every name" (i.e., Lord).

The language of the hymn is not characteristic of Paul. The expressions "possessing the form of "God"equality with God," and "emptied himself" are unusual in the New Testament. Nevertheless, the hymn's meaning is not inconsistent with Paul's own Christology. Further, the meaning is appropriate to Paul's purposes in writing to the Philippians. The hymn draws on Old Testament images and adapts a poetic style similar to that found in the Psalms. This hymn probably originated in early Jewish-Christian liturgies. Its use here strengthens the unity of the Christian creed, especially since Paul deemed it suitable for this predominantly gentile church. Of particular interest is the hymn's development of Old Testament messianic images. The primary images developed here are of the Suffering Servant who redeems the sins of many, the Son of man who receives cosmic-universal honor and dominion, and the preexistent Wisdom who creates and orders the world. These images do appear elsewhere in Paul's writings and provide the basis for Paul's developing Christology.

Never a popular image for the Messiah in Judaism, the Suffering Servant described in Isaiah 52–53 nevertheless provides a key for Paul's and the early church's presentation of the mission of Jesus. Christ, who possessed the form of God, exchanged it to take on the form of a slave. There is a double contrast expressed in this hymn, between the form of God and the form of the slave, and between Christ's servanthood and the lordship by which Christ is finally exalted.

The hymn's allusion to Christ's abasement (*cf.* 2 Cor 8:9, Heb 5:8) employs the image of the servant of Yahweh, who appears in Isaiah 52:14 described as "so marred and beyond human semblance, and his face beyond that of the sons of man." Of the servant's role Isaiah 53:8–12 says: "He was oppressed and afflicted, . . . stricken for the transgression of my people; . . . /he makes himself an offering for sins, . . . he bore the sins of many." Ideas drawn from this image occur also in Galatians 4:4 and Romans 8:3.

The "form of God" that Christ possessed implies the external appearance of God, analogous to the glory of God in the Hebrew scriptures (*cf.* Exod 16:10, 24:15; Lev 9:6, 23). The "form of a servant" expresses not only Jesus' human appearance but his complete obedience to God. The final stage of this obedient servanthood is expressed in Jesus' death. Paul adds to this hymn the phrase "even unto death on the cross," a phrase that does not fit into the regular rhythm of the hymn. For Paul, this humiliating form of death is at the center of the proclamation and provides the critical factor in God's vindication of Jesus. Death on the cross is cursed by the Jewish Law, according to Galatians 3:13 (*cf.* Deut 21:23). By causing Christ to be raised from the dead, God went beyond the Law and its condemnation, robbing both death and the Law of their verdict and their power. Christ's obedient death freed the many (i.e., "all") from death and the Law and opened the way of the resurrection for all. This pre-Pauline hymn that employs non-Pauline terms is thus appropriated and adapted by Paul to remind the Philippians of the humble, suffering Messiah who triumphed over sin and the Law and whose death freed them from the Law's demands. This image presents the Philippians not only with an example to follow but also with the power, won by Christ, to overcome all divisions, anxiety, and fear as they await Christ's return while proclaiming his lordship.

The Suffering Servant image is joined to the apocalyptic figure, featured in Daniel 7:13–14, of one "like a son of man" who receives power, dominion, and universal and everlasting honor from God, depicted as the "Ancient of Days." The second part of the hymn considers the divine reaction to Christ's obedient death. Normally Paul dwells on the resurrection as the expression of God's vindication of Jesus. The Philippians' hymn rather focuses on Christ's exaltation, his ascent and appearance in the heavenly court, where he is celebrated as Lord by all. This exaltation does not make Christ competitive with the Father but serves to give God glory. This glory is the accomplishment of Jesus' mission to reconcile the whole world and return it to God (*cf.* 1 Cor 15:28; 2 Cor 5:19). The apostle participates in this mission of reconciliation by seeking to take captive every spirit, indeed, every thought, for obedience (*cf.* 2 Cor 10:5). Thus the kingdom of God is proclaimed by those who acknowledge the lordship of Christ. Although the title of Son of man is absent from Paul, its use was evidently prevalent in the early church.

Finally the image of Wisdom, preexistent and ordering all of creation, forms part of the background for this hymn. Wisdom is personified as a woman, creator and nurturer, delighting God even before the foundation of the world (Prov 8:22–31). She helps in the creation of all that comes into being (*cf.* Wis 9:9). Both Paul and John assign these attributes to Christ (*cf.* Jn 1:1–18). Meditation on divine wisdom evoked Paul's exalted celebration at the close of Romans 11 (vv. 34–36). For Paul, the wisdom of the cross is the message of the gospel, and Christ is the wisdom and the power of God (1 Cor 1:24, 30).

THE WARNING ABOUT JUDAIZERS

Paul wrote to a predominantly gentile-Christian community at Philippi, and his warning is not against Jews but against Judaizers, a term that has been coined to describe Christian teachers who wished to impose at least a minimum of requirements of the Jewish Law on the gentile converts to Christianity (*cf.* Gal 2:14). The first-century Jewish-Christian missionary church struggled with the issue of the applicability of the Law's requirements for gentile converts. Paul was reacting to the assertion by some Jewish-Christian missionaries that gentile converts had to fulfill basic requirements (e.g., circumcision, dietary restrictions, and feast observances). Paul does not argue against practice of the Jewish Law for Jews, but he opposes the notion that gentiles must be circumcised or required to fulfill other requirements of the Law. Apparently missionaries from Jewish-Christian churches (*cf.* Gal 2:4–5, 11–21) were following after Paul, agitating gentile converts with the assertion that Paul had not completed his mission to them, saying that now the basics of the Jewish Law had to be fulfilled.

Some interpreters have alleged that Paul's negative and even bitter reaction is against Judaism and was born of his own frustration with fulfilling the Law. But Philippians 3:3–7 acts as a corrective to this psychological approach to Paul's "conversion." Paul says in Philippians 3:6: "I was blameless under the law." Paul does not react against a false religion of legalism, which was hardly characteristic of a truly religious person and probably unrecognizable either to Paul or to his Jewish contemporaries. Rather, he develops his dichotomy between justification by faith and justification by certain works of the Law first in dialogue with other Jewish Christians (*cf.* Gal 2:15–16). His reaction is against the need to convert gentiles to Judaism. The dichotomy occurs again in Philippians, where Paul draws on his personal experience.

"In Christ," Paul has learned to view all reality in a new way (Phil 3:7–9). His own personal advantage as a Jew is now seen as waste, his excellence in knowledge and fulfilling the Law as illusion. Christ has taught him the wisdom of the cross, viewed by the Jews as scandal and the gentiles as folly (1 Cor 1:23). Now Paul reevaluates loss and gain, death and life, in a way that reverses the values of the world, including what is valued by the Law. It is not that the Law cannot be fulfilled nor that it leads to frustration. Fulfilling the Law is simply of no value for the gentiles; it is not a prerequisite for faith. Otherwise, grace would not be grace. It is not that Paul reacts against the Jewish religion but that he now sees Christ as the determining factor in being saved or perishing (3:19). "Their god is the belly" could refer to the idolatry of portraying dietary laws as essential to salvation.

Philippians provides a prime example of Paul's character, and he represents a model not only for that particular community but also for believers today. In Philippians we see at work the dynamic between the coherent center of Paul's apocalyptic thought and the contingency of the specific circumstances experienced by this beloved church. The use of the christological hymn, the virtues recommended to the Philippians, and the warning against the Judaizers all contribute to an appreciation of Paul's ecclesiology and his pastoral style. Philippians can serve both as an introduction to Paul and as a closing chapter on the implications of his life and thought.

Bibliography

Beker, J. Christiaan. *Paul the Apostle: The Triumph of God in Life and Thought.* Philadelphia, 1980.

———. *Paul's Apocalyptic Gospel.* Philadelphia, 1982.

Bruce, F. F. *Paul and His Converts.* Downers Grove, Ill., 1985.

Fitzmyer, Joseph A. "Philippians." In *Jerome Biblical Commentary.* Vol. 2. Englewood Cliffs, N.J., 1968. Pp. 247–253.

Getty, Mary Ann. *Philippians/Philemon.* Wilmington, Del., 1980.

Hock, Ronald F. *The Social Context of Paul's Ministry.* Philadelphia, 1980.

LaVerdiere, Eugene. *Invitation to the New Testament Epistles II.* Garden City, N.Y., 1980.

Meeks, Wayne. *The First Urban Christians: The Social World of the Apostle Paul.* New Haven and London, 1983.

Schüssler Fiorenza, Elisabeth. *In Memory of Her: A Feminist Reconstruction of Christian Origins.* New York, 1983.

MARY ANN GETTY

Colossians

ANYONE WHO TRAVELS to ancient Colossae, just south of the Lycus River in western Turkey, is surprised and pleased to see a town near the site. The modern town is about three miles south of and up the slope of Mount Cadmus from the ancient city founded before the conquests of Alexander. It is known in Turkish as Honaz (ancient Chonae). There is little to interest the visitor in the dusty place except for Turkish village life and the Roman bricks still to be found in many houses, as the guidebooks say. Colossae, mentioned by the Greek historian Xenophon, began to decline with the rise of the rival nearby cities of Laodicea (founded by Antiochus II in the third century B.C.E. and named for his sister-wife) and Hierapolis (possibly founded in the second century B.C.E. by Eumenes II, king of Pergamon). They are a few miles west and northwest of Colossae, respectively, forming a triangle in which Laodicea sits astride the river. An earthquake in 60 C.E. may well have destroyed Colossae; in any case it was the frequent victim of earth tremors. Despite its rebuilding up the hillside within a few years, it never regained its former importance in the ancient world. The Byzantine-Turkish wars of the Middle Ages brought its status lower still. The present traces of the ancient city that received a letter from Paul or a disciple are faint and few.

About ten miles west of Colossae, on a little hill, is the site of ancient Laodicea. Founded in the second century B.C.E. by Antiochus II, it was known anciently as Laodicea ad Lycum, "Laodicea on the Lycus," a tributary of the Meander. Mithridates, king of Pontus, besieged and held it between 88 and 84 B.C.E. Laodicea later suffered serious damage in the same earthquake as Colossae, according to Tacitus, but was then rebuilt. A sizable Jewish population lived there, which probably provided the core of the Christian community. The letter addressed to it in Revelation (3:14–22) stigmatized the recipients as "lukewarm" because of their complacency wealth. The city's ruins have been excavated by a team from Laval University in Quebec starting in 1961. They show a stadium, the remains of a gymnasium or bath, a theater, an amphitheater, and the ruins of what may be a temple to Isis (in use from the second to the fifth century C.E.). Traces of a Roman aqueduct and bridge also remain.

Hierapolis, the third city of the triangle, was destroyed by an earthquake in 17 C.E. but rebuilt. A tradition going back to the late first century conflated the careers of the apostle Philip and the evangelist Philip, one of the Seven (Acts 6:5, 21:8), and resulted in the erection of a *martyrium* there in the fifth century. Papias, who was active in Hierapolis about 125 as its *episkopos* ("bishop," "overseer"), is known for the *Exposition of the Lord's Oracles* attributed to him by Eusebius.

Below the plateau on which ancient Hierapolis

stood, the town of Pamukkale ("Cotton Castle") is situated, a modern tourist resort. Its attraction is not archaeology, pagan or Christian, but the baths available in salt springs and motel pools, and a quite spectacular salt deposit on the face of a travertine cliff to be seen for miles. The ruins of an early-sixth-century basilica are still to be found there, probably the cathedral when Hierapolis was named as a diocese of the church. The marble columns of another huge basilica still stand near the main city gate.

The letter to the Colossians, which should be scrutinized together with Ephesians because the latter is probably based on it, identifies Epaphras, whom Paul calls his "fellow servant" (literally, "fellow slave"), as the one who was the first teacher of the Christians at Colossae (Col 1:7). Paul is described as knowing their faith and love by hearsay (1:4), having been told of it by Epaphras himself (1:8).

The Laodiceans come in for the writer's concern in this letter also. They are referred to as a group who like the Colossians have not seen Paul's face (2:1–3) but are to have this letter read to them in their assembly (4:16). Nympha, in whose house the church meets, and Archippus are to be given a special greeting (4:15, 17). Epaphras, says the writer, has worked as hard for the believers in Laodicea and Hierapolis as for those in Colossae (4:13). The letter is clearly directed to the Christians of the three cities in the Phrygian mountains and assumes that they will not be surprised to hear from the apostle Paul, whose ministry (i.e., service) of the gospel impelled the efforts of Epaphras, Tychicus, Onesimus, Aristarchus, Mark, Jesus Justus, Luke, and Demas (4:7, 9–11, 14).

Numerous characteristics of Colossians have caused many scholars to argue that the letter was not written by Paul himself but by one of his followers. A difficulty about the many greetings the author asks to be transmitted toward the end of this letter (4:7–17) is that most of the names occur in the brief, unquestionably authentic letter to Philemon. Paul and Timothy are, together, named as the senders of Colossians and Philemon. Both letters are sent from prison in some unspecified place (Phlm 1, 13, 23; Col 4:2, 10, 18). Only Apphia appears in Philemon but not Colossians, only Tychicus, Jesus Justus, and Nympha in Colossians but not Philemon. These details would not in themselves be suspicious. One might write from prison to certain close friends and fellow workers at the same time and in the same frame of mind. The problem of Colossians is not so much that a good part of its last chapter seems to have been appended in order to authenticate it (especially 4:18, "I, Paul, write this greeting with my own hand," the signature of 1 Corinthians), nor even that its vocabulary and style are not characteristic of Paul, but that it responds to a challenge of cosmic, pagan religion faced by people acknowledged as unknown to Paul (2:1). Eighty-seven words used in Colossians do not appear in any of the undisputed Pauline letters. Twenty-five of these are also found in the equally disputed letter to the Ephesians. The totals are not conclusive, especially in light of the matters being discussed where the unique words occur (the hymn of 1:15–20 and the polemic of 2:6–23); but they are indicative. Even more significant are the terms and concepts that are characteristic of Paul that never turn up in Colossians: sin (in the singular), revelation, law, righteousness and related words, freedom, promise, boast, believe, obedience, and salvation. This argument is not probative either, however, for certain of these terms are not frequent in one or another authentic letter of Paul. It could be and has been maintained that since the subject matter of Colossians differs from that of the indisputably Pauline letters, this factor would account sufficiently for the vocabulary differences.

All this is true, but one would not expect Paul to desert the characteristic styles in which he addresses the recipients of a letter or by which he structures sentences. For example, the direct address "Brethren" or "My brethren," common in all the undisputed letters of Paul, does not occur in Colossians, Ephesians, or the "Pastoral" epistles, 1 and 2 Timothy and Titus. Similarly missing from Colossians are familiar Pauline connective phrases like "if anyone" and "but not only," and the Greek particles meaning "on which account," "therefore," and "because." Furthermore, numerous stylistic peculiarities of Colossians differ from Paul's style in the undisputed letters. For example, Colossians often uses synonyms in close conjunction or joins them by a non-declined "which is," a phrase never used by Paul in the undisputed letters. Colossians especially multiplies the use of dependent genitive constructions, often translated by the preposition "of" (for example, "the riches of the glory of this mystery" [1:27], or "to all riches of assurance of understanding, to the knowledge of the mystery of God, [namely] of Christ" [2:2; translations by the author except as noted]). Colossians also regularly attaches a noun to the preposition "in" ("in truth," "in spirit," "in power," "in the light").

The most convincing argument for the authorship of Colossians by a Pauline disciple and not the apostle himself, however, is the content of this epistle. The author seems to be faced with an expression of the current cosmic religion of paganism that is not testified to on these terms in Paul's extant correspondence. Paul knew the challenge of paganism in the Galatian churches but never, it seems, quite as it is described here. In Colossians we encounter a rival to the gospel for those to whom it had been preached in the generation after Paul, which he never had to face among members of his churches. Luckily, we know from pagan sources a good deal about the *philosophia* that the letter calls "empty deceit" (2:8). It was no hole-and-corner religion, no cult practiced by the few. It was, rather, the prevailing popular religion of the empire. There were elements in it of what would later be called gnosticism, but this religion professed no simple spirit-matter dichotomy. It was convinced there was a struggle for the human spirit being waged by the "elemental spirits" on the plane of earth.

Hellenist Judaism was both Paul's religion and the one he encountered wherever he met Jews and gentiles (the latter probably converts to Judaism or admirers of it) living in proximity. If he experienced pagan populations uninfluenced by Judaism, he never makes that clear. He wrote to Thessalonica as if its new believers had once worshiped idols (1 Thess 1:9) and to some communities in the province of Galatia as if, not being "under the law"—certainly not Jews but perhaps also not a certain type of observant Jew—they wished to be "under the law" (Gal 4:21). Nowhere, however, in an extant letter does he spell out the lure that the prevailing paganism exerted on those gentiles who had felt no attraction to Judaism as they came to hear the gospel. Paul reports on a judaizing movement, possibly the work of gentiles. Colossians conversely tells of a backsliding into an expression of paganism with which Paul does not elsewhere show familiarity. It hence provides an important missing link of religious history because it shows how a teacher of the generation after Paul tried to draw on Paul's heritage while presenting the gospel to a different population than the one Paul evangelized.

Rather than trying to defend Paul's authorship of this document either in his own person or through a secretary like Timothy to whom he conveyed its content, and rather than regretting how unlike Paul certain features are, we shall try to appreciate the insights it promises. The ancient literary convention of pseudepigraphy, which attributed authorship of a document to a great figure of the past in order to get a hearing for its message, has proved a happy fault more than once. Colossians can tell us something we need to know about the generation after Paul, for through its false attribution this letter has preserved in the name of Paul a window on the conflict between a gospel that had come out of Hellenist Judaism and the Hellenist popular religion by which the greatest part of the population lived. To take that popular paganism on was the chief wonder of the late-first-century spread of the gospel. We have few records of this great struggle other than the letters to the Colossians and Ephesians.

Cynic and Stoic ethics had recommended themselves to pagan and Jewish teachers alike, to the latter when the precepts of the pagans coincided with the teachings of the Torah. The theism of Platonism and its various daughter schools had popular influence but was not a pure theism like that of the Bible. It usually featured a deity who was the One or the All marked by "fullness" (*plērōma*), a God who at the same time surmounted a hierarchy of spirits. Between deity and the inhabitants of the earth were a whole host of intermediary beings with whom humanity had more to do than with deity itself. This heavily populated universe of popular paganism happened to coincide with postexilic Jewish belief in both a heavenly court and legions of troublesome unclean spirits. In first-century Judaism not only the devils of hell were to be feared (see Matt 25:41) but the capricious "powers" as well. Among those in the highest ranks were tutelary spirits to whom were entrusted the movements of the planets and stars (Uriel, in the postbiblical apocalyptic writings) and the destiny of the people Israel

(Michael). These angels were viewed as doing God's bidding, but of a whole host of lesser "powers" the Jews of this period could not be sure. It can be seen how Christian neophytes from paganism could find a set of symbols in popular Jewish religion to put them at their ease.

The two bands of spirits of popular paganism and nonbiblical Jewish angelology, lumped together as *stoicheia* (cosmic powers), could be thought of as a necessary supplement to belief in the one God. They were worshiped by ordinary devotees whose daily lives gave them every reason to be anxious, under the generic title "elemental spirits of the universe" (*stoicheia tou kosmou*, Col 2:8, 20). The hope was that they would give access to the divine, the "fullness" spoken of above. "In other words," as Edward Schillebeeckx puts it, "the aim of the angel cult was the experience of being filled with divinity (2:10)" (1980, 183). It is not possible to reconstruct the exact "philosophy" (2:8) that Colossians was taking exception to, if indeed there was anything exact about it. The word "philosophy" in this context did not mean rigorous critical thought but any of various religious ways of life. Even Hellenist Judaism would describe itself as a philosophy to gain respectability (4 Macc 5:11; Philo, *Legation to Gaius* 156). The Jewish historian Josephus spoke of the Pharisees, Sadducees, and Essenes as philosophical schools within Judaism (*War* 2.119, *Antiquities* 18.11). The one understanding of philosophy that late-first-century Jewish teachers would not have approved was as a description of induction into the pagan mystery cults, even though Judaism was not without its esoterica.

A basic understanding underlying late-first-century paganism was that the world was out of joint. Some primordial catastrophe had set the heavens and the earth at odds. The things that were in the heavens, or "above" were by definition less flawed than "things that are on the earth" (Col 3:1–2). The "heavenly places" (*ta epourania*) would describe this celestial sphere quite accurately for the author of Ephesians (2:6). Even Paul thought that the heavenly bodies like the planets and stars were celestial (the same word as above is used adjectivally in 1 Corinthians 15:40), not simply because they were "up there" but because they were thought to be composed of more subtle matter. The human race on the earth

below, sharing in the consequences of the cosmic fault, was in need of reconciliation—with what or whom is not clear, but probably the heavens. In the Christian solution provided by Colossians a reconciliation with the divine "fullness" (*plērōma*) is only to be achieved through reconciliation with Christ, in whom this fullness dwelt (1:19–20; see the *Hermetic Corpus* 6.4 for God as "the *pleroma* of good").

Pagan religious thought found ample evidence for a primeval decline of the earthly and human condition to its present state: wretchedness of body and spirit, the overwhelming force of destiny, and anxiety over uncertain deeds left certainly undone. The desire to do good that ends in failure and the involuntary doing of evil has always been a problem for humanity. This problem was carefully articulated in Mediterranean antiquity. The meaninglessness of existence was not an idle phrase for the ancient world but a lived reality. Various pagan religions sought meaning or "salvation" through discovery of the lost unity of the cosmos. The integrating link between the heavens and the earth was to be found, they were convinced, by wisdom, insight, and knowledge. Colossians reflects this search by speaking of "wisdom" (*sophia*, 1:9, 28; 2:3, 23; 4:5), "understanding" (*synesis*, 1:9, 2:2), and "knowledge" (*gnōsis*, 2:3 or the roughly equivalent *epignōsis* 1:6 [in verb form], 9, 10; 2:2; 3:10). Often the adjective "all" precedes these nouns or they are used to describe a word like "treasures." In popular religion total faith was put in these states of intellect and spirit as the keys to unlock the riddle of the universe.

The chief things to be known were the "elements of the universe" (*stoicheia tou kosmou*). From the usage of this phrase in the New Testament, these are not just basic components in a series, the literal meaning of the word *stoicheia* (according to Plato the primary elements of which all is composed, *Theaetetus* 201e), but animated spirits, or, in Jewish understanding, angelic ones. Earth, fire, water, and air were the traditional "elements" in ancient cosmology, but by a syncretistic process they became the "cosmic rulers of darkness" in a number of religions, variously seven (for the "planets"), twelve (for the signs of the zodiac), or thirty-six. In popular Hellenist Judaism they became angels related to the stars (1 Enoch 43:1–2) and to the seasons and the years (2 Enoch

19:1–4). They were worshiped not as deities but as divine powers—ministering spirits who because of their intimate relation to the stars had a say in human destiny.

Hellenistic thought related the microcosm to the macrocosm by maintaining that humans were formed of the same elements as the cosmos. To know of the stars and the powers behind them, furthermore to reverence them, was to have a measure of control over one's destiny. It is unclear how much this cosmic speculation influenced the ordinary Hellenist Jew. Most of the pious and the learned surely fled it, but a few of the latter wrote treatises indicating that it was the prevailing cosmology and to their minds not at odds with Jewish faith. Just as astrology and various half-digested Asian religions absorb many nominal Christians and Jews of today, so ancient, uninstructed Jews living in a sea of paganism might incline toward cultic practices that seemed to them compatible with Israelite faith. Colossians identifies a threat to integral Christian living without providing enough clues to identify the ethnic or religious makeup of the recipients of the admonition. They may have been Jewish in part (witness the references to circumcision and uncircumcision, 2:11, 13; 3:11) but, if so, heavily under the influence of syncretistic attempts to overcome the threats of an unfriendly universe.

The epistle opens with a traditional Pauline greeting and thanksgiving, but when it speaks of hope in 1:5, it does so in a way that distinguishes it from the usage of Paul. Hope meant much to him, but always in terms of the fulfillment of God's promises in the future. Here its object is fulfillment in a place, the heavens. First Peter contains the same usage at 1:4, Ephesians will echo it in 1:18. In Hebrews hope is an "anchor of the soul . . . that enters into the inner shrine beyond the curtain" (6:19; RSV). For his part, Paul waits for God's Son to come from the heavens (1 Thess 1:10) and can wish to be "away from the body and at home with the Lord," to "receive good" after appearing before "the judgment seat of Christ" (2 Cor 5:8, 10; RSV). He nonetheless never describes this life as the object of his hope. The Christian conception of heaven as an abode to look forward to in hope may take its beginnings from Colossians.

When this letter prays that its recipients may have "knowledge of [God's] will in all spiritual wisdom and understanding" (1:9; RSV) it resembles the opening prayer in Philippians 1:9 for "knowledge and all discernment." God's will, says the author, is that the Colossian community should bear fruit in good works. It must grow in the knowledge of God, achieving patience by dint of the "power" that is a divine gift. The phrasing of verses 9–11 is very Jewish with its stress on the might to endure. The invitation to give thanks that follows (1:12–13) enjoins the Colossians to have a part and lot with the holy ones in light, who are the angels of the heavenly inheritance spoken of in 1:5. While that sharing lies ahead, there is a transfer of realms that has already been achieved for the baptized. They have gone from the dominion of darkness to the dominion of the Son of God's love (1:13).

This antithesis of light and darkness is found in the Dead Sea Scrolls and is a major motif in John. Ephesians also contains it (Eph 5:8), perhaps derived from the present epistle. Luke's Gospel has the phrase "the dominion of darkness" (Luke 22:53); Paul sets light and darkness in opposition (2 Cor 6:14); and 1 Peter refers to a transfer from darkness to light by way of divine calling quite like that of Colossians (1 Pet 2:9). When we encounter the antithesis in 1 Clement (59:2) at the end of the first century, it could come from any of these sources or from common oral usage. It is important to observe here the progression from Paul's description of the temporary reign of Christ until God becomes "all in all" (1 Cor 15:24–25, 28) to Colossians' conception of Christ's rule of the world as an accomplished fact. In Colossians, contrary to the Pauline position, Christ is already "all, and in all" (3:11; RSV). Believers possess redemption in him and have the remission of sins (1:14). The tentativeness of an earlier age has been supplanted by a new assurance. Salvation in Christ is understood as a present reality by the time Colossians is written, whereas for Paul salvation always lies in the end-time future.

The verses of thanksgiving (1:12–14) lead into a hymn (1:15–20) that was presumably familiar in some form to the Christians of Phrygia. The "us" and the "we" of verses 13–14 are slightly at odds with the "you" of verse 12 and lead into a hymnic, third-person description of the Son, introduced by the relative pronoun "who" (1:15), a fact masked by most translations. The hymn was probably an original Christian composition, although some have argued that if the phrases "of the church" (1:18a) and "through the blood of his cross" (1:20) were removed, a perfectly satisfactory pagan Logos hymn would remain. Other elements, however, indicate a Christian origin—as, for example, the phrase "firstborn from the dead" (1:18), the biblical phrase "was pleased to dwell" (1:19), and the theme of creation and reconciliation. If the hymn had pagan antecedents, they had been well christianized by the time the author of Colossians got hold of it as a source.

The lordship of Christ is spelled out in the hymn as his mastery of the cosmos. He is neither inferior nor subordinate to anything in it. The phrases "image of the invisible God" and "firstborn of all creation" might well be used of the Logos described by Philo the Jewish philosopher. The idea of the creation of all things "visible and invisible" through the Son, which would find a place in the creed of Nicaea, occurs for the first time in Christian writings here (1:16). As "firstborn of all creation," although himself preexistent to it (vv. 15, 17), the Son surmounts even the cosmic powers, called "thrones," "dominions," "principalities," and "authorities" in a classification familiar to Jewish angelology (see 1 Cor 8:5, 15:24; Rom 8:38; 1 Enoch 61:10). They have all been created in him. Like Wisdom in the sapiential writings (Prov 8:22; Sir 1:4, 24:9; Wis 9:4, 9) he is the mediator of their creation. Christ is the bond who holds the universe together (Col 1:17; cf. Sir 43:26).

The church as a body (Col 1:18) is a figure Paul uses (1 Cor 11:29, 12:13–27; Rom 12:4–9) but there is no cosmic dimension to his usage. It is the familiar Stoic comparison of the functions and services of persons in a group to the members of a human body. In the Colossians hymn the reference is to the cosmos ("all things," vv. 16, 17) as a body whose head is Christ. Philo puts the Logos in a directive function over the body of the heavens in this way, as the Stoic and Orphic traditions had done before him. But, unexpectedly, in Colossians the headship of Christ is not immediately over the cosmos but over the church (1:18). Total preeminence is given to him, however, for the reconciliation of the heavens and the earth (1:20). This can only mean that the fullness of deity dwelling in Christ is using Christ's headship of the church as a means to assert his headship of the cosmos. The cosmos is evidently his body only where it is the church, that is, a universe under the guidance of those who have freely subjected themselves to Christ.

Colossians asserts that the blood of Christ's cross (1:20), that is, his death (1:22)—an event in history —has achieved the restoration of order to the earth and the heavens (1:20). Human estrangement and hostility are over (1:21). For the author this is the solution the Christian faith puts forward for the alienation the pagan world has experienced. Believers, if they remain steadfast in the gospel they have heard, have irreproachability or blamelessness as their new condition (1:22–23). This is a kind of invulnerability Paul does not habitually attribute to his converts, but it does not contradict his conviction that faith in the cross and resurrection is God's answer to the human plight.

Paul's afflictions and energetic strivings (1:24, 29) are familiar from his correspondence, but not the idea that Paul's sufferings "complete what is lacking in Christ's afflictions for the sake of his body" (1:24; RSV). The notion so repels certain loyal interpreters of Paul that they have engaged in a variety of athletic exercises to establish that the author, having said it, could not have meant it. A solidarity in suffering between Christ and his apostle, however, must not have been so repulsive to the writer of this epistle as to a modern theologian protecting the "one mediator" of 1 Timothy 2:5. All the sufferings endured by Paul for the sake of the church up to the time of the writing could be what are "lacking in Christ's afflictions." To say they are of no effect on the church's behalf is to deny without reason what Colossians affirms. To say that they achieve nothing salutary for the church is to protect a dogmatic principle against the written evidence. If Paul himself can assert that he endures affliction "for your comfort and salvation" (2 Cor 1:6), he must have in mind a salvific value of some sort. It seems better to ponder what Paul and his disciple meant than to say that a mystical union in suffering is unthinkable, or to say that Paul's prophetlike sufferings as an apostle for exemplary purposes are all that can be intended. Colossians seems to be claiming something beyond this, namely, that Paul's sufferings effect a divine benefit for the church. At the very least the agency of an apostle (the "divine office" of 1:25) aligned with the agency of Christ is at work for God on the church's behalf.

"To make God's word fully known" (literally "to complete the word of God") is the Colossians author's claim regarding Paul's task and primary duty (1:25–26; *cf.* 1 Cor 4:1). It is presented as the disclosure of a mystery long hidden "but now" disclosed (1:26). Paul had discussed the revelation the church had received as a secret and hidden wisdom of God (see 1 Cor 2:6–16 and the possibly derived Rom 16:25–27). The language of divine mystery or secret design comes from Jewish apocalyptic. This author sees it as something now revealed to the saints, including non-Jews (Col 1:26–27). The mystery is Christ proclaimed among them as their hope of glory. The statement is both apocalyptic in tone and more Pauline than the previous mentions of hope in the epistle because the hope centers on the age to come. As to the "mystery" made known, it is like the Hebrew concept of the mystery (*raz*) of the divine decree about the end time (1:26, 2:2–3). Conveniently, however, *ta mysteria* (mysteries) describes the induction of devotees into a pagan cult. Colossians also asserts that Christ proclaimed among the gentiles is the revelation of God's design that can make every believer "mature" or "perfect" in Christ, thereby using another watchword of members of pagan mystery cults. Knowledge of Christ is the key to all for the author; anything else is deluding, beguiling speech (2:3–4).

It is evident that a cult of a divine "fullness" that can only be approached by the mediation of angelic powers was making headway in Colossae, Laodicea, and Hierapolis. The apostolic-age writer hopes to undermine its attractiveness by resorting to its vocabulary and claiming that Christ alone is the bodily (i.e., real or substantial) repository of the divine fullness (1:19, 2:9), the firstborn for whom everything was created (1:16). The angelic powers came into existence through him. Hence, their intermediary function is not needed. Christ is doing the work of godhead in his own person.

All the warmth of Pauline love and encouragement is present in this epistle despite its admonitory tone (2:2). Its author knows well the concept of apostolic presence (*parousia*) through letter (found explicitly in 1 Corinthians 5:3 and more obliquely in 1 Thessalonians 2:17). At a distance from the community he rejoices in its firm faith in Jesus as the Christ and Lord (2:5, 6). The faith (2:7) has become "faith which" by this time, a body of belief, not simply the primitive "faith by which," a trustful commitment. It is a confessional reality at ease in proclaiming Christ Jesus as the Lord (2:6). Nowhere are the recipients of Colossians excoriated for having apostatized from the faith they once received. Throughout, they are praised while being warned about dangers that may ensnare them in the future. On balance, however, one must conclude that the relationship between writer and hearers is not personal in the manner of Paul's genuine correspondence. The presumption is that they may fall prey to the attractive teachings surrounding them and hence need solemn warnings against them. The Colossians already have "fullness of life" in Christ, "the head of all rule and authority" (2:10). They need not seek it elsewhere. The notion of the church as the fullness of Christ indicates that the church is the sphere in which his power has full scope.

The use of the phrase "circumcision of Christ," which is achieved by "putting off the body of flesh" (2:11; RSV), to describe the Colossians' baptism is a clear echo of Paul's language (Gal 5:6, 12; 6:15; Rom 2:29). The author may also have in mind Paul's admonition to "Put on the Lord Jesus Christ, and make no provision for the flesh" (Rom 13:14; RSV). The description of burial with Christ in baptism, which results in forgiveness of trespasses (Col 2:12–13), replicates Romans 6:4–11. Although the adjective "made without hands" describes the figurative circumcision of baptism as a way to praise it—the Greek biblical adjective "made with hands" impugns the idol-manufacture of pagans—there is no detailed reference to the rite of circumcision beyond the analogy of "putting off the body of flesh" (Col 2:11; see also 3:9). This is a rejection not of life in the body but of "flesh" in the sense of the "former self" of Paul's writings. These few verses (2:11–13) give no ground for supposing that the Jewish rite of circumcision was being thrust upon the baptized as in Galatia, or that it had any part in pagan syncretism. The passage simply reminds the Colossians that they are already alive with Christ in baptism. It does so by way of a comparison of circumcision with baptism, which no other New Testament writing contains. Surprising from the standpoint of Paul's letters is the claim that a fullness in Christ has already been achieved and that believers are already raised with Christ (2:10, 12; but *cf.* 1 Cor 4:8).

Colossians uses two figures in succession to portray the forgiveness of sins that came with baptism—the cancelled invoice that tells what the believers owed and the triumphant procession that leads principalities and powers through the streets in a humiliating public display (2:14–15). In the first, "legal demands" is probably a description of the ordinances of pagan religion; Mosaic observance is a bare possibility. In any case, the itemized bill is cancelled, set aside, and nailed to the cross—a fairly graphic triad of negation! In the second image we have something like the psalmist's triumphant procession in which God leads captives in a train of disgrace (Psalm 68:18; see Ephesians 4:8 but also Paul's placement of apostles as the condemned, trailing along at the end, 1 Corinthians 4:9; 2 Corinthians 2:14–16 has a procession of triumph). The interior of the Arch of Titus in the Roman forum conveys the image well. Romans wreathed in laurel do not lead Jews in train but carry the huge menorah from the Temple in Jerusalem on their shoulders, a framed placard that once read "SPQR" (*Senatus Populusque Romanus*) going on before it. In Colossians, God has totally disarmed both principalities and powers; they are the disgraced who are carried in tow (2:15).

Because God's victory in Christ is total, no one who sets ritual observances at naught need fear judgment at anyone else's hands (see Rom 14:1–4). The rigid asceticism in diet of certain votaries and the avoidance or keeping of certain days in the calendar of the pagan "philosophy" are no longer important (2:16). They are but a foreshadowing of the true reality that lies ahead. That substance (Colossians uses the word *sōma*, "body," for reasons evident above) is Christ. A number of expressions of commitment to the cult are to be held in contempt: adherence to prescriptions regarding food, submission to angels who determine the movement of the cosmos, and visionary experiences (2:16, 18). These practices could well have marked the targeted "philosophy." They are all worthless, the author says; everything done as religion must be related to Christ the head.

The contempt shown for these shadows of true religion resembles that of modern preachers faced with excessive reliance on astrology or devotion to reincarnation among their congregants. A better example might be fear of a pantheon of spirits in *Vodun* or *Santería,* or excessive fear of diabolic influence among believers in the gospel. Such preachers would be likely to stress the fact, in the spirit of Colossians, that the Christ of God is superior to all angelic, satanic, or cosmic forces. The redemption of humanity once accomplished does not allow for a return to the condition that preceded it. If Christ is head of a body-church that receives its nourishment from him and that is in a condition of vigor because of its divine origins, how can anyone worry about conforming to a regimen of ascetic abstentions and diet that is human in its origins? Asceticism, if it does not derive from some psychic disturbance like anorexia, will always have the appearance of superiority. Colossians teaches that a false asceticism is valueless in checking the "indulgence [literally, satiation] of the flesh" (2:23; RSV). In this it will be followed by any modern director of the spiritual life. Anyone who boasts of a way of religious conduct superior to the demands of the gospel is headed for a fall, Colossians says, the more so as there is no basis in faith for ascetical practices directed toward intermediaries. The ultimate basis for the prescribed regulations is the notion of a heavenly "fullness" (*plērōma*) to which the elements of the cosmos are subjected. Submitting to their prescriptions is a means of winning their favor. But this basis is false, says the author. God alone is the divine fullness, whose will it is to dwell "bodily" (i.e., substantially, fully) in the Son. Christ's is the headship of a more than cosmic body, the church. Submission to his guidance is the only knowledge or insight worth possessing.

One derives from the letter the flavor of exaltation and enthusiasm the sectarians of Colossae were experiencing. The writer counters it with a picture of Christian life lived to the full. To that end he exhorts those already buried with Christ in baptism and raised to life in him (2:12–13) to seek not that which is of earth but the things that are above (3:1–3). It is a plea to follow the logic of the new situation. They should orient themselves to Christ in glory, with whom they one day hope to be revealed (3:4), not to mundane considerations, however lofty they seem. Note the future character of the end-time hope, as also of the wrath to come (3:6). There is a wicked thrust of irony here, for the adherents to the philosophy are convinced that their consideration could not be more directed to the "above" than it is. The writer deflates them with the charge that their aspirations reach no higher than the plane of earth. They should seek what is truly above. No contempt for the everyday or the material is being expressed here. The philosophy does not seem to be gnostic in the later dualistic sense, a fortiori; neither is the author. He asks only for obedience to the heavenly Christ, not to the powers that in his view drag down to earth.

A series of practical ethical demands follows. They are the logic of the life of the baptized. Two lists of vices categorize what the believer may not do (3:5, 8–9). All these things must be "put to death," "done away," "put off." In their place a whole new self (neon [anthrōpon] 3:10; cf. Gal 6:15) must be put on, constantly being "renewed in knowledge after the image of its creator" (3:10; RSV). The theme of moving from death to life in baptism harks back to Romans 6:11, 13. The idea that in such a renewed image of God all distinctions of ethnicity, peoplehood, and culture are eliminated derives from passages like Galatians 3:28 and 1 Corinthians 12:13. Curiously in a catalog otherwise so complete, there is no mention of the obliteration of difference between male and female that Paul lists in Galatians 3:28. Are the consequences of such early egalitarianism already causing anxiety? "Barbarians" were for the Greeks what "the gentiles" were for the Jews; Scythians had the caricature status of a particularly wild kind of non-Greek. The reign of Christ puts such distinctions behind and embraces all (Col 3:11; cf. 1:15–20).

In the discussion of death and new life, Colossians agrees with Paul's thought at every point except that, where Paul features death to sin (Rom 6:6), Colossians speaks of death to the elemental spirits of the universe (Col 2:20). It is strongly implied that this kind of death is a precondition for death to the immorality, impurity, covetousness, and so on that will merit God's wrath (3:6). Get your religion straight, the author seems to say, and your morals will follow, a not inapplicable warning to Christians of later centuries.

The consequences of putting on the "new na-

ture," exhorted to above, are then spelled out. God's chosen are expected to be compassionate, kind, mutually forbearing, forgiving (3:12–13; cf. Rom 8:33). Love is the dominant virtue; peace and gratitude are concomitants (3:14–15). The Christian calling is to a life of harmony in the one body. Since this body possesses the word of Christ, teaching and admonition based on it are to be expected, but the perfect expression of the life is song (3:16). The exhortation to do and speak always in the name of Jesus as Lord in a spirit of thanks to God is one of the church's most treasured counsels from the apostolic age (3:17). It may be said to have pride of place. Critical considerations of authorship are not likely to dislodge it as an expression of the authentic Pauline spirit.

Some commonplaces of the time specifying domestic morality follow. They are found in pagan sources like the writings of Polybius, Epictetus, and Seneca; hence no effort should be made to claim them as a specifically Christian creation. Mention of "the Lord" as motivation for this line of conduct shows that the church has espoused it fully (3:18, 20, 23, 24). These "household rules" reflect the ordinary morality of the Hellenist, slaveholding upper class. A few items in them startle modern ears, beginning with the assumption without comment of the institution of slavery. Further, to balance the famous admonition to wives (3:18) with "Husbands, be subject to your wives" would have struck the people of the time as a kind of wild anarchy destructive of domestic piety. The advice contained here can be accommodated to the social change of the intervening centuries—lamentably slow in coming, from a gospel viewpoint—and still be useful counsel. The slave-master relation, for example, has some analogies to the military and to employer-employee relations, especially in corporate life and industry, where something like the "Do what you're told" mentality of 3:22 still applies. The motives proposed, however, are more important than the specific advice. Do all that you do to please the Lord, that is, Jesus (3:18, 20, 22–24). This motivation takes precedence over the impartial reward and punishment of God that are the bedrock assumption of biblical morality (3:24–25).

The epistle ends with a characteristic Pauline plea for prayers so that the work of the gospel may go forward. The apostle's figure of the open door (4:3; *cf.* 1 Cor 16:9; 2 Cor 2:12) had meant opportunity for further proclamation, but here it may have the narrower, literal meaning of the prison door. The Paul of Colossians "wants out." He also wants those who are outside (*exō*, v. 5, nonmembers of the church), to be edified by the gracious speech of believers seasoned with wisdom (4:5–6). In this they are (literally) "to make purchase of the time" (4:5), that is, to seize every opportunity to communicate the word, in act, with outsiders.

The concluding paragraphs, largely dealt with in the discussion of authorship above, identify Onesimus as "one of yourselves" (4:9), whereas Paul's letter about him to Philemon gives no clue as to the location of slave or master. Finally, Aristarchus, Mark the cousin of Barnabas, and Jesus are named as the only Jews currently detained along with Paul (4:10–11).

A careful exploration of this letter in its own language reveals the mastery the author has of the authentic Pauline corpus, usually put at seven letters. To those who think that Paul himself is the best candidate for knowledge of his own ideas and phrases, one can only respond that none of the letters that are assuredly his has this quality of an anthology. Colossians is Pauline in everything but the anticipated risen life as a quality of the life of the baptized. This mastery of Paul is put at the service of combating the new problem of pagan religion as a threat to Christian faith. The author has more to say to our age than Paul does—at least in the sense that the struggle over Law observance has not been a lively issue since 135. Only by making Law observants surrogates for some favored Christian adversaries, absent the practice of circumcision on which the whole edifice of Law observance is built, can large portions of Pauline polemic be kept alive. Colossians can be put to the same argumentative use because it speaks of festivals, fastings, and intercessors short of Christ. But such use would seem to miss the point entirely. The modern enemies of faith in Christ whom this epistle can be seen addressing are the Christians who want it both ways: the things of earth concurrently with the things of heaven. They have chosen their supplements to faith in Christ. These are not esoterica, the palpable tokens (to a Christian) of false religion. They are the assurances of salvation that are no assurance: a comfortable life, a multitude of possessions (today's *plērōma*), the blessed assurance that all but they are "outside," and elemental spirits who preside not over the cosmos but over a jingoistic patriotism that would cheerfully bomb any supposed enemies of flag and pulpit to extinction.

Bibliography

Lohse, Eduard. *Colossians and Philemon.* Philadelphia, 1971.

Moule, C. F. D. *The Epistles of Paul the Apostle to the Colossians and to Philemon.* Cambridge, 1957.

Schillebeeckx, Edward. "Christ, the Fullness of God; the Church, the Fullness of Christ." In his *Christ: The Experience of Jesus as Lord.* New York, 1980, pp. 181–194.

Schweizer, Eduard. *The Letter to the Colossians.* Minneapolis, 1982.

GERARD S. SLOYAN

I and II Thessalonians

THE THESSALONIAN LETTERS, though theologically overshadowed by the longer and weightier letters that precede them in the canon, offer a rare glimpse of Paul in a relatively untroubled relationship with one of his churches. The letters also present, however, a number of puzzles: questions about the literary integrity of 1 Thessalonians, hints of forgery in 2 Thessalonians (2:2, 3:17), and a peculiar combination of striking literary similarities and deep-seated theological differences that simultaneously unite and separate the two letters. These puzzles raise fundamental questions about the original form, sequence, authorship, and literary relationship of these letters that must be addressed before their contents can be explored.

LITERARY ISSUES

Periodically, the literary integrity of 1 Thessalonians has been questioned. Do we have the letter as Paul originally wrote it? This question has two sources: the unusual form of the letter and the vituperative tone of 2:14–16. We need to look briefly at these issues.

Following an epistolary convention of his age, Paul usually opened his letters with an expression of thanksgiving, and 1 Thessalonians clearly conforms to that practice (1:2). What is unusual about this letter, however, is the remarkable length of the thanksgiving, which extends over three chapters with repeated references to Paul's gratitude for the people to whom he was writing (1:2, 2:13, 3:9). Indeed, over half of 1 Thessalonians is a thanksgiving, a proportion so striking that some scholars have suggested that the canonical letter is actually composed of a number of letters with their several thanksgivings combined into one. This hypothesis, however, no longer finds many supporters, since the various "letters" presumed to constitute 1 Thessalonians turn out to be themselves little more than extensive thanksgivings. It is more likely that the unusual form of this letter is a witness both to Paul's flexibility in adapting epistolary conventions to his own needs and to his deeply felt—and thus extensively expressed—gratitude for this sturdy church. Somewhat more tenacious is the charge that 2:13–16 is an intercalation into the original text, for the vindictive anti-Semitism of these verses stands in strong contrast to the warm sense of solidarity with the Jews that Paul expresses in Romans 9–11. A decision on the authenticity of this passage, however, must await its contextual analysis.

The questions generated by 2 Thessalonians are not so readily dismissed or deferred, and they strike at fundamental issues of authorship and purpose. The first question is raised by the intimations of forgery found at two points in the letter: 2:2 warns against a letter "purporting to be from us," and the closing words in 3:17 are clearly formulated to serve as a sign of authenticity against which any questionable letters could be checked. The suspicion of forgery is somewhat surprising, for no other Pauline letters betray this concern. Indeed, the idea of forgery seems to suggest that Paul's authority was so well entrenched that a direct rebuttal of his views would be futile, yet other letters suggest that the opposite was true (Rom 3:8; 2 Cor 10–13; Gal 1:6–9; Phil 1:15–18).

A further question is raised by the peculiar relationship of the two Thessalonian letters to each other. Some portions of the second letter are strikingly similar to the first. The opening greetings, for example, are virtually identical, whereas other Pauline letters show considerable variation. The extensive thanksgiving of 1 Thessalonians, with its repeated expressions of gratitude, is reflected in 2 Thessalonians, but not in Paul's other letters. Similar issues are taken up in the same sequence in both letters, using many of the same words. Indeed, an astonishing amount of 2 Thessalonians is a paraphrase of the first letter, and decisively new elements are found only in 1:5–10 and 2:1–12.

Taken by itself, and assuming Pauline authorship of both letters, this evidence would seem to suggest a very brief time lapse between the letters to allow the structure and phraseology of the first letter to be fresh in Paul's mind as he wrote the second. (There is no evidence that Paul kept copies of his letters for later reference, and his expectation of Jesus' imminent return [4:15] as well as the time and expense involved in hand-copying a document would make this unlikely.) Yet there are also some striking discrepancies between these letters, especially in their eschatological perspectives and in the situation that each presupposes in the church at Thessalonica. Both letters, for example, assume a situation of conflict and persecution, but 1 Thessalonians seems to look back on a period of affliction (1:6), while 2 Thessalonians clearly addresses a church in the midst of it (1:4). Both letters focus on the Parousia, the return of Christ, but they do so from different perspectives. First Thessalonians assumes that this return is imminent and that Paul himself, as well as many members of the Thessalonian church, will live to see the event (4:15, 17). In 2 Thessalonians the author emphatically rejects the idea that this event is imminent, that is, that the Day of the Lord has come (2:1–2), and insists

that a force is in effect that restrains and indefinitely postpones the Parousia (2:3–7). Here we encounter the central dilemma posed by these letters. Could the situation in Thessalonica have changed so rapidly? Could Paul's eschatological perspective have changed so much? Various proposals have emerged to address these questions.

Some have suggested that 2 Thessalonians was written before 1 Thessalonians, for this sequence suggests a more logical progression of the persecution of the church. Yet Paul in 1 Thessalonians reviews in great detail his past connections with the church (2:1–3:10), and nowhere does he hint at an earlier letter (cf. 2 Thess 2:2, 15). The canonical sequence must be correct. Others have explained the close literary relationship between the letters by arguing that they were written at the same time, but to different groups within the church. Yet nothing in the letters themselves lends weight to this hypothesis. Nor is there any supportive evidence for the hypothesis that 2 Thessalonians was written to a different church (Beroea or Philippi) and acquired the Thessalonian address only through a later scribal mistake.

All of these proposals assume Pauline authorship of 2 Thessalonians, and all, as we have seen, are radically flawed. Quite a different hypothesis, and yet a persistent one, is that 2 Thessalonians is not by Paul at all. According to this hypothesis, some years after Paul's death an anonymous writer appropriated the name and reputation of the apostle to deal with a crisis threatening the church. The different situations and divergent eschatological perspectives are thus readily explained. This explanation, however, involves a complex forgery hypothesis, for 2 Thessalonians, itself pseudonymous (a forgery, if you will), hints at yet another forged letter. Some scholars have suggested that this is actually a reference to 1 Thessalonians, which the author of 2 Thessalonians would like to see rejected. But why would an author who esteemed Paul enough to use his name attempt to discredit Paul's own letter? The imminent eschatology of 1 Thessalonians may have contributed to the problem that 2 Thessalonians addresses, namely, the conviction that the Day of the Lord has arrived. The author of the second letter thus faced a dilemma: he could not refute this conviction without undermining Paul's authority, unless his letter were received as Paul's only authentic word on the subject.

Obviously the hypothesis of pseudonymity is not without conjectural difficulties, and no consensus is in sight on the question of authenticity. Yet because this hypothesis seems to deal best with the data, we will assume here the pseudonymity of 2 Thessalonians.

1 THESSALONIANS: A SURVEY

This first letter to the church in Thessalonica is also the earliest of all the extant Pauline letters. Probably written from Corinth in 50 or 51, during the so-called second missionary journey, it was addressed to a church Paul and his coworkers, Timothy and Silvanus, had founded not many months before. The persecution that dogged Paul's footsteps had driven him from the city somewhat prematurely (2:17; *cf.* Acts 17:1–10), and concern for the church, which continued to experience persecution after Paul's departure, prompted the apostle to make repeated efforts to return (2:17–18). When these efforts were frustrated, he sent Timothy back to strengthen and encourage it (3:1–5). Timothy's return to Paul with the news that the church was holding firm in faith despite its afflictions evoked this letter, which overflows with a sense of relief and gratitude.

Paul opens the letter with the usual epistolary conventions and then launches into a prolonged statement of thanksgiving (1:2–3:13). This becomes an occasion for rehearsing not only the exemplary faith of the Thessalonians (1:2–10), but also Paul's own actions when he was with them (2:1–16) and his anguished concern since his departure (2:17–3:10). These themes are repeated in the prayer that closes this section of the letter (3:11–13) and provides a transition to the exhortations that follow (4:1–5:22). In these exhortations Paul does not so much correct as encourage, focusing his attention on some eschatological issues that seem to be troubling the church (4:13–18, 5:1–11). Paul closes the letter with a second intercessory prayer (5:23–24) and the usual epistolary conclusions (5:25–28). The letter thus provides little in the way of dogmatic content (thereby provoking occasional, ill-conceived challenges to its authenticity), but it reveals much about the pastoral side of Paul's apostolic ministry.

ANALYSIS OF THE LETTER

Prescript (1:1)

Paul follows contemporary epistolary conventions in mentioning first the sender and then the recipients of the letter. In later letters Paul amplified this formula with comments about his own office (Gal 1:1) or about the status of the recipient church (1 Cor 1:2), so that the brevity of this prescript is striking. The reference to co-senders is, however, a common feature of Paul's letters. It does not signify shared authorship, however, but a shared concern for the church by Paul's associates. Timothy is particularly prominent in this role (1 Cor 16:10f.; 2 Cor 1:1; Phil 1:1; Phlm 1; Rom 16:21), while Silvanus ("Silas" in Acts) seems to have played a more limited part in Paul's missionary activities (2 Cor 1:19; *cf.* Acts 15:22–18:5).

The church is defined geographically and theologically. It is located in a prominent Macedonian city, but its true identity is constituted "in God the Father and the Lord Jesus Christ." As was his custom, Paul replaced the secular term "Greetings" that usually completed a prescript with the more theological phrase "Grace to you and peace." Already, then, in the phraseology of this brief prescript, the letter is given a liturgical cast that facilitated its being read aloud in the church (5:27).

Thanksgiving for the Church (1:2–10)

Where secular letters sometimes contained a formalized thanksgiving for a safe journey, a recovery from illness, or the like, Paul made the statement of thanksgiving almost a trademark of his letters, infusing it with theological content and expressive warmth. Here the object of Paul's gratitude is described expansively: the Thessalonians' faith, love, and hope as expressed in their work, labor, and steadfastness. The first triad is a familiar one, often used to summarize the Christian life (5:8; *cf.* 1 Cor 13:13), but by linking it here with the second triad, Paul emphasizes the active quality of this life. Yet such active faith, steadfast in the face of afflictions, can only come from God, Paul implies, and so it serves as a sign of election. This steadfast faith confirms the power of the gospel, which is not a static but an effective word that changes both those who receive it (1:3) and those who proclaim it (1:5b, 2:1–12). As recipients, the Thessalonians accepted the word of faith in affliction and yet with joy, thereby becoming imitators of Paul and also of Christ. Moreover, as the news of their exemplary faith spread, they became indirect proclaimers of the word, coworkers, as it were, with Paul in his missionary endeavors. As Paul summarizes the report about the Thessalonians that has become widespread among the churches, he uses a creedal formula that focuses on eschatological issues (1:9b–10). He will address these issues later in the hortatory portion of the letter, but here Paul uses the words to encourage continued steadfastness. If the current period is one of waiting, punctuated by affliction, the waiting will not be in vain. The God who chose them will deliver them, through Jesus, from the wrath to come.

Paul's Behavior Among the Thessalonians (2:1–12)

The tone of this section is defensive, as if Paul had to justify his actions against detractors. Yet the defense lacks Paul's usual passion (*cf.*, e.g., Gal 4–5), and the situation that provokes Paul's response is vaguely defined. Clearly Paul was concerned to distinguish himself and his associates from the questionable practices of other itinerant (non-Christian) preachers, but his primary concern here seems to be to show how his actions embodied the message he brought.

These verses are filled with allusions to what the Thessalonians already know and have experienced (vv. 2, 5, 9, 10, 11); Paul seeks here to remind and interpret, not to impart new teaching. He especially reminds them that his visit was not empty or powerless or "in vain," though the subsequent afflictions of the congregation may have suggested that it was. It is not a life free of trouble that reveals the divine power behind Paul's ministry, but rather courage in the face of persecution and opposition (2:1–2). In a series of antitheses (2:3–7) Paul contrasts his behavior with that of other itinerant preachers. Only Paul and his associates were tested and approved by God; only they were entrusted with God's gospel. Whereas others are oriented toward gaining p rsonal honor and authority, Paul and his coworkers were oriented toward pleasing God. As apostles of Christ their actions must

reflect Christ, and that correspondence provides the decisive authentication. They were gentle, self-giving, constant in toil, yet blameless in behavior. Thus not only by their words, but by actions that embodied these words, Paul and his coworkers encouraged the Thessalonians to live a life worthy of God, who calls them into the glorious kingdom. Once again Paul closes on an eschatological note, to which he will later return.

Renewed Thanksgiving (2:13–16)

Having reminded the church of the nature and import of his actions, Paul now expresses renewed thanks that they accepted these actions and his message as the very word of God. But when they accepted this word, they accepted also a pattern of affliction that is the signature of the Christian gospel. Paul embodied this pattern while he was among them (2:2), as did the Judean church before him, Christ himself, and even the prophets. Afflictions, then, do not compromise the truth of the gospel, with its promise of salvation (1:10), but they provide evidence that one stands within the authentic trajectory of the good news that began with the cross.

The general context of these verses is thus consistent with Paul's argument in this portion of the letter. What is problematical is the sharp, anti-Semitic tone that emerges in verses 15–16 and the finality of the closing words: "God's wrath has come upon them at last." This sentiment seems incompatible with the more positive opinion Paul has expressed elsewhere, most notably in Romans 9:1–5 and 11:25–32. The words also seem to reflect the destruction of the Jewish Temple in 70 C.E., which was viewed as a sign of God's wrath against the Jews (Matt 21:33–22:14). Thus while there is no textual evidence of an interpolation here, the historical and theological evidence does suggest a post-70 author for these verses, yet one sensitive to the movement of Paul's thought in this chapter.

Paul's Actions After His Departure (2:17–3:13)

Though the long section that relates Paul's concerns after leaving Thessalonica formally resembles the descriptions of travel plans that are a frequent feature of Paul's letters (Rom 15:22–29; 1 Cor

16:5–9), Paul's strong emotions during past travels, not his future plans, dominate these verses. Paul has referred to his relationship to the church at Thessalonica as that of a nurse or father to children (2:7, 11), but now he abandons family imagery and speaks theologically, even apocalyptically, of the church as his hope, joy, glory, and crown. The anxiety that led him to send Timothy is palpable, as is his relief at Timothy's message that all is well. It is life itself to Paul to hear of their faith and love (3:6–8), though the third member of the triad, hope, is noticeably missing. Paul's mood of thanksgiving returns (3:9), as does his desire to see this church and to "supply what is lacking in [their] faith" (3:10). In the light of Paul's effusive praise, this cannot be taken as a reproach, but it does signal some problem, the nature of which emerges only later. With these goals in mind, Paul raises a prayer to God that ends, once more, on an eschatological note (3:11–13).

Two Areas of Ethical Concern (4:1–12)

The general tenor of the hortatory section in chapter 4 is established in these opening verses: continue "just as you are doing" (4:1, *cf.* 4:10). Only minor corrections seem necessary in this church. It is not clear if the advice in these verses is in response to questions sent by the church. Even less clear is the nature of the sexual problem that Paul addresses (4:3–8), for the language is quite obscure. What is clear is the concern for holiness that is to distinguish the Thessalonian Christians from their neighbors. Scholars debate whether the admonition to "live quietly, mind your own affairs, and work with your hands" (4:11) reflects a concrete situation in the church. Some view this as a piece of traditional exhortation, while others read it in the light of the discussion of the Parousia that follows (4:13–18) and conclude that excitement over the impending Parousia has caused some members of the congregation to neglect their daily responsibilities. Such actions would exacerbate the tense situation in Thessalonica, and Paul summons the church to a quiet and diligent orderliness that reflects his own behavior among them (2:9).

The Parousia (4:13–5:11)

The opening words about concern for the dead suggest that this discussion of eschatological issues directly addresses "what is lacking" in their faith (3:10). Certainly Paul has been preparing for this discussion for some time with his frequent eschatological comments, and the seriousness of the problem is underscored by the length of the discussion as well as by Paul's formal appeal to a "word of the Lord" (4:15).

The Thessalonians have raised two questions: What becomes of those who have died ("are asleep"; 4:13)? And when will the Parousia occur (5:1)? These two questions, however, derive from a single issue: the delay of the Parousia. The Thessalonians were perhaps so convinced that the Parousia, the Day of the Lord, would come soon that they had not expected any deaths in the community to intervene. Thus they were unprepared when a death did occur and were uncertain about the status of the dead at the Parousia. It is striking that Paul had not addressed this question during his stay with them, but perhaps his own expectations of the imminent coming of Christ, still so evident in the letter (4:15, 17), precluded this. Now, however, Paul assures them that the dead in Christ suffer no disadvantage on the Day of the Lord. Indeed, there is no disadvantage for living or dead (4:17, 5:10), so the concern about "times and seasons" is unwarranted (5:1). The attempt to calculate the Day of the Lord is unnecessary for other reasons too. The Day is inherently incalculable (5:2), unavoidable (5:3), and for Christians it is, in a fundamental way, already present (*cf.* 2 Cor 5:17, 6:2). Paul thus redirects their thinking from the future to the present. They are already sons and daughters of the light, and their actions are already determined by the Day. Thus Paul repeats the triad with which he opened the letter (5:8; *cf.* 1:3), with hope now restored to its proper place. Paul closes with a final, familiar note of encouragement to keep up the good work (5:11).

Final Exhortations (5:12–22)

Many of Paul's closing exhortations are very general, applicable to any Christian community and therefore not indicative of special problems in Thessalonica. An exception may be the advice to "admonish the idlers" (perhaps better translated as the "disorderly"; 5:14), for this suggests a connection with the social irresponsibility described earlier (4:11–12).

References to the "fainthearted" and "weak" possibly point to the situation of persecution in Thessalonica; they may, however, simply reflect the general concern for the downtrodden that is central to the Christian message (Matt 5:3–12, Luke 6:20–23).

Closure of the Letter (5:23–28)

Paul closes his letter with a second intercessory prayer that, like the first (3:11–13), envisions a church kept blameless for the Parousia. Once again the connection between present actions and future goal is established, with the notion of God's election call providing the guarantee. According to his custom, Paul ends the letter with greetings, though these are elsewhere more extensive (see, e.g., 1 Cor 16:19–20). The "holy kiss" seems to have been a Christian ritual (Rom 16:16; 1 Cor 16:20; 2 Cor 13:12), and together with the final benediction it completes the liturgical framing of this letter.

2 THESSALONIANS: A SURVEY

If this letter is authentic, it was written shortly after 1 Thessalonians, and together with that letter reflects a very unstable situation in the church. If, however, it is pseudonymous (see above), it was probably written sometime after 70. In any case, its purpose is clear: to refute the claim that "the Day of the Lord has come" (2:2). The significance of this claim, however, and thus the situation the author addresses, is not at all clear. "The Day of the Lord" is an apocalyptic term referring to the moment of divine intervention on behalf of God's people, accompanied by cosmic convulsions and, in Christian thought, the return of Jesus to gather the elect. If such a Day had truly come, there would be no question about it, and no refutation of it. Thus some interpreters weaken the force of the verb "has come" to mean that the Day of the Lord is *imminent.* Others retain the natural sense of the verb but believe that the Thessalonians had eliminated its apocalyptic content by internalizing the Day of the Lord as a personal spiritual resurrection. Whatever the actual situation, the author responds in apocalyptic terms: the Day of the Lord has not come and cannot come unless certain other events occur first (2:1–12). This argument constitutes the heart of the letter, but in the surrounding verses the author

addresses some attendant issues. In the thanksgiving, for example, he explains the eschatological significance of the church's present afflictions (1:3–12), and in the hortatory section (3:6–15), he focuses on some disruptive behavior that seems to derive from the refuted claim. The letter closes in the usual way (3:16–18), but with a strange emphasis on the authenticity of "Paul's" signature. Overall, the letter lacks the warmth that characterizes 1 Thessalonians, even while using much of the same language. Missing also are allusions to the cross and the Resurrection, and little is said about the power behind the Christians' present existence. Instead this letter focuses quite resolutely on what the future holds.

ANALYSIS OF THE LETTER

Prescript (1:1–2)

The prescript is virtually identical to that of 1 Thessalonians, with the exception of the somewhat awkward repetition of the words "from God the Father and the Lord Jesus Christ" in the blessing.

Thanksgiving (1:3–12)

The influence of 1 Thessalonians is evident in the opening verses, but the mood of immediacy that Paul's original words conveyed is replaced by a sense of formality and obligation ("we are bound," "as is fitting"). The object of the author's thanksgiving is the congregation's faith and love, in which an echo of the original triad of 1 Thessalonians can be heard.

The mood shifts from thanksgiving to boasting as the author considers the circumstances of affliction and persecution in which the church's faith has been tested. In the first letter this affliction evoked the image of the cross as the paradigm for Christian existence (1:6); here, however, the focus is on the future, when God will reverse the present circumstances. This will confirm God's justice, which seems compromised by the afflictions of the faithful. The promise of future vindication, which is described in vivid apocalyptic language, anticipates the argument of chapter 2 by distinguishing the future Parousia, with all its blazing glory and fierce justice, from the present circumstances of affliction. To be sure, the present is not without meaning, for it serves as a time for proving one's worth, and thus as a proleptic vehicle for God's justice. By this means, however, the apocalyptic scenario serves not only as a promise but also as a warning to the church. In verses 11–12, the author evokes a mood of prayer as he returns to the terminology of the first letter, but the warning note is retained because the prayer to make them worthy of God's call points to a future goal, not a past (1 Thess 1:4) or present (1 Thess 2:12) reality.

Apocalyptic Instructions (2:1–12)

Though formally part of the thanksgiving, these verses are clearly the heart of the letter; yet they raise many problems for the interpreter. Not only is the significance of the Day of the Lord obscure (see above), but there are enigmatic references to a forged letter (2:2), an unnamed "man of lawlessness" (2:3), and a mysterious restraining force (2:6). In spite of these difficulties, however, the purpose and direction of the argument are clear.

The church has been shaken by a message whose original significance is lost but which the author renders apocalyptically: "The Day of the Lord has come" (2:2). The source of this disturbing news is left vague: "by spirit or by word or by letter purporting to be from us" (RSV). The author rejects Pauline authorship of such a message, even though this could mean rejecting Pauline authorship of 1 Thessalonians (see above). He also mounts a counterargument that is couched in apocalyptic language. The Day of the Lord has not come because it must be preceded by visible signs that have not yet occurred: rebellion and apostasy led by "a man of lawlessness." Indeed, these events cannot happen, for a mysterious force is, at the present moment, restraining them. The purpose of this rather complex apocalyptic timetable is clear: each element postpones further the advent of the Day. Yet the intervening events are described in such obscure terms that further attempts to pin down the Day are discouraged. This has not, however, discouraged contemporary interpreters, who offer a multitude of explanations concerning the identity of the various figures. The ambiguity surrounding the future Day, however, encourages a focus on the present instead, for one's decisions now will have consequences on that Day (2:9–12), and steadfast faith is the only security against the mystery of lawlessness that is even now at work.

Renewed Thanksgiving and Prayers (2:13–3:5)

After the distinctive message of 2:1–12, these verses echo once again the format and language of the first letter. As in 1 Thessalonians 2:13, the thanksgiving is renewed and focused on the status of the Thessalonian Christians. Their election and call by God and their "belief in the truth" (2:13) set them apart from those described in the preceding verses as deluded, deceived, and destined to perish (2:10–12). The tone here is thus one of gratitude and confidence, yet the actual purpose of these verses is paraenetic, as the warning to "stand firm" (v. 15) clearly indicates. The emphasis on authoritative traditions and letter (2:15) emerges again (3:6, 14, 17), strengthening the contrast with the false tradition and the "forged" letter rejected earlier (2:2).

An intercessory prayer, modeled on 1 Thessalonians 3:11–13, follows in 2:16–3:5, but here it is interrupted with a request for prayers on "Paul's" behalf (3:1–2). This interruption renews the contrast between the faithless and the faithful and confirms the urgency of the admonitory tone implicit throughout this section (2:15, 17; 3:4).

Exhortations (3:6–15)

The latent hortatory intent of 2:13–3:5 becomes explicit in these verses, which are primarily directed toward the problem of idle or disorderly behavior. It is difficult to determine if an actual problem is reflected here, for the verses could be simply an expansion of 1 Thessalonians 5:14. On the other hand, the disruptive behavior described here could easily be related to the anxiety aroused by the claim that the Day of the Lord has come. At any rate, in developing the argument against such behavior, two motifs are drawn from the first letter: imitation of Paul (1 Thess 1:6) and the apostle's constant toil and labor (1 Thess 2:9). But whereas the first was originally adduced to exemplify a life of affliction in imitation of the cross and the second was associated with the proclamation of the gospel, here both are given a purely ethical application, an example of responsible behavior to imitate. The unit closes with a final warning about the importance of heeding this particular letter, a warning that applies to the apocalyptic teaching as well as the ethical advice.

Letter Closing (3:16–18)

As in 1 Thessalonians 5:23, this letter closes with a second intercessory prayer, addressed to the "Lord of peace," and a final benediction. The author also remarks that the greeting comes from his ("Paul's") own hand. Paul himself made a similar comment in several letters (1 Cor 16:21; Gal 6:11), but the emphasis it receives here is striking. Clearly it is intended to flush out the suspected forgeries (2:2), but we have already seen that the suggestion of forgery points to late, pseudonymous authorship. Several scenarios thus suggest themselves. If the church had retained the original letter, a comparison of signatures would force it to decide which to accept as authentic, the first or the second letter. The author of 2 Thessalonians clearly hoped that the emphatic closure would gain credence for his letter, which would then replace 1 Thessalonians as Paul's only authentic letter to that church. If the church had only a copy of the original, and perhaps copies of other Pauline letters as well, the most the author could hope for is that his letter would be accepted alongside the others. The content of the letter seems to support the first scenario; it is the second, however, that has come to pass.

Bibliography

1 Thessalonians

Collins, Raymond F. *Studies on the First Letter to the Thessalonians*. Louvain, 1984.

Holtz, Traugott. *Der erste Brief an die Thessalonicher*. Zürich, 1986.

Malherbe, Abraham J. *Paul and the Thessalonians*. Philadelphia, 1987.

Marxsen, Willi. *Der erste Brief an die Thessalonicher*. Zürich, 1979.

Pearson, Birger. "I Thessalonians 2:13–16: A Deutero-Pauline Interpolation." *Harvard Theological Review* 64 (1971): 79–94.

2 Thessalonians: Authentic

Best, Ernest. *A Commentary on the First and Second Epistles to the Thessalonians*. London, 1972.

Bruce, Frederick F. *1 & 2 Thessalonians*. Waco, Tex., 1982.

Giblin, Charles H. *The Threat to Faith: An Exegetical and Theological Re-examination of 2 Thessalonians 2*. Rome, 1967.

Jewett, Robert. *The Thessalonian Correspondence: Pauline Rhetoric and Millenarian Piety*. Philadelphia, 1986.

Marshall, I. Howard. *1 and 2 Thessalonians*. Grand Rapids, 1983

2 Thessalonians: Pseudonymous

Bailey, John A. "Who Wrote II Thessalonians?" *New Testament Studies* 25 (1978–1979): 131–145.

Krodel, Gerhard. "2 Thessalonians." In *Ephesians, Colossians, 2 Thessalonians, the Pastoral Epistles*, edited by G. Krodel. Philadelphia, 1978. Pp. 73–96.

Lindemann, Andreas. "Zum Abfassungzweck des zweiten Thessalonicherbriefes." *Zeitschrift für die neutestamentliche Wissenschaft* 68 (1977): 35–47.

Marxsen, Willi. *Der zweite Thessalonicherbrief*. Zürich, 1982.

Trilling, Wolfgang. *Der zweite Brief an die Thessalonicher*. Zürich, 1980.

JOUETTE M. BASSLER

I and II Timothy, Titus

I and II Timothy, Titus

COLLECTIVELY, THE THREE documents discussed here, because of their concern about matters related to church order and regulations, including the exercise of church leadership, have traditionally (since the early eighteenth century) been referred to as the "Pastoral epistles." Although they purport to be letters written by the apostle Paul to two of his closest associates in the Christian mission, since the nineteenth century there has been a growing consensus among scholars that neither the terminology and literary style, the historical situation, nor the socioreligious perspective of the Pastorals supports Pauline authorship.

Terminology and Literary Style

Numerous studies have established the differences between the terminology and literary style of the Pastorals and that of other letters attributed to Paul. Not only are a considerable number of terms shared by the Pastorals not found in other letters attributed to Paul, but those terms that are used in the Pastorals to describe matters of great significance to the Pauline churches are used in fundamentally different ways. For example, "faith" (*pistis*) in the undisputed letters of Paul almost always refers to a disposition that should characterize the proper relationship between human beings and God. In the Pastorals, however, the term refers mostly to a creedal formula or tradition (1 Tim 3:9, 6:10; 2 Tim 4:7; *cf.* the formula "in the faith," 1 Tim 1:2, 2:7). The title "God our Savior" (Titus 2:10; *cf.* Titus 3:4) is used in no other letter of Paul. The description of Christian existence as "religion" or "godliness" is not found in the other Pauline letters, but occurs throughout the Pastorals (1 Tim 2:2; 3:16; 4:7–8; 6:3, 5, 11; 2 Tim 3:5; Titus 1:1) and is common in the literature of the second century and beyond. The description of Christian preaching as "sound doctrine" (1 Tim 1:10; 2 Tim 4:3; Titus 1:9, 2:1) or "sound words" (1 Tim 6:3; 2 Tim 1:13) and the call to be "sound in the faith" (Titus 1:13, 2:2) are very uncharacteristic of Paul. In fact, many of the terms in the Pastorals that are not found in the other Pauline letters are not attested anywhere else in Christian literature before the second century, long after the end of Paul's life.

Even in those passages in which the Pastorals present personal references to the apostle Paul, Pauline authorship must be questioned. For example, it is unlikely that in making reference to his life before being called to be an apostle to the gentiles, Paul would have said that he had "formerly blasphemed and persecuted and insulted [Christ]" and had "acted ignorantly in unbelief . . . " (1 Tim 1:13; RSV). Given 1 Corinthians 15:9, Galatians 1:13, and Philippians 3:6, the language of this reference appears to be uncharacteristically hyperbolic. (Only here does Paul indicate that he blasphemed and insulted Christ.) In addition, when Paul attempts to account for his former life, only in this passage does he blame it on ignorance, suggesting that such a life was totally misguided. In other passages his former life is seen as praiseworthy, if only in a relative sense (Gal 1:14, Phil 3:4–7).

The Historical Situation of the Letters

If these letters are in fact authentic, it is practically certain that they were not written during the period *before* Paul's imprisonment in Rome, as recorded in Acts 28. Although the account in Acts leaves open the possibility that Paul was released from prison in Rome, it nowhere provides for his later return to the area around the Aegean Sea where Timothy and Titus were located. If Paul was released, it is of course possible that he reached Spain, his intended destination (Rom 15:24; *1 Clement* 5:7). He might then have returned to the Aegean area before being imprisoned again in Rome. There he might have corresponded with Timothy (2 Tim 4:9–21) and suffered martyrdom. But corroboration for almost all of this scenario can be found or assumed *only* in the Pastorals. Since the entire period of Paul's life that the Pastorals assume is not supported by other evidence, their Pauline authorship must be questioned.

Socioreligious Perspective

The socioreligious perspective of the Pastorals, as they argue against the muted but discernible voices of their "opponents," also tells against Pauline authorship. It is not so much the religious perspective and orientation of the opponents that point to the later date of these letters, but rather the perspective of the Pastorals themselves. Each of the Pastorals characterizes its opponents—with only slight variations—as a type of Jewish-Christian gnostic heresy. The opponents belong to the "circumcision party," that is, to those who hold that all believers should observe the Jewish laws and traditions, especially circumcision (*cf.* Titus 1:10). They fancy themselves teachers of the Law (1 Tim 1:7), but are inclined to engage in quarrels and debates over mere "myths" and human proscriptions (Titus 1:14, 3:9). They boast of possessing a superior knowledge or insight into the myster-

ies of the universe (1 Tim 1:4, 4:7, 6:20; Titus 3:9). They practice a rigorous type of sexual and dietary asceticism as an index of their radical separation from the world (1 Tim 4:3; Titus 1:14–15). Canons of respectable social behavior are being undermined by attempts to convince women, especially, to abandon their traditional social roles and responsibilities in the household and to pursue strange new teaching (2 Tim 3:6–7; Titus 1:11). Some are said to hold as a creedal position that the resurrection has already been realized, signifying perhaps that the power of the resurrection is evident in their demonstration of great spiritual powers (2 Tim 2:18).

There is little in the characterizations of the opponents in the Pastorals that makes a dating during the time of the Pauline mission impossible. The gnostic or speculative and syncretist tendencies and the radical social behavior were characteristics of some of the opponents of the apostle Paul (*cf.* 1 Cor and Gal), as well as of some followers of Paul, such as the authors of Colossians and Ephesians. But what distinguishes the polemic of both Paul and the deutero-Pauline documents from the Pastorals is that in the former there is an attempt to demonstrate where the opponents have gone wrong, and in what direction the truth lies. This is done through a detailed argument of some salient issues. In the Pastorals, however, no issues are engaged in any sustained manner; it seems enough for the writer to discredit the motives and morals of the opponents. He simply asserts that they are opposed to tradition and to sound teaching and behavior, as though the assertion would obviate the need for more discussion and defense. This type of response to opposition stands in sharp contrast to the vigorous debate of Paul's letter or those under immediate Pauline influence.

It is the particular religious perspective of the writer of the Pastorals, however, that more clearly argues against Pauline authorship and dating before the turn of the second century. Each document reflects the tendency to accommodate, even to imitate, some of the traditions and ways—the ethos—of the larger social world, particularly of the aristocratic classes. Especially important are the values and character profiles attached to leadership classes (political and military) in the Greco-Roman world. The writer of the Pastorals exhorts all Christians to "renounce impiety and base desires, and live prudent and upright lives in the world" (Titus 2:12; RSV). Such exhortation was not intended to result in separation from the world, but in a type of worldly ethic. They are counseled to marry and be faithful in marriage, to care for their children and household, to be hospitable, to avoid quarrels and debates about religion, to care for the weak and needy—in short, as Christians, to be respectable and upright citizens. No longer is Christianity seen as a radically different and separate movement on the fringes of Greco-Roman society; it has taken note of, and has been noticed by, the surrounding social environment. Its response was to embrace firmly, but not absolutely and uncritically, the ethos and ethical norms of respectable Greco-Roman society. There is in the undisputed letters of Paul evidence that he was, especially for the sake of the success of the gentile mission, sensitive to the views of outsiders (*cf.* 1 Thess 4:10b–12). But this sensitivity never led him to call for acceptance of the norms and ethos of Greco-Roman society. To be sure, the writer of the Pastorals does not advocate unqualified acceptance of these norms (2 Tim 3:12). But he does seem to feel the need, in response to the teachings and behavior of the opponents, to emphasize the appropriateness of the worldly aspect of faith.

The socioreligious perspective and worldview of the writer of the Pastorals is also evidenced in the type of church organization that is taken for granted. The church is no longer thought of in an organic sense as the "body of Christ," but rather as the "household of God," which enjoys a hierarchy of leadership—bishops, presbyters, and deacons, along with the orders of deaconesses and widows. Whether it was a reaction to the radicalizing of the implications of the gospel in the form of attempts to realize some degree of social and political egalitarianism, or a result of the waning of eschatological enthusiasm and the concomitant "routinization of charism," the tendency toward organization and hierarchy bespeaks a post-Pauline situation. In the Pastorals much greater importance is attached to bishops and presbyters as administrators of church affairs and as teachers and guardians of church traditions and respectability, especially against the "heretics." Less important are spirit-filled prophets; their contributions are mentioned only in passing (1 Tim 1:18, 4:14), no doubt out of sensitivity to the perceived dangers of the opponents' claims to spirit possession.

The evidence in the Pastorals is not immediately clear as to whether the "bishop" or "overseer" (*episkopos:* 1 Tim 3:2; Titus 1:7) was thought of as the monarchical office or as the chief officer of the board of ruling "presbyters" or "elders" (*presbyteroi:* 1 Tim 5:17, 19; Titus 1:5). But the interchange of terms (offices) with the same set of responsibilities, namely, management (1 Tim 3:4–5, 5:17; *cf.* also Titus 1:7), suggests that "bishop" and "presbyter" were used to refer to the same office—presbyter-bishop—which was not yet monarchical. The roles of Timothy and Titus in connection with these designations of office are also not immediately clear—whether they are super-presbyter-bishops with responsibilities beyond the local level, or merely messengers and representatives for the apostle Paul as writer. Without attaching to them any of the terms above, the documents themselves state that the responsibility of Timothy and Titus is to hand down "sound" teaching and tradition as received from Paul (1 Tim 1:11; 6:20; 2 Tim 1:14; 2:2, 8).

Although it is not impossible that Paul turned his attention to concerns about church management and officers, he is unlikely to have done so in the way evidenced in the Pastorals. Not only is much of the terminology in which church government is discussed foreign to other letters of Paul, but the type of church leadership and government assumed in the Pastorals is more typical of a post-Pauline period in the church's history. Such a model of governance requires a more comfortable relationship between church and society, as well as a more worldly self-understanding on the part of the church than was evident during Paul's missionary career. The Pastorals' emphasis on church order and management, which some scholars have termed "bourgeois" Christianity or "worldly" Christianity, very likely does not belong to a period contemporaneous with Paul.

The Pastorals also reflect a similar attitude toward social relations within the church. Gender and social status are especially significant. The writer directs the ruling presbyters not to allow women to teach or exercise any authority over men in the church (1 Tim 2:12)—as women probably did among the opponents (2 Tim 3:6–7). He also expects all women "who profess religion" to be modest and sensible in their dress and behavior (1 Tim 2:9–11) and understands their (public) role in the church to be gender-specific, in line with the traditions of aristocratic Greco-Roman society. The possession of slaves by Christians is upheld by the writer. Christian slaves are bidden to be respectful of both pagan and Christian masters. They are especially to respect the latter, "since those who benefit by their service are . . . beloved" (1 Tim 6:1–2). The "rich in this world" are welcome in the church, and are merely charged not to be haughty, but to be liberal and generous with fellow church members in order to reap a spiritual reward (1 Tim 6:17–19). This ethos was foreign to Paul and his generation of Christians. The Christian churches of the middle of the first century were probably not yet constituted in a manner that would justify the Pastorals' sensitivity to the world in general and to bourgeois morality and values in particular (cf. 1 Cor 1:26–27).

AUTHORSHIP, DATE, PROVENANCE

If the arguments above speak against Pauline authorship, the question of authorship, dating, and provenance remains open. Nothing at all is known about the identity of the author. The argument by von Campenhausen that the author was Polycarp of Smyrna in the early second century is not defensible in light of the great similarity in literary style among the three Pastoral epistles, on the one hand, and the striking stylistic differences between Polycarp's *Epistle to the Philippians* and the Pastorals, on the other hand. But the shared terminology, as well as common ideas about church government, does suggest some affinity with Polycarp, or with the second-century Christianity in Asia Minor in which Polycarp played a significant part.

It is also unwarranted to date the Pastoral epistles beyond the first half of the second century on the basis of the argument that they reflect polemics against Marcion's *Antitheses*, written near the middle of the century (1 Tim 6:20). Not only is there little evidence in the Pastorals of polemic specifically against Marcion, but the polemic in evidence seems hardly directed against an advanced or systematically understood and articulated "gnosis" of the type associated with Marcion or with other figures in the late second

century. Given the language of conservative church government and positive social-political orientation, on the one hand, and the language of polemic against a not very advanced gnosticism, on the other hand, a general dating of the Pastorals between 100 and 140 would be appropriate. The peaceful and prosperous reigns of Emperors Hadrian and Antoninus Pius would have provided the climate and rationale for the social accommodationism; the absence of any well-organized, systematically articulated "heresy," which could account for the unsystematic, personalized polemic in the documents, warrants the earliest possible dating within the proposed chronological limits.

The earliest clear quotations from the Pastorals come from Irenaeus, the bishop of Lyons, who wrote in the 180s. The Muratorian Canon (*ca.* 200) also includes the Pastorals in its list of New Testament canonical writings. The Pastoral Epistles must, therefore, be dated before the last quarter of the second century.

As for provenance, the fact that all the geographical references in the Pastorals—Corinth, Crete, Dalmatia, Ephesus, Galatia, Miletus, Nicopolis, and Troas—point to areas around the Aegean Sea and Asia Minor is very suggestive.

Thus, the three "Pastorals" only purport to be writings of the apostle Paul. In a fertile area of the Pauline mission field, these (pseudonymous) documents were written by a student of Paul in order to enlist the authority of the apostle in the fight against "opponents" and their rigorously ascetic and socially disruptive tendencies, as well as to establish the church in Greco-Roman society in Asia Minor and the areas around the Aegean Sea.

DIFFERENCES WITHIN THE COLLECTION

The similarity of literary style and socioreligious perspective of the three documents notwithstanding, there are differences among them that must be noted if their function is to be understood. First, why are there *three* documents (as opposed to one), each internally consistent in terms of occasion, but difficult to square with the occasions for the writing of the others? Attention must be paid to each document—its genre, occasion, and special emphases.

1 Timothy

Traveling westward, "Paul" writes a "letter" to his young colleague "Timothy," who has been left behind in Ephesus (1:3). With intentions to return to Ephesus, the writer sends written instructions to his young colleague concerning proper conduct in the church, which is imaged as "the household of God" (3:14–15). These "instructions" have to do with prayer (2:1–2), the role of women in worship (2:8–15), qualifications of local church leaders (3:1–13), concern for widows (5:3–16), remuneration of local church leaders (5:17–19), procedures for the resolution of conflict with leaders (5:19–22), and the proper deportment of slaves (6:1–2) and the rich (6:17–19).

These instructions for church order were intended to help the entire church in Ephesus to counter the false teaching said to be in vogue there (1:3, 7, 19–20; 4:1–3; 6:5, 20). Direct correspondence between the instructions given to the church and the allegations of false teaching is difficult to establish. But directives for church order appear to have been a response to behavior and tendencies, especially on the part of women and slaves, deemed antisocial by the respectable society of Asia Minor. Such directives were intended to ensure that sensitive Christians might have good public relations and lead a "quiet life" in the world (2.2).

2 Timothy

Written from prison (1:8, 16; 2:9) and addressed to a young colleague in the ministry situated somewhere in Asia Minor (*cf.* 4:13), the "letter" known as 2 Timothy is a farewell discourse or final testament from a revered religious figure who feels himself abandoned by friends (4:16–17) and near death (4:6–7). He writes not simply to bid farewell to "Timothy" but to encourage him and to lend him advice about the correct conduct and indoctrination of a young Christian minister (2:1–2). He reminds Timothy of his heritage (1:5), offers himself as a model of ministerial conduct (1:11–13), and warns him against "opponents" whose false teaching and bad conduct provide a negative example for exhortation (1:15; 2:16–18, 23–26; 3:6).

Titus

The "letter" to Titus presupposes that Paul has left his young colleague Titus in Crete so that the work of building the apparently young and fragile community there might continue (1:5, 3:12). Communication is sent to direct Titus primarily in matters of church order—qualifications for the office of bishop (1:5–9)—and in matters pertaining to household and public conduct (2:1–3:11). There is some polemic against opponents of Jewish background (1:10, 14, 16; 3:9), whose understanding of Christianity and the ethic it demands is tied to observance of the Law. Such opponents seem to be identified with those who are accused of being profligate, insubordinate, not of sound doctrine, and home wreckers (1: 6, 9, 11). A type of Christianity requiring the assumption of certain social roles within and outside of the household, or with good citizenship in general, seems to be at stake. This "letter," as a primitive church order (compared not only to later examples of the genre, but also to 1 Tim) and rule book for good Christian citizenship, is the response.

Even these brief observations indicate the danger inherent in too quickly lumping these documents together. Not only is each document a response to a particular fictional situation, each also fits a particular literary genre (church order or testament). That both 1 Timothy and Titus can be considered church orders of sorts poses the problem of the significance of *two* such documents supposedly from the same hand. Titus, the less elaborate, more primitive church order, seems to have been written before 1 Timothy. The latter may have been provoked by the continuation of the situation that provoked Titus. Second Timothy, as an example of exhortation within the final testament of the dying apostle, could, for the purpose of making the fiction more dramatic and believable, have been intended from the beginning to be the third of three documents (4:18).

SIGNIFICANCE WITHIN EARLY CHRISTIANITY

In both their similarity (of literary style, terminology, and socioreligious perspective) and dissimilarity (occasions, internal "historical" situations, literary type, special emphases), the Pastorals should be understood in the context of movements within early Christianity from the late first century to the middle of the second century in areas around the Aegean Sea. They advance bold interpretations of Christian existence in this social context by reinterpreting and consolidating Christian (especially Pauline) traditions and making the Christian communities a part of the social world. They stress attention to church order and to the social conduct both of church leaders and of Christians in general. The social constitution of the churches in the area at this time was apparently changing to include more of the well-to-do and socially prominent. At the same time, some Christian teachers were advocating an interpretation of Christian existence that differed radically from the social and political conservatism of the author. The church orders and rules of social conduct embodied in the Pastorals were understood to be a necessary response.

The Pastorals, then, represent, along with the *Didache*, the beginning of a type of Christian literature that continued with such church orders as the *Didascalia Apostolorum* and the *Apostolic Constitutions*. These works advanced an interpretation of Christian existence in opposition to a gnostic-type asceticism of otherworldliness, as an acceptance of the world as the legitimate locus of Christian piety. This interpretation required critical discernment about what Christian piety must mean in the world. The Pastorals expressed that discernment through the rules of conduct within and outside the household.

The hallmark of the Pastorals as part of the early Christian movements toward accommodation to the world is not their social conservatism, but their boldness in experimenting with, and then offering, a way of being Christian *in* the world, as opposed to escaping from it. The codification and canonization of their social teachings in response to their specific sociopolitical context was accomplished by later generations.

Bibliography

Bassler, Jouette M. "The Widow's Tale: A Fresh Look at 1 Tim. 5:3–16." *Journal of Biblical Literature* 103 (1984): 23–41.

Campenhausen, Hans von. *Ecclesiastical Authority and Spiritual Power in the Church of the First Three Centuries.* Translated by J. A. Baker. Stanford, 1969.

———. "Polykarp von Smyrna und die Pastoralbriefe." In *Aus der Frühzeit des Christentums.* Tübingen, 1963. Pp. 197–252.

Davies, Stevan L. *The Revolt of the Widows: The Social World of the Apocryphal Acts.* Carbondale, Ill., 1980.

Dibelius, Martin, and Hans Conzelmann. *The Pastoral Epistles.* Edited by Helmut Koester, translated by P. Buttolph and A. Yarbro. Philadelphia, 1972.

Harrison, P. N. *The Problem of the Pastoral Epistles.* London, 1921.

Karris, R. J. "The Background and Significance of the Pastoral Epistles." *Journal of Biblical Literature* 92 (1973): 549–564.

Köster, Helmut. *Introduction to the New Testament.* Vol. 2, *History and Literature of Early Christianity.* Philadelphia, 1982. Pp. 297–305.

Kümmel, W. G. *Introduction to the New Testament.* Rev. ed. Translated by H. C. Kee. Nashville, 1975.

MacDonald, Dennis R. *The Legend and the Apostle: Battle for Paul in Story and Canon.* Philadelphia, 1983.

Schüssler Fiorenza, Elisabeth. *In Memory of Her: A Feminist Theological Reconstruction of Christian Origins.* New York, 1983.

Schweizer, E. *Church Order in the New Testament.* London, 1961.

Verner, David C. *The Household of God: The Social World of the Pastoral Epistles.* Chico, Calif., 1983.

VINCENT L. WIMBUSH

Philemon

ALTHOUGH PAUL WRITES the short personal letter to Philemon in his own hand, he includes Timothy as coauthor (Phlm 1). Paul's "imprisonment" probably refers to his house arrest in Rome between 61 and 63, shortly before his death. In other letters Paul refers to himself in his greetings as both slave of Jesus Christ and apostle, designating at once his service and his authority. In Philemon, however, Paul describes himself simply as a prisoner for Jesus Christ, a designation that includes his being under arrest and his dedication to the gospel.

Philemon was a leader of a house church, probably in Colossae. This location is substantiated by mention of Epaphras, Mark, Aristarchus, Demas, and Luke in Philemon 23 and Colossians 4:10–14. Onesimus, subject and bearer of the letter, is mentioned in Colossians 4:9, an indication that perhaps both Philemon and Colossians were written about the same time.

This letter is addressed to Philemon (pronounced Phi•'lē•mon), Apphia, Archippus, and "the church in your house." The Christians usually met in the homes of some of the wealthier members of the community, who would have had houses large enough to accommodate the group. These "house churches" celebrated the liturgy, read the Scriptures, and reflected on the instructions or letters of teachers and leaders. By thus building up a common tradition of faith—teaching and learning from each other—

the Christians gradually developed a new society distinct from the world around them. According to Acts, they "held all things in common" and took responsibility for the poor in their midst. In such a context, problems that developed among them were given new solutions based on the common faith of the members. So it is with the troubled relationship between the runaway slave Onesimus and his former master, Philemon. They are now no longer merely slave and master but "brothers," related in such a way that the former manner of handling problems (punishment or retaliation) is no longer possible. Implied in addressing various members of the household and the whole community that meets there is Paul's hope that the whole church will together discern a Christian way of resolving the problematic issues in the relationship of Onesimus and Philemon. The public and religious nature of this letter is further substantiated by the mention of all those who send greetings (Phlm 23–24), as well as by the liturgical language, which implies that Philemon would share the letter's contents and make his decision about Paul's proposal in consultation with the whole church.

Although Philemon is the only one of Paul's letters not concerned with doctrinal or ecclesiastical issues, its importance should not be overlooked. The ecclesiology reflected in the epistle and the critical nature of the ethical issues raised illustrate a developing Christian social consciousness.

On the one hand, the general practice in early Christianity was the conversion of whole households to the faith (see Acts 10:17–48). Living in an alien and often hostile society, Christians are often advised in the epistles not to seek revolutionary change but to remain as they were when they received the call (1 Cor 7:17, 20, 24). Some groups of people were especially vulnerable in the Greco-Roman society of the first century. Citizens, wives, children, and slaves were generally expected to follow the will of their rulers, husbands, parents, and masters. Piety included loyalty to authority. Thus the apostolic advice to members of those households that did convert en masse was to show a new deference to authority prompted by a new depth of motivation (cf. Eph 5:22–6:9; Col 3:18–4:1; 1 Pet 2:13–3:7). Citizens, wives, children, and slaves were exhorted to "be submissive," implying that they should remain within the roles they had when they were converted, awaiting the coming of the Lord while leading exemplary Christian lives.

On the other hand, Christianity introduced some revolutionary concepts, not the least of which was the notion of egalitarian discipleship and the possibility for individuals, regardless of their state in the world, to experience freedom in Christ. Baptism creates anew, and this creation is effective not only in the inner life of the individual but also in establishing new relationships among all.

Philemon indicates an ethical development beyond the instruction of Colossians, where the author exhorts slaves to "obey in everything your masters" (see Col 3:22–24). In Colossians 4:1, masters are instructed to "treat your slaves justly and fairly, knowing that you also have a Master in heaven." Paul goes further in Philemon. There the master is instructed to welcome back Onesimus, treating him as a "brother" and forgiving the wrongs Onesimus has done. Paul further appeals to Philemon to go beyond obedience, doing even more than asked.

In other letters, 1 and 2 Corinthians for example, Paul frequently appeals to his apostolic authority, commanding his addressees to carry out definite actions. His appeal to Philemon is on different grounds, and even the exact nature of his request is uncertain. It is not certain that Paul is seeking freedom for Onesimus. Paul subtly refers to his own example, adding that should Philemon seek redress for wrongs Onesimus has done, Paul himself will make retribution (v. 18). Paul appeals as one to whom Philemon himself is indebted (v. 19). Paul refers to his age (v. 10), suggesting that he deserves esteem and obedience on that account. Paul's affection for Onesimus is clear, recognizing no barriers of status distinction. He also indicates that Onesimus now enjoys the same relationship to Paul as Philemon himself does, that is, as son to father in the faith. And indeed Onesimus is even closer to Philemon, having become his brother "in the Lord" as well as "in the flesh" (v. 16). This apparently refers to Onesimus as a member of the household of Philemon.

The letter to Philemon, therefore, illustrates how much has changed for the Christian; relationships are to be judged on a different basis. Retaliation is not to be exacted. There is a new ethic and a new method of decision-making in the context of the liturgy, with trust, freedom, and generosity operative despite personal risk. The short letter to Philemon illustrates a dilemma with crucial and transforming implications for the community of believers.

Bibliography

Fitzmyer, Joseph A. "Philemon." In *Jerome Biblical Commentary*, vol. 2. Englewood Cliffs, N.J., 1968. Pp. 332–333.

Getty, Mary Ann. *Philippians/Philemon*. Wilmington, Del., 1980.

Peterson, Norman. *Rediscovering Paul: Philemon and the Sociology of Paul's Narrative World*. Philadelphia, 1985.

(*For additional bibliography, see the titles listed after the essay on Philippians in the present volume.*)

MARY ANN GETTY

hebrews

THE EPISTLE TO the Hebrews is the nineteenth book of the New Testament, following the letters of Paul to churches and to individuals and preceding the catholic, or general, epistles. This position does not reflect a unanimous judgment of the early church on its status in the canon. In the Western church, it was known and perhaps used, though without direct quotation or attribution, by Clement of Rome (*ca.* 96 C.E.; *1 Clement* 36:1–5) and enthusiastically appealed to by Tertullian of Carthage (*ca.* 160–200), but it subsequently fell into disuse in the West. In the important Eastern church of Alexandria, however, it was well known to Tertullian's contemporary, Clement, and continued to be used by his successors. In the period of the Christian empire (after 313), increased contact and exchange of views between churches led to a revival of knowledge of Hebrews in the West; Augustine (354–430) and Jerome (*ca.* 342–420) accepted it explicitly on Eastern authority, and it was thereafter in general use.

Doubts about the book's authority were raised again in the Reformation period: Luther judged it to be "nonapostolic," and relegated it to the end of his New Testament canon. His express reason for so doing was that the rigorism of Hebrews and its rejection of a second repentance from sin (6:4–6, 10:26–27, 12:16–17) were in conflict with his belief in the availability of God's grace to the sinner through faith, which was for him the central doctrine of all apostolic Scripture

(*Preface to the Epistle to the Hebrews*, 1522). Calvin, like Luther, did not believe that Paul was the author of the epistle, but he nevertheless highly commended it because it fully explained how Christ was the end of the Law. His commendation, and the fact that the tradition of reading Hebrews proved stronger than Luther's preference, has ensured that Hebrews has retained its place in the Protestant canon, as in all other branches of the Christian church.

AUTHORSHIP

The question of Hebrews' authority and its place in the canon of the New Testament was bound up with the question of its authorship. Although the text refers to Paul's companion Timothy (13:23), it makes no claim to have been written by Paul himself; nor do the early Western readers of the epistle. Tertullian (*On Modesty* 20) believed that it had been written by another of Paul's companions, Barnabas, probably because its use of priestly and sacrificial imagery seemed consistent with the description of Barnabas as a "Levite" and because it would be appropriate for this "son of exhortation" (Acts 4:36; RV) to write a "word of exhortation" (Heb 13:22; RSV; all subsequent quotations will be from the RSV translation unless otherwise stated). In Alexandria, however, acceptance of the epistle was based on the assumption that Paul was its author. Eusebius' canon list includes "the fourteen epistles of Paul" (*Ecclesiastical History* 3.3.5; hereafter cited as *E.H.*), and Athanasius lists Hebrews after Paul's letters to churches and before his personal letters to individuals (*Festal Letter* 39, for 367 C.E.). In the important third-century Egyptian papyrus manuscript of the Pauline epistles known as P[46] Hebrews appears between Romans and 1 Corinthians and thus among the major letters to churches. The Alexandrians were, however, far too good scholars not to recognize the considerable differences in style and language between Hebrews and the explicitly Pauline letters, and suggested explanations for this. Clement thought that it had been translated into Greek by Luke, from Paul's original Hebrew (Eusebius, *E.H.* 6.14.2), whereas Origen suggested that it might have been composed from notes made on Paul's teaching by an unknown disciple of the apostle, representing therefore Paul's thoughts but not his words (*E.H.* 6.25.13).

In questioning the epistle's canonical authority, Luther also rejected its Pauline authorship: his own guess was that it was written by Apollos, and this theory has been revived in some modern scholarship (Spicq 1952; Montefiore 1964). It has some plausibility. Apollos is described in Acts 18:24 as "an eloquent man, well versed in the scriptures," which would be consistent with the importance given in Hebrews to the exposition of Scripture. He was also a Jew from Alexandria, a city renowned for its intellectual and philosophical tradition, in which Apollos' older Jewish contemporary Philo shared. The literary quality and probable philosophical knowledge found in Hebrews might be attributed to Apollos the Alexandrian. We also know that Apollos became a Christian teacher whom some in the church in Corinth regarded as having an authority and attracting a loyalty equal to that of Paul and Peter (1 Cor 1:12; 3:4–5, 21–22), and the Epistle to the Hebrews is a sustained piece of argument by an author who clearly believes that his words will be heeded. We have, however, no example of Apollos' teaching with which the epistle might be compared, and its attribution to him must remain a speculation. Adolf von Harnack (1851–1930) suggested instead Apollos' instructors Aquila and Priscilla as coauthors, with Priscilla the dominant partner. If true, this would make the Epistle to the Hebrews the only document in the New Testament with a female author.

Most modern scholars have been content to rest with Origen's judgment that "who wrote the epistle, in truth God knows" (reported by Eusebius, *E.H.* 6.25.14). Few if any scholars, Catholic or Protestant, would now argue for Pauline authorship. As well as the differences in style and language noted by patristic and Reformation scholars, there are major differences in thought between Paul and Hebrews. Paul makes no use of priestly imagery for Christ, and very little use of sacrificial imagery for his work; while on the other hand dominant Pauline ideas, such as justification by grace through faith and the Christian experience of being "in Christ," have no place in Hebrews. The final established place of the epistle in the New Testament, after the letters bearing Paul's name but before those of any other letter-writers, represents both the long tradition of some form of association with Paul and the fact that as it stands the epistle is anonymous.

PLACE AND DATE

The author does not identify himself, and he does not identify his readers either, since the epistle carries no opening address. The title "To the Hebrews" is familiar both to Tertullian in the West and to Clement in the East, and was therefore attached to the epistle at a very early stage. Its adoption no doubt represents a judgment on the contents of the book, its extensive reliance on quotations from the Old Testament and in particular its exposition of scriptural models of priesthood and sacrifice, which are still thought by many modern scholars to be appropriate in writing to Jewish, but not to gentile, Christians.

The question of the geographical location of author and readers, however, receives a wide range of answers and is complicated by the question of the document's genre. If it is a real letter, sent from one place to another, then the locations of author and readers are different; if it is not, they may have been living in the same place, in immediate contact with each other. Chapter 13, which gives the document the character of a letter, includes greetings from "they of Italy" (13:24; RV). The phrase is ambiguous. It could denote people in Italy, along with the author, sending greetings to readers elsewhere; and an Italian place of origin for the epistle could be consistent with the fact that it was first known and used in Rome. More probably, though, the phrase denotes expatriates from Italy sending greetings back home: hence the RSV translation, "Those who come from Italy send you greetings." The epistle would then have been sent to Italy, again consistent with its early use in Rome, but have had its origin elsewhere. If, however (for reasons to be discussed below), chapter 13 is not regarded as an integral part of the epistle, its evidence either way will be set aside, and decisions about origin will rest on considerations about the overall character of chapters 1–12. Those who find a high level of Hellenistic culture in these chapters, along with a familiarity with the language and ideas of contemporary philosophy, may opt for Alexandria as a likely place for the epistle to have been written. Certainly it was in Alexandria that the ideas of Hebrews were to prove most congenial. Others, however, who feel that the discussion of Levitical priesthood and sacrifice presupposes a knowledge of their practice in the Temple of Jerusalem, will argue that the epistle must have been written close to the Temple, that is, in Palestine or Jerusalem itself (Spicq 1952; Buchanan 1972).

The question of the date of the epistle is similarly debatable. It must have been written before the end of the first century, when Clement of Rome knew it; the question is, how early in that century? This question would of course be preempted if Pauline authorship were accepted, the question then being at what stage in his career Paul might have written it. If the authorship is unknown, we are again left to interpret internal evidence. The readers' church is not a new foundation, but has a past, and an honorable one, to look back on (6:10, 10:32–34). Despite its past struggles, the author can write that "you have not yet resisted to the point of shedding your blood" (12:4). This would seem inappropriate for addressing Christians in Rome at any time after Nero's attack on them in 64 C.E.; and inappropriate for Christians in Jerusalem except in the very early days of the church there, before Herod's execution of James (Acts 12:1–2) or the death of Stephen (Acts 7:58–8:2).

The question of the relation of the Temple of Jerusalem to the argument of the epistle is again relevant. The Temple was destroyed in 70 C.E., at the end of the Jewish revolt. If the author intended to attack its practices, he would hardly have written that the old covenant that embodied them was "ready to vanish away" (8:13), or asked rhetorically whether its sacrifices "would not have ceased to be offered" (10:2) after that event. The fall of the Temple would have proved his point; the sacrifices would indeed have ceased and the covenant been rendered obsolete. In fact, his knowledge of the Levitical system is derived from the reading of Scripture rather than from empirical experience, but even so it seems unlikely that he could have ignored the catastrophic ending of an institution that purported to put the scriptural regulations into effect. Many scholars therefore date Hebrews before 70 C.E. It might just be arguable that the whole epistle is a response to the fall of the Temple, its purpose being to show shocked Jewish Christians who had retained their loyalty to the Temple that its catastrophe was necessary, indeed inevitable, since the system had already been superseded by Christ; but then the reason for writing would remain, curiously, an unspoken fact.

CONTENTS

The author opens with a declaration both of the finality of Christ's work and of his unique, preexistent character as God's Son (1:1–3). There follows a comparison between Christ the Son and the angels, demonstrating his superiority to them in a string of quotations (1:4–14). His superiority makes it imperative that Christ's message of salvation, even more than the message given by angels, not be neglected (2:1–4). The author then turns to consider the relationship of Christ and humanity, showing how he fulfills God's promise to humanity given in Psalm 8:4–6, and how he is himself fully identified with humanity (2:5–18). He is also superior to Moses, and the failure of Moses' followers is a warning to Christ's followers against failure of confidence in him (3:1–4:2). The promise that is open to Christ's followers is of entry into God's "rest," as indicated in Psalm 95:11 and Genesis 2:2 (4:3–13). We may be encouraged to approach God, confident in the assistance of Christ, the high priest who knows human weakness from his own experience (4:14–5:10). The readers are, however, reproached for their failure to grow in their faith, warned that apostasy is an unforgivable sin, and reminded of their worthier past (5:11–6:12).

God's promise stands, guaranteed by Christ, the "priest for ever after the order of Melchizedek" (Ps 110:4); and this claim leads to an exposition of the role of Melchizedek. What is distinctive about his priesthood and makes it a model for Christ's is that it is wholly separate from and superior to the Levitical order; and, because Melchizedek has no predecessor or successor, he symbolizes a priesthood that is permanent and eternal (6:13–7:22). The crucial features of Christ's own priesthood are that he is always available; that he needs to act only once because his action is effective; that because he is sinless he does not need to offer for himself, but can himself be his own offering; and that he operates in the right place: heaven, not earth (7:23–8:5). All this adds up to the enactment of God's promised new covenant (8:6–13, quoting Jeremiah 31:31–34).

The old covenant, although ineffective and now superseded, had nevertheless expressed in its institutions a true appreciation of human need. The author singles out the ritual of the Day of Atonement (Lev 16), in which the high priest, on that one day of the year only, took the blood of sacrifice into the Holy of Holies of the tabernacle (Heb 9:1–10). Christ, following this pattern, but giving it real effectiveness, has entered once for all into the true Holy of Holies, heaven, bearing the blood of his own sacrifice (9:11–28). The animal sacrifice prescribed by the Law had only served as reminders of the need to deal with sin; Christ's sacrifice of himself has answered that need (10:1–18). Once again the author draws out the consequences of his argument for the readers: the full and final effectiveness of Christ's act means that they may confidently draw near to God, but it also demands that they must continue to live up to their faith, as they have in the past, for as his work is unrepeatable, so there is no second chance for those who fall from their faith (10:19–39).

There then follows an exposition of the nature of faith, as exemplified by the heroes of the past, from Abel to the Maccabees (11:1–12:2). Faith is a commitment to God's promises, and to another world than this, "the assurance of things hoped for, the conviction of things not seen" (11:1). Jesus, the final example of faith (12:2), is also an example of endur-

ance of suffering, which is a necessary part of Christian experience and calls for mutual support (12:3–17). Christians have attained to the heavenly city, but must be prepared to face God's final convulsion of heaven and earth (12:18–29). The final chapter contains a variety of admonitions for the proper behavior of the community, warnings about false teachings, a magnificent closing prayer, and personal news and greetings (13:1–25).

GENRE

The impression gained from a reading of the epistle as a whole is that of a carefully worked-out argument, conducted in considerable detail and showing little sign of the haste and even incoherence that often mark Paul's epistles. This impression is enhanced by the author's mastery of the Greek language, which is of considerable literary quality. There are, however, two major literary-critical questions about the epistle: its genre and its integrity. Hebrews is known as an "epistle," and it concludes with the messages and greetings appropriate to a letter. It opens, though, by contrast, with no conventional address from author to readers, but with a polished, alliterative statement of the place of Christ in the history of God's communication with the world. This concentration on expounding the person and work of Christ has led some to describe it as a christological essay or treatise, with the ad hominem warnings being artificial devices to underline the importance of the theme. Alternatively, in 13:22 the author describes his work as a "word of exhortation," and this is the term used for Paul's sermon in Acts 13:15. In view of the prominence given by Hebrews to the exegesis of scriptural texts, the work might be described as a sermon, a *midrash* or synagogue homily on a text, subsequently translated into written form. Specifically, Hebrews may be seen as a *midrash* on Psalm 110, the text that leads the author into his exposition of the character and work of Christ as priest, the contrast between his priesthood and the Levitical order, and the analogy with the priesthood of Melchizedek (Buchanan 1972).

The problem of genre is in part posed by the inconsistency of chapter 13 with the rest of the document. Its ethical admonitions, especially against sexual sins (v. 4); its direct attack on false teaching and on a separate and opposed society "who serve the tent" (vv. 9–10); and its characterization of Jesus as "the great shepherd of the sheep" (v. 20) have no precedent in the main body of the epistle; and the reference to Jesus' coming "from the dead" (v. 20) is unusual in a document that thinks in terms of his exaltation to God's presence rather than of his resurrection. On the other hand, the statements that "Jesus Christ is the same yesterday and today and forever" (v. 8), and that "here we have no lasting city" (v. 14) echo themes found in the main argument (Filson 1967). It is possible that chapter 13 was added to the original document, to give it the character of a letter and something of a Pauline veneer, at a time when its authority was beginning to come into question.

Even without chapter 13 it is not easy to classify the genre of the document, but it is probably safe to say, first, that it was originally a written product rather than a spoken message later recorded in writing; second, that it was written to address a specific situation; and third, that that address is to a situation with which the author is in immediate contact: he writes to and for the community to which he belongs, rather than sending a message elsewhere.

SITUATION

The author criticizes his readers for failing in their Christian faith. This is in part an intellectual failure to grow in the faith, so that those who should by now be teachers still have to be treated like children (5:11–14). It is also a failure of community, so that some no longer bother to meet together (10:23–25). This contrasts markedly with their former enthusiasm and mutual support, and puts in question their ability to endure any future trial (10:32–36; cf. 12:3–4). The failure is serious, because it raises the possibility of passing beyond the scope of forgiveness (6:4–6, 10:26–27, 12:15–17), although the author reassures his readers that that point has not yet been reached. He does not describe in concrete terms what he sees to be this unforgivable sin. It is unlikely to be the espousal of new, and to him heretical, doctrine, for only in 13:9 is there any attack on false teachings, and the readers seem to be more prone

to flagging zeal than to misdirected enthusiasm. Their danger is more usually seen as one of relapse, a loss of their Christian convictions and a return to their former—presumably Jewish—faith. Even so, it is remarkable that there is no explicit attack on an alternative religious system, and it may be that the problem is primarily that of the failure of the Christian community in itself to maintain its own convictions and cohesion, rather than of a deliberate choice between options. At any rate, the author's response is to call for a renewal of their own confidence (4:14, 6:11, 10:19–23, 12:12–13) and to base this upon a demonstration both of the superiority of Christ to any other of God's agents, whether angels (1:4, 2:2–3), Moses (3:1–6), or the Levitical priests (7:23–25); and of the finality of his work (10:11–14).

CULTURAL AND RELIGIOUS BACKGROUND

If the danger that the author sees as threatening his readers is one of relapse into their past faith, this of course poses the question of what that past was. Lacking, as we do, explicit identification of author and readers, we have to ask what is indicated about their origins by the content and character of the epistle as a whole; what terms it is natural for this author to think in and argue with; what imagery he chooses to express his ideas; what axioms and presuppositions seem to be taken for granted as common ground between author and readers.

In the course of the epistle a number of distinctive features emerge. Its argument is marked by frequent appeal to Scripture, in simple quotation, in catenas, or strings of texts, and in detailed exposition of major passages. The Psalms are quoted more frequently than any other section of Scripture. Quotations are always from the Septuagint, the Greek translation of the Old Testament, which sometimes enables the author to make points he would be unable to make from the Hebrew text (e.g., 10:5–7; cf. Ps 40:6–8). Again, underlying the argument at many points is the conviction of a correspondence between earth and heaven, so that things on earth are copies and shadows of things in heaven (8:5, 9:23–24, 10:1), and there is a corresponding interest in the present work of Christ in heaven as well as in his past work on earth. The most characteristic image for Christ is that of the high priest, performing his work of sacrifices and of intercession. Certain axioms are taken for granted: for instance, that blood sacrifice is essential in dealing with sin (9:22); and that if an action is effective, it must be unrepeatable, since repetition is a sign of failure (9:25–26; 10:1–2, 11–14). The repeated warnings of the danger of neglecting the gospel are related to this, for there can be no second chance of redemption. The whole argument of the epistle is conducted in Greek of considerable literary quality, showing an extensive vocabulary and some acquaintance with the techniques of Hellenistic rhetoric.

All these features need to be taken into account in considering the cultural background of author and readers. The frequency and variety of use of the Old Testament Scriptures, and the exposition of their models of priesthood and sacrifice has naturally led many scholars to conclude that the background of author and readers lies in Judaism, and that it is into that former faith that the readers are tempted to relapse. Such temptation may have arisen at a time when old loyalties were particularly evoked, perhaps during the Jewish revolt of 66–70 C.E., or when Christian communities were themselves under pressure, and some may have wished to recover that measure of protection which Roman law had given to Judaism; or it may have arisen simply from a desire for the old certainties of an ancestral religion with established structures, after the first enthusiasm of Christian conversion had passed.

One major difficulty with this reconstruction is that the author does not deal with the empirical institutions of Judaism, such as Sabbath, synagogue, or circumcision; and even when he deals with sacrifice, priesthood, and holy place, his language is archaic and bookish, drawn from Scripture rather than from experience (Bruce 1964). He always writes of the "tent" (RV, "tabernacle"), and never of the Temple; and his list of the contents of the Holy of Holies in 9:2–5 may be checked off from the Pentateuch, but bears no relation to the contents of the Holy of Holies in the Temple in first-century Jerusalem, which Pompey entered in 63 B.C.E. to find empty of virtually all of them, most notably the Ark of the Covenant (Josephus, *Antiquities* 14.71–72; *Jewish*

War 1.152–153). This might be because the author is separated from the Temple in some way: in time, if he wrote after its destruction in 70 C.E.; in space, if he wrote in the Jewish Diaspora and could rarely if ever have visited Jerusalem; or in sympathy, if he belonged to an area of Judaism hostile to the priestly aristocracy of Jerusalem (for Judaism at the time of the beginnings of Christianity was not a single and homogeneous entity).

One area of Judaism with which it has been common to associate Hebrews is the Hellenistic Judaism of Philo of Alexandria (e.g., Spicq 1952; also Scott 1922). Philo (*ca.* 20 B.C.E. – *ca.* 50 C.E.) sought to harmonize Greek, especially Platonic, philosophy and the Jewish religion, finding in the Pentateuch an allegorical expression of philosophical ideas, while remaining loyal to the requirements of its law. In particular, he expounded the idea of two creations, of the eternal and material worlds, and of the Logos as the mediator between them, finding scriptural warrant for these two creations in the two narratives of Genesis 1 and 2. There are obvious analogies here with Hebrews. The author of Hebrews is similarly convinced of the coexistence of two orders, the one perfect, heavenly, and permanent, the other imperfect, transitory, and of this world; and he describes the relationship between them in terms of the latter being a "shadow" or "copy" of the former (8:5, 9:23–24, 10:1). This is strongly reminiscent of Platonic metaphysics, and the language even echoes the imagery used by Plato in his allegory of the cave to express the relationship between the material world and the world of forms (*Republic* 514A–517A). Hebrews' axiom, too, that anything that is repeated is necessarily ineffective (10:1–2) is also consistent with the Platonic assumption that time, movement, and change are characteristic of the imperfect material order. If the author of Hebrews, like Philo, seems to adopt philosophical ideas, he also, like Philo, finds warrant for them in Scripture, for God's command to Moses to "make everything according to the pattern which was shown you on the mountain" (Exod 25:40) demonstrates for him that the earthly practices of the Levitical order are an imperfect representation of the order of heaven (8:5).

Another similarity is that both Philo and the author of Hebrews make use of the figure of Melchizedek, Philo as an image of the Logos (*Legum Allegoriae* 3.79–82) and Hebrews as an image of Christ. However, Philo's Logos is not a person as is Hebrews' Christ, and though his Logos may reveal God to humanity, it does not redeem from sin in a once-for-all act. Philo's juxtaposition of his two worlds is fixed and permanent: he has nothing of the eschatological expectation expressed in Hebrews 12:25–29 (and indeed in 10:1, where the Law has a shadow of the good things "to come"). These contrasts may exist because Hebrews' new Christian convictions have altered his original Philonic presuppositions, but they may also instead indicate some basic differences between the thought world of Philo and that of the epistle. It is still possible, however, as we shall see, that the author of Hebrews is in his own way engaging in an enterprise similar to Philo's: that of commending his faith to the intellectual Hellenistic world.

A greater appreciation of the eschatological element in Hebrews, its expectation of change and of future event (with 12:25–29 cf. 8:13, 9:27–28, 10:25), has led other scholars to associate Hebrews with apocalyptic Judaism rather than with the philosophical world of Philo (Barrett 1956). The conviction of two world orders, earlier seen to be a prime indication of the philosophical, especially Platonic, background of Hebrews as of Philo, might instead derive from the apocalyptic idea of entities kept in heaven to be revealed at the end of time (as the heavenly city is prepared and descends in the Christian apocalypse; Rev 21:2). One particular branch of Judaism where eschatological expectation was strong was the Essene movement, as known from the writings of the community of Qumran. Here, too, analogies have been drawn (Bruce 1963; Hughes 1977). The Essenes of Qumran were interested in angels, were much engaged in the exegesis of Scripture so that it applied directly to the community, and repudiated the priesthood and sacrifices of the Jerusalem Temple. Most strikingly, they hoped for the coming of two Messiahs, one of whom—"the Messiah of Aaron"—has a priestly role to perform. The publication of scroll 11Q Melchizedek suggested another interesting comparison, for in it Melchizedek, so important an image for Christ in Hebrews, is apparently described as an angel and thought of as a redeemer who defeats Satan (Horton 1976). The Qumran community,

however, looked for the future establishment of a purified priesthood and temple service, which would for Hebrews be incompatible with and excluded by the one sufficient priesthood and sacrifice of Christ; and it sympathized with, and may have been actively involved in, the efforts of Jewish nationalists to obtain Israel's independence from Rome—an interest that is wholly foreign to the author of the epistle.

Yet another area of Judaism that has recently received attention as a possible background to Hebrews is that of *merkavah* ("throne") mysticism (Schenke 1973; Williamson 1976). This was characterized by the desire of the mystic to penetrate through contemplation the various heavens with their ministering angels and ultimately attain a vision of the throne of God. The documentary evidence for *merkavah* mysticism itself is later than the New Testament period, the fifth and sixth centuries, but a mystical tradition in Judaism may well go back over a considerable time. Paul writes in 2 Corinthians 12:2–4 of his being "caught up to the third heaven" and hearing "things that cannot be told," and the ultimate antecedent of *merkavah* mysticism is Ezekiel's vision of the chariot-throne of God (Ezek 1:4–28). This background would be consistent with the author of Hebrews' call to approach the throne of God (4:16; cf. 10:19–22), and his conviction of the reality and accessibility of heaven, while his description of Jesus as having "passed through the heavens" (4:14; cf. 7:26) and entered the heavenly holy place (8:1, 9:11–12) would make him the archetypal and exemplary mystic. The analogies are certainly striking, but questions must remain because of the date of the material for comparison, and because mysticism is a matter of individual religious experience rather than of the shared tradition of a community, and it is with his community, its situation and its dangers, that the author is concerned.

There have been some attempts to find the background of Hebrews outside Judaism altogether, and to place it firmly in the context of gentile Christianity. The Old Testament scriptures were, of course, the holy book for Jewish and gentile Christians alike. There are certainly some elements in the epistle that are uncharacteristic of Jewish religion and culture. The celebration of heroes in chapter 11 has little analogy in Jewish literature save for the—itself uncharacteristic—praise of famous men in Sirach 44:1–50:24. The identification of the "conscience" as that part of human nature that needs to be freed from sin (9:9, 14; 10:22) belongs to the language of Stoic rather than Jewish morality. The presentation of Jesus as one who through effort and suffering achieves perfection (2:10, 5:8–10) is similar to the heroes of Hellenistic religious imagination, such as Herakles; and the specific designation of him as "pioneer" (2:10, 12:2) and "forerunner" (6:20) has parallels in the celebration of these heroes (Knox 1941). The origins of the epistle's thought have even been traced in pagan gnosticism, the Jesus of Hebrews being the gnostic divine-man redeemer, who enters the world and returns whence he came (Käsemann 1938); but this has found little support, if only because Hebrews does not, in fact, describe Jesus' entry into the world, although it is much concerned with his exaltation beyond it.

To conclude, despite the common possession of the inherited Scripture, it is difficult to imagine that a Christian author would conduct a debate with his readers so much in terms of exegesis and of the imagery of Levitical practice unless they and he shared something of a Jewish cultural and religious heritage. The various suggestions that have been put forward caution against too precise an identification of that heritage, but it must be a Judaism that was both interested in speculation about another world, heaven, its inhabitants, and its accessibility, and also open to adopt ideas and language from the Hellenistic world. Such speculation was widespread, and the interpenetration of Judaism and Hellenism took place in many different contexts, in Judaism as well as in the Diaspora; indeed, both owe more to a general cultural climate and social attitudes than to the organization of specific groups.

What remains remarkable, as already noted, is Hebrews' lack of concern with empirical, contemporary Jewish practice, and the lack of polemic against an alternative community or teachings. There is nothing of Paul's argument against the practice of circumcision by Jewish converts or his invective against the Judaizers who promote it (Gal 5:2–12). A comparison is sometimes drawn between the viewpoint of Hebrews and that of Stephen, as known from Luke's account of his speech in Acts 7:2–53 (Manson

1951). Stephen is associated with those Jewish Christians described as "Hellenists" (Acts 6:1–6), and Hebrews, with its Jewish and Hellenistic characteristics, might seem to carry on his tradition. Like the author of Hebrews, Stephen emphasizes the role of angels as mediators of the Law (7:38, 53); the character of the patriarchs as sojourners but not settlers in the promised land (7:2–6); and the tabernacle as the place of worship copied by Moses from the original that he had seen (7:44). However, in Stephen's speech these themes are harnessed, as they are not in Hebrews, into a fierce attack on the man-made house, the Temple, and on the Jewish leaders who maintain it (7:47–53). It may be that the Christian community represented by Hebrews had continued to live as Jews, without feeling any tension; or that their Judaism was now some way in their past, so that such disputes were no longer relevant. If there is a debate about their Jewish past, it seems to be more concerned with the interpretation of a hallowed tradition than with their relation to a living and alternative Jewish community.

THE EPISTLE IN EARLY CHRISTIANITY

The intention of the author is to recall a flagging Christian community to the confidence of its original faith, but, whether intentionally or not, he may be seen to perform a number of other functions in the context of the development of Christianity. First, he performs a hermeneutical function, giving Christian readers ways in which they may appropriate the Scriptures that they have inherited from Judaism as their own. All Scripture is God's speech, and prophetic (Heb 1:1), yet much that is prescribed in it, especially in terms of priesthood and sacrifice, is rendered obsolete by Christ (8:13). This apparent paradox was realized and resolved in various ways in early Christianity. Marcion (*ca.* 144) came to reject the Old Testament altogether, maintaining that it did not bear witness to the God of Jesus, and established his own collection of Christian scriptures. Others adopted the expedient of allegorical interpretation, treating the Old Testament as a complex of interchangeable symbols for Christian truths. The author of Hebrews solves the paradox in three ways. First, although the old institutions of priesthood, sacrifice, holy place, and covenant were ineffective, they were still valid models, and are fulfilled in Christ. The role of the priest, the function of sacrifice, and the aspiration to enter the presence of God, as presented in Scripture, are all properly perceived. The old ways of putting them into action are discarded, but the patterns themselves are maintained and given new content by Christ, the effective priest who offers the only sufficient sacrifice and enters the true holy place. In effect, the imagery of the Old Testament becomes reality only in Christian terms, but its images are true and lasting images, not arbitrary symbols that might be chosen or discarded.

In another approach, the author demonstrates that the inadequacy of the old institutions is implied in Scripture itself. If Joshua's entry into the promised land had given the Israelites true rest, God would not have still held open the promise of entry into his rest in Psalm 95:11 (4:1–9); if the Levitical priesthood had been adequate, God would not have promised, in Psalm 110:4, another priest "after the order of Melchizedek" (7:11–19); and if the whole framework of the old covenant had been effective, God would not have promised, in Jeremiah 31:31–34, a "new covenant" (8:7–13). It is not that judgment is passed on Scripture from outside: Scripture contains its own judgments and points to the replacement and effective fulfillment of its institutions. The Christian way of reading Scripture is thus true to Scripture itself.

A further and striking way of appropriating the Old Testament is provided in the roll call of heroes in chapter 11. This makes it possible for Christian readers to claim the saints of the Old Testament, from Abel to the Maccabean martyrs, as their own ancestors, since the author establishes their relationship on the basis not of physical descent or national identity but of a common faith characterized as "assurance of things hoped for, . . . conviction of things not seen" (11:1). Faith is, however, a criterion for contrast as well as identity, for the Israelites of the wilderness wanderings are a warning to the Christian readers against a similar failure to attain God's promises "because of unbelief" (3:12–19).

Just as the argument of the epistle thus gives to its readers ways of appropriating their tradition and making Christian sense of it, so it also establishes bridges to the outside, Hellenistic world. Christian faith is beginning to be articulated in the language not only of Scripture and tradition but also of philosophy. When the author expresses his sense of the contrast between the material and heavenly worlds in terms of the former being "copies and shadows" of the latter, he is using language that would be familiar at the level of popular philosophy, even if he does not adopt the full metaphysics of a philosophical system. In his references to conscience and his characterization of the "heroic" Christ (and heroic or athletic Christians; see 10:32; 12:1, 12), he is using ideas that would be familiar to non-Jewish contemporaries. He accuses his readers of failing to apply their minds to their faith, and of intellectual immaturity (5:11–14), and in the way he writes he is himself beginning the process of making Christianity intellectually respectable and of commending it to the educated Roman world. He stands at the beginning of the line of Christian apologists, the predecessor in this enterprise of such thinkers as Justin Martyr, Tertullian, and Origen (Thompson 1982).

The author of Hebrews also gives his readers ways of affirming their distinctive Christian identity. In their contemporary society, the essential marks of a religion were that it was ancestral and that it possessed a sacrificing priesthood. In the era of persecution, Christians were to be called "atheists" because they lacked these characteristics. As we have seen, the author makes it possible for his readers to claim the saints of the Old Testament as their true ancestors. They have no allegiance to the sacrifices and priesthood of Judaism, nor indeed to those of Hellenistic religions, but the author argues that they have both priesthood and sacrifice, and have them in the only effective way: in the once-for-all sacrifice of Christ and in his continuing ministry in the heavenly sanctuary (7:23–25, 10:11–14). This argument is given a polemical and exclusive edge in 13:10, but in the bulk of the epistle it could be used positively to build up the readers' confidence in their faith, and maybe also to enable them to commend it to outsiders (Moule 1950).

The readers may well have felt, in their new faith, out of place in their society; they had experienced some hostile pressure in the past (10:32–34) and would probably have to face it again (12:3–4).

The author enables them to come to terms with this situation by showing that they very properly do not belong in this world, for their true place is in heaven. They stand in the succession of the patriarchs who refused to settle down permanently, even in the "land of promise," because they looked for another and better "homeland" or "city" (11:8–10, 13–16). Similarly, then, the Christian readers are also "strangers and exiles on the earth" (11:13), accepting that "here we have no lasting city, but we seek the city which is to come" (13:14); but with the difference that they already have contact with and access to that heavenly city (12:22), because Jesus has opened up the way to heaven for them. Again, Hebrews stands at the beginnings of a tradition in which Christians understand themselves as a people "not of this world," an interpretation of their identity expounded notably in the second-century *Epistle to Diognetus* ("every foreign country is a fatherland to them, and every fatherland is foreign" [5:5], and they "have their abode in the world, and yet they are not of the world" [6:3]) and also having parallels in the Gospel of John (17:14, 16).

THE EPISTLE IN THE NEW TESTAMENT

When the Epistle to the Hebrews was accepted into the canon of the New Testament, the text acquired a new context. It could then be considered not only in the context of its own original situation, but also in the context of the holy book, in relation to the other accepted texts, and in terms of what it has to say not just to its first readers but to the continuing generations of Christian readers.

Within the New Testament the epistle speaks with a highly distinctive voice, contributing imagery for understanding the person and work of Christ that has little parallel elsewhere. In particular, the presentation of Christ as priest has no clear analogy in the New Testament, except perhaps in the image of the Son of man in Revelation 1:13, where he wears priestlike vestments, and in the references to Christ's intercession in Romans 8:34 and 1 John 2:1. The understanding of his work as making sacrifice for sin has more widespread parallels: (John 1:29, 19:36; Rom 3:25; 1 Cor 5:7; 1 Pet 1:19), but it is nowhere

expounded with the systematic detail of Hebrews, nor do the other authors apparently draw as he does on the imagery of the sacrificial ritual of the Day of Atonement (Lev 16; unless John 1:29 alludes to the scapegoat of Lev 16:20–22, the one feature of the Day of Atonement ritual in which the author of Hebrews takes no interest). The usual Christian image is that of the Passover of Exodus 12, perhaps following the precedent of Jesus' own interpretation of his death in terms of the Passover sacrifice (Matt 26:26–28, Mark 14:22–24, Luke 22:17–20); but Hebrews makes only a passing reference to this, in 11:28.

In terms of the development of Christology, the epistle also makes a notable contribution. First, it insists upon the total humanity of Christ, "like his brethren in every respect," not only in the physical nature of humanity, but in the human experiences of suffering and temptation (2:17; cf. 4:15, 5:7–8). There is no room here for a superman redeemer or for a docetic Christ who is God merely pretending to be human. The author insists that the total humanity of Christ is essential to his work: it is only if he is fully identified with his "brethren" that he can be the "pioneer of their salvation" (2:10–11); only if he is equally susceptible to death can he break the devil's power of death (2:14); only if he is fully as they are can he be the high priest who is his people's representative before God (2:17–18, 4:15–5:1). He insists, however, that Christ as man was sinless (4:15, 7:27, 9:14). This has seemed to some theologians a difficulty, since it is hard to conceive of a sinless human being, and Christ's sinlessness might seem to set him so far apart from sinful humanity as to make it impossible for him really to sympathize with them; but the author sees clearly that while physical life, death, suffering, and temptation are proper to human experience and so to Christ's, sin is not (Williamson 1974).

Second, the author, like all other New Testament authors, affirms the basic pattern of Christian preaching of the life, death, and new life of Christ. He gives, however, a distinctive interpretation of the third part of that pattern. He never (unless in 13:20) writes in terms of resurrection, with its connotations of return to this world and questions of the bodily nature of the risen Lord. There is no allusion to the empty tomb or to the resurrection appearance narratives. In Hebrews, Jesus moves straight from suffering to glorification and entry into heaven (1:3, 2:9, 4:14, 6:19–20, 7:26–27, 9:11–12, 10:12). He is known as the living Lord not because of any event or encounter on earth, but from his opening up of access to heaven and his presence there. The same pattern of preaching is found in Philippians 2:8–9, in what may be a pre-Pauline hymn, and in a creedal passage in 1 Timothy 3:16, and it may be an early and alternative way of expressing what would elsewhere be called "the resurrection faith."

It is consistent with this last point that, third, the author's understanding of the work of Christ relates both to his past and to his present role. In other interpretations, the focus is almost exclusively upon the past event of his death, with his present state being apparently one of waiting until his second coming or the final resolution of all things (e.g., Acts 3:20–21). For Hebrews, however, the sacrificial work of Christ consists not only in his death but in the presentation of the sacrifice before God in heaven (9:12); and his work as priest consists not only in offering the one sacrifice but in opening up the continuing possibility of access to God and providing perpetual representation and intercession in heaven (7:24–25). The phrase "once for all," which is so characteristic of Hebrews (7:27; 9:12, 26, 28; 10:10; cf. 6:4), does not describe an act that has been done once and so lies in the past, but an act that has been done completely and so has established a permanent, present situation. What Christ has done, is done.

Fourth, like the author of the Fourth Gospel (John 1:1–3) and Paul (Col 1:15–17), the author of Hebrews affirms the preexistence of Christ, his unique relationship to God, and his participation in the work of creation. He does so in a highly formal opening statement (1:1–3). Surprisingly, after such an opening, the subject of Christ's preexistence is not discussed again in the epistle, though it may perhaps be alluded to in 10:5–9 and 11:26; and where creation is spoken of again, in 2:10 and 11:3, there is no reference to Christ's involvement in it. The opening statement, indeed, stands in some tension with the main thrust of the author's presentation of Christ in terms of his total humanity, for if it is difficult to think of the sinless Christ as able fully to sympathize with his brethren, it is much more difficult to claim that the one who was with God in creation is "like his

brethren in every respect" (2:17). The author makes no attempt to reconcile these two statements about Christ, but clearly feels that both must be made: they provide, as it were, the raw material of Christology, which it is left to later generations of theologians to formulate.

Because it deals so much with the imagery of priesthood and sacrificial ritual, the Epistle to the Hebrews has usually appealed more to those Christian churches which place a high value on liturgy, sacraments, and an ordained ministry than to those whose emphasis is more on preaching and the priesthood of all believers. This may be misleading. The author shows little, if any, interest in the Christian sacraments. The reference in 6:2 to instruction about "ablutions" (RSV) is usually taken to refer to the practice of baptism (hence RV, JB, and TEV, "baptisms"), but the plural noun is odd in that connection, and other interpreters have thought that the author may be referring instead to regular ritual cleansings such as those practiced at Qumran (cf. NEB, "instruction about cleansing rites"). There is no explicit reference to the Eucharist, even in contexts where it might be expected: for instance, in expounding the analogy between Melchizedek and Christ, the author does not take up the point that when Melchizedek came to meet Abraham he "brought out bread and wine" (Gen 14:18). Phrases that might elsewhere have eucharistic connotations are used exclusively of the one sacrifice of Christ: thus 10:10, "the offering of the body of Jesus Christ"; 10:29, "the blood of the covenant." The insistence in 13:10 that "we have an altar from which those who serve the tent have no right to eat" is sometimes taken to allude to the Christian eucharistic table, from which outsiders were excluded, but it could equally allude to the altar in the heavenly sanctuary, to which believers alone are given access; and in any event, if chapter 13 is the work of a later editor of the epistle, it may not provide a reliable guide to the interests of the original author (Williamson 1975).

Similarly, the author shows no interest in prescribing for a distinctively Christian order of ministry. His exposition of the qualifications and functions of the priest is solely concerned with the priesthood of Christ, and at least one of his arguments in this connection militates strongly against the establishment of any Christian priesthood. The Levitical succession was a sign of the fundamental failure of the Levitical model of priesthood: those priests were constantly replaced because they invariably failed to achieve their aim and their job had to be done again (7:11, 23; 10:1, 11). It is the sign of the unique effectiveness of Christ's priesthood that he stands outside this order of succession. Conversely, and by implication, for any priesthood to follow Christ's would be taken to suggest that his priesthood too was inadequate. The priesthood of Christ in Hebrews logically excludes a Christian priesthood. The author's principle that repetition is a sign of failure is diametrically opposed to the underlying principle of all liturgical practice, whether Jewish or Christian, which is that something is repeated because it is right, because it works. If the author's aim was to revive a failing and discouraged community, one way of doing so might have been by strengthening its institutions and giving it a sense of identity based on its distinctive practices; but that is not a solution that the author adopts.

The epistle may provide no guidance, then, for the development of Christian ministry and sacraments (and may be indeed a warning against their overemphasis), but it has certainly left a legacy in Christian art. The portrayal of Christ as the high priest, in crown-miter and vestments, is one of the dominant images of Christ in the icons of the Orthodox churches. It is less common in the West, but one notable example is the portrayal of Christ in the guise of Melchizedek in the celebrated twelfth-century altarpiece of the abbey of Klosterneuberg near Vienna.

Bibliography

Barrett, C. K. "The Eschatology of the Epistle to the Hebrews." In *The Background of the New Testament and Its Eschatology*, edited by W. D. Davies and D. Daube. Cambridge, 1956. Pp. 363–393.

Bruce, F. F. "'To the Hebrews' or 'To the Essenes'?" *New Testament Studies* 9 (1963): 217–232.

———. *The Epistle to the Hebrews*. Grand Rapids, 1964.

Buchanan, George W. *To the Hebrews*. Anchor Bible, vol. 36. Garden City, N.Y., 1972.

———. "The Present State of Scholarship on Hebrews." In *Christianity, Judaism, and Other Greco-Roman Cults*, edited by Jacob Neusner. Vol. 1. Leiden, 1975. Pp. 299–330.

Filson, Floyd V. *"Yesterday": A Study of Hebrews in the Light of Chapter 13*. London, 1967.

Horton, F. L. *The Melchizedek Tradition: A Critical Examination of the Sources to the Fifth Century A.D. and in the Epistle to the Hebrews*. Society for New Testament Studies Monograph Series 30. Cambridge, 1976.

Hughes, Graham. *Hebrews and Hermeneutics*. Society for New Testament Studies Monograph Series 36. Cambridge, 1979.

Hughes, P. E. *A Commentary on the Epistle to the Hebrews*. Grand Rapids, 1977.

Käsemann, Ernst. *Das wandernde Gottesvolk* (1938). Translated as *The Wandering People of God: An Investigation of the Epistle to the Hebrews*. Philadelphia, 1984.

Knox, W. L. "The 'Divine Hero' Christology in the New Testament." *Harvard Theological Review* 41 (1948): 229–249.

Manson, William. *The Epistle to the Hebrews*. London, 1951.

Montefiore, H. W. *A Commentary on the Epistle to the Hebrews*. London, 1964.

Moule, C. F. D. "Sanctuary and Sacrifice in the Church of the New Testament." *Journal of Theological Studies* 1 (1950): 29–41.

Schenke, H.-M. "Erwägungen zum Rätsel des Hebräerbriefes." In *Neues Testament und christliche Existenz*, edited by H. D. Betz and L. Schottroff. Tübingen, 1973. Pp. 421–437.

Scott, E. F. *The Epistle to the Hebrews: Its Doctrine and Significance*. Edinburgh, 1922.

Spicq, Ceslaus. *L'Épître aux Hébreux*. 2 vols. Paris, 1952, 1977.

Thompson, James W. *The Beginnings of Christian Philosophy: The Epistle to the Hebrews*. Catholic Biblical Quarterly Monograph Series 13. Washington, D.C., 1982.

Vanhoye, A. *Structure littéraire de l'Épître aux Hébreux*. Paris, 1976.

Williamson, Ronald. "Platonism and Hebrews." *Scottish Journal of Theology* 16 (1963): 415–424.

———. "Hebrews 4:15 and the Sinlessness of Jesus." *Expository Times* 86 (1974): 4–8.

———. "The Eucharist and the Epistle to the Hebrews." *New Testament Studies* 21 (1975): 300–312.

———. "The Background of the Epistle to the Hebrews." *Expository Times* 87 (1976): 232–237.

SOPHIE LAWS

James

THE EPISTLE OF James is a work of paraenesis (exhortation) whose exact author and date of composition are unknown. All the author chooses to tell us about himself is imparted in the book's opening verse: "James, a servant of God and of the Lord Jesus Christ" (RSV). He is probably invoking the authority of the most famous James in early Christianity, James "the brother of the Lord" (Gal 1:19; Mark 6:3). This man, though apparently not a disciple of his brother during Jesus' lifetime (Mark 3:31–35, John 7:3–5), became a believer after the resurrection (1 Cor 15:7, Acts 1:14) and went on to head the Jerusalem church until suffering a martyr's death in the early sixties of the first century (Josephus, *Antiquities* 20.200).

Scholars are divided as to whether or not the author of the letter is indeed James, the Lord's brother, but the high literary quality of the Greek, the apparently indirect nature of the author's knowledge of Paul's teaching, and the difficulties the letter had in gaining acceptance in the emerging New Testament canon push the probabilities away from the hypothesis of authorship by James. The author's use of James's persona, however, is an important indication of his background, for "James the Just" was a hero into the third century for groups of Jewish Christians who insisted that the Mosaic law, the Torah, was still binding on believers in Jesus. This prominence, which stemmed from James's strict observance of the Torah during his lifetime (Gal 2:12, Acts 21:17–25),

suggests that the author, himself a Torah-observant Jewish Christian, is wrapping himself in the mantle of a Jewish Christian hero in order to gain a better hearing with his addressees, other Jewish Christians who live outside Palestine ("the twelve tribes in the Dispersion," 1:1; *cf.* the reference in 2:2 to their place of assembly as a "synagogue"). It is probable that the author, too, is a Jewish Christian who lives in the Diaspora. The date of writing is difficult to pinpoint, but the distance from Paul and the closeness to *1 Clement* and the *Shepherd of Hermas* suggest composition in the late first or early second century.

The Jewish Christian background of the author and addressees is responsible for many of the letter's peculiarities. James sees no contradiction between Law and gospel; for him, the Law *is* good news, "the perfect law, the law of liberty" (1:25, 2:12), because observance of the Torah is the path of freedom. Although James is a Christian, then, for him the Torah rather than Jesus is the starting point for doing theology; hence his letter contains only glancing references to Jesus (1:1, 2:1) and to Christian concepts and practices (rebirth, 1:18; baptism, 2:7). The memory of Jesus is principally present not, as in the rest of the New Testament, through reflection on his person and deeds, but through recollection of his teachings (*cf.* the similiarities between Jas 3:12 and Matt 7:16 or between Jas 5:12 and Matt 5:39–37). Even these recollections of Jesus' words, however, take second place to allusions to the Old Testament and to intertestamental Jewish traditions.

The author sees himself as a teacher (3:1) and probably also as a wise man (3:13). What he teaches is the way in which one ought to live; that is, he provides paraenesis. It is significant that there are fifty-four imperative verbs in the 108 verses of his letter. Paraenetic traditions, it should be noted, are the ones in which early Christianity is most in continuity with Judaism. Parallels between 1 Peter and James contribute to the impression that James is heir to a developed body of paraenesis that has been substantially inherited from Judaism (Jas 1:2–3 and 1 Pet 1:6–7; Jas 1:10–11 and 1 Pet 1:24; Jas 4:6, 10 and Pet 5:5–6; Jas 5:20 and 1 Pet 4:8).

James, however, is not only a teacher; he is also something of a prophet. The excoriation of the rich in 5:1–6, which calls for them to howl because of the miseries coming upon them, is prophetic in its superb rhetoric. James is a champion of the widows, the orphans, the defrauded, and the poor generally. He champions those who have no one else to defend them and who therefore look to God as their only hope. He thus stands within a tradition of "poverty theology" that is particularly pronounced in the prophets, some psalms (e.g., Pss 10, 34, 37), certain apocalyptic writings (e.g., *1 Enoch* 91–108), and certain New Testament traditions (e.g., the Beatitudes and the "canticles" of the Lucan infancy narrative). James's uncompromisingly unworldly viewpoint places him on a collision course with emerging sociological trends in some of the Christian communities he is addressing, where Christians were beginning to show a partiality for the rich and were being tempted to settle down comfortably in the world (2:1–7, 4:4).

LITERARY FEATURES AND GENRE

In literary terms, James is a paradox many times over. Although it purports to be a letter, all features that would identify it as such drop out after the first verse, and the work lacks the sort of conclusion that is typical of letters. This incomplete adoption of the letter form is probably itself an indication of the work's late date, for use of the letter form to express theological truth was popularized in Christian circles by Paul and his followers, and other late New Testament documents (Hebrews, 1 and 2 Peter, Jude) reflect this popularization when they, like James, adopt some epistolary conventions without really being letters.

The "letter" (I will continue to use the term for convenience) is also paradoxical in its combination of literary sophistication and literary awkwardness. The sophistication is visible in the richness of its vocabulary and in its use of literary devices (e.g., puns, alliteration, rhetorical questions, unusual word order). The letter also uses images drawn not only from everyday life and Jewish literature but also from popular Hellenistic philosophy (e.g., "crown of life," 1:12; "wheel of becoming," 3:6). The awkwardness is visible in the lack of a carefully worked out structure in the letter as a whole. It is often difficult to see any thematic connection between individual passages, which are linked in the most superficial way by catchwords. For example, 1:26 and 1:27 are linked by the catchword "piety," but actually move in rather different directions; 1:26 defines true piety as bridling the tongue, while 1:27 defines it as visiting orphans and widows and keeping oneself unstained from the world. Here two originally independent sayings have probably been connected by means of the catchword.

There is indeed a loose structure to the letter. The central section consists of three longer discourses: 2:1–13, against partiality; 2:14–26, faith and works; and 3:1–12, the tongue. Around this central section the author assembles two sections of more loosely structured material (1:1–27, 3:13–5:20). There is perhaps a rough logic as well in the placement of references to baptism near the beginning of the letter (2:7; *cf.* 1:18, 21) and of references to the coming of the Lord near the end (5:7–11). But in general it is difficult to see a structured movement in the argument. Why, for example, does James say that "above all" one should not take an oath (5:12), and what sort of conclusion is 5:19–20?

This very lack of discernible structure, however, combined with the prominence of paraenesis, is a key to the genre of the letter. The Book of Proverbs in the Old Testament and the Book of Sirach in the Apocrypha exhibit a similar loose arrangement and give similar prominence to the imperative. Proverbs and Sirach are both wisdom writings, works of admonition and instruction in living a good life, and this is probably the genre of James also. James first speaks of wisdom in 1:5 and then gives it a place of prominence in the important passage 3:13–18. As is the case with other wisdom writings, the underlying theology of James is structured on the contrast between two paths: the path of wisdom, which leads to life, and the path of sin, which leads to death. I will look at some of the more important ways in which James depicts the two paths and the people who follow them in the three main sections of the letter.

THE WAY OF THE EVIL IMPULSE AND THE WAY OF WISDOM (1:1–27)

Immediately after the greeting in 1:1, James exhorts his readers to follow the path of patient endurance when they fall into temptation, outlining a chain of consequences: the testing of their faith leads to endurance, and endurance leads to perfection (1:2–4). ("Perfection," however, does not imply total faultlessness for James; see 3:2a.) This chain of wise action has its negative counterpart in the chain of foolish behavior described later in the section: desire leads to sin, and sin leads to death (1:14–15).

The culprit here, "desire," corresponds to the Jewish concept of "the evil impulse," a semi-personified entity within human beings that impels them to sin. The existence of this impulse removes direct responsibility for temptation and evil from God (1:13). True, as James will imply later, the evil impulse is a "spirit which [God] has made to dwell in us"; yet God also gives to people "the greater grace" necessary to defeat it (4:5–6). This grace is synonymous with the divine wisdom that God gives freely to all who ask for it (1:5), and probably also with the Law, which enables human beings to distinguish the path of death from the path of life (1:25).

Sadly, however, most human beings do not avail themselves of the divine aid that is available, but vacillate between following God's wisdom and following the lure of evil desire. They thus end up in a state of deep internal division; though they may have some commendable intentions, they are not even in control of their own tongues (3:1–12), and there is a "war" going on in their bodily members (4:1). James calls such people "doubleminded" (literally, "two-souled";

1:8, 4:8), and warns them that they cannot expect to receive anything from the Lord (1:7). James expresses no doubt (as Paul does in Rom 7) that a person who sets his mind to it can put an end to his own vacillation and defeat the evil impulse (1:6); as he says in 3:10, "These things do not have to be this way!" (Au. trans.). Yet on the other hand, he does not believe that one can pull oneself up by one's boot-straps; every good gift, including the ability to defeat evil desire, comes from God (1:16–18). It is God's word, not human action in itself, that saves souls, though human beings are exhorted to accept that word (1:21).

THE WAY OF PARTIALITY AND THE WAY OF THE TORAH (2:1–3:12)

In the first of the three central discourses (2:1–13), James paints a vivid portrait of the social consequences of following the evil impulse. The bejeweled, elegantly dressed rich man is given a place of honor when he enters a Christian assembly, while the poor man is shunted out of the way or even humiliated (2:2–4). James denounces this partiality by saying that it is a violation of the Law, specifically a violation of the commandment to love one's neighbor as oneself (2:8–9, citing Lev 19:18; the whole of Lev 19 is important background for James). James's argument is that the *whole* Torah must be obeyed; one cannot pick and choose among the commandments (2:10–11; cf. 4:11). James's adoption here of the Jewish principle of the unity of the Torah seems to rule out any hypothesis that "Law" for him means only the Decalogue, or only the ethical (as opposed to the cultic) portions of the Torah. "Law," rather, retains the sense that it has in the Old Testament and in Judaism: the full Mosaic Torah, which is God's greatest gift to humanity, since it points out the pathway to life.

In the second discourse (2:14–26), James reveals that some of the heartless Christians he is denouncing justify their indifference to the poor by saying that they are saved by faith alone, apart from works. James replies that, though faith and works are *separate* things, they are not *separable*, just as the body and the spirit are separate entities but not separable except in death (2:26). In making this argument, however,

James is adopting a terminology with which he himself is not fully comfortable; the terms of discourse have been set by James's opponent, a "certain someone" who separates faith and works (2:18). When James is expressing his own viewpoint, however, he uses the word "faith" in a different, totally Jewish way that *includes* the concept of "works"; faith means faithfulness, adherence to God in the midst of trial (1:3, 6; 2:5).

Who is this "certain someone" against whom James argues, and whose vocabulary he adopts? Paul is the first person we know of who separated faith from works, and indeed James 2:24 ("a person is justified by works, and not by faith alone") sounds at first like a polemic against Pauline passages such as Romans 3:28 ("for we hold that a person is justified by faith apart from works of the Law"). On the other hand, Paul would have been as appalled as James was by a theology that reduced faith to mere intellectual assent (*cf.* Jas 2:19). For Paul, faith is a life-changing reorientation of one's whole being toward God's action in Jesus Christ, and it works itself out in love (Gal 5:6). It is probable, then, that James's opponent is not Paul himself; rather, he is someone who has adopted the Pauline slogan of "justification by faith," but has distorted Paul's true message.

James goes on to say that Abraham, the father of God's people, was justified by his works, which perfected his faith (2:20–24). James is relying here on an established Jewish exegetical tradition that interpretes Genesis 15:6 (Abraham's faith was reckoned to him as righteousness) in terms of Genesis 22 (the sacrifice of Isaac). It is interesting that in Galatians 3:6 and Romans 4:3, Paul uses Genesis 15:6 to make precisely the opposite point, that Abraham was justified by *faith*; Paul is probably arguing against the exegetical tradition inherited by James.

THE WAY OF THE WORLD AND THE WAY OF GOD (3:13–5:19)

In the final section of the letter, the most radical antithesis of all emerges: the person who becomes a friend of the world thereby makes himself an enemy of God (4:4). The way of God, then, is in total contradiction to the way of the world. "World" is a wholly negative term in James. The world is a source of potential contamination, from which one must keep oneself "unstained" (1:27). Its standards are the opposite of faith (2:5). The unruly tongue, which wreaks havoc on everything around it, does so as the representative within the body of "the world of unrighteousness," which almost seems to be a synonym for hell (3:6).

For James, then, the world is a hell. It has fallen under the spell of a delusive wisdom, a demonic counterfeit of the true wisdom of God (3:13–18). The difference between these two forms of wisdom is readily apparent in the sorts of behavior to which they lead. The "earthly, physical, demonic" (3:15) wisdom creates jealousy and selfish ambition; it leads to a situation in which the focus of everyone's ingenuity is concern for self. Indeed, the result of such worldly wisdom is precisely the sort of destruction of human community that is so vividly portrayed in 2:2–4 and 5:4–6. It is possible that James is delivering a polemic here against a gnostic conception of wisdom that had infiltrated Christian communities known to him; the word "physical" used in 3:15 was a technical term among the gnostics, who emphasized their possession of heavenly wisdom and were often accused of the sort of moral indifference that so outraged James. "*This* is not the wisdom which comes from above," says James (3:15; Au. trans.); rather, the true wisdom shows its presence in peaceableness, mercy, and meekness, the sort of meekness that does not even resist the violence of the oppressor (5:6).

But is it *wise* to let oneself be killed? And is the world irremediably and forever a hell? James 5:1–11 hints that the world will not be a hell forever. God, the judge who will set all things right, is standing at the doors (5:8–9). At his coming, which will happen soon, the delusiveness of the wisdom that cared only for one's own comfort will be revealed, because the very instruments of luxury will become weapons of torture against the rich (5:1–3). On the other hand, God's coming will mean vindication for the poor and oppressed; *then* the lowly brother will be able to boast in his exaltation, while the rich person will fade away in his pursuits (*cf.* 1:9–11). Like Jesus' Beatitudes, then, James's paradoxical assertion of the blessedness of those who suffer unjustly is based primarily on his belief in the impending judgment that will reverse earthly realities (5:7–11).

JAMES AS PART OF THE CANON

Martin Luther's negative evaluation of James is well known: it is "an epistle of straw . . . for it has nothing of the nature of the gospel about it." Luther's verdict, which is based primarily on James's apparent contradiction of the Pauline principle of justification by faith, raises the question of the place of James in the canon of Scripture. How can the same New Testament contain both Galatians and James? As we have seen, part of the conflict is more apparent than real; James is arguing not against Paul but against a distorted form of Paulinism. On the other hand, it is probable that Paul and James would find much to argue about if they had an opportunity to sit down together. Paul would never agree with James that works perfect faith (Jas 2:22, 24), he probably would ascribe less freedom to the human will than would James (Jas 3:10b), and he probably would be disturbed by James's failure to ground his paraenesis explicitly in the death and resurrection of Jesus Christ.

As part of the canon of Scripture, however, the Epistle of James takes on a meaning that is different from its author's original intention. In the canon as it has come down to us, James occurs near the end, after the Gospels and after Paul's letters. Christians who read James have first read the Gospels, with their description of the life, death, and resurrection of Jesus. They have also read Paul's letters, with their ringing affirmation of salvation by God's grace through faith in Christ. In this canonical context, James becomes on the one hand a description of people who have been taken up by faith into Jesus' victorious battle against the evil in this world, and on the other hand a warning against the perils of a cheapened concept of justification by faith that would rob Paul's own insight of its life-changing power.

Bibliography

Commentaries

Davids, Peter H. *The Epistle of James.* Grand Rapids, 1982. A thoroughly researched, recent commentary on the Greek text. Davids emphasizes Jewish backgrounds and argues for authorship by James, the brother of Jesus.

Dibelius, Martin, and Heinrich Greeven. *A Commentary on the Epistle of James.* Philadelphia, 1976. Dibelius' classic German work, originally written in 1920, has been revised by Greeven and translated into English, and is a gold mine of information about the paraenetic traditions used by James. It is less helpful for determining the way in which James uses those traditions.

Laws, Sophie. *The Epistle of James.* New York, 1980. A sensible, well-written commentary that deals responsibly with the scholarship, yet is accessible to the layperson.

Mussner, Franz. *Der Jakobusbrief.* Freiburg, 1981.

Schrage, Wolfgang. "Der Jakobusbrief." In *Die katholischen Briefe*, edited by Horst Balz and Wolfgang Schrage. Göttingen, 1980.

Studies

Johnson, Luke. "The Use of Leviticus 19 in the Letter of James." *Journal of Biblical Literature* 101 (1982): 391–401.

Luck, Ulrich. "Der Jakobusbrief und die Theologie des Paulus." *Theologie und Glaube* 61 (1971): 161–179.

Marcus, Joel. "The Evil Inclination in the Epistle of James." *Catholic Biblical Quarterly* 44 (1982): 606–621.

Schoeps, Hans Joachim. *Jewish Christianity.* Philadelphia, 1969.

JOEL MARCUS

I Peter

AUTHORSHIP

FIRST PETER, ONE of the seven "catholic epistles" (so called because they are not addressed to specific churches; the others are James; 2 Peter; 1, 2, 3 John; and Jude), presents itself to the reader as a letter written by the apostle Peter to Christians living in five Roman provinces located in the northern half of Asia Minor (modern Turkey). Apart from the opening reference to Peter, however, there is nothing to connect the letter to the historic career of that apostle. Rather, several of its characteristics, including the style of language in which it is composed, the area to which it was addressed, and the social situation it presumes, make it unlikely that its author was Peter, the disciple of Jesus.

The language in which the letter is written bears a much closer resemblance to that of the educated defenders of Christianity who wrote in the second century than to the language of the canonical Gospels or the letters of Paul. Several grammatical constructions (the optative mood, conjunctive participles, and future participles) that appear in 1 Peter point rather to an educated author than to one who used ordinary Greek spoken in the market or the street. The large number of imperatives, the intense and intimate tone of the language, the abundance of abstract substantives, and the frequency of metaphorical language, however, separate 1 Peter from the popular style of the diatribe, a type of discourse used for instruction of students of philosophy, as in the *Discourses* of the Stoic philosopher Epictetus. On the other hand, while there are no obvious Semitisms that derive from direct translation of Hebrew into Greek, 1 Peter quotes frequently from the Septuagint (the Greek translation of the Old Testament), and that translation is reflected in the language of the letter even when direct quotations are absent. Since similar linguistic characteristics can be found in such writings as the Wisdom of Solomon and Sirach, the Greek of 1 Peter appears closest to that of "the edifying language of the hellenized synagogue" (Wifstrand 1948, 180).

Because of the polished Greek in which 1 Peter is written, many scholars conclude that it cannot have been written by the apostle Peter, who is described as "unlettered" and "uneducated" (Acts 4:13). The reference to Silvanus (1 Pet 5:12) has often been used to explain difficulties standing in the way of Peter as the author of the letter: what does not belong to Peter is attributed to Silvanus, to whom Peter supposedly dictated the letter. Yet the phrase used in 1 Peter 5:12 ("through" or "by means of" Silvanus) is not used elsewhere to indicate one who actually wrote down a letter (for such language, see Rom 16:22). Rather, the phrase is used to describe the one who delivers the letter (e.g., Acts 15:23: "with the following letter" [all quotations from RSV except as noted]; see also the letters of Ignatius: "To the Romans" [10:1]; "To the

Philadelphians" [11:2]; and "To the Smyrneans" [12:1]; and the *Epistle of Polycarp* [14:1]). Defense of Petrine authorship by appealing to references that would require an eyewitness to the events of Christ's life, such as his suffering or his transfiguration (5:1), bears little weight, since the historical Peter was not present at the crucifixion, and other references to the suffering of Christ owe more to the Old Testament than to personal reminiscence (*cf.* 2:22–25 and Isa 53:5–12). The reference to the author's being a "sharer in the glory to be revealed" (1 Pet 5:1) fits the general eschatological tone of the letter; a specific reference to the transfiguration would probably not be cast in so general a form (*cf.* 2 Pet 1:18).

There have been attempts to identify more exactly the author of the letter, but with little success. Silvanus has been proposed as the author, a conjecture based on the "hint" left in 5:12. Aside from the fact that the Greek does not mean "written by," such a conjecture is also rendered questionable by what would then be a blatant self-commendation by Silvanus (calling himself "a faithful brother"). Appeal to the added phrase "as I regard him" as a modest disclaimer of such self-acclamation has failed to convince most scholars of the correctness of this conjecture. There is in fact no real evidence that can lead us to the identity of the author. The writer remains for us an anonymous Christian who, following a custom known in the ancient world, especially in the Old Testament–Jewish milieu (e.g., 2 Macc 1:1–9, 1:10–2:18; Jer 29:4–23; *2 Baruch* 78:1–86.1), wrote a general letter to be copied and read by a group of churches all of whom faced similar difficulties (Brox 1979, 23).

The picture that emerges is, therefore, of a letter written in the name of Peter and delivered by Silvanus to churches in Asia Minor undergoing difficulties as a result of their faith. Following an ancient custom, the unknown author, surely a follower of Peter, writes in the name of his teacher to churches where Peter was revered, applying to their situation insights about the faith learned from Peter himself. The fact that Silvanus (sometimes called "Silas") is associated in the New Testament with Paul rather than with Peter (e.g., Acts 15:40; 2 Cor 1:19; 1 Thess 1:1), combined with the many reflections of Pauline theology in 1 Peter conveys the impression of the unity of theological approach between the two major apostles of the early church, Peter and Paul. Note, for example, the emphasis on the suffering and crucifixion of Christ in 1 Peter 2:21–24, 3:18 (*cf.* Rom 3:25; 1 Cor 2:2), on Christ's resurrection in 1 Peter 1:3, 21 (*cf.* Rom 10:9; 1 Cor 15:17), on the salvation of the gentiles in 1 Peter 2:10, 4:3 (*cf.* Rom 10:12, Gal 3:8), on faith in 1 Peter 1:5, 7, 8, 9 (*cf.* Rom 1:17, Gal 3:25–26), on grace in 1 Peter 1:10, 3:7 (*cf.* Rom 3:24; 2 Cor 8:9), and the advice to be subservient to qualified political authority in 1 Peter 2:13–14 (*cf.* Rom 13:1–2). The epistle thus represents an attempt to give advice on withstanding persecution to Christians under severe pressure, drawing on the unified approach of early tradition (from both Peter and Paul) to give weight to the material in the letter.

UNITY

An examination of the content of the letter, in addition to revealing material quite similar to that found in the Pauline letters, reveals an emphasis on the "newness" of Christians ("born anew," 1:3, 23; "newborn babes," 2:2) and a reference to baptism as the means of salvation (3:21). One can also note that the only material that identifies this as a letter is found in 1:1–2 and 5:12–14; in the remainder, there are no indications of anything but a general address to Christians in peril of martyrdom for their faith. Even that emphasis on suffering seems to be cast in two forms: as a future possibility (3:17) and as a present reality (4:12); furthermore, there is a benediction just prior to the second reference to suffering (4:11). All of these hints have led some scholars to posit the theory that the body of the letter (1:3–4:11) had its origin as a baptismal homily, used in connection with the baptism of new converts into the Christian faith. That homily was then adapted into a letter to be sent to people actually undergoing persecution by the addition of 1:1–2 and 4:12–5:14, to encourage them in the name of the martyred Peter (*cf.* Beare 1947, 6; Selwyn 1955, 19).

Although this explanation of the origin of the letter was widely held at one time, it came increasingly into question in later studies of 1 Peter. The reference to baptism is hardly the central point of the letter, and is no more prominent in this discussion than is Paul's reference to baptism in his discussion in Romans (6:1–4); yet no one has proposed that Romans was adapted from a baptismal homily. Such references are simply part of common early Christian tradition. The same is true of the emphasis on the newness of the Christians (cf. 2 Cor 5:17, Gal 6:15, Heb 5:12–13) in relation to their world. The presence, furthermore, of a benediction in the midst of an epistle is not all that uncommon (cf. Rom 1:25, 11:36). The references to suffering in 1 Peter 1:3– 4:11 are not at all hypothetical or future: 1:6 presumes suffering as a present reality, and 3:17 emphasizes not the possibility of suffering, but the fact that some suffering is in accordance with God's will. Finally, there is a unity of theme that runs throughout the letter. As one example, note that the problem of conflict brought on by the faith is mentioned in 1:6–7; 2:4–8, 12, 18–20; 3:1–2, 9, 14, 15, 17; 4:1–2, 12–19; and 5:8–10. Such lines of continuity indicate that the letter is not a composite creation, but rather was originally written as a letter and composed as a unity.

All of this evidence indicates that the letter owes more to common early Christian tradition than it does to any dependence on other New Testament writings or to an attempt to adapt an early liturgical form or homiletical writing into a letter. Drawing on the common fund of early Christian tradition, which included emphases on such matters as faith, grace, love, discipline within the Christian community, and the significance of baptism, the unknown author has written a general letter to fellow Christians in Asia Minor to encourage them in a difficult time.

DATE

If the author was not the disciple Peter, then a date for the letter need not be found prior to 64 C.E., the traditional date of the martyrdom of Peter. Evidence for a date has often been sought in the references to the persecutions the readers are undergoing specifically as Christians (4:14, 16). We know of the persecution of Christians in Rome during the reign of Nero, about the year 64, following the disastrous fire that he blamed on the Christians. There is, however, no evidence that such persecution

was a regular procedure from then on even in Rome, and there is no evidence that it ever extended beyond the bounds of the city during Nero's reign. There are also references to persecutions under the emperor Domitian in the last years of the first century, but they were visited as much on fellow Romans as on any other group, and were apparently more the result of Domitian's own brutal and suspicious nature than any desire to extirpate the Christian faith.

Again, there is a good deal of discussion about persecution of Christians early in the second century in the correspondence between the Roman emperor Trajan and Pliny the Younger, whom the emperor had sent as his legate to the provinces in northern Asia Minor to straighten out tangled financial affairs that were causing trouble there. Once more, however, the purpose of Pliny's trip was not to persecute members of the new religious sect; his correspondence makes clear that the prosecution of Christians was to Pliny, and his request to Trajan for advice on how to proceed shows there was no official policy at time to seek out Christians and destroy them. In the end, Christians were treated like any other individuals who, for whatever reason, failed to show proper respect to the emperor, and hence to the Roman empire.

Finally, the fact that systematic persecution of Christians as Christians was not undertaken until the reign of Decius in the middle of the third century (249–251), coupled with the ambiguous evidence we have about the policy of earlier procedures against Christians, simply means that evidence of persecution of Christians will not help us much in dating the letter. There is one interesting bit of information in the Pliny-Trajan correspondence, however, that may shed some light on this problem. Pliny, who wrote soon after 110, mentions to Trajan that some people accused of being Christians had recanted about twenty-five years earlier (Pliny, *Letters* 10.96). In addition to providing evidence for the existence of Christian communities in Asia Minor, specifically in Pontus and Bithynia, in the last decades of the first century, that information may well indicate that, in about 85, a persecution had broken out against Christians that had caused some to renounce their faith. It is attractive to speculate that it may indeed have been the earlier persecution that prompted the unknown author to write 1 Peter, which would give us a date sometime in the mid to late 80s for its composition. If that is the case, then the continued existence of Christians in that area a quarter of a century later would indicate that 1 Peter was successful in encouraging some Christians at least to continue in faithfulness to Christ.

However one may want to decide the matter of date, it is clear that 1 Peter was written to Christians under threat of persecution, to encourage them to remain faithful to their Lord. Such persecution, as we have seen, need not have been the result of official policy. Indeed, it never was the policy of the Roman government to persecute religions as such. The scholarly fiction that the Romans recognized certain religions as "legal" (*religio licita*) and labeled others as "illegal" ought finally to be abandoned. Neither phrase occurs in non-Christian Latin literature; the first appearance of the phrase *religio licita* is in Tertullian (*Apology* 21.1), and does not refer to Roman policy. Romans were indifferent to cultural or religious customs in the provinces as long as their observance did not disrupt the flow of taxes to Rome.

CHRISTIANS OUTSIDE SOCIETY

The problem for the kind of Christians to whom 1 Peter is addressed is that their faith prohibited them from the worship or acknowledgment of any Lord but Jesus. Yet such acknowledgment was part of the normal civic and religious celebrations held regularly throughout the Roman empire. In addition to the festivals for local gods, there appears to have been an empire-wide celebration in honor of the emperor on January 3 (see Tacitus, *Annales* 4.17). At such festivals, everyone, young and old, was expected to participate. There were processions, feasts, games, and, of course, sacrifices to various deities. Those not in the processions were expected to erect small altars in front of their houses and offer sacrifices as the procession passed by (Price 1984, 101, 111–112). Modern Western readers need constantly to keep in mind that in the Roman empire of the first and second centuries of our era, religion and politics were simply inseparable for the average person, and both were intimately related to the social fabric of the communi-

ty. Hence, to be a religious nonconformist was at the same time to attack the political stability of the community. It was for this kind of nonconformity that Christians generally, and specifically those addressed by 1 Peter, suffered. Once converted, they could no longer participate in the normal events of their communities (*cf.* 1 Pet 4:4), and that withdrawal branded them as outsiders (*cf.* 2:11).

It was this failure to take part in normal community activities that got Christians into trouble and made them the butt of accusations as evildoers. To counter such accusations, 1 Peter urges its readers to maintain exemplary conduct (2:12, 15; 3:16; 4:15–16) and to be ready to explain to anyone who asks why it is they act as they do (3:15). Christians are to live in every way as exemplary citizens, both to counter the charge that Christians are evil people and to show that their goal is not the downfall of the social fabric of their communities. As long as their observance of political and social customs did not lead them to deny their faith, they were to do what was expected of all law-abiding citizens (2:13–3:7).

PAST, PRESENT, AND FUTURE

To make the point of the need to remain steadfast in the face of persecution, the author employed two devices. The first was to contrast the past with the present and to employ a corollary contrast of the present with the future. The second device was to adopt for the church the controlling metaphor of Israel as chosen people in order to stress both the importance of the Christian faith and the need to remain steadfast.

The contrast between past and present appears in nineteen passages that are scattered throughout the letter. Typically, they are centered on the contrast between Christ who suffered (past) and the Christ who is now glorified (present). Although people rejected him in his condemnation (past), his resurrection (present) shows that he was chosen beforehand by God (2:4, *cf.* 1:20). Again, as a result of his exaltation (past), all supernatural powers are now subjected to him (present; 3:22). Using that Christ as a model, the author then contrasts what happened in the past to Christ with what is happening currently to the readers. As Christ suffered (2:21, 4:1–2), was wounded (2:24), and died (3:18), so the readers now suffer, but are also healed, made alive, and brought to God. The author also draws on other Old Testament figures to point to a similar contrast. The events that prophets foretold in the past are now fulfilled (1:10–12): as Noah was saved in the past, Christians are being saved in the present (3:20–21); as Sarah did what was right in the past, so are the readers now to do what is right as well (3:6).

Having used these examples, the author then turns to compare the readers' own past with their present, showing how great and beneficial that change has been. Their past (physical) birth is contrasted with their new birth into the Christian faith (1:3), a past characterized by ignorance as the present is characterized by holiness (1:14). They are now ransomed by Christ from their formerly futile ways (1:18), have been moved from darkness to light (2:9), and as formerly straying sheep, have now been brought to their true shepherd (2:25). Once as bereft of God as the gentiles in whose numbers they were found, they have now been constituted a people, and have been freed from the profligate behavior of their former state (4:3–4, 2:10). Having received this gift, they must now employ it in remaining faithful to the God who called them through Christ (*cf.* 4:10).

Yet the contrast between past and present, important as it is, has a parallel contrast between present and future. Appearing twenty times in the letter, this contrast, like that between past and present, is found in all parts of the letter. The present suffering ("testing") of the Christians will gain them praise, honor, and glory at Christ's (future) return (1:7; *cf.* 1:13), just as their present good conduct in the face of false accusations will allow them to glorify God at the time of the (future) final judgment of God (2:12, *cf.* 4:11–12). Presently humbled under God's mighty hand, they will be exalted in the future by that same God (5:6). Thus, those who have been born anew into the Christian faith will in future receive their new and imperishable inheritance (1:3–4, *cf.* 2:2), a salvation that awaits those who remain faithful in the midst of a difficult present (1:5–6, *cf.* 1:9; 3:9, 10–11, 14; 4:12–13; 5:1, 2–4). By their remaining faithful and doing what is right, the ignorance now responsible for their persecution will be put to silence (2:15),

since the "gentiles" too will one day have to give an account to God for their present profligate ways (4:4–5, *cf.* 4:17).

The formal parallelism between the past-present contrast and the present-future contrast informs the argument of the entire letter. The past-present contrast provides the reader with assurance that the present-future contrast will be as sure and as complete as the former has shown itself to be. The contrast between once and now serves to buttress the main purpose of the letter, namely to strengthen the readers in the "now" of their suffering and persecution by assuring them that the future glory will transform their present condition as surely as their present situation transformed their past.

THE CHOSEN PEOPLE

It is interesting to note that the author, in using these contrasts, has compared the behavior of his readers with that of the "gentiles," even though his readers were also drawn primarily from gentile rather than Jewish Christians (4:3–4 makes that clear, as does the Greek word for "inherited from your fathers" in 1:18, a word that never occurs in the Greek translation of the Old Testament but is used frequently in secular Greek writings). Clearly, our author is using the word "gentiles" metaphorically, and that usage points us to the second device our author employs to stress the need to remain faithful. That device is the use of images of the chosen people from the Old Testament as the controlling metaphor for the Christians as the new people of God.

That metaphor makes its appearance in the very first verses, where, in language that recalls Israel's Babylonian exile, the Christian readers are addressed as "dispersed exiles" who have been constituted a new people of God by the sprinkling of the blood of the new covenant sacrifice, namely Christ (1:1–2), just as Israel at its formation had been sprinkled with the blood of the covenant sacrifice (*cf.* Exod 24:8). This is the context within which the references to "newness" are to be understood, rather than within the context of baptism, as formerly thought. As the new people of God, prophesied in the Old Testament (1 Pet 1:10–12) and constituted by the gospel preached to them (1:23; *cf.* Isa 40:6–9), they are described with the same words used to describe Israel as the chosen people (1 Pet 2:4, *cf.* Ps 118:22; Isa 28:16; 1 Pet 2:6, *cf.* Isa 28:16; 1 Pet 2:7, *cf.* Ps 118:22; 1 Pet 2:8, *cf.* Isa 8:14–15; 1 Pet 2:9–10, *cf.* Isa 43:20–21, Exod 19:6, Exod 23:22, Hos 2:23). They also have the same task as that original people of God, to become holy because their God is holy (1 Pet 1:16, *cf.* Lev 11:44–45, 19:2, 20:7, 20:26).

Other terms originally applied to Israel are also applied to Christians in the course of this letter. They are "exiles and aliens" (1 Pet 2:11, *cf.* Gen 23:4, Ps 39:12; this phrase occurs only in Greek writers influenced by one or the other of those passages; it never appears in secular writers). They are God's flock (1 Pet 5:3, *cf.* Ps 23), God's household (1 Pet 4:17), whose task it is to offer acceptable ("spiritual") sacrifices to God (1 Pet 2:5), something only God's special people can do. The metaphor of church as new Israel continues right to the end of the letter, where the author's reference to "Babylon" (5:12) is surely intended to remind the readers of the exile language with which the letter began (1:1) and is thus intended to enclose the entire letter in that controlling metaphor. The term Babylon is very likely a metaphorical reference to Rome, the capital of the culture that has pitted itself against the Christians (*cf.* Rev 14:8, 16:19, 17:5, a writing addressed to the same area as 1 Peter). Equally important, the key statement about the fate of Christ, by which fate the new people of God are constituted, is also couched in terms taken from the Old Testament (2:22–25, *cf.* Isa 53:5–9).

The fact that that key statement about Christ occurs in advice addressed to slaves probably means that "slave" is also to be understood metaphorically for all Christians. Just as they, like Israel before them, were exiles and aliens in the culture they lived in, so, socially, their status was closer to that of slaves than of any other class. Like slaves, Christians could expect to be abused, unjustly punished, and even despised, but they were to know that when they endured this treatment they were faithful to their master, who also underwent such abuse, and thus they ensured themselves of sharing one day in his glory (2:18–25).

By using such a controlling metaphor, and by employing the parallel contrasts of past-present and present-future, the unknown author of this letter, alternating proclamation with exhortation, seeks to enable his readers to withstand the abuse of a culture that finds in their very faithfulness evidence of hostility to everything it stands for. The threat was formidable, and the continuing survival of the Christian community within the Roman empire points to the effectiveness of the witness of this letter.

Bibliography

Balch, David L. *Let Wives Be Submissive: The Domestic Code in 1 Peter.* Chico, Calif., 1981. A discussion of 1 Peter 2:13–3:17, which the author sees as advising Christians to be more accommodating to the cultural milieu, a difficult position to maintain in light of the letter's manifest desire to urge Christians to resist just such accommodation.

Beare, Francis Wright. *The First Epistle of Peter.* Oxford, 1947. A classic expression of what 1 Peter would mean if it were an adaptation of an early baptismal homily, written during the time of the persecutions instituted by Pliny about 110 C.E.

Brox, Norbert. *Der erste Petrusbrief.* Cologne, 1979. Perhaps the best current commentary. It presents a balanced picture of the cultural background and of the theological points the author of 1 Peter wishes to make.

Elliott, John H. *A Home for the Homeless.* Philadelphia, 1981. An investigation of the evidence in this letter for the social status of the Christians to whom it was addressed. Although the author does not take sufficient account of the controlling metaphor of 1 Peter, he has written a valuable study of the way 1 Peter seeks to solve the cultural crisis of its readers.

Furnish, V. P. "Elect Sojourners in Christ: An Approach to the Theology of 1 Peter." *Perkins School of Theology Journal* 28 (1975): 1–11. An excellent, compact survey of the major theological themes of 1 Peter. It presents a clear picture of the unity of the message of this letter.

Price, S. R. F. *Rituals and Power: The Roman Imperial Cult in Asia Minor.* Cambridge, 1984. A careful analysis of both archaeological and literary evidence relating to the development of the emperor cult in Asia Minor. It outlines the cultural background against which 1 Peter is to be understood.

Selwyn, Edward Gordon. *The First Epistle of St. Peter.* 2d ed. London, 1955. Still the best commentary in English, it gives an exhaustive treatment of the traditions underlying 1 Peter and how the author has woven them into the letter as we now have it.

Talbert, Charles H., ed. *Perspectives on First Peter.* Macon, Ga., 1986. A collection of essays by a number of scholars who have contributed significantly to recent discussion of 1 Peter. An excellent orientation to current scholarship and source for further bibliography.

Wifstrand, Albert. "Stylistic Problems in the Epistles of James and Peter." *Studia Theologica* 1 (1948): 170–182. A detailed study of the Greek used in 1 Peter compared with that in other kinds of contemporary literature.

PAUL J. ACHTEMEIER

II Peter
Jude

II PETER

THE SECOND LETTER of Peter is classified as a catholic, or general, epistle because it is supposedly addressed to the universal church. It claims the apostle Peter as its author, but most scholars doubt that it was composed by the historical Peter. Instead, it is believed, a late-first-century or early second-century Christian writes here in the name of Peter to warn the church of false teachers who deny the reality of the Parousia (the return of Christ at the end of the ages). The author (whom I shall refer to as "Peter") employs the genre of a farewell discourse. He says that the Lord has shown him that he will soon die (1:14). Therefore, he writes to remind his readers how to live the Christian life (1:12–15) and to warn them about false teachers (2:1–22) who will come at the end of the ages, scoffing at the teaching of the apostles concerning the Parousia (3:3–4).

There are several reasons for judging 2 Peter to be pseudonymous. Among the most important are the author's use of Jude (much of which is incorporated into chapter 2); the Hellenistic coloring of the author's language and concepts; and a reference to Paul's letters (3:15–16), which suggests a late-first-century date since it appears that the letters have been collected. The choice of the word "pseudonymous," however, is unfortunate because the prefix "pseudo" gives the mistaken impression that the writings are false. In fact, to write in the name of an important person was a practice that occurred with some regularity in the ancient world. Some wrote in the name of great figures such as Peter and Paul because they believed that they represented the authentic tradition of that person. Indeed, by eventually accepting 2 Peter into its canon of sacred Scripture, the church made a judgment that the text witnesses to authentic apostolic tradition.

Second Peter is one of the latest writings, if not the latest, of the New Testament. Estimates of its time of origin range from the late first century to the middle of the second. Because it is pseudonymous, it is difficult to determine its place of origin. Many scholars, however, believe that it was intended for the gentile churches of Asia Minor. It is difficult to say whether the author wrote to a particular community or to a group of churches.

CONTENT

Chapter One. The author of the letter identifies himself as Simeon Peter. The recipients of the letter are not named, but they are described as possessing a "faith of equal standing with ours," that is, with the church apostolic. Thus "Peter" establishes a firm relationship between himself and his audience. The introduction to the letter is noteworthy because it is one of the few places in the New Testament where Jesus is called God: "in the righteousness of our God and Savior Jesus Christ" (1:1–2; all translations from RSV).

As Christians, the readers have authentic knowledge of Christ, who has called them to his own glory and excellence. This knowledge stands in contrast to the false knowledge offered by the teachers described in chapter 2. The glory and excellence of the readers lead to the divine promises by which they can escape the corruption of this world and share in the "divine nature." This last term has a Hellenistic ring and probably comes from Greek mystical philosophy.

The privileges that the believer possesses should not be taken for granted. In verses 5–8, therefore, "Peter" describes a ladder of conduct for his readers to ascend: from faith to virtue to knowledge to self-control to steadfastness to godliness to brotherly affection to love. Qualities such as these will confirm the call and election of the believer (1:10) and provide entrance into the kingdom of Jesus, the Savior and Lord (1:11). For 2 Peter, the Kingdom of God lies in the distant future; it is something Christians will enter after the end of this world, which "Peter" sees as tainted by corruption.

In 1:12–15, "Peter" explains his reasons for writing. The Lord has revealed to him that his death is at hand (probably an allusion to John 21:18–19). Before departing from this world, therefore, he wants to remind his readers of certain truths, even though they are firmly established in them, so that when he departs they will be able to recall them. These verses enable the letter to function as a farewell discourse assuring that no other letters can be written in Peter's name after this one.

In 1:16, "Peter" switches from the first-person singular to the first-person plural as he recalls Jesus' transfiguration, which he, James, and John witnessed. He protests that he and his fellow apostles were not following "cleverly devised myths" when they made known the power and coming (*parousia*) of Jesus Christ. They were eyewitnesses (*epoptai*) of what they reported. The tone of the verse suggests that "Peter" is responding to charges that the promise of the Parousia was a story fabricated by the apostles. To defend himself against this charge, he refers to himself and his fellow apostles as *epoptai*, a Greek term that can

refer to one initiated into the mystery religions. This is Peter's way of saying that whereas he was initiated into the mystery of the Parousia by the transfiguration, the false teachers were not.

In 1:17–18, "Peter" narrates the transfiguration in language similar to that found in the accounts of the synoptic Gospels. The choice of the transfiguration has to do with the author's reason for writing, the defense of the Parousia. In the synoptic Gospels, the transfiguration occurs after Jesus' promise that some of the disciples will not die until they have seen the Parousia of the Son of man (Matt 16:28, Mark 9:1, Luke 9:27). The transfiguration, therefore, functions as a foretaste of the Parousia. "Peter" can guarantee the Second Coming because he, James, and John were eyewitnesses of the event that prefigured it.

In 1:19, the author turns to yet another witness, the prophetic word of the Old Testament, which also points to the Parousia and so confirms the witness provided by the transfiguration. The believer must wait for the fulfillment of the prophetic word, therefore, until the day of the Parousia, when Christ himself, like the morning star, will rise in the hearts of believers. The interpretation of Scripture is not a private affair, however, since the prophets spoke under the inspiration of the Holy Spirit. Scripture must be authoritatively interpreted. Given the circumstances under which the letter was composed, it appears that "Peter" is pointing to official church interpretation of prophecy in order to combat the false teachers.

Chapter Two. "Peter" momentarily sets aside his defense of the Parousia and turns to his opponents. He predicts that just as false prophets arose in ancient Israel, so false teachers will appear, causing destructive factions. "Peter" speaks in the future tense, but the false teachers who are described are already disturbing the church. That they are (or were) Christians is apparent from the author's statement that they even deny the Master who bought them, that is, Christ (2:1).

Although "Peter" knows that many within the church will follow these false teachers, he wants to assure his readers that God will eventually punish such people and rescue the righteous. Therefore in 2:4–10 he employs three examples from the Old Testament to make his point. First, long ago God punished the angels who disobeyed (an allusion to the Nephilim of

Genesis 6:1–4) by casting them into hell. Second, at the time of the Flood, God rescued Noah and seven others from a sinful world (Gen 6:5–8:22) because Noah was a preacher of righteousness. Third, at the time of the destruction of Sodom and Gomorrah (Gen 19:1–28), the righteous Lot was rescued. From these examples, "Peter" concludes that God does know how to save the godly and punish the unrighteous (especially those who challenge authority), a fact that Peter's readers may have begun to doubt.

In 2:10b–22, "Peter" unleashes one of the most vitriolic attacks found in the New Testament. His intent is to expose the error of the teachers and to assure his readers that these deceivers will be destroyed. He characterizes them as "bold and wilful" people who do not hesitate "to revile the glorious ones." The term "glorious ones" (*doxas*) may refer to church leaders or celestial beings; its interpretation is disputed. But the main point is clear: the false teachers do not respect authority, be it human or divine. "Peter" sees them as licentious individuals who extend their carousing to broad daylight, a level of debauchery frowned upon even in Roman society. They have gone so far as to train their hearts in greed. In this regard, they are like Balaam of the Old Testament, who because of his avarice was induced by the king of Moab to curse the Israelites (Num 22–24).

Having compared the false teachers to Balaam, "Peter" likens them to "waterless springs" and "mists driven by a storm" (2:17). The first image suggests that the teaching of these people disappoints, just as a dry spring frustrates a thirsty traveler. The second points to the ephemeral nature of their teaching.

Promising freedom, these teachers manage to convince some, especially those who have recently turned to the faith. This promise of freedom (2:19) suggests that the teachers may have been libertines, persons who saw themselves as beyond the moral order. In the author's view, they are "slaves of corruption," the very corruption from which the believer must flee if he or she hopes to share in "the divine nature" (1:4). In the remaining verses (2:20–22) it is difficult to say whether "Peter" is referring to the false teachers or to those who have been deceived by them. In either case, it would be better for them never to have escaped the world's defilements rather than, having once escaped, return to them.

Chapter Three. Having dealt with the opponents, "Peter" returns to the question that occasioned his letter, the delay of the Lord's coming. Continuing the genre of the farewell discourse, he says that this is the second letter he has written (the other being 1 Peter). He predicts that in the last days (the days in which the readers are living) scoffers will question the plausibility of the Second Coming. Clearly this is already happening; the false teachers point to the immutability of the world to argue that God will not intervene for the sake of judgment. If everything has remained the same, why should it change? The question faced by "Peter" is one of theodicy: Does God punish the wicked and reward the just?

The author's response is fourfold. First, the scoffers forget that at the time of Noah the world was destroyed. The destruction of the present order, therefore, is not impossible. Second, he quotes Psalm 90:4 to show that God reckons time differently from human beings. What seems a long period by human calculation is a brief time in God's sight. The delay of the Parousia derives from God's patience and is intended to lead sinners to conversion. Fourth, in words reminiscent of 1 Thessalonians 5:2, "Peter" reminds his audience of the suddenness of the Parousia. The Lord will come unexpectedly like a thief. Then the heavens will pass away with a loud noise, the physical elements of the world will burn away, and the earth will no longer be found. The description of the world's destruction seems dependent upon the Stoic notion that the world suffers periodic conflagrations. From these arguments, "Peter" draws an important lesson. Since the world will be destroyed, Christians must live lives of holiness and goodness as they await "new heavens and a new earth." Such behavior can even hasten the coming of the Parousia.

In 3:15–16, "Peter" calls upon the witness of Paul to substantiate his third argument, that God's patience should be seen as salvation. When "Peter" refers to obscure things in Paul's letters that the ignorant and unstable misinterpret, he may be alluding to Paul's teaching about the Parousia or about Christian freedom. It appears that the false teachers have appropriated the apostle for their own purposes and that the battle over the correct interpretation of Scripture has begun.

2 PETER AND THE CANON OF SCRIPTURE

Although 2 Peter was one of the last books to be accepted into the canon of Scripture, it is an important witness to the growth of the canon. The author writes at a time when the church must make judgments about the extent of sacred Scripture and the correct interpretation of it. Thus in employing Jude, 2 Peter eliminates the references to the *Assumption of Moses* and *1 Enoch*, works our author does not consider authoritative Scripture. In 2 Peter, the letters of Paul are beginning to receive the status of inspired Scripture (3:16), and like the prophets (1:20) they must be interpreted correctly, that is, in the light of apostolic tradition.

THE LETTER OF JUDE

The Letter of Jude is closely associated with 2 Peter, since nineteen of its twenty-two verses appear wholly or partially in 2 Peter. Various theories of literary dependence have been proposed, but the most plausible is that 2 Peter employs Jude as a source. If this is the case, Jude was composed earlier than 2 Peter, and the author of 2 Peter recognizes Jude as sound teaching.

The author identifies himself as "Jude, a servant of Jesus Christ and brother of James." The "James" mentioned here is probably the brother of the Lord (Gal 1:19, Mark 6:3). If so, "Jude" is the brother of the Lord mentioned along with James in Mark 6:3. The cultivated Greek of this letter, however, suggests that the historical Jude, an Aramaic-speaking peasant, was not its author. Rather, a Christian of the late first century writes in the name of Jude, thereby deriving some authority from a name associated with Jesus' family. Since the author does not identify his audience, this letter is also categorized as a general, or catholic, epistle. In fact, as in the case of 2 Peter, it was probably written to gentile churches in Asia Minor.

According to the letter, "Jude" had intended to write to his readers about the salvation he shares with them, but the sudden appearance of false teachers infiltrating the community has led him to write the present letter. The false teachers are libertines, people who have turned "the grace of our God into licentiousness" (v. 4). Their behavior is characterized by a rejection of authority, even to the point of reviling angelic beings (v. 8). Although they present themselves as visionaries, "Jude" identifies them as divisive people "devoid of the Spirit" (v. 19). These "heretics" have even found acceptance within the community: "Jude" calls them "blemishes on your love feasts" (v. 12).

In response to this crisis, "Jude" turns to the Old Testament as well as to a number of noncanonical writings to show how God dealt with such people in the past, thereby assuring his readers that the same fate awaits these evildoers. In verses 5–8 he gives three examples from the Old Testament. First, after the Lord saved the people from Egypt, he destroyed those who did not believe. Second, when the angels rebelled (Gen 6:1–4), God consigned them to the nether gloom. Third, when Sodom and Gomorrah sinned by unnatural lust, God destroyed them and the surrounding cities with fire. The agitators who have infiltrated the community will suffer a similar fate.

In verse 11, Jude compares these false teachers to Cain, Balaam, and Korah. The first murdered his brother (Gen 4:8), the second was tempted by greed to utter false prophecy against Israel (Num 22–24), and the third led a rebellion against Moses and Aaron in the wilderness (Num 16). These rebellious and greedy individuals will lead the community to death and destruction if they are not uprooted.

Finally, "Jude" points to the prophecy of Enoch, and the prediction of the apostles that saw the coming of these individuals. Quoting from the noncanonical *Book of Enoch* (*1 En* 1:9), he assures his readers that God and his angels will execute judgment upon such deceivers (vv. 14–15). Then, turning to a saying of the apostles (*cf.* 2 Tim 3:1), he reminds his audience that the apostles predicted such scoffers would come in the last times (vv. 17–20). The task of the community, therefore, is to build itself upon the faith "once for all delivered to the saints," and to save those it can from these agitators (vv. 20–23).

Although brief, the letter of Jude provides an important picture of the postapostolic church. Assailed from within by false teachers of a libertine persuasion, the church must appeal to apostolic authority, its received tradition, and the Scriptures. In the case of Jude, the appeal even extends to non-canonical literature such as the *Book of Enoch* (vv. 14–15) and the *Assumption of Moses* (v. 9). Within the canon of Scripture, the letter of Jude is a reminder that there are moments when false teaching must be exposed if the community is to remain faithful to its traditions.

Bibliography

Bauckham, Richard J. *Jude, 2 Peter*. Waco, Tex., 1983.

Farkasfalvy, Denis. "The Ecclesial Setting and Pseudepigraphy in Second Peter and Its Role in the Formation of the Canon." *The Second Century: A Journal of Early Christian Studies* 5 (1985/1986): 3–29.

Fornberg, Tord. *An Early Church in a Pluralistic Society: A Study of 2 Peter*. Lund, Sweden, 1977.

Käsemann, Ernst. "An Apologia for Primitive Christian Eschatology." In *Essays on New Testament Themes*. Translated by W. J. Montague. Naperville, Ill., 1964. Pp. 169–195.

Kelly, J. N. D. *A Commentary on the Epistles of Peter and of Jude*. London, 1969.

Neyrey, Jerome H. "The Apologetic Use of the Transfiguration in 2 Peter 1:16–21." *Catholic Biblical Quarterly* 42 (1980): 504–519.

———. "The Form and Background of the Polemic in 2 Peter." *Journal of Biblical Literature* 99 (1980): 407–431.

Schelkle, Karl Hermann. *Die Petrusbriefe, der Judasbrief*. Freiburg im Breisgau, 1970.

FRANK J. MATERA

I, II, and III John

THE THREE LETTERS known as First, Second, and Third John are "Johannine" in the sense that they display affinities with the Gospel of John, traditionally ascribed to John the Apostle. However, they do not appear to have been written by the "John" who is identified as the author of the Fourth Gospel. Their author speaks of himself only as "the elder" (2 John 1; 3 John 1). Scholars think that there was a "school" of teachers in the Johannine churches who were disciples of the "beloved disciple" (cf. John 21:7, 20). The author of the letters was a member of this group of teachers, as indicated by his reference to the "we" whose testimony the community accepts (1 John 1:1–4).

Literary form. Although we speak of all three writings as "letters," only 2 and 3 John are in letter form. Second John is from an individual who refers to himself as "the elder" (Gr., *presbyteros*) to members of a Johannine church, which he addresses as "the elect lady and her children" (2 John 1; all translations from RSV exept as noted). Third John is addressed to an individual, Gaius. They have similar openings and closings (cf. 2 John vv. 1, 4 and 3 John vv. 1, 3; 2 John v. 12 and 3 John v. 13). Further, each letter has a request to make of its addressee(s), one that in each case is linked to a crisis being faced by the community. In 2 John 7 the writer refers to persons who have left the Johannine churches for "the world." They refuse to acknowledge "the coming of Jesus Christ in the flesh." The presbyter warns the addressees against being deceived by such teachings and then requests that the church take drastic action against its exponents. They must refuse to offer any form of hospitality, even a greeting, to persons who hold such views.

In 3 John, the crisis is a different one. Diotrephes, apparently a wealthy Christian in whose house a group of Christians meets, has refused to offer hospitality to missionaries who come from the elder. He has also been saying things about the elder that the latter claims are untrue, and has used his influence to keep other Christians from welcoming the Johannine missionaries (3 John 9–10). The presbyter has heard that hospitality has been offered to traveling missionaries by Gaius, presumably a prominent Christian who lives in the same region as Diotrephes but is not under the latter's influence (3 John 5–6, 11). The letter seeks to establish a permanent relationship in which Gaius will continue to receive the missionaries. The conclusion of the letter shifts from a letter of request to a letter of recommendation, commending Demetrius, probably the person who was carrying the letter (v. 12).

The second and third letters follow the patterns of private letters. The opening of 2 John 2 presents a benediction such as one finds in the epistles of Paul and other early Christian letters. In 3 John 3 a wish is expressed for the health of the recipient, as would be common in secular letters. Letters often contain expressions of joy in the opening (2 John 4; 3 John 3). Letters of petition do not immediately state the request but rather establish the background or the relationship between the petitioner and the addressee. The request is to be granted in light of that relationship. In 2 John 5–6, the background to the request is described as the commandment to love one another, an injunction characteristic of the Johannine community. In 3 John 5–6 the writer uses less characteristically Johannine language but refers to Gaius' reputation for hospitality as the background. Verses 7–8 expand on the background with a conventional theme of missionary theology: that those who aid missionaries share their "good works." In addition to the formal statement of the background, the statement of verse 3, "I rejoiced . . . ," has been expanded with the information that associates of the elder have come and told him about Gaius.

Each of the letters concludes with a reference to a possible visit by the elder (2 John 12; 3 John 13–14) and a greeting from the elder and his associates to the addressees and others associated with them (2 John 13; 3 John 15). Both of these features are common in Pauline letters. Therefore, 2 and 3 John, though close to the pattern of a private letter in this period, already suggest that a special type of "Christian" letter form was emerging under the influence of the Pauline epistles. These letters are not simply communications between individuals. They establish, just as the traveling missionaries did, bonds of fellowship that hold the scattered "house church" communities together as one larger church.

First John is clearly not a letter, and some scholars have pointed out that it may even have been written by someone other than "the elder." However, the crisis referred to in 2 John and the emphasis on the love command as the background to the author's request are scarcely intelligible without 1 John. Therefore, most exegetes assume that the same person wrote all three letters. A copy of 1 John may even have been sent along with 2 John. First John is a treatise or homiletic exhortation by the "elder," a witness or teacher in the Johannine tradition, to a community of fellow Christians. The author speaks to them as "my little children" (2:1), "beloved" (2:7, 3:2, 21; 4:1, 7, 11), "little children" (2:12, 28; 3:7, 18; 4:4; 5:21), "fathers, young men, children" (2:13),

"children" (2:18), "brethren" (3:13). Thus the author suggests both a close fellowship with his addressees and a function on his part of responsibility for their faith.

Throughout 1 John the author appeals to traditions that he says his audience will recognize as having been taught "from the beginning" (1:1; 2:7, [18], [21], 24; 3:11; see also 2:18, 21; 3:5, 14; 4:3, 5; 5:18–20). These references to what the recipients already "know" suggest that the author is drawing upon a common fund of exhortation within the Johannine churches. The basic themes and images from which 1 John argues may have been those presented to new Christians when they joined the community. However, the treatise is not just a reminder of that initial catachesis. It is also polemic, since the occasion for its composition is the emergence within the community of dissident teachers, whom the author identifies as the predicted "antichrists." They have fractured the unity of the Johannine churches by separating from the "us" of 1 John, that is, the elder and those associated with him, (2:18–19, 26; 4:1, 3, 5). It is clear that the dissidents are also claiming to be part of the Johannine tradition. The author sees their separation from the community as evidence that they are not really part of that tradition. Instead, he argues that they have violated the fundamental commandment of the Johannine churches, "Love one another" (2:3–11, 3:10–11, 4:20–21).

The interpreter of 1 John must constantly keep an eye out for the earlier catechetical tradition that the author is using, the hints that the author gives about the way in which the dissidents are distorting the Christian message, and any new interpretation of the tradition that the author gives. We are not always certain how to separate tradition, interpretation, and polemic in 1 John. Attempts to solve the difficulty by constructing a pre-epistle form of exhortation that the author has modified and expanded to arrive at the present text remain unconvincing. Therefore, we assume that the author composed the treatise as a whole, relying on his experience as a teacher in the Johannine community and not on some written source for the traditional material that is used in 1 John.

Outline of 1 John. Because 1 John uses traditional material and often reformulates the same theme in different ways, no two exegetes agree on how it should be divided. The following outline presumes that the author is primarily concerned with exhorting his audience to lead a life worthy of those who are "children of God." If they do, they will also have to reject the teaching of the dissidents and will not depart from the community. It also presumes that much of the treatise is based upon traditional paraenesis, which has not been substantially changed to attack the dissidents.

A. Prologue (1:1–4)
B. Walking in light (1:5–2:29)
  1. God is light (1:5)
  2. Freedom from sin (1:6–2:2)
  3. Keeping the commandments (2:3–11)
  4. Address to the three groups (2:12–14)
  5. Reject the world (2:15–17)
C. Reject antichrists (2:18–29)
  1. Division signals the last hour (2:18–19)
  2. Anointing preserves true faith (2:20–27)
  3. Confidence at judgment (2:28–29)
D. Love as the mark of God's children (3:1–24)
  1. God has made us children now (3:1–10)
  2. Christians must love one another: like Christ, not like Cain (3:11–18)
  3. The confidence we have before God, who is greater than our hearts and abides in us (3:19–24)
E. Reject the antichrists (4:1–6)
  1. They do not confess Jesus (4:1–3)
  2. They have not overcome the world (4:4–6)
F. God is love (4:7–21)
  1. Christ has shown God's love (4:7–12)
  2. We know God's love through the spirit (4:13–16a)
  3. Our confidence: abiding in God's love (4:16b–21)
G. Belief in the Son (5:1–12)
  1. Faith overcomes the world (5:1–5)
  2. Testimony: the Son came in water and blood (5:6–12)
H. Conclusion (5:13)
I. Epilogue: sayings and rules (5:14–21)
  1. Confidence in prayer (5:14–17)
    (a) God hears our requests (5:14–15)
    (b) Prayer for sinners (5:16–17)
  2. Confidence sayings (5:18–20)
    (a) One born of God does not sin (5:18)
    (b) We are of God (5:19)
    (c) We know the true God and have eternal life (5:20)
  3. Keep from idols (5:21)

The letters and the Fourth Gospel. Echoes of the Fourth Gospel occur throughout 1 John, but the Gospel is never quoted directly; the Gospel's emphasis on the unique relationship between Jesus and God never appears, and the author of these letters refers to himself as "the elder" (2 John 1; 3 John 1), and to himself as part of a larger group of witnesses (1 John 1:2–3). He does not refer to the Beloved Disciple as the source of Johannine tradition, as in John 19:35 and 21:24. In 1 John the fact is emphasized that the death of Jesus is an atonement for sin (1 John 1:7, 2:2, 5:6). This interpretation of Jesus' death arose very early (see the pre-Pauline formula in Romans 3:24–26). It is mentioned in the Gospel's image of Jesus as "lamb of God" (John 1:29). But the Fourth Gospel connects salvation and the death of Jesus in a completely different way. The death of Jesus is the exaltation of the divine Son to the "glory" that he has with the Father. Those who believe, who see it as Jesus' glorification, are drawn to him and have eternal life (e.g., John 3:13–15, 8:28, 12:32–34, 13:31–32). In the Gospel, the Paraclete functions as a successor to the departed Jesus, renewing Jesus' "lawsuit" against an unbelieving world (16:7–11) and guiding the community in all that Jesus has revealed from the Father (14:15–16, 25–26; 16:12–14). First John uses the Greek word *parakletos* (paraclete) in a more conventional sense for Jesus as heavenly intercessor (1 John 2:1–2; RSV translates as "advocate"). It only speaks in general terms of an "anointing" that helps the community discern the truth and is the means by which God "abides in" the community (2:20–21, 27; 3:24; 4:13).

At some points the tradition on which 1 John draws may represent an earlier form of expression and reflection than that called upon in the Gospel. Some scholars have suggested that 1 John was written before the Gospel in its present form was completed. Others have tried to link 1 John with the divisions behind the later farewell discourses (chaps. 15–17). But such proposals have their own difficulties. First John speaks to a very different situation than the Gospel. In the Gospel the threat to the unity of the community comes from without, from the "Jews" who have expelled Christians from the synagogue, who insist that the Johannine claims for Jesus as the unique revelation of God are blasphemous, and who may be continuing to persecute Christians (John 16:1–4a). Both the specific concerns with Jewish polemic and the threat of external polemic are absent from 1, 2, and 3 John. The letters focus upon internal difficulties faced by the community from persons who had been part of its ranks. We also see that the group over against which Christians set themselves is one of "pagans" (1 John 5:21; 3 John 7), not Jews. The three letters suggest a situation later than that of the Gospel. That 1 John does not draw upon all of the theological developments of the Gospel may be the result of several interacting factors. First, the Johannine teacher who writes is a disciple of the evangelist and is not as theologically articulate as the latter. Second, the author is drawing upon traditions from the community that reflect an earlier stage in its theological development, one that continued to be used in the instruction of new members of the community. Finally, at least some of the views of the dissidents were based upon interpretations of Gospel material that the author wished to avoid.

We can also identify a practice of reusing expressions from the Gospel to apply to the new situation of the epistles. Such reapplication makes it difficult to tell whether the dissidents held all of the views that are attributed to them (especially when they are accused of not "confessing Jesus"), or whether they are being accused of being "as bad as" persons who denied their faith in Jesus during the earlier period of persecution. The Gospel uses expressions like "the world" and "children of the devil" to refer to the Jews who are seeking Jesus' life and persecuting his disciples (e.g., 8:44, 15:18–19). For 1 John, the dissidents are children of Satan who belong to "the world" (3:10, 4:5). Just as the dissidents are children of Satan, so they are also given the other attributes mentioned in the Gospel's description of Jesus' Jewish opponents as children of the devil: they are murderers and liars (2:22, 3:8–15, 4:1–6). The Gospel uses "darkness" to represent what is hostile to and will not accept Jesus (1:5; 3:19–21; 12:35). By contrast, 1 John uses the contrast between light and darkness as it was frequently used in Jewish and Christian ethical exhortation: darkness refers to living a sinful life, that is, hating one's brother or sister (2:9–11). Whereas the Gospel reflects a very early Christian tradition in speaking of the Jews who rejected Jesus as "blinded" (as Isaiah 6:10 had predicted; John 12:39–40), 1 John, in a passage that alludes to this use of darkness in the Gospel, speaks of those who hate their brothers and sisters as "blinded," stumbling in darkness (2:11).

Elsewhere, allusions to the language of the Gospel are not polemical but reflect the new situation of Johannine Christians in the epistles period. Compare the opening verses of the Gospel (John 1:1–5) with the opening of 1 John (1:1–4). The Gospel speaks of "beginning" as prior to the creation of the cosmos, while the epistle uses "beginning" for the beginning of the testimony about the life and ministry of Jesus (a usage of *archē* also found in the Gospel, e.g., 2:11, 6:64, 15:27, 16:4). The Gospel speaks of the Word and life in the presence of the Father, thus establishing the basis for its claim that Jesus is the manifestation of that Word and life. First John, on the other hand, speaks of the "word of life" as equivalent to the Gospel message that the witnesses of the Johannine community pass on to the readers. In that context the "word of life" would refer to the life-giving ministry of Jesus.

Being a child of God. The designations "children" and "beloved," which the author of 1 John frequently uses to address his audience, also have their origins in traditions that are represented in the Gospel. The Gospel makes it clear that those who believe in Jesus as God's Son become "children of God" through the Spirit at baptism (John 1:12–13, 3:3–12). First John does not refer to baptism directly, though the allusions to what Christians have heard "from the beginning" suggests that context. Instead, 1 John focuses on the new relationship that exists between those who are "children of God" and God. Even though "the world" cannot see this relationship, it is a reality, and it governs the way in which Christians live their lives (1 John 2:29–3:2). The author can even speak of the "child of God" as having the "seed" (*sperma*) of God (3:9; RSV, "nature"). Such a person does not sin (5:18).

Another Johannine expression for the special

relationship between Christians and God uses the images of "remaining" or "abiding" in God (2:24–29, 3:6, 3:24, 4:13, 5:20). As the Gospel also makes clear, this is a reciprocal relationship. God or Christ can be said to "abide in" the Christian (John 6:56, 15:4–7). But these expressions have an additional significance for Johannine Christians, since they also express the relationship that exists between the Father and the Son (John 17:21–23). Believers have the same relationship to the Father that they have to the Son.

The love command. For the Johannine tradition this relationship of "abiding in" God has to be demonstrated in love of others. The Gospel speaks of the love command as the "new commandment" that Jesus gives to his true disciples at the supper after Judas has departed (13:34–35, 14:21, 15:9–17). First John makes it clear that Christians were constantly exhorted to show such love to one another (1 John 2:7–11, 3:10–18, 4:7–5:5). Further, 1 John 3:10–18 even recalls the Gospel's formulations of the love command in John 15:9–17 by reminding the reader that the love that Christians show and that serves as the sign that they "abide in" God is really based on the love that Christ showed in offering his life for us. In 1 John 16–17 the reader is reminded that if Christ gave himself for us, then we should be willing to lay down our lives for others. But, barring that, we should certainly not close our hearts to others who are in need. The Gospel had insisted that Christ's coming was a sign of God's love for the world (John 3:16). In 1 John 4:7–21 this theme is picked up and combined with that of the obligation of Christians to show love to others. The author's reflection upon love leads him to the insight that in Christ we learn that "God is love." He goes on to argue that if Christians make this love the basis of their lives, they do not have to worry about divine judgment (4:17–21). This insight picks up another theme from the Gospel: Jesus' mission was one of salvation, not judgment and condemnation (John 3:17–21).

Conflict with the dissidents. Although much of the exhortation in 1 John belongs to the community's tradition and has not been shaped by the crisis that the author faces, we are never allowed to forget that some people have left this community and are trying to get others to do the same. When the author con-

trasts true Christian love with "hating one's brother," he is not only thinking of persons who "hate their brothers" by not showing charity for the needy. He is also thinking of those who "hate their brothers" by dividing the community. He insists that anyone who does that cannot claim to "know God" or to "remain in" or "be a child of" God (2:4, 9, 19; 3:10–15; 4:8, 20).

False perfectionism. The dissidents are clearly having some success in winning people over to their views (2:18; 4:1, 5). The measures to be taken against them, as given in 2 John 7–11, suggest that they were engaged in propagandizing in Johannine churches. The first clues that 1 John gives about their position suggest that they made claims to sinlessness that were deceptive (1:8, 1:10, 3:3–4). Since the Johannine tradition did speak of the Christian as "born of God" and as "sinless" in contrast to a world of sin and darkness, the dissidents probably based their views upon an interpretation of that tradition. They may have held that the Spirit that Christians receive wipes out all sin.

First John agrees that there is a sense in which the Christian is "free from sin." However, the author develops two arguments against the opponents' conclusions. One argument, as we have seen, is that no one can claim to be a "child of God" and fail to "love others." In fragmenting the community, the dissidents have shown that they are not living in a sinless unity with God as they claim. The second argument appears in the acknowledgment of 1 John that Christians do sin and need God's continued forgiveness. In 1 John 2:1–2 the reader is reminded that Christ serves as a heavenly intercessor for the sins of Christians, so that forgiveness is always available. The collection of sayings and rules at the end of 1 John suggests that the community may even have had a formal way of seeking God's forgiveness for the sinful Christian. To a saying on the certainty of prayer (1 John 5:14–15; *cf.* John 14:13; 15:16; 16:23, 26–27) 1 John 5:16–17 appends a practice of praying for a fellow Christian who sins. Such prayer will be answered except in the case of the "sin which is mortal" (literally, "sin unto death"). The author does not explain what this sin is, though parallels with Old Testament and Essene legislation suggest a sin that requires expulsion from the community (Num 15:30–

31, 18:22; Isa 22:14; *1 Qumran S* viii, 22–ix, 2). Comparison with Hebrews 10:26 would suggest that such a sin would be denial of one's faith in Christ (as had occurred during the period of persecution). The author may also have the apostasy of the dissidents in view.

False understanding of Christ. A second set of warnings is linked with what persons confess to be the truth about Jesus. We have already seen that the belief in Jesus as heavenly intercessor, or Paraclete, was tied to forgiveness of sin. Another conviction about Christ and forgiveness, that Jesus' death is an atonement for sin (1 John 1:7, 2:2, 3:16, 4:10), is repeatedly emphasized. We have seen that although this tradition is mentioned in the Gospel, it is not the primary understanding of Jesus' death. The dissidents appear to have denied any atoning significance to Jesus' death. The insistence in 1 John 5:6 that Jesus came in "water and blood" is perhaps an indication that the opponents granted the significance of water and the coming of the Spirit from the exalted Jesus (e.g., John 7:38–39) but denied that Jesus' death had any significance. Interpreters of the Gospel have suggested that the reference to "water and blood" flowing from the dead Jesus in John 19:34–35 was added to the story in response to the views rejected by 1 John. Some interpreters think that the dissidents may have begun to formulate theories about the death of Jesus that appear in later docetic and gnostic accounts, according to which the true, heavenly reality that has come to earth in Jesus departs to heaven, leaving its bodily shell on the cross. Naturally, persons who think of Jesus in that way cannot speak of Jesus offering himself "for us."

First John does not indicate how the dissidents described Jesus' life and death, though its emphasis upon the tangibility of what the witnesses to the tradition have seen and touched does point to the physical reality of Jesus (1:1–4). The author also refers to the opponents as denying that Jesus is Christ (5:1) or Son of God (1:7; 2:23; 3:8, 23; 4:9–10, 15; 5:5, 9–13, 20). Some of these slogans may be conventional declarations of faith that had been used when Johannine Christians were threatened with persecution. But in two instances the formula that the author says the opponents deny is not a common christological formula. He reports that they reject the confession "Jesus Christ is come in the flesh" (1 John 4:2; 2 John 7). In both passages, he is calling on a community to "discern" and avoid the spirit of "antichrist" that is evident in the opponents. These peculiar expressions do suggest that the opponents denied some facet of the human reality of Jesus.

Eschatology in 1 John. First John consistently reassures Christians that if they are faithful to its teaching, they need not worry about the judgment (2:28; 3:2–3, 19–21; 4:17–18). The conclusion to the body of 1 John, which echoes that of the Gospel, emphasizes the message that the audience should know that they have eternal life (5:13; cf. John 20:31). In 1 John 3:14 the mutual love among Christians is affirmed as evidence that they have passed "from death to life." It appears that the perfectionism of the opponents may have evoked fears of condemnation. First John also uses an apocalyptic metaphor of the Christian's faith as a victory over Satan (2:13–14), "the world" (5:4), and the dissidents who belong to the world (4:4). In addition, the author speaks of his opponents as "antichrists," a multiple manifestation of the end-time opponent of the Messiah (1 John 2:18; 4:3; 2 John 7), as well as calling them false prophets and deceivers. Similar apocalyptic scenarios can be found in Mark 13:14–22 and 2 Thessalonians 2:1–12 (cf. Dan 11:31–36), though the expression "antichrist" appears to have been coined by the author of 1 John. Although apocalyptic imagery is used to describe the crisis facing the community, 1 John also affirms the present reality of salvation and union with God for the Christian who remains in the community, confesses Jesus as Messiah, loves others, and has an expiation of sin available in the death of Christ. Within that context the "child of God" is sinless, has eternal life, and has overcome Satan. Therefore the eschatological language of 1 John does not represent an outcropping of apocalyptic "enthusiasm" and preoccupation with the end of the world. Just as the Gospel had done before him, the presbyter insists upon the concrete reality of salvation for those "born of God."

Bibliography

Scholarly Commentaries

Brown, Raymond E. *The Epistles of John.* Anchor Bible, vol. 30. Garden City, N.Y., 1982. The standard reference for future study of the Johannine letters.

Bultmann, Rudolf Karl. *The Johannine Epistles.* Philadelphia, 1973.

Schnackenburg, Rudolf. *Die Johannesbriefe.* Freiburg im Breisgau, 1978. Contains extensive thematic excursuses.

General Commentaries

Dodd, C. H. *The Johannine Epistles.* London, 1946.

Grayston, Kenneth. *The Johannine Epistles.* Grand Rapids, 1984.

Houlden, J. L. *A Commentary on the Johannine Epistles.* New York, 1973.

Marshall, I. H. *The Epistles of John.* Grand Rapids, 1978.

Smalley, Stephen S. *1, 2, 3 John.* Waco, Tex., 1984.

Special Studies

Bogart, John. *Orthodox and Heretical Perfectionism in the Johannine Community as Evident in the First Epistle of John.* Missoula, 1977.

Brox, Norbert. "'Doketismus'—Eine Problemanzeige." *Zeitschrift für Kirchengeschichte* 95 (1984): 301–314.

Cooper, E. J. "The Consciousness of Sin in 1 John." *Laval théologique et philosophique* 28 (1972): 237–248.

Donfried, K. P. "Ecclesiastical Authority in 2–3 John." In *L'Évangile de Jean,* edited by M. de Jonge. Gembloux, 1977.

Malherbe, A. J. "The Inhospitality of Diotrephes." In *God's Christ and His People,* edited by J. Jervell and W. A. Meeks. Oslo, 1977.

Perkins, Pheme. "Koinonia in 1 John 1:3–7." *Catholic Biblical Quarterly* 45 (1983): 631–641.

Wengst, Klaus. *Häresie und Orthodoxie im Spiegel des ersten Johannesbriefes.* Gütersloh, 1976.

PHEME PERKINS

Revelation

THE LAST BOOK of the Bible is known by its first Greek word as Apocalypse or by its Latin equivalent as Revelation. This name is derived from the book's opening statement: "This is the revelation [apokalypsis] God gave to Jesus Christ in order to show God's servants what must happen very soon" (Au. trans.).

INTRODUCTION

Although the book claims to be the apocalypse or revelation of Jesus Christ, it is generally known as the "Revelation of John." This title was only added when the book was accepted into the canon and seems to be derived from the first three verses. It is probably formulated in analogy to the titles of other Jewish or Christian "apocalypses" that were attributed to great figures of the past, such as Abraham, Enoch, or Peter. Tradition has therefore ascribed Revelation to the apostle John, although the author does not claim such a title for himself but refers to the twelve apostles as great figures of the past (21:14). Today, most scholars believe the book was written by a Jewish Christian seer who wrote down "the words of prophecy" under the reign of the Roman emperor Domitian (81–96 C.E.). This date is first attested by Irenaeus (ca 180), who was born in Asia Minor. Some ancient traditions and modern commentators claim that Revelation was written under the regime of Trajan (98–117) or of Nero (54–68).

Literary Genre

Since the last century the first word of Revelation, apokalypsis, has also been used to characterize a whole group of Jewish and Christian writings that flourished between 200 B.C.E. and 300 C.E. Examples of such apocalyptic literature include the Book of Daniel in the Hebrew Bible and 2 Esdras 3–14 (=4 Ezra) in the Apocrypha. Other such Jewish apocalyptic writings include the books of Enoch, 2 and 3 Baruch, the Apocalypse of Abraham, and some writings of Qumran. In the New Testament we find not only apocalyptic sections (e.g., the so-called synoptic apocalypse of Mark 13 and parallels or 2 Thess 2) but also basic apocalyptic categories and perspectives. Without question, Revelation belongs to this type of ancient literature.

The first apocalyptic literary expression, found in the Book of Daniel, was written in response to the religious persecution of Antiochus IV Epiphanes (ca. 165 B.C.E.). Apocalyptic literature, therefore, is generally considered to be revelatory "crisis literature." The religious crisis at the heart of apocalyptic literature is the matter of theodicy created by the conflict between the experience of suffering and the conviction of Israel's election. Such a conflict is expressed in the following prayer:

And now, O Lord, behold these nations which are reputed as nothing, lord it over us and crush us. But we, thy people, whom thou hast called thy first-born, thy only begotten, thy beloved, are given up into their hands. If the world has indeed been created for our sakes, why do we not enter into possession of our world? How long shall this endure? (2 Esdr 6:57–59)

At the same time, apocalyptic literature asserts that, despite all evidence to the contrary, God is in control and will soon intervene. The overall religious perspective of apocalyptic literature, therefore, is eschatological, that is, it concerns the end of the world or the state of the soul after death. The apocalyptic frame of mind distinguishes between this age and the age to come and at the same time asserts that this age is under the power of Evil: the wicked prosper and the righteous suffer. But through the intervention of God this age will soon come to an end by means of a catastrophe of cosmic proportions instigated by demonic and angelic forces. Indeed, before the end there will occur a period of extreme tribulation. After the cataclysm a new salvation will appear by means of a mediator. Some apocalyptic writers expect a messianic reign of bliss and happiness for the elect on earth to precede the final cataclysm.

The literary genre and stylistic features of apocalyptic writings are specified differently by different scholars, but some features can be said to typify apocalypses: (1) The author has received a secret revelation that is to be written down. (2) It involves another, heavenly world and envisions eschatological salvation. (3) This revelation is imparted in dreams, visions, auditions, and interpretations by a heavenly guide or angelic interpreter.

Such visionary accounts are the results of literary technique rather than the transcript of ecstatic experience, for apocalyptic literature is essentially a written rather than an oral literature. It utilizes standard imagery and symbolism and requires a shared code between seer and reader in order to be understood. Major literary techniques are periodizations of history and pseudonymity; that is, the reception of the revelation is attributed to a figure of the past. Such methods allow the author to project past historical periods as accurate predictions of the future.

The mysterious character of apocalyptic literature is achieved through fantastic symbolizations and mythical imagery that must be read on two levels. Numbers do not designate quantifiable amounts but are symbolic statements: For example, 7 means perfection and 6 means less than perfect; 3 stands for the divine and 4 for the created world; 12 is the number of Israel. Multiplication enhances the meaning of the root number ($144,000 = 12 \times 12 \times 10 \times 10 \times 10$); division lessens it ($3\frac{1}{2} = $ period of evil). Colors similarly must be read as statements of meaning: red means war and fighting, white stands for victory, and pale is the color of death.

Interpretive Approaches

Because of their bizarre character, ambiguity in form and imagery, and often grotesque language, apocalyptic writings allow for farfetched interpretations. Not only are they baffling to us today, but they were intended to be so even to people at the time they were written. It is not surprising, therefore, that Revelation is the most enigmatic writing in the New Testament.

Although scholarship has explored various ways for reading this difficult book, Revelation's world of vision and its symbolic universe have remained strange and difficult for many modern readers. It still is for many Christians a book with "seven seals" (6:1), seldom read and relegated to a curiosity in the Bible. Historicocritical scholarship also has neglected this book because its theology is suspect and its grotesque images elude any rational explanation. Scholars generally agree that the book should be understood in the context of the first century and the cultural ambience of its first readers. However, they often claim that the book is more Jewish than Christian and far below the theological level of the letters of Paul or the Gospel of John. As so-called apocalyptic literature, it is only slightly Christianized and contributes little to our understanding of early Christian life and theology.

In contrast, Revelation, more than any other book of the New Testament, has profoundly influenced Western art and literature. Although the text of Revelation defies visualization, works of art have nevertheless drawn their inspiration from it: from the decoration of the early Christian basilicas through the medieval manuscript illuminations of Queen Eleanor's Apocalypse, the Angers tapestry, Dürer's woodcuts, or the miniatures of the Flemish Apocalypse to Blake's etchings and Picasso's *Guernica*. The fact that so many artists have attempted to visualize the dazzling succession of Revelation's images indicates how effective are the mythic symbols of the book.

Moreover, Revelation has not only inspired revolutionary movements for justice, past and present, but also fostered the conservative or reactionary politics of disenfranchised groups. For many Christians, therefore, Revelation is still one of the most important, if not *the* most important, of the books of the Bible, providing information about our contemporary situation and fashioning predictions for what is to come in the very near future. They view their present situation and the future through Revelation's lenses. Such books as Hal Lindsey's *The Late Great Planet Earth*, which provide detailed applications of Revelation's visions to contemporary events, enjoy widespread popularity.

Throughout the history of interpretation the following basic approaches for reading the book—used often in some combination with each other—have prevailed.

Allegorical exegesis of Revelation has been practiced from its earliest interpretation. Throughout history Christians have maintained that the beast, identified by the number 666 (Rev 13:18), symbolizes well-known leaders, for example, the Roman pontiff, Hitler, or Stalin, or more recently the leaders of Islam. In the 1984 election campaign President Ronald Reagan, for instance, alluded to Revelation when he called the Soviet Union the "evil empire" and spoke of Armageddon; at the same time a flyer circulated asserting that the number of the beast, 666, was the code name for Ronald Wilson Reagan, because each of the president's three names consisted of six letters.

Such allegorical readings are already suggested by the author of the book when he declares, for instance, that "the one who has understanding" can reckon the number of the beast because it is a human number: 666. The ancient Greeks and Hebrews used the letters of the alphabet to represent numbers. The first nine letters were given the values 1–9; the second nine letters were given the values 10–90; and the last letters were valued in the hundreds. There were no letters *j* and *w* in Greek but *chi* between *n* and

o substitutes for *q*. To get the number of a name, one has to add up the number value of the letters. The numerical value of Jesus in Greek is 888. The English name Mary Smith would have the number 848. However, the number varies depending on which alphabet is utilized: the Greek, Hebrew, or English. Despite centuries of puzzling over the problem, scholars have not come to an agreement whether 666 refers to Nero, Caligula, or Domitian; the original readers, however, probably knew who was meant.

Spiritual interpretations take a different approach. They do not understand 666 as a code referring to a particular first-century Roman ruler. Rather they insist that the call for wisdom is not a call to decipher the number but to recognize its deeper meaning and significance. This interpretive approach understands 666 as the intensification of 6, which as one short of 7—the number of perfection—stands for imperfection. Generally this spiritual interpretation claims that Revelation speaks not about history but about timeless principles, inner spiritual realities, or psychological archetypes. It holds, for instance, that Babylon embodies the essence of urban civilization or that the opposition between Babylon and the New Jerusalem is the archetypal antithesis of Woman as whore and virgin. The whole book reveals those basic principles on which God acts in history, or it depicts the ageless struggle between the forces of Good and Evil.

According to a third approach, Revelation, at least since the twelfth century, has been predominantly understood as prophetic prediction. The so-called *preterist or contemporary historical interpretation* claims that it foretold the coming events in John's own time. Major prophecies of the book are seen as fulfilled in the fall of Jerusalem (70 C.E.), in the Bar Kokhba rebellion (132–135), or in the fall of Rome (476). It is then argued, for example, that chapters 4–11 describe the church's conflict with Judaism, chapters 12–19 refer to its conflict with paganism, and chapters 19–22 describe the present triumph of the church, which began with Constantine.

This church-historical interpretation, therefore, has insisted that Revelation forecasts the course of church and world history. For instance, Nicholas of Lyra (*d. ca.* 1340) held that the book contained the prediction of a continuous series of events from the apostolic age to the return of Christ. Others suggest that Revelation portrays the progress of the Christian faith or the progress of world history and the course of Western civilization.

Futuristic-eschatological interpretations in turn maintain that Revelation does not refer to history but that it predicts the coming events of the final days of humanity. Whereas chapters 1–3 refer to the history and present of the church, chapters 4–22, the eschatological chapters proper, predict the eschatological future. Millenarians believe that Christ will return before the thousand-year reign on earth and that the present is the time just before the final cataclysm. According to this interpretive approach the number 666 refers to the Antichrist, who in the near future will appear on earth. Or it can assert that John prophesied the unavoidable atomic annihilation of the world through fire in the very near future, a catastrophe from which only the elect will be saved.

Since the advent of the *historicocritical* interpretation scholars no longer search Revelation for predictions of future events but study it as an admittedly clouded window to its own time and community. Historicocritical interpretation utilizes the same methods—philology, source, form, redaction, cultural, and history of religions analysis—that were developed for the study of the Gospels or the narrative literature of the Hebrew Bible in order to establish the historicity of persons and events about which they speak. In the 1980s source and compilation theories, but not the history of religions approach developed at the beginning of the century, have widely been relinquished in favor of form and redaction critical readings.

The historicocritical approach has proved most fruitful in delineating the historicocultural setting of Revelation and especially in illuminating the sociocultural-religious context of the so-called seven letters (Rev 2:1–3:22). This approach, however, generally separates the letters as referring to the historical situation of Revelation from the apocalyptic, visionary part of the book. Yet, when the letters are divorced from the overall work and understood as actual historical letters, not only is their apocalyptic-literary character overlooked, but their integral function for the overall composition of Revelation is also misjudged.

Liturgical-dramatic interpretations assume that because of the worship setting of Revelation's visions, its hymnic language, and its liturgical-dramatic depiction of heaven, the whole book is patterned either after Christian and Jewish liturgical celebrations or after Roman imperial cultic drama and ritual. Some have suggested that its outline is patterned after the Jewish calendar of feasts, the Temple liturgy, or the Christian Sunday eucharistic celebration. Others stress the dramatic aspect of Revelation and maintain that it is constructed as a Greek drama or patterned after the imperial games celebrated at Ephesus. Others see it as a dramatic myth that transforms reality and facilitates the "cultic coming" of Christ in the worship of the community. This approach has paid increasing attention to the literary function of Revelation but suffers from the drawback of reducing the work to individual psychological-spiritual experience.

Since around the late 1970s scholars have come to appreciate anew the literary power of the work, although this appreciation has not yet permeated popular interpretations and teaching. In the following discussion of the form and content of Revelation, I will utilize a *rhetorical approach* that seeks to integrate historical, literary, and theological analysis. This implies a shift in interpretative paradigm from an allegorical-spiritual, predictive-literalist, or historical-factual to a rhetorical analysis that can do justice to the sociohistorical as well as to the literary-dramatic character of the book.

Revelation's rhetorical vision serves prophetic functions. However, it would be a misunderstanding of biblical prophecy if it were understood as prediction and foretelling of the future. Rather, early Christian prophecy is directed toward the interpretation of the present and seeks to encourage and strengthen the religious commitments of its audience. In order to delineate this visionary rhetoric of Revelation, I will seek first to interpret its language and imagery and to trace its composition and structure. Then I shall discuss and assess the rhetorical function of Revelation's world of vision.

LITERARY IMAGES AND COMPOSITION

The rhetorical character of Revelation is indicated by the fact that the apocalyptic visions of revelation are communicated in the form of an open letter to seven communities in Asia Minor. The "words of prophecy" that are "the revelation of Jesus Christ" are to be read in the assembly of the community. As a Christian prophet, the author does not engage in esoteric speculations or simply give injunctions and admonitions. Rather he constructs a symbolic universe and "plausibility structure" in order to make sense out of the experience of Christians who believe that the ultimate sources of political power are God and Christ but who experience daily poverty, persecution, and execution.

John portrays the experience and predicament of Christians who are powerless in terms of the political powers of the time. Therefore, he expresses his vision of the Christian symbolic universe in socioeconomic language and political-mythological imagery. In short, John does not write a tractate or sermon "on the last things," but seeks to persuade the reader/hearer with the evocative power of his images and visions. They not only provoke an intellectual response but also elicit emotional reactions and religious commitments.

Language and Imagery

Although Revelation's classification as apocalyptic literature is widely accepted, such a generic delineation is often perceived as a theological evaluation rather than as a literary categorization. As so-called apocalyptic literature Revelation is often deemed not to be a Christian prophetic work but a work that is only slightly Christianized and therefore one that has little to contribute to our understanding of Christian life, community, and theology.

However, if "apocalyptic" is understood not as a theological but as a literary-rhetorical qualification, then it is important to pay attention to the apocalyptic rhetoric of the work. Apocalyptic language is not predictive-descriptive language but mythological-imaginative. Apocalyptic language is not like a cloak that can be stripped down to its theological essence or principle; it is more like an onion with layers and layers of meaning. It does not appeal to our logical facilities but to our imagination and emotions. It uses mythological-fantastic language: stars fall from heaven, and the world is imagined as a palace with three stories—heaven, earth, and underworld. Animals speak and dragons spit fire, a lion is a lamb, and angels or demons engage in warfare.

As was pointed out, Jewish apocalyptic literature speaks about the past, present, and future in mythological language and images. For example, Daniel has a vision of four wild beasts emerging from the sea that are later identified as four great kings (Dan 7). The bizarre and terrifying features of these beasts indicate that they are not conceived as real beasts but as mythological symbolizations. The first beast, for instance, is likened to a lion with eagle's wings, while the third is compared to a leopard with four heads and four bird wings on its flanks (Dan 7:4–7). Thus in apocalyptic literature, which is a fantastic literature, world empires have become beasts, nations are symbolized by birds, and serpents start to speak.

Apocalyptic literature can be compared to the future-oriented genre of science fiction, which constructs the future out of the experience and fears of people in the present. Anyone enjoying the tales and future projections of science fiction writers, however, would readily agree that this literature does not predict the future but illuminates our present situation by projecting present hopes and fears into the future.

Revelation's classification as apocalyptic literature thus signals that its images and visions should not be understood in terms of historical description; nor should they be understood in terms of future prediction. The author who in 1:1 identifies himself as John does not have much more information about the end time than do the authors of the Synoptic apocalypse in Mark 13 (and parallels) or of 1 Thessalonians 4:13ff., 1 Corinthians 15:20ff., and 2 Thessalonians 2:1ff. However, his dramatic presentation elaborates these early Christian expectations with the help of traditional language and contemporary images.

Like science fiction, apocalyptic literature in general, and Revelation in particular, seeks to make sense of the world and present time in terms of the future or of the transcendent. At the same time it pictures the future with the help of knowledge and language gleaned from the past and the present. Like other apocalyptic authors John describes the future in terms of the knowledge available to him in the present. He speaks about heavenly or demonic realities in human language and imagery derived from the mythological traditions and scientific knowledge of his own time.

In creating this mythological symbolization John does not freely invent his images and symbols but derives them from Jewish and Greco-Roman literature and tradition. In working with associations and allusions to very divergent mythic and religiopolitical traditions, he appeals to the imagination of people steeped in Jewish and Hellenistic culture and religion. Apocalyptic language, in other words, does not invent its images and myth but uses "traditional" language.

We still can observe how the author "composes" his language and imagery when we compare his text with that of the Hebrew Bible, which he utilized as one of his language reservoirs. Although the author knows how to write "correct" Greek, the whole book is written in a hebraizing idiom that gives its language a hieratic traditional character. Moreover, he never quotes or interprets the Hebrew Bible or any of his other sources specifically; rather, he uses them as a "language." A careful look at the inaugural vision (1:10–20) can demonstrate why it is justified to call Revelation a "literary vision." It is impossible to picture or draw this vision. Its images and symbols function more like words and sentences in a composition. One could say that the author constructs his sentences and paragraphs with symbols and images rather than with abstract concepts and theological statements.

A comparison of the figure in Daniel 10 with that of Christ in Revelation 1 indicates that John works in an associative literary fashion insofar as he closely follows the text of Daniel 10. But he differs from it in several instances in ways that stress his own emphases. Whereas Daniel 10:5 refers to a human person, Revelation refers here and in 14:14 to someone *like* a human person. The descriptions of the hair (*cf.* Dan 7) and of the voice (*cf.* Ezek 1:24, 43:2) stress the affinity of this "someone like a human" with God. Moreover, while the human figure in Daniel 10 is clothed in linen and wears the girdle around the hips, the Christ figure in Revelation 1 is clothed like the Jewish high priest, in a long robe (*cf.* Ezek 9:2; Exod 28:4, 31), and girded around the breast (*cf.* Ezek 44:18). These explicit changes seem intended to stress Christ's royal/priestly character, an emphasis

not found in the Daniel text that served John as basic literary pattern for the composition of this vision.

Revelation's language and images are derived not only from the Hebrew Jewish tradition but also from Babylonian, Zoroastrian, Greco-Roman, and Asian mythologies. Although difficult for modern readers to understand, these traditions were readily available and unconsciously present to the original recipients of the book. The "traditional" language of Revelation can be illustrated for instance with reference to chapter 12.

The myth of the queen of heaven with the divine child was internationally known at the time of John. Variations of it are found in Babylonia, Egypt, Greece, and Asia Minor. The elements of this myth —the goddess with the divine child, the great red dragon and his enmity to mother and child, and their protection—are also incorporated in Revelation 12. As in some versions of the myth, the dragon seeks the child not yet born in order to devour and kill it. In other forms of the myth either the pregnant woman is carried away to give birth in a protected place or she gives birth in a miraculous way and escapes with the newborn the onslaught of the dragon. In Revelation 12 the child is exalted to heaven and the woman is carried to the desert for her own protection.

Some features of this myth are also found in the Roman imperial cult. A coin of Pergamum portrays the goddess Roma with the emperor. Roma, the queen of heaven, was worshiped as the mother of the gods in the cities of Asia Minor, and her oldest temple stood in Smyrna. Her imperial child was celebrated as the world's savior and the sun-god, Apollo. Such an allusion to the imperial cult and to the goddess Roma is probably intended here, since the "woman clothed with the sun" clearly is the anti-image of Babylon, signifying Rome and its allies in chapters 17 and 18.

John reinterprets this ancient myth in terms of Jewish expectations. The stress on the travail of the woman is not found in the ancient myth but is inspired by the Hebrew Bible's image of Israel-Zion in messianic times. The symbolic language of the ancient pagan myth evokes the image of the messianic child being born in the birth pangs of the messianic woes. In Revelation this child is without question Jesus Christ, who is exalted and receives the powers of the messianic king (*cf.* Ps 2:9 and Rev 11:15, 12:10, 19:15). The birth of the Messiah here is not the historical birth of Jesus but his exaltation and enthronement as "the firstborn of the dead" (1:5) and "the beginning of a new creation."

The figure of the dragon, serpent, crocodile, or sea monster also is familiar from ancient mythology and the Hebrew Bible. In Hebrew Jewish writings the dragon frequently serves as the symbol for an oppressor nation such as Egypt (Ps 74:14) and its ruler, pharaoh (Ezek 32:3ff.); or Syria and Babylon (cf. Isa 27:1). In Daniel it is the symbol of the last great anti-divine nation and the ruler opposing Israel (7:1–7). In this symbolic context the red dragon is immediately understood as the ultimate foe of the people of God.

The multivalent symbol of the "woman clothed with the sun," whose fate is announced in 12:6 and expanded on in the last section, has received very different interpretations. She has been identified as the Israel of the Hebrew Bible, as the heavenly or earthly church, or as Mary, the mother of Jesus. If we observe how the figure of woman functions in the symbol system of Revelation, we recognize that this symbol is used either for the "great harlot Babylon" or for the New Jerusalem coming down from heaven like a bride adorned for her husband (cf. 19:7ff; 21:2, 9ff.). As an eschatological reality the symbol of Woman signifies not only the eschatological salvation of the people of God but also the future of a renewed world.

The mythological symbolization of "war in heaven" serves to explain in the language of Jewish myth that Satan, the accuser and prosecutor of Christians, has for a short time received the opportunity to exercise oppressive power on earth after being thrown down from heaven at the exaltation of Jesus Christ. Thus the central section of Revelation 12:7–12 reveals the deepest cause for the persecution and oppression experienced by Christians at the time of John. At the same time this vision assures the reader/hearer that eschatological salvation is not jeopardized.

In sum, in working with associations and allusions to divergent mythic and religiopolitical traditions Revelation appeals to the imagination of people steeped in Jewish and Greco-Roman culture and religion. John achieves the literary-symbolic power of his work by taking traditional symbols and mythological images out of their original contexts and by placing them into a new literary composition.

Revelation must be read and contemplated as a symphony of images if one wants to experience the book's full emotional impact. Its symbolizations elicit emotions, feelings, and convictions that cannot, and should not, be fully conceptualized. The phrasing of the images and symbols in propositional, logical, factual language robs them of their power of persuasion. Literary and historical analyses can deepen the book's persuasive mythological language but not replace it. An analysis of Revelation's sources and traditions helps to elucidate the possible meanings of Revelation's images, but such an analysis does not "explain" them. Their meaning cannot be derived from the tradition but only from their present position within the overall symbolic framework and narrative of the book. Therefore, Revelation can be fully understood only when analyzed as a literary composition because each vision and symbol derives its import from its relation to the overall architecture of the work.

Literary Composition

The artistic-poetic character of Revelation can best be experienced when one hears the book read aloud in its entirety. The hearer is impressed by the archaic rhythmic language, by the repetition of sounds and formulas, and by the wealth of its colors, voices, and image association. This dramatic and symbolic character of Revelation defies exact analysis and definite interpretation. It would therefore be a serious mistake to reduce the visionary rhetoric of Revelation to an abstract system or theological argument. We have to approach the book in the same manner as we approach a work of art.

To appreciate a symphony, for example, one has to listen to the whole work in order to grasp the full impact of its tonalities, musical forms, motifs, and relationships. After listening to the work as a whole, one can go on to analyze the elements and details of its composition and to study the techniques employed by its composer.

As distinct from other apocalypses, Revelation makes a very unified and well-organized impression, even though the author mixes traditional symbols and obscure patterns of disparate origin. That Revelation is not encyclopedic but dramatic in character is a function of the author's literary techniques and compositional skills that integrate the various elements into a unified literary movement.

A primary means to achieve unity is John's use of a common stock of symbols and images. The individual visions of the book rely on symbols and images that are distributed over the whole work—for example, the symbol of the throne or the image of prostration. The author also achieves a unified narrative structure by employing image clusters and symbol associations that reinforce each other and, like musical leitmotifs, connect the individual visions with each other (e.g., the image of the throne achieves its full impact and "volume" through its association with other symbols of imperial power and reign). Further techniques of literary integration are (1) pre-announcements (e.g., the promises to the victor at the end of the seven messages are developed in chaps. 21–22), (2) cross-references (christological characteristics of the inaugural vision are repeated not only in chaps. 2–3, but also in 14:14ff. and 19:11ff.), and (3) contrasts (e.g., the great Babylon in chaps. 17–18 and the New Jerusalem of chaps. 12 and 21f.).

Unity of effect is also enhanced by the interwoven texture of numbers and numerical patterns. Basic numerical-structural component forms are the four "cycles of seven" of the messages and plagues; the two book visions, which symbolize a new prophetic commissioning; and the two visions of Christ with the sword, the symbol of judgment (cf. 1:13ff., 19:11ff.). The seven cycles in turn are structured into groupings of four and three. This numerical interweaving of visions has the effect of combining a cyclic form of repetition with a continuous forward movement, which characterizes Revelation as end-oriented rather than cyclic or encyclopedic.

The forward surge of the narrative is interrupted by interludes (e.g., 7:1–17, 11:15–19, 12:10, 14:1–5, 15:2–4, 19:1–9, 20:4–6) that are generally visions of eschatological protection and salvation. By interrupting the patterns of continuous narrative and cyclic repetition through the insertion of these anticipatory visions of salvation, the author underlines the connection between the present state of oppression and the eschatological future of salvation. At the same time he maintains structurally that the eschatological future gives meaning to the present struggle.

Very important for the understanding of Revelation are the literary techniques of intercalation and of interlocking that make a diagraming of the successive sections and development of Revelation almost impossible. Intercalation, or sandwiching, involves the insertion between two related episodes or symbols or images (A and A') of another element (B), which emphasizes the link between A and A' and thus requires the reader to see the text as an indivisible whole. For example, the seven-trumpet series is introduced by the following inclusion:

A "Next I saw seven trumpets being given" (8:2)
B "Another angel who had a golden censer" (8:3–5)
A' "The seven angels who had the seven trumpets" (8:6ff.)

Many sections of Revelation are structured in the form of an inclusion.

The technique of interlocking or interlacing is a combination of the ABA' pattern and the interlude. The author inserts into the preceding passage a section or vision that clearly belongs also to the following section. For example, the section 10:1–11:14 is an interlude before the opening of the seventh trumpet and at the same time is clearly characterized as a part of chapters 12–14.

Intercalation represents the greatest obstacle to our Western minds because we are trained to divide a text into sections that follow each other in a logical, linear fashion. The author of Revelation, however, does not separate the narrative structure into clear-cut segments or logical sequences but seeks to join the individual visions and cycles together by interweaving them with each other through the techniques of intercalation and inclusion. Although scholars usually look for the "dividing marks" of Revelation, it is more fruitful to concentrate on the joints that link the different cycles of visions.

There are as many outlines and structurations of Revelation's surface structure as there are scholars studying the book. Since we are trained in linear thinking, we assume that it is possible to come up with a definite outline that can chart the temporal sequence of the visions. Therefore, we are startled by anticipatory interludes and hymns, apparent repetitions, and the repeated announcements that the end is here.

Nevertheless, Revelation is not cyclic: its narrative moves forward. Insofar as the promises of the seven messages all recur in the last section of the book, this forward movement proceeds from promise to fulfillment. Yet the movement of the narrative is not simply logical or temporal. It can best be envisioned as a conic spiral moving from the present to the eschatological future. This forward movement of the narrative is not a flight into a utopian future but is anchored in the present of the communities. The total literary vision of Revelation is set within the epistolary framework of an open pastoral-prophetic letter on the one hand, and exhortations, beatitudes, and warnings referring the apocalyptic images and visions to the present experience of the Christian community on the other.

The following outline of the surface structure of Revelation is determined by the forward movement of the narrative and the concentric pattern of the epistolary inclusion. Its development of symbol and thought is not chronological but topical and thematic. Such a concentric structure of composition is also found in Jewish and Greco-Roman literature and art. It indicates that the whole book is conceived as an inclusion that could be compared to the several layers of an onion. Its individual elements may be sketched in the following way (with Roman numerals indicating the four "cycles of seven"):

A Epistolary frame and prologue (1.1–8)
   Title (1:1–3)
   Greetings (1:4–6)
   Motto (1:7–8)
B The community under judgment (1:9–3:22)
   Author and situation (1:9–10)
   Prophetic inaugural vision (1:11–20)
   (I) Prophetic messages (2:1–3:22)
C The reign of God and Christ (4:1–9:21, 11:15–19)
   Heavenly court and sealed scroll (4:1–5:14)
   (II) Cosmic plagues: seven seals (6:1–8:1)
   (III) Cosmic plagues: seven trumpets (8:2–11:19)
D The "war" against the community (10:1–15:4)
   Prophetic commissioning (10:1–11:13)
   Prophetic interpretation (12:1–14:5)
   Eschatological liberation (14:6–15:4)
C' Judgment of Babylon/Rome (15:1, 5–19:10)
   (IV) Cosmic plagues: seven bowls (15:1–16:21)

Babylon/Rome and its power (17:1–18)
Judgment of Babylon/Rome (18:1–19:10)
B' World judgment and salvation (19:11–22:9)
   Parousia and judgment (19:11–20:15)
   The new world of God (21:1–8)
   The new city of God (21:9–22:9)
A' Epilogue and epistolary frame (22:10–22:21)
   Revelatory sayings (22:10–17)
   Epistolary conclusion (22:18–21)

Revelation's narrative movement does not work with a plot but can best be envisioned as a concentric spiral moving from the present to the eschatological future. It may be likened to that of a film whose individual scenes portray characters or actions from different perspectives, each of which adds some new insight to the whole. It also could be likened to a musical composition that varies the musical themes in different ways, each variation enhancing and moving the total composition.

Sonia Delaunay's expressionist paintings can be used to visualize the development of symbol and movement in Revelation. Her picture *Rhythm*, for instance, contains a number of different-colored circles or half circles from which radiate lines of colors like light that seems to be splintered by a prism. The picture is not static, but its lines indicate a forward movement of the circles of color like a revolving planet. While the evolving circles of color suggest simultaneity, the contrasting colors create a sense of light and movement.

THE RHETORICAL FUNCTION OF REVELATION'S WORLD OF VISION

John develops Revelation's dynamic composition not for art's sake but for the sake of prophetic motivation and interpretation. In writing down the "words of prophecy" to be read in the worship assembly of the community, John seeks to motivate and encourage Christians in Asia Minor who have experienced harassment and exploitation. He does this not simply by writing a letter of exhortation but by creating a new plausibility structure and symbolic universe within the framework of a prophetic letter. Apocalyptic vision and explicit admonition have the same functions. Revelation provides the vision of an alternative world intended to encourage Christians and to enhance their staying power in the face of suffering and harassment.

Rhetorical Situation and Sociopolitical Occasion

The "crisis" interpretation of Revelation has been questioned recently by scholars who point out that we have no evidence of an official persecution of Christians under Domitian. Such an objection overlooks the fact that the rhetorical situation that evokes the visionary response of Revelation is generated not just by the urgency of the sociopolitical-religious situation of harassment and denunciation but also by conflicting symbolic universes.

Although Christians were not officially persecuted under Domitian or Trajan, the correspondence between Pliny the Younger, the provincial governor of Asia Minor, and the emperor Trajan at the beginning of the second century testifies to the fact that Christians were denounced and executed in Asia Minor even before Pliny arrived on the scene, since he mentions that some had left the Christian group "as many as twenty-five years ago." Those who were denounced as Christians and who confessed were either tried and executed immediately or, when Roman citizens, sent to Rome. Those who recanted or claimed never to have been Christian had to invoke the gods, to sacrifice before statues of the gods and the image of the emperor, and to curse Christ (Pliny, *Epistle* 10.96–97). A number of minor charges to which Christians were particularly vulnerable could apparently be construed as treason.

Pliny states in plain words what Revelation expresses with the images of the beasts and the great harlot. Yet Revelation 13:17 reflects another hardship in stressing that those who do not have the mark of the beast cannot buy or sell. Not only threat of harassment, imprisonment, and execution but also economic deprivation and destitution are to be suffered by those who refuse to take the mark of the beast. Although exegetes are not quite able to explain the mark of the beast and its number, its economic significance is plain. The "beast," signifying Roman imperial cultic power, not only threatens the followers of the lamb with death but also makes it impossible for them to live.

Thus it appears that Christians of Asia Minor suffered a deep tension between their faith and their experience. They believed in the ultimate power of God and Christ, but at the same time they experienced daily their powerlessness in the face of harassment, exploitation, and persecution. Their everyday experiences ran counter to their belief in God's power and undermined their hope in God's empire, glory, and life-giving power.

This tension between the conviction of faith and the negative experience of everyday life must have provoked difficult theological questions: If God and Christ have the real power in the world, why do their loyal believers have to suffer? Why does Christ not return in glory and without delay to prevent further suffering and to establish justice? If the divinity of the emperor is just a constitutional fiction, why resist it? Is such behavior not dangerous illusion? Why not work out a compromise with the imperial powers and cults of Asia Minor and Rome? True, Jesus was executed by the Romans as a political criminal, but this was a theological misunderstanding of his claim to Messiahship. Did not Paul, the great apostle, preach that Christians ought not to resist civil authorities but to give honor to whom honor is due (Rom 13)? To behave otherwise is religious fanaticism and foolishness.

It seems that some established Christians in the churches of Asia Minor argued in such a theological vein. Since John rails against such Christians, whom he calls by nicknames drawn from the Hebrew Bible —Balaamites or followers of Jezebel or Nicolaitans (2:6, 14, 15, 20)—it is difficult to distill their genuine teachings from John's biting polemics. It is interesting that one of their renowned prophets was a woman who could claim the official title "prophet," while John never applies this title to himself, probably because his prophetic office was not officially acknowledged by all the churches. However, John does not argue against this woman prophet because she was a woman claiming prophetic office and leadership but because of her teachings.

This alternative Christian prophetic group seems to have approved of Christian participation in pagan cultic meals and in the imperial cult, a practice that John consistently labels as "fornication." The expressions "eating meat sacrificed to idols" and to "know the deep things of Satan" give some clues about their theological argument and its legitimization. Like the Corinthians and Paul, they probably argued that "idols are nothing" and that an idol has no real power over those whom Christ has redeemed from the cosmic powers of this world. Therefore, participation in the everyday life of Greco-Roman society and in the formalities of the imperial cult is perfectly harmless for a spirit-filled Christian.

God's and Christ's powers are of an order completely different from the politico-religious order of Rome (cf. John 18:36ff.). Like the author of the First Letter of Peter, who also wrote to Christians in Asia Minor toward the end of the first century, they might have insisted: "Be subject for the Lord's sake to every human institution, whether it be to the emperor as supreme, or to governors. . . . Fear God. Honor the emperor" (1 Pet 2:13, 17; RSV).

It seems that the difference in theological perspective is not so much doctrinal as it is rooted in a quite different assessment of Roman power and influence in Asia Minor. Although we do not know the social status of the prophetic Christian group against which John competes, we do know that some of the communities to whom he writes have experienced poverty, banishment, violence, and assassination. He has only praise for those communities that are poor and have experienced harassment from their Greco-Roman, Asian, and Jewish neighbors (Smyrna, 2:8–11; Philadelphia, 3:7–13), but he has harsh criticism for the community of Laodicea (3:14–22), which considers itself to be rich and prosperous.

In short, John advocates an uncompromising theological stance toward the imperial cult and Christian assimilation because for him and his followers the dehumanizing power of Rome and its vassals has become so destructive that a compromise with them would mean an affirmation of the power of those "who destroy the earth." Therefore Revelation stresses that Christ is alive even though he was killed. Those who resist letting the powers of death determine their lives will share in the power and glory of the New Jerusalem. To those who are poor, harassed, and persecuted the promises to the "victorious" assure the essentials of life for the eschatological future: food, clothing, home, citizenship, security, honor, power, glory.

In constructing the symbolic universe of Revelation, John attempts to show the superiority of his view of human and divine reality. Since Roman political power was understood in cultic terms, the symbolic universe of Revelation needed to appeal to cultic-religious symbols in order to alienate his audience from the magnificent symbols and cultic drama of the imperial cult. Yet such an appeal was difficult, since Christians lacked such formal institutions as priests and sacrifices and temples. Therefore, John adopts the cultic language and institutional symbols of Israel. In taking over traditional Jewish cultic symbols such as temple, altar, priests, sacrifice, vestments, hymns, incense, or ritual purity, John seeks to construct an alternative to the splendor of the imperial cult and to appeal to Jews and Jewish Christians who "own" the tradition to accept his alternative vision. These cultic symbols and institutions of Israel serve as evocative language in Revelation but do not describe the actual cultic practices of Christians in Asia Minor.

Revelation's World of Vision

Although Revelation's world of vision is articulated in cultic language, such language serves to symbolize the struggle between divine and imperial power. The central theological question of Revelation thus is not the course of history or the provision of an exact timetable for the events of the end time, but it is the question of power and justice. In 6:9–11 those who were slaughtered and killed because of their witness to God and Christ ask the key apocalyptic question: How long, O Lord? They ask the centuries-old question of those who suffer unbearable injustice and oppression: When, O God, will you vindicate our faith and restore justice to us? The central theological symbol of Revelation is therefore the throne, which signifies the power of divine liberation or demonic death dealing. While Christians are the representatives and agents of the power and empire of God and Christ here on earth, the universal Roman empire and its imperial powers are the agents of the demonic and destructive power of Satan.

Revelation is thus a deeply politicotheological work. Its central theological question is: To whom does the earth belong? Who is the ruler of this world? The Christian claim that Jesus Christ is not a mere cultic God but the Lord of the world necessarily had to come into conflict with the proclamation of the

Roman civil religion: Caesar is Lord! Revelation maintains that the one who "makes all things new" (21:5) and the one who is "Lord of Lords and King of Kings" are one and the same. God's and Christ's coming and reign mean salvation not only for Christians but also for all those now slaughtered and oppressed by political powers. At the same time, the book maintains that God's and Christ's judgment engenders the destruction of all "who corrupt the earth."

The power behind the political domination of Rome, which "corrupts the earth," is not merely human. It is Satan, the anti-divine power par excellence. Whereas the heavens rejoice over the devil's downfall, the earth is in anguish:

> Woe to you, O earth and sea, for the devil has come down to you in great wrath, because he knows that his time is short. (12:12; RSV)

The dragon-devil has given to the beast from the sea, the Roman emperor, "his power and his throne and great authority" (13:2). This power appears to be absolute and universal and affects Christians and non-Christians alike:

> Also it [the beast] was allowed to make war on the saints and to conquer them. And authority was given it over every tribe and people and tongue and nation, and all who dwell on earth will worship it. (13:7–18)

As the designated heirs of God's power on earth (1:6, 5:10), Christians are by definition enemies of the totalitarian Roman empire and its allies. The "dwellers of the earth," the free and the slaves, the merchants and kings of the earth submit to the power of this empire, which corrupts and devastates the land. Therefore the outcries of Christians for judgment and justice (6:9, 15:4, 18:20) are also on behalf of the earth. God's justice and human salvation coincide (21:1–7).

However, as the first seven series of the messages at the beginning of the book signal, judgment begins with the church. Just as the church of Laodicea can be condemned when it says, "I am rich and have grown wealthy, and have need of nothing" (3:17; Au. trans.), so Christians can loose their freedom again by becoming slaves to the earth-destroying power of

Babylon/Rome. Revelation gives great prominence to the ethics of commitment. Such ethical-political commitment prohibits Christians from projecting evil only unto others while holding themselves exempt from it. Revelation not only speaks of judgment against the dehumanizing powers but also warns Christians not to succumb to their very concrete pressures.

The book, therefore, begins and ends with a section of censure and exhortation to faithfulness. Only later the work describes in mythological symbolization the threat and destructive force of Roman imperial power and cult. It highlights in mythological language that God, the creator, and Christ, the liberator, are the legitimate regents of the world. Therefore the "eternal gospel" (14:6) calls all the earth dwellers to repentance and Christians to loyal resistance against the beast and its pressures.

God's coming in judgment means justice for those who have rejected the oppression of the great world power Babylon/Rome (19:2). It brings judgment on those who have usurped God's and Christ's reign over the earth. Both aspects of God's coming to judgment are expressed in the eschatological victory hymn in 11:17–18 (RSV):

> We give thanks to thee, Lord God Almighty,
>   who art and who wast,
> that thou has taken thy great power and begun
>   to reign.
> The nations raged, but thy wrath came,
> and the time for the dead to be judged,
> for rewarding thy servants, the prophets and saints,
> and those who fear thy name, both small and great,
> and for destroying the destroyers of the earth.

God's judgment and reign, which are here announced in hymnic praise, are imaged in the final visions of the book. Babylon, the two beasts, and finally the dragon are overcome and punished. The last enemies to be judged are Hades and Death. The new earth is an earth without any life-destroying and oppressive powers. God's judgment means liberation and salvation for the earth and humanity.

The new earth and world are envisioned as the alternative to the present world of suffering, exploitation, and death. God's reign cannot be conceived of as coexisting with any dehumanizing power that destroys the earth. The first heaven and the first earth, the antagonistic dualism between divine and demonic power, will give way to a world centered around the "tree of life." John does not envision as Paul had done that on the Last Day Christians shall be "caught up together with [the dead] in the clouds to meet the Lord" (1 Thess 4:17), but he sees instead the New Jerusalem, the holy city of humanity, "coming down out of heaven from God" (21:2). The voice from the throne pronounces final salvation on earth:

> Behold, the dwelling of God is with human beings. God will dwell with them and they shall be the people of God. And God Self will be with them; God will wipe every tear from their eyes, and death shall be no more, neither shall there be mourning nor crying nor pain any more. For the former things have passed away. (21:3–4; Au. trans.)

In short, the last section shows the glory, life, light, and happiness of God's empire of salvation, which is open to all the nations and free from all oppressive powers and dehumanizing forces. Revelation's politico-mythological symbolization does not "spiritualize" human oppression but fully unmasks it as being against God's intention. The injunctions, beatitudes, warnings, and promises, which run like a red string through the book, have the function of motivating the audience, and the book's symbolic universe of vision seeks to give meaning and hope in a situation of political harassment and exploitation.

Theological Assessment and Evaluation

Revelation's visionary symbolization of eschatological salvation and well-being and its denunciation of all destructive powers have throughout Christian history mostly inspired chiliastic movements rather than establishment Christianity. Whereas mainline Christianity has often co-opted or neutralized Revelation's politicoreligious language and vision by identifying God's empire with the institutional church or with the interior salvation of the soul, messianic-prophetic Christian movements have again and again affirmed Revelation's vision of salvation as total humanization and wholeness. They have stressed that Revelation's message spells liberation from oppressive ecclesiastical structures and from the destructive domination of those who have power in this world. The empire of God means salvation for this world and not merely salvation from this world or salvation of the soul. Oppressive political, societal, and religious powers and the life-giving empire and power of God cannot coexist. The outcry of Revelation for justice and judgment can only be fully understood by those who hunger and thirst for justice.

John's attempt to formulate the reality and meaning of eschatological salvation in universal and political symbols gains greater significance again, at a time when those who share Revelation's assessment of oppression and exploitation attempt to formulate their own theology of liberation and to stake their life on it. Archbishop Desmond Tutu has underlined this affinity between the key theological question of Revelation and liberation theology: "Liberation theology more than any other kind of theology issues out of the crucible of human suffering and anguish. It happens because people cry out, 'Oh God, how long?' 'Oh God, but why? . . .' All liberation theology stems from trying to make sense of human suffering when those who suffer are the victims of organized oppression and exploitation" (Tutu 1979, 163).

The Guatemalan poet in exile Julia Esquivel utilizes the language of Revelation in her poem "Thanksgiving Day in the USA" to denounce the United States as a Babylonian state whose false prophets "twist the truth, calling their intervention into Central America and the Caribbean 'peace and development' in order to silence the outcry of the thousands being crucified in El Salvador and Guatemala" (1982, 89). It might very well be that we will feel as helpless or resentful vis-à-vis such a prophetic liberation theological rhetoric as we feel vis-à-vis the theology of Revelation. We will not be able to appreciate the poet's vision unless we also share the theological analysis of those who experience American culture, society, and religion as destructive and oppressive.

Martin Luther King, Jr.'s "Letter from a Birmingham Jail" is another example of such a utilization of the language and vision of Revelation. It reflects experiences and hopes similar to those that determine the theology of Revelation. In the crude outline of this letter scribbled on toilet paper in jail, the

379

following three topics emerge: first, the ethics of Christian commitment; second, the judgment of God upon the dehumanizing power of white America; and third, a glimpse of the New Jerusalem, echoing King's famous "I have a dream."

Admittedly Martin Luther King was influenced by the visionary rhetoric of Revelation, just as John's vision was nourished by Jewish apocalyptic writings. Nevertheless, it was his experience of the oppression of his people and his own imprisonment that led him to underscore the political implications of Christian theology. His indictment of racist white America must not be construed as "hatred of civilization" or as "envy deficient of Christian love" or as psychological displacement and repression of the "will to power," as scholars have misconstrued the theology of Revelation. Moreover, whoever has understood the dehumanizing power of racism as life-destroying evil power cannot adopt the perspective of well-to-do white Americans, which says that no harassment, denigration, discrimination, or oppression of blacks existed, and this, even though Martin Luther King was killed. In a similar fashion, the author of Revelation has adopted the "perspective from below" and expressed the experiences of those who were poor, powerless, and in constant fear of denunciation.

This does not mean that we should uncritically adopt Revelation's language and world of vision. For example, the symbols of Revelation for both the oppressive and the eschatologically redemptive communities are female because Israel was imaged as bride and wife of Yahweh in the Hebrew Bible and because in antiquity, as today, a city was personified as a woman. Revelation symbolizes idolatry with the prophetic and cultic language of the Hebrew Bible as "whoring" or "defilement with women" (14:4). Today we have become aware of the destructive impact of such misogynist religious language and its socializing functions. These words no longer move readers to persistent resistance against political idolatry but appeal to quite different emotions. Such language engages contemporary readers to perceive women in terms of good or evil, pure or impure, divine or demonic, helpless or powerful, bride or temptress, wife or whore. Rather than instilling a hunger and thirst for justice, such language perpetuates prejudice and injustice if it is not adequately translated to communicate the author's vision.

Revelation's adoption of language and imagery rooted in Near Eastern court protocol and Roman imperial cult also calls for theological evaluation. In likening God's glory and power to Roman imperial power and splendor, in portraying Christ as divine warrior and "King of Kings," Revelation is in danger of conceiving divine power as "power over, as dominating power" in terms of Roman domination. True the author sought to transform this language and imagery, but it is doubtful whether he was able to do so for many readers. Nurturing and compassionate images of God, such as Revelation 7:16–17 and 21:3–4, function as correctives, but they are not sufficiently strong to determine the image of God and Christ in the overall symbolization of the book. Since Revelation is not the only biblical writing that promotes the image of an Almighty Ruler-King God fostering militarism and destruction, we need to replace such New Testament theological and christological language with symbols and images of God and Christ that can foster human responsibility and care for the earth and its future.

Finally, Revelation's apocalyptic insistence on God's foreordained plan to destroy the present world of suffering and death in an imminent last judgment should be critically evaluated. Whereas in the rhetorical situation of Revelation this apocalyptic pattern serves to encourage those who are completely powerless, in a democratic society it can lead to political defeatism and abrogation of the responsibility for the future of the earth and of humanity.

In short, contemporary readers of Revelation need to learn not only to read Revelation's strange language and imagery and to appreciate its world of vision, but also to assess the moral-political persuasion of its visionary rhetoric.

Bibliography

Blevins, James L. *Revelation*. Atlanta, 1984.

Collins, Adela Yarbro. *The Apocalypse*. Wilmington, Del., 1983.

———. *Crisis and Catharsis: The Power of the Apocalypse*. Philadelphia, 1984.

———. "Reading the Book of Revelation in the Twentieth Century." *Interpretation* 40 (1986): 229–242.

———. ed. *Early Christian Apocalypticism: Genre and Social Setting.* Decatur, Ga., 1986.

Esquivel, Julia. *Threatened with Resurrection.* Elgin, Ill., 1982.

Hellholm, David, ed. *Apocalypticism in the Mediterranean World and Near East.* Philadelphia, 1983.

Hemer, Colin J. *The Letters to the Seven Churches of Asia in Their Local Setting.* Winona Lake, Ind., 1986.

Jeske, Richard. *Revelation for Today: Images of Hope.* Philadelphia, 1983.

Minear, Paul S. *I Saw a New Earth.* Washington, D.C., 1968.

———. *New Testament Apocalyptic.* Nashville, Tenn., 1981.

Mounce, R. H. *The Book of Revelation.* Grand Rapids, 1977.

Pilch, John J. *What Are They Saying About the Book of Revelation?* New York, 1978.

Schüssler Fiorenza, Elisabeth. "The Revelation of John." In *Hebrews, James, 1 and 2 Peter, Jude, Revelation.* Proclamation Commentaries. Philadelphia, 1977. Pp. 99–120.

———. *Invitation to the Book of Revelation.* Garden City, N.Y., 1981.

———. *The Book of Revelation: Justice and Judgment.* Philadelphia, 1985.

Sweet, J. P. M. *Revelation.* Philadelphia, 1979.

Tutu, Desmond. "The Theology of Liberation in Africa." In *African Theology en Route,* edited by Kobi Appiah-Kubi and Sergio Torres. Maryknoll, N.Y., 1979.

Van der Meer, Frederick. *Apocalypse: Visions from the Book of Revelation in Western Art.* London, 1978.

ELISABETH SCHÜSSLER FIORENZA

List of Contributors

PAUL J. ACHTEMEIER   Herbert Worth and Annie H. Jackson Professor of Biblical Interpretation at Union Theological Seminary in Virginia. Author of numerous scholarly books and articles. Editor of *Harper's Bible Dictionary* and of *Interpretation: A Journal for Bible and Theology*.
1 Peter

JOUETTE M. BASSLER   Associate Professor of New Testament at Perkins School of Theology, Dallas, Texas. Author of *Divine Impartiality: Paul and a Theological Axiom* and of numerous essays in journals and in *Harper's Bible Dictionary* and the *Anchor Bible Dictionary*.
1 and 2 Thessalonians

J. CHRISTIAAN BEKER   Richard J. Dearborn Professor of Biblical Theology at Princeton Theological Seminary. Author of *The Church Faces the World, Paul the Apostle: The Triumph of God in Thought and Life*, and *Paul's Apocalyptic Gospel: The Coming Triumph of God*.
Romans

RAYMOND E. BROWN, S. S.   Auburn Distinguished Professor of Biblical Studies at Union Theological Seminary. Author of *The Gospel and Epistles of John, The Churches the Apostles Left Behind*, and *The Community of the Beloved Disciple*. Editor of the *Jerome Biblical Commentary*.
Introduction to the New Testament

TONI CRAVEN   Associate Professor of Old Testament at Brite Divinity School, Texas Christian University. Author of many articles on the Book of Judith and the forthcoming *Judith*.
Judith

R. ALAN CULPEPPER   James Buchanan Harrison Professor of New Testament Interpretation at the Southern Baptist Theological Seminary. Author of *The Johannine School, Anatomy of the Fourth Gospel: A Study in Literary Design, John, the Son of Zebedee: The Life of a Legend*, and numerous articles and teaching guides.
John

ROBERT DORAN   Associate Professor of Religion at Amherst College. Author of *Temple Propaganda: The Literary Character of 2 Maccabees, Simeon Stylites: The Biographies*, and various studies of the interaction of Jews and Gentiles in the Hellenistic period.
1 and 2 Maccabees

MARY ANN GETTY   Associate Professor of New Testament Studies at Catholic University of America. Author of commentaries on various letters of Paul. Associate editor of the *Catholic Biblical Quarterly* and *The Bible Today*. Editor of Zacchaeus Studies, New Testament Series.
Philippians; Philemon

DONALD JUEL   Professor of New Testament at Luther Northwestern Theological Seminary. Author of *Messianic Exegesis, Luke-Acts: The Promise of History*, and *Messiah and Temple*.
Luke-Acts

HOWARD CLARK KEE   William Goodwin Aurelio Professor of Biblical Studies at Boston University. Author of *Medicine, Miracle, and Magic in New Testament Times, Understanding the New Testament*, and *Miracle in the Early Christian World* among other books and articles. Editor of *Journal of Biblical Literature*.
Mark

JACK DEAN KINGSBURY   Aubrey Lee Brooks Professor of Biblical Theology at Union Theological Seminary in Virginia. Author of *Conflict in Mark: Jesus, Authorities, Disciples; Matthew as Story; The Christology of Mark's Gospel*; and numerous other books and articles. Contributor to *Harper's Bible Dictionary* and *The Oxford Companion to the Bible*. Member of the editorial board of *Ex Auditu*.
Matthew

RALPH W. KLEIN   Dean and Christ Seminary/Seminex Professor of Old Testament at the Lutheran School of Theology at Chicago. Author of *Textual Criticism of the Old Testament, Israel in Exile*,

1 Samuel, and *Ezekiel: The Prophet and his Message* among others.
1 Esdras

SOPHIE LAWS   Lecturer in New Testament Studies, King's College, University of London.
Hebrews

BURTON L. MACK   Professor of New Testament at the School of Theology at Claremont and the Claremont Graduate School. Author of works on Hellenistic Judaism, Greek education, and early Christianity; most recently *A Myth of Innocence*, on the Gospel of Mark and Christian origins.
Sirach (Ecclesiasticus)

JOEL MARCUS   Assistant Professor of New Testament, Princeton Theological Seminary. Author of *The Mystery of the Kingdom of God* and numerous articles.
James

J. LOUIS MARTYN   Edward Robinson Professor Emeritus of Biblical Theology at Union Theological Seminary. Author of *History and Theology in the Fourth Gospel*, *Proclamation of Easter*, *The Gospel of John in Christian History: Essays for Interpreters*, and many articles. Coeditor of *Studies in Luke-Acts*.
Galatians

FRANK J. MATERA   Associate Professor of New Testament at the Catholic University of America. A priest of the Archdiocese of Hartford.
2 Peter and Jude

GEORGE W. E. NICKELSBURG   Professor of Christian Origins and Early Judaism at the University of Iowa. Author of *Jewish Literature Between the Bible and the Mishnah* and *Resurrection, Immortality, and Eternal Life in Intertestamental Judaism*. Coauthor of *Faith and Piety in Early Judaism* among many other writings. Past chairman of the Society of Biblical Literature Pseudepigrapha Group.
Introduction to the Apocrypha

KATHLEEN M. O'CONNOR   Associate Professor of Biblical Studies at the Maryknoll School of Theology. Author of *The Wisdom Literature*, *Message of Biblical Spirituality 5*, and *The Confessions of Jeremiah: Their Interpretation and Role in Chapters 1–25*.
Baruch, Letter of Jeremiah, and Prayer of Manasseh

PHEME PERKINS   Professor of New Testament at Boston College. Author of commentaries on the Gospel

and Epistles of John and other books and articles on the New Testament, gnosticism and biblical theology. Member of the editorial boards of the *Catholic Biblical Quarterly* and the *Journal of Biblical Literature*.
1, 2, and 3 John

NORMAN RICHARD PETERSEN, JR. Washington Gladden Professor of Religion at Williams College, Williamstown, Massachusetts. Author of *Literary Criticism for New Testament Critics*, *Rediscovering Paul*, and *The Sociology of Paul's Narrative World*.
Tobit

J. PAUL SAMPLEY   Professor of New Testament and Christian Origins at the School of Theology and the Graduate School at Boston University. Author of *The Pauline Parallels* and *Pauline Partnership in Christ*.
1 and 2 Corinthians

ELISABETH SCHÜSSLER FIORENZA   Krister Stendahl Professor of Divinity at Harvard Divinity School. Author of *In Memory of Her*, *Bread Not Stone*, and *The Book of Revelation: Justice and Judgment* among many others. Co-founder and editor of *The Journal of Feminist Studies in Religion*. Editor of *Religious Studies Review* and *Concilium*. Former president of the Society of Biblical Literature. Member of the board of the Women's Alliance for Theology, Ethics, and Ritual and of the Women's Ordination Conference.
Revelation

GERARD S. SLOYAN   Professor of Religion at Temple University. Author of *Jesus on Trial*, *A Commentary on the New Lectionary*, *Jesus in Focus*, and *Is Jesus the End of the Law?* Author of *John* in the *Interpretation* Bible commentary series. He is a priest of the Diocese of Trenton.
Ephesians; Colossians

MICHAEL E. STONE   Professor at Hebrew University, Jerusalem. Author of *Armenian Apocrypha Relating to Patriarchs and Prophets* and *Scriptures, Sects, and Visions*; Coauthor of *Faith and Piety in Early Judaism* and *Armenian Art Treasures of Jerusalem*. Editor of *Jewish Literature of the Second Temple Period*.
2 Esdras

VINCENT L. WIMBUSH   Assistant Professor at the School of Theology at Claremont and Claremont Graduate School. Author of *Paul the Worldly Ascetic: Response to the World and Self-Understanding According to 1 Corinthians 7* and various articles. Editorial board member of *Semeia*. Member of Research Council of the Institute for Antiquity and Christianity at Claremont.
1 and 2 Timothy

Comprehensive Index

A

genealogy of, **1:**123a, 125a, 126a, 151a, 160b, 161b, 267a

as Philistine mercenary, **1:**133a, 135a, 165b

psalms of, **1:**136a, 139b, 216a, 216b

reign of, **1:**13b, 16b, 84a, 128a, 133b, 134a, 135a–137b, 141a–b, 145a, 147a, 149b, 156a, 160b, 165a, 249a, 258a, 268b, 269a, 270a, 276a, 376a

religious policies, **1:**79a, 110a

return of Ark to Jerusalem by, **1:**130a, 136a–b

reverence toward God, **1:**141b, 149a

rise of, **1:**132a–133b, 134b

and Saul, **1:**133b, 135a–b, 137b, 165a–b, 166b, 303b

Sheba's revolt against, **1:**139a, 165b

Temple founding by, **1:**156a, 166a–b

see also Jesus, genealogy of

Day of Atonement. *See* Yom Kippur

Day of Judgment. *See* Judgment Day

Day of the Lord. *See* Judgment Day

Day of Yahweh. *See* Judgment Day

Dead Sea, **1:**116a, 376b

Dead Sea Scrolls, **1:**89b, 177b, 329b–330a, 338b, 340a–341a, 341b, 343b, 392b, 395b; **2:**5a, 8b, 9b, 10a, 35b, 41b, 53b, 54a, 58b, 70a, 101b, 108b, 157a, 158a, 164a, 197a, 205a, 279a, 305b, 333a, 337b

foundation documents, **2:**151b–152a

Death

dirges for, **1:**303a–304b, 307a

Qohelet's view of, **1:**233a–234b, 235b

Satan associated with, **2:**57b–58a, 336b

significance of Pelatiah's, **1:**322b, 325a

Sirach on, **2:**58b

see also Afterlife, Heaven; Hell; Immortality; Judgment Day; Resurrection; *Sheol*

Debir, **1:**115b

Deborah, **1:**115a, 116a–117b

Decalogue. *See* Ten Commandments

Decapolis, **2:**129a, 152b, 161b, 163b

Decius (Roman emperor), **2:**347b

Delaunay, Sonia, **2:**375b

Demas, **2:**302a, 325a

Demetrius I (Seleucid ruler), **2:**99b, 100b–101a, 111b–112a, 113a

Demetrius II (Seleucid ruler), **2:**99b, 102a

Demons

and false messiah, **2:**126a–b

Jesus' exorcism of, **2:**132a, 149b, 153b, 158a, 161b, 162b, 163b

in Tobit story, **2:**38b–39a, 40a, 40b, 41a

Derbe, **2:**271a

Deuterocanonical writings. *See* Apocrypha

Deuteronomistic historian, **1:**13a, 108a–b, 120b, 128b–129b, 132a, 134a–b, 137a, 142b, 284a–b, 286a

Deuteronomy, Book of, **1:**2b, 11a, 23a, 23b, 24a, 38a,

67a, 69a, 69b, 73a, 75b, 77a, **89a–101a,** 106b, 108b, 109a, 110b, 142b, 146a, 199a, 218a, 229b, 284a, 289a, 291b, 292b, 294b, 323a, 329b, 353b, 376a, 388b, 399a, 402b; **2:**88a, 95a, 165b

Devil. *See* Demons; Satan

Diana (Roman goddess), **2:**285a

see also Artemis

Diaspora, **1:**92b, 93a, 94b, 100a, 215b, 336a, 339a, 342b, 351b, 402a; **2:**7b, 8a, 9a, 35a, 36b, 51b

see also Babylonian captivity; Hellenization

Diatessaron, **2:**122b, 123a

Dibelius, Martin, **2:**187b, 189a, 198b

Didascalia Apostolorum, **2:**91a, 324a

Dies irae, **1:**400b

Dietary code, **1:**67a–68a, 68b, 334b; **2:**47b, 190a–b, 195a–b, 197a, 271b, 275b, 298b, 399a

Diognetus, Epistle to, **2:**336a

Dionysius of Alexandria, **2:**120b, 121b

Diotrephes, **2:**359b

Dirges, **1:**303a–304b, 307a

Disasters. *See* Afflictions; Flood; Plagues

Disciples

conditions and life of, **2:**162a–b, 164a–b

Isaiah's, **1:**264a–b, 271b

Jesus' sermon to, **2:**142a–145a

persecution of, **2:**212a

power struggle among, **2:**165a

rights of, **2:**253a

roles of, **2:**219a–221a

see also Acts of the Apostles; Beloved Disciple; specific names

Disease. *See* Afflictions; Sickness and health; specific conditions

Divine promise. *See* Messiah; Promise; Yahweh, promises to Israel

Divorce, **1:**413a

prohibition on remarriage after, **2:**143a, 150a, 154a, 156a, 165a, 251a–b

Dnil (Canaanite hero), **1:**334a

Docetists, **2:**121b

Documentary Hypothesis, **1:**25b, 26a, 26b

Domitian (Roman emperor), **2:**29b, 198a, 347b, 369b, 376a

Doves, **1:**245a; **2:**23a, 216a

Dragon

Bel and, **1:**338b, 339b–340a, 391b; **2:**3a, 7a, 7b

symbolism of, **2:**373a

Dreams

Daniel's, **1:**334b–335a

in Joseph story, **1:**38b–40b

Judas Maccabeus', **2:**112a

Mordecai's, **1:**178a

to save Jesus from Herod, **2:**134b

Drunkenness, **1:**147b; **2:**17a, 17b, 104b, 290a

Dura Europos synagogue, **1:**331a

Q

Shalmaneser V (king of Assyria), 1:351a–b
Shalmaneser (in Tobit). *See* Sargon II
Shamgar, 1:115a
Shaphan, 1:287b
Shavu'ot, 1:126a
Shealtiel, son of. *See* Zerubbabel
Shear-jashub, 1:252b–253a
Sheba, Queen of, 1:166b
Sheba (Benjaminite), 1:139a, 165b
Shechem, 1:13a, 36b, 95a, 103a, 118a
Shema, 1:89b, 95a, 99a, 101a; 2:26a, 234b
Shenazzar. *See* Sheshbazzar
Sheol (netherworld), 1:185b; 2:54a, 54b, 289b
    see also Hell
Shepherd imagery
    Judah's relationship with Yahweh, 1:411b–412a
    Peter as shepherd, 2:220b, 227a
Sheshbazzar, 1:161a, 162a; 2:14a, 18b
Sheshonk I (pharaoh), 1:350a
Shibboleth, 1:119a
Shiloh, 1:120b, 284b, 286a, 287a
Shimei, 1:145a
Sickness and health
    God as healer metaphor, 1:92b
    healings by Jesus, 2:133b–134a, 158a, 161b–162a,
        178a
    in Psalms, 1:207b, 209a
    skin (scale) disease prohibitions, 1:67b, 79b, 80a
    see also Blindness; Leprosy; Plagues
Sidon, 1:363b; 2:129a, 159a
Sign-names, 1:252b, 253b
Sihon (king of Amorites), 1:74a, 75b, 90a
Silvanus, 2:245a, 313a, 313b, 345b, 346a
Simchat Torah, 1:93b
Simeon, 1:52b, 116b; 2:174b–175a, 176a, 177b, 181a,
    189a
Simon Peter. *See* Peter the Apostle
Simon II (high priest), 2:66b, 67a, 81b
Simon Maccabeus, 2:95a, 97a, 97b, 99b, 101a–104b,
    109a, 113a
Simon of Bilgah, 2:107b, 111b
Sin. *See* Serpent; Sins
Sinai, Mount
    burning bush at, 1:52a
    covenant at, 1:21b, 28a, 49a, 95b, 98b, 150b; 2:10b,
        32b, 80b–81a, 277b, 278a
    Israelites' arrival and encampment at, 1:55a–b, 69b,
        71a, 93a; 2:162b–163a
    Moses' speech to Israelites at, 1:89b–90a, 91a, 92a,
        100b
    tabernacle as extension of, 1:59a
    theophany at, 1:55a–55b, 59a
Sinai Covenant. *See* Covenant Code
Sinai region, 1:28a, 55a, 73b, 74b, 75b–76a, 76b–77a,
    360a

Sins
    blood sacrifice for, 2:332a
    Christians as free from, 2:363b
    Christian vs. Jewish view of, 1:41b
    confession of, 1:210a, 296a–b, 306a, 340b, 401b;
        2:25a, 87b, 88b, 91a
    forgiveness of, 1:382a–383a, 385a, 390a; 2:90b,
        91a–92a, 157a, 158a–b, 159a, 184a, 185a, 187a,
        189a, 234a–b, 274b, 287a; *see also* Jesus Christ,
        forgiveness of sins by
    grace relationship, 2:235b, 236b–237b, 327a
    impulse motivating, 2:341a
    revelation countering, 2:215b, 224b
    seven deadly, 1:340a
    suffering linked to, 1:185a–186b
    see also Retribution; Theodicy
Sirach, Book of, 1:5b, 223a, 229b, 238a; 2:3a, 6a, 6b,
    53b, 55b, 56a, **65a–85a,** 87b, 340b
Sirach, Jesus ben (son of Sirach), 1:177b, 225a,
    226b–227a; 2:7a, 8a, 9a, 58b
Sisera, 1:116b–117a
Sistine Chapel, 1:338a
666 (mystical number), 1:345a; 2:369b–370a
Skehan, Patrick, 1:223b, 224a–b
Skin (scale) disease, 1:67b, 79b, 80a
    see also Leprosy
Slander. *See* False accusations
Slavery, 1:368a
    associated with fall of Jerusalem, 1:309a
    Christians' right to hold slaves, 2:322a
    Covenant Code laws governing, 1:56a, 60a–b
    as metaphor for early Christians' plight, 2:350a
    Onesimus and Philemon relationship, 2:325a–326b
    Paul on, 2:291b, 309b
    in Solomon's reign, 1:144a
    see also Exodus, Book of
Snake. *See* Serpent
Sodom and Gomorrah, 1:6a, 35a, 275b; 2:355a, 356b
Solomon (king of Israel), 1:79a, 105b, 217a; 2:9b, 15a,
    15b, 98b, 106a
    association with Ecclesiastes, 1:231b, 238b
    infidelity of, 1:166b–167a
    kingship's transfer to, 1:166a
    association with Proverbs, 1:224b, 238b
    reign of, 1:50a, 143b–144a, 145a, 146a, 150b, 286a
    association with Song of Solomon, 1:238b, 241a–b
    in Succession Narrative, 1:13b, 134b, 138a–139a,
        139b
    tabulation of royal officials, 1:140b–144a
    as *torah* keeper, 1:110a
    wedding of, 1:242b
    wisdom of, 1:231b, 339b
    see also Wisdom of Solomon
Song of Solomon, 1:6a, 11b, 14b, 156b, 238b,
    241a–245b; 2:4b, 7a, 65a